Readings in Philosophy of Religion

For Martha, who continues to show me that when words
and reasons fail, love remains

Readings in Philosophy of Religion

East Meets West

Edited by Andrew Eshleman

Blackwell
Publishing

Editorial material and organization © 2008 by Blackwell Publishing Ltd

BLACKWELL PUBLISHING
350 Main Street, Malden, MA 02148-5020, USA
9600 Garsington Road, Oxford OX4 2DQ, UK
550 Swanston Street, Carlton, Victoria 3053, Australia

The right of Andrew Eshleman to be identified as the author of the editorial material in this work
has been asserted in accordance with the UK Copyright, Designs, and Patents Act 1988.

First published 2008 by Blackwell Publishing Ltd

1   2008

Library of Congress Cataloging-in-Publication Data

Readings in philosophy of religion : East meets West / edited by Andrew Eshleman.
     p. cm.
  Includes bibliographical references.
  ISBN 978-1-4051-4716-3 (hardcover : alk. paper) — ISBN 978-1-4051-4717-0 (pbk. : alk. paper)
1. Religion—Philosophy.   I. Eshleman, Andrew.

  BL51.R324 2008
  210—dc22

                                                                          2007038436

A catalogue record for this title is available from the British Library.

Set in 9.5/11.5pt Minion
by Graphicraft Limited, Hong Kong
Printed and bound in Singapore
by Utopia Press Pte Ltd

The publisher's policy is to use permanent paper from mills that operate a sustainable forestry
policy, and which has been manufactured from pulp processed using acid-free and elementary
chlorine-free practices. Furthermore, the publisher ensures that the text paper and cover
board used have met acceptable environmental accreditation standards.

For further information on
Blackwell Publishing, visit our website at
www.blackwellpublishing.com

Contents

Acknowledgments

For some time now I have used a self-selected compilation of readings for use in my philosophy of religion course, so I wish to begin by thanking my students over the years for helping to guide my sense of what should be in this book. I'd like to especially thank those who took my course in 2006 and 2007 – as well as those in Julie Piering's philosophy of religion course in 2006 at Northern Arizona University – for working through a draft of the present volume and providing me with valuable feedback.

I am also grateful to my home institution, the University of Arkansas at Little Rock, for: a wonderfully supportive department within which to work; the administrative assistance of Stacia Sauls; a helpful interlibrary loan staff who fulfilled a great many requests on my behalf; granting me a sabbatical to work on the book during the fall semester of 2005; and travel monies for research that semester at the East–West Center in Honolulu. *Mahalo* as well to the East–West Center for office space during my sabbatical semester, administrative support, and library privileges at the University of Hawaii, Manoa.

For guidance, comments, and general support throughout the process of completing the book, I heartily thank (in alphabetical order): Smaranda Aldea, Roger Ames, Craig Berry, Timothy Bilbruck, Christopher Blakey, Peter Byrne, Joshua Counce, James Deitrick, John Martin Fischer, Avery Fouts, Richard Frothingham, Kevin Hart, Micah Hester, John Hick, Angela Hunter, Steven Jauss, Harvey Luber, Jay McDaniel, Matthew Mullins, Robert Musser, Julie Piering, Daryl Rice, Polly Sanders, Daniel Speak, Jan Thomas, William Brent Turney, William J. Wainwright, Keith Ward, Linda Zagzebski, and several anonymous referees who provided helpful comments in the early review of the book proposal.

Finally, for their excellent professional support and guidance, I thank the Blackwell editorial team of Jeff Dean, Danielle Descoteaux, Justin Dyer, and Jamie Harlan.

Preface to the Instructor

The aim of this anthology is to present a broader range of philosophical reflection than one finds in most anthologies in philosophy of religion. In particular, it aims to supplement some of the best contemporary work in Western philosophy of religion with some of the best recent discussions of Hindu, Buddhist, Daoist, and Confucian philosophies. Though the emphasis here is on contemporary philosophy of religion, influential historical selections have been included as well to provide background for the contemporary discussion.

Though this anthology prizes diversity, it neither seeks to be comprehensive (which would be impossible), nor values diversity simply for diversity's sake. Every non-Western selection here has been chosen because of the way it supplements a current conversation in the Western literature, by either: (a) illustrating the way that some issues seem to arise across cultural divides (e.g., concerns about the continuation of personal identity in an afterlife); (b) introducing a new slant on a trans-cultural issue (e.g., Nagarjuna's treatment of the limitations of reason); or (c) challenging a central assumption in Western thinking (e.g., that all consciousness must involve an object of awareness).

Since most students and many instructors may have had little exposure to non-Western religious philosophies, clarity has been made a high priority in the selection of texts included. The authors of contemporary selections about

Eastern views are familiar with the Western tradition and write with the Western reader in mind. A glossary is also provided for key terms. Substantial introductions to each section provide helpful background to the reader and help orient him or her to the defining issues of the section. In these introductions, a short précis for each upcoming contemporary selection is provided as well. By situating them next to one another rather than at the beginning of the reading selections themselves, I hope the reader will gain a clearer sense of how the readings within each section relate to one another. The introductory material for each section may be assigned as a whole to provide an overview before the section's readings. Alternatively, my own preference is to assign the relevant portions of the section introduction along with the individual reading selections and then to recommend that students re-read the introduction as a whole at the conclusion of the section as a means of review.

Finally, let me address a concern that some instructors may have about the structure and content of the book. The text is largely structured according to a set of questions roughly modeled on those that have grown out of a tradition of reflection on Western brands of monotheism: What is Ultimate Sacred Reality?; Can the existence of an Ultimate Sacred Reality be demonstrated by argument?; Can belief in an Ultimate Sacred Reality be rational despite the absence of evidence?; Does evil undermine belief in an Ultimate Sacred Reality?, etc. Also, each section begins by examining how this question is addressed from the theistic perspective. One might wonder about the wisdom of this approach – given that the goal is to broaden the approach to doing philosophy of religion – for in doing so, do we not risk re-making non-Western views in our own image? Nevertheless, although approaching Eastern views in this way may have something of a distorting effect, inquiry must begin somewhere, and the somewhere for most readers of this book will include some level of familiarity with Western brands of monotheism as well as the questions that have been raised about them (even if they have never practiced such a religion). Therefore, pedagogically, it has seemed best to proceed in this fashion.

I hope that you find the book in you hands to be a valuable teaching tool, as I have in my own classes. If you would like to comment on your experience with the text, I would be happy to hear from you.

Andrew Eshleman
University of Arkansas at Little Rock

A Note on the Treatment of Non-English Names and Terms

Increasing Western readers' familiarity with non-Western views entails that they be exposed to a range of names and terms from other languages. Often, there is no completely standardized way of representing such words in English. When doing so, some authors choose to add diacritical marks – marks intended to help indicate the proper pronunciation of a word – and some authors choose to dispense with such marks – e.g., the Persian name of one of Islam's greatest philosophers is sometimes rendered "al-Ghāzālī" and at other times "al Ghazali." Alternate spellings are also common – e.g., the Sanskrit name for one of India's most famous philosophers is rendered by some authors as "Shankara" and by others as "Samkara." Compiling selections for an anthology of this kind will almost inevitably result in a collection of authors who have made different decisions about how best to render such foreign names and terms. Therefore, as the editor of such a volume, I have faced decisions about how to treat such variations. The purpose of this note is to highlight the decisions made and some of the considerations that bear on those decisions.

Diacritical marks are one way of preserving some of the distinctiveness of a word's linguistic origin in the process representing it in another language. This concern for preservation is an important one. Also, one must respect the choices made by the individual scholars whose work appears in this volume about how best to render the relevant words. Thus, while a fully standardized treatment of the use of diacritics and of spellings used across the volume would no doubt be easier for readers, it was not realizable given these competing concerns.

However, since diacritical marks are of very limited value for the reader who does not know how to make use of them, and this book is principally intended for use in college and university classrooms by students who will lack this expertise, it seemed best to forgo the use of diacritical marks in the book's editorial matter – e.g., the introductory material provided for students with each section and the glossary. The exception to this rule is when reference is made in the introductory material to the title of a work which itself includes diacritical marks. Also, I have sought whenever possible to alert the reader parenthetically to alternate spellings of key terms and names – e.g., *karma* (*kamma*).

In this way, I hope to have struck a reasonable balance between respect for the distinctiveness of languages and choices of authors/translators, as well as the desire to make unfamiliar material accessible.

Section I
What is Philosophy of Religion?

A. Introduction to the Section

This book concerns the attempt to think philosophically about religion. However, this simple characterization is unlikely to help anyone not already familiar with philosophy of religion. In the end, philosophical thinking of any kind is best understood by engaging in it, but it may prove helpful – especially for the newcomer – to be given some idea of what is to follow. As part of this general introduction to the book, I first provide a characterization of religion as the target, or object, of reflection in philosophy of religion. Then I introduce the kind of thinking brought to bear here on that target by situating it in relation to two other influential approaches to thinking about religion. Finally, I conclude with some comments about the scope of the book, in particular, the use of the words, "East"/"Eastern" and "West"/"Western," as they appear in the title and throughout the text.

B. *Religion*

B1. *Seeking the Substance and Function of Religion*

Offering a characterization of religion that is both helpful and accurate is no easy task. Some readers might initially be surprised that this is so. Following the lead of Edward Herbert (1582–1648),[1] one might think that religion can straightforwardly be defined by something like the following set of beliefs:

1 A supreme God exists.
2 God deserves to be worshipped.
3 True worship must be coupled with a life of moral virtue.
4 All must repent of their sin.
5 There will be rewards and punishments in a life after this one.[2]

Here Herbert seeks to spell out the substance, or essence, of religion, so we might call this a "substantive" definition of religion. There are several instructive problems with attempting to define religion in this way. First, though he was familiar with the histories of a number of different religious traditions, his understanding of what is essential to religion seems to have been shaped predominantly by those monotheistic religions that played a central role in shaping Anglo-European culture (i.e., principally Christianity, but also Judaism and Islam). As a result, his characterization fails to capture a number of traditions that are widely recognized today as religions – most notably, some forms of Hinduism, Buddhism, Daoism, and Shinto in which the object of religious concern is not God (at least not any sort of personal God – see section II). It also fails to include religions that do not maintain belief in the sort of afterlife presupposed in Herbert's definition.

Second, a definition of this sort is too narrow insofar as it suggests that religion is defined primarily by what people believe. This, too, is a common assumption in many Western circles, illustrated by the widespread practice of referring to religious persons as "believers." Though belief of some sort may be central to most, if not all, religion and certainly is the fundamental aspect of religion scrutinized in philosophy of religion, it is important to recognize that the priority given to right belief varies considerably across religious traditions. For example, for many religious persons, communal ritual practices and their accompanying experiential states seem at least as important as, if not more important than, holding particular religious beliefs. Thus, in defining religion, one should try to capture some of the diverse elements that commonly constitute what we regard as a religion. Again, this is important even though one's attention in philosophy of religion will be directed primarily toward religious belief, for a proper understanding of a

---

[1] Dates throughout this book will be presented using the following conventions. Unless accompanied by the abbreviation, "BCE" ("Before the Common Era"), dates are from the Common Era ("CE"). When exact dates are uncertain, they will be accompanied by the abbreviation, "c." ("circa," or approximately).

[2] Edward Herbert, *De Veritate*, trans. Meyrick H. Carre (Bristol: J. W. Arrowsmith, Ltd, 1937), pp. 291–303. In what follows, I refer to this as Herbert's definition of religion, but it's not entirely clear whether he intended to define religion or prescribe what genuine religion ought to be.

particular religious belief might in the end require that we understand how it is connected to other aspects of a religious tradition.

Third, Herbert's definition neglects the function or role of religion in people's lives – for example, the way that it serves to provide comfort and/or strength in the face of life's challenges. Here there has been some controversy about whether one should try to specify the allegedly *real* (often purportedly hidden) function of religion as opposed to its only *apparent* function as experienced by those who practice it. For example, some theorists have suggested that the primary function of religion is to serve as a crutch in managing feelings of helplessness[3] or to reinforce social rules and structures of authority.[4] It would be premature to rule out such theories, but since our task in what follows will be to take the claims of religious persons seriously at face value in order to judge their merits for ourselves, it seems that we should begin by seeking to characterize the function of religion in a way that most, if not all, religious persons could endorse.

Finally, it is worth highlighting that a considerable degree of consensus has emerged amongst scholars of religion that it is not possible – or perhaps even desirable – to define religion so as to completely remove any and all ambiguity about whether a particular thing is a religion or not. The point here is similar to one Aristotle wished to emphasize about ethical theorizing – that one should not expect greater precision in one's theoretical treatment of a topic than there is to be found in the phenomena that one is theorizing about.[5] While there are clear cases of what we call religion and clear cases of things that are not a religion, there are also ambiguous cases. For example, there have been disagreements about whether Confucianism is or is not a religion (a topic we will return to in section VIII). Also, state-institutionalized Marxism has tended

(ironically given its often aggressive opposition to religion) to resemble a religion in important respects, and, in general, the rituals and accompanying emotions associated with the symbols of modern nation states often take on a religious quality (e.g., the ritual ceremonies surrounding a nation's flag). So, while it is useful to formulate a working definition of religion in order to better focus our attention on the relevant object of study, it is important to remember that the boundary between what is or is not a religion is sometimes not entirely clear.

B2.   A Definition of Religion

Given the above, it seems that we should aim for a definition of religion that: (a) is wide enough to capture those things that are commonly recognized as religions; (b) is sufficiently narrow to distinguish the former from what is clearly not a religion; and (c) allows for some ambiguous cases. (Ideally the definition would also shed some light on why the latter are ambiguous cases.) Here is an attempt at such a definition:

> By means of an interwoven set of symbols, narratives, doctrines, rituals, ethical prescriptions, and social institutions, a religion aims to provide an appropriate way of being related cognitively, emotionally, and behaviorally (both individually and collectively) to that which is conceived of as Ultimate Sacred Reality.[6]

The substantive aspect of this definition refers to the interconnected components of a religious tradition (symbols, narratives, beliefs, etc.) and the way these are organized around a conception of Ultimate Sacred Reality. The functional aspect stresses that religion aims to bring human beings into proper alignment with that which is conceived of as Ultimate Sacred Reality. What constitutes "proper alignment" will vary across religious

---

[3]   Sigmund Freud, "The Future of an Illusion" (1927), in the *Standard Edition of the Complete Psychological Works of Sigmund Freud*, trans. James Strachey, Vol. 21 (London: Hogarth Press, 1964).

[4]   Émile Durkheim, *The Elementary Forms of the Religious Life*, trans. J. W. Swain (London: George Allen & Unwin, 1915).

[5]   *Nicomachean Ethics*, Book I, section 3.

[6]   Here I have expanded the content of and added a functional component to a definition provided by Michael Peterson, William Hasker, Bruce Reichenbach and David Basinger, *Reason and Religious Belief*, 3rd edition (New York: Oxford University Press, 2003), p. 7.

traditions. The phrase "Ultimate Sacred Reality" is likewise intended to be broad enough to capture the diverse ways traditions have characterized this reality – for example, as God, Brahman, Emptiness, Dao, etc. – as well as indicating something of its alleged distinctiveness. That which is sacred is set apart, in the sense that it evokes (or is said to deserve) a special attitude of reverence. Many different kinds of things in a religion may be regarded as sacred – for example, particular individuals, locations, and ritual objects. The word "Ultimate" seeks to capture the sense in which, "Religion, in the largest and most basic sense of the word, is ultimate concern."[7] That is, according to religion, there is a sacred reality or aspect of reality that, given its nature, deserves our very highest concern and commitment.

C. *Philosophy of* Religion

As should be clear by now, religions are complex phenomena. Philosophy of religion is not equally concerned with every aspect of religion, though, as I've suggested, it is important to keep in mind the interconnected nature of those aspects. The primary – though not exclusive – focus of reflection in philosophy of religion is on what might be called the "cognitive" component of religion – that which concerns belief. The cognitive component is expressed directly in a religion's doctrines and often indirectly in its symbols and narratives. These aspects of religion recommend that certain beliefs be held or rejected – for example, beliefs about the nature of Ultimate Sacred Reality, how that reality is related to the world, the fundamental nature of human beings, what constitutes their highest good, etc. The philosopher of religion is concerned to understand what is believed by the religious person and to assess the grounds for thinking that those beliefs are true or false. To better understand this process of inquiry, we will now compare and contrast it with some other approaches to the study of religion.

C1. *Philosophy of Religion and Religious Philosophy*

Though what is assembled in this book under the heading "philosophy of religion" has a long and culturally diverse history, the phrase itself did not gain widespread acceptance in the Western academic setting until the latter half of the twentieth century. On the one hand, it has developed in the contemporary setting as a label to demarcate an area of study within philosophy. Here, it stands alongside phrases of parallel construction – for example, "philosophy of science," "philosophy of law," "philosophy of literature," "philosophy of art," etc. In each of these subfields, philosophers apply their conceptual tools in an effort to illuminate and evaluate the philosophical issues that underlie or arise within these distinct areas of human activity.

On the other hand, the phrase "philosophy of religion" also currently serves to distinguish one approach to the study of religion from two other influential approaches (though, as we shall see, there are important ways in which these approaches overlap). The first of these, in some form or another, arguably belongs to the history of every religion that has succeeded in sustaining itself over many generations. It is a form of thinking that takes place from a standpoint *within* a particular religious tradition. For example, one might begin by accepting certain doctrines on the basis of the sacred texts in one's tradition and reflect on how those doctrines might best be understood so as to cohere with a wider swath of experience and other doctrines, thereby maximizing their explanatory power. These are the sort of goals that become increasingly important for a tradition as it encounters competing traditions or other socio-historical factors that demand that the tradition articulate its relevance anew. Call this, broadly speaking, "religious philosophy."

Traditions vary greatly in the extent to which their religious philosophy is carried out in abstraction from their central texts and practices. In the history of Western thought, theology may be thought of as a form of religious

---

[7] Paul Tillich, *Theology of Culture,* ed. Robert C. Kimball (New York: Oxford University Press, 1964), p. 8.

philosophy as described above – in which one works from a set of scriptural texts and reasons toward a more systematic understanding of the God spoken of there and God's relation to the world. Owing in part to the influence of Greek philosophy on their development, Western forms of theology – especially forms of Christian theology – have historically pursued high levels of abstraction and systematization, so much so that Christian theology was once regarded in the medieval European university as the "Queen" of all the sciences, or pursuits of rational inquiry.

While those engaged in religious philosophy and philosophy of religion often seek to address the same sorts of issues, many who practice philosophy of religion today see themselves as engaged in a practice that is distinct from that of the former. When doing philosophy of religion, one seeks a standpoint of reflection on religious claims *outside* that of a particular tradition. This is so even though the claims themselves may originate from a particular religion (and even though the one engaged in that reflection may belong to that religion or some other religion). This distinguishing feature of philosophy of religion is illustrated by the fact that one can do philosophy of religion whether one is a religious person or not. No commitment to particular religious presuppositions is required to establish the relevant standpoint for reflection, as is the case in religious philosophy. The point here is a methodological one and connected to how philosophy arose historically.

In ancient Greece, several individuals began to distinguish themselves based on the way they approached fundamental questions about the origin, nature, and functioning of the world. Rather than accepting the culturally authoritative accounts on these matters that had been handed down from the earlier Homeric narratives, they began to offer naturalistic theories of their own. For example, Anaxagoras (c. 530–469 BCE) denied that the sun was a glowing chariot driven across the sky by the god Apollo, claiming instead that it was a redhot rock. Later, Socrates (469–399 BCE) famously revealed just how poorly his fellow leading Athenians understood some of their central guiding ideals,

ideals that they often accepted without much scrutiny. In challenging the culturally authoritative views of their day, early Greek philosophers exemplified an important characteristic of philosophical thinking: such thinking recognizes the independent authority of a special form of human reason. This means that an individual's capacity to think both critically and constructively via such reason is recognized as a legitimate and independent guide on the path to truth.

A much older inkling of this philosophical impulse is recorded in a remarkable passage in India's ancient religious text, the *Rig Veda* (c. 1200 BCE). After puzzling over some of the received views concerning the origin of the cosmos, the unknown author registers perplexity and perhaps some skepticism as well:

Who really knows? Who will here proclaim it? Whence was it produced? Whence is this creation? The gods came afterwards, with the creation of this universe. Who then knows whence it has arisen? Whence this creation has arisen – perhaps it formed itself, or perhaps it did not – the one who looks down on it, in the highest heaven, only he knows – or perhaps he does not know.[8]

By the time of the later and more obviously philosophical *Upanishads* (c. 900–300 BCE), Indian thinkers had already begun to formalize the debating of competing views. And though some disagree over the extent to which Confucius (or Kungzi, c. 551–479 BCE) sought to revolutionize as opposed to simply re-vitalize the views of earlier authorities, it is clear that the subsequent generation of Chinese thinkers (e.g., Mozi and Zuangzi, fifth to fourth century BCE) were fully prepared to challenge the prevailing authoritative views of their day on the basis of reason and experience.

In contrast to appeals to sacred or cultural authority – which carry force only with those who accept the same authority – philosophical thinking seeks to appeal to what we might call "public reason." Reason is public when it tries to tap into a capacity to reason and a body of experience that is assumed to be shared amongst human beings. That is, it aspires to appeal to that

---

[8]   From *Rig Veda* 10.129, as translated by Wendy Doniger O'Flaherty in *Textual Sources for the Study of Hinduism* (Totowa, NJ: Barnes and Noble Books, 1988), p. 33.

which, in principle, any person could – upon due attention – comprehend and recognize as worthy of consideration.[9]

We are perhaps now in a position to understand better the distinction drawn earlier between doing religious philosophy from a standpoint *within* a tradition and doing philosophy of religion from a standpoint *outside* a tradition. Both are exercises of reason and possible guides to truth. The standpoint of reflection is determined by the type of considerations to which one allows oneself to appeal. When one engages in the thinking characteristic of philosophy of religion, one attempts to restrict oneself to the considerations of public reason alone. Using reason of this sort, one seeks to understand and assess religious claims – for example, claims about the existence and nature of an Ultimate Sacred Reality or the destiny of human beings after death. Insofar as we approach such claims from the standpoint of philosophy of religion, the fact that a certain sacred text teaches that a personal God exists or that human beings are reborn after death as part of a series of lives will not function as a reason for us to accept it as true or as an adequate response should there be an objection to the possibility that this is so.

The practice of religious philosophy also grants authority to public reason (thus the label "philosophy"), but it does not restrict itself to the considerations of public reason alone. This is the sense it which religious philosophy is practiced from a standpoint *within* a particular tradition. From this standpoint within a tradition, one may appeal to considerations – for example, the teachings of a sacred text or a type of religious experience – the force of which only those who already share one's religious perspective are likely to recognize.

Understanding philosophy of religion as a matter of adopting a certain standpoint of reflection allows us to recognize that one and the

same thinker may adopt different standpoints on different occasions depending upon his or her interests and/or audience. In this regard, the following image might be helpful. Imagine a thinker with two hats. When she dons one, she is a religious philosopher. When she dons the other, she is a philosopher of religion. Given a thinker's ability to switch standpoints in this way, we need not for our purposes get bogged down with questions of the following sort: "Is thinker *X* a religious philosopher or a philosopher of religion?"; or "Is this text a work of religious philosophy or philosophy of religion?" If on a particular occasion the individual is engaged in the exercise of public reason, then it is material with which we can do philosophy of religion.

For example, in the work of both Thomas Aquinas (a twelfth-century Christian thinker) and Ramanuja (a twelfth-century Hindu thinker), support for views is provided both by appeal to scripture and by arguments grounded in public reason. Unless we share the author's confidence in the scriptural authority of the relevant text (the Christian Bible in the first case and the *Upanishads* in the second) we will be unmoved by their appeals to scripture. However, we can entertain the force of their arguments made from the standpoint of public reason. In the latter case, they and we are doing philosophy of religion.

C2. Philosophy of Religion and other Academic Approaches to the Study of Religion

In the preceding section, the approach to the study of religion characteristic of philosophy of religion was defined by its emphasis on public reason. However, philosophy of religion is not the only approach to the study of religion in which forms of public reason are predominant. In the past century, another broad interdisciplinary cluster of approaches has gained prominence.

---

[9] At various points in this book, a more nuanced treatment of public reason will be required. For example, it will become important (in sections III and IV) to distinguish the constructive vs critical roles that public reason might play – for example, when it is being used to support a claim as opposed to being turned on itself to reveal its own limitations (perhaps to make room for an alternate source of truth). Questions will also be raised (especially in section VIII) about the adequacy of this notion of public reason itself, given the way our reasoning may seem always to be situated, or contextualized, by factors such as our gender and sociohistorical setting. However, the notion of public reason is an important place to begin a discussion of philosophical thinking about religion, and most of the authors of the selections contained herein as well as the historical figures they discuss are committed to the usefulness of some forms of such reasoning.

Some of those within this cluster emphasize the research tools and methodologies of disciplines in the humanities – e.g., history, literature, linguistics, etc. – while others utilize the methodologies of the social sciences – e.g., sociology, psychology, and anthropology. The aim of these approaches is to better understand both the contemporary expression and historical evolution of religious traditions. There is no generally accepted overarching term for this group of approaches. In the United States, they are sometimes grouped together under the heading of "religious studies."[10] In these approaches scholars think it important to aspire to an empathetic sort of objectivity in the study of religion and so seek, like the philosopher of religion, to set aside temporarily whatever religious commitments – if any – that they have in order to reflect on religion from a standpoint outside that of any particular religious tradition.

Though philosophers of religion share with these other scholars a standpoint of reflection on religion defined by a commitment to public reason, they also differ in at least two important respects. First, there is a difference in the scope of reflection. As mentioned above, philosophy of religion focuses primarily on those aspects of religion of cognitive import – those that concern religious belief. This component is not ignored by scholars engaged in these other academic approaches to the study of religion, but their interests are not limited to this component. In these other approaches, all aspects of religion and their interconnections are legitimate objects of study. This broader work is proving to be increasingly valuable to philosophers of religion as they seek a better understanding of the context within which religious belief functions.

A second and more important difference between philosophy of religion and these other academic approaches is that scholars engaged in the latter often hold that an aspiration to objectivity in the study of religion requires not only that one seek a standpoint of reflection outside that of religion, but also that one not entertain questions about the truth or falsity of the claims made by religious persons. For example, one might say that from this standpoint of inquiry, one is more interested in understanding *how* belief in God structures the life of an individual or community rather than in the question of whether that belief might be true – i.e., whether God, in fact, exists. In this respect, the philosopher of religion is more like the religious philosopher, for the question of whether a particular religious belief is true is of fundamental importance. Thus the philosopher of religion wishes not only to understand what it means for a person to believe that God exists but also whether the considerations that might count in favor of such a belief outweigh those that might count against it.

To sum up, "philosophy of religion," as it will be conceived here, designates a subfield within the discipline of philosophy and so is an approach to the study of religion that focuses primarily on the cognitive component of religion – that which concerns religious belief. The approach is distinguished from the approach taken in religious philosophy insofar it restricts itself to examining religious belief from the standpoint of public reason. However, like the religious philosopher, the philosopher of religion is ultimately concerned with whether particular religious beliefs are true. In this respect, then, the approach differs from that taken by many other scholars engaged in the academic study of religion.

D.   On "East"/"Eastern" and "West"/"Western"

The principal aim of this book is to expand the approach often taken in colleges and universities to the study of philosophy of religion, which often focuses exclusively on topics that arise from reflection on beliefs central to Western brands of monotheism. Here the idea is to augment those materials with some reflection on Eastern religious thought. In addition to simply increasing awareness of and respect for diverse views, there are at least two ways in which this can prove to be

---

[10] Other terms with some currency include the "history of religions" (though not all such work is historical), or "comparative religion" (though not all such work is comparative), or the German term "*Religionswissenschaft*, or "systematic study of religion."

fruitful. First, the study of culturally diverse texts sometimes reveals significant cultural continuities, suggesting that distant human beings may grapple with similar questions in similar ways. Second, the study of such texts may on other occasions reveal important discontinuities, suggesting that human beings may answer the same question in interestingly different ways or that they are interested in different – but perhaps equally important – questions. In either case, whether the question remains the same or is altered, our perspective is enlarged in a productive manner. In philosophy, as in other areas of inquiry, one seeks to answer a pressing question, but sometimes in the process of seeking an answer, one may come to believe that one has been asking the wrong question.

Up to this point, I have been invoking the distinction between East (or Eastern) and West (or Western) as if it was unproblematic. Having reached the conclusion of this general introduction, it is now worth pausing to reflect on these nouns and their associated adjectives in order to be aware of their limitations. First, it is important to observe the directional nature of the labels. This reveals the fact that they derive historically from the preoccupations of Anglo-European thinkers several centuries ago, in relation to whom countries like India, China, and Japan lay to the East.[11] Thus, in adopting these labels, we are at least implicitly situating ourselves in a particular socio-historical perspective.

This initially may seem to be a mundane point, until one recalls that much of these lands to the east of Europe were at one time or another colonized by Anglo-Europeans (and then Americans). The significance of this is that whenever we define others in relation to ourselves – and especially when we are in a position to exercise power over the other – we need be aware that there is the danger of distorting the other in a way that serves our own purposes. So, for example, it seems clear historically that what was labeled "Eastern" by some came to be viewed as that which was contrary to the rationality and order allegedly characteristic of Western culture. This essentialist conception of peoples of the West and East provided support for colonial aspirations since it suggested that colonization was for the good of native peoples, even if they themselves were not capable of recognizing it as such.[12]

A little reflection also reveals that the directional nature of the labels "Eastern" and "Western" can be misleading. For example, Judaism, Christianity, and Islam are today often classified by scholars of religion as "Western" traditions, but all three originated in what we now call the "Middle East." Also, today the greatest concentration of Muslims in one place is neither in the West nor in the Middle East (contrary to popular perception) but rather in Indonesia. The question of Islam's place in this East–West scheme is further highlighted by the way in which many of its members have come to see themselves (and be seen by others) as critics of contemporary Western culture. The point to remember for the purposes of this book is that, as utilized here, the labels refer primarily to the way in which a group of traditions have exerted influence on one another in the course of their development and/or shared some original resources. Thus, the so-called "Western" religions of Judaism, Christianity, and Islam share a long history of mutual and cultural influence in the broad multi-cultural region now referred to as the "West." Likewise, largely because of the way ideas traveled with goods along a connected series of trade routes (including the famous Silk Road), the so-called "Eastern" religions – most notably, Hinduism, Buddhism, Daoism, and Confucianism – share a high level of mutual and cultural influence in the broad and multi-cultural region referred to as the "East."

In suggesting that the labels "Eastern" and "Western" point to some overlapping history and mutual influence, it is important that one not assume uniformity amongst those that share one of these broad labels or discontinuity between those falling under different labels. For example, at times some of our authors will discuss a

---

11   The original labels employed by Anglo-European scholars were "Occident"/"Occidental ("where the sun sets") for "West"/"Western" and "Orient"/"Oriental" ("where the sun rises") for "East"/"Eastern." The latter originally included what we now regard as the "Middle East."

12   This argument is made forcefully in the contemporary classic, *Orientalism*, by Edward Said (New York: Vintage Books, 1979).

view of God that they take to be shared by most Western monotheists – i.e., most Jews, Christians, and Muslims. Even if they are correct in their generalization, this is not to deny that there are other important differences between members of these Western religious traditions. Nor should the labels for the various religious traditions themselves be taken to imply that every member of those traditions thinks about God the same way. Every religion contains a wealth of diversity (and some an embarrassment of such riches!), much of which cannot be represented in this or any single book. Given the internal diversity of religious traditions, it may turn out, for example, that some Christians think about God in a way that is more similar to the view held by some Hindus than to that of their fellow Christians (or vice versa). As should be clear by now, the problem to be wary of here is one that accompanies the use of any general term to classify a group of people. Since the use of some such

terms is probably unavoidable, the point is simply to be careful to monitor one's accompanying assumptions.

Finally, it is important to recognize that the terms "Eastern" and "Western" are not meant to function as exhaustive categories. Not all religions can be classified as either Eastern or Western. This is true not only of some that seem to sit on the border of the classification – e.g., Sikhism – but also for some that seem completely outside the scheme – e.g., the religions of native peoples of Africa, the Americas (North, Central, and South), and the Pacific Islands, amongst others. Thus, not only does this book not pretend to give a comprehensive treatment of Western and Eastern views, it also does not aim to be fully global in its treatment of religion.

With these cautionary comments and qualifications behind us, let us now turn to our first philosophical task – the attempt to characterize Ultimate Sacred Reality.

Section II
Characterizing Ultimate Sacred Reality

Introduction

A. General Introduction to the Section

Before a religious worldview can be evaluated, one must understand it. Thus, one important aspect of doing philosophy of religion is the explication and clarification of religious claims. The most pivotal of these claims concern the nature of that Ultimate Sacred Reality around which the religion is organized. Perhaps most familiarly, this sacred reality may be conceived of as God, so we begin with that conception of sacred reality, both as it has been conceived traditionally by thinkers in Western religions, and with some reformulations of that view that have been offered more recently.

The concept of a god, or supernatural personal being to whom one owes devotion, can be found in a great many religious traditions. Worldwide, it is perhaps the most common form of religious belief. Some believe that there are many gods (*polytheism*), while others hold that there is but one supreme God (*monotheism*). Though all traditions organized around the concept of a deity or deities are, strictly speaking, *theistic* (*theos* = god/God), I will hereafter follow the widely accepted convention of using "theism" as a synonym for "monotheism."

Most of the discussion of God in this and later sections derives from reflection on a concept of the divine that is shared by many varieties of Judaism, Christianity, and Islam. It is perhaps not surprising that this concept of sacred reality has occupied center-stage in the West, for it is these religious traditions that have exerted and continue to exert the greatest influence on Western cultures. The similarity in how God is conceived across these traditions is due to several factors. First, they derive from a common narrative – the story of Abraham, a Semitic man who responds faithfully to a divine call. The God of this narrative begins to come into sharper focus with the rise of the Hebrew prophets (c. 900–500 BCE), who emphasize God's oneness, supremacy, justice, love, and universal providence – themes that receive further refinement in the teachings of Jesus, Paul of Tarsus, and the Prophet Muhammad. Finally, in similar fashion, later Jewish, Christian, and Muslim thinkers eventually turned to ancient Greek philosophy in an attempt to better articulate the nature of God as depicted in their respective sacred texts.

Despite the focus here on how God is conceived in these traditions, it is important to recognize that they are not alone in endorsing theism. For example, many Hindus and members of the influential Yoruba religion of Africa are theists (though members of both believe that the one God is manifested in a multitude of divine forms).

B. The God of Theism

B1. The Attributes of God

In the first selection of this section, "The Divine Attributes: What is God Like?," the authors – Peterson, Hasker, Reichenbach, and Basinger (hereafter, Peterson *et al.*) – discuss a cluster of attributes associated with the traditional theistic concept of God. Many of these will be familiar to readers with some exposure to theistic traditions. Others may seem not only unfamiliar, but also strange because of the way they have been abstracted away from their more concrete religious context.

For example, members of theistic religions (theists) commonly believe that God is perfect. Traditionally, philosophers who aim to explicate and clarify the claim that God is perfect have concluded that a perfect God must have certain attributes, attributes that many theists may not themselves have considered. In particular, philosophers have traditionally held that God's perfection consists partly in virtue of the distinctive *kind* of existence God enjoys and that this helps explain the more familiar belief that God exists eternally. According to this line of thought, God's existence is wholly unlike our own because the idea of God is the idea of a self-existent and necessary being. This means that if God exists at all (the authors intend this to remain an open question), then God exists in a very robust and unusual way. That is, if God exists, then God's existence is unlike our own in that it does not depend upon anyone or anything else, so it would be impossible for anything ever to bring God into existence or to end God's existence. God must have always existed and will always exist, if God exists at all. This, says Anselm of Canterbury (1033–1109), follows from the concept of God as a supreme being, for if God's existence derived from that of another being, God would not be supreme (see "How the Supreme Nature Exists through Itself"). Further, from this claim about God's necessary existence, Avicenna (or Ibn Sina, 980–1037) derives the claim that God must be one, for two such beings could not be distinguished from one another (see "Of the Unicity of God").

According to Thomas Aquinas (1225–74), the extraordinary difference between a perfect God and ourselves requires that language about such a being be used analogically (see "Thinking and Speaking about God by Analogy"). Peterson *et al.* survey several claims about God's nature associated with the view that God is a personal agent and thus engaged in activities and characterized by attributes that we may understand by analogy based on our own experience. For example, God is said to create, sustain, and govern the world. As the authors highlight, *how* God creates – *ex nihilo*, or "out of nothing" – is a distinctive feature of this brand of theism. It supports the central contention that God and the created world are absolutely distinct and, further, that while the existence and nature of the world are entirely dependent upon God, God's existence and nature are in no way dependent upon the world.

The God of classical theism is also said to be all-powerful (ominipotent), all-knowing (omniscient), and perfectly good (omnibenevolent). As Peterson *et al.* discuss, exactly how these "omni" attributes should be understood has been a fertile area of philosophical reflection. For example, should we say that there are absolutely no limits on what an omnipotent being can do, or say, following Aquinas, that an omnipotent being can do whatever is logically possible (see "The Omnipotence of God") and consistent with its own nature? These debates are significant both because of questions about the internal coherence of the concept of God and because of the implications of accepting a particular interpretation for other issues in theology and philosophy. As we shall see in section V, how the attribute of omnipotence is interpreted is especially important in relation to the question of whether the existence of evil is consistent with the existence of God.

B2. God and Sexism

A religious tradition cannot persist over time as the same tradition without a considerable degree of continuity in how it conceives of Ultimate Sacred Reality. However, a tradition's conception of the sacred is often challenged both from within and from without. In response to a challenge, one may seek to defend the existing framework of belief, reject it, or seek to reshape it in what is perceived to be a more suitable fashion.

One important challenge faced by theistic traditions is reflected in feminist concerns that God is conceived in a patriarchal fashion in those traditions. The charge here is that humans have made God in their own image – in particular, that they have attributed to God those masculine traits that have typically been prized in their male-led families and societies. As a result, religion functions to reinforce those existing social structures that keep women in subordinate positions and limit their life prospects. Though the scope of feminist inquiry in philosophy of religion has widened in recent years (more on this in our final section), questioning the presence of sexism in the very concept of God remains a central concern. In "The Female Nature of God," Rosemary Radford Ruether raises this concern and evaluates three possible ways of responding to it. According to the first, one attempts to supplement the existing conception of God by recovering from within the tradition the suppressed attribution of characteristically feminine traits to God. A second, more radical strategy involves the wholesale rejection of traditional theism in favor of a Goddess-centered religion. Ruether argues that both such strategies are problematic and urges that one must move to a conception of the divine that is beyond gender characterization.

B3.   God as Responsive Co-Creator

In "God as Creative-Responsive Love," John B. Cobb, Jr and David Ray Griffin fault traditional theism for the way it has valued absolute independence – reflected in the view that while the world is dependent on God, God is in no way dependent on the world. The result, they contend, is a God incapable of being genuinely responsive to the needs of the created cosmos. Following Alfred North Whitehead (1861–1947), they attempt to correct this picture by proposing that God's nature is dipolar, or comprised of two aspects. Under one aspect, God is independent and unchanging – for example, God's aim to realize goodness remains constant. However, God's second aspect is very much dependent upon and thus constantly changing in relation to the cosmos. It is this emphasis on change, or process, that gives rise to the label "process philosophy/theology" for this view. God not only acts upon the world, but the world also acts upon God. This mutual dependence is made possible because the world is internally related to God rather than radically distinct, on this view. The metaphor sometimes

used by process thinkers for this panentheist ("all-in-God") view is to think of God as the all-pervading soul of the universe and the universe itself as God's body. As in the model of the human person it draws upon, the two mutually depend upon and constantly influence one another.

Though process thinkers like Cobb and Griffin often characterize God as having many of the same attributes – perfect knowledge, goodness, and power – as found in the traditional theistic model, it is important to notice the difference in how these attributes are understood. To give just one important example, God's power, on this view, is not the unilateral controlling power to bring about whatever is logically possible. Rather, what transpires in the world is co-created by God and the world's individuals, each of which possesses its own measure of creative power. Perfect power, on this model, is thus persuasive power, the expression of God's desire to draw individuals toward the realization of goodness. This is significant, for persuasive power – unlike absolute controlling power – can be thwarted, with the result that, on this view, how things ultimately play out in the universe depends much more on how individuals respond to God's call.

C.   Some Eastern Conceptions of Ultimate Sacred Reality

C1.   Brahman According to Hindu Vedanta

The roots of contemporary Indian culture extend to at least the second millennium BCE. Many religions have originated in India, and today it continues to be one of the world's most religiously diverse cultures. Hinduism is often regarded as the principal religious expression of this diverse culture and is by far the largest religious group in contemporary India. However, the term "Hinduism" is perhaps best understood as an umbrella term that refers to a cluster of views and practices that is itself very diverse. As Sushanta Sen suggests in "The Vedic-Upanisadic Concept of Brahman," one important factor lending historical unity to this loosely affiliated cluster is a commitment to the authority of a set of sacred texts, the *Vedas*.

Some of the diversity to be found within Hinduism can be illustrated by looking at just one of its schools of philosophical thought: Vedanta. Vedanta (literally, "end of the *Veda*") is named for the way it took the later Vedic texts, the *Upanishads* (900–300 BCE), to be the highest expression of religious understanding. As Sen explains, in the *Upanishads*, hints of a unity behind the many gods discussed in previous Vedic texts are pursued in earnest. Also, whereas the earlier form of Vedic religion stressed the significance of right ritual, the authors of the *Upanishads* emphasized the need to pursue a spiritual path involving a set of meditative practices aimed at fostering a personal realization of the true nature of one's own deepest self, or *atman*, and, through this, a realization of the true nature of the one Ultimate Sacred Reality. Finally, the *Upanishads* introduced the interrelated doctrines of *karma* and rebirth (*samsara*), maintaining that how one lives determines one's place in a continuing cycle of lives until one is liberated through spiritual realization (more on *karma* and rebirth in sections V and VI).

Though Vedanta thinkers share a common focus, they divide into sub-schools based on disagreements about the nature of the one Ultimate Sacred Reality, or Brahman. Some Vedanta thinkers are theists and so conceive of Brahman as a personal God distinct from the cosmos and other selves, much like Western theists. Others are panentheists and so endorse a model similar to that held by process theists. However, according to Advaita, or "Non-dual," Vedantists like Sen, Brahman is the only one true reality. Thus we are mistaken insofar as we perceive the world to consist of many independently existing objects and selves. On this pantheist (all-is-God) view, our own true and most fundamental self as *atman*, and, in fact, everything else that exists, is Brahman. Though Brahman may appear to human selves as a personal God (for example, as *Isvara*) in religious practice, Brahman's true self is non-personal insofar as it transcends all such human categories of thought (also note Sen's discussion of how Brahman's creative act and thus ongoing relation to the world is typically conceived differently than in Western theism).

Responding to some objections to this brand of monism, Shankara (Samkara) (788–820), one of the founding thinkers of Advaita Vedanta, maintains that the distinctions we draw between individual objects and selves are only apparent.

They are, he says, analogous to the apparent but ultimately unreal distinction between a wave and the ocean of which it is a part or the air inside a clay jar with the air outside the jar (see "Everything Has Its Self in Brahman"). Lastly, though Brahman, on the Advaita Vedanta view, is sometimes characterized as "Pure Consciousness" and so seems to be attributed with a mental life of some sort, it is important to realize that this consciousness is conceived as lacking those individuating kinds of mental states that we typically associate with a personal being – e.g., wishes, desires, beliefs, etc. (For further discussion of this kind of awareness and whether humans can at least temporarily achieve it, see Robert K. C. Forman's "Mystical Knowledge: Knowledge by Identity" in section IV.) Again, in all schools of Vedanta, the spiritual goal is to achieve a realization of the divine through a deeper realization of one's own true self, or *atman* – either by realizing that one's *atman* reflects, or is an image of, Brahman's divine nature on the theistic model, or by realizing that it is identical to Brahman on the pantheist model.

C2.   Emptiness as Ultimate Sacred Reality in Mahayana Buddhism

Though the details of his life are difficult to confirm, Siddhartha Gautama (also sometimes referred to as "Shakyamuni," or the sage of the Shakya clan) was likely born in the sixth century BCE and spent most of his life in a region that now encompasses southern Nepal and Northeast India. According to tradition, Gautama became the Buddha (literally, the "Awakened One") after an extended spiritual quest. After his death, disputes eventually arose over how best to interpret some of his teachings, leading to a division between what is now referred to as Theravada and Mahayana Buddhism (as well as many subdivisions within the latter). Though Buddhism gradually lost much of its influence in India, it became a powerful migrating religion. In its Theravadan form, it came to exert tremendous influence over Southeast Asia (e.g., Sri Lanka and Thailand), while the Mahayana forms made their greatest impact on North and Far Eastern Asia (e.g., Tibet, China, Korea, and Japan).

Given their proximity in time and place, it is not surprising that the Buddha's teachings are in important respects similar to the teachings of the authors of the *Upanishads*. Both sought to address the experience of *dukkha*, a word often translated as "suffering" but one whose central meaning is perhaps better rendered as "disease," a sense that one's aims in life are misaligned and consequently ultimately unsatisfying. Also according to both, the experience of *dukkha* was extended over a cycle of lives (*samsara*) governed by the principle of *karma*. Finally, both diagnosed that one's *dukkha* was fueled by a misdirected form of desire and that the way to free oneself from this desire was to come to a realization of one's true self through meditative practice.

What, then, distinguished the Buddha's teaching from that of others so that the religious tradition founded on his teachings eventually came to be regarded as distinct from what we know now as Hinduism? The central reason appears to lie in the rejection by him and his followers of the authority of the Vedic teachings on several topics, including its endorsement of a caste-structured society. For our purposes, it will be useful to focus on two additional ways he departed from the teachings of those texts. First, given the prominence of creation stories in both the early and late Vedic texts, it is striking that the Buddha seemed to find the question of the world's origin an unhelpful distraction and the notion of a supreme deity spiritually irrelevant. Second, and perhaps more importantly, the Buddha rejected the notion of self as *atman* that lies at the heart of much Hindu thinking both about human selves and about the divine Self.

Atman in classical Hindu thought is the notion of an unchanging and independently existing self. In teaching *anatman*, or "no-self," the Buddha denied that our true selves are unchanging and independently existing *things*. Instead, he taught that we are a collection of ever-changing *processes* existing momentarily as part of *pratitya-samutpada*, or "dependent co-origination" – a wider causally interdependent web of such processes. According to the Buddha, attachment to the notion of our ego-selves as *atman* is what generates those mis-directed desires leading to *dukkha*. Given this diagnosis, the answer to the human predicament lies in an experiential grasp of one's nature as *anatman*, leading to an elimination of those ego-driven

desires generating *dukkha*. The extinction of such desires is known as *nirvana* and is said to yield genuine fulfillment and compassion. Final liberation from the rebirth cycle is said to await the enlightened person at death.

The Buddha's teaching suggests that *nirvana* is made possible by grasping something about the fundamental character of reality – in particular, the ever-changing and interdependent nature of our selves. As Christopher Ives explains in "Emptiness in Mahayana Buddhism," some early interpreters of the Buddha's teachings concluded that at least some of the constituents (*dharmas*) of the interdependent process of *pratitya-samutpada* must have an independent and non-changing existence. At the very least, they surmised, *nirvana* itself must be a reality that stands in opposition to the realm of ceaseless change and rebirth (*samsara*), making liberation from that realm possible. From our own perspective, we can see how the normal way words are used might naturally encourage such an interpretation, for the very phrase "experience of nirvana" suggests that nirvana is a *something* to be experienced, and so perhaps not so unlike God or Brahman. Nagarjuna (second century) saw this way of thinking as threatening to undermine the very heart of the Buddha's teaching. His attempt to return to what he regarded as the original insight of the Buddha became the cornerstone of most subsequent Mahayana Buddhist thought.

Like his Western counterparts, Nagarjuna made use of the best available conceptual and logical tools at his disposal. However, unlike most Western thinkers, who often use philosophical tools in a constructive attempt to lend further clarity to descriptions of the sacred, Nagarjuna's use of such tools was predominantly negative. That is, for him, they serve primarily to reveal faulty ways of thinking (see "An Analysis of Nirvāṇa"). According to Nagarjuna, analysis reveals that *nirvana* is not a realm distinct from *samsara* to which one is attempting to escape or an independently existing thing of any sort. As Ives explains, Nagarjuna borrows the notion of emptiness (*sunyata*) to convey this point. Our selves and all other constituents of reality are empty. To realize *nirvana* is thus to realize the emptiness of all reality. This does not mean that *nothing* at all exists, only that what exists is empty of a particular kind of existence. No *things* exist, where "things" are understood to be changeless and capable of existing apart from one another. This emptiness of reality is at the same time portrayed as functioning positively (like the emptiness of a bell). Here, emptiness is said to be a dynamic fullness – the ground, or foundation, of the universe's endless creative becoming. Like the two faces of a coin, these two faces of Emptiness constitute the religious ultimate in Mahayana Buddhism.

C3.   Ultimate Sacred Reality in Chinese Philosophy

Though Buddhism received a cold shoulder when it first made contact with the ancient and already highly developed Chinese culture (near the beginning of the Common Era), it eventually worked its way into the Chinese mindset and flourished for many centuries. In large part, this was due to the way its teachings came to be viewed as complementing China's own religious philosophies. Daoism (Taoism) and Confucianism are commonly regarded as the two principal forms of indigenous Chinese religious philosophy, but in "Reality and Divinity in Chinese Philosophy," Chung-Ying Cheng presents these two traditions as an outgrowth of an even older tradition of thought. This older tradition of thought is expressed in the *Zhouyi*, the earliest strata of the text more commonly known as the *Yijing* (*I-Ching*), or *Book of Changes* (c. 1200 BCE).

The *Zhouyi* itself is a resource for divination. That is, it developed in conjunction with a practice used to answer questions about the future. First used exclusively by members of the emperor's court to answer questions vital to the empire's well-being (e.g., "Will we be attacked?" or "Will the prince have a son?"), the practice originally involved carving questions onto animal bones or tortoise shells and then baking them until cracks appeared. These cracks would be interpreted as answers to the questions posed. Later, the practice involved a "reading" of a set of plant (yarrow) stalks or coins that had been cast and so became more widely used by the populace (and is still used worldwide by some today). The *Zhouyi* evolved as a manual for how to read

these castings; thus it is not a book of philosophy in a straightforward sense. The text is structured around a set of sixty-four abstract figures composed of lines, known as "hexagrams" (which, in turn, are composed of another set of figures known as "trigrams"). These hexagrams represent the possible outcomes of the casting process. Their components and the manner of their construction are symbolic. Some of these symbolic meanings refer to fundamental forces and principles that govern the behavior of the universe. It is in this sense, then, that the *Zhouyi* can be said to express, or presuppose, a theory of reality. Cheng refers to this ancient strand of Chinese thought as the *Yizhuan* theory of reality because it is discussed in the later *Yizhuan* commentary on the *Zhouyi*.

Like some of the previous views discussed here, the *Yizhuan* theory of reality is non-theistic insofar as Ultimate Sacred Reality is not depicted as a personal being (though, as Cheng mentions, a brand of theism did exist in China for a period of time alongside it). According to this ancient line of thought, change is the fundamental character of reality. Mapping the forms of change and understanding the principles behind it becomes the central philosophical endeavor, for successful living and human fulfillment depend upon one's ability to navigate these transformations. According to the *Yizhuan* theory of reality, the root and inexhaustible source of all transformations is *taiji*, the Great Ultimate.

The continual origination of new events from the Great Ultimate is governed by the alternating polar principles of *yin* and *yang*. The former is associated with qualities such as stillness, darkness, and softness; whereas the latter is associated with qualities like activity, brightness, and hardness. These forces interact at multiple levels and function to constitute the make-up of all that exists, each individual containing some mixture of the two. However, this constitution itself is constantly in flux, ebbing first in one direction, then recursively flowing back in the other. The *dao* (tao) is the way things come to be and behave according to *yin* and *yang*.

Two texts are central to the early (c. 500–300 BCE) formation of Daoism: the *Daodejing* (Tao-te-Ching) and *Zuangzi* (Chuang-tzu). Though there are interesting differences between them, they together share a view that, while clearly founded on the *Yizhuan* theory of reality, is also distinctive in some respects. As the name of the tradition suggests, it is the notion of the *dao* (already present in the earlier view but playing a subsidiary role) that occupies center-stage, taking on many of the attributes of the *taiji*. The *dao* is now both the power, or force, that gives rise to everything and the way, or manner, in which things naturally function and transform themselves. As the internal source of all, the *dao* is said to be empty (note the parallel with Mahayana Buddhism), for it is itself not any determinate thing but rather the power through which things become determinate.

As Cheng suggests, the teachings of Confucius (or Kongzi, 551–479 BCE) presuppose much of the *Yizhuan* theory of reality as background, but unlike the Daoists, Confucians focus their attention on the *dao* of human interaction within the framework of existing social roles and conventions. Discussion of the religious dimension of Confucianism is postponed until later in our text (section VIII).

C4. Orthodoxy vs Orthopraxy

Finally, it is important to note the following tendency in many forms of Far Eastern religion. While it is common in the West for religious persons to identify themselves and other religious persons as a member of a particular religion (e.g., as Jewish, Christian, or Muslim), this has been less common in countries like China and Japan. There are several reasons for this. First, unlike members of a Western tradition like Christianity, members of these traditions have historically been less inclined to identify themselves by reference to right religious belief, or *orthodoxy*. Though the form of their religious life may presuppose particular religious beliefs, the focus is often instead on right practice, or *orthopraxy* (in this respect, the traditions may be said to resemble some forms of Judaism). Second, given this emphasis on practice rather than belief, it has often been true that the practices of several different traditions are combined in a single life, with each perhaps dominating in a different sphere of that person's life. For exam-

ple, it would not have been surprising for a Chinese person to practice a combination of Daoism – in relation to nature – Confucianism – in relation to family and society – and Buddhism – in relation to death (or, similarly, for a Japanese person to practice Shinto, Confucianism, and Buddhism). Lastly, while disagreement between schools of thought has sometimes been vigorous in these cultures, there has often been a counterbalancing tendency to work toward a philosophical synthesis. A prime example of this tendency is seen in the work of the Neo-Confucian Zhou Dunyi (or Zhou Lianxi, 1017–73), who sought to reconcile the insights of Daoism and Confucianism (see "Non-Polar and Yet Supreme Polarity!").

Suggestions for Further Reading

Abe, Masao, *Zen and Western Thought*, ed. William R. LaFleur (Honolulu: University of Hawaii Press, 1985).

Basinger, David, *Divine Power in Process Theism: A Philosophical Critique* (Albany, NY: State University of New York Press, 1988).

Clooney, Francis X., *Theology after Vedanta: An Experiment in Comparative Theology* (Albany, NY: State University of New York Press, 1993).

Daly, Mary, *Beyond God the Father: Toward a Philosophy of Women's Liberation* (Boston: Beacon Press, 1973).

Deutsch, Eliot, *Advaita Vedanta: A Philosophical Reconstruction* (Honolulu: University of Hawaii Press, 1973).

Gowans, Christopher, *Philosophy of the Buddha* (New York: Routledge, 2003).

Hartshorne, Charles, *Omnipotence and Other Theological Mistakes* (Albany, NY: State University of New York Press, 1984).

Hasker, William, *God, Time, and Knowledge* (Ithaca, NY: Cornell University Press, 1989).

Huntington, C. W., Jr, *The Emptiness of Emptiness* (Honolulu: University of Hawaii Press, 1989).

Kasulis, T. P., *Zen Action, Zen Person* (Honolulu: University of Hawaii Press, 1981).

Kenney, Anthony, *The God of the Philosophers* (Oxford: Clarendon Press, 1979).

Leftow, Brian, *Time and Eternity* (Ithaca, NY: Cornell University Press, 1989).

Liu, JeeLoo, *An Introduction to Chinese Philosophy* (Malden, MA: Blackwell Publishing, 2006).

Loy, David, *Non-Duality: A Study in Comparative Philosophy* (New York: Humanity Books, 1988).

McFague, Sallie, *Models of God: Theology for an Ecological, Nuclear Age* (Philadelphia: Fortress Press, 1987).

Murti, T. R. V., *The Central Philosophy of Buddhism* (London: George Allen & Unwin, 1955).

Runzo, Joseph, "The Symbolism of Sex and the Reality of God," in *Love, Sex and Gender in the World Religions*, ed. Joseph Runzo and Nancy M. Martin (Oxford: Oneworld Publications, 2000).

Swinburne, Richard, *The Coherence of Theism* (Oxford: Clarendon Press, 1977).

Ward, Keith, *Images of Eternity: Concepts of God in Five Religious Traditions* (London: Darton, Longman, and Todd, Ltd, 1987).

Wierenga, Edward, *The Nature of God: An Inquiry into the Divine Attributes* (Ithaca, NY: Cornell University Press, 1989).

1

The Divine Attributes
What is God Like?

Michael Peterson, William Hasker, Bruce Reichenbach, and David Basinger

"Throw this salt in the water, and sit with me on the morrow."

So he did. He said to him, "Well, bring me the salt that you threw in the water last night." He looked for it, but could not find it as it was dissolved.

"Well, taste the water on this side. – How does it taste?"

"Salty,"

"Taste it in the middle. – How does it taste?"

"Salty."

"Taste it at the other end. – How does it taste?"

"Salty."

"Take a mouthful and sit with me." So he did.

"It is always the same."

He said to him, "You cannot make out what exists in it, yet it is there.

"It is this very fineness which ensouls all this world, it is the true one, it is the soul. *You are that*, Shvetaketu."

– Chandoya Upanishad[1]

In this text from the sacred writings of India, Shvetaketu and his father are probing a topic of intense interest to religious people – they are considering the *nature of God*. The answer they arrive at, to state it all too simply, is that God is the Being which is the inner reality of everything whatever. The salt is imperceptible to touch or vision; nevertheless it pervades every drop of the water. Similarly, God – or Being, or Brahman – is imperceptible to human senses, yet nevertheless completely pervades all of reality, including the inquirer who raises the question concerning the nature of God: "*You are that*, Shvetaketu."

"The Divine Attributes: What is God Like?" from *Reason and Religious Belief*, 3rd edition, by Michael Peterson, William Hasker, Bruce Reichenbach, and David Basinger (Oxford: Oxford University Press, 2003), pp. 58–75. By permission of Oxford University Press Inc.

[1] Eliot Deutsch and J. A. B. van Buitenen, *A Source Book of Advaita Vedanta* (Honolulu: University Press of Hawaii, 1971), pp. 14–16.

This question concerning the nature of God will occupy us throughout the present chapter. We shall not, however, concern ourselves primarily with the specific answers found by Shvetaketu and his father, and by others in the Hindu religious tradition. Rather, we shall focus most of our attention on a view of God known as *traditional theism*; this is the conception of God that has been held, with some variations, by the vast majority of thinkers in the great "theistic" religions of Judaism, Christianity, and Islam. But the view of God seen in the selection from the Upanishads, often termed *pantheism*, will not be neglected entirely; instead, it will be introduced from time to time as a contrast and an alternative to classical theism. We also, from time to time, explain and comment on another sort of conception of God that has recently become popular in some Christian and Jewish circles, a view known as *process theism*.

At this point, however, a question may be occurring to the reader. What is the point, it may be asked, of inquiring about the *nature* of God when, as yet, we have not even established whether there *is* any such being as God? Would it not make more sense first to show that there *is* a God, and then to discuss his (or her, or its) attributes or characteristics?

There is certainly some point to this, but consider a counter-question: if we have no idea *what* God is, then what sense is there in asking whether God *exists* or not? Lewis Carroll wrote a marvelous poem titled "The Hunting of the Snark," but it would make little sense to ask whether there really are snarks, because Carroll never tells us clearly what sort of creature a snark is supposed to be. If we are similarly "in the dark" as to God's nature, what meaning can we attach to the question whether God exists or not?

Probably the reason why the question of God's existence seems to most of us to make reasonably clear sense is that we *do* have an idea of what God is like, and when we ask whether God exists it is *that kind* of being whose existence is being asked about. Many readers [. . .], furthermore, will have a background of familiarity with the theistic religious traditions, and the conception of God's nature these readers will be presupposing is one which is at least fairly close to the traditional theism we will be studying in this chapter. Therefore it is important to become as clear as

possible about that conception of God before we proceed with other matters.

The right way to understand what is going on in this chapter, then, is this: we are not meaning to assert at this point that there *really* is a being, called God, with the various characteristics discussed throughout the chapter. Rather, we are *presenting a hypothesis* concerning the nature of a being whose existence will be investigated later on. The questions we will be asking are of two kinds: First, what is the conception of God's nature held by traditional theism (and, from time to time, the conceptions held by pantheism and by process theism)? Second, is this conception one that is *coherent* and *logically consistent*? If it should develop that a certain idea of God suffers from unreconcilable internal contradictions, then with regard to *that* conception we need proceed no further: a "God" whose nature can be stated only in contradictions cannot possibly exist, and to suppose that there is such a God as that is nonsense.

How will we arrive at the characteristics we attribute to God? In part, the question is one of history and tradition: the attributes considered here are some of those that *in fact* have been ascribed to God by theistic thinkers. Many such thinkers, however, would assert that there is more to it than this; they would claim that the theistic concept of God possesses an *internal unity and coherence* that goes far beyond any list of characteristics that merely happen to be ascribed to God in a certain tradition. An important source of this unity and coherence lies in the attributes considered in the next section.

Perfect and Worthy of Worship

In developing our conception of God, it would be foolish to overlook the fact that, above all, *God is a being who is the object of worship*. God's "worshipability" – or, to use a word that is no longer very familiar, his "worshipfulness" – is of primary religious importance, so that a conception of God that is lacking at this point is unacceptable regardless of other merits it may possess. Whatever else may be true of God, it must at least be said that *God is worthy of worship*.

But what sort of God is required, if God is to be worthy of our worship? The attitude or activity of worship is no doubt complex and difficult to describe completely and accurately. But there can be little doubt that worship, in the full sense of the term, is supposed to involve *total devotion* of the worshiper to the one worshiped. In worship we totally dedicate ourselves to God; we place ourselves at God's disposal completely and without reservation. Any hint of "bargaining" with God, any mental reservation by which, however subtly, we "keep our options open" with respect to a possible shift of allegiance detracts severely from the complete commitment that worship properly requires of us.

If this is the case we can ask, What must be true of God in order to make such unreserved devotion appropriate – in order, that is, for God to be "worthy of worship"? It is fairly clear, to begin with, that *God must be the greatest of all beings*. How could it be reasonable, or even plausible, to offer to God such total devotion if there exist other beings equally or even more worthy of our adulation, obedience, and so on? Under such circumstances as these, the response of a reasonable person would seem to be that God might, indeed, be entitled to a measure of honor and obedience because of his superiority to all others in the immediate vicinity – but not unreserved trust and honor and obedience, not total devotion. One would give to God his due, while keeping in mind the possibility that someone else might appear to whom even more was due. God would merit respect, honor, and a degree of obedience, but not worship.

God, then, must be the greatest of all beings. But we can go farther than this. Suppose it is plain to us that, though God is *in fact* the greatest of all beings, it is entirely possible that there should have been a being *superior* to God in one or several ways. Would this not inevitably detract from the unreserved devotion which is required for worship? As a matter of fact, we are supposing, God is the greatest of all beings, and there is nothing else in existence that could supplant him in our esteem. But things could have been different; there might very well have been some other being able to rival or even excel the God whom we worship. If so, then even in the midst of our worship, would we not occasionally find ourselves with a touch of regret for the greater things which might have been?

With this line of thought in mind, we are ready to appreciate the point of a definition of God offered by the great medieval Christian thinker Anselm (1033–1109). Addressing God, he said, "We believe that thou art a being than which nothing greater can be conceived."[2] He was saying, in effect, that God is so great that *no being is conceivable that would surpass God in any way*. God, in other words, is the *absolutely perfect being*. Not only is there in fact no other being equal or superior to God, but there could not be any such being, for God contains in himself all possible perfection and excellence.

This conception of God, as the *absolutely perfect being*, is one that, upon reflection, many religious persons have found to be deeply satisfying. It is, as we have seen, plausibly thought to be implied by the very idea of worship, and it lays the foundation for a conception of God that is very hard to challenge as inadequate.

"Perfect-being theology" (or "Anselmian" theology, as it is also called), can then be seen as a "binding thread" that ties together and unifies the discussion of the various attributes ascribed to God by traditional theism. Can we, indeed, go further and say (as Anselm himself seems to say) that the notion of God as the perfect being gives us all the guidance we need in setting forth the divine attributes, so that our whole conception of God can be, as it were, woven in its entirety from this single thread?

Probably not, for several reasons. For one thing, although the idea of God as the perfect being has strong intuitive appeal, it is by no means the case that different theologians, even from the same religious tradition, will always agree on which conception of God's attributes has the effect of portraying God as "more perfect" than another. For example, it seemed clear to Anselm, as to Augustine (354–430) and most other ancient and medieval theologians, that in order to be perfect God must be *impassible* – that is, God must be incapable of emotion, and in particular incapable of feeling any sorrow or suffering as a result of the afflictions of his creatures. Since

---

[2]   *St Anselim: Basic Writings*, tr. S. N. Deane (La Salle, Ill.: Open Court, 1962), p. 7 [see also "Truly There is a God," p. 141 below].

suffering is negative, a harm to the being which undergoes it, a perfect being must be *incapable* of suffering. More recently, however, many theologians have rebelled against the notion of an "impassible" God, insisting that God's perfection, and in particular his attributes of love and sympathy, positively require that he be capable of suffering along with his creatures. Clearly, we have here a major disagreement, and one that will not readily be settled by further discussions about the meaning of "perfect" as applied to God.

It should also be realized that in setting forth God's attributes we cannot possibly ignore the religious and theological tradition within which any given theology operates. If, for instance, one were to offer to the Jewish religious community a conception of God radically at variance with that which is found in the Hebrew Bible and in Jewish tradition, that conception would not be warmly received no matter how plausible a case one could make for the "perfection" of God so conceived. An interesting historical example of this is the philosopher Baruch de Spinoza (1632–77). Born a Jew, he was excommunicated from the synagogue for his "heretical" conception of God, which was in fact closer to pantheism than to traditional Jewish theism. As we have noted, intuitions about perfection may vary, and a philosopher of religion who is seeking to apply that notion would do well to pay attention to the conception of God that actual religious communities have found best to represent perfection and worshipfulness.

A further consideration that must guide our application of the notion of divine perfection is that of *logical consistency and coherence*. As was already noted, any conception of God that is supposed to represent an actual being must at least meet the requirement of logical consistency. To be sure, a set of divine attributes that are logically inconsistent could not possibly be part of the description of a perfect being, so this criterion may already be included in the very idea of "perfect-being" theology. But while this reasoning may be valid, it is also true that humans can be quite ingenious in imagining and ascribing to God seemingly marvelous characteristics that in fact are logically inconsistent. It is important, then, to carefully investigate the logical consistency of the various attributes we wish to ascribe to God.

Necessary and Self-Existent

We begin with a pair of attributes that at first may seem abstract and difficult to grasp, yet are important for pointing out the fundamental difference, according to traditional theism, between God and everything else whatsoever. First, consider *self-existence*. It is a familiar thought to us that for many things – especially living creatures of all kinds – it may take energy and often effort simply for the thing to remain in existence. We live our lives "from within," and when the inner vitality needed to do this becomes weak we feel our own existence to be imperiled and insecure. But we also depend on external beings and circumstances in various ways for our existence. Other beings brought us into existence, and we depend on food, water, air, and so on, to sustain us in existence. Furthermore, we are all too aware of various things that might damage or destroy our existence; in a sense, then, we are dependent on the *non*occurrence of these sorts of things for our continued life and well-being.

Now, consider the idea of a being that is dependent on other things in none of these ways. It owes nothing to any other being for its origin or sustenance, and it is entirely incapable of being threatened, harmed, or destroyed by anything else whatsoever. Such an entity would exist wholly "from within," entirely "on its own steam." It would be, in a word, self-existent.

Now we introduce two additional terms: *necessary* and *contingent*. To say something is contingent is to say that it depends on things or circumstances other than itself: contingency plans are plans for what may or may not be done, depending on other things that may or may not happen. If on the other hand a being is not contingent in any way and it will exist regardless of anything that may happen to other things or circumstances, then its existence is inevitable, inescapable. It is, in other words, a *necessary being*, a being that *depends on nothing but itself, and, given that it exists, its nonexistence, either in the past or in the future, is absolutely impossible.*

It is very clear that God, as conceived by traditional theism, is a necessary and self-existent being in the senses I have just explained. God is eternal; no other being is relevant to his coming into existence, since he never in fact came into existence, and nothing whatever can in any way threaten or endanger God's existence. It is, then, simply impossible that God should not exist. We further note that God's necessity and self-existence are essential elements in his perfection; it seems clear that God is greater if he depends on nothing outside himself than if he were so dependent.

These characteristics of necessity and self-existence fundamentally distinguish God from all other things in existence. In particular, there is nothing in the natural world, the world revealed to us by the sciences, about which it is at all plausible to say that it is necessary and self-existent. All the familiar things of everyday life – people and animals, cars and houses, trees and mountains, stars and galaxies – come into being and pass away, and are clearly contingent beings. Even the fundamental constituents of matter – the so-called "elementary particles" – are not immutable but form, disappear, and are changed into others, as attested by high-energy physics. According to the Big Bang theory (now a consensus view among cosmologists), it seems that the very matter-energy of the universe itself had an origin. So if there is anything at all other than God that is necessary and self-existent, we have no idea what it might be and no reason to suppose that anything of the sort exists at all.

[. . .]

Personal and Free Creator

We now turn to some attributes that are more familiar to ordinary religious people. To say that God is *personal* is to say at least the following things: God has *knowledge and awareness*; God *performs actions*; God is *free* in the actions he performs; and God can *enter into relationships* with persons other than himself. These requirements seem minimal, in that a God lacking in any of them would seem *not* to be fully personal; on the other hand, if God does meet these requirements then it would seem appropriate to describe God as "personal" even though there may be many respects in which God is very different from the human persons we know.

From the standpoint of theism it seems evident that personality, or personhood, should be considered as a perfection of God. Many of the finest things we know – love, intelligence, creativity, and moral goodness, for example – are attributes exclusively of persons, and if God were not personal he would be debarred from possessing any of these excellences. There is also the extremely important point that for many theists worship, and the religious life generally, are conceived in terms of a *personal relationship* with God; thus if God were *not* personal their entire idea of the religious life would collapse.

God, according to traditional theism, is also the *creator* of all things other than himself. The idea of creation is important in all the theistic faiths, and it seems essential to the idea of an absolutely perfect being that, if there are beings other than God in existence, God should be their creator. God's status as creator ensures his superiority, mastery, and ownership over all the things he has created in a way that could hardly be done otherwise. God is said, furthermore, to have created "out of nothing" (Latin, *ex nihilo*). This is not to be understood as if "nothing" were the name of some sort of mysterious "stuff" out of which God created the universe. Instead, to say that creation is out of nothing means that there was no material out of which God created; rather, all things other than God exist solely because he wills them to exist and have no other basis at all for their existence. Creation out of nothing contrasts with, and is superior to, two other modes in which the production of things might be imagined. It is superior to production from pre-existing materials because in the latter case God's act of creating would be dependent upon, and probably to some extent limited by, the materials he had to work with. (There would also be the question of how to account for the existence of the materials.) It also is superior to creation *ex Deo*, "out of God's own being," because this would tend to compromise the absolute distinction between creator and creature that is the hallmark of theistic metaphysics.

The God of classical theism is not only the creator but also the *sustainer* of finite things, which is to say that created things are *totally dependent on God for their existence from moment to moment*. A dramatic but not inaccurate way of putting this is to say that, were God for a single instant to completely forget about his creation, in that instant the entire creation would collapse into nothingness.

God, furthermore, enjoys *freedom* in creating, sustaining, and governing the world. To say that God is free means that God cannot be forced, constrained, or controlled by anything outside of himself. Unlike creatures, God has no need to adjust himself to an environment; rather, all environments exist only in virtue of his creating and sustaining activity. Moreover, God has the freedom to *choose* what sort of world to create and how to dispose of that world. To be sure, given God's essential goodness, it is impossible that God should choose anything that conflicts with that goodness. But this leaves God still with a very wide range of possibilities, among which he chooses the ones he will bring about. Indeed, it has generally been held that God was perfectly *free either to create a world or to refrain from creating*; prior to creation, there were no creatures to whom the "right to exist" was owed, nor would the goodness of creation "add to" the greatness and goodness of God in such a way that creating was for him necessary and inevitable. Thus, the decision to create was itself a free and generous choice on God's part.

These attributes fundamentally distinguish the theistic God from God as conceived in pantheism. To see this, we will consider briefly an especially interesting form of pantheism, the *advaita vedanta* of the Hindu thinker Shankara (788–820). The sole ultimate reality, according to Shankara, is Brahman, which is wholly non-empirical, entirely beyond ordinary human experience, though its existence and nature can be grasped intuitively through yogic meditation. Our ordinary experience, to be sure, indicates that both the world of nature and individual human personalities exist as independent realities. Such experience, however, is to be viewed as we view dream experiences: within the dream, we cannot help but consider the objects of the dream experiences as real, but once we awaken this is seen to have been an illusion. Similarly, in our ordinary state of ignorance we cannot help regarding the objects and persons of everyday life as real, but from the higher, enlightened standpoint, all of this – including one's own personal existence! – is seen to be illusory. Indeed, this "ignorance"

is the principal obstacle that needs to be overcome in order to reach true spiritual illumination.

Brahman, then, is *not* personal; rather, it is the ultimate, impersonal "true being" that is the reality behind all the illusory appearances of the world. Other versions of pantheism describe the situation somewhat differently, but for none of them is God the creator, for creation implies a distinction between God and the universe that is alien to pantheism. Furthermore, an impersonal "being" cannot *act* and therefore cannot be *free* in its actions; rather, it simply and changelessly *is*.

The God of process theism is like the God of traditional theism in being personal. But the relationship between God and the universe is considerably different. Process theism rejects both the idea of creation *ex nihilo* and the radical distinction between God and the world posited by traditional theism. Process theism's conception of God's relation to the world is best expressed by saying that the world is *God's body*, through which he lives his life as we live our lives through our bodies. This means that God and the universe are not wholly distinct from each other, as for classical theism; rather, all finite things, including human beings, are in a sense included in God's own being. Perhaps the best way of conceiving this is to imagine that each individual cell in a human body is possessed of its own consciousness and awareness, however limited, of what is happening to it and what is going on around it Then imagine that these individual "cell-consciousnesses" are, as it were, caught up and included in the *unified* consciousness that is the "mind" of the entire body, a consciousness that both transcends and includes each one of them. In some such way as this, each of us is a "cell" in the body of God, and because of this God is able literally to *share*, in a most intimate way, in all of our experiences, our joys and our sorrows. In the words of A. N. Whitehead (1861–1947), the philosopher whose works inspired process theism, "God is the great companion – the fellow-sufferer who understands."[3]

All of this means that the relationship between God and the universe is conceived very differently

---

[3]   Alfred North Whitehead, *Process and Reality*, ed. David Ray Griffin and Donald W. Sherburne, Corrected ed. (New York: Free Press, 1978), p. 351.

in process theism than in traditional theism. In traditional theism, there is a *one-sided dependence* of the universe upon God, whereas in process theism the relationship is better described as one of *interdependence and mutuality* between God and the universe. Whitehead went so far as to say, "It is as true to say that God transcends the World, as that the World transcends God. It is as true to say that God creates the World, as that the World creates God."[4] Since God needs his body through which to live, even as we need our bodies, it must be concluded that *God can never be without a body* – that is, without a universe. That does not necessarily mean that the present universe is, like God, without beginning and without end, though this is a possibility. But if, as scientific evidence seems to suggest, our present physical universe had a beginning in time, we may be assured that before it there was another universe, or perhaps an endless series of universes, so that God has never been without a body – without a world.

All-Powerful, All-Knowing, and Perfectly Good

God is *all-powerful*, or *omnipotent*, he is *all-knowing*, or *omniscient*, and he is *perfectly morally good*. All of these attributes are fundamental to the theistic view of God, and each of them involves difficulties in understanding and formulation.

Apparently the natural way to understand God's omnipotence is simply to say that God can do anything whatever. But this quickly runs into difficulties. Can God create a square circle, or cause it to be true that $1 + 2 = 1$? At least since the time of Thomas Aquinas (1225–74), it has been recognized that the exercise of God's power must be limited to what is *logically possible*. The expression *square circle* is one that could not possibly apply (correctly) to anything, and so the fact that God cannot make one implies no defect in God's power. Other limitations on what God can do stem from God's own nature: God cannot do things that require embodiment (such as climbing Mount Everest) or that imply limitations

(such as, for instance, forgetting something). Perhaps more significant, it is generally held that God cannot do things that imply a moral fault, such as breaking one of his promises. In view of such considerations as these, we may say that God's omnipotence means that *God can perform any action the performance of which is logically consistent, and consistent with God's own nature.*

[. . .]

The most immediately obvious way of expressing God's *omniscience* is to say that God knows everything, or, better (since only *true* propositions can be *known*), that God knows all true propositions. A difficulty arises, however, in that it seems there are propositions that are true at some times but not at others. Consider the proposition "Martha was married last Sunday." Assuming that Martha does indeed marry on a Sunday, this proposition is true for exactly one week, from midnight on the Sunday of the wedding to Sunday midnight one week later. God, presumably, *knows* this proposition for exactly as long as the proposition itself is true – though to be sure, he would know *after* the time period in question that this proposition *had been true* during that period. In view of this, we can modify our definition to say that at any time God knows all the propositions which are true at that time.

But do we also need a clause, similar to the one in the definition of omnipotence, excluding true propositions which are such that it is *logically impossible* that God should know them? Are there any true propositions of this sort? One possible candidate consists of propositions about decisions God himself is going to make. It seems likely that it is not possible for anyone, including God, to be in the process of making a decision and also, while making it, already to know what the decision will be. So if God *does* make decisions (as theism says he does), there may be truths God logically cannot know while he is making those decisions. To be sure, it might be held that God does not decide things in time, but rather, in some peculiar way, before time or outside of time. But even if this is true, it does

---

[4] Ibid., p. 348.

not entirely blunt the force of the point made: there would still be an "aspect" of God's life, even if not a period of time, in which he must operate without knowledge of certain true propositions. [. . .]

There is one further point to be made, before we present our full definition of omniscience. We humans not only *know* things, we also *believe* things; some of the latter are true, and others are false. Now, it may be that God has *no* beliefs over and above his knowledge, and certainly he holds no false beliefs. But then our definition of omniscience needs to be crafted so as to exclude explicitly God's holding false beliefs.

With these considerations in mind, we can define God's omniscience as follows: *At any time, God knows all propositions which are true at that time and are such that God's knowing them at that time is logically possible, and God never believes anything that is false.* The most controversial element in this definition is the clause stating that God knows only what it is logically possible for him to know. But this really should not cause any difficulty: if there are no truths that are logically impossible for God to know, then the clause in question will exclude nothing from God's knowledge, but that does not mean that the definition is incorrect or inadequate.

It is a matter of consensus among theists that God is *perfectly morally good*. Whatever character traits, principles of action, and so on, it may take to qualify a being as morally perfect must definitely be held to characterize God. What needs to be clarified here mainly involves two things: What is the *content* of perfect moral goodness? Furthermore, what is the *relation* between moral goodness and God?

The specific content of moral goodness – whether, for instance, love is more important as a divine attribute than holiness and justice, or the reverse, or whether they are all equally important – is something theists find it hard to agree about. One's answers to these kinds of questions are apt to depend in important ways on particular theological views about the ways in which God acts and deals with people, and so these matters are perhaps best left to be dealt with within the various theological traditions. In what follows we

shall speak generally of God's "goodness," "love," "justice," and the like, without claiming to specify exactly what each of these means or how they are related to each other.

With regard to the relation between goodness and God, an initial question is whether God is capable of acting contrary to moral goodness. A few philosophers have thought that, in order for God to be morally praiseworthy, he must be capable of doing evil, even though he never in fact does so. The vast majority of theistic thinkers, however, have held that God is *essentially* morally perfect – that his very nature is such that it is impossible for him to act in a way that is morally wrong. This view was, in fact, anticipated in our discussion of omnipotence, when we assumed that God is *incapable* of breaking one of his promises.

Another question about the relation between goodness and God concerns the source of the standard of moral goodness. Does there exist, independently of God, a standard of goodness to which God, like all other persons, is morally obligated to conform? On the other hand, do moral good and evil owe their existence entirely to the will and command of God? Or is there some further possibility for the relation between God and the standard of moral goodness? [. . .]

None of the attributes discussed in this section can properly apply to God as conceived in pantheism. The pantheistic God can, to be sure, be said to possess "all power" and "all knowledge," since whatever power and knowledge there may be are, by definition, *its* power and knowledge; it is the ultimate substance, the "inner soul," of everything that exists. But the pantheistic God possesses no *individual mind* that would enable it either to *know* or to *act* as we understand these notions. According to Spinoza, "Neither intellect nor will pertain to God's nature," and if we were to attribute intellect and will to God, they "would have nothing in common with [human intellect and will] but the name; there would be about as much correspondence between the two as there is between the Dog, the heavenly constellation, and a dog, an animal that barks."[5] Perhaps the most striking point to be made,

---

5   *Chief Works of Benedictus de Spinoza*, vol. 2, tr. R. H. M. Elwes (New York: Dover, 1955), pp. 60–1.

however, is that *the God of pantheism cannot distinguish between good and evil.* All actions performed in the universe are *equally* manifestations of the power of God; the notion that some of these actions are in an ultimate sense "good" and others "evil" must in the end be dismissed as an illusion. Pantheists may be, and often are, extremely upright and scrupulous in their personal ethics, but in the ultimate perspective good and evil – or what *we call* good and evil – are transcended. This contrasts the pantheistic God very sharply with the God of theism, who is a fighting God, a God who is unambiguously *for* good and *against* evil.

There is no reason why the God of process theism need be greatly different from the God of traditional theism with respect to knowledge and goodness. The process theist's attitude toward divine power, on the other hand, is markedly different, as shown in the title of a book by Charles Hartshorne (1897–2000): *Omnipotence and Other Theological Mistakes.*[6] Why is omnipotence a mistake? Because traditional theism depicts God as having the power to impose his will unilaterally on things and persons in his creation, as exercising coercive power over them. Process theism, on the other hand, maintains that *God's power can never be coercive, but must always be persuasive.* God does not have the power to unilaterally impose his will on nature, thus, the process God performs no miracles. Furthermore, he is not able to compel human beings to do his will – rather, he "lures" them, as Whitehead said, by holding before their minds the highest and best possibilities to which they can attain by voluntarily complying with his intentions.

Traditional theists typically see this as greatly diminishing the power and greatness of God, as making God distinctly less "worthy of worship" than if he were omnipotent. The reply to this is that, because of the inherent moral superiority of persuasive over coercive power, God's greatness is enhanced, not diminished, by his inability to use coercive power. However that may be, it is clear that this stance places process theism

sharply in conflict with the theological traditions of all the theistic faiths, all of which clearly portray God as capable of exercising *both* persuasive and coercive power.

God Eternal – Timeless or Everlasting?

That God is eternal is a common conviction among theists. But how is this to be understood? The most straightforward and readily understandable way to interpret God's eternity is simply to say that *God always has existed and always will exist.* God, then, exists *through time* like other persons and things, but unlike the others, his existence has neither beginning nor end. In a word, God is *everlasting.*

Some philosophers and theologians, however, have found this to be an inadequate interpretation of God's eternity. They have said, rather, that God is *timeless, outside of time altogether.* God, on this view, does *not* experience the world moment by moment as we finite persons do; rather, he experiences the world's history all at once, in a total simultaneous present. For God, they say, there is neither past, nor present, nor future; God simply *is.* All of time is present to God, all at once and changelessly, in his eternal present. Augustine put it like this:

Nor dost Thou by time, precede time: else shouldest Thou not precede all times. But Thou precedest all things past, by the sublimity of an ever-present eternity; and surpassest all future because they are future, and when they come, they shall be past; but Thou art the Same, and Thy years fail not. Thy years neither come nor go; whereas ours both come and go, that they all may come. Thy years stand together, because they do stand; nor are departing thrust out by coming years, for they pass not away; but ours shall all be, when they shall no more be. Thy years are one day; and Thy day is not daily, but To-day, seeing Thy To-day gives not place unto tomorrow, for neither doth it replace yesterday. Thy To-day, is Eternity. . . .[7]

6 Albany: SUNY Press, 1984.
7 *The Confessions of St. Augustine*, tr. Edward B. Pusey (New York: Random House, 1949), bk 11, pp. 252–3. [. . .]

The most fundamental reason why the doctrine of timelessness has appealed to many seems to be the conviction, which has its roots in Greek philosophy and especially Neoplatonism, that the *changeability* that must characterize God if he exists through time is unacceptable as an attribute of the "most real being." A recent defense of divine timelessness puts it this way:

> Such radically evanescent existence [as that of temporal beings] cannot be the foundation of existence. Being, the persistent, permanent, utterly immutable actuality that seems required as the bedrock underlying the evanescence of becoming, must be characterized by genuine [i.e., timeless] duration, of which temporal duration is only the flickering image.[8]

[. . .]

The doctrine of divine timelessness continues to be a topic of controversy among philosophers of religion. In recent years there has been a trend away from this view and toward accepting the view that God is everlasting, which is both easier to understand and apparently more in agreement with the scriptures of theistic religions, which depict God as acting in time and history. Nevertheless, timelessness continues to find able defenders and advocates. The discussion of the various divine attributes earlier in this chapter has been carried on in terms of the idea of God as everlasting, since this is the more familiar and easily understood concept. But the same attributes can, with appropriate modifications, be restated as attributes of a timeless God. The issue between these rival conceptions, then, remains very much in doubt.

Here, then, we bring to a conclusion our exposition of the theistic concept of God. The concept seems to be logically consistent, though in view of its complexity it is difficult to be absolutely certain about that. It is one that has fascinated and intrigued generation after generation of philosophers and theologians. But is it more than this? Is the concept one which applies to a *real being*, one who in very truth is the creator and sustainer of all things other than himself, and who enters powerfully and intimately into the world-process and especially into the lives of his worshipers? [. . .]

---

[8]   Eleonore Stump and Norman Kretzmann, "Eternity," *Journal of Philosophy* 79 (1981): 444–5.

2

The Female Nature of God
A Problem in Contemporary Religious Life

Rosemary Radford Ruether

The exclusively male image of God in the Judaeo-Christian tradition has become a critical issue of contemporary religious life. This question does not originate first of all in theology or in hermeneutics. It originates in the experience of alienation from this male image of God experienced by feminist women. It is only when this alienation is taken seriously that the theological and exegetical questions begin to be raised.

1. What is the Problem?

The problem of the male image of God cannot be treated as trivial or an accidental question of linguistics. It must be understood first of all as an ideological bias that reflects the sociology of patriarchal societies; that is, those societies dominated by male, property-holding heads of families. Although not all patriarchal societies have male monotheist religions, in those patriarchal societies which have this view of God, the God-image serves as the central reinforcement of the structure of patriarchal rule. The subordinate status of women in the social and legal order is reflected in the subordinate status of women in the cultus. The single male God is seen not only as creator and lawgiver of this secondary status of women. The very structure of spirituality in relation to this God enforces her secondary status.

What this means quite simply is the following. When God is projected in the image of one sex, rather than both sexes, and in the image of the ruling class of this sex, then this class of males is seen as consisting in the ones who possess the image of God primarily. Women are regarded as relating to God only secondarily and through inclusion in the male as their "head". This is stated very specifically by St Augustine in his treatise *On the Trinity* (7, 7, 10).

The male monotheist image of God dictates a certain structure of divine–human relationship. God addresses directly only the patriarchal ruling class. All other groups – women, children, slaves – are addressed by God only indirectly and through the mediation of the patriarchal class. This hierarchal order of God/Man/Woman appears throughout Hebrew law. But it also re-appears as a theological principle in the New Testament. Thus Paul (despite Gal. 3:28) in I Cor. 11:3 and 7 reaffirms this patriarchal order of relationships:

But I want you to understand that the head of every man is Christ, the head of a woman is her husband, and the head of Christ is God. . . . For a man ought not to cover his head, since he is the image and glory of God; but the woman is the glory of man.

"The Female Nature of God: A Problem in Contemporary Religious Life" by Rosemary Radford Ruether, *Concilium* 143 (1981): 61–6. Reprinted by permission of Stichting Concilium.

Thus the woman is seen as lacking the image of God or direct relation to God, in herself, but only secondarily, as mediated through the male.

2. The Suppressed "Feminine" in Patriarchal Theology

Recognising the fundamentally ideological, and even idolatrous, nature of this male-dominant image of God, some recent scholars have sought to show that this was never the whole story. God is not always described as a male. There is a small number of cases where God is described as a female. These texts occur in the Scriptures, particularly in the context of describing God's faithfulness to Israel and suffering on behalf of Israel. Here the labours of a woman in travail, giving birth to a child, and the fidelity of a mother who loves the child unconditionally, seemed to be more striking human analogies for these attributes of God than anything to be found in male activity. Thus in Isaiah we find:

Yahweh goes forth, now I will cry out like a woman in travail, I will gasp and pant. (Isa. 42:13, 14)

For Zion said, "Yahweh has forsaken me; my Lord has forgotten me. Can a woman forget her suckling child, that she should have no compassion on the son of her womb? Even these may forget, yet I will not forget you." (Isa. 49:14, 15)

These analogies of God as female in Scripture have been collected in Leonard Swidler's *Biblical Affirmation of Woman* (Philadelphia: Westminster 1979).

There is a second use of the female image for God in Scripture. The female image also appears as a secondary *persona* of God in the work of mediation to creation. In biblical thought this is found primarily in the Wisdom tradition. Here Holy Wisdom is described as a daughter of God through whom God mediates the work of creation, providential guidance, revelation, and reconciliation to God. In relation to the Solomon, the paradigmatic royal person, Wisdom is described as a "bride of his soul". Of her Solomon says:

I loved her and sought after her from my youth, and I desired to take her for my bride, and I

became enamoured of her beauty. . . . Therefore I determined to take her to live with me, knowing that she would give me good counsel. (Wisd. of Sol. 8:2, 9)

The same view of Wisdom as mediating creatrix is found in Proverbs (8:23–31). Here she is imaged as the mother who mediates wisdom to her sons.

Behind this powerful image of Divine Wisdom undoubtedly lies remnants of the ancient Near Eastern Goddess, Isis or Astarte. These Goddesses were imaged as creators and redeemers. They are linked particularly with Wisdom, defined as both social justice and harmony in nature, over against the threatening powers of Chaos. Raphael Patai, in his book, *The Hebrew Goddess* (Ktav 1967), has delineated the heritage of this ancient Near Eastern Goddess as she appeared in suppressed form in Hebrew theology.

Although the Sophia image disappears in rabbinic thought after the advent of the Christian era, possibly because of its use in gnosticism, a new image of God's mediating presence as female appears in the form of the *Shekinah*. The *Shekinah* is both the mediating presence of God in the midst of Israel, but also the reconciler of Israel with God. In rabbinic mystical speculation on the *galut* (exile), the *Shekinah* is seen as going into exile with Israel when God-as-father has turned away his face in anger. Each Shabbat celebration is seen as a mystical connubial embrace of God with his *Shekinah*, anticipating the final reuniting of God with creation in the messianic age. The exile of Israel from the land is seen ultimately as an exile within God, divorcing the masculine from the feminine "side" of God.

In Christianity this possibility of the immanence of God as feminine was eliminated. Christianity translated the Sophia concept into the Logos concept of Philo, defined as "son of God". It related this masculine mediating *persona* of God to the human person, Jesus. Thus the maleness of Jesus as a human person is correlated (or even fused into) the maleness of the Logos as "son of God". All possible speculation on a "female side" of God within trinitarian imagery was thus cut off from the beginning.

Some Sophia speculation does get revived in the Greek Orthodox tradition in relation to creation, the Church and Mariology. One somewhat maverick modern Orthodox thinker (Sergius Bulgakov, *The Wisdom of God*, London 1937) even relates this sophiological aspect of God to the *ousia* or Being of God. Sophia is the matrix or ground of Being of the three (male) persons of God! But it is doubtful if most Orthodox thinkers would be comfortable with that idea.

In western thought speculation on feminine aspects of God were probably rejected early because of links with gnosticism. Some recent Catholic thinkers (i.e., Leonard Swidler) have tried to revive the Sophia/*Shekinah* idea and link it with the Holy Spirit. But this does not have roots in western trinitarian thought. Basically the Spirit is imaged as a "male", but non-anthropomorphic principle. As the power of God that "fecundates" the waters at creation and the womb of Mary, its human referent would seem to be closer to the male semen as medium of male power.

This means that in western Christian theology, the female image is expelled from any place within the doctrine of God. It appears instead on the creaturely side of the God/creation relation. The female is used as the image of that which is created by God, that which is the recipient of God's creation; namely, Nature, Church, the soul, and, finally, Mary as the paradigmatic image of the redeemed humanity.

One partial exception to this rule is found in the Jesus mysticism of the middle ages that finds its culmination in Juliana of Norwich. Here Jesus, as the one who feeds us with his body, is portrayed as both mother and father. Eucharistic spirituality particularly seems to foster this mothering, nurturing image of Jesus. However, since both the divine and the human person of Jesus is firmly established in the orthodox theological tradition as male, this feminine reference to Jesus remains an attribute of a male person. Female-identified qualities, such as mothering and nurturing, are taken over by the male. But the female is not allowed "male" or "headship" capacities.

What I wish to argue then is that all of these suppressed feminine aspects of God in patriarchal theology still remain fundamentally within the context of the male-dominant structure of patriarchal relationships. The female can never

appear as the icon of God in all divine fullness, parallel to the male image of God. It is allowed in certain limited references to God's faithfulness and suffering for Israel. Or it appears as a clearly subordinate principle that mediates the work and power of the Father, much as the mother in the family mediates to the children (sons) the dictates of the father. She can be daughter of the divine king; bride of the human king; mother of his sons; but never autonomous person in her own right.

The "feminine" in patriarchal theology is basically allowed to act only within the same limited, subordinate or mediating roles that women are allowed to act in the patriarchal social order. The feminine is the recipient and mediator of male power to subordinate persons; i.e., sons, servants. In Christianity even these covert and marginal roles of the feminine as aspects of God disappear. Here the feminine is only allowed as image of the human recipient or mediator of divine grace, not as an aspect of the divine. In every relationship in which this "feminine" aspect appears in patriarchal theology, the dominant sovereign principle is always male; the female operating only as delegate of the male.

3. "Pagan Feminism": The Revolt against the Biblical Patriarchal God

In the 1970s the feminist movement, particularly in the United States, began to develop an increasingly militant wing that identified patriarchal religion as the root of the problem of women's subordination. These women saw that efforts to create a more "androgynous" God within the biblical tradition would be insufficient. The female aspect of God would always be placed within this fundamentally male-centred perspective. They concluded that biblical religion must be rejected altogether.

In its place they would substitute a Goddess and nature religion that they believe to be the original human cult of matriarchal society before the rise of patriarchy. They believe that the witches of the European middle ages preserved this Goddess-centred nature religion. They were persecuted for this faith by the Christian Church, who falsely accused them of malevolence and "devil worship". Feminist Wicca (or witchcraft) believes itself to be reviving this ancient Goddess religion. The book by Starhawk (Miriam Simos), *The Spiral Dance* (New York 1979), is a good expression of this feminist Goddess movement.

It is possible that we are witnessing in this movement the first strings of what may become a new stage of human religious consciousness. This possibility cannot be ruled out by the critical Christian. It may be that we have allowed divine revelation through the prophets and through Jesus to be so corrupted by an idolatrous androcentrism that a fuller understanding of God that truly includes the female as person must come as superseding and judging patriarchal religion. However, Goddess religion in its present form manifests a number of immaturities that are open to criticism, even from the point of view of feminism.

Following outdated matriarchal anthropology from the nineteenth century, much of the pedigree claimed by this movement is of doubtful historicity. In fact, the patterns of Goddess religion reveal very clearly their roots in nineteenth-century European romanticism. The dualistic world view that sets the feminine, nature and immanence on one side, and the masculine, history and transcendence on the other, is fundamentally preserved in this movement. It simply exalts the feminine pole of the dualism and repudiates the masculine side. One must ask whether this does not entrap women in precisely the traditional stereotypes. The dualisms are not overcome, but merely given a reverse valuation. But, in practice, this still means that women, even in "rebellion", are confined to a powerless Utopianism in which males own and run "the world".

Moreover, within their own community, instead of transforming the male monotheist model, they have reversed it. Now the great Goddess is the predominant image of the Divine. Woman then becomes the one who fully images the Goddess and communicates directly with her. Males are either excluded or given a subordinate position that is analogous to the position traditionally accorded women in the patriarchal cult. This *coup d'état* may feel satisfying in the short run, but in the long run would seem to reproduce the same fundamental pathology.

4.   Does the Ancient Goddess Represent the Feminine?

Both biblical feminists, who search for the suppressed feminine in the Judaeo-Christian tradition, and Goddess worshipers, who wish to exalt the feminine at the expense of the masculine, share a common assumption. Both assume that the recovery of the female as icon of the divine means the vindication of the "feminine". Neither ask the more fundamental question of whether the concept of the feminine itself is not a patriarchal creation. Thus the vindication of the "feminine", as we have inherited that concept from patriarchy, will always be set within a dualistic scheme of complementary principles that segregate women on one side and men on the other. Even if this scheme is given a reversed valuation, the same dualism remains.

A recent study by Judith Ochshorn, *The Female Experience and the Nature of the Divine* (Indiana University Press 1980), raises some important questions about the appropriateness of identifying this patriarchally-defined feminine with the ancient goddesses of polytheistic cultures. What Ochshorn has discovered is that, in polytheistic cultures of the Ancient Near East, gods and goddesses do not fall into these stereotyped patterns of masculinity and femininity. A God or Goddess, when addressed in the context of their own cult, represents a fullness of divine attributes. The Goddess represents sovereignty, wisdom, justice, as well as aspects of sexual and natural fecundity. Likewise the God operates as a sexual and natural principle, as well as a principle for social relations. The Goddess displays all the fullness of divine power in a female image. She is not the expression of the "feminine". Ochshorn also believes that this more pluralistic schema allows women to play more equalitarian and even leading roles in the cultus.

The subordinate status of women, in which relation to God is mediated only through the patriarchal class, is absent from religions which have a plurality of divine foci in male and female forms. Although such a lost religious world is probably not revivable as an option today, such studies may help to point us to the relativity of our patriarchally-defined patterns of masculine or feminine. They alert us to the dangers of simply surfacing the suppressed "feminine side" of that dualism as part of the image of God, without further criticism.

5.   Towards an Image of God beyond Patriarchy

If we are to seek an image of God(ess) beyond patriarchy, certain basic principles must be acknowledged. First we must acknowledge that the male has no special priority in imaging God(ess). If male roles and functions, i.e., fathering, are only analogies for God, then those analogies are in no way superior to the parallel analogies drawn from female experience, i.e., mothering. God(ess) as Parent is as much Mother as Father.

But even the Parent image must be recognised as a limited analogy for God(ess), often reinforcing patterns of permanent spiritual infantilism and cutting off moral maturity and responsibility. God(ess) as creator must be seen as the Ground of the full personhood of men and women equally. A God(ess) who is a good parent, and not a neurotic parent, is one that promotes our growth towards responsible personhood, not one who sanctions dependency. The whole concept of our relation to God(ess) must be reimaged.

If God(ess) is not only creator, but also redeemer of the world from sin, then God(ess) cannot be seen as the sanctioner of the priority of male over female. To do so is to make God the creator and sanctioner of patriarchy. God becomes the architect of injustice. The image of God as predominantly male is fundamentally idolatrous. The same can be said of an image of God(ess) as predominantly female.

The God(ess) who can be imaged through the experience of men and women alike does not simply embrace these experiences and validate them in their traditional historical form. We cannot simply add the "mothering" to the "fathering" God, while preserving the same hierarchical patterns of male activity and female passivity. To vindicate the "feminine" in this form is merely to make God the sanctioner of patriarchy in new form.

God(ess) must be seen as beyond maleness and femaleness. Encompassing the full humanity of both men and women, God(ess) also speaks as judge and redeemer from the stereotyped roles in which men as "masculine" and women as "feminine" have been cast in patriarchal society. God(ess) restores both men and women to full humanity. This means not only a new humanity, but a new society, new personal and social patterns of human relationships. The God(ess) who is both male and female, and neither male or female, points us to an unrealised new humanity. In this expanding image of God(ess) we glimpse our own expanding human potential, as selves and as social beings that have remained truncated and confined in patriarchal, hierarchical relationships. We begin to give new content to the vision of the messianic humanity that is neither "Jew nor Greek, that is neither slave nor free, that is neither male nor female" (Gal. 3:28) in which God(ess) has "broken down the dividing wall of hostility" (Eph. 2:14).

3

God as Creative-Responsive Love

John B. Cobb, Jr. and David Ray Griffin

God as Responsive Love

[T]raditional theism said that God is completely impassive, that there was no element of sympathy in the divine love for the creatures. The fact that there was an awareness that this Greek notion of divine impassibility was in serious tension with the Biblical notion of divine love for the world is most clearly reflected in this prayer of the eleventh-century theologian Anselm:

> Although it is better for thee to be . . . compassionate, passionless, than not to be these things; how art thou . . . compassionate, and, at the same time, passionless? For, if thou art passionless, thou dost not feel sympathy; and if thou dost not feel sympathy, thy heart is not wretched from sympathy for the wretched; but this it is to be compassionate. (Anselm, *Proslogium*, VI and VII, in *Proslogium; Monologium; An Appendix, In Behalf of the Fool, by Gaunilon; and Cur Deus Homo*, tr. by S. N. Deane [The Open Court Publishing Company, 1903,1945], pp. 11, 13)

Anselm resolved the tension by saying: "Thou art compassionate in terms of our experience, and not compassionate in terms of thy being" (Ibid., p. 13). In other words, God only *seems* to us to be compassionate; he is not *really* compassionate!

In Anselm's words: "When thou beholdest us in our wretchedness, we experience the effect of compassion, but thou dost not experience the feeling" (Ibid.). Thomas Aquinas in the thirteenth century faced the same problem. The objection to the idea that there is love in God was stated as follows: "For in God there are no passions. Now love is a passion. Therefore love is not in God" (*Summa Theologica* I, Q. 20, art. 1, obj. 1). Thomas responds by making a distinction between two elements within love, one which involves passion and one which does not. He then says, after quoting Aristotle favorably, that God "loves without passion" (Ibid., ans. 1).

This denial of an element of sympathetic responsiveness to the divine love meant that it was entirely creative. That is, God loves us only in the sense that he does good things for us. In Anselm's words:

> Thou art both compassionate, because thou dost save the wretched, and spare those who sin against thee; and not compassionate, because thou art affected by no sympathy for wretchedness. (*Proslogium*. VII, *loc. cit.*, pp. 13–14)

In Thomas' words: "To sorrow, therefore, over the misery of others belongs not to God, but it

"God as Creative-Responsive Love" by John B. Cobb, Jr and David Ray Griffin in *Process Theology: An Introductory Exposition* (Philadelphia: Westminster Press, 1976), pp. 44–57; 61–2.

does most properly belong to Him to dispel that misery" (*Summa Theologica* I, Q. 21, art. 3, ans).

Accordingly, for Anselm and Thomas the analogy is with the father who has no feeling for his children, and hence does not feel their needs, but "loves" them in that he gives good things to them. Thomas explicitly states that "love" is to be understood in this purely outgoing sense, as active goodwill: "To love anything is nothing else than to will good to that thing." He points out that God does not love as we love. For our love is partly responsive, since it is moved by its object, whereas the divine love is purely creative, since it creates its object (*Summa Theologica* I, Q. 20, art. 2, ans).

This notion of love as purely creative has implications that are in tension with the Biblical idea of God's equal love for all persons. All persons are obviously not equal in regard to the "good things of life" (however these be defined) that they enjoy (especially in the context of traditional theism, where the majority are consigned to eternal torment). And yet, if God's love is purely creative, totally creating the goodness of the beings loved, this implies that God loves some persons more than others. As Thomas said: "No one thing would be better than another if God did not will greater good for one than for another" (*Summa Theologica* I, Q. 20, art. 3, ans). This is one of the central ways in which the acceptance of the notion of divine impassibility undercuts the Biblical witness to the love of God.

Since we mold ourselves partly in terms of our image of perfect human existence, and this in turn is based upon our notion of deity, the notion of God as an Impassive Absolute whose love was purely creative could not help but have practical consequences for human existence. Love is often defined by theologians as "active goodwill." The notion of sympathetic compassion is missing. Indeed, one of the major theological treatises on the meaning of agape, or Christian love, portrays it as totally outgoing, having no element of responsiveness to the qualities of the loved one (Anders Nygren, *Agape and Eros* [The Westminster Press, 1953], pp. 77–8). This notion of love has promoted a "love" that is devoid of genuine sensitivity to the deepest needs of the "loved ones." Is this not why the word "charity," which is derived from *caritas* (the Latin word for agape), today has such heavily negative connotations? Also, the word "do-gooder" is a word of reproach, not because we do not want people to do good things, but because people labeled "do-gooders" go around trying to impose their own notions of the good that needs doing, without any sensitive responsiveness to the real desires and needs of those they think they are helping. This perverted view of love as purely active goodwill is due in large part to the long-standing notion that this is the kind of love which characterizes the divine reality.

This traditional notion of love as solely creative was based upon the value judgment that independence or absoluteness is unqualifiedly good, and that dependence or relativity in any sense derogates from perfection. But [. . .] while perfection entails independence or absoluteness in some respects, it also entails dependence or relativity in other respects. It entails ethical independence, in the sense that one should not be deflected by one's passions from the basic commitment to seek the greatest good in all situations. But this ethical commitment, in order to be actualized in concrete situations, requires responsiveness to the actual needs and desires of others. Hence, to promote the greatest good, one must be informed by, and thus relativized by, the feelings of others. Furthermore, we do not admire someone whose enjoyment is not in part dependent upon the condition of those around them. Parents who remained in absolute bliss while their children were in agony would not be perfect – unless there are such things as perfect monsters!

In other words, while there is a type of independence or absoluteness that is admirable, there is also a type of dependence or relativity that is admirable. And, if there is an example of absoluteness that is *unqualifiedly* admirable, this means that there is a divine absoluteness; and the same holds true of relativity. Process thought affirms that both of these are true. While traditional theism spoke only of the divine absoluteness, process theism speaks also of "the divine relativity" (this is the title of one of Hartshorne's books).

Process theism is sometimes called "dipolar theism," in contrast to traditional theism with its doctrine of divine simplicity. For Charles Hartshorne, the two "poles" or aspects of God are the abstract essence of God, on the one hand, and God's concrete actuality, on the other. The abstract essence is eternal, absolute, independent, unchangeable. It includes those abstract attributes of deity which characterize the divine existence at every moment. For example, to say that God is omniscient means that in every moment of the divine life God knows everything which is knowable at that time. The concrete actuality is temporal, relative, dependent, and constantly changing. In each moment of God's life there are new, unforeseen happenings in the world which only then have become knowable. Hence, God's concrete knowledge is dependent upon the decisions made by the worldly actualities. God's knowledge is always relativized by, in the sense of internally related to, the world.

[. . .]

This divine relativity is not limited to a "bare knowledge" of the new things happening in the world. Rather, the responsiveness includes a sympathetic feeling with the worldly beings, all of whom have feelings. Hence, it is not merely the content of God's knowledge which is dependent, but God's own emotional state. God enjoys our enjoyments, and suffers with our sufferings. This is the kind of responsiveness which is truly divine and belongs to the very nature of perfection. Hence it belongs to the ideal for human existence. Upon this basis, Christian agape can come to have the element of sympathy, of compassion for the present situation of others, which it should have had all along.

God as Creative Love

If sympathetic responsiveness is an essential aspect of Christian love, creative activity is no less essential. Whether it be considered a theme or a presupposition, the notion that God is active in the world, working to overcome evil and to create new things, is central to the Biblical tradition. To be in harmony with the God of Israel and of Jesus is to be involved in the struggle to overcome the various impediments to the fullness of life. In Luke 4:18, Jesus quotes from Isaiah, who indicates that the Spirit of the God he worships impels one to "set at liberty those who are oppressed."

The impetus in Western civilization for individual acts and social programs aimed at alleviating human misery and injustice has come in large part from the belief that God not only loves all persons equally, and hence desires justice, but also is directly acting in the world to create just conditions. The reason is that the basic religious drive of humanity is not only to be in harmony with deity, it is also to be in contact with this divine reality. It is because God is personally present and active in the world that contact with the sacred reality does not necessitate fleeing from history. Our activity aimed at creating good puts us in harmony and contact with God. Indeed, this activity can be understood in part as God's acting through us.

Accordingly, the loss of belief in the creative side of God's love would tend to undermine the various liberation movements that have been originally inspired by belief in divine providence, since it is largely this belief which has lent importance to these movements. Cultures in which the sacred is not understood as involved in creating better conditions for life in the world have had difficulty in generating the sustained commitments necessary to bring about significant change.

It is precisely this notion of divine creative activity in the world which has been most problematic in recent centuries, both within theological circles and in the culture at large. In traditional popular Christian thought, God was understood as intervening here and there in the course of the world. The notion of "acts of God" referred to events which did not have natural causes, but were directly caused by God. In traditional theological thought, all events were understood to be totally caused by God, so all events were "acts of God." However, most events were understood to be caused by God through the mediation of worldly or natural causes. God was the "primary cause" of these events, while the natural antecedents were called "secondary causes." However, a few events were thought to be caused directly by God, without the use of secondary causes. These events were "miracles." Accordingly, while all events were in one sense acts of God, these miracles were acts of God in a special sense. Thus, both in popular and theological circles, there was meaning to be given to the idea that God was creatively active in the world.

However, there are two major problems with this notion. First, it raises serious doubt that the creative activity of God can be understood as *love*, since it creates an enormous problem of evil by implying that *every* event in the world is *totally* caused by God, with or without the use of natural causes. Second, since the Renaissance and Enlightenment, the belief has grown that there are no events which happen without natural causes. Accordingly, the notion of "acts of God" has lost all unambiguous referents. Every event termed an act of God was said also, from another perspective, to be totally explainable in terms of natural causation. This rendered the notion of "act of God" of doubtful meaning. If an event can be totally explained in terms of natural forces, i.e., if these provide a "sufficient cause" for it, what justification is there for introducing the idea of "another perspective"? This seems like special pleading in order to retain a vacuous idea.

Deism was a manifestation of the felt difficulty of speaking of divine activity in the world. God's causation was put totally at the beginning of the world process. Once created, the world was said to run autonomously, without any additional divine input. Insofar as some form of this idea has become pervasive in the culture (not to mention complete atheism), the idea that one's activity in the world could put one in harmony and contact with deity has faded.

Twentieth-century theology has reaffirmed the centrality of the idea of God's activity in history. But it has generally lacked the conceptuality for consistently explicating this belief. [...] Also, in the light of the tremendous evil unleashed in the twentieth century, the assertion that the God who is in control of the whole process is loving or gracious seems just that – a bare assertion.

[...]

In Western culture generally, the problem of evil, and the widespread belief that the nexus of natural cause and effect excludes divine "intervention," have combined to render the notion of divine creative love problematic. When the leading secular thinkers then see that the leading theologians have provided no intelligible means for speaking of God's activity in the world, they are confirmed in their suspicion that this belief belongs to the myths of the past. Process theology provides a way of recovering the conviction that God acts creatively in the world and of understanding this creative activity as the expression of divine *love* for the world. The notion that there is a creative power of love behind and within the worldly process is no longer one which can only be confessed in spite of all appearances to the contrary. Instead it illuminates our experience.

Divine Creative Love as Persuasive

... [T]raditional theism portrayed God as the Controlling Power. The doctrine of divine omnipotence finally meant that God controlled every detail of the world process. Some traditional theologians, such as Thomas Aquinas, muted this implication of their thought as much as possible (in order to protect the doctrine of human freedom). Others, such as Luther and Calvin, proclaimed the doctrine from the housetops (in order to guard against both pride and anxiety). But, in either case, the doctrine followed logically from other doctrines that were affirmed. The notion that God knows the world, and that this knowledge is unchanging, suggests that God must in fact determine every detail of the world, lest something happen which was not immutably known. The doctrine that God is completely independent of the world implies that the divine knowledge of it cannot be dependent upon it, and this can only be if the world does nothing which was not totally determined by God. The doctrine of divine simplicity involves the assertion that all the divine attributes are identical; hence God's knowing the world is identical with God's causing it. The Biblical record is quite ambivalent on the question of whether God is in complete control of the world. There is much in the Bible which implies that divine providence is not all-determining. But the interpretation of the Biblical God in terms of valuations about perfection derived from Greek philosophy ruled out this side of the Biblical witness, thereby making creaturely freedom vis-à-vis God merely apparent.

Process thought, with its different understanding of perfection, sees the divine creative activity as based upon responsiveness to the world. Since the very meaning of actuality involves internal relatedness, God as an actuality is essentially related to the world. Since actuality as such is partially self-creative, future events are not yet determinate, so that even perfect knowledge cannot know the future, and God does not wholly control the world. Any divine creative influence must be persuasive, not coercive.

Whitehead's fundamentally new conception of divine creativity in the world centers around the notion that God provides each worldly actuality with an "initial aim." This is an impulse, initially felt conformally by the occasion, to actualize the best possibility open to it, given its concrete situation. But this initial aim does not automatically become the subject's own aim. Rather, this "subjective aim" is a product of its own decision. The subject may choose to actualize the initial aim; but it may also choose from among the other real possibilities open to it, given its context. In other words, God seeks to persuade each occasion toward that possibility for its own existence which would be best for it; but God cannot control the finite occasion's self-actualization. Accordingly, the divine creative activity involves risk. The obvious point is that, since God is not in complete control of the events of the world, the occurrence of genuine evil is not incompatible with God's beneficence toward all his creatures.

A less obvious but equally important consequence is that, since persuasion and not control is the divine way of doing things, this is the way we should seek to accomplish our ends. Much of the tragedy in the course of human affairs can be attributed to the feeling that to control others, and the course of events, is to share in divinity. Although traditional theism said that God was essentially love, the divine love was subordinated to the divine power. Although the result of Jesus' message, life, and death should have been to redefine divine power in terms of the divine love, this did not happen. Power, in the sense of controlling domination, remained the *essential* definition of deity. Accordingly, the control of things, events, and other persons, which is to some extent a "natural" human tendency, took on that added sense of satisfaction which comes from participating in an attribute understood (more or less consciously) to be divine.

Process theology's understanding of divine love is in harmony with the insight, which we can gain both from psychologists and from our own experience, that if we truly love others we do not seek to control them. We do not seek to pressure them with promises and threats involving extrinsic rewards and punishments. Instead we try to persuade them to actualize those possibilities which they themselves will find intrinsically rewarding. We do this by providing ourselves as an environment that helps open up new, intrinsically attractive possibilities.

Insofar as the notion that divine love is persuasive is accepted, the exercise of persuasive influence becomes intrinsically rewarding. It takes on that aura of extra importance that has too often been associated with the feeling of controlling others. This change has implications in all our relations, from one-to-one I–thou encounters to international relations. It does not mean that coercive control could be eliminated, but it does mean that such control is exercised as a last resort and with a sense of regret rather than with the thrill that comes from the sense of imitating deity.

Divine Creative Love as Promoting Enjoyment

In traditional Christianity, God has been understood as a Cosmic Moralist, in the sense of being *primarily* concerned with the development of moral behavior and attitudes in human beings. Negatively, this meant that the promotion of creaturely enjoyment was not God's first concern. In fact, in most Christian circles enjoyment has been understood as something that God at best tolerated, and often as something that he opposed. Thus the pleasure of sexual relations is tolerated, as long as it is only a concomitant of the primary function of sex, which is the morally sound intention to have children. The use of contraceptives has been frowned upon, since their use would mean the explicit admission that sexual intercourse was being engaged in solely for the enjoyment it brings.

This attitude toward sex is only the extreme example of the church's traditional attitude toward enjoyment in general, which has been taken to be a reflection of God's attitude. The result has been a stern, lifeless Christianity, being in tension with rather than supportive of the natural drive to enjoy life. The man whom Christians have called the Christ was called by some a "glutton and a drunkard" (Matt. 11:19; Luke 7:34) and could be quoted by one of the Evangelists as saying, "I came that they may have life, and have it abundantly" (John 10:10). But the Christian church has been perceived, not as the community that encourages the enjoyment of the abundant life, but as the institution that discourages most forms of enjoyment in the name of "being good." To put it crudely, one does not attend church to have a good time, but to atone for the good time one had the night before! God has been understood as commanding us to suppress our desire for most of those experiences which we find *intrinsically* good in favor of being *morally* good. And moral goodness has primarily been understood negatively, that is, as involving the suppression of many of the natural forms of enjoyment.

This notion of God as Cosmic Moralist is not unrelated to the idea of God as Controlling Power. The problem of evil would too evidently disprove the existence of God, if God be understood not only as controlling all events but also as willing the maximum enjoyment of his creatures. If the primary focus is on the creatures' enjoyment of existence, the great amount and variety of suffering and the great inequalities involved would easily suggest that God was either malevolent or incompetent, if not both. Hence, the notion that God is competently in control of all things can be saved by saying that creaturely enjoyment is not a high priority. In fact, the sufferings of life, and even the inequalities in this regard, can be regarded as divinely intended means to promote the desired moral and religious attitudes.

[. . .]

Process theology sees God's fundamental aim to be the promotion of the creatures' own enjoyment. God's creative influence upon them is loving, because it aims at promoting that which the creatures experience as intrinsically good. Since God is not in complete control, the divine love is not contradicted by the great amount of intrinsic evil, or "disenjoyment," in the world. The creatures in part create both themselves and their successors.

God's creative love extends to all the creatures, since all actualities, as experiential, have some degree of enjoyment. The promotion of enjoyment is God's primary concern throughout the whole process of creative evolution. The contrary doctrine, which sees God's primary concern to be the development of moral attitudes, is in the uncomfortable position of maintaining that over 99 percent of the history of our planet was spent in merely preparing the way for beings who are capable of the only kind of experience that really interests God.

Enjoyment is God's primary concern even with those beings who are capable of developing moral attitudes. But this is not in conflict with an emphasis on morality. God wants us to enjoy, true.

But he wants us *all* to enjoy. Accordingly, he wants us to enjoy in ways that do not unnecessarily inhibit enjoyment on the part of others. That puts it negatively. Positively stated, God wants our enjoyment to be such as to increase the enjoyments of others. To be moral is to actualize oneself in such a way as to maximize the enjoyments of future actualities, insofar as these future enjoyments can be conditioned by one's present decision. Hence, although the development of moral attitudes is of extreme importance, it is a derivative concern, secondary to the primary value, which is enjoyment itself.

[. . .]

God as Creative-Responsive Love

The traditional concept of God is in many respects stereotypically masculine. God was conceived to be active, unresponsive, impassive, inflexible, impatient, and moralistic. This being had none of the stereotypically feminine traits – it was not at all passive, responsive, emotional, flexible, patient, and it did not balance moral concern with an appreciation of beauty. This has led to a one-sided and hence unhealthy Christianity.

An overreaction resulting in a concept of God devoid of the stereotypically masculine attributes would also be destructive of authentic Christian existence. Losing the active or creative side of the divine love would undercut much of the good that Biblical faiths have brought into history, as we have already suggested. The same is true of the strong element of moral concern that has been attributed to God in the cultures decisively influenced by the Biblical faiths. Likewise, the loss of the notion of a divine purpose that at its most general level is inflexible would lead to a complete relativism. The positive aspects of these "masculine" attributes can be retained, without their destructive implications, if they are incorporated into a revolutionized concept of God into which the stereotypically feminine traits are integrated. For, in the integrated result, the former traits are changed qualitatively.

[...]

The process dipolar notion of deity has some affinity with the Taoist notion of the Tao, in which the "feminine" and "masculine" (yin and yang) dimensions of reality are perfectly integrated. The Tao is spoken of as a power that works slowly and undramatically, but is finally the most effective agency in reality. Whereas there are aspects of the notion of the Tao which have unfortunate implications, the Taoist vision of deity does contain an important element which should all along have been part of the Christian vision.

4

The Vedic-Upanisadic Concept of *Brahman* (The Highest God)

Sushanta Sen

Introductory Remarks

In India, unlike the West, the line of demarcation between philosophy and religion is so very thin that the one often flows into the other, making her philosophy as much religious as her religion philosophical. This is particularly true of Hinduism and is evident from the fact that the Vedas, the foundational scriptures of the Hindu religion, stand as the unquestionable authority for all the six orthodox systems of Hindu philosophy (*āstika darsana*). In these systems the Vedas are often invoked as the final court of appeal in matters of philosophical controversy, or a well reasoned conclusion arrived at by a valid logical argument is sought to be corroborated by some textual citations from the Vedas as a plea for its acceptance. Indeed, the very definition of Hindu orthodoxy (*āstikya*) which distinguishes it from other non-Hindu heterodox (*ñastika*) systems of Indian religions, like Buddhism and Jainism, affirms its unqualified faith in the truth of the Vedas. This is borne out by the fact that though Hinduism in the course of time branched off into a bewildering variety of conflicting sects,

none of them quarrels over the authority of the Vedas; and the Vedas are claimed to command such infallible authority because their contents are believed to be the records of direct revelation of Truth received by the pure-hearted saints and seers of remote antiquity. This persistent allegiance to the essential teachings of the Vedas explains why Hinduism is justifiably called *vaidika dharma* or the religion of the Vedas. Hence the Hindu concept of God primarily means the Vedic concept of God.

The Vedic-Upanisadic Teachings on God: The Idea of Self-God (*Ātman-Brahman*) Identity

But it is not a very easy task to distill the essence of the Vedic teachings on God out of their huge bulk and their rich diversity of metaphors and allegories. The thematic division of the Vedas into three different parts – the Saṁhitās, Brāhmanas and the Upanisads[1] – makes the matter more difficult, because the theme of the one part seems to contradict the theme of

---

"The Vedic-Upanisadic Concept of *Brahman* (The Highest God)" by Sushanta Sen in *Concepts of the Ultimate*, ed. Linda Tessier (New York: St Martin's Press, 1989), pp. 83–97.
[1] Traditionally the Vedas are divided into four parts – Saṁhitās, Brāhmanas, Aranyakas and Upanisads. But since the Āranyakas intend to be the philosophical interpretations of Brāhmanic ritualism, these may be treated as parts of the Brāhmanas and not as a separate branch of the Vedas.

the other. Thus, to a casual reader cursorily glancing over the pages of the Vedas, the polytheistic overtone of the Saṃhitās and the Brāhmanas in admitting a number of gods (*devas*) and offering sacrificial oblation to them appears to be flatly incongruous with the strictly monotheistic conception of God that permeates the whole corpus of the Upaniṣadic literature. The countless passages of the Upaniṣads seek to elaborate one fundamental theme in a variety of ways: "There is but one Being, not a second" (*Ekam eva advitiyam*).[2] This one universal Being has been variously termed in the Upaniṣads as *Brahman, Isvara, Paramātman*, and so on, for all of which the blanket English term "God" may be used, though each one of them has a characteristic shade of meaning distinct from the others. Now, this sort of thematic discrepancy of the one part of the Vedas with the others makes it rather difficult to ascertain which one of these two parts is to be accepted as truly representing the Vedic idea of God – the polytheism of the Saṃhitās and the Brāhmanas or the monotheism of the Upaniṣads. This is a problem which we shall discuss in detail in the next section. But for the present purpose let us see if the Saṃhitā portion of the Vedas, where polytheism is most prominently displayed, can suggest any intelligible hint toward its solution.

We have it on the authority of the Vedas themselves as well as on the evidence of other Sanskrit writings that the "Gāyatri" verse of the Vedas,[3] through the impartation of which a Hindu of the upper three castes is initiated for the first time into spiritual life, contains the quintessence of the entire mass of Vedic literature. In the *Atharva-Veda*, the Gāyatri has been described as the "mother of the Vedas" (Veda-mātā)[4] containing their essential spirit. This particular cryptic verse of the Ṛg-Veda, therefore, should be taken as the main trunk of the great Vedic tree of which the other elements are its dispensible ramifications. In this Gāyatri verse it has been said

that there is one Universal Being who is self-luminous and manifests himself in this and many other worlds; and this Being dwells in our heart as our Inner Ruler. It has been translated into English as follows:

> We meditate on the most resplendent and adorable light of the self-luminous Spirit who dwells in the heart as its inner ruler and manifests Himself as the earth, and sky and the heavens; may He guide our thoughts along the right path.[5]

This Gāyatri conception of a self-luminous Universal Spirit and of His residence in the human heart was later crystallized in the Upaniṣads, the concluding part of the Vedas, into the doctrine of an all-pervading *Brahman* (God) and His identity with the individual Self (*Ātman*). The individual self, however limited and imperfect it may appear, is in its final depths Divine in nature, because "the most resplendent and adorable light of the self-luminous spirit" dwells in it. This doctrine of the essential identity of the self (*Ātman*) with God (*Brahman*) – first suggested in the Gāyatri verse but fully developed in the Upaniṣads – is, therefore, the central creed of the Vedas, and indeed of Hinduism in general. The four "great sayings" (*mahāvākyas*) of the Upaniṣads, like "that thou art" (*tat tvam asi*),[6] I am Brahman (*aham Brahmāsmi*), and so on, as well as countless other passages, point to this central doctrine. Since the Self and God are ultimately identical, enquiry into the nature of God resolves itself into an enquiry into the nature of the Self. This explains why the concept of *Ātman* or the Self is the pivot around which all the doctrines of the Upaniṣads revolve. "What is that, Venerable Sir, which being known everything else is known?" – an eager seeker asked Angīra, the great sage of the Upaniṣadic period.[7] The Upaniṣads found the answer to this question in the knowledge of the true nature of the Self.

[2] *Chāndogya Upaniṣad*, VI.2.1.
[3] *Ṛg-Veda*, III.62.10.
[4] *Atharva Veda*, XIX.7.12.
[5] S. K. Chatterjee, *The Fundamentals of Hinduism* (Calcutta: University of Calcutta, 1970), p. 6.
[6] *Chāndogya Upaniṣad*, VI.8.7.
[7] *Muṇḍaka Upaniṣad*, I.1.3.

The Self (*Ātman*) is, according to the Upanisads, the inner essence of humanity – a permanent substance which remains fixed and constant amidst all sorts of change of the body, sense-organs and the mind. The body of a person may change beyond recognition, the sense-organs may be mutilated and the mind may be (and in fact is) in a state of incessant flux – its sensations, emotions, ideas, images, and such like, are continuously gliding away one after another. But the fact that one never loses one's self-identity to oneself proves that somewhere within this ceaseless phantasmagoria there exists an abiding reality which simply witnesses these changes but does not become affected by them. This permanent immutable substance in humanity is called the *Ātman* or Self. This *Ātman*, however, is thought to be not only the *inner essence* of humanity but also the outer essence of the Universe. The Upanisads do not make any distinction between within and without. We read in the *Kathopanisad*: "What is within us is also without. What is without is also within. He who sees difference between what is within and what is without goes evermore from death to death."[8] When viewed as the ultimate metaphysical principle of the outer Universe, the *Ātman* is termed *Brahman*. There is endless change without in the shape of movement, growth, decay and death, and at the heart of these changes there is an abiding reality called *Brahman*. Again, at the heart of endless changes within our body-mind complex there is an abiding reality called *Ātman*, and these two principles are treated as one and the same. *Ayam Ātmā Brahman* – "this Self is the Brahman" – is one of the "great sayings" (*mahāvākyas*) in which the Upanisads sum up this teaching.

But a crucial question can be raised here: if an immutable changeless *Ātman* is the sole reality of humanity and the Universe, then how are we to view the phenomena of change and becoming which characterize the world of our everyday experience? The reply of Upanisadic Hinduism to this question would be that whatever undergoes change and is unstable, fleeting and evanescent cannot have any intrinsic value and reality of its own. Hence, change or becoming is to be regarded as more or less unreal and as the source of all pain and suffering of our life. It is the *Ātman* only that lies beyond any possibility of change and suffering. But though itself devoid of any suffering and change, the *Ātman*, under the spell of a cosmic nescience (*avidyā*), forgets its real nature and wrongly identifies itself with the changing phenomena of its body and mind. These latter are not parts of the Self itself but are its *Kosas*, or the sheaths within which it is wrapped. This mistaken identification of the *Ātman* with what it is not, that is, its bodily and mental sheaths, is held to be responsible for all the sorrows and sufferings of human life, because the Self wrongly imagines that various affections and afflictions which really belong to the body-mind complex are aspects of its own nature. Only when the *Ātman* is able to abstract itself from these sheaths by a long and rigorous spiritual training under the guidance of a Guru or spiritual guide does it shine forth in its pristine divine glory as the same with God (*Brahman*). But so long as this does not happen the Self suffers from the illusion that it is subject to all the evils, imperfections and limitations of its external sheaths and thus makes itself a miserable victim of the distressing sense of finitude, suffering and death.

But at the same time the fact that each conscious individual instinctively desires to escape suffering and resist death proves that this miserable and wretched existence is neither one's essential nature nor final destiny. For if some foreign element enters our body, such as a particle of dust in the eye or a thorn in the flesh, the body immediately reacts to it and tries to rid itself of it; likewise, every person wants to get rid of the sorrows and sufferings of human life, which therefore shows that these do not belong to the essence of the Self but are foreign elements which have become imposed on it. This suggests again that the natural condition of the Self is a state of perfect and unalloyed peace or bliss (*ānanda*) absolutely free from all sufferings and imperfections. This painless perfect state of the Self has been variously termed in the Upanisads *mukti*, *moksa*, *kaivalya*, *apavarga*,

8   *Kathopanisad*, II.l.10.

and so on, and the attainment of this state is described as the supreme end of human life (*carana purusārtha*).

But how is one to attain this ideal state? Only by tearing off the veil of cosmic nescience (*avidyā*) and thus realizing the essential identity of one's inner Self with *Brahman*: this is the invariable answer of the Upanisads. When one realizes this identity one knows the truth that "the Self is free from evil, free from old age, free from death, free from grief, hunger and thirst . . .",[9] that is free from all temporality, affections and afflictions of body and mind. That is why humans are described in the Upanisads as the "sons of Immortality" (*amrtasya putrāh*).

This doctrine of the essential identity of the human Self (*Ātman*) with God (*Brahman*) represents the central spiritual insight of the Vedic-Upanisadic seers and gives Hinduism its distinctive character. It is interesting to note here that this ancient Upanisadic doctrine of *Ātman-Brahman* identity finds a parallel expression in the medieval Christian mystic Eckhart: "To gauge the Soul we must gauge it with God, for the Ground of God and the Ground of the Soul are one and the same."[10] To know the Self, therefore, is to know God: and to know God is to know everything, because everything in the Universe is pervaded by God, "all this is enveloped by God".[11] Thus the strange question – what is that which, being known, everything else becomes known? – finds its answer in the human Self: *Ātmānam Viddhi*: "know your own Self". It is for this reason that all the Upanisadic writings together go by the name, *ātmavidyā*, a study of the nature of the Self.

The Status of Minor Gods (*Devas*) in Hinduism

As the Upanisads are called *ātmavidyā*, so the Samhitās, the first and oldest part of the Vedas, may aptly be designated as *devavidyā*, a study of the nature of gods, because these are collections of hymns and prayers addressed to different gods, or the *devas* as they are called. A particular Rg-Vedic verse (VIII.28.1) and the traditional commentaries on the Vedas allude to 33 such *devas*, viz. Indra, Varuna, Usha, Agni, and so on. These gods are said to be the supernatural and luminous personalities through whose active agency and guidance different objects of nature and phenomena are able to function. Understood in this sense Indra is the god of rain, thunder and storm, Varuna the god of sky, Usha the goddess of dawn, Agni the deity of fire, and so on. Though the relation of these Vedic gods with nature is very intimately conceived, they are not mere natural forces *personified*, as often interpreted by Western scholars. It would be truer to understand them as *personalities* presiding over different phenomena of nature (*abhimāna-devatās*) and guiding and controlling them. Prayers for favour could be addressed to them, for they were deities more powerful than ourselves and had control over nature, and as personalities they could be gracious.

But a very crucial question which we have already raised immediately crops up here: how can the existence of many gods (*devas*), as we find it in the Samhitā portion of the Vedas, be reconciled with the basic Upanisadic doctrine that God (*Brahman*) is one and only one and that the individual Self (*Ātman*) is essentially identical with God? Unless this question is satisfactorily answered, a critic of Hinduism might argue, the entire bulk of Vedic literature on which Hinduism is based remains a senseless mumbo-jumbo of irreconcilable contradictions.

To an objection of this kind a typical Hindu reply would be that there is no pure and unmixed polytheism in Hinduism. What appears to be polytheism in the verses of the Samhitās is really monotheism, only clothed in polytheistic guise. This leads us to a more basic enquiry into the nature of the existence of these Vedic deities (*devas*) and their metaphysical status.

If we take the pre-Christian pagan religion of the classical Greeks and the Romans to be typical examples of pure polytheism, it is not difficult to see why Hinduism cannot be subsumed

---

9   *Chāndogya Upaniṣad*, VIII.7.1.
10   Quoted in Aldous Huxley, *Perennial Philosophy* (London: Chatto & Windus, 1974), p. 19.
11   *Isopaniṣad*, 1.

under this category. In Graeco-Roman paganism the main difference between gods and humans is that the former are immortal while the latter are not, and a mortal can never attain to the status of a god. But in Hinduism humans and gods share a common fate in that both are created by an omnipotent creator God and as creatures both are subject to birth and death. Like human beings, the destiny of these gods is determined by the karmic law of cause and effect, and this law sets a beginning and an end to their status as gods. In accordance with the law of *karma*, a pervasive assumption in Indian religio-philosophical thought, the joys and sufferings of human life are strictly conditioned by and proportionate to the merits (*punyas*) and demerits (*pāpas*) of actions (*karmas*) performed by the individual: virtuous actions are rewarded by appropriate happiness and evil deeds are punished by befitting misery. Now if the merits of actions earned by someone are of such immense magnitude that all earthly pleasures are too paltry to provide rewards proportionate to these merits, then after physical death he or she is reborn as a god (*deva*) in heaven to enjoy uninterrupted heavenly bliss, and remains there as an extraordinarily powerful being to govern certain courses of nature. Unmixed pleasure and superhuman power characterize the lives of these heavenly gods. Again, when someone dies who has acquired the highest merit by performing some special kinds of penance and Vedic sacrifice (*yajña*), that person is reborn again not only as a god but as the king of gods, Indra, whose commands the lesser gods obey. But the lives of all these gods including Indra come to a definite end when their accumulated merits become exhausted by the enjoyment of heavenly pleasures and privileges; and after that they have to die from heaven as gods and be reborn again on earth as ordinary human beings within the process of repeated reincarnations known as *samsāra*. This cycle of births and deaths, either as humans or gods, goes on until they realize their essential identity with *Brahman*.

It is interesting to note here that these Vedic gods are declared to be cosmic officials holding certain positions (*padas*) and having certain duties. Thus the term "Indra", the king of gods, is not the name of a person but designates an office or a post (*Indra-pada*). Anyone who has rendered oneself worthy of it by virtue of meritorious deeds becomes entitled to this post and occupies it. But when the merits of these good *karmas* are exhausted, one has to abdicate this office and another Indra at once steps into one's place. Thus, though these godly offices (*padas*) are constant, the individual beings that carry out the duties of Indra, Agni and the rest change.

Now considering these two peculiarities of the Vedic gods – their mortality and the ability of humans to rise to the status of gods – it is not permissible to equate the so-called Vedic polytheism with the pure polytheism of the ancient Greeks and Romans. But the most important feature to be noticed about these Vedic gods is that, though they are powerful enough to control the forces of nature and to some extent the destiny of worldly individuals, they are never described as creators of humanity and nature. Creatorship in Hinduism is an exclusive property of an Omnipotent God (*Īśvara*) who is one and uncreated. The gods (*devas*) of the Hindu pantheon correspond rather to the angels and saints and share the feature of not having possessed their high status from all eternity. The angels were created by God at the time of creation; saints attained to sainthood only after their lives on earth. The difference, however, is that unlike angels and saints these Vedic deities (*devas*) lose their status again at a later stage, whereas the former retain it by divine decree for all time. Technically, the angels and saints are sempiternal creatures, that is, they have a beginning but (apart from divine annihilation) no end. And just as the introduction of a variety of these sempiternal beings does not affect the fundamental mono-theism of Christianity, so the existence of different gods (*devas*) does not in any way deprive the "One God" theory of the Upanisads of its basic monotheistic character.

But this is not the whole story concerning the Vedic gods, and Hinduism has gone much deeper than this in its treatment of them. Among the great variety of gods it has discovered a fundamental unity, a unity which has prevented it from degenerating into a crude form of polytheism. This point has been made abundantly clear by Swami Vivekananda, a saint and savant of Hinduism, in a comparative study of other non-Hindu polytheistic mythologies.[12] In these mythologies, says Vivekananda, it is usually found that one particular god competes with other gods, becoming prominent and assuming the supreme position over others, while the other gods gradually die out. Thus, in the Jewish mythology, Jehovah becomes supreme of all the Molochs, and the other Molochs are forgotten or lost forever; Jehovah becomes the God of gods. In the same way, in Greek mythology, Zeus comes to the forefront and assumes a great magnitude, becoming the God of the Universe, and all the other gods are degraded into minor angels. This seems to be a worldwide process. But in the Hindu polytheistic mythology we find an exception. Among the Vedic gods any one is raised to the status of the Omnipotent God for the time being when that god is praised and worshipped by the Vedic sages. Thus, when Indra is worshipped it is said that he is the all-powerful and all-knowing Supreme Lord, and the other gods, like Baruna, Usha, Agni and so forth, only obey his commands. But in the next book of the same Veda, or sometimes in the same book, when hymns are addressed to Varuna it is said that he is the Almighty and Omniscient God, and Indra and others only obey his command. In this way all other gods occupy the position of the Supreme Lord of all in turns. Observing this peculiarity of the Vedic pantheon, Professor Max Müller, instead of characterizing the Vedic faith as polytheism, coined a new name for it and called it "henotheism". But to give a new name to a new situation does not explain the situation itself. Hence Max Müller's use of the new term "henotheism" instead of polytheism does not really explain why the different Vedic gods are elevated one after another to assume the status of Almighty and Omniscient God of the Universe. The explanation, however, is there in the Vedic texts themselves. It has been expressly stated in one of the hymns of the Vedas: *Ekam sat viprā vahudhā vadanti*[13] – "That which exists is one: sages call It by various names". Hence only the names or concepts of gods are different, but the Reality underlying these concepts is one and

the same. Multiple ways of conceiving Reality are not incompatible with the unity of the Reality conceived. Varying degrees of intellectual capacity of different individuals in apprehending one and the same Reality result in the formation of various concepts of gods. But at the heart of all these variations the same Reality reigns: "That which exists is one: sages call it by various names." And this is obviously not polytheism. What appears to be polytheism in the Saṁhitā portion of the Vedas is really monotheism, only dressed in polytheistic language. And though the language of polytheism clamours to draw our attention in these Saṁhitā verses, whispering notes of monotheism are not altogether absent in them, as is evident from the Gāyatri verse of the Rg-Veda already quoted. This undercurrent of monotheism in the first and oldest part of the Vedas, that is, the Saṁhitās, becomes dominant in the Upanisads of a later period when the Upanisadic sage declares in unequivocal terms: *Ekam eva advitīyam* – "There is but One Being, not a second." This "One-God" theory, therefore, is the uncompromising creed of the Vedas, and the Hindu concept of God should be divined in terms of it. Hinduism has never been a pure polytheistic religion.

The Immanent and Transcendent Aspects of God

Though God is one and only one in Hinduism, God's nature has been conceived in the Vedas in two different aspects – immanent and transcendent. In the immanent aspect God is said to be creator, preserver and destroyer of the world (*srsti-sthiti pralaya kartā*). The notion of a Creator God constitutes a fundamental category in almost all the major religious traditions of the world, and Hinduism is no exception. But one distinctive feature of the Hindu conception of the Creator God lies in that, after creating the world, God does not stand outside but remains within it. The concept of a God residing in Heaven above the universe and occasionally interfering with the affairs of the world at

---

[12] See Swami Vivekananda, *Hinduism* (Sri Ramakrishna Math, Mylapore, Madras-4, India, 1968), pp. 23–4.
[13] *Rg-Veda*, I.164–6.

moments of crisis is quite alien to the Hindu mind. God, according to Hinduism, remains in the very bosom of the Universe, pervades and permeates the whole of it, and controls it while remaining within it.[14] Hence God has been described in the Hindu scriptures as the inherent creator and inner controller of the world, or the *Antaryāmin*. To appreciate properly why God is said to be inherently embedded in the Universe we need to understand the Hindu theory of creation, a detailed discussion of which is reserved for the next section. However, for the present purpose it is sufficient to note that God in the immanent aspect is no other than the Personal God of religion who, in the later Bhakti cult of Hinduism, has been invested with six attributes, viz., majesty (*aiśvarya*), omnipotence (*vīrya*), glory (*yaśa*), beauty (*srī*), knowledge (*jñāna*), and dispassion (*vairāgya*). This immanent God with attributes (*saguna Brahman*), who can be worshipped and prayed to, is specifically termed *Īśvara* in the Upanisadic literature.

But though God resides within the world and pervades the whole of it, God's being is not wholly exhausted in it; God is also beyond the world. God is both immanent and transcendent in relation to the world. This is suggested by a famous hymn of the Rg-Veda known as Purusa-sukta: "God pervades the whole world by a quarter of His being, while the three fourth of Him stands over as immortal in the sky."[15] The language of this hymn is of course metaphorical: we shall see later that God in the transcendental aspect defies all human measurement – both in terms of quality and quantity. But what it really suggests is that God's being cannot be unresidually equated with the world, that God is not merely the totality of the objects of the world but something more: God is also beyond the world. This "beyond-aspect" of God is called *Brahman* just as God's immanent aspect is known as *Īśvara* in the Upanisads. Not only in the Rg-Veda but in other Hindu scriptures also the concept of God as "beyond" is repeatedly emphasized.[16]

Now, from God's transcendence follows God's necessary inaccessibility to the human mind and to linguistic description. To quote from an Upanisad: *Brahman* is that "from where mind and speech recoil, baffled in their quest".[17] Since *Brahman* transcends the limits of all phenomenality, the concepts of our discursive reason and the words of our language through the instrumentality of which we interpret the phenomenal world do not have any legitimate application: and any attempt to apply these to *Brahman* will distort and falsify the nature of *Brahman*. Hence conceptual thought cannot grasp the real nature of *Brahman*, nor can language describe *Brahman* by any positive terms. *Brahman* can only be described negatively as "not this, not this" (*neti neti*).[18]

But a long process of spiritual practice (*Yoga*) is able to free our minds from these concepts and transform our discursive reason into a direct state of transcendental intuition. This transformed, de-conceptualized state of our minds is known as *samādhi* in the *Yoga-Sūtra* of Patanjali, and it is said that the knowledge of the true nature of *Brahman* dawns in this state. In the light of such intuitive transcendental experience (*samādhi*), the Upanisads describe the essential nature of *Brahman* as pure existence, consciousness and bliss (*sat-cit-ānanda*). Yet all these references of the scriptures do not and cannot describe the real nature of *Brahman*. These are at best suggestive hints of the great Transcendent Reality. All that we may gather from these is that *Brahman* is not void or blank (*śūnya*), nor an insentient something, but that *Brahman* is the source and support of every object and experience in nature; One without a second.

This *Brahman* when conceived as the creative energy (*śakti*) of the Universe is called Īśvara, and there is no substantial difference between the two. In fact Īśvara is the highest possible reading of the *Brahman* by the finite human mind; but beyond that mental measurement God stands as the highest, transcendental and impersonal Absolute which, however, is too

---

[14]   *Bhagavad Gita*, XV.13.
[15]   *Rg-Veda*, I.90.3.
[16]   *Brhadāranyaka Upaniṣad*, III.9.26; *Bhāgavad-Gita*, X.42 and XV.16–17.
[17]   *Taittiriya Upaniṣad*, II.9.1.
[18]   *Brhadāranyaka Upaniṣad*, III.9.26.

much an abstraction to be loved and worshipped. So a religious devotee chooses the immanent aspect of God in order to establish a personal relationship. Thus, from the religious point of view, the concept of *Īśvara* is more important than the concept of *Brahman*. In the concluding section of this chapter let us concentrate on this and see in what sense Īśvara is said to be the creator and destroyer of the world.

God (*Īśvara*) and Creation

The Vedic-Upaniṣadic theory of creation rests on the explicit rejection of two other rival theories – creation *ex nihilo* and creation out of the pre-existing materials of the Universe. According to the former theory, nothing but God existed before creation and God created the universe out of nothing by sheer creative will. We find this theory of creation being mentioned and rejected in one of the principal Upaniṣads, and the argument on the strength of which it is rejected is that an existent entity can never be produced out of nothing (*katha-masaiah sajjāyeteti*).[19] This argument rests on a particular view of causation known as *sat-kārya-vāda* in the Saṃkhya system of Hindu philosophy. According to it the effect (*kārya*) must exist (*sat*) in its material cause in an extremely rarefied form before it is actually produced. One gets oil from seeds, because oil is somehow contained within the seeds before these are squeezed and crushed. A thousand efforts on the part of the agent will not produce a single drop of oil from the crushing of sand, because sand does not already contain oil. Hence what is called production or creation really means the evolution of a thing which was already involved in its material cause. What was involved becomes evolved; what was enveloped becomes developed; what was latent becomes patent; and this is all that creation means in Hinduism. Hence a thing cannot be created or produced out of sheer "nothing" in which it was not involved before. To say, therefore that God created the world *ex nihilo* is to flout this fundamental principle of creation.

As an antidote to this theory, another theory of creation is put forward by some cosmologists and philosophers which may be designated as the "Design" theory of the world. According to this theory, God created the universe not out of sheer nothing but out of pre-existing materials like atoms (*paramānus*), space (*dik*), time (*kāli*), and so on, which are co-eval entities with God. These materials were already present before and outside God, and God as a conscious efficient agent merely shaped or designed the world out of them. On this theory God is not so much a creator as a designer or architect of the Universe. But Hinduism rejects this theory, finding it as faulty as the theory of creation *ex nihilo*. The chief defect of this theory is that it reduces God to a dependent, limited and finite being. An architect has to depend on the materials available and can only do what these materials make possible. In this way God becomes restricted by the materials of creation, and God's omnipotence is lost. Thus, though the Design theory avoids the defects of the *ex-nihilo* theory of creation, it does so at the cost of an omnipotent God. Hence it cannot be accepted as a satisfactory solution to the problem of creation.

Having rejected these two extreme views, Upaniṣadic Hinduism puts forward its own theory of creation in positive terms. According to it, God created the world not out of sheer nothingness, nor out of pre-existing materials lying outside God, but from within God. God is both the material cause and the efficient cause of the world (*abhinnanimittopadānā*). In ordinary empirical cases of production, the material cause (*upādāna kārana*) and the efficient cause (*nimitta kārana*) are two different things, and the material cause lies outside the efficient cause. In the case of the production of a clay pot, the clay out of which the pot is made is its material cause and the potter who consciously makes the pot is its efficient cause. After the pot is produced it continues to have an independent existence apart from and outside the potter. But this is not so with the creation of the world. Here God (Īśvara) is said to be both the efficient cause and the material cause of the world. God creates the

[19] *Chāndogya Upaniṣad*, VI.2.1–2.

world out of God's own inner nature. God is both the creator and the stuff of the world at the same time. Hence after creating the world, God does not stand outside it but is involved in every bit of it. God pervades and permeates the whole Universe, because it is God that has become the Universe; the Universe is an extension of God's own being, a projection of God's inner nature (*prakṛti*). To quote from an Upanisad: "Just as a spider throws out the web from within itself and again draws it in . . . so also does God (*akṣara*) create the Universe."[20]

Another interesting feature of the Hindu theory of creation is that created Nature is said to be eternal, without any absolute beginning and absolute end. No point in time is imaginable at which God existed but not yet a world. The world has a beginning and an end only in a relative sense, to be explained shortly. It is not that the Universe was created a few thousand years ago for the first time and that it will be destroyed forever a few thousand years hence. It is not that at a particular point of time God created the world, and since then God has been resting in peace except for occasional interference in its affairs. The creative energy is still going on; God is eternally creating and is never at rest. In the *Gita*, Śrikrsna, who is believed by a sect of the Hindus to be the incarnation (*avatāra*) of God, declares: "If I remain inactive for a single moment, the entire universe will fall into pieces."[21]

But how can the idea of eternal creation without beginning and end be reconciled with the notion of cyclical dissolution of the world, or the *pralaya* as it is called in different Hindu scriptures? The answer is as follows. According to Hindu metaphysics the created universe is a mass of vibrations remaining at a certain level of frequency. But there are periods when this whole mass of vibrations becomes extremely rarefied, starts receding and finally gets reabsorbed into God from where it was projected forth. This unmoved mass of vibrations of the Universe within God is known as *pralaya* or the cosmic dissolution. But it should not be taken to mean the absolute destruction of the Universe. The Universe during *pralaya* does not explode into absolute non-being forever. Having reached the lowest level of frequency it merely exists as an unmanifested condition within God. What was evolved from God becomes again involved within God. But after a period of such temporary involution the whole world again evolves forward at the beginning of a new cycle. This process of involution and evolution of the world goes on backward and forward like ocean-waves through all eternity. Again this sort of *pralaya* does not take place simultaneously in all parts of the Universe. A particular solar system like ours may be disintegrating but thousands of others will continue to exist in their manifested condition. Thus creation taken as a whole is eternal in the sense that it has neither an absolute beginning nor an absolute end. Whenever in the Hindu scriptures the words "beginning" and "end" of the world are used, they should be taken to mean the beginning and end of one particular cycle, and no more than that.

---

[20] *Muṇḍaka Upaniṣad*, I.1.7.
[21] *Bhāgavad-Gītā*, III.24.

5

Emptiness in Mahayana Buddhism

Christopher Ives

"Emptiness" has its true connotations in the process of salvation, and it would be a mistake to regard it as a purely intellectual concept, or to make it into a thing, and give it an ontological meaning. The relative nothing ("this is absent in that") cannot be hypostatized into an absolute nothing, into the non-existence of everything, or the denial of all reality and of all being.[1]

The search for the "ultimate" in Mahayana Buddhism leads inevitably to emptiness (*śūnyatā*). Emptiness first emerges as a key Buddhist concept in the *Prajñāparamitā Sūtras* (Perfection of Wisdom Sutras), Mahayana Sanskrit writings of the 1st century BCE. On the basis of this group of sutras, the great Indian philosopher Nagarjuna (2nd century CE) gives emptiness a systematic philosophical expression. In his writings, especially the *Mūlamadhyamika-kārikās* (Stanzas on the Middle Way), Nagarjuna sets forth emptiness as a thorough-going negation of independent self-existence and a refutation of substantialist conceptual approaches to reality, with the intention of dissolving human attachment and consequent suffering. Later Mahayana thinkers develop these aspects of emptiness as an ontologically descriptive term and, more importantly, a

soteriological device, a skillful means (*upaya*) of leading people beyond ignorance to liberation. It is primarily in the latter sense that emptiness functions as the "ultimate" in Mahayana Buddhism.

The Sanskrit term *śūnyatā* derives from the root *śvi*, which means to swell. That which is swollen appears full when viewed from the outside, but is often empty within.[2] Such emptiness is not necessarily negative, however, for it can function constructively, as does the hollowness that enables a temple bell to ring or a gourd to function as a water vessel. (As we will see, emptiness also refers to the metal of the bell and the walls of the gourd.) In conjunction with this connotation of the term, *śūnyatā* is also the Sanskrit word for zero, the "empty" number in mathematics. As mathematicians well know, "in the

"Emptiness in Mahayana Buddhism," a selection from "Emptiness: Soteriology and Ethics in Mahayana Buddhism" by Christopher Ives in *Concepts of the Ultimate*, ed. Linda Tessier (New York: St Martin's Press, 1989), pp. 113–22; 125–6.

[1]   Edward Conze, *Buddhist Thought in India* (Ann Arbor: University of Michigan Press, 1967), p. 61.
[2]   Edward Conze, *Buddhism: Its Essence and Development* (New York: Harper & Row, 1975), p. 130.

total (holistic) system of digits, the zero is a necessary starting point as well as conclusion . . .".[3]

Nagarjuna draws on these connotations of *śūnyatā* in responding to *Abhidharma* Buddhist thought, especially as conveyed in the *Abhidharma Pitaka*, the "basket" of the Pali Canon that elaborates on the ethical, psychological and ontological concepts in Gautama Buddha's talks. *Abhidharma* thinkers follow the historical Buddha in his negation of an eternal, independent self (*ātman*). They assert that the "self" is an everchanging process, not a thing, and arises through the dependent co-origination (*pratītya-samutpāda*) of numerous *dharmas*, the physical and mental factors constituting reality. The traditional formula of dependent co-origination is, in the Buddha's words,

> When this is present, that comes to be;
>   from the arising of this, that arises.
> When this is absent, that does not come to be;
>   on the cessation of this, that ceases.[4]

To clarify the constitution of subjectivity and the emergence of ignorance and suffering, *Abhidharma* Buddhists analyze and classify the various *dharmas*, which can be "this" or "that" in the above formula. At times, *dharmas* are discussed as independent, atomistic entities. The *Sarvastivada* ("everything exists") school of *Abhidharma* thought argues that space and Nirvana are unconditioned *dharmas*.

Nagarjuna criticizes this hypostatization of the elementary factors or *dharmas*, labelling it a metaphysical error, a form of ignorance (*avidyā*) which conduces to attachment and further suffering. He contends that not only composite entities but also their compositional elements come into being through the interaction of various conditions in a constantly changing field of interaction. In other words, *all* things lack own-being (*svabhāva*);[5] they are empty (*śūnya*), devoid of independent self-existence. Nagarjuna is not arguing that nothing exists or that we live in an illusory nihilistic void, but that there are no independent, unchanging, permanent essences. As he writes, "Since there is no *dharma* whatever originating independently, no *dharma* whatever exists which is not empty."[6] Simply put, Nagarjuna proceeds a step beyond the earlier Buddhist notion of "personal selflessness" and expounds the "selflessness of dharmas". Of course, in the process he reconceptualizes the Theravadin notion of dependent co-origination, for "in the context of emptiness (*śūnyatā*), co-originating dependently loses its meaning as the link between two 'things'; rather it becomes the form for expressing the phenomenal 'becoming' as the lack of any self-sufficient, independent reality".[7] Thus Nagarjuna states, "The 'originating dependently' we call 'emptiness'."[8]

Emptiness as the negation of independent self-existence pertains not only to the human self, the array of things in our world, and the compositional factors, but to the religious ideal of *nirvāna* as well. Unlike *Sarvastivadin Abhidharma* thought, Nagarjuna does not regard *nirvāna* as an independent, unconditioned state. Convinced of universal relatedness, he considers such an independent reality a mental fabrication and argues that true *nirvāna* is not found apart from living-dying (*samsāra*), but realized in its midst:

> There is nothing whatever which differentiates the
>   existence-in-flux (*samsāra*) from *nirvāna*;
> And there is nothing which differentiates
>   *nirvāna* from existence-in-flux.[9]

[3] Kenneth K. Inada, "The America Involvement with Sunyata", in *Buddhism and American Thinkers*, eds Kenneth K. Inada and Nolan Jacobson (Albany: State University of New York Press, 1984), p. 82.

[4] David J. Kalupahana, *Buddhist Philosophy: A Historical Analysis* (Honolulu: University Press of Hawaii, 1976), p. 28.

[5] According to Richard Robinson and Willard L. Johnson, *svabhāva* indicates "something (1) existing through its own power rather than that of another, (2) possessing an invariant and inalienable mark, and (3) having an immutable essence". *The Buddhist Religion: An Introduction*, 3rd edn (Belmont, CA: Wadsworth, 1982), p. 69.

[6] *Mūlamadhyamika-kārikās*, XXIV, 19, tr. Frederick Streng, in *Emptiness: A Study in Religious Meaning* (Nashville: Abingdon, 1967), p. 213.

[7] Frederick Streng, *Emptiness: A Study in Religious Meaning*, p. 63.

[8] *Mūlamadhyamika-kārikās*, XXIV, 18, in Streng, p. 213.

[9] Ibid., XXV, 19, in Streng, p. 217 [see also, "An Analysis of *Nirvāna*," p. 77 below].

From the standpoint of unawakened, conventional knowledge, *samsāra* and *nirvāna* are seen as thoroughly opposite, whereas in absolute knowledge they are grasped as non-dual. Further, in the realization of emptiness, one is not attached to either of the realms conceptualized in conventional knowledge: *samsāra* or *nirvāna*, the secular or the sacred. This non-attachment constitutes religious freedom. "In the realization of emptiness through complete detachment from both the secular and the sacred worlds one can freely move back and forth between the two worlds without hindrance."[10]

Nagarjuna even argues that emptiness itself is empty. "Emptiness" does not refer to a transcendent, substantial Reality. As one scholar remarks, "when emptiness is described as inexpressible, inconceivable, and devoid of designation, it does not imply that there is such a thing having these as characteristics".[11] Again, emptiness is synonymous with dependent co-origination, with the continuous changing system of relationships called "becoming". It is not apart from actuality, as indicated by the famous line in the Heart Sutra, "Form is emptiness and emptiness is form".

Emptiness, then, is not a religious ultimate in the sense of a transcendent Being or eternal Oneness. In fact, emptiness negates the reification of *anything* as an ultimate. This point is of crucial soteriological significance. "Only by realizing that the *dharma* [the historical Buddha's teaching], the Path, and the Buddha were not ultimate entities to be grasped by intellectual or meditative techniques could one be free from the attempt to possess an Ultimate as well as be free from the sorrow resulting from not attaining that illusory 'Ultimate'."[12] Nagarjuna's articulation of emptiness thus serves to dissolve ignorant structures of experience and lead us toward a realization of liberating wisdom (*prajñā*). "Epistemologically, emptiness is *prajñā*, an unattached insight that truth is absolutely true."[13] But what is the nature of attachment and suffering?

As the historical Buddha discussed in his talks on the Four Holy Truths, human suffering is caused primarily by desire or craving (*trsna*). Through ignorance (*avidyā*) of dependent co-origination and impermanence, a person takes the objectified self and other experiential objects to be independent, enduring entities, and through this mode of experience grows attached to them positively (desire and love) or negatively (aversion and hatred). This ignorance of the conditioned nature of the self and its world derives in large part from hypostatizing that which we experience and giving it a convenient designation, such as "me", "you", "us", "them", "career", "fame", or "wealth". To the degree subjectivity positions itself as some thing or self, identifies with that position and whatever bolsters it, becomes negatively attached – through aversion, fear and hatred – to entities threatening it, and works to protect and maintain its position relative to the non-self, subjectivity becomes alienated from its world, the very context and source of its be-ing. Moreover, in objectifying itself through self-consciousness, subjectivity becomes split into a reflective subject and reflected-upon object, and thus becomes estranged even from itself.

To loosen attachment to the boundaries created by the "thinking-thinging"[14] process, Nagarjuna explicates the relational character of reality. In the *Mūlamadhyamika-kārikās*, he sets forth emptiness to negate the reification of the convenient constructions (*prajñapti*) of language and the projection of them onto reality. He

asserts that the so-called essence is nothing but a hypostatization of word-meaning. The word, he says, is not of such a nature that it indicates a real object. Instead of being a sure guarantee of the existence of an ontological essence, every word is itself a mere baseless mental construction whose meaning is determined by the relation in which it stands to other words. Thus

[10]   Masao Abe, "Substance, Process, and Emptiness", *Japanese Religions*, Vol. 11 (September 1980), Nos 2 and 3, p. 26.
[11]   Op. cit., Streng, p. 80.
[12]   Ibid., p. 158.
[13]   Hsueh-li Cheng, *Nagarjuna's "Twelve Gate Treatise"* (Dordrecht, Holland: D. Reidel, 1982), p. 14.
[14]   Ken Wilber, *No Boundary* (Boulder, CO: Shambhala, 1981), p. 41.

the meaning of a word immediately changes as soon as the whole network of which it is but a member changes even slightly.[15]

Essentially, "emptiness is a non-referring word about referring words".[16] That is to say, "Emptiness is not a term outside the expressional system, but is simply the key term within it . . . Like all other expressions, it is empty, but it has a peculiar relation within the system of designations. It symbolizes non-system, a surd within the system of constructs."[17]

Further, through a dialectical analysis of various philosophical viewpoints, Nagarjuna demonstrates the inherent contradictions of any doctrinal standpoint that attempts to grasp reality conceptually. This analytical method is called *prasanga*, a type of *reductio ad absurdum*. One form this dialectical method takes is the negation of a tetralemma. Nagarjuna argues that a *dharma* is

neither 1. existent
  nor 2. non-existent
  nor 3. both existent and non-existent
  nor 4. neither existent nor non-existent.

This is echoed in Nagarjuna's eightfold negation:

I salute the Buddha,
The foremost of all teachers;
He has taught
The doctrine of dependent co-arising,
[The reality of all things is marked by]
No origination, no extinction;
No permanence, no impermanence;
No identity, no difference;
No arrival, no departure.[18]

In this way, Nagarjuna negates (empties) the ontological categories of being and non-being, and rejects both naive realism and nihilism. Reality eludes discursive, discriminating thought and its dualistic categories of being and non-being, subject and object, identity and difference, cause and effect. It cannot be objectified or articulated by any word, theory or thought process; any attempt to grasp it conceptually is doomed to failure and, more crucially, suffering. Again, this does not imply that there is an independent, substantial "thing" eluding us. Rather, reality is beyond all distinctions of thing and no-thing, being and non-being, immanent and transcendent, or eternal and temporal. As the open, dynamic context of becoming, "it" gives rise to all things, though never apart from them. Emptiness hence signifies that (1) nothing in the world has any self-existence, and (2) no concept or theory, nor the cognitive process that creates and uses it, can grasp the nature of reality.

A mere intellectual understanding of these two senses of emptiness is not sufficient to bring about a cessation of suffering, for ignorance colours not only the intellectual but also the emotional and volitional aspects of human existence. To understand emptiness non-objectively in its full religious significance, ignorant subjectivity must be sloughed off. This emptying requires more than a mere philosophical dialectic, so Nagarjuna's logic must be linked with an engaged religious quest. Through meditation and other religious practices, or through despair of the ego-self and a realization of the human predicament, one arrives at what Zen refers to as Great Doubt and Great Death, in which dualistic ego-consciousness is broken through. More specifically, subjectivity entangled in the ignorant reification and attachment process reaches an impasse and ultimately drops away, an event the Japanese Zen master Dogen (1200–53) calls "the dropping off of mind and body". Simultaneously, unattached liberated subjectivity awakens. This subjectivity is not attached to or identified with any particular self-definition or form, and hence has been termed the "Formless Self" by a modern Zen master, Shin'ichi Hisamatsu. And since emptiness understood as absolute subjectivity is beyond the grasp of

[15] Toshihiko Izutsu, *Toward a Philosophy of Zen Buddhism* (Boulder, CO: Prajna, 1982), pp. 105–6.
[16] Douglas D. Daye, "Major Schools of the Mahayana: Madhyamika", in *Buddhism: A Modern Perspective*, ed. Charles S. Prebish (University Park, PA: Pennsylvania State University Press, 1978), p. 92.
[17] Richard H. Robinson, *Early Madhyamika in India and China* (New York: Samuel Weiser, 1978), p. 49.
[18] Translated by Hsueh-li Cheng, *Nagarjuna's "Twelve Gate Treatise"*, pp. 15–16.

language and conceptual thought, it is said to be "unattainable" (*anupalambha*), or unobjectifiable. This aspect of emptiness generates such metaphors as a sword unable to cut itself or an eye unable to see itself while functioning effectively in actuality.

The goal of Nagarjuna's dialectic and the accompanying quest, then, is a transcendence of subjectivity that reifies things or states of affairs and becomes attached to that which has been reified. In Nagarjuna's writings and before him "in the *Prajñāpāramitā*, supreme enlightenment is identified with the attainment of *śūnyatā*. In other words, the object of the Buddhist life is to find an unattached abode in this realization. This abode is called *apratishthita*, not-abiding."[19] In Mahayana Buddhism, non-abiding, liberated subjectivity is equipped with the wisdom (*prajñā*) that "sees" the arising of all things in emptiness (dependent co-origination). Such wisdom does not indicate a retreat from actuality into annihilation or a void, but a dynamic realization that emptiness is none other than form, that is, the world of events. This dynamic regrasping of actuality in terms of open, processive emptiness is empowered by the energy formerly blocked in the attempt to maintain a delineated self and its boundaries. "To maintain this integrated self, enormous *binding force*, or *clinging*, is required. Setting loose the binding force of ego-clinging thus releases the tremendous potential energy within, and this constitutes what Buddhism calls Enlightenment and liberation."[20]

In conjunction with this transformation, subjectivity has shifted epistemologically from conventional, practical knowledge and truth (*samvṛti-satya*) in which the person was entangled, to liberated religious knowledge and truth (*paramārtha-satya*), the insight into universal emptiness. On the basis of the latter, the person is able to make use of conventional knowledge in the everyday practical realm without causing suffering by reifying the convenient concepts used in such knowledge. Epistemologically, "all dualism or conceptual distinction is reconstructed

in the realization of Emptiness without any possibility of clinging to distinction".[21] And in making the shift to the second truth, the anxiety, pain and dis-ease previously experienced disappear as subjectivity stops clinging and opens up to empty, dependent co-arising. Paradoxically (at least when seen from our ordinary perspective), salvation is achieved not by realizing an eternal, unchanging reality outside of becoming, but by overcoming the subjectivity that seeks permanence apart from actuality and thus entering fully into becoming Here and Now. In this way, the problem of the search for permanent being outside of becoming is dissolved, rather than "solved" through the discovery of a permanent Reality, the way normal subjectivity imagines the problem to be solvable. One's whole being shifts from substantialist, dualistic thought, to non-substantial thought, or, in the words of one Buddhist scholar, from the "*Svabhava*" way of thinking to the "*Nihsvabhava*" ("no-own-being", empty) way of thinking, as delineated in the following:

The *Svabhava* Way	The *Nihsvabhava* Way
independent	interdependent
unitary	structural
entity and substance	events and actions
static	dynamic
fixed	fluid
bound	free
definitely restricted	infinite possibilities
clinging and attachment	release and detachment
thatness	thusness[22]

It must be noted here, however, that the empty (*Nihsvabhava*) way of thinking or experiencing is not a theory advanced in opposition to theories based on substantialist *svabhavic* thought. Rather, it cuts through all cognition, all theoretical standpoints that attempt to objectify reality and grasp its nature conceptually. Emptiness serves to circumvent such thought, not to give it a correct object to ponder. Nagarjuna asks us to empty ourselves of such objectification,

[19]   Daisetz Teitaro Suzuki, *Studies in the Lankavatara Sutra* (London: Routledge & Kegan Paul, 1975), p. 94.
[20]   Garma C. C. Chang, *The Buddhist Teaching of Totality: The Philosophy of Hwa Yen Buddhism* (University Park, PA: Pennsylvania State University Press, 1971), pp. 78–9.
[21]   Masao Abe, "God, Emptiness, and Ethics" (unpublished), p. 5.
[22]   Op. cit., Chang, p. 85, partially adapted here.

discrimination, and conceptualization – and then experience in terms of *prajñā*.

In addition to the critical, soteriological and epistemological aspects of the term, emptiness also plays a positive "ontological" role in Nagarjuna's thought. To Nagarjuna, emptiness is not merely a negation of own-being (*svabhāva*), for it is only by virtue of emptiness that things can "be". As discussed earlier, to be is to co-originate with other things through mutual conditioning. And to be open to the various conditions, the relational entity must be *empty* of any independent, self-contained status. Thus, as one Buddhist scholar tells us, "things exist by virtue of their true emptiness. . . . If things were not empty of a substance or essence, they could not exist even for a second; conversely, without things, there can be no emptiness. This is not hard to understand if it is remembered that emptiness refers only to the mode of being of existents."[23] In Nagarjuna's words,

When emptiness "works", then everything in existence "works". If emptiness does not "work", then all existence does not "work".[24]

Since universal interrelating provides the necessary condition for things to "be", all apparently enduring entities (me, you, the piece of paper before us) are constantly "open" to constitutive factors; accordingly, an independent entity with own-being cannot even begin to exist. It is not that things exist *even though* they are empty, but that things exist *precisely because* they are empty. On this basis we express schematically the meaning of the aforementioned couplet from the Heart Sutra, "Form is emptiness, emptiness is form":

form is emptiness	no own-being (*svabhāva*); "things" arise only through dependent co-origination
emptiness is form	the dependent co-origination by virtue of which "things" arise is not apart from them

Thus it is not the case that emptiness or dependent co-origination exists temporally or ontologically prior to actuality; rather, emptiness as dependent co-origination is the actual dynamics of reality in its very becoming.

In awakening to emptiness as the dynamics of becoming, as the mode of be-ing, we realize the convergence of ontology, epistemology and ethics. Ontologically, the emptied self ceases to posit itself as an enduring, bounded entity standing in opposition to the objects of its experience (including itself as objectified in dualistic knowing). It experiences the world as a system of dynamic, processive interrelationships (temporal) and mutual constitution (atemporal and structural in the now). More exactly, the emptied self *is* its experience. That is to say, it is not that we *have* an experience of something, but that we *are* our experience. In the immediacy of direct experience prior to later reflection, the experiencer, experiencing and experienced are not separate. Epistemologically, this openness and direct experience is *prajñā*, defined here as experiencing in the mode of emptiness, that is, nihsvabhavically. Psychologically, "the dawning of *prajñā*, by which one sees the emptiness of things, is an act of absolute encompassing whereby one's boundaries expand to include everything. To see emptiness is to become emptiness, or, . . . to become empty is to see emptiness."[25] To use the terminology of one Zen philosopher, this openness is the "boundless expanse of Awakening" (*Kaku-no-hirogari*).[26] This can be understood only when the reflective, hypostatizing ("thinging") ego-self is emptied and formless subjectivity (Awakening) opens up. In Nagarjuna's parlance, this is the shift from *samvṛti-satya* to *paramārtha-satya*.

Given that the "self" is precisely the dynamism of experiencing, human knowing and being converge. More exactly put, emptiness indicates the level at which knowing and being (and doing) are still undivided. Understood in this way, "emptiness" functions as the ground of Mahayana Buddhist ethics. When we conceive of *śūnyatā*

---

[23] Francis H. Cook, *Hua-yen Buddhism: The Jewel Net of Indra* (University Park, PA: Pennsylvania State University Press, 1977), p. 102.
[24] *Mūlamadhyamika-kārikās*, XXIV, 14, in Streng, p. 213.
[25] Op. cit., Cook, p. 107.
[26] Masao Abe coined this term to express the open, inclusive nature of Awakening.

as "emptying", that which is emptied is the self-centred, defensive, boundary-forming ego-self. Emptying is a liberating expansion, in which emptied subjectivity becomes a context for fullness. It is not unlike the sky, the other meaning of the Chinese ideograph for *śūnyatā*. As one Zen master states, "We should always live in the dark, empty sky. The sky is always the sky. Even though clouds and lightning come, the sky is not disturbed."[27]

Through this emptying of the ego-self, the artificial distinctions and discriminations made with regard to others are emptied as well. The other is now seen for what he or she is. In Buddhist terminology, the person is seen in his or her suchness, or "as-it-is-ness". And at a deeper level, our sense of self expands to include others. One contemporary Zen master writes,

> The practice of "being with them" [realizing mutual constitution] converts the third person, *they, it, she, he*, into the first person *I*, and *we*. For Dogen Zenji, the others who are "none other than myself" include mountains, rivers, and the great earth. . . .

This is compassion, suffering with others. "Dwell nowhere, and bring forth that mind" [Diamond Sutra]. "Nowhere" is the zero of purest experience, known inwardly as fundamental peace and rest. To "come forth" is to stand firmly and contain the myriad things.[28]

In conjunction with the realization of such subjectivity, we are emptied of rigid attachment to personal notions of truth and falsehood, right and wrong. We realize that all views, including our own, are tentative and partial. Here the road to tolerance, inclusiveness and participation opens before us, and we begin to serve each other as we inter-act and inter-create in the open context of emptiness. We shift from a svabhavic, self-centred outlook to a holistic, organic view of actuality. No longer frightened and defensive, we can act freely and creatively in the web of interrelationship. "Not holding on to a notion of self, we are invited to engage ourselves courageously in the world, to see the nature of suffering clearly, and with discriminating awareness to undertake the task of liberating all sentient beings."[29] [. . .]

[27]   Shunryu Suzuki, *Zen Mind, Beginner's Mind* (New York: John Weatherhill, 1973), p. 86.
[28]   Robert Aitken, *A Mind of Clover* (San Francisco: North Point, 1984), p. 173.
[29]   Fred Eppsteiner, "In the Crucible: The Tiep Hien Precepts", in *The Path of Compassion: Contemporary Writings on Engaged Buddhism*, eds Fred Eppsteiner and Dennis Maloney (Buffalo: White Pine, 1985), p. 101.

Reality and Divinity in Chinese Philosophy

Chung-Ying Cheng

The Chinese Approach to the Theory of Reality

In the *Xici Commentary* on the *Zhouyi*, we witness the emergence of the two basic concepts characterizing the ultimate reality of human experience. These two basic concepts are, respectively, that of the great ultimate (*taiji*) and that of the way (*dao*). Both concepts are derived from human experience of the formation and transformation of things in nature, which are referred to as "*bianyi*" or "*bianhua*" (change).

[...]

It is this theory of *taiji* and *dao* that represents the main stream of metaphysical thinking in the 3,200-year history of Chinese philosophy, and which thus should be regarded as the fundamental theory of reality in Chinese philosophy. [...] However, in order to distinguish this ancient view from the later Daoist approach to reality of Laozi (whose exact dates are uncertain, but who lived about the middle of the sixth century BCE) and Zhuangzi (circa 370–300 BCE), and their elaboration of the philosophy of the *dao*, we may refer to it as the "*Yizhuan* theory of

reality", since the theory is suggested and implicitly formulated in the Commentaries on the *Zhouyi* known as *Yizhuan* [...].

In order to understand the *Yizhuan* theory of reality, we should take note of the following characterization of our experience of change:

(1) *Reality as inexhaustible origination.* We can trace the presentation and development of the world's reality to a root-source. This root-source, called "the great ultimate" (*taiji*), is the absolute beginning of all things, but it is also the sustaining base for all things in the present, because all changes in the world are based on it and contained in it. In this sense, the *taiji* is the primordial and inexhaustible source of creative and transformative energy, a fact conveyed by its designation as the "creativity of creativity" or "generation of generation" (*shengsheng*) [...]. In this sense, reality is not something static underneath a world of fleeting phenomena; nor is it a realm of forms or ideas reflected in a world of imitations. Neither is it something accessible only to abstractive human reasoning, or through divine revelation. Reality is concrete, vivid and holistic, not merely in the sense that all things are interrelated within a whole originally defined by

"Reality and Divinity in Chinese Philosophy" by Chung-Ying Cheng in *A Companion to World Philosophies*, ed. Eliot Deutsch and Ron Bontekoe (Malden, MA: Blackwell Publishers, Inc, 1997), pp. 185–97. Reprinted by permission of the publishers, Blackwell Publishing.

the oneness of the *taiji*, but in the sense that changes and the non-changes underlying these changes are organically part and parcel of the same thing, and there cannot be any strict demarcation or bifurcation between appearance and reality. Changes and the constant and continuous regeneration of things are what reality consists of. Any scheme to divide or stratify reality can only serve a limited purpose. This means that all theories of reality share with reality itself the fact of change and are subject to the continuous challenges of an ongoing process of formation and transformation. Therefore, we may understand *taiji* as not just primary origination but constant and ceaseless origination. In a Whiteheadean spirit, we may say that the world is in-the-making, and is constantly and forever in-the-making.

(2)   Reality as a polar-generative process. When the *taiji* gives rise to things in the world, it does so by introducing polarities: the positive and the negative, or the *yang* (the brightening/the moving/the firm) and the *yin* (the darkening/the restive/the soft). These polarities are sub-contraries, which exist simultaneously and are conspicuous on one level. At the same time, they are also contraries which are hidden on the more concrete levels of things. In this latter sense, they are identifiable with the *taiji*, because the *taiji*, as the source of change, is always hidden beneath all things. The generation of new things occurs on the basis of the coexistence and interaction of these polarities. Thus, in this model novelties arise from the internal dynamics of a bifurcating of reality into *yin* and *yang* and the subsequent commingling of *yin* and *yang*. Thus the novelty of things is inherent in the very source of the world itself, and also in the creative potential of a thing, which requires the interaction of forces to bring it about.

(3)   Reality as a multi-interactive harmony. An individual thing or an individual class of things always has two aspects: the *yin*, which pertains to its stationary state of existence (its given nature) and its receptivity to the outside world, and the *yang*, which pertains to its dynamic state in developing its propensities in interaction with the outside world. As the *yin*–*yang* polarities are definitive of individual things or individual classes of things, that a thing must interact with

the outside world is in the nature of the thing itself. It is in this process of interaction that a thing fulfills its potentialities and runs its course of bounded existence. It is with respect to a thing's maintaining itself as a given nature that we speak of the "centrality" of a thing, and with respect to its properly taking from and giving to other things that we speak of "harmony" between or among things. There could be non-centrality and disharmony in the formation and transformation of a thing, which would constitute a crisis for its identity and its survival in the world of reality as things. And thus we see the importance of the thing's natural abilities both to maintain itself and to enter into proper give-and-take relations with other things. In the case of human beings in particular these two aspects of existence must be cultivated in order to enhance and realize human potentiality.

It is said that "One *yin* and one *yang* is thus called the *dao*. To follow it is goodness and to complete it is nature" (*Xici-shang*, 5). How are we to understand this in reference to individual things? The *dao* is how things come into being and how they grow and develop over time, and the process of one *yin* and one *yang* consists of the alternation, conjunction and mutual interaction of the positive and negative forces and positive and negative activities of the individual things, which results in the formation and transformation of things.

(4)   Reality as virtual hierarchization. The world is made of many levels, each of which exhibits the combination of the *yin* and *yang* forces or activities of things. For the *taiji* and *dao* model of cosmogony and cosmography (and hence ontocosmology), there are numerous general features of *yin* and *yang*, such as rest/motion, darkness/brightness, invisibility/visibility, softness/firmness, closedness/openness, and retrospective propensities/prospective propensities. Although these properties are basically described in phenomenal and experiential terms, there is no reason why they could not be described in a logical and scientific language of abstract and primary properties. One could, as many people have already done, for example, identify the *yin* and *yang* elements or processes in the genetic code and the theory of subatomic particles. Similarly, there is no reason why human values, emotions

and intentions could not be described in the language of *yin* and *yang*. In this light, *yin* and *yang* should be regarded as neutral and variant functors or operators, which interact to generate relationships and changes. The important point to remember is that, as there are levels of simplicity and complexity in the structures and activities of a scheme of things in being and becoming, so there are various levels of *yin* and *yang*. [. . .] But individual things must be understood as manifesting a complex hierarchy of levels of *yin* and *yang* background as well as a complex world of *yin* and *yang* interactions. This means that the individual thing or person can only be understood as acting within the context of a field or web of forces, and within this context it is still capable of having a creative impact and making a contribution to the formation and transformation of the world.

(5) Reality as recursive but limitless regenerativity. Although the Commentaries on the *Zhouyi* do not mention the recursive and regenerative nature of the *yi*, the presentation of nature in eight trigrams and of the world in 64 hexagrams in the original 1200 BCE symbolism, and the appended judgments of divination clearly suggest that nature is a process of both collective and distributive balance and that it functions as a process of return and reversion – as we see in the rotation of seasons and celestial cycles. [. . .]

In the *taiji* and *dao* model of reality what is shown in the symbolism of the *yi* is a regenerative recursion by reversion – which is to say, the *yin* stage has to revert to a *yang* stage and vice versa in order for creative change to be realized. It is in the nature of time that *yin* and *yang* interact through alternation. Because of this, one is entitled to expect that reaching the worst implies of necessity a return to a better condition. Although in practice, of course, it is difficult to know whether one has in fact reached the worst or how long the improvement will last, it is nevertheless possible to conceive of reality as an alternation between good and bad as a natural process of change.

(6) Reality as an organismic totality. From the above description, it should be clear that the world of reality on the model of the *taiji* and *dao* is totalistic in the sense that all things are

included and there is nothing beyond it. It is said that, "*The Book of Changes* is extensive and all-comprehensive. It contains the way of heaven, the way of man and the way of earth" (*Xici-xia*, 10). For the early Chinese, the real world is confined to heaven, earth and the ten thousand things, among which humanity stands out as the most intelligent and the one capable of forming a tri-partnership with heaven and earth. Everything in this reality comes from the *taiji* and follows or embodies the *dao*. This implies, then, that there is no transcendent reality beyond this world. When we come to Laozi, we find that even when the notion of emptiness (*wu*) is introduced, what the term "*wu*" stands for is part and parcel of the universe of the *dao*. The *dao* in Laozi is simply enriched by something called the void or non-being (*wu*). Similarly, when Zhou Dunyi (1017–73) speaks of the ultimateness (*wuji*) giving rise to the great ultimate, he is simply extending the *dao* to cover both void and non-void. There is no break between the void and the non-void and hence one does not have a transcendent nothingness or emptiness apart from reality. In this non-transcendence, we do not speak merely of immanence, but also of totality. Immanence refers to values and powers inherent in the things themselves, but totality refers to all of the interrelated parts of all things in the real world. The reason why things belong or hang together, is because in the ultimate reality things are not simply contained, but rather are interrelated or even interpenetrating. It is the organismic nature of the totality that not only can there not be any object "outside," but that all things exist together by way of mutual support and even mutual grounding. This is how the immanence of heaven in the nature of man leads to an interminable exchange between, as well as a unity of, man and heaven.

Although the *Yizhuan* developed the fundamental metaphysics of the *taiji* and *dao* in Chinese philosophy, which inspires or perhaps grounds the Confucian view on the moral propensity of man, it is in Laozi's *Daodejing* ("The Classic of Dao and De") that we find a better thematized theory of the *dao*. It might be said that a fuller and more distinctive theory of reality was formulated in the *Daodejing*. We may call it the Daoist theory of reality.

[. . .]

There are four major features of the Daoist theory of reality which can be regarded as differentiating it from the *Yizhuan* theory of reality. In the first place, the *Daodejing* introduced a unique notion of the *dao* which cannot be conveyed by language. The first sentence of the *Daodejing* declares, "The *dao* can be spoken, but it is not the constant *dao*; The name can be named, but it is not the constant name." What then is the *dao*? It is apparently the power or force underlying all changes and transformations of things in the world. The key here is that even though each thing has its own manner of change, they all share a common moving or motivating force for change. They also share in being in a common time and a common space with one another. This oneness is further manifested in the interrelatedness of all things in the world. But this power of change and this oneness are not separate from each other; nor are they separate from the world or from each individual thing in the world. It is difficult to express this all-encompassing oneness, comprehensiveness and moving/motivating power. When we choose the word "*dao*" to indicate or refer to this power, we cannot identify it with any of the things in the world, because it is not any of the things that our language describes. It is rather like an inaccessible object, such as the moon, to which we may point with a finger. Hence the *dao* is to be experienced, reflected upon, intended in our speech, but it cannot be identified. But this is not to say that the *dao* is non-existent, although it is invisible, inaudible, and intangible. Nor is it to say that its existence is non-efficacious, although it is non-substantial. On the contrary, the *dao* is full of power and functions in all of the natural activities of things in the world. More specifically, one can say that the *dao* is a power giving rise to all things without owning them, sustaining all things without dominating them, enabling things to act on their own without claiming their work. (See *Daodejing*, chapters 10, 34, 51.) The *dao* (which we might call "the creative spirit of the world") therefore is real and profound and can be considered the absolute beginning and primordial source of all things. In this sense, the *dao* can be said to exist before heaven and earth, and is the forerunner of all

things and the mother of all lives. It is also the naturally-of-its-accord spontaneity of things. Thus Laozi observes, "While man follows earth, earth follows heaven, heaven has to follow the *dao* and the *dao* would act of its own accord" (*Daodejing*, 25).

With all of this said, the important thing to keep in mind is that, although not the same as anything in the world, the *dao* is not separate from and does not transcend the world. Moreover, although it is the source of change and the ground of being for all things, it is not to be conceived of as God in any sense that a Western religion might understand this. It is rather the very nature of things when they are considered as an interrelated whole, as a unity of multiplicity, which exhibits its creativity and novelty through multifarious change and the abundance of life. One sees in the *dao* a dialectical unity of transcendence and immanence – which is to say, the transcendence of immanence and the immanence of transcendence in the relationship between nature and individual lives in nature. This understanding is intensified in the work of Zhuangzi, which stresses the idea of *dao* as the self-transformation (*zihua*) of things and the interpenetrating power of oneness (*dao-tong weiyi*).

We come now to the second point about the Daoist theory of reality. Because the *dao* is indescribable and non-substantial, it is conceived as void or empty (*chong, xu*). It is said that "*Dao* is void and its function is infinite" (*Daodejing*, 4). This voidness of the *dao* is also referred to as non-being (*wu*) by Laozi, when he says, "*Wu* names the beginning of heaven and earth, and *yu* [being] names the mother of ten thousand things" (*Daodejing*, 1). In fact, in order to appreciate how *wu* is a process of being's emergence from non-being, one might also see *wu* as a process of non-being's emergence from being. To become non-being is to void existence of all determinate characteristics and to go back to a state when all determinations of characteristics are in the offing. Things come into being, in other words, from a nebulous and indeterminate state of non-being, in which non-being could even be understood as indeterminacy of being. There are many passages offering this view. (See, for example, chapters 14 and 21.) In this sense, *wu* can be regarded as one aspect of the *dao*, the other aspect of which is simply *yu*. *Wu* is no-thing (*wuwu*), and *yu* is having-things (*yuwu*). As *dao* is a power creative of all things as well as the process of creative production, it has both the activity of *wu* and the activity of *yu*, just as all things have both the *yin* (emptying) and *yang* (substantiating) functions. It is through the interaction of these two functions and their conjunction that things become what they are and reach a state of harmony. [. . .]

One way to reach the state of *wu*, and hence the state of the natural functioning of the *dao*, is to have no desires (*wu-yu*) and no action (*wu-wei*) on the part of a person. This is important for the Daoist theory of reality because the theory is not simply a matter of abstract speculation, but of close personal embodiment of ontocosmological principles in one's life experience. In fact, without such an embodiment, Laozi (the Old One) would not have been able to describe so vividly the reality and creativity of the *dao*. From this, one may correctly conclude that, according to the Daoist, any human being can come to an intimate knowledge and understanding of the *dao* so long as he reduces his desires, knowledge and actions to a state of oneness. (See chapter 39.) This also means that, at a minimum, one should not let one's desires and knowledge block the open vision of the whole process of change and transformation in the *dao*. The idea that one's vision could be blocked by one's desires and knowledge is a result no doubt of a close observation of reality. Hence Laozi advises that one should keep oneself free from diversions of the senses, and the burdens of learning. For the *dao* reveals itself to those in a free state of mind or in an open state of the non-fixation of belief. This point is also strongly stressed in Zhuangzi.

We come to a third point in the Daoist theory of reality. Reality under the name "*dao*" is always a matter of return (*fu*) and reversion (*fan*). It is said that,

To reach for the ultimate of emptiness and to abide by the utmost of tranquility, ten thousand things will agitate at the same time. I would therefore be able to observe the process of return. There are many things and each would return to its root. To return to the root is called "tranquility" and this is called "return to destiny" (*fuming*). (*Daodejing*, 16)

It is interesting to note that, whereas the *Yizhuan* approach to reality stresses the ceaselessness of productive creativity (*shengsheng buyi*), the Daoist approach to reality stresses the constancy of return. In this sense, then, the *Yizhuan* approach is dynamic and the Daoist approach is static. However, the Daoist stress on return as a distinctive feature of reality was already implicit in the *Zhouyi* symbolism of trigrams and hexagrams.

[. . .]

The fourth point is a brief one. Not only can man observe the *dao* both outside of himself and within his own person, and thus come to an understanding of it, he can also cultivate the *dao* (participating in it or imitating it) in order to achieve a desirable and ideal state of life. For the Daoists, just as for the Confucianists, there are ample grounds for speaking of the unity of man and heaven or the unity of the human person and the *dao*. This unity is important for both schools in so far as ethics, social action and political life are all dependent upon it.

We now have a composite picture of reality as it is understood in classical Chinese philosophy by way of the *Yizhuan* approach and the Daoist approach. Their different points of emphasis should not overshadow their common roots and common vision of reality as a world of interrelated things in a creative process of change and transformation. [. . .]

The Chinese Approach to the Theory of Divinity

Any theory of divinity must be grounded on or presuppose a theory of reality. A notion of divinity might appear on the scene first, but in time it must disclose the theory of reality presupposed by it. It may happen, of course, that the theory of divinity in question could itself offer an account of reality, so that the notion of divinity is, as it were, logically prior to the notion of reality. It may also happen, however, that an early notion of divinity (and the notion of reality implicit in it) comes to be supplanted by a new, perhaps more sophisticated, theory of reality, which in turn makes possible a new and perhaps more sophisticated understanding of divinity.

We can see the development of Christianity in the West as a classical example of the former case – of transition from a specific theory of God's nature to a theologically grounded theory of reality. On the other hand, we can see the development of Confucian and Daoist metaphysics as an example of the latter case – of transition from a theory of *tian* (heaven) or *di* (lord on high) to an ontocosmological theory of reality which traces the activity of the divine in the creative productiveness and transformativeness of things.

[...]

As early as the beginning of the Xia Era in 2000 BCE, there were already references to the Lord on High (*di*) who would supervise and oversee human affairs and who controls human destiny from above. This notion of *di* could be regarded as a spiritual projection of a powerful and venerated ancestor who played the role of ruler and governor in his lifetime. The word "*di*" is also said to symbolize the bud of a flower, and hence the source of life. The Lord on High, then, as he is presented in the *Book of Documents* (*Shujing*) and the *Book of Poetry* (*Shijing*), is to be seen as a supreme being who combines the source of life and the source of power in one person, and who cares for the well-being of people (as his posterity) and the ordering of the state. He was thought of and worshipped as a personal god who could issue commands and mandates. In time, however, the idea of *di* fused with the notion of *tian* (heaven or sky, a term to be understood spatially rather than temporally). *Tian* too is to be conceived of as powerful and life-giving, although now the conception of infiniteness is added. (In the *Shijing* we read that "The great heaven has no limit.") It seems probable that a more sophisticated sense of reality made possible the transformation from a worship of *di* to a worship of *tian*. [...]

This more sophisticated sense of reality diluted the personalistic character of *tian* as a supreme ruler on high and a supreme creator of life. As the Chinese sense of reality focused increasingly on the unity of man and heaven, understood in terms of a common bond of creative activity, *tian* eventually came to be regarded as the Way of Heaven (*tiandao*). We find this depersonization of *tian* already in Confucius, although

Confucius still occasionally spoke of *tian* as if it were the Lord on High or a supreme moral being. The full naturalization and depersonalization of *tian* occurs in Daoism, where *tian* is seen as having been given rise to by the great *dao* (not the *dao* of any given thing, but the *dao* itself as a creative process and reality which generates things in the world and imparts to them the power of self-autonomy and self-transformation).

The transformation of *di* to *tian* and then to *dao* embodies a movement from a theory of personal divinity to a theory of depersonalized reality. Even though a personalistic notion of divinity is lost, which accounts for the fact that China, unlike the West, has not sustained a monotheistic religion, the sense of divinity is still present in the form of a profound understanding of reality itself as the process of creative change and as the inexhaustible source of novelty and life. This [...] is a kind of "divinity without theology."

What, then, is divinity in Chinese philosophy? The Chinese term "*shen*" is used to refer to all natural spirits, which may be conceived of as personalized entities vested with life and special powers. In fact, *shen* is the living presence of power which may be said to exist in all of those living things of nature that can exert their influence upon other things. More specifically, the term "*shen*" applies to human persons in their possession of this living presence of power to influence others. Thus a person who accomplishes great deeds and achieves exemplary virtues, and who is consequently respected and wields great influence during his life, leaves upon his death his *shen* (or influence, heretofore referred to as "spirit") to be worshipped or sought after. In this sense, the *shen* of a person is the natural extension of his life and the power of his influence projected into the present and the future even after the physical person is no longer present. When an unworthy person dies, however, his spirit is not sought after but rather avoided, and he is known not as a *shen*, but as a *gui* or ghost – something belonging (one hopes) only to the past. If *shen* is to be explained as the beneficial power of a person extending to the future from the present, *gui* is to be conceived of by contrast as the traces of a past human life. But even the *gui* of a person can affect the present, although a deceased person's coming back to the present would be a surprising and alarming event.

This conception of *shen* is well developed in both the classical Confucian and the classical Daoist philosophies of the constitution of the human person. [...] The human person is conceived of as formed of three or four levels of existence. On the first level, there is the physical reality which is his body (*shen*). On the second level, there is his essence of life (*jing*) or the essential elements of his life as an organism. On the third level, there is his energy and the circulating powers of life, which are referred to as vital breath (*qi*). Finally, there is the level of *shen*, which can be regarded as the quintessence of life and vital energy, or the *qi* of *qi*. It is the freest element of life, but an element which also survives physical life in a free manner in that it can be expressed in the arts and deeds, the work and the words of a person.

According to this conception, human existence is not a conjunction of mind and body, as Cartesian dualism would have it, but rather a holistic unity of interpenetrating life-elements, each of which is itself to be conceived holistically. The holistic conception of life differs from the atomistic conception in that there are no absolute simple elements postulated, but rather nebulous wholes, and these interactively support each other. Thus it is not simply that the higher levels depend on the lower levels, but the lower levels also depend on the higher levels. In this sense, any lower level of existence can be thought of as having a higher level which is its *shen*. Whether the *shen* stands out depends on the special influence or presence of power a thing has. Thus for the ancient Chinese, all major mountains and rivers have their *shen* or spirits which are worthy of worship and respect. On the other hand, the *shen* of a human being who achieved great power of influence would be more vividly entertained in the minds of the relevant people and would thus become more clearly an object of worship.

With respect to the last point, it is interesting to note that Confucius says in the *Analects* that we must "sacrifice to the spirits as if the spirits are present; if I am not engaging myself (*yu*) in the sacrifice, it is like not holding a sacrifice" (3:12). How does one feel that the spirits are present? To feel the presence of the person or the object involves using one's feelings and imaginative powers in a projection of the known person or object. In the case of an unknown person or object, it is to think of the person or object of worship. It is a total engagement of one's person in the projected construction of the object, and as a consequence the object becomes the subject, because it is infused with the best spirit and essence of life of the person engaged. A person who does not engage in sacrifice in this manner is not considered to have genuinely performed a sacrifice.

When we enlarge on and extend the notion of *shen* as explained above, we see that the whole universe has its *shen*, particularly when we reflect and observe the life-generating and life-preserving power of the universe conceived as an organic whole. The whole universe is then seen as a progenitor, maintainer and preserver of life. As we have seen, it is in this way that the idea of the "Way of Heaven" was developed, in which heaven is both a concretion and an abstraction of the whole of nature focused upon in its powers of life-generation and life-maintenance. *Tian* is conceived of as both the whole of nature and the whole process of life production, in which both birth and death are regarded as part and parcel of the life-maintaining and life-generating process. In this sense, death is absorbed into the larger process and circulation of life and must be faced by a person with equanimity and peace of mind, a point which Confucianism and Neo-Confucianism have specifically stressed.

When we speak of the *shen* of the whole of nature or the universe, we speak of the divine. The divine, in this sense, is an elevation of the spiritual, because in becoming the divine the spiritual is no longer confined to any projected or formerly existing person or thing, but pertains to the ever-present and ever-active life and vitality of the whole of nature. In essence it pertains to the ever-creative creativity of the source of life. Therefore, the power of influence becomes the power of the generation and transformation of life. We find this sense of divinity presented in the writings of Mencius and the *Doctrine of the Mean*. Mencius writes,

> What is desirable is goodness. One holding to oneself [in self-knowledge] is integrity. To fulfil one's potentiality is beauty. To have

self-fulfillment and shining out [and being influential] is greatness. Being great and capable of transforming life is called sagely (*sheng*). When the sagely power is beyond the measure of knowledge, it is called the divine (*shen* – in the deeper sense of the spiritual or creative). (7B:25)

It should be noticed that the spiritual creative power which is the divine is to be built up from the basic desires of life whose fulfillment is a form of goodness, according to Mencius. Only when one attains goodness based on one's genuine desire for goodness, will one achieve integrity in the sense that the self is not just a physical event but a value of importance. This integrity would then be the starting point for the enlargement and extension of a transforming power that raises other beings and persons onto a higher level of existence. The key phrase here is "great and transforming", which is taken as the mark of the divine.

The divine is conveyed by the notion of sageliness (*sheng*), which culminates in the limitless influence and transformation it may entail. The combination of "sageliness" and "divinity" in the phrase "*shengshen*" (divine and sagely) can be said to capture the meaning of the sacred or holy in the best spirit of the Western religious tradition without assuming its concomitant theology. Thus there are two forms of "divinity without theology": the Confucian and the Daoist.

7

How the Supreme Nature Exists through Itself

Anselm of Canterbury

Since the same meaning is not always attached to the phrase, "existence through" something, or, to the phrase, "existence derived from" something, very diligent inquiry must be made, in what way all existing beings exist through the supreme Nature, or derive existence from it. For, what exists through itself, and what exists through another, do not admit the same ground of existence. Let us first consider, separately, this supreme Nature, which exists through self; then these beings which exist through another.

Since it is evident, then, that this Nature is whatever it is, through itself, and all other beings are what they are, through it, how does it exist through itself? For, what is said to exist through anything apparently exists through an efficient agent, or through matter, or through some other external aid, as through some instrument. But, whatever exists in any of these three ways exists through another than itself, and it is of later existence, and, in some sort, less than that through which it obtains existence.

But, in no wise does the supreme Nature exist through another, nor is it later or less than itself or anything else. Therefore, the supreme Nature could be created neither by itself, nor by another; nor could itself or any other be the matter whence it should be created; nor did it assist itself in any way; nor did anything assist it to be what it was not before.

What is to be inferred? For that which cannot have come into existence by any creative agent, or from any matter, or with any external aids, seems either to be nothing, or, if it has any existence, to exist through nothing, and derive existence from nothing. And although, in accordance with the observations I have already made, in the light of reason, regarding the supreme Substance, I should think such propositions could in no wise be true in the case of the supreme Substance; yet, I would not neglect to give a connected demonstration of this matter.

[. . .]

That this Nature, then, without which no nature exists, is nothing, is as false as it would be absurd to say that whatever is is nothing. And, moreover,

"How the Supreme Nature Exists through Itself" from *Monologion*, section VI, by Anselm of Canterbury, in *Proslogium; Monologium; an Appendix in Behalf of the Fool by Gaunilon; and Cur Deus Homo*, trans. Sydney Norton Deane (Chicago: Open Court Publishing, 1903, reprinted 1948), pp. 46–9. Reprinted by permission of Open Court Publishing Company, a division of Carus Publishing Company, Peru, IL, from *St Anselm Basic Writings*, trans. S. N. Deane, copyright © 1903 (reprinted 1948) by Open Court Publishing.

it does not exist through nothing, because it is utterly inconceivable that what is something should exist through nothing. But, if in any way it derives existence from nothing, it does so through itself, or through another, or through nothing. But it is evident that in no wise does anything exist through nothing. If, then, in any way it derives existence from nothing, it does so either through itself or through another.

But nothing can, through itself, derive existence from nothing, because if anything derives existence from nothing, through something, then that through which it exists must exist before it. Seeing that this Being, then, does not exist before itself, by no means does it derive existence from itself.

But if it is supposed to have derived existence from some other nature, then it is not the supreme Nature, but some inferior one, nor is it what it is *through itself*, but through another.

Again: if this Nature derives existence from nothing, through something, that through which it exists was a great good, since it was the cause of good. But no good can be understood as existing before that good, without which nothing is good; and it is sufficiently clear that this good, without which there is no good, is the supreme Nature which is under discussion. Therefore, it is not even conceivable that this Nature was preceded by any being, through which it derived existence from nothing.

Hence, if it has any existence through nothing, or derives existence from nothing, there is no doubt that either, whatever it is, it does not exist through itself, or derive existence from itself, or else it is itself nothing. It is unnecessary to show that both these suppositions are false. The supreme Substance, then, does not exist through any efficient agent, and does not derive existence from any matter, and was not aided in being brought into existence by any external causes. Nevertheless, it by no means exists through nothing, or derives existence from nothing; since, through itself and from itself, it is whatever it is.

Finally, as to how it should be understood to exist through itself, and to derive existence from itself: it did not create itself, nor did it spring up as its own matter, nor did it in any way assist itself to become what it was not before, unless, haply, it seems best to conceive of this subject in the way in which one says that *the light lights* or is *lucent*, through and from itself. For, as are the mutual relations of *the light* and *to light* and *lucent* (*lux, lucere, lucens*), such are the relations of *essence*, and *to be* and *being*, that is, *existing* or *subsisting*. So the supreme *Being*, and *to be* in the highest degree, and *being* in the highest degree, bear much the same relations, one to another, as *the light* and *to light* and *lucent*.

8

Of the Unicity of God

Avicenna (Ibn Sina)

It is not possible in any way that the Necessary Being should be two. Demonstration: Let us suppose that there is another necessary being: one must be distinguishable from the other, so that the terms "this" and "that" may be used with reference to them. This distinction must be either essential or accidental. If the distinction between them is accidental, this accidental element cannot but be present in each of them, or in one and not the other. If each of them has an accidental element by which it is distinguished from the other, both of them must be caused; for an accident is what is adjoined to a thing after its essence is realized. If the accidental element is regarded as adhering to its being, and is present in one of the two and not in the other, then the one which has no accidental element is a necessary being and the other is not a necessary being. If, however, the distinction is essential, the element of essentiality is that whereby the essence as such subsists; and if this element of essentiality is different in each and the two are distinguishable by virtue of it, then each of the two must be a compound; and compounds are caused; so that neither of them will be a necessary being. If the element of essentiality belongs to one only, and the other is one in every respect and there is no compounding of any kind in it, then the one which has no element of essentiality is a necessary being, and the other is not a necessary being. Since it is thus established that the Necessary Being cannot be two, but is All Truth, then by virtue of His Essential Reality, in respect of which He is a Truth, He is United and One, and no other shares with Him in that Unity: however the All-Truth attains existence, it is through Himself.

"Of the Unicity of God" by Avicenna (Ibn Sina) from *Avicenna on Theology*, trans. and ed. Arthur J. Arberry (Westport, CT: Hyperion Press, Inc. 1951), pp. 25–6.

9

The Omnipotence of God

Thomas Aquinas

[...] All confess that God is omnipotent; but it seems difficult to explain in what His omnipotence precisely consists: for there may be a doubt as to the precise meaning of the word "all" when we say that God can do all things. If, however, we consider the matter aright, since power is said in reference to possible things, this phrase, *God can do all things*, is rightly understood to mean that God can do all things that are possible; and for this reason He is said to be omnipotent. Now according to the Philosopher *(Metaph. v. 17)*, a thing is said to be possible in two ways. First in relation to some power, thus whatever is subject to human power is said to be possible to man. Secondly absolutely, on account of the relation in which the very terms stand to each other. Now God cannot be said to be omnipotent through being able to do all things that are possible to created nature; for the divine power extends farther than that. If, however, we were to say that God is omnipotent because He can do all things that are possible to His power, there would be a vicious circle in explaining the nature of His power. For this would be saying nothing else but that God is omnipotent, because He can do all that He is able to do.

It remains, therefore, that God is called omnipotent because he can do all things that are possible absolutely; which is the second way of saying a thing is possible. For a thing is said to be possible or impossible absolutely, according to the relation in which the very terms stand to one another, possible if the predicate is not incompatible with the subject, as that Socrates sits; and absolutely impossible when the predicate is altogether incompatible with the subject, as, for instance, that a man is a donkey.

It must, however, be remembered that since every agent produces an effect like itself, to each active power there corresponds a thing possible as its proper object according to the nature of that act on which its active power is founded; for instance, the power of giving warmth is related as to its proper object to the being capable of being warmed. The divine existence, however, upon which the nature of power in God is founded, is infinite, and is not limited to any genus of being; but possesses within itself the perfection of all being. Whence, whatsoever has or can have the nature of being, is numbered among the absolutely possible things, in respect of which God is called omnipotent. Now nothing is opposed to the idea of being except non-being. Therefore, that which implies being and non-being at the same time is repugnant to the idea of an absolutely possible thing, within the scope of the divine omnipotence.

"The Omnipotence of God," Part I, Question 25, 3rd article of *The Summa Theologica* by Thomas Aquinas, trans. Fathers of the English Dominican Province, 2nd revised edition (London: Burns Oates & Washbourne, 1920), pp. 350–2.

For such cannot come under the divine omnipotence, not because of any defect in the power of God, but because it has not the nature of a feasible or possible thing. Therefore, everything that does not imply a contradiction in terms, is numbered amongst those possible things, in respect of which God is called omnipotent: whereas whatever implies contradiction does not come within the scope of divine omnipotence, because it cannot have the aspect of possibility. Hence it is better to say that such things cannot be done, than that God cannot do them. [. . .]

10

Thinking and Speaking about God by Analogy

Thomas Aquinas

[. . .] Univocal predication is impossible between God and creatures. The reason of this is that every effect which is not an adequate result of the power of the efficient cause, receives the similitude of the agent not in its full degree, but in a measure that falls short, so that what is divided and multiplied in the effects resides in the agent simply, and in the same manner; as for example the sun by the exercise of its one power produces manifold and various forms in all inferior things. In the same way, [. . .] all perfections existing in creatures divided and multiplied, pre-exist in God unitedly. Thus, when any term expressing perfection is applied to a creature, it signifies that perfection distinct in idea from other perfections; as, for instance, by this term *wise* applied to a man, we signify some perfection distinct from a man's essence, and distinct from his power and existence, and from all similar things; whereas when we apply it to God, we do not mean to signify anything distinct from His essence, or power, or existence. Thus also this term *wise* applied to man in some degree circumscribes and comprehends the thing signified; whereas this is not the case when it is applied to God; but it leaves the thing signified as incomprehended, and as exceeding the signi-fication of the name. Hence it is evident that this term *wise* is not applied in the same way to God and to man. The same rule applies to other terms. Hence no name is predicated univocally of God and of creatures.

Neither, on the other hand, are names applied to God and creatures in a purely equivocal sense, as some have said. Because if that were so, it follows that from creatures nothing could be known or demonstrated about God at all; for the reasoning would always be exposed to the fallacy of equivocation. Such a view is against the philosophers, who proved many things about God, and also against what the Apostle says: *The invisible things of* God *are clearly seen being understood by the things that are made* (Rom. i. 20). Therefore it must be said that these names are said of God and creatures in an *analogous* sense, that is, according to proportion.

Now names are thus used in two ways: either according as many things are proportionate to one, thus for example *healthy* is predicated of medicine and urine in relation and in proportion to health of body, of which the former is the sign and the latter the cause: or according as one thing is proportionate to another, thus *healthy* is said of medicine and animal, since medicine is the

"Thinking and Speaking about God by Analogy," Part I, Question 13, 5th article of *The Summa Theologica*, by Thomas Aquinas, trans. Fathers of the English Dominican Province, 2nd revised edition (London: Burns Oates & Washbourne, 1920), pp. 159–61.

cause of health in the animal body. And in this way some things are said of God and creatures analogically, and not in a purely equivocal nor in a purely univocal sense. For we can name God only from creatures [. . .]. Thus, whatever is said of God and creatures, is said according to the relation of a creature to God as its principle and cause, wherein all perfections of things pre-exist excellently. Now this mode of community of idea is a mean between pure equivocation and simple univocation. For in analogies the idea is not, as it is in univocals, one and the same, yet it is not totally diverse as in equivocals; but a term which is thus used in a multiple sense signifies various proportions to some one thing; thus *healthy* applied to urine signifies the sign of animal health, and applied to medicine signifies the cause of the same health.

11

Everything Has Its Self in Brahman

Shankara (Samkara)

[An] objection, based on reasoning, is raised against the doctrine of Brahman being the cause of the world. [. . .] The distinction of enjoyers and objects of enjoyment is well known from ordinary experience, the enjoyers being intelligent, embodied souls, while sound and the like are the objects of enjoyment. Devadatta, for instance, is an enjoyer, the dish (which he eats) an object of enjoyment. The distinction of the two would be reduced to non-existence if the enjoyer passed over into the object of enjoyment, and vice versa. Now this passing over of one thing into another would actually result from the doctrine of the world being non-different from Brahman. But the sublation of a well-established distinction is objectionable, not only with regard to the present time when that distinction is observed to exist, but also with regard to the past and the future, for which it is inferred. The doctrine of Brahman's causality must therefore be abandoned, as it would lead to the sublation of the well-established distinction of enjoyers and objects of enjoyment.

To the preceding objection we reply, "It may exist as in ordinary experience." Even on our philosophic view the distinction may exist, as ordinary experience furnishes us with analogous instances. We see, for instance, that waves, foam, bubbles, and other modifications of the sea, although they really are not different from the sea-water, exist, sometimes in the state of mutual separation, sometimes in the state of conjunction, &c. From the fact of their being non-different from the sea-water, it does not follow that they pass over into each other; and, again, although they do not pass over into each other, still they are not different from the sea. So it is in the case under discussion also. The enjoyers and the objects of enjoyment do not pass over into each other, and yet they are not different from the highest Brahman. And although the enjoyer is not really an effect of Brahman, since the unmodified creator himself, in so far as he enters into the effect, is called the enjoyer (according to the passage, "Having created he entered into it," Taitt. Up. II, 6), still after Brahman has entered into its effects it passes into a state of distinction, in consequence of the effect acting as a limiting adjunct; just as the universal ether is divided by its contact with jars and other limiting adjuncts. The conclusion is, that the distinction of enjoyers and objects of enjoyment is possible,

"Everything has its Self in Brahman" from *Brahmasutrabhasya*, II.1.13–14 by Shankara (Samkara), in *A Sourcebook of Advaita Vedanta*, ed. Eliot Deutsch and J. A. B. van Buitenen (Honolulu: University of Hawaii Press, 1971), pp. 177–9. Reprinted by permission of Professor Eliot Deutsch.

although both are non-different from Brahman, their highest cause, as the analogous instance of the sea and its waves demonstrates (II, 1, 13).

The refutation contained in the preceding Sūtra was set forth on the condition of the practical distinction of enjoyers and objects of enjoyment being acknowledged. In reality, however, that distinction does not exist because there is understood to be non-difference (identity) of cause and effect. The effect is this manifold world consisting of ether and so on; the cause is the highest Brahman. Of the effect it is understood that in reality it is non-different from the cause, i.e. has no existence apart from the cause. – How so? – "On account of the scriptural word 'origin' and others." The word "origin" is used in connexion with a simile, in a passage undertaking to show how through the knowledge of one thing everything is known; viz. Ch. Up. VI, 1, 4, "As, my dear, by one clod of clay all that is made of clay is known, the modification (i.e. the effect; the thing made of clay) being a name merely which has its origin in speech, while the truth is that it is clay merely; thus," &c. – The meaning of this passage is that, if there is known a lump of clay which really and truly is nothing but clay, there are known thereby likewise all things made of clay, such as jars, dishes, pails, and so on, all of which agree in having clay for their true nature. For these modifications or effects are names only, exist through or originate from speech only, while in reality there exists no such thing as a modification. In so far as they are names (individual effects distinguished by names) they are untrue; in so far as they are clay they are true. – This parallel instance is given with reference to Brahman; applying the phrase "having its origin in speech" to the case illustrated by the instance quoted we understand that the entire body of effects has no existence apart

from Brahman. . . . We therefore must adopt the following view. In the same way as those parts of ethereal space which are limited by jars and waterpots are not really different from the universal ethereal space, and as the water of a mirage is not really different from the surface of the salty steppe – for the nature of that water is that it is seen in one moment and has vanished in the next, and moreover, it is not to be perceived by its own nature (i.e. apart from the surface of the desert) – ; so this manifold world with its objects of enjoyment, enjoyers and so on has no existence apart from Brahman. [. . .]

The following passage [. . .], "That is the Self; thou art that, O Śvetaketu!" teaches that the embodied soul (the individual soul) also is Brahman. (And we must note that) the passage distinctly teaches that the fact of the embodied soul having its Self in Brahman is self-established, not to be accomplished by endeavour. This doctrine of the individual soul having its Self in Brahman, if once accepted as the doctrine of the Veda, does away with the independent existence of the individual soul, júst as the idea of the rope does away with the idea of the snake (for which the rope had been mistaken). And if the doctrine of the independent existence of the individual soul has to be set aside, then the opinion of the entire phenomenal world – which is based on the individual soul – having an independent existence is likewise to be set aside. But only for the establishment of the latter an element of manifoldness would have to be assumed in Brahman, in addition to the element of unity. – Scriptural passages also (such as "When the Self only is all this, how should he see another?" Bṛh. Up. II, 4, 13) declare that for him who sees that everything has its Self in Brahman the whole phenomenal world with its actions, agents, and results of actions is non-existent.

12

An Analysis of *Nirvāṇa*

Nagarjuna

1 [An opponent says:] If all existence is empty, there is no origination nor destruction.

Then whose *nirvāṇa* through elimination [of suffering] and destruction [of illusion] would be postulated?

2 [Nāgārjuna replies:] If all existence is non-empty, there is no origination nor destruction.

Then whose *nirvāṇa* through elimination [of suffering] and destruction [of illusion] would be postulated?

3 *Nirvāṇa* has been said to be neither eliminated nor attained, neither annihilated nor eternal,

Neither disappeared nor originated.

4 *Nirvāṇa* is certainly not an existing thing, for then it would be characterized by old age and death.

In consequence it would involve the error that an existing thing would not become old and be without death.

5 And if *nirvāṇa* is an existing thing, *nirvāṇa* would be a constructed product (*saṃskṛta*),

Since never ever has an existing thing been found to be a non-constructed-product (*asaṃskṛta*).

6 But if *nirvāṇa* is an existing thing, how could [*nirvāṇa*] exist without dependence [on something else]?

Certainly *nirvāṇa* does not exist as something without dependence.

7 If *nirvāṇa* is not an existing thing, will *nirvāṇa* become a non-existing thing?

Wherever there is no existing thing, neither is there a non-existing thing.

8 But if *nirvāṇa* is a non-existing thing, how could [*nirvāṇa*] exist without dependence [on something else]?

Certainly *nirvāṇa* is not a non-existing thing which exists without dependence.

9 That state which is the rushing in and out [of existence] when dependent or conditioned –

This [state], when not dependent or not conditioned, is seen to be *nirvāṇa*.

10 The teacher [Gautama] has taught that a "becoming" and a "non-becoming" (*vibhava*) are destroyed;

Therefore it obtains that: *Nirvāṇa* is neither an existent thing nor a non-existent thing.

11 If *nirvāṇa* were both an existent and a non-existent thing,

Final release (*mokṣa*) would be [both] an existent and a non-existent thing; but that is not possible.

12 If *nirvāṇa* were both an existent and a non-existent thing,

"An Analysis of Nirvāṇa," by Nagarjuna, from the *Mūlamadhyamakakārikās*, chapter XXV, in *Emptiness: A Study in Religious Meaning* by Frederick Streng (New York: Abingdon Press, 1967), pp. 215–17.

There would be no *nirvāṇa* without conditions, for these both [operate with] conditions.

13 How can *nirvāṇa* exist as both an existent thing and a non-existent thing,

For *nirvāṇa* is a non-composite-product (*asaṃskṛta*), while both an existent thing and a non-existent thing are composite products (*saṃskṛta*).

14 How can *nirvāṇa* exist as both an existent and a non-existent thing?

There is no existence of both at one and the same place, as in the case of both darkness and light.

15 The assertion: "*Nirvāṇa* is neither an existent thing nor a non-existent thing"

Is proved if [the assertion]: "It is an existent thing and a non-existent thing" were proved.

16 If *nirvāṇa* is neither an existent thing nor a non-existent thing,

Who can really arrive at [the assertion]: "neither an existent thing nor a non-existent thing"?

17 It is not expressed if the Glorious One [the Buddha] exists after his death,

Or does not exist, or both or neither.

18 Also, it is not expressed if the Glorious One exists while remaining [in the world],

Or does not exist, or both or neither.

19 There is nothing whatever which differentiates the existence-in-flux (*saṃsāra*) from *nirvāṇa*;

And there is nothing whatever which differentiates *nirvāṇa* from existence-in-flux.

20 The extreme limit (*koṭi*) of *nirvāṇa* is also the extreme limit of existence-in-flux;

There is not the slightest bit of difference between these two.

21 The views [regarding] whether that which is beyond death is limited by a beginning or an end or some other alternative

Depend on a *nirvāṇa* limited by a beginning (*pūrvānta*) and an end (*aparānta*).

22 Since all *dharmas* are empty, what is finite? What is infinite?

What is both finite and infinite? What is neither finite nor infinite?

23 Is there anything which is this or something else, which is permanent or impermanent,

Which is both permanent and impermanent, or which is neither?

24 The cessation of accepting everything [as real] is a salutary (*śiva*) cessation of phenomenal development (*prapañca*);

No *dharma* anywhere has been taught by the Buddha of anything.

13

Non-Polar and Yet Supreme Polarity!

Zhou Dunyi (Zhou Lianxi)

Non-Polar (*wuji*) and yet Supreme Polarity (*taiji*)! The Supreme Polarity in activity generates yang; yet at the limit of activity it is still. In stillness it generates yin; yet at the limit of stillness it is also active. Activity and stillness alternate; each is the basis of the other. In distinguishing yin and yang, the Two Modes are thereby established.

The alternation and combination of yang and yin generate water, fire, wood, metal, and earth. With these Five [Phases of] *qi* harmoniously arranged, the Four Seasons proceed through them. The Five Phases are simply yin and yang; yin and yang are simply the Supreme Polarity; the Supreme Polarity is fundamentally Non-Polar. [Yet] in the generation of the Five Phases, each one has its nature.

The reality of the Non-Polar and the essence of the Two [Modes] and Five [Phases] mysteriously combine and coalesce. "The Way of *qian* becomes the male; the Way of *kun* becomes the female"; the two *qi* stimulate each other, transforming and generating the myriad things. The myriad things generate and regenerate, alternating and transforming without end.

Only humans receive the finest and most spiritually efficacious [*qi*]. Once formed, they are born; when spirit (*shen*) is manifested, they have intelligence; when their fivefold natures are stimulated into activity, good and evil are distinguished and the myriad affairs ensue.

The sage settles these [affairs] with centrality, correctness, humaneness, and rightness (the Way of the Sage is simply humaneness, Tightness, centrality, and correctness) and emphasizes stillness. (Without desire, [he is] therefore still.) In so doing he establishes the ultimate of humanity. Thus the sage's "virtue equals that of Heaven and Earth; his clarity equals that of the sun and moon; his timeliness equals that of the four seasons; his good fortune and bad fortune equal those of ghosts and spirits." The superior person (*junzi*) cultivates these and has good fortune. The inferior person rejects these and has bad fortune.

Therefore [the *Classic of Changes* says], "Establishing the Way of Heaven, [the sages] speak of yin and yang; establishing the Way of Earth they speak of yielding and firm [hexagram lines]; establishing the Way of Humanity they speak of humaneness and rightness." It also says, "[The sage] investigates beginnings and follows them to their ends; therefore he understands death and birth." Great indeed is [the *Classic of*] *Changes*! Herein lies its perfection.

"Non-Polar and Yet Supreme Polarity!" by Zhou Dunyi (Zhou Lianxi), in *Sources of Chinese Tradition*, 2nd edition, Vol. 1, ed. W. T. de Bary and Irene Bloom (New York: Columbia University Press, 1999), pp. 673–6. Copyright © 1999 Columbia University Press. Reprinted with permission of the publisher.

The Diagram of the Supreme Polarity

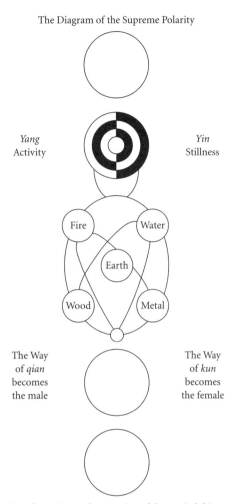

Transformation and generation of the myriad things

Figure 13.1

Section III

The Role and Limits of Reason in Supporting Belief in an Ultimate Sacred Reality

Introduction

A. General Introduction to the Section

In the previous section, we surveyed several ways that Ultimate Sacred Reality has been characterized in various religious traditions. Here, we turn to the question of whether belief in the existence of such a sacred reality can be supported by reason. The issue of reason's role in relation to religious belief is one with which thinkers of most, if not all, religious traditions have grappled. There are a number of positions that can be taken on this general issue, resting on a continuum that ranges from forms of rationalism to irrationalism. According to evidentialism, perhaps the most influential form of rationalism since the onset of the modern era, one ought to believe only those things that can be supported by sufficient evidence. At the other end of the spectrum lie forms of irrationalism. For example, the fideist holds that reason has absolutely no role to play in relation to religious belief and that the latter by its nature is opposed to reason. On this view, religious belief is to be adopted on the basis of faith alone. Most thinkers – including most

of those represented in this book – have held positions somewhere between these two extremes.

For example, many theistic thinkers in both the West and India have held a position similar to that which Thomas Aquinas articulated. According to Aquinas, some religious truths can be known through reason while others can be known only through revelation accepted on faith (and some by both means). To know by faith, on his view, is to give one's voluntary assent to something revealed as true in scripture and for which one otherwise lacks sufficient evidence.[1] For Aquinas and a good number of other theistic thinkers, the existence of God is one of those religious truths that can be demonstrated to be true by reason alone. Much of the focus of this section is on such arguments.

Arguments for the existence of God have taken many forms over the ages. Some – for example the ontological argument for God's existence – seek to establish that God must exist based on the very idea of what God is (see Anselm's "Truly There is a God"). Though the ontological argument continues to elicit

---

[1] For Aquinas's view, see *Summa Contra Gentiles*, Book I. Despite there being two routes to religious truth, it is important to note that truth is still unified for Aquinas. That is, though some truths can be known only through faith, even these truths cannot contradict what we know through the proper exercise of reason. Citing a slogan popularized in recent years by the philosopher Arthur Holmes, one might say that on this view, "All truth is God's truth."

philosophical discussion, we will focus here on two other types of arguments for God's existence: the cosmological and design arguments. After examining these arguments, we will introduce views – both Eastern and Western – that are situated closer to the irrationalist end of the continuum described above. According to these views, the existence (let alone nature of) Ultimate Sacred Reality cannot be grasped through the exercise of reason.

B.   Cosmological Arguments

Rather than beginning with the idea of God as in the ontological argument, cosmological arguments begin with some very general observations about the universe – for example, simply that it exists at all or that it seems as though it must have had a beginning – and work toward the conclusion that God must exist in order to account for what is observed. The argument has been popular throughout much of the history of Western thought beginning with Aristotle and appears in the work of some Indian theists as well. Part of the argument's persistence is no doubt attributable to the way that it taps into a kind of natural wonder expressed in the question: "How did all of this come to be?"

B1.   The Cosmological Argument from Contingency

In "A Cosmological Argument for God's Existence" Richard Taylor presents a contemporary version of the cosmological argument that was articulated by Muslim philosophers of the medieval period, later picked up by Aquinas (see his discussion of the "third way" in "Whether God Exists?"), and then further refined subsequently by G. W. Leibniz (1646–1716). We might call this the "cosmological argument from contingency." The force of the argument is driven by two primary considerations. First, there is appeal to a general principle known as the "principle of sufficient reason." According to this principle, there must be an explanation for everything that exists. Second, a distinction is drawn between what exists contingently and what exists by necessity. Something exists contingently if it might not have existed but for the fact that

something else brought it into existence. In contrast, recall from the discussion of God's nature in the previous section that to say that something exists necessarily is to say that it must have always existed and will always exist (if it exists at all), thus its existence depends upon nothing else.

With these notions in hand, the proponent of the cosmological argument from contingency argues that the universe, or cosmos, itself exists contingently. If this is true, then according to the principle of sufficient reason, there must be an explanation for its existence. Of course, this explanation could refer to something else that exists contingently, but that would only give rise to the question – what explains the existence of *that* contingent thing? According to Taylor, explanations referring to contingently existing things must eventually reach an endpoint, or we really have not been provided with a sufficient explanation at all. That endpoint is that there must be something, call it "God," which exists necessarily – and so is self-existent, needing no explanation by reference to something other than itself – and which serves as the ultimate explanation for all that exists contingently.

B2.   The Kalam *Cosmological Argument*

A second type of cosmological argument has recently been championed by William Lane Craig and others. In "al-Ghāzāli and the *Kalām* Cosmological Argument," Craig focuses on a version of the argument articulated by the Muslim philosopher al-Ghazali (or Abu Hamid, 1058–1111). Unlike the argument from contingency, this argument does not rest on the claim that the universe might not have existed, or is contingent, but rather on the claim that the universe *began* to exist at some particular time. The general principle applied to those things that have a beginning in time says that everything that begins to exist at some time must have a cause in time. The reasoning of this argument thereby continues to push the inquiry into the origin of things backward in time. Then, in a move that parallels the one made in the contingency version of the cosmological argument, the proponent of this argument maintains that at some point, the series – in this case, the series of temporal causes extending backward in time – must end.

According to the defender of this argument, there cannot be such an infinite series of temporal causes, because the notion of an actually existing infinite number of things is itself contradictory. Thus, the argument concludes, there must be a being that has no beginning in time, namely God, who first initiated the temporal series of causes.

B3. Evaluating the Cosmological Arguments

In "Cosmological Arguments," J. L. Mackie raises objections to both forms of the cosmological argument discussed above. His criticisms of the contingency version of the argument are of two main sorts. He first raises questions about the notion of necessary existence itself, suggesting that either the notion is incoherent or that we have no reason to reject the possibility that the universe itself might exist necessarily. The latter, if true, would undermine the need to conclude that there is a necessary being that exists apart from the universe and that functions as its sufficient explanation. His second line of criticism targets the principle of sufficient reason. Though he is willing to grant the usefulness of the principle as a practical guide to inquiry, he wonders why we are entitled to suppose that the principle expresses anything more than our "preference" that the universe be intelligible. Perhaps, he suggests, the existence of the universe is simply a brute unintelligible fact.

In response to the *kalam* cosmological argument, Mackie first raises questions about whether an actual infinite and thus an actual infinite series of temporal causes (in other words, an eternally existing universe) is impossible, as the argument's proponent claims. Then setting this debate aside, he highlights again the difficulty of comprehending the notion of a necessary being. In particular, he asks us why we should suppose that it is any less mysterious to conclude that such a necessary being exists and has initiated a temporal series of physical causes out of nothing than to conclude that the temporal series itself simply began from nothing.

C. Arguments from Design

Like the cosmological arguments, arguments from design begin with observations about the world and conclude that God's existence is needed to account for these observed features. However, the relevant observations in this case are more specific insofar as they tend to focus on the way that the properties of some things in the universe appear to serve a function, or purpose. The argument then seeks to capitalize on the fact that we know from our experience that function, or purpose, is a characteristic effect of the intentional creative acts of an intelligent being. Since these function-serving properties contribute to the achievement of an end, or goal (see Aquinas's discussion of the "fifth way" in, "Whether God Exists?"), these arguments are also sometimes known as "teleological arguments" (*telos* = "goal," or "end").

Here, for example, is a brief statement of the argument by the tenth-century Indian philosopher Udayana:

> From effects . . . we can prove the existence of the all-knowing, imperishable God. . . . Things like the earth must have a cause. Because they are effects. Like a pot.
>
> By having a cause, I mean active production by someone possessed of the intent to produce, and a direct knowledge concerning the matter from which the production is to be.[2]

Udayana's reasoning invokes an analogy. The earth is likened to a pot, something exhibiting properties – e.g., its shape – that allow it to serve a particular function, or purpose. The pot's existence and shape are the effects of the work of an intelligent creator. Likewise, Udayana suggests by analogy that the earth exhibits the characteristics of an intelligently produced product. Historically, some of the most popular forms of the argument from design have argued on the basis of such analogies, so we will begin our discussion of this type of argument by focusing on the role of analogy.

---

[2] *Flower Offerings of Logic (Nyayakusumanjali)* by Udayana in *Hindu Theology: A Reader*, ed. José Pereira (New York: Image Books, 1976), p. 116.

C1.   Analogical Arguments from Design

In "How the Existence of God Explains the World and Its Order," Richard Swinburne begins by likening human and animal bodies to machines. That is, biological organisms of this type, like humanly designed machines, exhibit a complex organization of parts that function together to serve certain identifiable purposes – e.g., the parts of the eye function together to provide sight. What is the best explanation for how such biological organisms have come to exhibit this functional complexity? According to Swinburne, this cannot ultimately be accounted for by appeal to chance alone, so it is reasonable to conclude that God is the foundational source of such complexity.

As Swinburne notes, this line of thought was most influential in the eighteenth century due in great part to the efforts of William Paley (1743–1805), one of the most successful popularizers of the argument during that period (see his "Evidence of Design"). Paley famously likened many biological organisms and organs to a watch. According to Paley, since we know that the parts of a watch are able to accomplish their purpose only because they were created and arranged to do so by an intelligent being, we can conclude by analogy that the existence of complex biological organisms whose parts function together to accomplish a purpose is also an effect of the creative design of an intelligent being, though one vastly more intelligent and powerful than human agents.

Two factors contributed to the eventual decline in influence of strictly analogical versions of the design argument. The first of these was a set of objections raised against the argument by David Hume (1711–76), presented in his work *Dialogues Concerning Natural Religion* (see his "On the Argument from Design"). The work is presented as a series of conversations between three characters: (1) Cleanthes, a proponent of the design argument and, more generally, the project of "natural theology" – i.e., theology based on reason alone; (2) Demea, a fideist who mocks Cleanthes' attempt to support religious belief through reason and expresses fear that by appealing to reason Cleanthes is playing into the hands of skeptics; and (3) Philo, a character who, like Demea, is critical of Cleanthes' endeavor but who seeks to meet him on his own chosen terms by raising objections and mounting counterarguments.

Many of Philo's objections to the design argument aim to show that the premises do not provide a high degree of confidence in the truth of the conclusion. For example, Philo raises questions about the degree of similarity between natural complexity and the complexity found in objects of human design, argues that we have insufficient grounds for drawing inferences about nature as a whole from analogical reasoning about its parts, and contends that even if the general form of reasoning is accepted, we are not in a position to rule out alternative design conclusions which would be unacceptable to the traditional theist – e.g., that the world was designed by a committee of gods or that it was designed by an imperfect deity after several previous botched attempts.

In addition to the objections raised by Hume through the mouthpiece of Philo, the design argument faced another important challenge shortly thereafter with the gradual acceptance of the evolutionary theories developed by Charles Darwin (1809–82) and Alfred Russel Wallace (1823–1913). Recall that the strength of the above design argument rests on an inference about how best to account for a kind of complexity often found in nature – in particular, the purpose-serving complex structures in biological organisms. Upon the widespread acceptance of evolutionary theory, it became easier to articulate explanations for how organisms came to acquire such complex structures through wholly natural processes, thereby weakening for many people the perceived need to account for their existence with supernatural explanations.

C2.   The Fine-tuning Design Argument

Hume's objections in conjunction with the widespread acceptance of evolutionary theory led to a general decline in the influence of design reasoning for almost a century. However, such reasoning is currently enjoying something of a renaissance. Swinburne's argument illustrates two important characteristics of one of the more recent versions of the design argument known as the "argument from fine-tuning." First, though he doesn't repudiate the earlier analogy between biological organisms and machines, the force of his argument no longer rests on the analogy. This thereby enables the proponent of such an argument to avoid some of Hume's central objections. Second, Swinburne accepts evolution as the mechanism by which biological organisms came to have their complex structure but refocuses attention on more fundamental features of the universe that had to be in place in order for evolutionary processes to ever give rise to life, let alone a complex form of life like that of a human being. Thus, for proponents of this form of design argument, evolutionary theory need pose no obstacle to design reasoning.

Swinburne and other proponents of this new version of the design argument draw upon recent advances in chemistry, astronomy, and astrophysics to highlight the way in which it seems that the eventual evolution of life – especially our form of life – required that the laws of physics and initial conditions of the universe at the Big Bang be "fine-tuned." In other words, if the physical laws or initial conditions had been just slightly different, life would never have arisen. Given the alleged high improbability that these laws and initial conditions would happen by chance to fall within the narrow range necessary for life, the proponent of the fine-tuning design argument concludes that the best explanation for the universe's being fine-tuned for life is that an intelligent and vastly powerful creator God exists.

C3. The Probability of Fine-Tuning

Robin Le Poidevin assesses the fine-tuning argument in "Are We the Outcome of Chance or Design?" He notes that much in the argument hinges on how one conceives of the relevant notion of chance since this will determine the probability calculations that the argument asks one to compare – that is, how likely it is that conditions at the beginning of the universe would be conducive to eventually give rise to conscious life on the hypothesis that God exists vs the

hypothesis that God does not exist. After introducing two competing theories about how to understand chance – the frequency and propensity models – he contends that proponents of the fine-tuning argument cannot successfully make use of either model of chance in order to yield the probability calculations required to support the argument's conclusion. Thus, he argues, the argument fails.

C4. Irreducible Complexity and the Intelligent Design Movement

Before leaving the topic of design arguments, another recent version of the argument deserves mention, though space will not allow for discussion of it. This version of the argument confronts the challenge posed to design reasoning by evolutionary theory not by bypassing it – as the fine-tuning argument seeks to do – but by arguing that current evolutionary theory cannot by itself account for a particular kind of complexity found in some biological organisms. Proponents of this version of the design argument have deemed this phenomenon "irreducible complexity" since, they allege, its presence cannot be explained solely by appeal to the naturalistic process of random selection.[3]

Finally, it is important to distinguish both the fine-tuning and irreducible complexity arguments from a wider social-political movement in recent years that has come to be known as the "Intelligent Design Movement." Members of this movement have urged that students in public school settings in the United States be allowed to regard the claim that a designing intelligence lies behind the origination of biological life as a legitimate scientific hypothesis. Some proponents of the contemporary design arguments discussed above have aligned themselves with this broader movement but others have not. Philosophically, the design arguments for God's existence stand or fall independently of one's convictions about whether the conclusion of the argument should be considered a scientific hypothesis.

---

[3]   The leading proponent of this argument is Michael Behe. See, for example, *Darwin's Black Box: The Biochemical Challenge to Evolution* (New York: Free Press, 1996).

D. Reasoning about Reason's Limits

The arguments above aim to establish the existence of God. It is no accident of history that
thinkers in religious traditions like Advaita
Vedanta, Buddhism, and Daoism have generally
not sought to offer similar arguments in support
of their own conception of Ultimate Sacred
Reality. If, as is maintained in these traditions,
Ultimate Sacred Reality is in some sense non-dual,
then not only do all characterizations of such
reality fall woefully short (a claim that thinkers
in all religious traditions have commonly made
about Ultimate Sacred Reality), it is literally
beyond conceptualization. To conceptualize something is to delimit it in relation to something
else that it is not. Thus, in saying that Ultimate
Sacred Reality is non-dual, one is denying in
one way or another that there is anything over
against which it can be distinguished.

In general, the use of language necessitates the
drawing of conceptual distinctions. Reasoning
capitalizes on these distinctions in the drawing
of inferences. More specifically, the reasoning in
arguments for God's existence explicitly depends
upon a central conceptual distinction denied by
non-dualists – that is, the ability to distinguish
between the universe of existing things and a
being that might exist apart from it (and is perhaps the cause of its existence). Therefore, given
the nature of their view, we should not expect
proponents of non-dualist views to utilize arguments in the same fashion as theistic thinkers. On
non-dual views, to approach a grasp of Ultimate
Sacred Reality in this manner would be both
misleading and ineffective.

However, this does not mean, as some have
assumed, that such views are by their nature
irrationalist, allowing no legitimate role for conceptualization and reason in relation to Ultimate
Sacred Reality. A famous Zen saying cautions
one to not mistake the finger pointing at the
moon for the moon itself, where the "moon"
represents *nirvana* and the "finger" represents
the linguistic-conceptual attempt to refer to
nirvana. For our present purposes, it is important simply to note that the Zen master did not
say to stop pointing.[4] This section concludes

with two selections that illustrate some of the roles
reason might have for those who are otherwise
skeptical about reason's ability to provide direct
access to truths about Ultimate Sacred Reality.

D1. Pointing at Non-dual Consciousness

In "The Message of the Māṇḍūkya Upaniṣad,"
Ramakrishna Puligandla asks us to reflect on a
puzzling fact about the experience of deep
dreamless sleep. By definition, this is a state
involving no mental activity in the form of
representations of objects. While we are in such
a state, we are not aware of it. Yet later, when asked
how we slept, we might claim to know that we
were in such a state. "How could such knowledge
be possible?" he asks, since we cannot be said
to remember being in a state that involved no
mental activity.

It is common in Western thought to assume
that all knowledge is through mental activity,
where mental activity is defined in relation to
objects of awareness. Puligandla seeks to undermine this assumption. If this were so, he argues,
then when we know that we've had a dreamless
sleep we know it through the activity of our
minds. But dreamless sleep just is a state where
our minds are not active, so we do not know this
through mental activity. The puzzle is solved,
Puligandla proposes, if we distinguish between
the mind and pure consciousness and grant that
we can know something directly through our
consciousness – in this case, that we have persisted as ourselves through dreamless sleep.
Here, Puligandla is using reason in a negative
fashion (i.e., to undermine a prevailing view) in
an attempt to point toward the existence of
atman – that non-dual self that is, according to
Advaita Vedanta, both our own most fundamental nature and identical to Brahman, the
Ultimate Sacred Reality.

D2: A Comparative Look at Two Forms of Antirationalism

In "Antirationalism in Zhuangzi and Kierkegaard" Karen Carr and Philip Ivanhoe compare
two thinkers – the Daoist philosopher Zhuangzi

---

[4] Similarly, the *Daodejing* famously opens (in the first of eighty-one sections!) by saying that the *dao* which can
be spoken of is not the real *dao*.

(Chuang-tzu) and the Christian philosopher Søren Kierkegaard – both of whom are notoriously skeptical about the power of reason to reveal and support religious truth. Nevertheless, the authors argue that these thinkers are best understood not as irrationalists but rather as antirationalists. "Antirationalism" here refers to a "principled objection to rationalism." That is, an antirationalist believes that reason has at least negative value insofar as it can be turned against itself to show that one cannot rely on reason alone to grasp the most important truths in life. They point out that an antirationalist might also hold that reason has some limited positive value as well in directing one's attention to religious and ethical truths, though this positive value is not likely to be expressed in the form of explicitly formulated arguments like the arguments for God's existence discussed above.

As our authors note, the Chinese philosopher Zhuangzi (c. 369–298 BCE) seemed to enjoy poking fun at reason, sometimes using reason itself to do so. Not only was he skeptical about its power to reveal what was most important, he thought over-reliance on the general principles upon which it operates could actually hamper one's ability to accurately perceive and respond to the fluid expression of the *dao* through the working of *yin* and *yang*. Zhuangzi's positive theses are not supported through argumentation but illustrated in carefully crafted stories that together aim to provide a consistent model of how the *dao* operates and how to live in conformity with it.

Kierkegaard (1813–55), a Danish thinker, is sometimes interpreted as endorsing fideism, but our authors argue that this would be to misrepresent his view. Interpreting Kierkegaard's work is complicated by the fact that he often wrote under the pseudonyms of fictional individuals. This sometimes makes it unclear whether Kierkegaard means to be expressing his own view on a particular occasion or is merely using the fictional character to express a view he wishes to discuss. For example, the passages that most strongly suggest fideism are found in a work under the pseudonym Johannes Climacus. For Climacus, it seems that faith in the form of a passionate subjective commitment is that which determines the truth of a religious belief, that reason inhibits passion, and that the primary object of Christian faith – the incarna-tion of God as man – presents itself to reason as an absurd paradox (see "Truth is Subjectivity"). However, as our authors point out, the irrationalist reading of Kierkegaard's own view is difficult to reconcile with the fact that he clearly did not think that passionately held Christian belief was no better than any other passionately held religious belief. Also, reason clearly seems to play a role for Kierkegaard in recognizing its own imperialistic tendency to dominate the self, thereby preventing one from acknowledging one's rightful dependence on God.

According to Carr and Ivanhoe, Zhuangzi and Kierkegaard both share a deep distrust in the power of reason to discover and justify religious belief. Yet they both grant reason an important role in diagnosing its own limitations and a modest role in directing one's attention toward a truth that must be grasped by alternative means. In the next section, we examine whether a religious belief might be rationally held even if it is not arrived at or sufficiently supported by reason but instead by such alternative means.

Suggestions for Further Reading

Clifford, William K., "The Ethics of Belief," in *Lectures and Essays* (London: Macmillan, 1879).

Craig, William Lane and Quentin Smith, *Theism, Atheism, and Big Bang Cosmology* (New York: Oxford University Press, 1993).

Davies, Paul, *Are We Alone?* (New York: Basic Books, 1995).

Dembski, William, *The Design Inference* (New York: Cambridge University Press, 1998).

Evans, C. Stephen, *Faith beyond Reason: A Kierkegaardian Account* (Grand Rapids, MI: William B. Eerdmans Publishing Company, 1998).

Fakry, Majid, "The Classical Islamic Arguments for the Existence of God," *The Muslim World* 47 (1957): 133–45.

Gale, Richard and Alexander R. Pruss, "A New Cosmological Argument," *Religious Studies* 35 (1999): 461–76.

Grimes, John, *Problems and Perspectives in Religious Discourse: Advaita Vedanta Implications* (Albany, NY: State University of New York Press, 1994).

Hayes, Richard P., "Principled Atheism in the Buddhist Scholastic Tradition," *Journal of Indian Philosophy* 16 (1988): 5–28.

Helm, Paul, *Faith and Reason* (New York: Oxford University Press, 1999).

Kenny, Anthony, *The Five Ways* (New York: Schocken Books, 1969).

Leslie, John (ed.), *Physical Cosmology and Philosophy* (New York: Macmillan, 1990).

Mackie, J. L., *The Miracle of Theism* (Oxford: Clarendon Press, 1982).

Manson, Neil (ed.), *God and Design: The Teleological Argument and Modern Science* (New York: Routledge, 2003).

Martin, Michael, *Atheism: A Philosophical Justification* (Philadelphia: Temple University Press, 1990).

Murray, Michael (ed.), *Reason for the Hope Within* (Grand Rapids, MI: Eerdmans, 1999).

Penelhum, Terence, *God and Skepticism: A Study in Skepticism and Fideism* (Dordrecht: D. Reidel Publishing Company, 1983).

Plantinga, Alvin, *God and Other Minds* (Ithaca, NY: Cornell University Press, 1967).

Putnam, Hilary, "God and the Philosophers," in *Midwest Studies in Philosophy, Volume XXI: Philosophy of Religion*, ed. Peter A. French, Theodore E. Uehling, Jr, and Howard K. Wettstein (Notre Dame, IN: University of Notre Dame Press, 1997).

Reichenbach, Bruce R., *The Cosmological Argument: A Reassessment* (Springfield, IL: Charles Thomas, 1972).

Rowe, William, *The Cosmological Argument* (Princeton, NJ: Princeton University Press, 1975).

Swinburne, Richard, *The Existence of God* (Oxford: Clarendon Press, 1979).

14

A Cosmological Argument for God's Existence

Richard Taylor

Suppose you were strolling in the woods and, in addition to the sticks, stones, and other accustomed litter of the forest floor, you one day came upon some quite unaccustomed object, something not quite like what you had ever seen before and would never expect to find in such a place. Suppose, for example, that it is a large ball, about your own height, perfectly smooth and translucent. You would deem this puzzling and mysterious, certainly, but if one considers the matter, it is no more inherently mysterious that such a thing should exist than that anything else should exist. If you were quite accustomed to finding such objects of various sizes around you most of the time, but had never seen an ordinary rock, then upon finding a large rock in the woods one day you would be just as puzzled and mystified. This illustrates the fact that something that is mysterious ceases to seem so simply by its accustomed presence. It is strange indeed, for example, that a world such as ours should exist; yet few people are very often struck by this strangeness but simply take it for granted.

Suppose, then, that you have found this translucent ball and are mystified by it. Now whatever else you might wonder about it, there is one thing you would hardly question; namely, that it did not appear there all by itself, that it owes its existence to something. You might not have the remotest idea whence and how it came to be there, but you would hardly doubt that there was an explanation. The idea that it might have come from nothing at all, that it might exist without there being any explanation of its existence, is one that few people would consider worthy of entertaining.

This illustrates a metaphysical belief that seems to be almost a part of reason itself, even though few ever think upon it; the belief, namely, that there is some explanation for the existence of anything whatever, some reason why it should exist rather than not. The sheer nonexistence of anything, which is not to be confused with the passing out of existence of something, never requires a reason; but existence does. That there should never have been any such ball in the forest does not require any explanation or reason, but that there should ever be such a ball does. If one were to look upon a barren plain and ask why there is not and never has been any large translucent ball there, the natural response would be to ask why there should be; but if one finds such a ball, and wonders why it is there, it is not quite so natural to ask why it should

"A Cosmological Argument for God's Existence" by Richard Taylor in *Metaphysics*, 4th edition (Englewood Cliffs, NJ: Prentice Hall, 1992), pp. 100–7. © 1992. Reprinted by permission of Pearson Education, Inc., Upper Saddle River, NJ.

not be – as though existence should simply be taken for granted. That anything should not exist, then, and that, for instance, no such ball should exist in the forest, or that there should be no forest for it to occupy, or no continent containing a forest, or no Earth, nor any world at all, do not seem to be things for which there needs to be any explanation or reason; but that such things should be *does* seem to require a reason.

The principle involved here has been called the principle of sufficient reason. Actually, it is a very general principle, and it is best expressed by saying that, in the case of any positive truth, there is some sufficient reason for it, something that, in this sense, makes it true – in short, that there is some sort of explanation, known or unknown, for everything.

Now, some truths depend on something else, and are accordingly called *contingent*, while others depend only upon themselves, that is, are true by their very natures and are accordingly called *necessary*. There is, for example, a reason why the stone on my window sill is warm; namely, that the sun is shining upon it. This happens to be true, but not by its very nature. Hence, it is contingent, and depends upon something other than itself. It is also true that all the points of a circle are equidistant from the center, but this truth depends upon nothing but itself. No matter what happens, nothing can make it false. Similarly, it is a truth, and a necessary one, that if the stone on my window sill is a body, as it is, then it has a form, because this fact depends upon nothing but itself for its confirmation. Untruths are also, of course, either contingent or necessary, it being contingently false, for example, that the stone on my window sill is cold, and necessarily false that it is both a body and formless, because this is by its very nature impossible.

The principle of sufficient reason can be illustrated in various ways, as we have done, and if one thinks about it, he is apt to find that he presupposes it in his thinking about reality, but it cannot be proved. It does not appear to be itself a necessary truth, and at the same time it would be most odd to say it is contingent. If one were to try proving it, he would sooner or later have to appeal to considerations that are less plausible than the principle itself. Indeed, it is hard to

see how one could even make an argument for it without already assuming it. For this reason it might properly be called a presupposition of reason itself. One can deny that it is true, without embarrassment or fear of refutation, but one is then apt to find that what he is denying is not really what the principle asserts. We shall, then, treat it here as a datum – not something that is provably true, but as something that people, whether they ever reflect upon it or not, seem more or less to presuppose.

The Existence of a World

It happens to be true that something exists, that there is, for example, a world, and although no one ever seriously supposes that this might not be so, that there might exist nothing at all, there still seems to be nothing the least necessary in this, considering it just by itself. That no world should ever exist at all is perfectly comprehensible and seems to express not the slightest absurdity. Considering any particular item in the world it seems not at all necessary that the totality of these things, or any totality of things, should ever exist.

From the principle of sufficient reason it follows, of course, that there must be a reason not only for the existence of everything in the world but for the world itself, meaning by "the world" simply everything that ever does exist, except God, in case there is a god. This principle does not imply that there must be some purpose or goal for everything, or for the totality of all things; for explanations need not be, and in fact seldom are, teleological or purposeful. All the principle requires is that there be some sort of reason for everything. And it would certainly be odd to maintain that everything in the world owes its existence to something, that nothing in the world is either purely accidental, or such that it just bestows its own being upon itself, and then to deny this of the world itself. One can indeed *say* that the world is in some sense a pure accident, that there simply is no reason at all why this or any world should exist, and one can equally say that the world exists by its very nature, or is an inherently necessary being. But it is at least very odd and arbitrary to deny of this existing world the need for any sufficient reason, whether independent of itself or not, while presupposing that there is a reason for every other thing that ever exists.

Consider again the strange ball that we imagine has been found in the forest. Now, we can hardly doubt that there must be an explanation for the existence of such a thing, though we may have no notion what that explanation is. It is not, moreover, the fact of its having been found in the forest rather than elsewhere that renders an explanation necessary. It matters not in the least where it happens to be, for our question is not how it happens to be *there* but how it happens to be at all. If we in our imagination annihilate the forest, leaving only this ball in an open field, our conviction that it is a contingent thing and owes its existence to something other than itself is not reduced in the least. If we now imagine the field to be annihilated, and in fact everything else as well to vanish into nothingness, leaving only this ball to constitute the entire physical universe, then we cannot for a moment suppose that its existence has thereby been explained, or the need for any explanation eliminated, or that its existence is suddenly rendered self-explanatory. If we now carry this thought one step further and suppose that no other reality ever has existed or ever will exist, that this ball forever constitutes the entire physical universe, then we must still insist on there being some reason independent of itself why it should exist rather than not. If there must be a reason for the existence of any particular thing, then the necessity of such a reason is not eliminated by the mere supposition that certain other things do *not* exist. And again, it matters not at all what the thing in question is, whether it be large and complex, such as the world we actually find ourselves in, or whether it be something small, simple, and insignificant, such as a ball, a bacterium, or the merest grain of sand. We do not avoid the necessity of a reason for the existence of something merely by describing it in this way or that. And it would, in any event, seem quite plainly absurd to say that if the world were composed entirely of a single ball about six feet in diameter, or of a single grain of sand, then it would be contingent and there would have to be some explanation other than itself why such a thing exists, but that, since the actual world is vastly more complex than this, there is no need for an explanation of its existence, independent of itself.

Beginningless Existence

It should now be noted that it is no answer to the question, why a thing exists, to state *how long* it has existed. A geologist does not suppose that she has explained why there should be rivers and mountains merely by pointing out that they are old. Similarly, if one were to ask, concerning the ball of which we have spoken, for some sufficient reason for its being, he would not receive any answer upon being told that it had been there since yesterday. Nor would it be any better answer to say that it had existed since before anyone could remember, or even that it had always existed; for the question was not one concerning its age but its existence. If, to be sure, one were to ask where a given thing came from, or how it came into being, then upon learning that it had always existed he would learn that it never really *came* into being at all; but he could still reasonably wonder why it should exist at all. If, accordingly, the world – that is, the totality of all things excepting God, in case there is a god – had really no beginning at all, but has always existed in some form or other, then there is clearly no answer to the question, where it came from and when; it did not, on this supposition, *come* from anything at all, at any time. But still, it can be asked why there is a world, why indeed there is a beginningless world, why there should have perhaps always been something rather than nothing. And, if the principle of sufficient reason is a good principle, there must be an answer to that question, an answer that is by no means supplied by giving the world an age, or even an infinite age.

Creation

This brings out an important point with respect to the concept of creation that is often misunderstood, particularly by those whose thinking has been influenced by Christian ideas. People tend to think that creation – for example, the creation of the world by God – *means* creation *in time*, from which it of course logically follows that if the world had no beginning in time, then it cannot be the creation of God. This, however, is erroneous, for creation means essentially *dependence*, even in Christian theology. If one thing is the creation of another, then it depends for its existence on that other, and this is perfectly consistent with saying that both are eternal, that neither ever came into being, and hence, that neither was ever created at any point of time. Perhaps an analogy will help convey this point. Consider, then, a flame that is casting beams of light. Now, there seems to be a clear sense in which the beams of light are dependent for their existence upon the flame, which is their source, while the flame, on the other hand, is not similarly dependent for its existence upon them. The beams of light arise from the flame, but the flame does not arise from them. In this sense, they are the creation of the flame; they derive their existence from it. And none of this has any reference to time; the relationship of dependence in such a case would not be altered in the slightest if we supposed that the flame, and with it the beams of light, had always existed, that neither had ever *come* into being.

Now if the world is the creation of God, its relationship to God should be thought of in this fashion; namely, that the world depends for its existence upon God, and could not exist independently of God. If God is eternal, as those who believe in God generally assume, then the world may (though it need not) be eternal too, without that altering in the least its dependence upon God for its existence, and hence without altering its being the creation of God. The supposition of God's eternality, on the other hand, does not by itself imply that the world is eternal too; for there is not the least reason why something of finite duration might not depend for its existence upon something of infinite duration – though the reverse is, of course, impossible.

God

If we think of God as "the creator of heaven and earth," and if we consider heaven and earth to include everything that exists except God, then we appear to have, in the foregoing considerations, fairly strong reasons for asserting that God, as so conceived, exists. Now of course most people have much more in mind than this when they think of God, for religions have ascribed to God ever so many attributes that are not at all implied by describing him merely as the creator

of the world; but that is not relevant here. Most religious persons do, in any case, think of God as being at least the creator, as that being upon which everything ultimately depends, no matter what else they may say about Him in addition. It is, in fact, the first item in the creeds of Christianity that God is the "creator of heaven and earth." And, it seems, there are good metaphysical reasons, as distinguished from the persuasions of faith, for thinking that such a creative being exists.

If, as seems clearly implied by the principle of sufficient reason, there must be a reason for the existence of heaven and earth – i.e., for the world – then that reason must be found either in the world itself, or outside it, in something that is literally supranatural, or outside heaven and earth. Now if we suppose that the world – i.e., the totality of all things except God – contains within itself the reason for its existence, we are supposing that it exists by its very nature, that is, that it is a necessary being. In that case there would, of course, be no reason for saying that it must depend upon God or anything else for its existence; for if it exists by its very nature, then it depends upon nothing but itself, much as the sun depends upon nothing but itself for its heat. This, however, is implausible, for we find nothing about the world or anything in it to suggest that it exists by its own nature, and we do find, on the contrary, ever so many things to suggest that it does not. For in the first place, anything that exists by its very nature must necessarily be eternal and indestructible. It would be a self-contradiction to say of anything that it exists by its own nature, or is a necessarily existing thing, and at the same time to say that it comes into being or passes away, or that it ever could come into being or pass away. Nothing about the world seems at all like this, for concerning anything in the world, we can perfectly easily think of it as being annihilated, or as never having existed in the first place, without there being the slightest hint of any absurdity in such a supposition. Some of the things in the universe are, to be sure, very old; the moon, for example, or the stars and the planets. It is even possible to imagine that they have always existed. Yet it seems quite impossible to suppose that they owe their existence to nothing but themselves, that they bestow existence upon themselves by their very natures, or that they are in themselves things of such nature that it would be impossible for them not to exist. Even if we suppose that something, such as the sun, for instance, has existed forever, and will never cease, still we cannot conclude just from this that it exists by its own nature. If, as is of course very doubtful, the sun has existed forever and will never cease, then it is possible that its heat and light have also existed forever and will never cease; but that would not show that the heat and light of the sun exist by their own natures. They are obviously contingent and depend on the sun for their existence, whether they are beginning-less and everlasting or not.

There seems to be nothing in the world, then, concerning which it is at all plausible to sup-pose that it exists by its own nature, or contains within itself the reason for its existence. In fact, everything in the world appears to be quite plainly the opposite, namely, something that not only need not exist, but at some time or other, past or future or both, does not in fact exist. Every-thing in the world seems to have a finite dura-tion, whether long or short. Most things, such as ourselves, exist only for a short while; they come into being, then soon cease. Other things, like the heavenly bodies, last longer, but they are still corruptible, and from all that we can gather about them, they too seem destined eventually to perish. We arrive at the conclusion, then, that although the world may contain some things that have always existed and are destined never to perish, it is nevertheless doubtful that it contains any such thing, and, in any case, everything in the world is capable of perishing, and nothing in it, however long it may already have existed and how-ever long it may yet remain, exists by its own nature but depends instead upon something else.

Although this might be true of everything in the world, is it necessarily true of the world itself? That is, if we grant, as we seem forced to, that nothing in the world exists by its own nature, that everything in the world is contingent and perishable, must we also say that the world itself, or the totality of all these perishable things, is also contingent and perishable? Logically, we are not forced to, for it is logically possible that the totality of all perishable things might itself be imperishable, and hence, that the world might exist by its own nature, even though it is composed exclusively of things that are contingent. It is not

logically necessary that a totality should share the defects of its members. For example, even though every person is mortal, it does not follow from this that the human race, or the totality of all people, is also mortal; for it is possible that there will always be human beings, even though there are no human beings who will always exist. Similarly, it is possible that the world is in itself a necessary thing, even though it is composed entirely of things that are contingent.

This is logically possible, but it is not plausible. For we find nothing whatever about the world, any more than in its parts, to suggest that it exists by its own nature. Concerning anything in the world, we have not the slightest difficulty in supposing that it should perish, or even that it should never have existed in the first place. We have almost as little difficulty in supposing this of the world itself. It might be somewhat hard to think of everything as utterly perishing and leaving no trace whatever of its ever having been, but there seems to be not the slightest difficulty in imagining that the world should never have existed in the first place. We can, for instance, per-fectly easily suppose that nothing in the world had ever existed except, let us suppose, a single grain of sand, and we can thus suppose that this grain of sand has forever constituted the whole universe. Now if we consider just this grain of sand, it is quite impossible for us to suppose that it exists by its very nature and could never have failed to exist. It clearly depends for its existence upon something other than itself, if it depends on anything at all. The same will be true if we con-sider the world to consist not of one grain of sand but of two, or of a million, or, as we in fact find, of a vast number of stars and planets and all their minuter parts.

It would seem, then, that the world, in case it happens to exist at all – and this is quite beyond doubt – is contingent and thus dependent upon something other than itself for its existence, if it depends upon anything at all. And it must depend upon something, for otherwise there could be no reason why it exists in the first place. Now, that upon which the world depends must be something that either exists by its own nature or does not. If it does not exist by its own nature, then it, in turn, depends for its existence upon something else, and so on. Now then, we can say either of two things; namely, (1) that the world depends for its existence upon something else, which in turn depends on still another thing, this depending upon still another, *ad infinitum*; or (2) that the world derives its existence from something that exists by its own nature and that is accordingly eternal and imperishable, and is the creator of heaven and earth. The first of these alternatives, however, is impossible, for it does not render a sufficient reason why anything should exist in the first place. Instead of supplying a reason why any world should exist, it repeatedly begs off giving a reason. It explains what is dependent and perishable in terms of what is itself dependent and perishable, leaving us still without a reason why perishable things should exist at all, which is what we are seeking. Ultimately, then, it would seem that the world, or the totality of contingent or perishable things, in case it exists at all, must depend upon something that is necessary and imperishable, and that accordingly exists, not in dependence upon something else, but by its own nature.

"Self-Caused"

What has been said thus far gives some intimation of what meaning should be attached to the concept of a self-caused being, a concept that is quite generally misunderstood, sometimes even by scholars. To say that something – God, for example – is self-caused, or is the cause of its own existence, does not mean that this being brings itself into existence, which is a perfectly absurd idea. Nothing can *bring* itself into existence. To say that something is self-caused (*causa sui*) means only that it exists, not contingently or in dependence upon something else but by its own nature, which is only to say that it is a being which is such that it can neither come into being nor perish. Now, whether in fact such a being exists or not, there is in any case no absurdity in the idea. We have found, in fact, that the principle of sufficient reason seems to point to the existence of such a being, as that upon which the world, with everything in it, must ultimately depend for its existence.

15

Al-Ghāzāli and the *Kalām* Cosmological Argument

William Lane Craig

In the *Incoherence*, Ghāzāli's position is one of attack, not construction.[1] His faith had gone through a crisis period of scepticism, and in the *Incoherence*, according to W. Montgomery Watt, Ghāzāli "is trying to show that reason is not self-sufficient in the field of metaphysics and is unable out of itself to produce a complete world-view".[2] Therefore, we should not expect to find him setting forth a reasoned case for theism. But he does argue for the temporal beginning of the universe, and, placed within the context of his total thought as expressed elsewhere, this does constitute an argument for God's existence. The logical context for the arguments in the *Incoherence* may be found in the *Iqtiṣād* and "The Jerusalem Letter" of Ghāzāli. In the first of these two works, Ghāzāli presents this syllogism: "Every being which begins has a cause for its beginning; now the world is a being which begins; therefore, it possesses a cause for its beginning."[3] Defining his terms, Ghāzāli states, "We mean by 'world' every being except God; and by 'every being which begins' we mean all bodies and their accidents."[4] Ghāzāli regards the first premiss as indubitable, calling it "an axiom of reason" in his "Jerusalem Letter".[5] But he does supply a supporting argument: anything that comes to be does so in a moment of time; but since all moments are alike prior to the existence of the thing, there must be "some determinant to select the time" for its appearance.[6] Thus, the cause demanded in the first premiss is really the determinant, as Beaurecueil explains,

> The first premiss of his syllogism furnishes a starting point which, in his eyes, presents no

"Al-Ghāzāli and the *Kalām* Cosmological Argument," from *The Kalām Cosmological Argument* by William Lane Craig (Eugene, OR: Wipf and Stock Publishers, 1979), pp. 43–9; 58–60.

1 Al-Ghāzāli, *Tahafut al-Falasifah* [Incoherence of the Philosophers], trans. Sabih Ahmad Kamali (hahore: Pakistan Philosophical Congress, 1958), p. 8.

2 W. Montgomery Watt, *Muslim Intellectual: A Study of Al-Ghazali* (Edinburgh: Edinburgh University Press, 1963), p. 58.

3 Al-Ghāzāli, *Kitāb al-Iqtiṣād fi'l-I'tiqād*, with a Foreword by Îbrahim Agâh Çubukçu and Hüseyin Atay (Ankara: University of Ankara Press, 1962), pp. 15–16; cf. p. 20. [. . .]

4 Al-Ghāzāli, *Iqtiṣād*, p. 24.

5 Al-Ghāzāli, "The Jerusalem Tract", trans. and ed. A. L. Tibawi, *The IslamicQuarterly* 9 (1965), p. 98.

6 Ibid.

difficulty at all . . . we must understand by *a being which begins* that which did not exist at one time, which was nothing, and which finally came to existence; as for the *cause* which he requires, it is precisely that which gives preference to the existence of one being over its non-existence. The coming to existence, established by the senses in the world of bodies, demands the intervention of a determinant principle among the possibles. . . .[7]

Ghāzāli now essays to prove in the second pre-miss that the world has come to be. This is the logical juncture at which the arguments in the *Incoherence* fit in, for it is evident that his argument from temporal regress is designed to prove that the world must have had a beginning. [. . .] Ghāzāli mounts two lines of attack on the thesis of the world's eternity: (1) that the philosophers fail to demonstrate the impossibility of the creation of a temporal entity from an eternal being and (2) that the beginning of the universe is demonstrable. It is to the second point that we shall now turn our attention. Ghāzāli summarises his proof as follows:

You reject as impossible the procession of a temporal from an eternal being. But you will have to admit its possibility. For there are temporal phenomena in the world. And some other phenomena are the causes of those phenomena. Now it is impossible that one set of temporal phenomena should be caused by another, and that the series should go on *ad infinitum*. No intelligent person can believe such a thing. If it had been possible, you would not have considered it obligatory on your part to introduce the Creator [into your theories], or affirm the Necessary Being in whom all the possible things have their Ground.

So if there is a limit at which the series of temporal phenomena stops, let this limit be called the Eternal.

And this proves how the possibility of the procession of a temporal from an eternal

being can be deduced from their fundamental principles.[8]

[. . .] Ghāzāli's terse summary [of this popular *kalām* argument for God's existence] may be outlined as follows:

1 There are temporal phenomena in the world.
2 These are caused by other temporal phenomena.
3 The series of temporal phenomena cannot regress infinitely.
4 Therefore, the series must stop at the eternal.

We shall now fill out the structure of this outline by a step by step analysis. The first point, that *there are temporal phenomena in the world*, is straightforward. We experience in the world of the senses the coming to be and the passing away of things around us. Ghāzāli takes the point as obvious.

Secondly, *these are caused by other temporal phenomena*. This step assumes the principle of secondary causation, which [. . .] Ghāzāli thoroughly repudiates. It is therefore odd for him to be propounding the principle here himself. Probably the best explanation is that it is a concession to his opponents. The argument is addressed to the philosophers, who believed in the existence of real causes in the world.[9] Rather than raise here an extraneous issue that could only sidetrack the discussion, he gives the philosophers their four Aristotelian causes operating in the world. Ghāzāli himself did not believe in the efficacy of secondary causes, and his argument for a beginning of the universe does not depend on their presence. For he could just as easily have argued that there are temporal phenomena in the world, these temporal phenomena are preceded by other temporal phenomena, and so forth. The proof is not dependent at this point upon the causal principle, and it seems likely that Ghāzāli admits it simply for the sake of his opponents, who

7   S. de Beaurecueil, "Ġazzālī et S. Thomas d'Aquin: Essai sur la preuve de l'existence de Dieu proposée dans l'*Iqtiṣād* et sa comparison avec les 'voies' Thomistes", *Bulletin de l'Institut Français d'Archaéologie Orientale* 46 1947): 212–13.
8   Al-Ghāzāli, *Tahafut*, p. 32.
9   Seyyed Hossein Nasr, *An Introduction to Islamic Cosmological Doctrines* (Cambridge, Mass.: Belknap Press of Harvard University Press, 1964), p. 230.

would not think to dispute it. Thus, he willingly acknowledges of temporal phenomena that these are caused by other temporal phenomena.

The third premiss, *the series of temporal phenomena cannot regress infinitely*, is the crux of the argument. Ghāzali supports the premiss by showing the absurdities involved in the supposition of the eternity of the world, that is, in an infinite regress of temporal phenomena. For example, it leads to the absurdity of infinites of different sizes.[10] For Jupiter revolves once every twelve years, Saturn every thirty years, and the sphere of the fixed stars every thirty-six thousand years. If the world were eternal, then these bodies will each have completed an infinite number of revolutions, and yet one will have completed twice as many or thousands of times as many revolutions as another, which is absurd. Or again, there is the problem of having an infinite composed of finite particulars.[11] For the number of these revolutions just mentioned is either odd or even. But if it is odd, the addition of one more will make it even, and *vice versa*. And it is absurd to suppose that the infinite could lack one thing, the addition of which would make the number of the total odd or even. If it is said that only the finite can be described as odd or even and that the infinite cannot be so characterised, then Ghāzali will answer that if there is a totality made up of units and this can be divided into one-half or one-tenth, as we saw with regard to the different ratios of revolutions per year on the part of the planets, then it is an absurdity to state that it is neither odd nor even.[12] If it is objected to this that the revolutions do not make up a totality composed of units, since the revolutions of the past are non-existent and those of the future not yet existent, Ghāzali will reply that a number must be odd or even, whether it numbers things that now exist or not.[13] Hence,

the number of the revolutions must be odd or even. Or again, there is the problem of souls.[14] If the world is eternal then there will be an infinite number of actually existing souls of deceased men. But an infinite magnitude cannot exist. Ghāzali implicitly assumes here the truth of Aristotle's analysis of the infinite, knowing that his opponents also accept it. Ghāzali's arguments may appear rather quaint, presupposing as they do the constancy of the solar system and the life of man upon earth. But the problems raised by the illustrations are real ones, for they raise the question of whether an infinite number or numbers of things can actually exist in reality. Ghāzali argues that this results in all sorts of absurdities; therefore, the series of temporal phenomena cannot regress infinitely.

The conclusion must therefore be: *the series must stop at the eternal.* The series of temporal phenomena must have a beginning. Therefore, according to the principle of determination (premiss one in the *Iqtiṣād*), an agent must exist who creates the world. Ghāzali states,

> ... the people of the truth ... hold that the world began in time; and they know by rational necessity that nothing which originates in time originates by itself, and that, therefore, it needs a creator. Therefore, their belief in the Creator is understandable.[15]

This also means for Ghāzali that time itself had a beginning and was created.[16] As Michael E. Marmura points out, Ghāzali does not challenge the Aristotelian definition of time as the measure of motion, nor does he question the legitimacy of the inference of the eternity of motion from the eternity of time.[17] For him if temporal phenomena, or things changing in time, have an

---

[10] Al-Ghāzali, *Tahafut*, p. 20.
[11] Ibid., pp. 20–1.
[12] Ibid., p. 21.
[13] Ibid., pp. 21–2.
[14] Ibid., p. 22.
[15] Ibid., p. 89.
[16] Ibid., p. 36.
[17] Michael E. Marmura, "The Logical Role of the Argument from Time in the Tahāfut's Second Proof for the World's Pre-Eternity", *Muslim World* 49 (1959): 306.

origin, then time, as the measure of such change, must have an origin as well. Prior to the beginning of the world was simply God and no other being. Time came into existence with the universe. It is only through the weakness of our imagination that we think there must be a "time" before time:

> ... all this results from the inability of the Imagination to apprehend the commencement of a being without supposing something before it. This "before," which occurs to the Imagination so inevitably, is assumed to be a veritable existent – viz., time. And the inability of the Imagination in this case is like its inability to suppose a finite body, say, at the upper level, without something above its surface. Hence its assumption that beyond the world there is space – i.e., either a plenum or a void. When therefore it is said that there is nothing above the surface of the world or beyond its extent, the Imagination cannot accept such a thing – just as it is unable to accept the idea that there is nothing in the nature of a verifiable being before the existence of the world.[18]

So just as we realise the universe is finite and nothing is beyond it, though we cannot imagine such a thing, we know that time, too, is finite and nothing is before it. Similarly, to suppose that God could have created the world earlier is simply "the work of the Imagination".[19] Ghāzāli is fond of emphasising that it is the imagination that leads one astray with regard to questions of time and space; we must accept the conclusions of reason despite the problems the imagination might confront. So with regard to the problem of God's creating the world earlier, this is obviously nonsensical since no time existed before the universe. Thus, it could not have been created sooner in time, and to think it might have is only to be deceived by the imagination.

Now placing this argument within the logical context of Ghāzāli's thought, we can see why Ghāzāli concludes that the world must have a

cause: the universe had a beginning; while it was non-existent, it could either be or not be; since it came to be, there must be some determinant which causes it to exist. And this is God. Thus, Ghāzāli says, "So either the series will go on to infinity, or it will stop at an eternal being from which the first temporal being should have originated".[20] Ghāzāli assumes that the universe could not simply spring into existence without a determinant, or cause. We may schematise his argument as follows:

1 Everything that begins to exist requires a cause for its origin.
2 The world began to exist.
   (a) There are temporal phenomena in the world.
   (b) These are preceded by other temporal phenomena.
   (c) The series of temporal phenomena cannot regress infinitely.
      (i) An actually existing infinite series involves various absurdities.
   (d) Therefore, the series of temporal phenomena must have had a beginning.
3 Therefore, the world has a cause for its origin: its Creator.

In conclusion, it is significant to note that Ghāzāli does not, like al-Kindi, base his argument on the finitude of time. Rather he argues from temporal *phenomena*, not time itself. These phenomena cannot regress infinitely, for this is absurd. We might also note that Ghāzāli, like Kindi, argues against the *real* existence of an infinite quantity. This is especially clear when in the *Iqtiṣād* Ghāzāli states that God's knowledge of infinite possibles does not refute his case against the infinite magnitude, for these "knowables" are not real, existent things, to which his argument is confined.[21] Finally, we should reiterate that the role of the causal principle is not in the relation between phenomena, but in the demand for a determinant which causes the

18 Al-Ghāzāli, *Tahafut*, p. 38.
19 Ibid., p. 43.
20 Ibid., p. 33.
21 Beaurecueil, "Ġazzālī et S. Thomas", p. 211.

phenomena to be. This fact alone serves to clearly demarcate Ghāzāli's proof from arguments relying upon the reality of secondary causes, for example, the first three ways of Aquinas. Since God is the only cause, a causal series of any sort cannot exist. In sum, Ghāzāli's cosmological argument is squarely based on two principles, as pointed out by Beaurecueil:

"There remain . . . to the scepticism of Ghāzāli two great limits, which appear now with a majestic clarity: one, the impossibility of the infinite number, and the other, the necessity of a principle of determination amongst the possibles."[22]

These are the two pillars of all Ghāzāli's reasoning in his proof for the existence of God: the impossibility of the infinite number permits him to establish that the world has a beginning; on the other hand, if it has begun, it is necessary that one being should give preference to its existence over its non-existence: this being is God, its creator.[23]

---

[22] Carra de Vaux, *Gazal:* (Amsterdam: Philo Press, 1974), pp. 80–1.
[23] Beaurecueil, "Gazzāli et S. Thomas", p. 222.

16

Cosmological Arguments

J. L. Mackie

[T]he cosmological argument [. . .] is *par excel-lence* the philosophers' argument for theism. It has been presented in many forms, but in one version or another it has been used by Greek, Arabic, Jewish, and Christian philosophers and theologians, including Plato, Aristotle, al Farabi, al Ghazali, ibn Rushd (Averroes), Maimonides, Aquinas, Spinoza, and Leibniz.[1] What is common to the many versions of this argument is that they start from the very fact that there is a world or from such general features of it as change or motion or causation – not, like the argument from consciousness or the argument for design, from specific details of what the world includes or how it is ordered – and argue to God as the uncaused cause of the world or of those general features, or as its creator, or as the reason for its existence. I cannot examine all the variants of this argument that have been advanced [. . .]. And although arguments to a first cause or a creator are more immediately attractive, and appeared earlier in history, than those which argue from the contingency of the world to a necessary being, the latter are in some respects simpler and perhaps more fundamental, so I shall begin with one of these.

(a) Contingency and Sufficient Reason

Leibniz gives what is essentially the same proof in slightly different forms in different works; we can sum up his line of thought as follows.[2] He assumes the *principle of sufficient reason*, that nothing occurs without a sufficient reason why it is so and not otherwise. There must, then, be a sufficient reason for the world as a whole, a reason why something exists rather than nothing. Each thing in the world is contingent, being causally determined by other things: it would not occur if other things were otherwise. The world as a whole, being a collection of such things, is therefore itself contingent. The series of things and events, with their causes, with causes of those causes, and so on, may stretch back infinitely in time; but, if so, then however far back we go, or if we consider the series as a whole, what we have is still contingent and therefore requires a sufficient reason outside this series. That is, there must be a sufficient reason *for* the world which is *other than* the world. This will have to be a necessary being, which contains its own sufficient reason for existence. Briefly, things must have a sufficient reason for their existence,

"Cosmological Arguments" from *The Miracle of Theism* by J. L. Mackie (New York: Oxford University Press, 1982), pp. 81–2; 84–7; 91–5. Reprinted by permission of Oxford University Press.
[1] W. L. Craig, *The Cosmological Argument from Plato to Leibniz* (Macmillan, London, 1980). [. . .]
[2] The clearest account is in "On the Ultimate Origination of Things", printed, e.g., in G. W. Leibniz. *Philosophical Writings* (Dent, London, 1934), pp. 32–41.

and this must be found ultimately in a necessary being. There must be something free from the disease of contingency, a disease which affects everything in the world and the world as a whole, even if it is infinite in past time.

This argument, however, is open to criticisms of two sorts, summed up in the questions "How do we know that everything must have a sufficient reason?" and "How can there be a necessary being, one that contains its own sufficient reason?" These challenges are related: if the second question cannot be answered satisfactorily, it will follow that things as a whole cannot have a sufficient reason, not merely that we do not know that they must have one.

[. . .]

Since it is always a further question whether a concept is instantiated or not, no matter how much it contains, the existence even of a being whose essence included existence would not be self-explanatory: there might have failed to be any such thing. This "might" expresses at least a conceptual possibility; if it is alleged that this being none the less exists by a metaphysical necessity, we are still waiting for an explanation of this kind of necessity. The existence of this being is not logically necessary; it does not exist in all logically possible worlds; in what way, then, does it necessarily exist in this world and satisfy the demand for a sufficient reason?

It might be replied that we understand what it is for something to exist contingently, in that it would not have existed if something else had been otherwise: to exist necessarily is to exist but not contingently in this sense. But then the premiss that the natural world as a whole is contingent is not available: though we have some ground for thinking that each part, or each finite temporal stretch, of the world is contingent in this sense upon something else, we have initially no ground for thinking that the world as a whole would not have existed if something else had been otherwise; inference from the contingency of every part to the contingency *in this sense* of the whole is invalid. Alternatively, we might say that something exists contingently if and only if it might not have existed, and by contrast that something exists necessarily if and only if it exists, but it is not the case that it might not have

existed. In this sense we could infer the contingency of the whole from the contingency of every part. But once it is conceded, for reasons just given, that it is not logically impossible that the alleged necessary being might not have existed, we have no understanding of how it could be true of this being that it is not the case that it might not have existed. We have as yet no ground for believing that it is even possible that something should exist necessarily in the sense required.

This criticism is reinforced by the other objection, "How do we know that everything must have a sufficient reason?" I see no plausibility in the claim that the principle of sufficient reason is known *a priori* to be true. [. . .] Even if, as is possible, we have some innate tendency to look for and expect such symmetries and continuities and regularities, this does not give us an *a priori* guarantee that such can always be found. In so far as our reliance on such principles is epistemically justified, it is so *a posteriori*, by the degree of success we have had in interpreting the world with their help. And in any case these principles of causation, symmetry, and so on refer to how the world works; we are extrapolating far beyond their so far fruitful use when we postulate a principle of sufficient reason and apply it to the world as a whole. Even if, within the world, everything seemed to have a sufficient reason, that is, a cause in accordance with some regularity, with like causes producing like effects, this would give us little ground for expecting the world as a whole, or its basic causal laws themselves, to have a sufficient reason of some different sort.

The principle of sufficient reason expresses a demand that things should be intelligible *through and through*. The simple reply to the argument which relies on it is that there is nothing that justifies this demand, and nothing that supports the belief that it is satisfiable even in principle. As we have seen in considering the other main objection to Leibniz's argument, it is difficult to see how there even could be anything that would satisfy it. If we reject this demand, we are not thereby committed to saying that things are utterly unintelligible. The sort of intelligibility that is achieved by successful causal inquiry and scientific explanation is not undermined by its inability to make things intelligible through and through. Any particular explanation starts with premises which state "brute facts", and although the brutally factual starting-points of one explanation may themselves be further explained by another, the latter in turn will have to start with something that it does not explain, *and so on however far we go.* But there is no need to see this as unsatisfactory.

A sufficient reason is also sometimes thought of as a final cause or purpose. Indeed, if we think of each event in the history of the world as having (in principle) been explained by its antecedent causes, but still want a further explanation of the whole sequence of events, we must turn to some other sort of explanation. [. . .] The principle of sufficient reason, thus understood, expresses a demand for some kind of absolute purposiveness. But if we reject this demand, we are not thereby saying that "man and the universe are ultimately meaningless".[3] People will still have the purposes that they have, some of which they can fulfil, even if the question "What is the purpose of the world as a whole?" has no positive answer.

The principle of sufficient reason, then, is more far-reaching than the principle that every occurrence has a preceding sufficient cause: the latter, but not the former, would be satisfied by a series of things or events running back infinitely in time, each determined by earlier ones, but with no further explanation of the series as a whole. Such a series would give us only what Leibniz called "physical" or "hypothetical" necessity, whereas the demand for a sufficient reason for the whole body of contingent things and events and laws calls for something with "absolute" or "metaphysical" necessity. But even the weaker, deterministic, principle is not an *a priori* truth, and indeed it may not be a truth at all; much less can this be claimed for the principle of sufficient reason. Perhaps it just expresses an arbitrary demand; it may be intellectually satisfying to believe that there is, objectively, an explanation for everything together, even if we can only guess at what the explanation might be. But we have no right to assume that the universe will comply with our intellectual preferences. Alternatively, the

supposed principle may be an unwarranted extension of the determinist one, which, in so far as it is supported, is supported only empirically, by our success in actually finding causes, and can at most be accepted provisionally, not as an *a priori* truth. The form of the cosmological argument which relies on the principle of sufficient reason therefore fails completely as a demonstrative proof.

(b) The Regress of Causes

There is a popular line of thought, which we may call the first cause argument, and which runs as follows: things must be caused, and their causes will be other things that must have causes, and so on; but this series of causes cannot go back indefinitely; it must terminate in a first cause, and this first cause will be God. This argument envisages a regress of causes in time, but says (as Leibniz, for one, did not) that this regress must stop somewhere. Though it has some initial plausibility, it also has obvious difficulties. Why must the regress terminate at all? Why, if it terminates, must it lead to a single termination, to one first cause, rather than to a number – perhaps an indefinitely large number – of distinct uncaused causes? And even if there is just one first cause, why should we identify this with God?

[. . .]

Why must the regress of causes in time terminate? Because things, states of affairs, and occurrences *depend* on their antecedent causes. Why must the regress lead to one first cause rather than to many uncaused causes, and why must that one cause be God? Because anything other than God would need something else causally to depend upon. Moreover, the assumption needed for this argument is more plausible than that needed for Leibniz's proof, or for Aquinas's. The notion that everything must have a sufficient reason is a metaphysician's demand, as is the notion that anything permanent must depend for its permanence on something else unless its essence

---

[3] Craig, op. cit., p. 287.

involves existence. But the notion that an effect *depends* on a temporally earlier cause is part of our ordinary understanding of causation: we all have some grasp of this asymmetry between cause and effect, however hard it may be to give an exact analysis of it.

Nevertheless, this argument is not demonstratively cogent. Though we understand that where something has a temporally antecedent cause, it depends somehow upon it, it does not follow that everything (other than God) *needs* something else to depend on in this way. Also, what we can call al Farabi's principle, that where items are ordered by a relation of dependence, the regress must terminate somewhere, and cannot be either infinite or circular, though plausible, may not be really sound. But the greatest weakness of this otherwise attractive argument is that some reason is required for making God the one exception to the supposed need for something else to depend on: why should God, rather than anything else, be taken as the only satisfactory termination of the regress? If we do not simply accept this as a sheer mystery (which would be to abandon rational theology and take refuge in faith), we shall have to defend it in something like the ways that the metaphysicians have suggested. But then this popular argument takes on board the burdens that have sunk its more elaborate philosophical counterparts.

(c) Finite Past Time and Creation

There is, as Craig explains, a distinctive kind of cosmological argument which, unlike those of Aquinas, Leibniz, and many others, assumes or argues that the past history of the world is finite.[4] This, which Craig calls, by its Arabic name, the *kalam* type of argument, was favoured by Islamic thinkers who were suspicious of the subtleties of the philosophers and relied more on revelation than on reason. Nevertheless, they did propound this as a rational proof of God's existence, and some of them used mathematical paradoxes that are descended from Zeno's, or that anticipate Cantor's, to show that there

cannot be an actual infinite – in particular, an infinite past time. For example, if time past were infinite, an infinite stretch would have actually to have been traversed in order to reach the present, and this is thought to be impossible. Then there is an ingenious argument suggested by al Ghazali: the planet Jupiter revolves in its orbit once every twelve years, Saturn once every thirty years; so Jupiter must have completed more than twice as many revolutions as Saturn; yet if past time were infinite they would each have completed the same (infinite) number; which is a contradiction [see "Al-Ghāzāli and the *Kalām* Cosmological Argument," p. 99 above]. The first of these (which Kant also uses in the thesis of his First Antinomy) just expresses a prejudice against an actual infinity. It assumes that, even if past time were infinite, there would still have been a starting-point of time, but one infinitely remote, so that an actual infinity would have had to be traversed to reach the present from there. But to take the hypothesis of infinity seriously would be to suppose that there was no starting-point, not even an infinitely remote one, and that from any specific point in past time there is only a finite stretch that needs to be traversed to reach the present. Al Ghazali's argument uses an instance of one of Cantor's paradoxes, that in an infinite class a part can indeed be equal to the whole: for example, there are just as many even numbers (2, 4, 6, etc.) as there are whole numbers (1, 2, 3, etc.), since these classes can be matched one-one with each other. But is this not a contradiction? Is not the class of even numbers both equal to that of the integers (because of this one–one correlation) and smaller than it (because it is a proper part of it, the part that leaves out the odd numbers)? But what this brings out is that we ordinarily have and use a criterion for one group's being smaller than another – that it is, or can be correlated one-one with, a proper part of the other – and a criterion for two groups' being equal in number – that they can be correlated one–one with each other – which together ensure that *smaller than* and *equal to* exclude one another for all pairs of finite groups, but not for pairs of infinite groups. Once we understand the relation

---

[4] Craig, op. cit., Chapter 3 [see also chapter 15 above].

between the two criteria, we see that there is no real contradiction.

In short, it seems impossible to disprove, *a priori*, the possibility of an infinite past time. Nevertheless, many people have shared, and many still do share, these doubts about an actual infinite in the real world, even if they are willing to leave mathematicians free to play their Cantorian games – which, of course, not all mathematicians, or all philosophers of mathematics, want to play. Also the view that, whatever we say about *time*, the *universe* has a finite past history, has in recent years received strong empirical support from the cosmology that is a branch of astronomy. So let us consider what the prospects would be for a proof of the existence of a god if we were supplied, from whatever source, with the premiss that the world has only a finite past history, and therefore a beginning in time, whether or not this is also the beginning of time. Here the crucial assumption is stated by al Ghazali: "[We] know by rational necessity that nothing which originates in time originates by itself, and that, therefore, it needs a creator" [see "Al-Ghāzāli and the *Kalām* Cosmological Argument," p. 99 above]. But *do* we know this by rational necessity? Surely the assumption required here is just the same as that which is used differently in the first cause argument, that anything other than a god needs a cause or a creator to depend on. But there is *a priori* no good reason why a sheer origination of things, not determined by anything, should be unacceptable, whereas the existence of a god with the power to create something out of nothing is acceptable.

When we look hard at the latter notion we find problems within it. Does God's existence have a sheer origination in time? But then this would be as great a puzzle as the sheer origination of a material world. Or has God existed for ever through an infinite time? But this would raise again the problem of the actual infinite. To avoid both of these, we should have to postulate that God's own existence is not in time at all; but this would be a complete mystery.

Alternatively, someone might not share al Ghazali's worries about the actual infinite, and might rely on an empirical argument – such as the modern cosmological evidence for the "big bang" – to show that the material world had a beginning in time. For him, therefore, God's existence through an infinite time would be unproblematic. But he is still using the crucial assumptions that God's existence and creative power would be self-explanatory whereas the unexplained origination of a material world would be unintelligible and therefore unacceptable. [. . .] [T]he notion, embedded in the ontological argument, of a being whose existence is self-explanatory because it is not the case that it might not have existed, is *not* defensible; so we cannot borrow that notion to complete any form of the cosmological argument. The second assumption is equally questionable. We have no good ground for an *a priori* certainty that there could not have been a sheer unexplained beginning of things. But in so far as we find this improbable, it should cast doubt on the interpretation of the big bang as an absolute beginning of the material universe; rather, we should infer that it must have had *some* physical antecedents, even if the big bang has to be taken as a discontinuity so radical that we cannot explain it, because we can find no laws which we can extrapolate backwards through this discontinuity.

In short, the notion of creation seems more acceptable than any other way out of the cosmological maze only because we do not look hard either at it or at the human experiences of making things on which it is modelled. It is vaguely explanatory, apparently satisfying; but these appearances fade away when we try to formulate the suggestion precisely.

17

How the Existence of God Explains the World and Its Order

Richard Swinburne

The orderliness of nature in the regular behaviour of objects over time, codified in natural laws, is not the only facet of the orderliness of the natural world. There is also the marvellous order of human and animal bodies. They are like very very complicated machines. They have delicate sense organs which are sensitive to so many aspects of the environment, and cause us to have true beliefs about our environment. We learn where the objects around us are, where our friends are and where our enemies are, where there is food and where there is poison – through our eyes turning light rays and our ears turning sound waves into nerve impulses. And by using these resultant beliefs we can move ourselves, our arms and hands and mouths – to climb and hold rocks and talk – as basic actions in ways which enable us to achieve all sorts of diverse goals (including those needed for our survival). The complex and intricate organization of human and animal bodies, which made them effective vehicles for us to acquire knowledge and perform actions in these ways, was something which struck the anatomists and naturalists of the eighteenth century even more than those of earlier centuries (partly because the invention of the microscope at the end of the seventeenth century allowed them to see just how intricately organized those bodies were).

Very many eighteenth-century writers argued that there was no reason to suppose that chance would throw up such beautiful organization, whereas God was able to do so and had abundant reason to do so – in the goodness, [...] of the existence of embodied animals and humans. Hence their existence, they argued, was good evidence of the existence of God. I believe this argument (as so far stated) to be correct [...]. God has reason for creating embodied persons and animals, and so for creating human and animal bodies. With such bodies we can choose whether to grow in knowledge and control of the world (given that it is an orderly world). God is able to bring about the existence of such bodies. That he does so, [...] is a simple hypothesis. Hence there is good reason to believe that God is the creator of human and animal bodies. Their existence provides another strand of evidence (additional to that provided by the existence of the universe and its conformity to natural laws) for the existence of God.

The best-known presentation of this argument was by William Paley in his *Natural Theology* (1806) [...]. [See "Evidence of Design," pp. 144–5 below].

"How the Existence of God Explains the World and Its Order" from *Is There a God?* by Richard Swinburne (New York: Oxford University Press, 1996), pp. 56–68. Reprinted by permission of Oxford University Press.

[. . .]

Paley's book is devoted to showing how well built in all their intricate detail are animals and humans, and so to concluding that they must have had God as their maker. This analogy of animals to complex machines seems to me correct, and its conclusion justified.

The argument does not, however, give any reason to suppose that God made humans and animals as a basic act on one particular day in history, rather than through a gradual process. And, as we now know, humans and animals did come into existence through the gradual process of evolution from a primitive soup of matter which formed as earth cooled down some 4,000 million years ago. In that process natural selection played a central role. Darwin's *Origin of Species* (1859) taught us the outlines of the story, and biologists have been filling in the details ever since. The clear simple modern presentation in Richard Dawkins's *The Blind Watchmaker* (1986) is deservedly popular.

Because the story is so well known, I shall summarize it in a quick and very condensed paragraph. Molecules of the primitive soup combined by chance into a very simple form of life which reproduced itself. It produced offspring very similar to itself but each of them differing slightly by chance in various respects. In virtue of these differences, some of the offspring were better adapted to survive and so survived; others were not well equipped to survive and did not survive. The next generations of offspring produced on average the characteristics of their parents, but exhibited slight variations from them in various ways. The more a characteristic gave an advantage in the struggle for survival, the more evolution favoured its development. Other things being equal, complexity of organization was a characteristic with survival value, and so more complex organisms began to appear on earth. A characteristic which gave an advantage to complex organisms was sexual reproduction, and so gradually today's male and female organisms evolved. Whatever characteristic of an animal you name, there is a story to be told of how it came to have that characteristic in terms of it being one of many characteristics which were slight variants on the characteristics of parents, and

it giving an advantage in the struggle for survival over the other characteristics. Once upon a time giraffes had necks of the same length as other animals of their bodily size. But by chance some giraffe couples produced offspring with longer necks than usual. These offspring with the longer necks were better able to reach food (e.g. leaves in the tree tops) than the others, and so they flourished and more of them survived to have more offspring than did those with shorter necks. The offspring of the longer-necked giraffes had on average necks of the same lengths as their own parents, but some had ones slightly longer and others had ones slightly shorter. There was an advantage in even longer necks, and so the average neck of the population became longer. But giraffes with very long necks proved less able to escape from predators – they could not escape from woods or run so fast when pursued by lions. So the length of giraffe necks stabilized at an optimum size – long enough for giraffes to get the leaves but not so long as to make them unable to escape from predators. That, or something like it, is the explanation of why the giraffe has a long neck. And there is a similar story to be told for every animal and human characteristic. A little sensitivity to light gave some advantage (to many animals in many environments) in the struggle for survival, a little more sensitivity gave more advantage, and hence the eye developed in many animals. And, above all, complexity of nervous organization in supporting a range of sense organs and bodily movements gave great advantage, and so we have the complexly organized animals and humans we have today.

So, in summary, the Darwinian explanation of why there are the complex animal and human bodies there are today is that once upon a time there were certain chemicals on earth, and, given the laws of evolution (e.g. reproduction with slight variation), it was probable that complex organisms would emerge. This explanation of the existence of complex organisms is surely a correct explanation, but it is not an ultimate explanation of that fact. For an ultimate explanation we need an explanation at the highest level of why those laws rather than any other ones operated. The laws of evolution are no doubt consequences of laws of chemistry governing the organic matter of which animals are made. And the laws of chemistry hold because the fundamental laws of physics hold. But why just those fundamental laws of physics rather than any others? If the laws of physics did not have the consequence that some chemical arrangement would give rise to life, or that there would be random variations by offspring from characteristics of parents, and so on, there would be no evolution by natural selection. So, even given that there are laws of nature (i.e. that material objects have the same powers and liabilities as each other), why just those laws? The materialist says that there is no explanation. The theist claims that God has a reason for bringing about those laws because those laws have the consequence that eventually animals and humans evolve.

Even given that the laws of physics are such as to give rise to laws of evolution of complex organisms from a certain primitive soup of matter, animals and humans will evolve only if there is a primitive soup with the right chemical constitution to start with. Some soups different in chemical constitution from that from which the earth actually began would also, given the actual laws of physics, have given rise to animals. But most soups of chemical elements made from differently arranged fundamental particles would not have given rise to animals. So why was there that particular primitive soup? We can trace the history of the world further backwards. The primitive soup existed because the earth was formed in the way it was; and the earth was formed in the way it was because the galaxy was formed in the way it was, and so on . . . until we come right back to the Big Bang, the explosion 15,000 million years ago with which apparently the universe began. Recent scientific work has drawn attention to the fact that the universe is "fine tuned". The matter-energy at the time of the Big Bang had to have a certain density and a certain velocity of recession to bring forth life. (For a simple account of some of this work, see John Leslie, *Universes* (1989).) Increase or decrease in these respects by one part in a million would have had the effect that the universe was not life evolving. For example, if the Big Bang had caused the chunks of matter-energy to recede from each other a little more quickly, no galaxies,

stars, or planets, and no environment suitable for life, would have been formed on earth or anywhere else in the universe. If the recession had been marginally slower, the universe would have collapsed in on itself before life could have been formed. If there is an ultimate scientific explanation, it will have to leave it as a brute fact that the universe began in such a state and had such natural laws as to be life evolving, when a marginal difference in those initial conditions would have ensured that no life ever evolved anywhere.

Of course, the universe may not have had a beginning with a Big Bang, but may have lasted forever. Even so, its matter must have had certain general features if at any time there was to be a state of the universe suited to produce animals and humans. There would need, for example, to be enough matter but not too much of it for chemical substances to be built up at some time or other – a lot of fundamental particles are needed but with large spaces between them. And only a certain range of laws would allow there to be animals and humans at any time ever. The recent scientific work on the fine-tuning of the universe has drawn attention to the fact that, whether or not the universe had a beginning, if it had laws of anything like the same kind as our actual ones (e.g. a law of gravitational attraction and the laws of the three other forces which physicists have analysed – electromagnetism, the strong nuclear force, and the weak nuclear force), the constants of those laws would need to lie within narrow bands if there was ever to be life anywhere in the universe. Again the materialist will have to leave it as an ultimate brute fact that an everlasting universe and its laws had those characteristics, whereas the theist has a simple ultimate explanation of why things are thus, following from his basic hypothesis which also leads him to expect the other phenomena we have been describing.

True, God could have created humans without doing so by the long process of evolution. But that is only an objection to the theistic hypothesis if you suppose that God's only reason for creating anything is for the sake of human beings. To repeat my earlier point – God also has reason to bring about animals. Animals are conscious beings who enjoy much life and perform intentional actions, even if they do not choose freely which ones to do. Of course God has a reason for giving life to elephants and giraffes, tigers and snails. And anyway the beauty of the evolution of the inanimate world from the Big Bang (or from eternity) would be quite enough of a reason for producing it, even if God were the only person to have observed it. But he is not; we ourselves can now admire earlier and earlier stages of cosmic evolution through our telescopes. God paints with a big brush from a large paintbox and he has no need to be stingy with the paint he uses to paint a beautiful universe.

Darwin showed that the universe is a machine for making animals and humans. But it is misleading to gloss that correct point in the way that Richard Dawkins does: "our own existence once presented the greatest of all mysteries, but . . . it is a mystery no longer . . . Darwin and Wallace solved it" (*The Blind Watchmaker*, [New York: Norton, 1986], p. xiii). It is misleading because it ignores the interesting question of whether the existence and operation of that machine, the factors which Darwin (and Wallace) cited to explain "our own existence", themselves have a further explanation. I have argued that the principles of rational enquiry suggest that they do. Darwin gave a correct explanation of the existence of animals and humans; but not, I think, an ultimate one. The watch may have been made with the aid of some blind screwdrivers (or even a blind watchmaking machine), but they were guided by a watchmaker with some very clear sight.

Stephen Hawking has suggested that the universe is not infinitely old, but that nevertheless it did not have a beginning, and so there was no need for it to begin in a particular initial state if animals and humans were to emerge. He suggests, as Einstein did, that space is closed – finite but without a boundary. Three-dimensional space, that is, is like the two-dimensional surface of a sphere. If you travel in any direction along the surface of a sphere, you will come back to your starting-point from the opposite side. It is indeed possible that three-dimensional space is also like this, though that remains a matter on which there is no scientific consensus. But Hawking also makes the paradoxical "proposal" that the same is true with respect to time (see *A Brief History of Time* [New York: Morrow, 1985], p. 136): time is closed because it is cyclical – if

you live long enough after 1995 into the future, you would find yourself coming from 1994 into 1995 (looking and feeling just like you do now). Hawking claims that the "real" test of his proposal is whether his theory which embodies it "makes predictions that agree with observation". But that is not the only test which his proposal must pass. [. . .] [A] theory which entails a contradiction cannot be true, however successful it is in making predictions. And the "proposal" that time is cyclical to my mind does entail a contradiction. It entails that tomorrow is both after and before today (because if you live long enough after tomorrow, you will find yourself back to today). That in turn entails that I today cause events tomorrow which in turn by a long causal chain cause my own existence today. But it is at any rate logically possible (whether or not possible in practice) that I should freely make different choices from the ones which I do make today; and in that case I could choose so to act today as to ensure that my parents were never born and so I never existed – which is a contradiction. Cyclical time allows the possibility of my acting so as to cause my not acting. And, since that is not possible, cyclical time is not possible. In saying this, I have no wish to challenge the correctness of Hawking's equations as parts of a theory which predicts observations. But I do wish to challenge the interpretation in words which Hawking gives of those equations.

The use to which Hawking puts his "proposal" is contained in this paragraph:

The idea that space and time may form a closed surface without boundary also has profound implications for the role of God in the affairs of the universe. With the success of scientific theories in describing events, most people have come to believe that God allows the universe to evolve according to a set of laws and does not intervene in the universe to break these laws. However, the laws do not tell us what the universe should have looked like when it started – it would still be up to God to wind up the clockwork and choose how to start it off. So long as the universe had a beginning, we could suppose it had a creator. But if the universe is really completely self-contained, having no boundary or edge, it would have neither beginning nor end: it would simply be. What place, then, for a creator? (*A Brief History of Time*, 140–1)

The theist's answer to this paragraph is twofold. First, whether or not God ever intervenes in the universe to break his laws, according to theism, he certainly can do so; and the continued operation of these laws is due to his constant conserving of them, his choosing not to break them. And, secondly, if the universe had a beginning, God made it begin one way rather than another. If the universe did not have a beginning, the only alternative is that it is everlasting. In that case, God may be held to keep it in being at each moment with the laws of nature as they are. It is through his choice at each moment that it exists at that moment and the laws of nature are as they are then. The grounds for believing this theistic answer to Hawking to be not merely possible but true are those being set out in this book.

An objector may invoke a form of what is known as the *anthropic principle* to urge that, unless the universe exhibited order of the kinds which I have described (simple laws operating on matter in such a way as to lead to the evolution of animals and humans), there would not be any humans alive to comment on the fact. (If there were no natural laws, there would be no regularly functioning organisms, and so no humans.) Hence there is nothing surprising in the fact that we find order – we could not possibly find anything else. (This conclusion is clearly a little too strong. There would need to be quite a bit of order in and around our bodies if we are to exist and think, but there could be chaos outside the earth, so long as the earth was largely unaffected by that chaos. There is a great deal more order in the world than is necessary for the existence of humans. So there could still be humans to comment on the fact, even if the world were a much less orderly place than it is.) But, quite apart from this minor consideration, the argument still fails totally for a reason which can best be brought out by an analogy. Suppose that a madman kidnaps a victim and shuts him in a room with a card-shuffling machine. The machine shuffles ten packs of cards simultaneously and then draws a card from each pack and exhibits simultaneously the ten cards. The kidnapper tells the victim that he will shortly set the machine to work and it will exhibit its first draw, but that, unless the draw consists of an ace of hearts from each pack, the machine will simultaneously set off an explosion which will kill

the victim, in consequence, of which he will not see which cards the machine drew. The machine is then set to work, and to the amazement and relief of the victim the machine exhibits an ace of hearts drawn from each pack. The victim thinks that this extraordinary fact needs an explanation in terms of the machine having been rigged in some way. But the kidnapper, who now reappears, casts doubt on this suggestion. "It is hardly surprising", he says, "that the machine draws only aces of hearts. You could not possibly see anything else. For you would not be here to see anything at all, if any other cards had been drawn." But, of course, the victim is right and the kidnapper is wrong. There is indeed something extraordinary in need of explanation in ten aces of hearts being drawn. The fact that this peculiar order is a necessary condition of the draw being perceived at all makes what is perceived no less extraordinary and in need of explanation. The theist's starting-point is not that we perceive order rather than disorder, but that order rather than disorder is there. Maybe only if order is there can we know what is there, but that makes what is there no less extraordinary and in need of explanation. True, every draw, every arrangement of matter, is equally improbable a priori – that is, if chance alone dictates what is drawn. But if a person is arranging things, he has reason to produce some arrangements rather than others (ten aces of hearts, a world fine tuned to produce animals and humans). And if we find such arrangements, that is reason for supposing that a person is doing the arranging.

Another objector may advocate what is called the *many-worlds* theory. He may say that, if there are trillions and trillions of universes, exhibiting between them all the possible kinds of order and disorder there can be, it is inevitable that there will be one governed by simple comprehensible laws which give rise to animals and humans. True. But there is no reason to suppose that there are any universes other than our own. (By "our universe" I mean all the stars and other heavenly bodies which lie in some direction at some distance, however large, from ourselves; everything we can see in the night sky, and everything there too small to be seen, and everything further away than that.) Every object of which we know is an observable component of our universe, or postulated to explain such objects. To postulate a trillion trillion other universes, rather than one God in order to explain the orderliness of our universe, seems the height of irrationality.

So there is our universe. It is characterized by vast, all-pervasive temporal order, the conformity of nature to formula, recorded in the scientific laws formulated by humans. It started off in such a way (or through eternity has been characterized by such features) as to lead to the evolution of animals and humans. These phenomena are clearly things "too big" for science to explain. They are where science stops. They constitute the framework of science itself. I have argued that it is not a rational

conclusion to suppose that explanation stops where science does, and so we should look for a personal explanation of the existence, conformity to law, and evolutionary potential of the universe. Theism provides just such an explanation. That is strong grounds for believing it to be true. [...] Note that I am not postulating a "God of the gaps", a god merely to explain the things which science has not yet explained. I am postulating a God to explain what science explains; I do not deny that science explains, but I postulate God to explain why science explains. The very success of science in showing us how deeply orderly the natural world is provides strong grounds for believing that there is an even deeper cause of that order.

18

Are We the Outcome of Chance or Design?

Robin Le Poidevin

Analogy and the Teleological Argument

Whereas the various versions of the cosmo-logical argument start from relatively general observations about the universe, teleological arguments for God's existence start with more specific observations: for example, that the universe is highly ordered, or that living things are well adapted to their environments. Another difference between the two kinds of arguments is that, whereas for the cosmological argument the crucial notion is that of causality, for the teleological argument the crucial notion is that of *purpose*. We can make the existence of some-thing intelligible by pointing to its antecedent cause, or we can make intelligible its existence by pointing to the purpose for which it was made, provided of course that we are talking of artefacts, i.e. things which are constructed by a conscious agent. The teleological argument for God is that naturally occurring features of the universe were constructed by a conscious agent with a certain end in mind. It is this aspect that gives the argu-ment its name, for the Greek word *telos* means "end" or "goal".

The period in which the teleological argu-ment, in its original form, was most influential was undoubtedly the eighteenth century. The developing sciences of astronomy, chemistry and biology – particularly the last of these – provided a wealth of examples of highly ordered systems whose complexity made it almost inconceiv-able that they could have been the outcome of chance. This gave rise to a new justification of theism, based on the idea that the path to belief was not through revelation, but rather through the contemplation of the wonders of the natural world. The teleological argument was presented in terms of an analogy between various naturally occurring things – in par-ticular, parts of living things – and human artefacts. Perhaps the most famous example of the analogy was the one articulated by William Paley: just as a watch is a complex mechanism, having parts which cooperate so as to achieve a certain end, namely the measurement of time, so, for example, the eye is a (highly) complex system, having parts which cooperate so as to achieve a series of ends, such as providing information about its environment to the organism. The watch bears *marks of design*: the fact that it can be used for the purpose of measuring time sug-gests that it was devised by an intelligence with that purpose in mind. Similarly, the eye bears (what can be interpreted to be) marks of design: the fact that it can be used for seeing suggests that it was devised by an intelligence with that purpose in mind. That living things are as they are is testimony to the existence of a creator.

That, in a nutshell, is the traditional teleological argument. Since the universe is full of apparent "marks of design", the argument may take as its first premise any of a number of observations about the universe, each supposedly requiring a creator to explain it.

[. . .]

The parts of the body clearly do have a function: the legs, or wings, for locomotion, the stomach for digestion, the circulatory system for the transport of gases and dissolved nutrients, etc. Does the fitness of the parts to their ends, and more generally the adaptation of living things to their environment, not indicate the existence of a creator who so constructed them? This rhetorical question, however, highlights the fact that the traditional teleological argument has not survived the advance of science. We now know, or think we know, why life is adapted to its environment: by the production of thousands of variations, some of which will better adapt the organism which has them to its environment and which will therefore provide it with a better chance of survival. Evolution through natural selection is the non-theological account of what, prior to Darwin, seemed an extraordinary fact requiring the hypothesis of a benevolent creator to explain it. The appearance of design, then, may simply be specious. Although we can, at one level, talk of the purpose of the eye – to provide information about the immediate environment – the facts underlying this talk are not themselves purposive. It is not that the eye developed in order that organisms would be all the better at adapting themselves to their environment, but rather that the adaptive consequences of having eyes ensured that the organisms possessing them would be more likely to reproduce. [. . .]

The analogy between artefacts and sense organs is a weak one, therefore. Although there are no laws which would explain the natural (i.e. non-artificial) production of accurate mechanical time pieces, there are laws which explain the natural development of sense organs.

Probability and the Teleological Argument

However, this is not the demise of the teleological argument, for, instead of focusing on the results of the laws of nature, we can focus on the laws themselves and ask why these laws, ones which permitted the evolution of life in the universe, should have been the ones to dictate what happened. The occurrence of life on earth seems to have depended upon some remarkably improbable features of the physical universe. For example, life as we know it is carbon-based: most of the important chemicals constituting the bodies of organisms are complex molecules in which carbon atoms join to form long chains. Where did this carbon come from? The currently favoured answer is that it is synthesised in large quantities in stars, and it was from the explosion of a star that the present universe was formed. But the fact that carbon is synthesised in significant quantities in stars depends upon two apparent coincidences. One concerns the relationship between the thermal energy of the nuclear constituents of stars and a property of the carbon nucleus; the other concerns the relationship between this same thermal energy and a property of the oxygen nucleus. Without the first relationship, little carbon would have been formed in stars in the first place, since not enough energy would have been available to form it. Without the second relationship, what carbon was formed would have been converted, through bombardment by helium, into oxygen, because too much energy would have been produced. Either way, carbon-based life would not have developed. If this is to be regarded as a coincidence, it is, it seems, a remarkably improbable one. How much more probable, says the contemporary teleologist, that the initial conditions of the universe were so arranged that the development of life as we know it was possible.

What we have here is a modern teleological argument, differing from the original form in two respects. First, the marks of design are to be looked for not in living things but in the fundamental constants: i.e. in basic physical values, such as the atomic mass of oxygen, which remain the same in all places and at all times; second, the reasoning is probabilistic rather than analogical: instead of drawing comparisons between artefacts and creation, the argument stresses the improbability of the coincidences to which atheism commits us. The analogy between the created order and human artefacts remains, but it is no longer required to bear the weight of the argument. The modern teleological argument is not an argument *from* analogy, but rather *to* analogy: it is because we are justified in positing a creator that we are justified in drawing an analogy between certain aspects of the universe and human artefacts.

Let us now spell out the probabilistic reasoning more explicitly. The argument appeals to the following principle: we have good reason to believe that some hypothesis is a true explanation of some phenomenon if (i) the probability of the phenomenon's occurring given that the hypothesis is true is much greater than the probability of its occurring given that the hypothesis is false, *and* (ii) if the hypothesis is true, then the probability of the phenomenon's occurring is much greater than the probability of its not occurring. This seems sensible enough, indeed it could be a rule for the rational scientist. How does it favour theism? The fact that, given theism, it was much more probable that the initial conditions would favour the development of life than that they would not, and the fact that the hypothesis of theism makes the life-favouring initial conditions of the universe vastly more probable than they would have been had theism been false, provide us with powerful arguments in favour of theism. (I am calling these "facts", but whether they really are so is something we shall need to examine.) We can now set out the modern, probabilistic teleological argument in full as follows:

The probabilistic teleological argument

1 The laws of the universe are such as to permit the development of life.
2 The probability of (1)'s being true on the hypothesis that there is a God who desires the development of life is much greater than the probability of (1)'s being true on the hypothesis that there is no such God.
3 If there does exist a God who desires the development of life, then the probability of (1)'s being true is much greater than the probability of its being false.

4 We have good reason to believe that some hypothesis is a true explanation of some phenomenon if (i) the probability of the phenomenon's occurring given that the hypothesis is true is much greater than the probability of its occurring given that the hypothesis is false, *and* (ii) if the hypothesis is true, then the probability of the phenomenon's occurring is much greater than the probability of its not occurring.

Therefore: We have good reason to believe that there is a God who desires the development of life.

If we are looking for an argument for a God who is recognisably the God of traditional theism, then the teleological argument takes us much further along the road than does the cosmological argument, because, whereas the latter only posits a cause for the universe without providing us with a reason for thinking of it as an *intelligent* cause, the former points to something which has intentions, for example the intention to bring about the evolution of life in the universe.

The teleological argument fills another gap in the case for theism. [...] it is only the *contingency* of the universe, or its features, which leads us to seek further explanation, then our search will be endless, for each contingent explanation will require further explanation. But the probabilistic argument suggests that it is the apparent *improbability* of the universe's being as it is which should incline us to look for an explanation, an explanation which would make it less improbable.

We might pause for a moment, before going on to assess the argument, to note that the conclusion of the teleological argument, as we have set it out, is quite different in form from that of the cosmological and ontological arguments. Those arguments have as their conclusion the proposition that God exists, whereas the probabilistic teleological argument has as its conclusion the weaker proposition that *we have good reason to believe* that God exists. If we are trying to construct a valid argument from probabilistic considerations, this is inevitable. There will always be a gap between what it is reasonable to believe and what is true. We may be perfectly justified in adopting a hypothesis, having correctly

applied reliable principles of probabilistic reasoning, and yet that hypothesis turn out to be false.
But the conclusion of the argument is still highly
significant, and, if the argument is a good one,
then we have what all but the most sceptical
would count as an adequate defence of theism.

The Concept of Chance

The probabilistic argument is valid. But are its
premises true? Let us look first at the principle set
out in premise (4):

4   We have good reason to believe that some
    hypothesis is a true explanation of some
    phenomenon if (i) the probability of the
    phenomenon's occurring given that the
    hypothesis is true is much greater than
    the probability of its occurring given that
    the hypothesis is false, *and* (ii) if the hypo-
    thesis is true, then the probability of the
    phenomenon's occurring is much greater
    than the probability of its not occurring.

Both conditions seem plausible because they
describe our reasoning about everyday situations. If a lamp does not come on when the
switch is operated, but all the other lights in the
house are working, we will naturally assume that
the bulb has blown. This is a familiar context
to which the rule above obviously applies, if it
applies anywhere. But the teleological argument
was not concerned with a familiar context such
as lights failing to come on, but rather with the
context of the laws and fundamental constants of
nature. Do the rules of probability still apply in
this less familiar context?

When we are considering the probability of a
phenomenon such as a lamp's failing to come on,
we do so against a background of information.
The lamp is plugged in, and switched on at the
mains, a bulb is fitted, the other lights are on. We
also include, in this background information,
some laws of physics – for example the fact that,
when electricity flows through a narrow tungsten
wire in a rarefied atmosphere containing no oxygen but some argon, the wire tends to glow. (We
can, if we know enough, derive this from more
fundamental laws.) Given all this information, we
will assume that the lamp is more likely to come

on than not. However, if we add the information
that there has been a power failure, then we
will assume that the lamp is more likely not to
come on. What determines the probability of
the lamp's coming on is a conjunction of the
various states of affairs obtaining and the laws
of physics. Altering any of these will alter the
probability. But if the probability of events is
determined in part by the laws of physics, what
can it mean to talk of the probability of the laws
of physics themselves? If we judge that it was
extremely improbable that the charge on the proton should have been $1 \cdot 602 \times 10^{-19}$ coulomb,
against what background are we making our
judgement? What do we suppose is determining
the probability of this value? Not, surely, the
other laws of physics, for any given law will
either have nothing whatsoever to do with the
charge on the proton, or otherwise will actually
entail that it has the value that it has.

The difficulty here is precisely analogous to
the difficulty [. . .] that causal explanation takes
place against a background of laws, so it is
inappropriate to talk of a causal explanation of
the laws themselves. Similarly, since statements
of probability take place against a background of
laws, it is inappropriate to talk of the probability
of the laws themselves.

The defender of the teleological argument has
a reply to this objection, which goes as follows.
Admittedly, when we are dealing with ordinary
situations, the probability of an event, such as a
fire, depends upon a whole series of background
conditions. Working out the probability in any
detail will, in fact, be a complex process. But
when we talk of the improbability of the universe's
favouring life we mean something much simpler. We imagine a series of possible universes,
some of which have laws which favour the
development of life as we know it, but the vast
majority of which will not favour life as we know
it. Given that only one imaginary universe will
correspond to the way things really are, it is
much more probable that the one which does
will be in the majority group (i.e. the life-hostile
universes) than in the minority group (i.e. the
life-favouring universes). However, if we hypo-
thesise that which imaginary universe corresponds to the way things are is actually determined
by a being who desires the evolution of life,
then the tables are turned, and it becomes vastly

more likely that the laws of the universe will be life-favouring ones. Since we know that the laws of the universe are life-favouring ones, we have a reason to suppose that there is such a being who made things turn out this way.

The concept of probability that is in play here is sometimes called *statistical probability* or *chance*. It is not the only kind of probability that there is, but it is the one most clearly relevant to this argument, and we should pause to examine it more carefully. We can illustrate statistical probability with the very familiar case of tossing a coin. Suppose we toss a coin 1,000 times and note the number of times the coin lands heads and the number of times it lands tails. Assuming that the coin is not "loaded" in any way, and that the tosses are fair, we would expect a roughly even distribution of outcomes, i.e. 500 times heads and 500 times tails, or some approximation to this, such as 455 heads and 545 tails. The greater the number of tosses, the greater would be the approximation to 50 per cent heads and 50 per cent tails. So we say that the statistical probability (hereafter "chance") of the coin's landing tails is 0.5.

This only tells us how chance is measured, however. It does not tell us what chance is, in the sense of providing a metaphysical account. And a metaphysical account of chance is what we need if we are to determine the legitimacy of using the concept in the context of the teleological argument. One, very influential, account is the *frequency theory*. According to the frequency theory, the chance of a given outcome is just the frequency of that outcome in a large enough sample. So, when we describe the chance of a coin's landing tails as 0.5, this is just equivalent to the assertion that in a large enough sample of tosses, 50 per cent of the tosses result in tails. Strictly, then, the frequency theorist would not allow that chance is *measured by* frequency: chance just *is* frequency. What the simple example of a coin obscures, however, is that frequency will be relative to a population. Thus the frequency of people dying within twenty years of a certain date in, for example, a population of people who were non-smoking, healthy teenagers at that date will be quite different from the frequency in a population of people who were heavy smokers, had parents who died of heart disease and were over 80 at that date. This, for the frequency

theorist, is what it means to say that the chances of your having a life expectancy of twenty years will vary according to your age, medical history, life-style, etc.

However, if this is the correct account of chance, the use of it by the teleological argument is quite illegitimate. The chance, it is said, of the universe turning out to be life-supporting is vanishingly small on the atheist hypothesis. That must mean, if the frequency theory is correct, that the frequency of universes capable of sustaining life is very small in the total population of universes. But the total population of universes contains exactly one member, namely the actual universe. It would seem to follow that the chance of there being a universe capable of sustaining life is actually very high; indeed, it is 1! This cannot be right. For chance to make sense on the frequency theory, the relevant population must contain more than one member. Perhaps, then, the relevant population is the population of *possible* universes, and this is the way in which we presented the argument when we talked earlier of "imaginary universes". But this cannot be right either, precisely because these other universes are not real: they are not there to be counted. [. . .]

The frequency theory suffers from two rather serious limitations, however. The first is that we do, intuitively, want a distinction between the measure of chance and chance itself. Frequency is, surely, only an indication of real chance. The second is that we want to be able to talk of chance in a single case. It is because we want to talk of chance in the single case, in fact, that we want the distinction between frequency and what it measures. Take this particular coin. It has never been tossed before and I intend to toss it just once. Do we not want to be able to say that there is a certain chance of its landing tails on that one toss? If we do say this, we do not mean, surely, just that if it were tossed enough times, the frequency of tails would be 50 per cent. Chance is, arguably, a property of the single case. It does not depend on whether the experiment is, or even could be, repeated. This is exactly what will be insisted on by the proponent of the teleological argument: although only one universe is realised, the fact that the one which is realised is capable of sustaining life has a certain chance.

So, in place of frequency theory, we may prefer *propensity theory*. Just as solubility is a disposition of a lump of sugar – the disposition to dissolve when placed in water – so, according to propensity theory, the chance of landing tails is a disposition of a coin. Some coins are fair, some are biased. The chances of their landing tails will therefore differ, and this is because of a real property of the coins themselves. This property we will call a *propensity*: a disposition which is, or determines, the chance of a certain outcome. Propensities are measurable, and frequency is what measures them. But the propensity does not depend on the actual frequency of an outcome in any population any more than solubility depends on being actually immersed in water.

It is widely thought that chance merely reflects our ignorance, and that, if we knew precisely the conditions of a given throw (the shape of the coin, the number of spins, the angle at which it hits the table, etc.), we would be able to work out whether it would land heads or tails. Or, even if we could never work it out, the initial conditions nevertheless determine the outcome, so that the *real* probability of landing tails on a given throw will in fact be either 1 or 0: i.e. it will either be necessary that it lands tails, or impossible. If everything in the world is determined in this way, it is argued, then there are in reality no probabilities between 1 and 0. The reason the frequency of tails is, in a large number of throws, 50 per cent, is simply that the conditions of each throw differ slightly from those of the other throws. If the conditions were repeated exactly in each case, then the frequency of tails would be either 1 or 0. We should therefore distinguish the chance which we assign to an outcome from the *real* chance of that outcome. Propensity theory is perfectly consistent with this distinction, because it allows that our measure of chance may not always accurately reflect real chance. But we can distinguish between measured chance and real chance without having to concede that the real chance of any event is either 1 or 0. The world itself may be indeterministic, so that the state of the universe at a particular time may only make it 90 per cent probable that a certain event will occur later. Are we then wrong to say that the chance of the coin's landing tails is 0.5? No, because this

reflects the fact that the coin itself (considered independently of the conditions in which it is thrown) has no greater propensity to land tails than land heads.

To return to the main discussion: can we appeal to propensity theory in making sense of the idea of a godless universe being the outcome of chance? No, we cannot. For the propensity theorist, the chance of an outcome resides in the circumstances which produce the outcome. The chance of landing tails is a property of the coin, or, more accurately, of the whole situation in which the coin is thrown. But the fact that this universe was realised is not, if the atheist is right, the outcome of any *process*. Only if we accept that a creator exists can we talk of a propensity in anything to produce universes. We may imagine God contemplating, for example, a whole series of values for the speed of light and eventually coming down in favour of one. If God did this completely at random, then we could perhaps talk of its being extremely improbable that the charge on the proton should have been $1 \cdot 602 \times 10^{-19}$ coulomb. But then, if we have to introduce a creator in order to be able to talk coherently of the probability of the laws of physics being what they are, we can hardly appeal to the supposed improbability of certain combinations of those laws as an argument for God's existence.

Where does this get us? The teleological argument asks us to compare the following: (i) the probability of there being laws which permit the development of intelligent life on the hypothesis that God does exist; and (ii) the probability of there being laws which permit the development of intelligent life on the hypothesis that God does *not* exist. Probability (i) is supposed to be far greater than probability (ii), and this provides a case for theism. Now we can certainly find some kind of value for (i), at least on the propensity theory of chance, because we can talk in terms of God's propensity to produce a universe of a certain type, just as we can talk of the propensity of a fruit machine to produce the jackpot. We are not, of course, imagining God playing a game of chance ("Heads I create the universe, tails I don't"). Rather, we will reason as follows. If it is in God's nature to be benevolent, we would imagine that he would realise this benevolence by creating an object which he could love, and which, moreover, was capable of being aware of that love. God, then, has good reason to create intelligent life. The probability of there being intelligent life given God's existence, then, is high, perhaps as high as 1. But this gets us nowhere, because we cannot intelligibly assign a value to (ii). If there is no creator, then there is nothing to which we can ascribe the propensity to produce a universe. Consequently, the notion of chance is inapplicable.

In stating the principles on which the teleological argument depends, we overlooked another important principle: do not choose a hypothesis which is itself very improbable. As in the lamp case, we may be faced with competing hypotheses, all of which make the phenomenon to be explained probable. The fact that one of the hypotheses is more likely to be true than another is one reason for adopting it. For example, suppose on entering a science museum we are confronted with a perplexing sight: a tap, apparently suspended in mid-air, connected to nothing at all, and yet spouting a vertical stream of water. We are faced with competing hypotheses: (a) we are having an hallucination at just that moment; (b) there is a hollow glass tube on which the tap is fixed, and through which water is being pumped from below, so that when the water overflows from the top, it runs down the tube in such a way as to disguise its presence. Both of these hypotheses make the phenomenon to be explained probable. Indeed, the first makes it absolutely certain, because the hallucination just *is* the phenomenon. But we will almost certainly not adopt the first in preference to the second, because the chance that the first hypothesis is true is so small. So it might seem that, in order to assess whether we should adopt theism as a hypothesis, we need to know the chance of God's existing. Now, for reasons given above, we cannot make sense of such a chance, for God is supposed to be the outcome of no process whatsoever. There is nothing, therefore, which can be said to have a certain propensity to produce God. But if there is no propensity, then there is no chance of God's existing or not existing.

The Weak Anthropic Principle

Despite its failure as an argument for theism, the teleological argument remains as a powerful statement of what puzzles us about the universe, and it appears, moreover, to offer an answer to that puzzlement. We may not be forced to acknowledge that we are the result of design, but we still want to have an explanation of why, for example, the fundamental constants of nature were so balanced as to allow large amounts of carbon to be available, this in turn making possible the development of life. If we are used to being able to explain things, it is very difficult simply to accept that there are certain things which are beyond explanation. But in recent years a principle has been articulated which, at least on one interpretation, offers an antidote to our puzzlement over the fact that the universe was such as to permit the development of life. Known as the *anthropic principle*, it can be stated simply, though ambiguously, as follows: "The fundamental constants are as they are because this is a possible world in which there is life." There are two quite different versions of the principle. One of them, [. . .] is called the *weak* anthropic principle. It goes as follows:

The weak anthropic principle

What we can expect to observe must be restricted by the conditions necessary for our presence as observers.

We might call it the "'What-else-would-you-expect-to-observe?' principle". As Descartes pointed out, we cannot doubt our own existence. So what we observe must be consistent with our own existence. So *of course* the fundamental constants will be such as to permit the development of life. Our puzzlement is groundless.

[. . .]

However, this attempt to defuse the mystery of existence has met with some resistance. Richard Swinburne, for example, has suggested that there must be a more substantive explanation of why the fundamental constants are as they are, and in order to drive the point home he appeals to the following analogy:

Suppose that a madman kidnaps a victim and shuts him in a room with a card-shuffling machine. The machine shuffles ten packs of cards simultaneously and then draws a card from each pack and exhibits simultaneously the ten cards. The kidnapper tells the victim that he will shortly set the machine to work and it will exhibit its first draw, but that unless the draw consists of an ace of hearts from each pack, the machine will simultaneously set off an explosion which will kill the victim, in consequence of which he will not see which cards the machine drew. The machine is then set to work, and to the amazement and relief of the victim the machine exhibits an ace of hearts drawn from each pack. The victim thinks that this extraordinary fact needs an explanation in terms of the machine having been rigged in some way. But the kidnapper, who now reappears, casts doubt on this suggestion. "It is hardly surprising", he says, "that the machine draws only aces of hearts. You could not possibly see anything else. For you would not be here to see anything at all, if any other cards had been drawn." But, of course, the victim is right and the kidnapper is wrong. There is indeed something extraordinary in need of explanation in ten aces of hearts being drawn. The fact that this peculiar order is a necessary condition of the draw being perceived at all makes what is perceived no less extraordinary and in need of explanation. [See "How the Existence of God Explains the World and Its Order," p. 111 above]

How good an analogy is this? Although Swinburne does not say so, the reason why the outcome of this fiendish experiment is so surprising is that it is extremely improbable. Given the number of combinations which the card-shuffling machine could have produced, the chance that it would produce ten aces is very small indeed – it is in fact $(1/52)^{10}$. That is why the victim naturally feels there should be some more substantive explanation than that offered by the kidnapper. But, as we are now in a position to see after the discussion of the previous section, this makes the analogy very suspicious. For the permutation of the fundamental constants is *not* the outcome of some random process, and the idea that such a permutation is very improbable is, therefore, quite inappropriate. In the language of propensity theory, whereas in the case Swinburne discusses there is an object to which one can ascribe a propensity, in the case of the fundamental constants there is no such object. No object, no propensity; no propensity, no chance.

[...]

Summary

In its traditional form in the writings of eighteenth-century theologians, the teleological argument attempted to construct an analogy between human artefacts and natural objects. Just as a watch bears the marks of its designer, so do such things as the eye. The eye has a particular purpose, that of conveying visual information. But we cannot talk of purpose here unless we can also talk of someone who designed the eye for that purpose. Hence, according to the argument, we can infer the existence of a creator.

What undermines the analogy is the discovery of a natural, non-theological explanation for phenomena like the eye, such as the theory of natural selection. However, we can construct a probabilistic version of the teleological argument which cannot be refuted by scientific developments. The probabilistic teleological argument exploits the idea that it is extremely improbable that the laws of the universe should be so balanced as to permit the development of life unless we adopt the hypothesis that these laws were fixed by a creator who desired the development of life. The argument, however, faces the same kind of objection as the one we brought against the cosmological argument [...]: it takes a certain concept out of a context in which it is obviously applicable, and applies it to a context in which that concept is not applicable. In the case of the cosmological argument, the crucial concept is that of causation; in the case of the teleological argument, it is statistical probability. Neither argument carries conviction because we can plausibly deny that the concept in question can be extended to cover extraordinary contexts.

Two theories of statistical probability were presented: the frequency theory and the propensity theory. The frequency theory equates probability with frequency in a sufficiently large population. The propensity theory equates probability with a real property in a situation to produce a particular outcome. On the basis of either theory, it makes no sense to talk of the probability of a life-sustaining universe in the absence of God.

19

The Message of the Māṇḍūkya Upaniṣad
A Phenomenological Analysis of Mind and Consciousness

Ramakrishna Puligandla

[T]he Māṇḍūkya Upaniṣad is the briefest but most important of all the Upaniṣads, in that it contains the gist, the heart, and the essence of the entire Upaniṣad teaching. It is also my considered judgement that, although a number of commentaries, ancient, modern, and contemporary, exist on this Upaniṣad, a thorough phenomenological investigation of some fundamental issues is lacking. Accordingly, the purpose of this paper is to undertake such an investigation and shed light on mind, consciousness, and the *turīya*.

[. . .]

In the waking state, we are aware of external objects; that is, we have external perceptions. In the dream state, we are aware of internal objects; that is, we have internal perceptions. In the deep-sleep state, we are aware of neither external objects nor internal objects; that is, we have neither external nor internal perceptions. The point to be made here, then, is that objects, whether external or internal, are perceived only when the mind is functioning. In other words, perception of objects is due to the working of the mind. This means that the state of deep sleep, where there is no perception of objects, external or internal, mind is not functioning. In a word,

mind is quiescent. During the state of deep sleep, one does not know that one is in deep sleep. However, when one awakes and is asked whether he slept well, he answers affirmatively by saying, "Yes, I have had a restful and blissful sleep." The question now is: how does one know that one had deep sleep on waking up, if one does not know that one is in deep sleep during the state of deep sleep? It simply does not make sense to answer by saying that one *remembers* that one had a deep sleep; for remembering implies knowing at an earlier time, but one does not know during deep sleep that one is in deep sleep. Let it be emphasized here that a person's claim to have had deep sleep can be objectively determined through neurophysiological investigation, just as his claim to have had a dream. If all knowing is through the activity of the mind through mental operations – including remembering – and the mind is quiescent during deep sleep, then one's claim to have had deep sleep becomes mysterious and inexplicable.

The only way to rationally answer this question is to grant that there is a knowing that does not involve any mental activity – mental operations – and the knower is consciousness itself; and there are many passages in the Upaniṣad where "consciousness" is used synonymously with

"The Message of the Māṇḍūkya Upaniṣad: A Phenomenological Analysis of Mind and Consciousness" by Ramakrishna Puligandla, *Indian Philosophical Quarterly* 26:2 (April 1999): 221–31.

"knower" and "knowledge." Let us here clarify the two senses in which consciousness is to be understood as knowledge: 1. consciousness is the ultimate necessary condition for any knowing, and 2. consciousness itself is knowledge. All knowing through the mind involves an *object*, the known; accordingly, knowing through mind necessarily involves the tripartite distinction of the knower, the known, and the activity of knowing; that is, this distinction is never absent and cannot be collapsed in any knowing through the mind. The upshot of these observations is that the Māṇḍūkya Upaniṣad recognizes and calls our attention to a knowing and hence knowledge which does not involve the mind – any mental operations. Here, the tripartite distinction mentioned above is wholly absent. In a word, in this kind of knowing consciousness itself is the knower and, whatever is known and the act of knowing cannot exist separately from consciousness. Thus, according to the Māṇḍūkya Upaniṣad, one knows, through consciousness itself, on awaking that one has had a deep sleep. It is true that on waking up mental activity resumes. Once one knows, no matter how, mind will simply report. I am fully aware that many philosophers will dismiss as absurd the whole idea of knowing anything at all without mental operations. But let me give a clear example of knowing without involving any mental operations. Thus ask someone, say John, "are you conscious now?" John immediately replies by saying, "Yes, of course I am conscious. What do you mean by asking such an absurd question?" Let me clarify the situation here. Yes, there certainly are mental operations enabling John to hear the question, just as there certainly are to enable him to answer the question. But this is not the point; rather, the point is, what mental operations are involved in John's *arriving at* the answer? I submit that there are none. But if someone thinks that there are mental operations by performing which John arrived at his answer, I would like to see the list. Let me emphasize that this is not a matter to be decided by arbitrary decisions and fiat of definitions, but by phenomenological investigation. I suggest that the reader inquire into this matter and determine for himself how he would arrive at his answer if he were asked this question; and if he does perform some mental operations, he should give me a list of

them. Let me assure him that there are absolutely no mental operations in arriving at the answer, "Yes, I am of course conscious." The reason for there being no mental operations in arriving at the answer to the above question is that here knowing and being are one and the same and the tripartile distinction is wholly absent. One *immediately* knows that one is conscious, not through some mental operations, such as inference. The point of the Māṇḍūkya Upaniṣad can now be stated as follows: during the state of deep sleep, the mind is quiescent, that is, there are no menial operations and hence there can be no knowing through the mind. Nevertheless, there is consciousness and it is through consciousness itself that the deep-sleep state is known; and on waking, mental activity resumes and the mind simply reports what is known, no matter how it is known.

Someone might now object by saying that one's claim that one has had deep sleep is based on inference. The objection runs as follows: on waking up, one feels relaxed, and one attributes the state of relaxation to having had deep sleep. This objection, however, cannot stand scrutiny. A state of relaxation can be had through means other than deep sleep. The person was awake before deep sleep and is awake after deep sleep and when he says he has had a deep sleep he means that he was not aware of any objects in between; and this claim he could not have made if he did not in some sense know he has had a deep sleep. He could just as well have said that someone injected into him a substance which induces relaxation. Someone might now object by saying that the person just got up from sleep and no wonder he says he has had deep sleep. But this objection begs the question, for the person did not say he has had sleep but a *deep* sleep. There is no difficulty with a person's saying on getting up that he has had a sleep, but it is quite a different matter when he says he has had a *deep* sleep. How did he know he has had a deep sleep? Appeals to feeling relaxed are of no avail, for as pointed above a state of relaxation can be had through means other than deep sleep. The inescapable conclusion, according to the Māṇḍūkya Upaniṣad, is that in some sense there is knowledge of being aware of no objects at all. It might be mentioned in passing that the EEGs of different persons in the waking state are similar, those of dreaming are similar, and those of deep sleep are similar. The import of this remark is that we do not have to take on faith a person's report that he dreamt or has had deep sleep; rather, such reports are open to objective confirmation or disconfirmation.

Another important phenomenological observation here is that when we ask someone whether he slept well, he does not begin his reply by saying, "now, well, let me see..." Rather, he immediately says that he had trouble sleeping, had to turn and toss in the bed for long, had bad dreams, or has a deep sleep. This observation confirms the claim that one knows without any inference that one has had a deep sleep.

If the state of deep sleep were one wholly devoid of consciousness, then there could be no continuity between going to sleep and waking up, and consequently the person could not draw any inferences. This is to say that the possibility for drawing inferences presupposes continuity of being; and, according to the Māṇḍūkya Upaniṣad, it is consciousness that provides the continuity. And given that the mind is quiescent during deep sleep, it is through consciousness itself (which persists even in deep sleep) that one knows directly, immediately (without having to draw any inferences) that one has had deep sleep. In short, the knower here is none other than consciousness itself.

The important question that now arises is: what happened to the mind during the deep-sleep state? The Māṇḍūkya Upaniṣad answers this question as follows: To say that the mind is quiescent during deep sleep is not to say that the mind simply vanished away and became non-existent; rather, it is to say that the mind is no longer manifest as an individual entity, but became one with consciousness. It is precisely for this reason that there are no perceptions – objects – at all during deep sleep. In other words, during deep sleep mind merges with consciousness, losing everything characteristic of it as an individual entity. However, on waking up, the mind re-emerges from consciousness, manifesting itself as an individual entity with all its specific characteristics such as thoughts, feelings, memories, etc. The point here, then, is that the knowledge that one has had deep sleep is present in consciousness and it is recovered by the mind as soon as one wakes up. If the knowledge were not present, the mind could not recover it. It

is clear from these observations that the mind is none other than consciousness with objects – intentionalities. Whatever is known through the mind, is always an intentionality, an object. In the state of deep sleep, there is no mental activity and consequently there are no intentionalities. The knowledge that one has had a deep sleep is therefore non-intentional knowledge, the knower here being non-intentional, objectless consciousness itself. It is clear, then, that according to the Māṇḍūkya Upaniṣad, there is non-intentional, objectless consciousness, which is also a knower. All non-intentional knowing, such as one's knowing that one is conscious, is knowing by non-intentional consciousness, not knowing by mind, which is intentional consciousness.

From the above considerations, it is clear that the Māṇḍūkya Upaniṣad draws a *phenomenological* distinction between mind and consciousness. Mind is *phenomenologocally* distinguished from consciousness as intentional knower – that is, whatever is known through the mind is always, unexceptionably, an object, an intetionally. And whatever is known non-intentionally is not an object, and it is known through non-intentional, objectless consciousness. However, mind is not *ontologically* different from consciousness; in fact, it *cannot* be different from consciousness, for consciousness – Ātman – is the ultimate, non-dual reality; that is, nothing other than the non-dual reality can exist. Whatever exists is a manifestation (appearances) of consciousness, and mind is but one of the manifestations of the ultimate non-dual reality. Manifestations can disappear and reappear but consciousness – ultimate reality – whose manifestations are all appearances, itself never disappears. It is this consciousness that persists through all the three modes of our being, namely, waking, dreaming, and deep sleep. It is also the non-intentional knower and makes possible intentional knowing through mind.

At this juncture, I wish to make some pertinent observations on the treatment of the topic of consciousness in the Western tradition. In this tradition, the terms "mind," "self," "I," and "consciousness" are used synonymously. Thus consider Descartes. He asks, "what then is it that I am?" and answers by saying, "A thinking thing ... and if I entirely cease to think, thereupon I shall altogether cease to exist" (*Meditation* II).

It is clear from this quote that Descartes does not phenomenologically distinguish mind and consciousness. I can easily imagine an Upaniṣadic rishi asking Descartes, "your teaching is interesting; however, I wish to ask as to how you *know* you cease to exist if you cease to think." The rishi will then offer deep sleep as an example of a state in which one certainly exists, although there is no thinking. This is the basis on which the Māṇḍūkya Upaniṣad phenomenologically distinguishes mind and consciousness. In deep sleep, there is just consciousness and absolutely no thinking; whereas in the waking and dream states there is consciousness with thinking, which is none other than mind; these correspond to non-intentional knowing and intentional knowing, respectively. Thus from the ontological standpoint, the Western use of "mind" and "consciousness" synonymously is not wrong; on the contrary, it is in full accord with the teaching of the Māṇḍūkya Upaniṣad. But failing to phenomenologically distinguish mind and consciousness has led the Western tradition into denying non-intentional consciousness – objectless consciousness. In sharp contrast, the Māṇḍūkya Upaniṣad, having phenomenologically distinguished mind and consciousness, consistently and correctly affirms non-intentional consciousness – Ātman. It is not surprising, then, that the Upaniṣadic tradition also developed various phenomenological techniques – Yogic disciplines – in order to realize non-intentional consciousness as the ultimate nondual reality. An observation concerning Western phenomenology: Husserl and all his followers regard consciousness as intentional; but from our discussion of the state of deep sleep, it should be clear by now that it is mind and not consciousness that is intentional. It is mind that pays attention to objects and therefore is intentional. Consciousness makes possible paying attention and having intentionalities – objects.

I come now to a discussion of *turīya*. "*Turīya*" literally means the fourth. It is worth noting that the Māṇḍūkya Upaniṣad does not refer to *turīya* as a state, but merely as the fourth, beyond the state of deep sleep. The reason for this is that "state" connotes duality, in particular the distinction between the knower and the known *turīya*, according to the Māṇḍūkya Upaniṣad, is the highest mode of being, beyond all dualities. But,

unfortunately, commentaries on the Māṇḍūkya Upaniṣad do not offer any phenomenological clarification of *turīya*; instead, they merely describe the *turīya* in vague terms and phrases, such as "realization of Brahman," "realization of Ātman," "realization of the ultimate non-dual reality," etc. I propose to offer here a phenomenological interpretation of *turīya*. From the phenomenological point of view, *turīya* is just like the state of deep sleep, except for one important difference: the difference is that whereas during deep sleep one does not know one is in deep sleep, in *turīya* one *does* know that one *is* in deep sleep. I shall now proceed to discuss the most significant implications of this interpretation.

In *turīya*, just as in deep sleep, there are no perceptions – objects; and one knows that one is in deep sleep; that is, one is aware that there are no objects at all. This means that one is aware of one's being even when there are no objects at all. This is the mode of highest wakefulness. Why is it the mode of highest wakefulness? Because "I am" persists even when there are no objects. This in turn means that there is a reality about each of us – the same reality, non-dual consciousness – whose existence is not contingent upon any objects. Such reality is indeed the necessary being – the reality that exists without depending for its existence upon anything other than itself. A word of caution here: In the phrase "I am" above, "I" is not to be understood as the ego, which is an object. The phrase is to be correctly understood as just consciousness (awareness) – Ātman, Brahman, the ultimate non-dual reality. Even if the entire world – all manifestations – disappears, there is a reality that never disappears and reappears. That reality is at once Ātman (objectless consciousness) and Brahman (*Sat*, Existence); realization of this reality is the highest philosophical and religious goal the sages exhort us to attain. He who attains this realization is the most wakeful one and the realization is the discovery that one is immortal. Immortality is not something we need to acquire but rather the attainment of *turīya* is the *discovery* that we have always been immortal. In short, it is an epistemological discovery, not acquiring something we did not have before. Having discovered that in one's true being one is immortal, not subject to birth and death, one is forever free of pain and suffering and lives in peace and joy. It is to be emphasized here that in the teaching of the Māṇḍūkya Upaniṣad there is no transcendental [. . .] God, the Devil, Judgement, heaven, hell, etc. The Upaniṣad is concerned with discovering, through thoroughgoing phenomenological inquiry, one's true being as non-intentional consciousness. And since consciousness persists through all of our modes of being, there is a sense in which we are always in *turīya*.

[. . .]

To conclude, 1. The Māṇḍūkya Upaniṣad is unique in its phenomenological investigation of our possible modes of being, in order to discover the reality that persists through all of them. 2. There is a knowing independently of any mental activity (mental operations); it is through consciousness itself that one knows directly and immediately on waking that one has had a deep sleep, not through any mental activities such as remembering and inferring. 3. This kind of knowing is non-intentional knowing, for it is not knowing any objects (phenomena) but rather knowing one's own mode of being. 4. The Māṇḍūkya Upaniṣad. *phenomenologically* distinguishes mind and consciousness and shows on clear phenomenological grounds that *ontologically* mind is non-different from Ātman, the non-intentional consciousness; the reason for this ontological claim is that the non-intentional consciousness is indeed the ultimate non-dual reality; it is ultimate because even when all objects disappear it continues to be; objects appear, disappear, and reappear, whereas the non-intentional consciousness *never* disappears; it is non-dual in two senses: a). it is impartite and b). nothing other than it can exist; whatever exists is this reality. It is for this reason that Ātman, the non-intentional consciousness, is also non-different from Brahman (*Sat*, Existence). 5. During deep sleep mind loses its individuality by merging – becoming one – with the non-intentional and therefore non-dual consciousness. Whatever consciousness knows in the state of deep sleep is simply reported by the mind on waking up, without having to perform

any operations. That is, once something is known, no matter how, the mind also knows. 6. It is clear from this analysis that mind is none other than *intentional* consciousness, and whatever is known by the non-intentional consciousness is directly and immediately accessible to the mind. 7. By failing to *phenomenologcally* distinguish mind and consciousness, the Western tradition denies non-intentional consciousness; in keen contrast, through its analysis of the state of deep sleep, the Māṇḍūkyā Upaniṣad affirms non-intentional consciousness. 8. *Turīya* is just like deep sleep, except for one most significant difference; the difference is that whereas during deep sleep one does not know that one is in deep sleep, in *turīya* one *does* know during deep sleep that one *is* in deep sleep; thus *turīya* is the mode of highest wakefulness; it is the mode of highest wakefulness, because one is fully aware of one's being even when the entire world has disappeared. 9. The attainment of *turīya* is the realization of one's true being as the ultimate non-dual reality (non-dual consciousness) which never disappears. 10. The realization of *turīya* is thus the discovery that one has always been immortal (attaining immortality is not acquiring something one did not have before, but rather discovering that one has always been immortal). 11. Thus the attainment of *turīya* and therewith immortality is an *epistemological* event; consequently, *turīya* is not a postmortem state to be looked forward to after death; instead, it is knowledge that is to be realized here and now, while fully embodied. 12. In the Upaniṣad tradition, the attainment of *turīya* is the highest philosophical and religious goal; for this reason, the Upanisdic sages exhort us to earnestly strive after it. 13. Each person has to achieve *turīya* by himself or herself, and not expect others to achieve it for him or her (just, as everyone has to take his or her own bath). 14. The realization of *turīya* leads one to fearlessness, wisdom, freedom, peace, and joy. 15. The teaching of the Māṇḍūkya Upaniṣad is grounded in thorough and sound phenomenological inquiry, and is wholly free of any and all theological baggage [. . .].

20

Antirationalism in Zhuangzi and Kierkegaard

Karen L. Carr and Philip J. Ivanhoe

Introduction

In order to set the stage for our discussions of Zhuangzi and Kierkegaard's particular forms of antirationalist thought, we shall first describe what we mean by the term *antirationalism* in general. Specifically, we want to emphasize how antirationalism differs from both rationalism and irrationalism, how our use of the term differs from that of the late A. C. Graham, and what some of the central problems are for religious thinkers who embrace and employ this philosophical view.[1]

Antirationalism is not a view opposed to or inconsistent with being rational; rather, it is a principled objection to rationalism. Rationalism is here taken to be the view or rather the family of views that holds that reason takes commanding precedence over other ways of acquiring true knowledge. In its strongest form, rationalism is the view that only reason can lead to true beliefs. Many intuitionists in esthetics or ethics, most sensibility theorists in ethics, and many other particular philosophical positions are all forms of antirationalism.

So conceived, antirationalism is a philosophical position about how one grounds certain kinds of truth claims, particularly those concerned with establishing the proper ends of human life. While antirationalism does not deny the value of reason even in this project, it denies that reason alone will enable one to chose and pursue the proper goal of life. Antirationalists believe in alternative sources of guidance. They maintain that we have a tendency to place too much trust in abstract, apersonal forms of reasoning and that this leads us to lose contact with these important, alternative sources of wisdom. Our excessive trust in reason thus hinders our ability to see things as they really are and to act properly and effectively in the world.

There is a parallel between the antirationalist belief that an excessive trust in reason often interferes with proper perception, thought, evaluation, and action and the belief, held by many philosophers (and more than a few psychologists as well), that excessive emotion interferes with these same cognitive, evaluative, and intentional processes. Antirationalists believe that if we allow ourselves to be exclusively or excessively

---

"Antirationalism in Zhuangzi and Kierkegaard" from *The Sense of Irrationalism: The Religious Thought of Zhuangzi and Kierkegaard* by Karen L. Carr and Philip J. Ivanhoe (New York: Seven Bridges Press, 2000), pp. 31–51; 54–7; 130–4.

[1]   We get the term *antirationalism* from Angus Graham, who used it throughout many of his works. His most complete statement of this notion can be found in his *Reason and Spontaneity* (London: Curzon Press, 1985) and *Unreason within Reason. Essays on the Outskirts of Rationality* (La Salle, IL: Open Court Press, 1992).

led by reason we will tend to focus on the wrong kinds of things. In particular, we will be led to attend to improper aims in life. Moreover, we will tend to think about what we do see in the wrong ways. Our thinking will be restricted to familiar and well-worn categories and styles of reasoning that prevent us from seeing alternative, more appropriate approaches. We will also tend to evaluate and judge the things and events we encounter incorrectly. Excessive rationality can prejudice our appreciation of important dimensions of life and upset a balanced judgment of what we should do. These various errors, in different combinations, lead us to act foolishly and even tragically.

The two thinkers who are the focus of the present study are not of one mind concerning the degree to which reason can aid one in the effort to gain a true grasp of the world and our place in it, but neither of them completely rejects reason. They both seem to believe that, at the very least, reason can help one to recognize the inadequacy of relying upon reason alone. In other words, careful analysis can reveal that accepted beliefs and well-attested styles of inquiry lead to logical inconsistencies or prove, upon close scrutiny, inadequate. We will refer to this as the *negative* value of reason. Zhuangzi and Kierkegaard also seem to believe that reason has *positive* value as well, for they present their religious visions in elaborate and vivid detail and in a logically consistent fashion. The very fact that they rely on language to describe or at least point to their religious ideals commits them to a tacit approval of at least some positive value to reason. Commonsense applications of practical reasoning pose no particular problem for these thinkers. As we shall see, this aspect of their thought presents unique and interesting challenges for them as authors and us as readers of their works.

Antirationalism is importantly different from irrationalism, which Graham describes as "the principled refusal to take account of facts which conflict with one's values or desires."[2] Irrationalism, Graham notes, "allows you to see things

as you like."[3] Graham also points out that antirationalist thinkers like Zhuangzi are very different from irrationalists such as the Western Romantics, in that the latter extol "the subjective vision in heightened emotion."[4] He further claims that *all* antirationalists regard excessive emotions as interfering with clear perception. While we agree with his view about the important difference between Zhuangzi and Western Romantics, we do not follow him in his general claim that all antirationalists reject excessive emotions. We find no good reason to commit antirationalists to such a view. One might hold that only certain intense, ecstatic states allow one to see things as they really are, but as long as one would be willing to offer some kind of rational defense of these insights, one would be an antirationalist.

Graham implies that the difference between antirationalists and irrationalists is that the latter extol "the subjective vision in heightened emotion." But calm or even emotionless individuals might hold to their personal visions with a "principled refusal to take account of facts which conflict with one's values or desires." This is equally irrational. The value of the intensity of one's emotions is still a significant issue among antirationalists, but the degree to which they are willing or refuse to defend their beliefs rationally is the salient difference in this case. The most distinctive features of antirationalist thinkers are that they do not wholly reject rationality but they also find it not only inadequate but potentially inimical to a proper appreciation of how things really are. Moreover, they insist that there are alternative and reliable sources of understanding, sources that by their very nature cannot be described in the objective, systematic, and precise language of rationality.

Antirationalism and irrationalism are both distinct from rationalism, by which Graham seems to mean the philosophical view that gives pride of place to a personal and precise description and logical analysis. A prime example of this kind of thinking would be geometric proof. Such a definition of rationalism to some degree

---

[2]   *Unreason within Reason*, 109.
[3]   *Unreason within Reason*, 99.
[4]   *Unreason within Reason*, 109.

underemphasizes the empirical side of most rationalist thinkers. That is, it stresses logical form and consistency and the role of analysis but does not link this directly with an appeal to facts and experimental demonstration. But beliefs can be formal and consistent and capable of careful analysis yet irrational in that they fly in the face of evident and irrefutable states of affairs. True propositions do not always describe real states of affairs. We will use the term rationalism to mean the philosophical view that bases its knowledge claims not only on systematic form, logical consistency, and rigorous analysis, but also on some form of realism and clearly established methods of demonstration.[5] This is important, for antirationalists share with rationalists a commitment to some form of realism and at least a tacit view of how one is to arrive at their purported state of understanding.

Part I: Zhuangzi

There can be no doubt that Zhuangzi saw reason as possessing what we are calling a negative value; much of his work consists of *reductio ad absurdum* arguments and logical paradoxes designed to challenge one's reliance on and confidence in rational analysis. Zhuangzi's criticisms of an overreliance on reason had many sources and different forms. For example, he argued that reason is always neutral with regard to ends and so can be employed with equal force in different and incompatible causes. Therefore, if one begins from incompatible premises, following reason often leads to nothing more than paradox. Moreover, there are significant differences in the way people weigh evidence and arrive at judgments – especially when it comes to questions of value – and this generates considerable skepticism concerning the supremacy of reason. As Zhuangzi says, "If right were really right,

it would differ so clearly from not right, that there would be no need for argument."[6] There is overwhelming evidence that not only do disagreements arise, they persist. Many arguments stubbornly resist resolution; appeals to reason seem incapable of reconciling well-entrenched differences.

> Suppose you and I have an argument. If you have beaten me instead of my beating you, then are you necessarily right and am I necessarily wrong? Is one of us right and the other wrong? Are both of us right or are both of us wrong? If you and I don't know the answer, then other people are bound to be even more in the dark. Whom shall we get to decide what is right? Shall we get someone who agrees with you to decide? But if he already agrees with you, how can he decide fairly? Shall we get someone who agrees with me? But if he already agrees with me, how can he decide? Shall we get someone who disagrees with both of us? But if he already disagrees with both of us, how can he decide? Shall we get someone who agrees with both of us? But if he already agrees with both of us, how can he decide? Obviously, then, neither you nor I nor anyone else can decide for each other. Shall we wait for still another person?[7]

Such doubts about reason's ability to set proper goals and settle disagreements were an important part of what led Zhuangzi to seek guidance elsewhere, specifically in our prerational intuitions and tendencies. But there was more to his distrust of reason than this. For Zhuangzi also worried that any sort of abstract reflection on how to conduct one's life eventually results in a stifling routinization and alienation. Whenever we attempt to generalize from specific situations we tend to lose the specificity and nuance required for proper assessment. Such an approach seems inexorably to lead to fixed and inaccurate conceptions of and clumsy and ineffective responses

---

[5]   We are not claiming that there is only one version of such an appeal, only that in order to have a legitimate version of such a view, one needs to embrace some view about the way things really are (i.e., one is committed to some form of metaphysical realism) and some notion of how one comes to know this (i.e., one cannot be a strong epistemological skeptic). This still leaves a good deal up for grabs.

[6]   Burton Watson (trans.), *The Complete Works of Chuang Tzu* (New York: Columbia University Press, 1968), 48–9.

[7]   Watson, *Complete Works*, 48.

to the world. In novel situations the breakdown between our conceptions of the world and how things really are can be complete, often comical, and sometimes tragic. Huizi regularly appears as an illustration of such a narrow-minded and inflexible approach. For example, [. . .] he is given seeds that produce marvelously large gourds. However, stuck in his view that gourds can be used only as vessels or ladles, he deems his huge gourds to be useless and smashes them. This draws a minilecture from Zhuangzi on the need to remain open-minded that ends with the rebuke, "Now you had a gourd big enough to hold five piculs. Why didn't you think of making it into a great tub so you could go floating around the rivers and lakes, instead of worrying because it was too big and unwieldy to dip into things! Obviously you still have a lot of underbrush in your head!"[8]

In addition to leading to a loss of flexibility and sensitivity, Zhuangzi feared that reason, by its very nature, has a tendency to divorce individual cases from their surrounding context and separate the agent from the situation at hand. When we see a given situation as "a case of x" we often lose sight of the distinctive features unique to its particular occurrence. And when we reason abstractly about a given situation, we attempt to bracket our individual responses to it and emphasize our role as unmoved, objective observers. These twin tendencies lead on the one hand to a fragmented view of the world and on the other to a sense of alienation from it. Zhuangzi's turn away from reason and toward prereflective intuitions and tendencies was in part motivated by his desire to achieve a sense of unity with the world. The spontaneously responsive Daoist sage interacts fluidly and without hesitation with a world that is an organismic whole, and the sage's responses themselves are simply natural features within this grand Heavenly system.

In addition to using reason to illustrate its own limitations, Zhuangzi also saw a positive value to reason, at least in the sense that he believed well-drawn and coherently developed stories about certain types of characters (humans, animals, and in some cases fantastic creatures) and their activities could convey a genuine sense of his Way and would help move people to follow it. In particular, Zhuangzi relied upon exquisitely composed descriptions of people who have attained a different and clearly desirable way of life. These exemplars of the Way differ in significant ways from what we might expect of other kinds of paragons: They subvert rather than reinforce the dominant social hierarchy of the day. Zhuangzi's heroes are more "under-heroes" than antiheroes: butchers, boatmen, and buckle makers; maimed criminals, crippled men, and hump-backed women. Almost everything about them – station, occupation, appearance, and gender – make them underappreciated, even outcasts in their own society. But these very people are the ones who are able to understand and live in accordance with the *dao*. In some sense their lowly position in the social hierarchy gives them a clearer view of Heaven.

Many of these exemplars of the Way are skillful people; individuals who have mastered a way of acting in the world that connects them in a harmonious manner with the greater natural *dao*. But the dazzling skills they display in themselves are not the goal; these are simply particular manifestations of what it is to live in accordance with the Way. Zhuangzi is not recommending that we do *what* these skillful people do; rather, he is encouraging us to *be* as they are, to live as they live. The particular skills and lifestyles of Zhuangzi's exemplars are not offered as a menu of suitable Daoist occupations; their specific content is largely a matter of the contingencies of each person's fate and particular opportunities. There are, however, distinctive features shared by these exemplars that do place definite restrictions on the range of appropriate activities. [. . .] [T]his explains why we do not find Zhuangzi offering us skillful exemplars engaged in anything other than benign activities. According to Zhuangzi, aggressive or vicious behavior is always motivated by humanly constituted views about value. Such views and their associated behavior have no place in the natural order of things and will disappear of themselves as the world turns to spontaneity.

---

[8]   For this story, see Watson, *Complete Works*, 34–5.

Merely perfecting some given skill is not the goal for Zhuangzi. Such a goal could only be yet another human desire to "master" Nature or impose one's personal view upon the world. This in itself would be sufficient to prevent one from harmonizing with the *dao*, which is Zhuangzi's ultimate goal. As the famous cook of Chapter Three of the *Zhuangzi* insists, "What I care about is the Way, which goes beyond skill."[9] This point is often lost in contemporary accounts of Zhuangzi's thought, and this oversight allows interpreters to ignore the meandering yet normative current that runs through the text. They fail to grasp the special nature of Zhuangzi's antirationalism. The shape and direction of his vision, like the shape and direction of the skills that embody it, is subtle and slippery and lies between the lines of any fixed description. The *dao* provides the standard for leading the good life, and its spontaneous manifestation in our prereflective and unforced tendencies and intuitions leads us to such a life. Rationality has a tendency to encroach upon and stifle these natural inclinations and thus is a constant threat to spiritual achievement.

The skillful individuals Zhuangzi describes are not acting mindlessly or haphazardly; they are following along the seams of a deep pattern that runs throughout the world and they are in accord with natural processes of which all people are to some degree aware. Following this pattern and harmonizing with these processes allows them and others to lead long, peaceful, contented, and highly effective lives. These goals – living out one's natural span of years, freedom from physical harm and psychological worry, acting effectively in the world whatever your station or occupation, and enjoying a deep and abiding sense of oneness and ease – are all positive values for Zhuangzi. Such freedom from suffering, strife, and anxiety on the one hand and the enjoyment of security and metaphysical comfort on the other describe the primary attractive features of Zhuangzi's spiritual goal. These are the marks of the well-lived life and the primary characteristics of his exemplars of the Way.

While the patterns and processes of Nature are regular and reliable, they also vary and can, on occasion, change. Their natural regularity is not the unwavering uniformity of mathematical entities or mechanically produced products. Such natural regularity can be found among human beings as well: They share the same general shape, possess similar kinds of abilities and capacities, and have many basic needs, desires, challenges, and fears in common. Those who understand the Way neither rejoice in nor sorrow over these given features of the human condition; they seek neither to embrace nor to avoid them and they are not concerned about understanding underlying causes. Their aim is to face and respond spontaneously to them.

> Life, death, preservation, loss, failure, success, poverty, riches, worthiness, unworthiness, slander, fame, hunger, thirst, cold, heat – these are the alternations of the world, the workings of fate. Day and night they change place before us and wisdom cannot spy out their source.[10]

Despite the significant similarities among people, Zhuangzi recognized that no two people are quite alike. There is infinite diversity in the ways our common features can be manifested, developed, and arranged. We travel individual paths within the vast and complex matrix of the *dao* and face unique sets of situations. These diverse factors combine to influence how we respond to the challenges we share. In order to navigate one's way through such variety and diversity, one needs sensitivity, flexibility, and skill. Only those who maintain and display open-minded flexibility toward the world can possibly succeed. As a consequence, the Way Zhuangzi promotes cannot be nailed down in any strict formula or algorithm. Because of certain unavoidable features of the world, Zhuangzi concludes that a mechanical kind of rationality will not serve us well. And so reason is not preeminent in the ideal Daoist life; skills, knacks, intuitions, keen perception, open-mindedness, and spontaneous action are much more highly valued. Reason plays no

---

9   Watson, *Complete Works*, 50.
10 Watson, *Complete Works*, 73–4.

direct or central role in identifying or generating the proper ends for human life. Our prereflective intuitions and tendencies are already moving us toward these proper ends. And since our rational faculties have a tendency to usurp and obscure these reliable, innate inclinations, we must keep our rational powers in check in order to keep in contact with these deep and subtle springs of knowledge.

In the introduction to this chapter we drew a parallel between the way antirationalist thinkers view reason and the way many philosophers have viewed emotions: An excessive trust in reason often interferes with proper perception, thought, evaluation, and action in the same way that excessive emotion can interfere with these same cognitive, evaluative, and intentional processes. While we maintain that all antirationalists hold this view of reason, this does not entail and we do not claim that they necessarily have a corresponding view of the emotions. For example, Kierkegaard does not appear to be concerned with the danger of excessive emotion. In fact, he seems to have something of the opposite concern: that many lack the passion needed for salvation. According to our definition, antirationalist thinkers can maintain consistently that certain intense emotional states offer a unique source of true knowledge. In any event, Zhuangzi is interesting in this regard, for he has parallel criticisms of excessive rationality and excessive emotion.

For Zhuangzi, the ideal state entails using the "mind like a mirror." In such a state, one is able to reflect accurately the way things really are, and one's spontaneous tendencies and intuitions will then lead one to respond appropriately. Zhuangzi's use of the mirror metaphor is different from what one might expect in that the "reflections" of the mirror-like mind of a sage entail appropriate responses to what it encounters. This last point is lost on several contemporary interpreters, and this leads them to see Zhuangzi as advocating a kind of spectator view of the self. As in many other respects, Graham stands out by avoiding this error. He emphasizes the point that our spontaneous tendencies are always already moving us toward certain ends and away from others.[11] Those who are led to the overly detached spectator view of the mind fail to appreciate certain widely held early Chinese beliefs about the nature of mirrors and their place in the world. For the early Chinese, mirrors were not simply passive "reflectors" of information; they offered accurate and appropriate *responses* to whatever came before them. When placed before the sun – the ultimate *yang* phenomenon in the world – they respond with fire: the pure essence of *yang*. When placed before the moon – the ultimate *yin* phenomenon in the world – they respond with water: the pure essence of *yin*. Thus mirrors offer the paradigm for *proper responsiveness*: They reflect the true essence of the ultimate *yin* and *yang* – the alpha and omega of phenomena in early Chinese cosmology.

According to Zhuangzi, the mind of the sage is not a passive observer of events. It offers a calm and imperturbable response to each situation and then moves on, without retaining any trace of the previous interaction. Moreover, since the sage's prereflective inclinations are themselves manifestations of the *dao*, in an important sense his actions are not his own: They do not manifest the individual intentions of an autonomous agent. Rather, the sage serves as a locus for the spontaneous operation of the Way. When acting in such a mode, the movements of a sage are all in complete harmony with the greater *dao*. This explains their preternatural effectiveness and ease. Excessive emotions, as well as rigid conceptual categories and set styles of reasoning, disrupt such clear perception and appropriate response; they act like wind on or sediment in water, distorting the image and interfering with proper action. Such "wind" must cease and "sediment" settle in order for water to mirror the world accurately and precisely. Thus, according to Zhuangzi, our emotions can interfere with proper perception, thought, evaluation, and action in the same way that excessive rationality can. What is more, like our rational capacity, they have a natural tendency toward such damaging excess.

---

[11] See Graham's "Taoist Spontaneity" and "Value, Fact and Facing Facts," in *Unreason within Reason*, 17–27.

When men get together to pit their strength in games of skill, they start off in a light and friendly mood, but usually end up in a dark and angry one, and if they go on too long they start resorting to various tricks. When men meet at some ceremony to drink, they start off in an orderly manner, but usually end up in disorder, and if they go on too long they start indulging in various irregular amusements . . . What starts out sincere usually ends up being deceitful. What was simple in the beginning acquires monstrous proportions in the end.

Words are like wind and waves; actions are a matter of gain and loss. Wind and waves are easily moved; questions of gain and loss easily lead to danger.[12]

One possible response to such a view would be to launch a concerted effort to eradicate one's emotions and thereby eliminate the source of the problem. This is a strategy one can find in religious traditions throughout the world, and some scholars have suggested that this is the course that Zhuangzi elects. One could understand irrationalism as displaying a similar dynamic – though in the opposite direction – to a negative view of excessive rationality, a kind of cognitive parallel to excessive emotion. Western Romanticism is one example of a particular form of such an alternative response. But Zhuangzi chooses neither of these routes. Just as he is not against reason *per se*, he is not in principle against the emotions. In fact, he believes that the emotions are a natural part of being human:

Joy, anger, grief, delight, worry, regret, fickleness, inflexibility, modesty, willfulness, candor, insolence – music from empty holes, mushrooms springing up in dampness, day and night replacing each other before us, and no one knows where they sprout from. Let it be! Let it be! [It is enough that] morning and evening we have them, and they are the means by which we live.[13]

Any attempt to completely eliminate one's emotions would fail. Moreover, since such a life

is obviously not the result of following the spontaneous tendencies of human nature, it is clearly unnatural and hence an inappropriate goal for Zhuangzi and those who would follow him. Instead, the Daoist suggests that one allow one's natural emotions to manifest themselves spontaneously in response to the things and events one encounters in the meandering course of life.

[. . .]

In rejecting appeals to traditional wisdom and rationality as definitive sources of knowledge, Zhuangzi is forced to present his views in novel ways. Instead of appeals to historical exemplars and discursive arguments, he relies on fantastic stories, *reductio* arguments, paradoxes, allegories, accounts of dreams, etc., as a kind of spiritual therapy. These stories jolt, cajole, and move us to loosen our commitment to tradition and rationality as the primary means for understanding how things are and navigating our way through the world. Zhuangzi then leads us to a greater appreciation of the spontaneous tendencies that are always behind our actions but that become obscured through layers of routine and rationalization. However, we are not to follow these innate tendencies blindly. We must tutor them through a process of reflective experience about how things are in the world. This allows us to match up our innate tendencies with the events and things in the world, or as Woodcarver Qing says, "I am simply matching up Heaven with Heaven."[14] This dual process – paring away layers of interference while seeking to find and follow underlying patterns and processes – provides the basic structure of Zhuangzi's method of self cultivation. [. . .]

Part II: Kierkegaard

On first blush, Kierkegaard might appear to be a prime example of the Western Romanticism labeled by Graham irrationalist, rather than anti-rationalist. His definition of truth, in *Concluding*

12   Watson, *Complete Works*, 60–1.
13   Watson, *Complete Works*, 37–8.
14   Watson, *Complete Works*, 206.

Unscientific Postscript, as "an objective uncertainty, held fast through appropriation with the most passionate inwardness"[15] has been interpreted by a number of commentators as a glorification of precisely that "subjective vision in heightened emotion" that, for Graham and for others, is a hallmark of irrationalism. Some argue that, for Kierkegaard, the sole determining factor in assessing the beliefs of an individual is the degree of passion with which the belief is held – the amount of evidence for or against any given belief is irrelevant. The passion factor measures, so this reading goes, not only the integrity of the believer but also the truth of his or her belief. In this vein, for example, Alasdair MacIntyre writes that, for Kierkegaard, "the criterion of both choice and truth is intensity of feeling."[16] The passage from his work most often cited to support this comes from *Concluding Unscientific Postscript*. In that work, Kierkegaard, writing as Johannes Climacus, asks:

If someone who lives in the midst of Christianity enters, with knowledge of the true idea of God, the house of God, the house of the true God, and prays, but prays in untruth [i.e., insincerely], and if someone lives in an idolatrous land, but prays with all the passion of infinity, although his eyes are resting upon the image of an idol – where, then, is there more truth? The one prays in truth to God although he is worshipping an idol; the other prays in untruth to the true God and is therefore in truth worshipping an idol.[17]

Viewed in isolation from both the *Postscript* as a whole and Kierkegaard's other works, this passage seems to suggest that as long as one believes sincerely – i.e., is committed 100 percent to the object of one's belief, with the "passion of infinity" – one believes truly. Thus there is no difference between the "fanatic" and the "true believer"; anyone who believes sincerely, believes truly.

This claim is usually combined with a second, that for Kierkegaard passion and reason are mutually exclusive, that the more "reasons" one has for believing something, the less passionate and emotional will be the resulting belief. Here, too, *Concluding Unscientific Postscript* is usually cited as the best source for this view. Kierkegaard's pseudonym, Johannes Climacus, argues that uncertainty is a necessary prerequisite for passionate belief, distinguishing quite sharply between reasonable knowledge and belief:

The almost probable, the probable, the to-a-high-degree and exceedingly probable – that he can almost know, or as good as know, to a higher degree and exceedingly almost *know* – but *believe* it, that cannot be done, for the absurd is precisely the object of faith and only that can be believed.[18]

Thus, on this reading, belief is linked with passion, and passion requires the absence of reasons or justification for the belief; hence in order to believe passionately, there must not be adequate grounds for holding that belief – one's belief must not be "probably true."

From this it is a short step to the third component of the irrationalist reading: that the degree of passion in belief is negatively correlated with its reasonableness. That is, the more reasonable a belief is, the less passionately it is held (and the less it can be said to be believed, strictly speaking), while the more unreasonable a belief is, the greater the passion binding it to the believer. Here interpreters can point to the many references made by Kierkegaard, through the voice of Climacus and other pseudonyms, to the "absurd" and the "absolute paradox" as the true object of belief. According to the logic of this argument, then, the most passionate, and by extension the (at least subjectively) truest belief, will be the least reasonable, bordering on, even passing over into, outright contradiction. The combined force of these three claims (first, that

15 *Concluding Unscientific Postscript*, trans. Howard V. Hong and Edna H. Hong (Princeton, NJ: Princeton University Press, 1992), 203 [see also p. 154 below].
16 In *The Encyclopedia of Philosophy*, ed. Paul Edwards (New York: Macmillan, 1967), Vol. 4, 338.
17 *Concluding Unscientific Postscript*, 201 [see also p. 152 below].
18 *Concluding Unscientific Postscript*, 211.

passion is the criterion of truth and belief; second, that reason is inimical to the intensity of passion; therefore, third, the best object for passion is absurd, a paradox) renders Kierkegaard a fairly strong irrationalist: reason cannot help you – indeed, it can only *hurt* you – in your search for truth, because truth is a function of the passion of the believer. By implication, whatever you intensely believe to be true, is true (at least for you), and the only things you can really *believe* (as opposed to "merely" know) to be true are irrational.

Although this reading does have some textual support, it has at least two serious shortcomings. First, this reading cannot account for the fact that Kierkegaard unquestionably believes that one path (the Christian religious path) is superior to all others and is indeed the only true path, not only for him but for others as well. Whatever praise Climacus might heap on the passion of the pagan, in the end for Kierkegaard only one objective absurdity, the Incarnation, corresponds to the truth. Despite the passage from the *Postscript* quoted above about the pagan, Kierkegaard – and for that matter, Climacus also – clearly distinguishes genuine passion from "aberrant" forms; the distinction does not rest upon the sincerity of the passion, but on the nature of its object. Don Quixote is cited several times within the *Postscript* as an example of "subjective lunacy." The irrationalist reading of Kierkegaard/Climacus cannot account for such a distinction other than to regard it as an unfortunate inconsistency in his position. Were Kierkegaard an irrationalist, he would be unable to distinguish between objects of faith – or, at the very least, between irrational objects of faith: Any irrational belief would be as good as any other. However, for Kierkegaard the truth of Christianity is not grounded in its being irrational, but only in its objective, empirical reality – only if God in fact became a man at a certain point in history is Christianity true, the subjective intensity of millions of believers notwithstanding. The fundamental, underlying realism of Kierkegaard's thought is made quite clear in the non-pseudonymous *On Authority and Revelation*:

Christianity exists before any Christian exists, it must exist in order that one may become a Christian, it contains the determinant by which one may test whether one has become a Christian, it maintains its objective subsistence apart from all believers . . . [E]ven if no one had perceived that God had revealed himself in a human form in Christ, he nevertheless has revealed himself.[19]

The second difficulty with the irrationalist reading is that it cannot account for the fact that Kierkegaard himself uses reason, in at least two ways. He uses it, first, to describe faith phenomenologically, i.e., without respect to the truth of its object. Kierkegaard cannot both reject reason as intrinsically hostile to religious truth and use it as a vehicle for characterizing faith without contradiction. If nothing else, the internal coherence of Kierkegaard's position and the tightness of many of his arguments demonstrate a healthy respect for reason, properly employed. He uses reason, second, to show why reason cannot be a primary means of attaining faith, that its function is purely negative in the acquisition and realization of faith, if certain assumptions about the nature of human beings and, in particular, about their relationship to the creator and to themselves are accepted as true. Kierkegaard's authorship can, in part, be understood as an attempt to offer a compelling and consistent model of religious faith in which reason, by definition, can play only a negative role. Thus, Kierkegaard uses reason on the meta-level, to describe *what* faith is and *how it is realized*; but part of that description, as we shall see below, involves a severe restriction and a redefinition of reason's role *vis-à-vis* faith.

That Kierkegaard is not an irrationalist, of course, does not automatically mean that he is an antirationalist. A number of scholars, dissatisfied with the irrationalist interpretation, offer a suprarationalist reading in which faith is described not as contrary to reason, but above it. Many proponents of this interpretation argue that the irrationalist reading relies too heavily on one pseudonymous author, Johannes Climacus, and identifies his words with those

---

[19] *On Authority and Revelation: The Book on Adler*, trans. Walter Lowrie (New York: Harper & Row, 1966), 168–9.

of Kierkegaard. Not only does such a move ignore Kierkegaard's explicit disclaimer that in the *Postscript* "there is not a single word by me,"[20] but it overlooks the fact that Johannes Climacus is a professed non-Christian, and thus views Christianity from the outside. Alastair McKinnon, for example, has argued at length that it is essential to treat the works written under the non-Christian pseudonyms quite differently from the Christian, and that when one does so one *sees* that the phrases so beloved of the Kierkegaard-as-irrationalist camp ("faith by virtue of the absurd," "the absolute paradox") essentially disappear in the Christian and non-pseudonymous works. On this reading, something fundamental happens to the Christian after he or she has embraced the cross, and what appears absurd to the unbeliever does not so appear to the believer: "The object of faith is the absurd or paradox but only for one who *sees* it from the outside, for one who does not yet have faith. For the man of faith it is no longer absurd or paradoxical."[21] Timothy Jackson makes essentially the same point when he writes ". . . faith does not violate the intellect but rather sets it aside or supersedes it . . . Kierkegaardian faith embraces in passionate inwardness what reason alone is unable to demonstrate is not a genuine antinomy. Reason is not contradicted, but neither is it given the last word."[22]

[. . .]

In order to understand Kierkegaard's position, one must supplement the treatment of reason and offense given in the *Fragments* with that given by the pseudonym Anti-Climacus in *Sickness unto Death* and *Practice in Christianity*, two works in which the concept of offense (reason's response to Christianity) is discussed at length.

When one further adds into the mix Climacus' discussion in the *Postscript* of how Christianity is distinct from "paganism," even the claim that Climacus is a suprarationalist becomes suspect. The conjunction of *Sickness unto Death*, *Practice in Christianity*, and the *Postscript* results in a reading that *sees* reason operating in continuing opposition to faith even after the truth of Christianity has been embraced by the believer.

The pseudonyms Anti-Climacus and Climacus clearly stand in a special relationship with one another. The fact that Climacus is expressly a non-Christian, while Anti-Climacus "regards himself as a Christian on an extraordinarily high level,"[23] coupled with a prefix usually suggesting antagonism, might lead one to infer that they represent divergent, even opposing points of view on the nature of faith. According to Howard and Edna Hong, however, "the prefix 'Anti-' . . . does not mean 'against.' It is an old form of 'ante' (before), as in 'anticipate,' and 'before' also denotes a relation of rank, as in 'before me' in the First Commandment."[24] This suggests that the works of Anti-Climacus and Climacus are complementary, possibly with a fuller and more complete picture of faith provided by Anti-Climacus. Kierkegaard himself stated explicitly that Climacus' *Postscript* and Anti-Climacus' *Sickness unto Death* and *Practice in Christianity* convey most clearly his understanding of Christianity.

Of the two works attributed to Anti-Climacus, *Sickness unto Death* is probably the more widely known. In it, the author develops first a psychological model of the self as a dynamic entity that is continually in the process of making and remaking itself, and then recasts the psychological model into a theological framework. Two assumptions drive Anti-Climacus's discussion: first, that most people fail to be selves, either by never attempting to become a self at all, or by

[20] *Concluding Unscientific Postscript*, 626. This disclaimer applies not only to the *Postscript*, but to all the pseudonymous works published in or before 1846.
[21] McKinnon, "Søren Kierkegaard," in *Nineteenth Century Religious Thought in the West*, ed. Ninian Smart et al. (Cambridge; Cambridge University Press, 1985), Vol. I, 197.
[22] "Kierkegaard's Metatheology," *Faith and Philosophy* 4:1 (1987), 81.
[23] *Journals and Papers*, trans. and ed. Howard V. Hong and Edna H. Hong (Princeton, NJ: Princeton University Press, 1967), Vol. 7 entry #6433.
[24] Introduction to *Sickness unto Death*, trans. Howard V. Hong and Edna H. Hong (Princeton, NJ: Princeton University Press, 1980), xxii.

attempting to become the wrong kind of self; second, that the human self is created by God ("the Power that posits it") and thus always stands in a dependent relationship to him. As a result, even though I may be striving to be a self as I understand it to be, if I am not constantly relating myself to God in this process, I am attempting to be the wrong kind of self – to be a self that is self-sustaining, rather than dependent upon God.

After developing a typology of despair at some length, Anti-Climacus turns to his primary theme: that despair, or the failure to be a self or to be the right kind of self, is sin. More precisely, sin is despair "before God." In connecting despair and sin he has provided a clarification of the classical Christian concept of sin as refusal to submit to God. In Anti-Climacus's terms, we disobey God by refusing (either through indolence, weakness, or defiance) to be the kind of self He created us to be, a self that is both free to define itself and bound by its relation to its creator. The introduction of God (as the "establisher" of all human beings, who thereby are in a dependent relationship with him) ensures that no individual is able to free him- or herself of despair through his or her own efforts. Any such attempt is an attempt to define oneself by oneself – i.e., any such attempt is an example of defiant despair. Although we are all responsible for our despair, ultimately it is only God who can free us of it.

Anti-Climacus develops his picture of sin as "despair before God" by introducing the category of "offense." Faced with Christianity – in particular, with its account of a God who so loves human beings that he died on the cross to atone for their sin – the despairing individual is offended: He proclaims the message of Christianity insane or ridiculous. He tells himself (and others) that Christianity makes no sense, that it is absurd. This is, for Anti-Climacus, a telling example of the defiance of the despairing individual – essentially, this person has set up his own intellect, his own reason, as the arbiter of what is possible and what is true; he has forgotten, to borrow a phrase used by both the

Anti-Climacus pseudonym and others, that with God "all things are possible." What Christianity demands, according to Anti-Climacus, is obedience and submission; any attempt to understand it, to comprehend it, is an attempt to gain mastery over it. "The secret of all comprehending is that this comprehending is itself higher than any position it posits."[25] Confronted with Christianity, the individual has, for Anti-Climacus, only two choices: "either it must be believed or one must be scandalized and offended by it"; ". . . all Christianity turns on this, that it must be believed and not comprehended."[26]

To clarify his account of despair as sin, and the distinctively Christian nature of sin, he contrasts his model with the Socratic, a strategy also employed by Climacus in *Philosophical Fragments*. On the Socratic model, sin is simple ignorance: One chooses evil out of the mistaken notion that it is really good. On the Christian model, by contrast, one chooses evil knowing it is evil – indeed, because it is evil. Sin is thus not a negation or a privation (as in the Socratic model, an absence of knowledge), but a position, an active force. There is a sense, Anti-Climacus suggests, in which Christian sin can be understood as ignorance, but it is a willed ignorance – and in that adjective lies a world of difference from the Socratic. To the extent that an individual believes his evil choice to be the right one, it is because he has persuaded himself that this is the case.

Anti-Climacus describes this process as the corruption of the mind by the will:

In the life of the spirit there is no standing still . . . therefore, if a person does not do what is right at the very second he knows it – then, first of all, knowing simmers down. Next comes the question of how willing appraises what is known . . . If willing does not agree with what is known, then it does not necessarily follow that willing goes ahead and does the opposite of what knowing understood . . . rather, willing allows some time to elapse, an interim called: "We shall look at it tomorrow." During all this time, knowing becomes more and more obscure, and the

---

25   *Sickness unto Death*, 97.
26   *Sickness unto Death*, 98.

lower nature gains the upper hand more and more . . . And when knowing has become duly obscured, knowing and willing can better understand each other; eventually they agree completely, for now knowing has come over to the side of willing and admits that what it wants is absolutely right.[27]

Sin, then, is essentially a form of self-deception in which the individual willingly turns away from the good (a life "grounded transparently in the power that posits it") and persuades himself that the evil he prefers is really good.

The parallel with self-deception is both important and instructive, for it helps to clarify why Anti-Climacus believes an individual to be incapable of thinking his or her way out of despair into faith. A person in the throes of self-deception is unable to heal him- or herself precisely because self-deception is a corruption of the reasoning process. Generally, we label another self-deceived because he or she believes something to be the case despite extremely compelling evidence to the contrary. We deem this other to be self-deceived, rather than simply ignorant (the Socratic model), because the contrary evidence seems impossible to ignore; thus we say the individual "knows," in some sense, the falsity of what he or she believes, even while denying this to be the case. A self-deceived person does not ignore the contrary evidence; he simply assesses it incorrectly (deeming it unimportant, for example), usually because of some great personal stake he has in what he believes being true. (Consider, for example, a woman who continues to assert that her husband "really" loves her despite his constant mental and physical abuse of her. She is not unaware of the abuse, but she may construct an elaborate justification scheme in which the abuse becomes actual evidence of his love, rather than the obvious counter-indication it seems to others.) Because the reasoning process is impaired – and indeed, perpetuates its own impairment through

its ongoing efforts at rationalization – the individual is simply not able to think his or her way to the truth so obvious to others. In the case of despair, the situation is, if anything, even worse, because the self-deception occurs at such a fundamental level: the very definition of who and what the self is. One's reasoning powers have always already been coopted by the sinning will; not only does reason fail to help us, it actively leads us astray through the pernicious influence of the will.

What, though, of an individual who has been transformed through grace by his or her confrontation with the Savior? Granted, prior to the acceptance of Christianity, its message is an offense to one's reasoning powers; but after one has responded with faith (after one's will has been retooled, in effect), does the same tension between reason and the Christian truth exist?

On our reading of Kierkegaard it does, and this is why we believe Kierkegaard is best thought of as an antirationalist, rather than as a suprarationalist or a rationalist. While it is true that the believer is not offended by the paradox – that "when the believer has faith, the absurd is not the absurd," to quote the journal entry often cited by proponents of the suprarationalist interpretation[28] – this does not mean that the believer comprehends the paradox, or that the tension between reason and faith is lessened. [. . .]

Anti-Climacus continues the discussion of offense initiated in *Sickness unto Death* in *Practice in Christianity*. Here offense is defined as "that which conflicts with all (human) reason." Such a thing cannot, by definition be proven or demonstrated true: "One can 'demonstrate' only that it conflicts with reason."[29] Does this then mean that the Christian knows nothing of Christ? In a word, yes: ". . . one cannot know anything at all about Christ; he is the paradox, the object of faith, exists only for faith."[30] Any attempt to come to a rational understanding of this object destroys it. "Jesus Christ is the

27 *Sickness unto Death*, 94.
28 *Journals and Papers*, entry #10, Vol. 1, pp. 7–8.
29 *Practice in Christianity*, trans. and ed. by Howard V. Hong and Edna H. Hong (Princeton, NJ: Princeton University Press, 1991), 26.
30 *Practice in Christianity*, 25.

object of faith; one must either believe in him or be offended; for to 'know' simply means that it is not about him ... knowledge annihilates Jesus Christ."[31] The sharp dichotomy between knowledge and faith, in other words, developed by Johannes Climacus – who is a self-professed non-Christian – is expressed in even stronger terms by the Christian author Anti-Climacus. Perhaps even more important, the battle between offense and belief is not presented by Anti-Climacus as a single event, after which faith, having conquered, reigns victorious, without opposition. Rather, the battle is portrayed as a constant struggle in the life of the believing Christian: "faith conquers the world by conquering at *every moment* the enemy within one's own inner being, the possibility of offense."[32] The continuing precariousness of faith – and its ongoing relationship with offense – is one of this work's most recurring themes. "Faith is carried in a fragile earthen vessel, in the possibility of offense."[33]

This clear indication that reason and faith remain in opposite and hostile corners even after one has committed oneself, in fear and trembling, to Christianity is reiterated by Kierkegaard in his journals. The same entry that acknowledges that the absurd "is not the absurd" to the believer also stresses that "the absurd and faith are inseparables," that "true faith breathes healthfully and blessedly in the absurd."[34] The nonbeliever, in other words, dismisses Christianity as nonsense, as sheer folly or madness; the believer does not do so, and yet while he "expresses just the opposite of offense ... he always has the possibility of offense as a negative category."[35]

The ongoing presence of the possibility of offense in the life of faith is closely connected to Kierkegaard's conviction that religious faith is, above all else, an act of obedience and submission to God. Offense before Christianity is essentially refusal to obey the higher authority of God; to be offended before Christianity is

to place one's own standard of truth and "reasonableness" ahead of the divine reality. For Kierkegaard, "the matter is very simple: will you or will you not obey, will you submit in faith to his divine authority, or will you take offense – or will you perhaps not take sides – be careful, for that, too, is offense."[36]

[. . .]

Conclusion

The forms of antirationalism embraced by Zhuangzi and Kierkegaard do not deny the value of reason, but they do insist that reason alone will never enable one to attain their respective spiritual ideals. Both thinkers further caution us that reason and its products often prove to be among the most formidable obstacles to the spiritual life and that reason has an almost irresistible tendency toward an imperialistic domination of the self. Reason – like a certain conception of magic – represents both a great power and a great danger.

For Zhuangzi, reason proves too crude to capture the variety, nuance, and texture of the world through which we must navigate. Rationally based methods for dealing with the world require generalization, and this process of abstraction effaces the particular nature and specific details of life. Rational approaches further give rise to routine, which stifles flexibility and originality and deadens perception. Moreover, the apersonal, objective perspective inherent to the ideal rational point of view leads us to misconceive our basic existential situation in the world. We lose sight of life's proper aims, are seduced by more immediate desires, and our spirits wither and decay. Thus rationality tends to lead us to misconceive the nature of both ourselves and the world. Those who understand and accord with the *dao* see through these widespread delusions.

---

[31] *Practice in Christianity*, 33.
[32] *Practice in Christianity*, 76, my emphasis.
[33] *Practice in Christianity*, 76.
[34] *Journals and Papers*, entry #10, Vol. 1, pp. 7–8.
[35] *Journals and Papers*, entry #9, Vol. 1, p. 6.
[36] *Journals and Papers*, entry #3026, Vol. 3, 366.

They realize that we do not stand apart from and work at the Way. Rather we stand within it while it works through us. By paring away the false, arrogant, and alienated views of both self and world that lure most of humankind to lead short, vexed, and unfulfilling lives, such individuals come to appreciate and accord with their true nature and fulfill their proper relationship to the grand and harmonious patterns and processes that are the *dao*.

For Kierkegaard, rationality constantly threatens to obscure the true nature of the self and its relationship to God. If we allow ourselves to be seduced by the false presumption that we can, on our own, come to understand and appreciate God, we commit the fatal sin of being in despair before God. For finite and essentially flawed creatures like us to arrogantly claim such an ability, we must in fact reject God. In making such a claim, we fail to be the kinds of creatures He made us to be: free to construct our own self-understanding yet unavoidably dependent on our creator. There is an unbridgeable and incomprehensible gap between our ability to know and God's true nature. At best, human reason can lead us to recognize this state of affairs, but it cannot cross this bridge and grasp God's true form. Christianity itself and in particular the paradox of Christ is beyond the compass of human understanding. Even those who commit themselves to Christianity in the appropriate attitude of fear and trembling must continue to struggle with the absurdity that it represents. But for such true believers, Christianity is not *just* absurd. Its truth guarantees that it is the one absurdity in which "faith breathes healthfully and blessedly."[37]

In order to work against the corrosive effects of an excessive trust in reason, Zhuangzi and Kierkegaard prescribe a kind of spiritual therapy. They first engage in what we have described as the "negative" project of loosening our determined obsession with reason. In this process, they themselves often deploy reason against itself in a variety of ways designed to show its limitations and potential dangers. As we free ourselves from our ill-advised rational routines, they lead us to recognize and appreciate those alternative sources of knowledge and guidance that are the key to the spiritual ideals they describe.

While the thought of Zhuangzi and that of Kierkegaard share these important features, significant differences exist in how each thinker develops and fills them out. For example, Zhuangzi is much more wary than is Kierkegaard of the threat that excessive emotions pose to the spiritual life. For Zhuangzi, human passions are a dangerous source of interference. This concern is captured well in Zhuangzi's metaphor of the ideal spiritual state: the mind as a mirror. The sage is to attain a mirror-like state in which no individual preference or prejudice obscures the accurate reflection of whatever comes before him. Like the placid surface of a calm pool of water, his mind attains this state only when unruffled by the distorting "winds" of excessive emotion. But the sage's "reflection" of each situation he encounters is not a cool accounting of information; his mirroring of the world entails a response as well. Just as a mirror responds with fire when stimulated by the light of the sun and dew when placed on the ground in the early morning, the sage's mind offers the proper response to any and all situations it encounters. And after so responding it retains no trace of its last encounter; no stain remains to interfere with its next interaction with the world.

We find no equivalent metaphor in Kierkegaard's writings, and indeed such a view is foreign and even anathematic to his way of thinking. Zhuangzi's metaphor reveals his greater faith in the underlying benign shape of both the self and the world. His conception of the world is one in which a lessening of individual willfulness leads to a lessening of pain, cruelty, and distress. With the elimination of human cleverness and our willful manipulation of the world, the *dao* resonates through and resides in all things, settling them down and leading each to its proper place in a greater harmonious balance.

Kierkegaard did not believe that the world would return to such a happy state if only we could abandon our attempts to reform it. [. . .] The Daoist approach could never lead one to Kierkegaard's spiritual ideal, which requires one to be constantly aware of oneself as an *individual*

---

[37] *Journals and Papers*, entry #10, Vol. 1, pp. 7–8.

seeking a personal relationship with an infinite and unknowable God. According to Kierkegaard, one must continually be engaged in the ongoing struggle of living a Christian life. Such a life can never be understood adequately in the terms of this world and is under the constant threat of leveling: the tendency to abandon one's self to the common point of view. Kierkegaard believed in an alternative source of knowledge and guidance, but one not in or of this world: God and His gift of grace. We find no such notions in Zhuangzi's writings. We can find the

"teachers" or wise men of what Kierkegaard called pagan religion – but not the savior of the one true faith. Zhuangzi's *dao* is not Kierkegaard's personal, all-powerful, all-knowing, loving, and incomprehensible God. And so, while these two thinkers shared important concerns and approaches, they took these in remarkably different directions. It is helpful to recognize that both Zhuangzi and Kierkegaard were antirationalists but that their antirationalisms are distinct in form, function differently, and lead toward profoundly dissimilar religious goals.

Truly There is a God

Anselm of Canterbury

And so, Lord, do thou, who dost give understanding to faith, give me, so far as thou knowest it to be profitable, to understand that thou art as we believe; and that thou art that which we believe. And, indeed, we believe that thou art a being than which nothing greater can be conceived. Or is there no such nature, since the fool hath said in his heart, there is no God? (Psalms xiv. 1). But, at any rate, this very fool, when he hears of this being of which I speak – a being than which nothing greater can be conceived – understands what he hears, and what he understands is in his understanding; although he does not understand it to exist.

For, it is one thing for an object to be in the understanding, and another to understand that the object exists. When a painter first conceives of what he will afterwards perform, he has it in his understanding, but he does not yet understand it to be, because he has not yet performed it. But after he has made the painting, he both has it in his understanding, and he understands that it exists, because he has made it.

Hence, even the fool is convinced that something exists in the understanding, at least, than which nothing greater can be conceived. For, when he hears of this, he understands it. And whatever is understood, exists in the understanding. And assuredly that, than which nothing greater can be conceived, cannot exist in the understanding alone. For, suppose it exists in the understanding alone: then it can be conceived to exist in reality; which is greater.

Therefore, if that, than which nothing greater can be conceived, exists in the understanding alone, the very being, than which nothing greater can be conceived, is one, than which a greater can be conceived. But obviously this is impossible. Hence, there is no doubt that there exists a being, than which nothing greater can be conceived, and it exists both in the understanding and in reality.

"Truly there is a God," by Anselm of Canterbury, from *The Proslogion*, chapter II, in *Proslogium; Monologium; an Appendix in Behalf of the Fool by Gaunilon; and Cur Deus Homo*, trans. Sydney Norton Deane (Chicago: Open Court Publishing, 1903, reprinted 1948), pp. 7–8. Reprinted by permission of Open Court Publishing Company, a division of Carus Publishing Company, Peru, IL, from *St Anselm Basic Writings*, trans. S. N. Deane, copyright © 1903 (reprinted 1948) by Open Court Publishing.

Whether God Exists?

Thomas Aquinas

[...] The existence of God can be proved in five ways.

The first and more manifest way is the argument from motion. It is certain, and evident to our senses, that in the world some things are in motion. Now whatever is in motion is put in motion by another, for nothing can be in motion except it is in potentiality to that towards which it is, in motion; whereas a thing moves inasmuch as it is in act. For motion is nothing else than the reduction of something from potentiality to actuality. But nothing can be reduced from potentiality to actuality, except by something in a state of actuality. Thus that which is actually hot, as fire, makes wood, which is potentially hot, to be actually hot, and thereby moves and changes it. Now it is not possible that the same thing should be at once in actuality and potentiality in the same respect, but only in different respects. For what is actually hot cannot simultaneously be potentially hot; but it is simultaneously potentially cold. It is therefore impossible that in the same respect and in the same way a thing should be both mover and moved, *i.e.*, that it should move itself. Therefore, whatever is in motion must be put in motion by another. If that by which it is put in motion be itself put in motion, then this also must needs be put in

motion by another, and that by another again. But this cannot go on to infinity, because then there would be no first mover, and, consequently, no other mover; seeing that subsequent movers move only inasmuch as they are put in motion by the first mover; as the staff moves only because it is put in motion by the hand. Therefore it is necessary to arrive at a first mover, put in motion by no other; and this everyone understands to be God.

The second way is from the nature of the efficient cause. In the world of sense we find there is an order of efficient causes. There is no case known (neither is it, indeed, possible) in which a thing is found to be the efficient cause of itself; for so it would be prior to itself, which is impossible. Now in efficient causes it is not possible to go on to infinity, because in all efficient causes following in order, the first is the cause of the intermediate cause, and the intermediate is the cause of the ultimate cause, whether the intermediate cause be several, or one only. Now to take away the cause is to take away the effect. Therefore, if there be no first cause among efficient causes, there will be no ultimate, nor any intermediate cause. But if in efficient causes it is possible to go on to infinity, there will be no first efficient cause, neither will there be an ultimate

"Whether God Exists?" Part I, Question 2, 3rd article of *The Summa Theologica* by Thomas Aquinas, trans. Fathers of the English Dominican Province, 2nd revised edition (London: Burns Oates & Washbourne, 1920), pp. 24–7.

effect, nor any intermediate efficient causes; all of which is plainly false. Therefore it is necessary to admit a first efficient cause, to which everyone gives the name of God.

The third way is taken from possibility and necessity, and runs thus. We find in nature things that are possible to be and not to be, since they are found to be generated, and to corrupt, and consequently, they are possible to be and not to be. But it is impossible for these always to exist, for that which is possible not to be at some time is not. Therefore, if everything is possible not to be, then at one time there could have been nothing in existence. Now if this were true, even now there would be nothing in existence, because that which does not exist only begins to exist by something already existing. Therefore, if at one time nothing was in existence, it would have been impossible for anything to have begun to exist; and thus even now nothing would be in existence – which is absurd. Therefore, not all beings are merely possible, but there must exist something the existence of which is necessary. But every necessary thing either has its necessity caused by another, or not. Now it is impossible to go on to infinity in necessary things which have their necessity caused by another, as has been already proved in regard to efficient causes. Therefore we cannot but postulate the existence of some being having of itself its own necessity, and not receiving it from another, but rather causing in others their necessity. This all men speak of as God.

The fourth way is taken from the gradation to be found in things. Among beings there are some more and some less good, true, noble, and the like. But "more" and "less" are predicated of different things, according as they resemble in their different ways something which is the maximum, as a thing is said to be hotter according as it more nearly resembles that which is hottest; so that there is something which is truest, something best, something noblest, and, consequently, something which is uttermost being; for those things that are greatest in truth are greatest in being, as it is written in *Metaph.* ii. Now the maximum in any genus is the cause of all in that genus; as fire, which is the maximum of heat, is the cause of all hot things. Therefore there must also be something which is to all beings the cause of their being, goodness, and every other perfection; and this we call God.

The fifth way is taken from the governance of the world. We see that things which lack intelligence, such as natural bodies, act for an end, and this is evident from their acting always, or nearly always, in the same way, so as to obtain the best result. Hence it is plain that not fortuitously, but designedly, do they achieve their end. Now whatever lacks intelligence cannot move towards an end, unless it be directed by some being endowed with knowledge and intelligence; as the arrow is shot to its mark by the archer. Therefore some intelligent being exists by whom all natural things are directed to their end; and this being we call God.

23

Evidence of Design

William Paley

In crossing a heath, suppose I pitched my foot against a *stone*, and were asked how the stone came to be there, I might possibly answer, that, for anything I knew to the contrary, it had lain there for ever; nor would it, perhaps, be very easy to show the absurdity of this answer. But suppose I had found a *watch* upon the ground, and it should be inquired how the watch happened to be in that place, I should hardly think of the answer which I had before given – that, for anything I knew, the watch might have always been there. Yet why should not this answer serve for the watch as well as for the stone? why is it not as admissible in the second case as in the first? For this reason, and for no other, viz., that, when we come to inspect the watch, we perceive (what we could not discover in the stone) that its several parts are framed and put together for a purpose, *e.g.* that they are so formed and adjusted as to produce motion, and that motion so regulated as to point out the hour of the day; that, if the different parts had been differently shaped from what they are, of a different size from what they are, or placed after any other manner, or in any other order than that in which they are placed, either no motion at all would have been carried on in the machine, or none which would have answered the use that is now served by it. [. . .]

This mechanism being observed (it requires indeed an examination of the instrument, and perhaps some previous knowledge of the subject, to perceive and understand it; but being once, as we have said, observed and understood), the inference, we think, is inevitable, that the watch must have had a maker: that there must have existed, at some time, and at some place or other, an artificer or artificers who formed it for the purpose which we find it actually to answer; who comprehended its construction, and designed its use.

[. . .]

[E]very indication of contrivance, every manifestation of design, which existed in the watch, exists in the works of nature; with the difference, on the side of nature, of being greater and more, and that in a degree which exceeds all computation. I mean that the contrivances of nature surpass the contrivances of art, in the complexity, subtilty, and curiosity of the mechanism; and still more, if possible, do they go beyond them in number and variety; yet, in a multitude of cases, are not less evidently mechanical, not less evidently contrivances, not less evidently accommodated to their end, or suited to their office, than are the most perfect productions of human ingenuity.

"Evidence of Design" from *Natural Theology: or the Evidences of the Existence and Attributes of the Deity* by William Paley (London: Griffin, Bohn, and Company, 1855), pp. 5–7; 17; 64–5.

[...]

Were there no example in the world of contrivance except that of the *eye*, it would be alone sufficient to support the conclusion which we draw from it, as to the necessity of an intelligent Creator. It could never be got rid of; because it could not be accounted for by any other, supposition, which did not contradict all the principles we possess of knowledge the principles according to which things do, as often as they can be brought to the test of experience, turn out to be true or false. Its coats and humours, constructed as the lenses of a telescope are constructed, for the refraction of rays of light to a point, which forms the proper action of the organ; the provision in its muscular tendons for turning its pupil to the object, similar to that which is given to the telescope by screws, and upon which power of direction in the eye the exercise of its office as an optical instrument depends; the further provision for its defence, for its constant lubricity and moisture, which we see in its socket and its lids, in its glands for the secretion of the matter of tears, its outlet or communication with the nose for carrying off the liquid after the eye is washed with it; these provisions compose altogether an apparatus, a system of parts, a preparation of means, so manifest in their design, so exquisite in their contrivance, so successful in their issue, so precious and so infinitely beneficial in their use, as, in my opinion, to bear down all doubt that can be raised upon the subject.

24

On the Argument from Design

David Hume

Not to lose any time in circumlocutions, said CLEANTHES, addressing himself to DEMEA, much less in replying to the pious declamations of PHILO; I shall briefly explain how I conceive this matter. Look round the world: contemplate the whole and every part of it: You will find it to be nothing but one great machine, subdivided into an infinite number of lesser machines, which again admit of subdivisions, to a degree beyond what human senses and faculties can trace and explain. All these various machines, and even their most minute parts, are adjusted to each other with an accuracy, which ravishes into admiration all men, who have ever contemplated them. The curious adapting of means to ends, throughout all nature, resembles exactly, though it much exceeds, the productions of human contrivance; of human designs, thought, wisdom, and intelligence. Since therefore the effects resemble each other, we are led to infer, by all the rules of analogy, that the causes also resemble; and that the Author of Nature is somewhat similar to the mind of man; though possessed of much larger faculties, proportioned to the grandeur of the work, which he has executed. By this argument *a posteriori*, and by this argument alone, do we prove at once the existence of a Deity, and his similarity to human mind and intelligence.

I shall be so free, CLEANTHES, said DEMEA, as to tell you, that from the beginning, I could not approve of your conclusion concerning the similarity of the Deity to men; still less can I approve of the mediums, by which you endeavour to establish it. What! No demonstration of the Being of a God! No abstract arguments! No proofs *a priori!* Are these, which have hitherto been so much insisted on by philosophers, all fallacy, all sophism? Can we reach no farther in this subject than experience and probability? I will not say, that this is betraying the cause of a Deity: But surely, by this affected candor, you give advantage to Atheists, which they never could obtain, by the mere dint of argument and reasoning.

What I chiefly scruple in this subject, said PHILO, is not so much, that all religious arguments are by CLEANTHES reduced to experience, as that they appear not to be even the most certain and irrefragable of that inferior kind. That a stone will fall, that fire will burn, that the earth has solidity, we have observed a thousand and a thousand times; and when any new instance of this nature is presented, we draw without hesitation the accustomed inference. The exact similarity of the cases gives us a perfect assurance of a similar event; and a stronger evidence is never desired nor sought after. But where-ever you depart, in the

"On the Argument from Design" from Part II and Part V of *Dialogues Concerning Natural Religion* by David Hume, in *A Treatise of Human Nature and Dialogues Concerning Natural Religion*, Vol. II, ed. T. H. Green and T. H. Grose (New York: Longmans, Green, and Co., 1898), pp. 392–8; 412–15.

least, from the similarity of the cases, you diminish proportionably the evidence; and may at last bring it to a very weak *analogy*, which is confessedly liable to error and uncertainty. After having experienced the circulation of the blood in human creatures, we make no doubt that it takes place in Titius and Mævius: but from its circulation in frogs and fishes, it is only a presumption, though a strong one, from analogy, that it takes place in men and other animals. The analogical reasoning is much weaker, when we infer the circulation of the sap in vegetables from our experience, that the blood circulates in animals; and those, who hastily followed that imperfect analogy, are found, by more accurate experiments, to have been mistaken.

If we see a house, CLEANTHES, we conclude, with the greatest certainty, that it had an architect or builder; because this is precisely that species of effect, which we have experienced to proceed from that species of cause. But surely you will not affirm, that the universe bears such a resemblance to a house, that we can with the same certainty infer a similar cause, or that the analogy is here entire and perfect. The dissimilitude is so striking, that the utmost you can here pretend to is a guess, a conjecture, a presumption concerning a similar cause; and how that pretension will be received in the world, I leave you to consider.

It would surely be very ill received, replied CLEANTHES; and I should be deservedly blamed and detested, did I allow, that the proofs of a Deity amounted to no more than a guess or conjecture. But is the whole adjustment of means to ends in a house and in the universe so slight a resemblance? The economy of final causes? The order, proportion, and arrangement of every part? Steps of a stair are plainly contrived, that human legs may use them in mounting; and this inference is certain and infallible. Human legs are also contrived for walking and mounting; and this inference, I allow, is not altogether so certain, because of the dissimilarity which you remark; but does it, therefore, deserve the name only of presumption or conjecture?

[. . .]

[PHILO:] Now, according to this method of reasoning, DEMEA, it follows (and is, indeed, tacitly allowed by CLEANTHES himself) that order, arrangement, or the adjustment of final causes is not, of itself, any proof of design; but only so far as it has been experienced to proceed from that principle. For ought we can know *a priori*, matter may contain the source or spring of order originally, within itself, as well as mind does; and there is no more difficulty in conceiving, that the several elements, from an internal unknown cause, may fall into the most exquisite arrangement, than to conceive that their ideas, in the great, universal mind, from a like internal, unknown cause, fall into that arrangement. The equal possibility of both these suppositions is allowed. But by experience we find, (according to CLEANTHES) that there is a difference between them. Throw several pieces of steel together, without shape or form; they will never arrange themselves so as to compose a watch: Stone, and mortar, and wood, without an architect, never erect a house. But the ideas in a human mind, we see, by an unknown, inexplicable economy, arrange themselves so as to form the plan of a watch or house. Experience, therefore, proves, that there is an original principle of order in mind, not in matter. From similar effects we infer similar causes. The adjustment of means to ends is alike in the universe, as in a machine of human contrivance. The causes, therefore, must be resembling.

I was from the beginning scandalised, I must own, with this resemblance, which is asserted, between the Deity and human creatures; and must conceive it to imply such a degradation of the Supreme Being as no sound Theist could endure. With your assistance, therefore, Demea, I shall endeavour to defend what you justly called the adorable mysteriousness of the Divine Nature, and shall refute this reasoning of CLEANTHES, provided he allows, that I have made a fair representation of it.

When CLEANTHES had assented, PHILO, after a short pause, proceeded in the following manner.

That all inferences, CLEANTHES, concerning fact, are founded on experience, and that all experimental reasonings are founded on the supposition, that similar causes prove similar effects, and similar effects similar causes; I shall not, at present, much dispute with you. But observe, I entreat you, with what extreme caution all just reasoners proceed in the transferring of experiments to similar cases. Unless the cases be exactly similar, they repose no perfect confidence in applying their past observation to any particular phenomenon. Every alteration of circumstances occasions a doubt concerning the event; and it requires new experiments to prove certainly, that the new circumstances are of no moment or importance. A change in bulk, situation, arrangement, age, disposition of the air, or surrounding bodies; any of these particulars may be attended with the most unexpected consequences: And unless the objects be quite familiar to us, it is the highest temerity to expect with assurance, after any of these changes, an event similar to that which before fell under our observation. The slow and deliberate steps of philosophers, here, if any where, are distinguished from the precipitate march of the vulgar, who, hurried on by the smallest similitudes, are incapable of all discernment or consideration.

But can you think, CLEANTHES, that your usual phlegm and philosophy have been preserved in so wide a step as you have taken, when you compared to the universe houses, ships, furniture, machines; and from their similarity in some circumstances inferred a similarity in their causes? Thought, design, intelligence, such as we discover in men and other animals, is no more than one of the springs and principles of the universe, as well as heat or cold, attraction or repulsion, and a hundred others, which fall under daily observation. It is an active cause, by which some particular parts of nature, we find, produce alterations on other parts. But can a conclusion, with any propriety, be transferred from parts to the whole? Does not the great disproportion bar all comparison and inference? From observing the growth of a hair, can we learn any thing concerning the generation of a man? Would the manner of a leaf's blowing, even though perfectly known, afford us any instruction concerning the vegetation of a tree?

But allowing that we were to take the *operations* of one part of nature upon another for the foundation of our judgement concerning the *origin* of the whole (which never can be admitted) yet why select so minute, so weak, so bounded a principle as the reason and design of animals is found to be upon this planet? What peculiar privilege has this little agitation of the brain which we call *thought*, that we must thus make it the model of the whole universe? Our

partiality in our own favour does indeed present it on all occasions; but sound philosophy ought carefully to guard against so natural an illusion.

So far from admitting, continued PHILO, that the operations of a part can afford us any just conclusion concerning the origin of the whole, I will not allow any one part to form a rule for another part, if the latter be very remote from the former. Is there any reasonable ground to conclude, that the inhabitants of other planets possess thought, intelligence, reason, or any thing similar to these faculties in men? When Nature has so extremely diversified her manner of operation in this small globe; can we imagine, that she incessantly copies herself throughout so immense a universe? And if thought, as we may well suppose, be confined merely to this narrow corner, and has even there so limited a sphere of action; with what propriety can we assign it for the original cause of all things? The narrow views of a peasant, who makes his domestic œconomy the rule for the government of kingdoms, is in comparison a pardonable sophism.

But were we ever so much assured, that a thought and reason, resembling the human, were to be found throughout the whole universe, and were its activity elsewhere vastly greater and more commanding than it appears in this globe; yet I cannot see, why the operations of a world, constituted, arranged, adjusted, can with any propriety be extended to a world, which is in its embryo-state, and is advancing towards that constitution and arrangement. By observation, we know somewhat of the economy, action, and nourishment of a finished animal; but we must transfer with great caution that observation to the growth of a fœtus in the womb, and still more, in the formation of an animalcule in the loins of its male parent. Nature, we find, even from our limited experience, possesses an infinite number of springs and principles, which incessantly discover themselves on every change of her position and situation. And what new and unknown principles would actuate her in so new and unknown a situation as that of the formation of a universe, we cannot, without the utmost temerity, pretend to determine.

A very small part of this great system, during a very short time, is very imperfectly discovered to us: and do we then pronounce decisively concerning the origin of the whole?

Admirable conclusion! Stone, wood, brick, iron, brass, have not, at this time, in this minute globe of earth, an order or arrangement without human art and contrivance: therefore the universe could not originally attain its order and arrangement, without something similar to human art. But is a part of nature a rule for another part very wide of the former? Is it a rule for the whole? Is a very small part a rule for the universe? Is nature in one situation, a certain rule for nature in another situation, vastly different from the former?

[...]

When two *species* of objects have always been observed to be conjoined together, I can *infer*, by custom, the existence of one where-ever I *see* the existence of the other: and this I call an argument from experience. But how this argument can have place, where the objects, as in the present case, are single, individual, without parallel, or specific resemblance, may be difficult to explain. And will any man tell me with a serious countenance, that an orderly universe must arise from some thought and art, like the human; because we have experience of it? To ascertain this reasoning, it were requisite, that we had experience of the origin of worlds; and it is not sufficient surely, that we have seen ships and cities arise from human art and contrivance....

[...]

Now, CLEANTHES, said PHILO, with an air of alacrity and triumph, mark the consequences. *First*, By this method of reasoning, you renounce all claim to infinity in any of the attributes of the Deity. For as the cause ought only to be proportioned to the effect, and the effect, so far as it falls under our cognisance, is not infinite; what pretensions have we, upon your suppositions, to ascribe that attribute to the divine Being? You will still insist, that, by removing him so much from all similarity to human creatures, we give in to the most arbitrary hypothesis, and at the same time weaken all proofs of his existence.

Secondly, You have no reason, on your theory, for ascribing perfection to the Deity, even in his finite capacity; or for supposing him free from every error, mistake, or incoherence in his undertakings. There are many inexplicable difficulties in the works of Nature, which, if we allow a perfect author to be proved *a priori*, are easily solved, and become only seeming difficulties, from the narrow capacity of man, who cannot trace infinite relations. But according to your method of reasoning, these difficulties become all real; and perhaps will be insisted on, as new instances of likeness to human art and contrivance. At least, you must acknowledge, that it is impossible for us to tell, from our limited views, whether this system contains any great faults, or deserves any considerable praise, if compared to other possible, and even real systems. Could a peasant, if the ÆNEID were read to him, pronounce that poem to be absolutely faultless, or even assign to it its proper rank among the productions of human wit; he, who had never seen any other production?

But were this world ever so perfect a production, it must still remain uncertain, whether all the excellences of the work can justly be ascribed to the workman. If we survey a ship, what an exalted idea must we form of the ingenuity of the carpenter, who framed so complicated, useful, and beautiful a machine? And what surprise must we feel, when we find him a stupid mechanic, who imitated others, and copied an art, which, through a long succession of ages, after multiplied trials, mistakes, corrections, deliberations, and controversies, had been gradually improving? Many worlds might have been botched and bungled, throughout an eternity, ere this system was struck out: much labour lost: many fruitless trials made: and a slow, but continued improvement carried on during infinite ages in the art of world-making. In such subjects, who can determine, where the truth; nay, who can conjecture where the probability, lies; amidst a great number of hypotheses which may be proposed, and a still greater number which may be imagined?

And what shadow of an argument, continued PHILO, can you produce, from your hypothesis, to prove the unity of the Deity? A great number of men join in building a house or ship, in rearing a city, in framing a commonwealth: why may not several deities combine in contriving and framing a world? This is only so much greater similarity to human affairs. By sharing the work among several, we may so much further limit the attributes of each, and get rid of that extensive power and knowledge, which must be supposed in one deity, and which, according to you, can only serve to weaken the proof of his existence. And if such foolish, such vicious creatures as man can yet often unite in framing and executing one plan; how much more those deities or daemons, whom we may suppose several degrees more perfect?

To multiply causes, without necessity, is indeed contrary to true philosophy: but this principle applies not to the present case. Were one deity antecedently proved by your theory, who were possessed of every attribute, requisite to the production of the universe; it would be needless, I own (though not absurd) to suppose any other deity existent. But while it is still a question, Whether all these attributes are united in one subject, or dispersed among several independent beings: by what phenomena in nature can we pretend to decide the controversy? Where we see a body raiscd in a scale, we are sure that there is in the opposite scale, however concealed from sight, some counterpoising weight equal to it: but it is still allowed to doubt, whether that weight be an aggregate of several distinct bodies, or one uniform united mass. And if the weight requisite very much exceeds any thing which we have ever seen conjoined in any single body, the former supposition becomes still more probable and natural. An intelligent being of such vast power and capacity, as is necessary to produce the universe, or, to speak in the language of ancient philosophy, so prodigious an animal, exceeds all analogy, and even comprehension.

But farther, CLEANTHES; men are mortal, and renew their species by generation; and this is common to all living creatures. The two great sexes of male and female, says MILTON, animate the world. Why must this circumstance, so universal, so essential, be excluded from those numerous and limited deities? Behold then the theogony of ancient times brought back upon us.

And why not become a perfect Anthropomorphite? Why not assert the deity or deities to be corporeal, and to have eyes, a nose, mouth, ears, &c.? EPICURUS maintained, that no man had ever seen reason but in a human figure; therefore the gods must have a human figure. And this argument, which is deservedly so much ridiculed by Cicero, becomes, according to you, solid and philosophical.

In a word, CLEANTHES, a man, who follows your hypothesis, is able, perhaps, to assert, or conjecture, that the universe, sometime, arose from something like design: but beyond that position he cannot ascertain one single circumstance, and is left afterwards to fix every point of his theology, by the utmost licence of fancy and hypothesis. This world, for aught he knows, is very faulty and imperfect, compared to a superior standard; and was only the first rude essay of some infant deity, who afterwards abandoned it, ashamed of his lame performance: it is the work only of some dependent, inferior deity; and is the object of derision to his superiors: it is the production of old age and dotage in some superannuated deity; and ever since his death, has run on at adventures, from the first impulse and active force, which, it received from him. You justly give signs of horror, DEMEA, at these strange suppositions: but these, and a thousand more of the same kind, are CLEANTHES's suppositions, not mine. From the moment the attributes of the Deity are supposed finite, all these have place. And I cannot, for my part, think, that so wild and unsettled a system of theology is, in any respect, preferable to none at all.

25

Truth is Subjectivity

Søren Kierkegaard

In an attempt to make clear the difference of way that exists between an objective and a subjective reflection, I shall now proceed to show how a subjective reflection makes its way inwardly in inwardness. Inwardness in an existing subject culminates in passion; corresponding to passion in the subject the truth becomes a paradox; and the fact that the truth becomes a paradox is rooted precisely in its having a relationship to an existing subject. Thus the one corresponds to the other. By forgetting that one is an existing subject, passion goes by the board and the truth is no longer a paradox; the knowing subject becomes a fantastic entity rather than a human being, and the truth becomes a fantastic object for the knowledge of this fantastic entity.

When the question of truth is raised in an objective manner, reflection is directed objectively to the truth, as an object to which the knower is related. Reflection is not focussed upon the relationship, however, but upon the question of whether it is the truth to which the knower is related. If only the object to which he is related is the truth, the subject is accounted to be in the truth. When the question of the truth is raised subjectively, reflection is directed subjectively to the nature of the individual's relationship; if only the mode of this relationship is in the truth, the individual is in the truth even if he should happen to be thus related to what is not true.[1] Let us take as an example the knowledge of God. Objectively, reflection is directed to the problem of whether this object is the true God; subjectively, reflection is directed to the question whether the individual is related to a something in such *a manner* that his relationship is in truth a God-relationship. On which side is the truth now to be found? Ah, may we not here resort to a mediation, and say: It is on neither side, but in the mediation of both? Excellently well said, provided we might have it explained how an existing individual manages to be in a state of mediation. For to be in a state of mediation is to be finished, while to exist is to become. Nor can an existing individual be in two places at the same time – he cannot be an identity of subject and object. When he is nearest to being in two places at the same time he is in passion; but passion is momentary, and passion is also the highest expression of subjectivity.

"Truth is Subjectivity" from *Concluding Unscientific Postscript* by Søren Kierkegaard, trans. David F. Swenson and Walter Lowrie (Princeton, NJ: Princeton University Press, 1941), pp. 177–82. © 1992 Princeton University Press. Reprinted by permission of Princeton University Press.

[1] The reader will observe that the question here is about essential truth, or about the truth which is essentially related to existence, and that it is precisely for the sake of clarifying it as inwardness or as subjectivity that this contrast is drawn.

The existing individual who chooses to pursue the objective way enters upon the entire approximation-process by which it is proposed to bring God to light objectively. But this is in all eternity impossible, because God is a subject, and therefore exists only for subjectivity in inwardness. The existing individual who chooses the subjective way apprehends instantly the entire dialectical difficulty involved in having to use some time, perhaps a long time, in finding God objectively; and he feels this dialectical difficulty in all its painfulness, because every moment is wasted in which he does not have God.[2] That very instant he has God, not by virtue of any objective deliberation, but by virtue of the infinite passion of inwardness. The objective inquirer, on the other hand, is not embarrassed by such dialectical difficulties as are involved in devoting an entire period of investigation to finding God – since it is possible that the inquirer may die tomorrow; and if he lives he can scarcely regard God as something to be taken along if convenient, since God is precisely that which one takes *a tout prix*, which in the understanding of passion constitutes the true inward relationship to God.

It is at this point, so difficult dialectically, that the way swings off for everyone who knows what it means to think, and to think existentially; which is something very different from sitting at a desk and writing about what one has never done, something very different from writing *de omnibus dubitandum* and at the same time being as credulous existentially as the most sensuous of men. Here is where the way swings off, and the change is marked by the fact that while objective knowledge rambles comfortably on by way of the long road of approximation without being impelled by the urge of passion, subjective knowledge counts every delay a deadly peril, and the decision so infinitely important and so instantly pressing that it is as if the opportunity had already passed.

Now when the problem is to reckon up on which side there is most truth, whether on the side of one who seeks the true God objectively, and pursues the approximate truth of the God-idea; or on the side of one who, driven by the infinite passion of his need of God, feels an infinite concern for his own relationship to God in truth (and to be at one and the same time on both sides equally, is as we have noted not possible for an existing individual, but is merely the happy delusion of an imaginary I-am-I): the answer cannot be in doubt for anyone who has not been demoralized with the aid of science. If one who lives in the midst of Christendom goes up to the house of God, the house of the true God, with the true conception of God in his knowledge, and prays, but prays in a false spirit; and one who lives in an idolatrous community prays with the entire passion of the infinite, although his eyes rest upon the image of an idol: where is there most truth? The one prays in truth to God though he worships an idol; the other prays falsely to the true God, and hence worships in fact an idol.

When one man investigates objectively the problem of immortality, and another embraces an uncertainty with the passion of the infinite: where is there most truth, and who has the greater certainty? The one has entered upon a never-ending approximation, for the certainty of immortality lies precisely in the subjectivity of the individual; the other is immortal, and fights for his immortality by struggling with the uncertainty. Let us consider Socrates. Nowadays everyone dabbles in a few proofs; some have several such proofs, others fewer. But Socrates! He puts the question objectively in a problematic manner: *if* there is an immortality. He must therefore be accounted a doubter in comparison with one of our modern thinkers with the three proofs? By no means. On this "if" he risks his entire life, he has the courage to meet death, and he has with the passion of the infinite so determined the pattern of his life that it must be

[2]   In this manner God certainly becomes a postulate, but not in the otiose manner in which this word is commonly understood. It becomes clear rather that the only way in which an existing individual comes into relation with God, is when the dialectical contradiction brings his passion to the point of despair, and helps him to embrace God with the "category of despair" (faith). Then the postulate is so far from being arbitrary that it is precisely a life-necessity. It is then not so much that God is a postulate, as that the existing individual's postulation of God is a necessity.

found acceptable – *if* there is an immortality. Is any better proof capable of being given for the immortality of the soul? But those who have the three proofs do not at all determine their lives in conformity therewith; if there is an immortality it must feel disgust over their manner of life: can any better refutation be given of the three proofs? The bit of uncertainty that Socrates had, helped him because he himself contributed the passion of the infinite; the three proofs that the others have do not profit them at all, because they are dead to spirit and enthusiasm, and their three proofs, in lieu of proving anything else, prove just this. A young girl may enjoy all the sweetness of love on the basis of what is merely a weak hope that she is beloved, because she rests everything on this weak hope; but many a wedded matron more than once subjected to the strongest expressions of love, has in so far indeed had proofs, but strangely enough has not enjoyed *quod erat demonstrandum*. The Socratic ignorance, which Socrates held fast with the entire passion of his inwardness, was thus an expression for the principle that the eternal truth is related to an existing individual, and that this truth must therefore be a paradox for him as long as he exists; and yet it is possible that there was more truth in the Socratic ignorance as it was in him, than in the entire objective truth of the System, which flirts with what the times demand and accommodates itself to *Privatdocents*.

The objective accent falls on WHAT is said, the subjective accent on HOW it is said. This distinction holds even in the aesthetic realm, and receives definite expression in the principle that what is in itself true may in the mouth of such and such a person become untrue. In these times this distinction is particularly worthy of notice,

for if we wish to express in a single sentence the difference between ancient times and our own, we should doubtless have to say: "In ancient times only an individual here and there knew the truth; now all know it, except that the inwardness of its appropriation stands in an inverse relationship to the extent of its dissemination.[3] Aesthetically the contradiction that truth becomes untruth in this or that person's mouth, is best construed comically: In the ethico-religious sphere, accent is again on the "how." But this is not to be understood as referring to demeanor, expression, or the like; rather it refers to the relationship sustained by the existing individual, in his own existence, to the content of his utterance. Objectively the interest is focussed merely on the thought-content, subjectively on the inwardness. At its maximum this inward "how" is the passion of the infinite, and the passion of the infinite is the truth. But the passion of the infinite is precisely subjectivity, and thus subjectivity becomes the truth. Objectively there is no infinite decisiveness, and hence it is objectively in order to annul the difference between good and evil, together with the principle of contradiction, and therewith also the infinite difference between the true and the false. Only in subjectivity is there decisiveness, to seek objectivity is to be in error. It is the passion of the infinite that is the decisive factor and not its content, for its content is precisely itself. In this manner subjectivity and the subjective "how" constitute the truth.

But the "how" which is thus subjectively accentuated precisely because the subject is an existing individual, is also subject to a dialectic with respect to time. In the passionate moment of decision, where the road swings away from objective knowledge, it seems as if the infinite

---

[3]   *Stages on Life's Way*, Note on p. 426. Though ordinarily not wishing an expression of opinion on the part of reviewers, I might at this point almost desire it, provided such opinions, so far from flattering me, amounted to an assertion of the daring truth that what I say is something that everybody knows, even every child, and that the cultured know infinitely much better. If it only stands fast that everyone knows it, my standpoint is in order, and I shall doubtless make shift to manage with the unity of the comic and the tragic. If there were anyone who did not know it I might perhaps be in danger of being dislodged from my position of equilibrium by the thought that I might be in a position to communicate to someone the needful preliminary knowledge. It is just this which engages my interest so much, this that the cultured are accustomed to say: that everyone knows what the highest is. This was not the case in paganism, nor in Judaism, nor in the seventeen centuries of Christianity. Hail to the nineteenth century! Everyone knows it. What progress has been made since the time when only a few knew it. To make up for this, perhaps, we must assume that no one nowadays does it.

decision were thereby realized. But in the same moment the existing individual finds himself in the temporal order, and the subjective "how" is transformed into a striving, a striving which receives indeed its impulse and a repeated renewal from the decisive passion of the infinite, but is nevertheless a striving.

When subjectivity is the truth, the conceptual determination of the truth must include an expression for the antithesis to objectivity, a memento of the fork in the road where the way swings off; this expression will at the same time serve as an indication of the tension of the subjective inwardness. Here is such a definition of truth: *An objective uncertainty held fast in an appropriation-process of the most passionate inwardness is the truth*, the highest truth attainable for an *existing* individual. At the point where the way swings off (and where this is cannot be specified objectively, since it is a matter of subjectivity), there objective knowledge is placed in abeyance. Thus the subject merely has, objectively, the uncertainty; but it is this which precisely increases the tension of that infinite passion which constitutes his inwardness. The truth is precisely the

venture which chooses an objective uncertainty with the passion of the infinite. I contemplate the order of nature in the hope of finding God, and I see omnipotence and wisdom; but I also see much else that disturbs my mind and excites anxiety. The sum of all this is an objective uncertainty. But it is for this very reason that the inwardness becomes as intense as it is, for it embraces this objective uncertainty with the entire passion of the infinite. In the case of a mathematical proposition the objectivity is given, but for this reason the truth of such a proposition is also an indifferent truth.

But the above definition of truth is an equivalent expression for faith. Without risk there is no faith. Faith is precisely the contradiction between the infinite passion of the individual's inwardness and the objective uncertainty. If I am capable of grasping God objectively, I do not believe, but precisely because I cannot do this I must believe. If I wish to preserve myself in faith I must constantly be intent upon holding fast the objective uncertainty, so as to remain out upon the deep, over seventy thousand fathoms of water, still preserving my faith.

Section IV

The Rationality of Religious Belief in the Absence of Evidence

Introduction

A. General Introduction to the Section

Recall that the evidentialist maintains that a rational belief is one that is supported by sufficient evidence. William Clifford (1845–79) famously summed up this view by saying that "it is wrong always, everywhere, and for anyone, to believe anything upon insufficient evidence."[1] At the end of the previous section, we began to examine the views of some thinkers who are skeptical about reason's ability to provide what the evidentialist insists is necessary to guarantee the rationality of religious belief. Suppose that their skepticism about reason's capacity to supply adequate justification is merited. Would this then entail that religious belief is irrational, as the evidentialist holds? In this section, we examine several attempts to deny that religious belief is irrational in the absence of supporting argument.

To challenge the evidentialist's demand is to maintain that there are at least some beliefs that are rationally held despite the fact that they are not based on other beliefs that justify them. One might approach this challenge in one of two ways. The first involves reflection on the foundations of our systems of belief. Following Descartes (1596–1650), one may pursue the suggestion that our many individual beliefs, like a building, rest on a foundation.[2] Following this strategy, one then argues that while such a foundation may provide justification or warrant for one's beliefs, it cannot itself be subject to the evidentialist demand. Finally, one seeks to establish that this foundation provides a rational basis for religious belief (in some cases because the foundation itself consists, in part, of religious beliefs).

A second approach to challenging the evidentialist demand is to appeal to religious experience. Here it is important to distinguish two different ways of thinking about the role of religious experience in relation to religious belief. According to one way of thinking about such experiences, a person might have a religious experience, and, on the basis of this experience, infer that some Ultimate Sacred Reality exists. If this is the proper way to think about religious experience, it does not involve a rejection of evidentialism for the experience is being interpreted as evidence for the relevant religious belief. The question then is simply whether such experiences provide sufficient evidence for religious belief.

---

[1] "The Ethics of Belief," in *The Ethics of Belief Debate*, ed. Gerald D. McCarthy (Atlanta: Scholars Press, 1986), p. 24.

[2] *Meditations on First Philosophy*, Meditation I.

The focus here will be instead on the attempt to conceive of the role of religious experience in a non-evidentialist manner. Those embracing this way of thinking argue that the relationship between religious experience and religious belief is not that the latter is inferred from the former. For example, many theistic thinkers have sought to liken the experience of God to sensory experience. In the case of beliefs formed through sense perception, for example: "There is a tree," it seems incorrect to say that my belief that there is a tree is the result of some reasoning that I have done. Likewise, these thinkers contend that it is inaccurate to say that the religious person infers the existence of God when she has a sense of being in God's presence. Instead, she is said to perceive God directly.

B.   The Foundations of Religious Belief

B1.   *William James and the Right to Believe*

Though William James (1842–1910) entitled his lecture (and subsequent essay) "The Will to Believe," he tells us early on that his aim is to provide "a defence of our right to adopt a believing attitude in religious matters, in spite of the fact that our merely logical intellect may not have been coerced" (p. 162). A contemporary of William Clifford, James felt the need to respond to Clifford's evidentialist dictum (quoted above). Though he was willing to grant the importance of abiding by the evidentialist principle in many areas of life, he argued that it was not appropriately applied in several important spheres, including that of religion.

James focuses on cases when one is forced to choose between two or more hypotheses that are of great significance for how one will lead one's life, even though the available evidence is indeterminate – i.e., the evidence doesn't settle for us the issue of which competing hypotheses is true. According to James, this is (at least for some) the nature of the confrontation between religious belief and atheism. If so, then James contends that we not only *may* but *must* opt for one hypothesis or the other based on our "passional" natures, not

on the basis of other supporting beliefs. In speaking of our passional natures, James intends to direct our attention to non-cognitive aspects of our psychological make-up – for example, our hopes, fears, and risk-taking dispositions. One might think that by stressing the significance of such aspects of our psychological make-up for religious belief James is severing the connection between religious belief and the issues of truth and rationality. However, this would be a mistaken reading, for James clearly seems to think that the rejection of evidentialism is the more rational position for one who seeks the truth: "*a rule of thinking which would absolutely prevent me from acknowledging certain kinds of truth if those kinds of truth were really there, would be an irrational rule*" (p. 170).

B2.   *Alvin Plantinga and Properly Basic Belief*

Like James, Alvin Plantinga has recently sought to defend the rationality of religious belief by denying the evidentialist standard of rationality. However, Plantinga's strategy differs from that of James insofar as he holds – like the evidentialist – that the rationality of a religious outlook will depend ultimately on the rationality of its constituent beliefs (rather than being grounded in non-cognitive aspects of our psychological make-up).

In "Is Belief in God Properly Basic?" Plantinga begins by pointing out that the evidentialist is typically a *classical foundationalist*. According to the foundationalist, the rationality of beliefs is linked to the way in which our beliefs form a structured web. At various points in this web, some beliefs are supported by other beliefs. It is this sort of structural connection that the evidentialist emphasizes. However, not all our beliefs are (or could be) supported by other more fundamental beliefs (for this would appear to generate an infinite regress of justification). In other words, some beliefs in the structure of the web are foundational, or basic. That is, they provide support for other beliefs but are themselves not based on any more fundamental beliefs. Basic beliefs that are rational to hold are said to be *properly basic*. Plantinga argues that belief in God may be properly basic.[3]

---

[3]   Plantinga attributes this view to several of the central Protestant Reformation thinkers, thus his view and others like it have come to be grouped together under the label "Reformed Epistemology."

Since basic beliefs are not supported by other beliefs, their rationality cannot be assessed using the evidentialist standard. Thus the classical foundationalist has sought to spell out separate criteria for the rationality of basic beliefs. For example, Descartes held that basic beliefs must be either self-evident to all rational persons and/or incorrigible (i.e., impossible to doubt). Belief in God is certainly neither self-evident in this sense nor incorrigible, but Plantinga contends that other beliefs that are plausibly taken to be properly basic also fail to meet the standards of the classical foundationalist – for example, perceptual beliefs, memory beliefs, and beliefs about the mental states of others. According to Plantinga, when we examine what it is that seems to underlie the rationality of these beliefs, we find that the same can be said to be true of belief in God. Therefore, if we are willing to regard the former beliefs as rational, we should regard belief in God as rational.

B3. Questioning the Foundations of Religious Belief

Michael Martin raises a number of objections to Plantinga's approach in the selection "Plantinga on Belief in God as Properly Basic." Though Plantinga's views are his critical target, many of his concerns are similar to those that have been raised about other non-evidentialist strategies. Perhaps chief amongst these concerns is that non-evidentialist views like Plantinga's seem to entail that the rationality of religious belief may be relative to the community of belief to which one belongs (or perhaps even relative to individual believers). That is, the same non-evidentialist standards of rationality that allow belief in God to be rational would seem to allow many other types of apparently incompatible beliefs to be justified as well. The force of this objection might be understood in two different ways. First, one might think that relativistic views are generally rationally suspect; thus, any view that entails relativism is itself problematic.

Second, regardless of what one might think about the rational merits of relativistic views in general, one might wonder whether theists themselves are willing to grant that both atheists and persons from other religious communities are likewise rationally justified in holding beliefs very different from their own.

C. Religious Belief and Religious Experience

C1. Perceiving God

William Alston is one of the most prominent recent defenders of the view that at least some religious experiences can be likened to perceptual experience and thus, as the title of his selection puts it, that "Religious Experience Justifies Religious Belief." According to Alston, an experience is perceptual in nature if something seems to present itself to the subject in the experience and is a *mystical* perceptual experience if that which seems to present itself is God.[4] Note that this way of understanding perceptual experience allows for the fact that one may be mistaken about what is perceived. Also note that in referring to mystical experiences as perceptual, Alston is assuming not that the experiences derive from the operation of our sensory organs (though some might), but rather that the character of the experience is analogous to sensory experiences. This parallel is suggested as well by the personal accounts of many mystics, for while they often say that they experience a strong sense of detachment from their physical bodies, they nevertheless invoke sensory metaphors in describing their experience of God – e.g., that God is "tasted," "heard," or "seen" (see Teresa of Ávila's "The Difference between Union and Rapture").

As Alston notes, we typically accept that one is *prima facie* rationally warranted in holding beliefs formed through sensory experience in the absence of reasons to think that one's perception

---

[4] Alston says that he intends for the word "God" to "range over any *supreme reality*, however construed" (p. 183), and so seems to assume that his account is equally applicable to the mystical experiences of those in non-theistic traditions as well. See the later selection, "Mystical Knowledge: Knowledge by Identity," by Robert Forman, for critical discussion of assumptions of this kind.

is mistaken. Using an analogy from criminal proceedings, one might say that these beleiefs are presumed innocent until proven guilty. According to Alston, if we accept this presumption of rationality in the case of beliefs derived from sensory perceptual experience, and some religious beliefs are derived from experiences that are likewise perceptual in character, then we should acknowledge the *prima facie* rationality of those religious beliefs as well.

C2.   Misperceiving God?

Since Alston's argument contends that mystical experience is analogous to sensory experience, an obvious strategy in challenging his approach is to claim that sensory experience and mystical experience are different in ways that undermine the force of the analogy. Also, recall that Alston's view is that religious beliefs deriving from mystical experience have presumptive rational warrant only in the absence of reasons to think that the perceptions are mistaken, so another means of challenging accounts like his is to argue that there are good reasons to think that such experiences are not veridical. Evan False pursues both these strategies in "Do Mystics See God?" That is, he first argues that sensory experience, unlike mystical experience, is subject to a kind of "cross-checking" about the causes of one's experience that helps to diminish, if not eliminate, the likelihood that one's perception is mistaken. Second, he argues that there are plausible naturalistic explanations for why people have mystical experiences; thus there is good reason to not take them as perceptions of God.

C3.   Religious Experience as Knowledge by Identity

In "Mystical Knowledge: Knowledge by Identity," Robert Forman objects to a general assumption that lies behind many accounts which seek to model religious experience on sensory experience. The problem, he contends, is that proponents of such accounts often assume that all experience must be intentional in character – that is, involve a consciousness of something distinct from oneself. Further, Forman objects to the fact that this assumption is often linked with a theory of human experience according to which the object of experience is never experienced directly but instead mediated or constructed through the lenses of the subject's existing conceptual framework. In other words, on this view all experience is interpreted experience (note the parallel between Forman and Puligandla's argument in the preceding section).

Forman's objections to the above are based on a type of experience he refers to as a "pure consciousness event." Reports of pure consciousness events suggest that it is a transient state wherein the subject remains aware and alert yet this awareness is devoid of mental content. That is, she or he is conscious, but there is no object of consciousness to which the subject is attending and so nothing that is being conceptually mediated or constructed. As Forman documents, this sort of religious experience – which involves the dissolution of the subject/object distinction and cessation of our normal habits of conceptual overlay – is reported in many traditions. Certainly, experiences of this type or similar to it play an especially prominent role in a number of Eastern traditions (though one should be careful not to assume that there is one type of experience shared across these traditions). So, for example, in characterizing enlightenment, the Zen philosopher Dogen (1200–53) says, "Inasmuch as this way, this place, is neither large nor small, self nor other, does not exist from before, does not come into being now for the first time, *it is just as it is*" (see "Manifesting Suchness," p. 224).

Forman argues that in states of pure consciousness one is capable of a kind of direct knowing of one's consciousness – knowledge arrived at by experiencing identity with it. From here, he acknowledges, mystics may vary in the significance attributed to this knowledge. Some will say that this consciousness is nothing other than Ultimate Sacred Reality, while others maintain that it merely reflects the essence of the divine (see, for example, the way that al-Ghazali cautions fellow mystics to correct the impression left by such experiences that one is identical to God in "Divine Intoxication").

In this and the previous section, we have been examining claims about the role of reason – or lack thereof – in providing rational warrant for religious belief. In the next section, we will turn to an important and influential challenge to the rationality of such belief based on the experience of evil.

Suggestions for Further Reading

Alston, William P., *Perceiving God: The Epistemology of Religious Experience* (Ithaca, NY: Cornell University Press, 1991).

Davis, Carolyn Franks, *The Evidential Force of Religious Experience* (Oxford: Clarendon Press, 1989).

Forman, Robert K. C. (ed.), *The Problem of Pure Consciousness: Mysticism and Philosophy* (New York and London: Oxford University Press, 1993).

Gellman, Jerome, *Experience of God and the Rationality of Theistic Belief* (Ithaca, NY: Cornell University Press, 1997).

James, William, *The Varieties of Religious Experience* (New York: Mentor Books, 1958).

Jantzen, Grace M., *Power, Gender, and Christian Mysticism* (Cambridge: Cambridge University Press, 1995).

Katz, Steven (ed.), *Mysticism and Philosophical Analysis* (Oxford: Oxford University Press, 1978).

Leaman, Oliver, "Philosophy vs Mysticism: An Islamic Controversy," in *Philosophy, Religion, and the Spiritual Life: Royal Institute of Philosophy Supplement: 32*, ed. Michael McGhee (Cambridge: Cambridge University Press, 1992).

McLeod, Mark S., *Rationality and Theistic Belief: An Essay in Reformed Epistemology* (Ithaca, NY: Cornell University Press, 1993).

Otto, Rudolf, *The Idea of the Holy*, 2nd edition (Oxford: Oxford University Press, 1957).

Phillips, Stephen, "Could there be Mystical Evidence for Non-dual Brahman?" *Philosophy East & West* 51 (2001): 492–506.

Pike, Nelson, *Mystic Union: An Essay in the Phenomenology of Mysticism* (Ithaca, NY: Cornell University Press, 1992).

Plantinga, Alvin, *Warranted Christian Belief* (Oxford: Oxford University Press, 2000).

Plantinga, Alvin and Wolterstorff, Nicholas (eds), *Faith and Rationality* (Notre Dame, IN: University of Notre Dame Press, 1983).

Proudfoot, Wayne, *Religious Experience* (Los Angeles: University of California Press, 1985).

Raphael, Melissa, "Feminism, Constructivism, and Numinous Experience," *Religious Studies*, 30 (1994): 511–26.

Stace, Walter T., *Mysticism and Philosophy* (London: Macmillan, 1961).

Swinburne, Richard, *The Existence of God*, revised edition (Oxford: Clarendon Press, 1991).

Wainwright, William J., *Mysticism: A Study of Its Nature, Cognitive Value, and Moral Implications* (Madison, WI: University of Wisconsin Press, 1981).

Yandell, Keith, *The Epistemology of Religious Experience* (New York: Cambridge University Press, 1993).

Yazdi, Mehdi Ha'iri, *The Principles of Epistemology in Islamic Philosophy* (Albany, NY: State University of New York Press, 1992).

Zagzebski, Linda (ed.), *Rational Faith: Catholic Responses to Reformed Epistemology* (Notre Dame, IN: University of Notre Dame Press, 1993).

26

The Will to Believe

William James

I have brought with me to-night something like a sermon on justification by faith to read to you, – I mean an essay in justification *of* faith, a defence of our right to adopt a believing attitude in religious matters, in spite of the fact that our merely logical intellect may not have been coerced. "The Will to Believe," accordingly, is the title of my paper.

I have long defended to my own students the lawfulness of voluntarily adopted faith; but as soon as they have got well imbued with the logical spirit, they have as a rule refused to admit my contention to be lawful philosophically, even though in point of fact they were personally all the time chock-full of some faith or other themselves. I am all the while, however, so profoundly convinced that my own position is correct, that your invitation has seemed to me a good occasion to make my statements more clear. Perhaps your minds will be more open than those with which I have hitherto had to deal. I will be as little technical as I can, though I must begin by setting up some technical distinctions that will help us in the end.

I.

Let us give the name of *hypothesis* to anything that may be proposed to our belief; and just as the electricians speak of live and dead wires, let us speak of any hypothesis as either *live* or *dead*. A live hypothesis is one which appeals as a real possibility to him to whom it is proposed. If I ask you to believe in the Mahdi, the notion makes no electric connection with your nature, – it refuses to scintillate with any credibility at all. As an hypothesis it is completely dead. To an Arab, however (even if he be not one of the Mahdi's followers), the hypothesis is among the mind's possibilities: it is alive. This shows that deadness and liveness in an hypothesis are not intrinsic properties, but relations to the individual thinker. They are measured by his willingness to act. The maximum of liveness in an hypothesis means willingness to act irrevocably. Practically, that means belief; but there is some believing tendency wherever there is willingness to act at all.

"The Will to Believe" from *The Will to Believe and Other Essays in Popular Philosophy by* William James (New York: Longmans Green and Co., 1902), pp. 1–20; 22–30.

Next, let us call the decision between two hypotheses an *option*. Options may be of several kinds. They may be – 1, *living* or *dead*; 2, *forced* or *avoidable*; 3, *momentous* or *trivial*; and for our purposes we may call an option a *genuine* option when it is of the forced, living, and momentous kind.

1. A living option is one in which both hypotheses are live ones. If I say to you: "Be a theosophist or be a Mohammedan," it is probably a dead option, because for you neither hypothesis is likely to be alive. But if I say: "Be an agnostic or be a Christian," it is otherwise: trained as you are, each hypothesis makes some appeal, however small, to your belief.

2. Next, if I say to you: "Choose between going out with your umbrella or without it," I do not offer you a genuine option, for it is not forced. You can easily avoid it by not going out at all. Similarly, if I say, "Either love me or hate me," "Either call my theory true or call it false," your option is avoidable. You may remain indifferent to me, neither loving nor hating, and you may decline to offer any judgment as to my theory. But if I say, "Either accept this truth or go without it," I put on you a forced option, for there is no standing place outside of the alternative. Every dilemma based on a complete logical disjunction, with no possibility of not choosing, is an option of this forced kind.

3. Finally, if I were Dr Nansen and proposed to you to join my North Pole expedition, your option would be momentous; for this would probably be your only similar opportunity, and your choice now would either exclude you from the North Pole sort of immortality altogether or put at least the chance of it into your hands. He who refuses to embrace a unique opportunity loses the prize as surely as if he tried and failed. *Per contra*, the option is trivial when the opportunity is not unique, when the stake is insignificant, or when the decision is reversible if it later prove unwise. Such trivial options abound in the scientific life. A chemist finds an hypothesis live enough to spend a year in its verification: he believes in it to that extent. But if his experiments prove inconclusive either way, he is quit for his loss of time, no vital harm being done.

It will facilitate our discussion if we keep all these distinctions well in mind.

II.

The next matter to consider is the actual psychology of human opinion. When we look at certain facts, it seems as if our passional and volitional nature lay at the root of all our convictions. When we look at others, it seems as if they could do nothing when the intellect had once said its say. Let us take the latter facts up first.

Does it not seem preposterous on the very face of it to talk of our opinions being modifiable at will? Can our will either help or hinder our intellect in its perceptions of truth? Can we, by just willing it, believe that Abraham Lincoln's existence is a myth, and that the portraits of him in *McClure's Magazine* are all of some one else? Can we, by any effort of our will, or by any strength of wish that it were true, believe ourselves well and about when we are roaring with rheumatism in bed, or feel certain that the sum of the two one-dollar bills in our pocket must be a hundred dollars? We can *say* any of these things, but we are absolutely impotent to believe them; and of just such things is the whole fabric of the truths that we do believe in made up, – matters of fact, immediate or remote, as Hume said, and relations between ideas, which are either there or not there for us if we see them so, and which if not there cannot be put there by any action of our own.

In Pascal's *Thoughts* there is a celebrated passage known in literature as Pascal's wager. In it he tries to force us into Christianity by reasoning as if our concern with truth resembled our concern with the stakes in a game of chance. Translated freely his words are these: You must either believe or not believe that God is – which will you do? Your human reason cannot say. A game is going on between you and the nature of things which at the day of judgment will bring out either heads or tails. Weigh what your gains and your losses would be if you should stake all you have on heads, or God's existence: if you win in such case, you gain eternal beatitude; if you lose, you lose nothing at all. If there were an infinity of chances, and only one for God in this wager, still you ought to stake your all on God; for though you surely risk a finite loss by this procedure, any finite loss is reasonable, even a certain one is reasonable, if there is but the possibility of infinite gain. Go, then, and take holy water, and have masses said; belief will come and stupefy your scruples, – *Cela vous fera croire et vous abêtira*. Why should you not? At bottom, what have you to lose?

You probably feel that when religious faith expresses itself thus, in the language of the gaming-table, it is put to its last trumps. Surely Pascal's own personal belief in masses and holy water had far other springs; and this celebrated page of his is but an argument for others, a last desperate snatch at a weapon against the hardness of the unbelieving heart. We feel that a faith in masses and holy water adopted wilfully after such a mechanical calculation would lack the inner soul of faith's reality; and if we were ourselves in the place of the Deity, we should probably take particular pleasure in cutting off believers of this pattern from their infinite reward. It is evident that unless there be some pre-existing tendency to believe in masses and holy water, the option offered to the will by Pascal is not a living option. Certainly no Turk ever took to masses and holy water on its account; and even to us Protestants these means of salvation seem such foregone impossibilities that Pascal's logic, invoked for them specifically, leaves us unmoved. As well might the Mahdi write to us, saying, "I am the Expected One whom God has created in his effulgence. You shall be infinitely happy if you confess me; otherwise you shall be cut off from the light of the sun. Weigh, then, your infinite gain if I am genuine against your finite sacrifice if I am not!" His logic would be that of Pascal; but he would vainly use it on us, for the hypothesis he offers us is dead. No tendency to act on it exists in us to any degree.

The talk of believing by our volition seems, then, from one point of view, simply silly. From another point of view it is worse than silly, it is vile. When one turns to the magnificent edifice of the physical sciences, and sees how it was reared; what thousands of disinterested moral lives of men lie buried in its mere foundations; what patience and postponement, what choking down of preference, what submission to the icy laws of outer fact are wrought into its very stones and mortar; how absolutely impersonal it stands in its vast augustness, – then how besotted and contemptible seems every little sentimentalist who comes blowing his voluntary smoke-wreaths, and pretending to decide things from out of his private dream! Can we wonder if those bred in the rugged and manly school of science should feel like spewing such subjectivism out of their mouths? The whole system of loyalties which grow up in the schools of science go dead against its toleration; so that it is only natural that those who have caught the scientific fever should pass over to the opposite extreme, and write sometimes as if the incorruptibly truthful intellect ought positively to prefer bitterness and unacceptableness to the heart in its cup.

> It fortifies my soul to know
> That, though I perish, Truth is so –

sings Clough, while Huxley exclaims: "My only consolation lies in the reflection that, however bad our posterity may become, so far as they hold by the plain rule of not pretending to believe what they have no reason to believe, because it may be to their advantage so to pretend [the word 'pretend' is surely here redundant], they will not have reached the lowest depth of immorality." And that delicious *enfant terrible* Clifford writes: "Belief is desecrated when given to unproved and unquestioned statements for the solace and private pleasure of the believer. . . . Who so would deserve well of his fellows in this matter will guard the purity of his belief with a very fanaticism of jealous care, lest at any time it should rest on an unworthy object, and catch a stain which can never be wiped away. . . . If [a] belief has been accepted on insufficient evidence [even though the belief be true, as Clifford on the same page explains] the pleasure is a stolen one. . . . It is sinful because it is stolen in defiance of our duty to mankind. That duty is to guard ourselves from such beliefs as from a pestilence which may shortly master our own body and then spread to the rest of the town. . . . It is wrong always, everywhere, and for every one, to believe anything upon insufficient evidence."

III.

All this strikes one as healthy, even when expressed, as by Clifford, with somewhat too much of robustious pathos in the voice. Free-will and simple wishing do seem, in the matter of our credences, to be only fifth wheels to the coach. Yet if any one should thereupon assume that intellectual insight is what remains after wish and will and sentimental preference have taken wing, or that pure reason is what then settles our opinions, he would fly quite as directly in the teeth of the facts.

It is only our already dead hypotheses that our willing nature is unable to bring to life again. But what has made them dead for us is for the most part a previous action of our willing nature of an antagonistic kind. When I say "willing nature," I do not mean only such deliberate volitions as may have set up habits of belief that we cannot now escape from, – I mean all such factors of belief as fear and hope, prejudice and passion, imitation and partisanship, the circum-pressure of our caste and set. As a matter of fact we find ourselves believing, we hardly know how or why. Mr Balfour gives the name of "authority" to all those influences, born of the intellectual climate, that make hypotheses possible or impossible for us, alive or dead. Here in this room, we all of us believe in molecules and the conservation of energy, in democracy and necessary progress, in Protestant Christianity and the duty of fighting for "the doctrine of the immortal Monroe," all for no reasons worthy of the name. We see into these matters with no more inner clearness, and probably with much less, than any disbeliever in them might possess. His unconventionality would probably have some grounds to show for its conclusions; but for us, not insight, but the *prestige* of the opinions, is what makes the spark shoot from them and light up our sleeping magazines of faith. Our reason is quite satisfied, in nine hundred and ninety-nine cases out of every thousand of us, if it can find a few arguments that will do to recite in case our credulity is criticised by some one else. Our faith is faith in some one else's faith, and in the greatest matters this is most the case. Our belief in truth itself, for instance, that there is a truth, and that our minds and it are made for each other, – what is it but a passionate affirmation of desire, in which our social system backs us up? We want to have a truth; we want to believe that our experiments and studies and discussions must put us in a continually better and better position towards it; and on this line we agree to fight out our thinking lives. But if a pyrrhonistic sceptic

asks us *how we know* all this, can our logic find a reply? No! certainly it cannot. It is just one voli-tion against another, – we willing to go in for life upon a trust or assumption which he, for his part, does not care to make.

As a rule we disbelieve all facts and theories for which we have no use. Clifford's cosmic emotions find no use for Christian feelings. Huxley belabors the bishops because there is no use for sacerdo-talism in his scheme of life. Newman, on the contrary, goes over to Romanism, and finds all sorts of reasons good for staying there, because a priestly system is for him an organic need and delight. Why do so few "scientists" even look at the evidence for telepathy, so called? Because they think, as a leading biologist, now dead, once said to me, that even if such a thing were true, scientists ought to band together to keep it sup-pressed and concealed. It would undo the uni-formity of Nature and all sorts of other things without which scientists cannot carry on their pursuits. But if this very man had been shown something which as a scientist he might *do* with telepathy, he might not only have examined the evidence, but even have found it good enough. This very law which the logicians would impose upon us – if I may give the name of logicians to those who would rule out our willing nature here – is based on nothing but their own natural wish to exclude all elements for which they, in their professional quality of logicians, can find no use.

Evidently, then, our non-intellectual nature does influence our convictions. There are passional tendencies and volitions which run before and others which come after belief, and it is only the latter that are too late for the fair; and they are not too late when the previous passional work has been already in their own direction. Pascal's argument, instead of being powerless, then seems a regular clincher, and is the last stroke needed to make our faith in masses and holy water complete. The state of things is evidently far from simple; and pure insight and logic, whatever they might do ideally, are not the only things that really do produce our creeds.

IV.

Our next duty, having recognized this mixed-up state of affairs, is to ask whether it be simply reprehensible and pathological, or whether, on the contrary, we must treat it as a normal element in making up our minds. The thesis I defend is, briefly stated, this: *Our passional nature not only lawfully may, but must, decide an option between propositions, whenever it is a genuine option that cannot by its nature be decided on intellectual grounds; for to say, under such circumstances, "Do not decide, but leave the question open," is itself a passional decision, – just like deciding yes or no, – and is attended with the same risk of losing the truth.* The thesis thus abstractly expressed will, I trust, soon become quite clear. But I must first indulge in a bit more of preliminary work.

V.

It will be observed that for the purposes of this discussion we are on "dogmatic" ground, – ground, I mean, which leaves systematic philosophical scepticism altogether out of account. The postulate that there is truth, and that it is the destiny of our minds to attain it, we are deliberately resolving to make, though the sceptic will not make it. We part company with him, therefore, absolutely, at this point. But the faith that truth exists, and that our minds can find it, may be held in two ways. We may talk of the *empiricist* way and of the *absolutist* way of believing in truth. The absolutists in this matter say that we not only can attain to knowing truth, but we can *know when* we have attained to knowing it; while the empiricists think that although we may attain it, we cannot infallibly know when. To *know* is one thing, and to know for certain *that* we know is another. One may hold to the first being possible without the second; hence the empiricists and the absolutists, although neither of them is a sceptic in the usual philosophic sense of the term, show very different degrees of dogmatism in their lives.

[...]

You believe in objective evidence, and I do. Of some things we feel that we are certain: we know, and we know that we do know. There is something hat gives a click inside of us, a bell that strikes twelve, when the hands of our mental clock have swept the dial and meet over the meridian hour. The greatest empiricists among us are only empiricists on reflection: when left to their instincts, they dogmatize like infallible popes. When the Cliffords tell us how sinful it is to be Christians on such "insufficient evidence," insufficiency is really the last thing they have in mind. For them the evidence is absolutely sufficient, only it makes the other way. They believe so completely in an anti-christian order of the universe that there is no living option: Christianity is a dead hypothesis from the start.

VI.

But now, since we are all such absolutists by instinct, what in our quality of students of philosophy ought we to do about the fact? Shall we espouse and indorse it? Or shall we treat it as a weakness of our nature from which we must free ourselves, if we can?

I sincerely believe that the latter course is the only one we can follow as reflective men. Objective evidence and certitude are doubtless very fine ideals to play with, but where on this moonlit and dream-visited planet are they found? I am, therefore, myself a complete empiricist so far as my theory of human knowledge goes. I live, to be sure, by the practical faith that we must go on experiencing and thinking over our experience, for only thus can our opinions grow more true; but to hold any one of them – I absolutely do not care which – as if it never could be reinterpretable or corrigible, I believe to be a tremendously mistaken attitude, and I think that the whole history of philosophy will bear me out. There is but one indefectibly certain truth, and that is the truth that pyrrhonistic scepticism itself leaves standing, – the truth that the present phenomenon of consciousness exists. That, however, is the bare starting-point of knowledge, the mere admission of a stuff to be philosophized about. The various philosophies are but so many attempts at expressing what this stuff really is. And if we repair to our libraries what disagreement do we discover! Where is a certainly true answer found? Apart from abstract propositions of comparison (such as two and two are the same as four), propositions which tell us nothing by themselves about concrete reality, we find no proposition ever regarded by any one as evidently certain that has not either been called a falsehood, or at least had its truth sincerely questioned by some one else.

[. . .]

For what a contradictory array of opinions have objective evidence and absolute certitude been claimed! The world is rational through and through, – its existence is an ultimate brute fact; there is a personal God, – a personal God is inconceivable; there is an extra-mental physical world immediately known, – the mind can only know its own ideas; a moral imperative exists, – obligation is only the resultant of desires; a permanent spiritual principle is in every one, – there are only shifting states of mind; there is an endless chain of causes, – there is an absolute first cause; an eternal necessity, – a freedom; a purpose, – no purpose; a primal One, – a primal Many; a universal continuity, – an essential discontinuity in things; an infinity, – no infinity. There is this, – there is that; there is indeed nothing which some one has not thought absolutely true, while his neighbor deemed it absolutely false; and not an absolutist among them seems ever to have considered that the trouble may all the time be essential, and that the intellect, even with truth directly in its grasp, may have no infallible signal for knowing whether it be truth or no. When, indeed, one remembers that the most striking practical application to life of the doctrine of objective certitude has been the conscientious labors of the Holy Office of the Inquisition, one feels less tempted than ever to lend the doctrine a respectful ear.

But please observe, now, that when as empiricists we give up the doctrine of objective certitude, we do not thereby give up the quest or hope of truth itself. We still pin our faith on its existence, and still believe that we gain an ever better position towards it by systematically continuing to roll up experiences and think.

[. . .]

VII.

One more point, small but important, and our preliminaries are done. There are two ways of looking at our duty in the matter of opinion, – ways entirely different, and yet ways about whose difference the theory of knowledge seems hitherto to have shown very little concern. *We must know the truth*; and *we must avoid error*, – these are our first and great commandments as would-be knowers; but they are not two ways of stating an identical commandment, they are two separable laws. Although it may indeed happen that when we believe the truth *A*, we escape as an incidental consequence from believing the falsehood *B*, it hardly ever happens that by merely disbelieving *B* we necessarily believe *A*. We may in escaping *B* fall into believing other falsehoods, *C* or *D*, just as bad as *B*; or we may escape *B* by not believing anything at all, not even *A*.

Believe truth! Shun error! – these, we see, are two materially different laws; and by choosing between them we may end by coloring differently our whole intellectual life. We may regard the chase for truth as paramount, and the avoidance of error as secondary; or we may, on the other hand, treat the avoidance of error as more imperative, and let truth take its chance. Clifford, in the instructive passage which I have quoted, exhorts us to the latter course. Believe nothing, he tells us, keep your mind in suspense forever, rather than by closing it on insufficient evidence incur the awful risk of believing lies. You, on the other hand, may think that the risk of being in error is a very small matter when compared with the blessings of real knowledge, and be ready to be duped many times in your investigation rather than postpone indefinitely the chance of guessing true. I myself find it impossible to go with Clifford. We must remember that these feelings of our duty about either truth or error are in any case only expressions of our passional life. Biologically considered, our minds are as ready to grind out falsehood as veracity, and he who says, "Better go without belief forever than believe a lie!" merely shows his own preponderant private horror of becoming a dupe. He may be critical of many of his desires and fears, but this fear he slavishly obeys. He cannot imagine any one questioning its binding force. For my own part, I have also a horror of being duped; but I can believe that worse things than being duped may happen to a man in this world: so Clifford's exhortation has to my ears a thoroughly fantastic sound. It is like a general informing his soldiers that it is better to keep out of battle forever than to risk a single wound. Not so are victories either over enemies or over nature gained. Our errors are surely not such awfully solemn things. In a world where we are so certain to incur them in spite of all our caution, a certain lightness of heart seems healthier than this excessive nervousness on their behalf. At any rate, it seems the fittest thing for the empiricist philosopher.

VIII.

[...]

Wherever the option between losing truth and gaining it is not momentous, we can throw the chance of *gaining truth* away, and at any rate save ourselves from any chance of *believing falsehood*, by not making up our minds at all till objective evidence has come. In scientific questions, this is almost always the case; and even in human affairs in general, the need of acting is seldom so urgent that a false belief to act on is better than no belief at all. Law courts, indeed, have to decide on the best evidence attainable for the moment, because a judge's duty is to make law as well as to ascertain it, and (as a learned judge once said to me) few cases are worth spending much time over: the great thing is to have them decided on *any* acceptable principle, and got out of the way. But in our dealings with objective nature we obviously are recorders, not makers, of the truth; and decisions for the mere sake of deciding promptly and getting on to the next business would be wholly out of place. Throughout the breadth of physical nature facts are what they are quite independently of us, and seldom is there any such hurry about them that the risks of being duped by believing a premature theory need be faced. The questions here are always trivial options, the hypotheses are hardly living (at any rate not living for us spectators), the choice between believing truth or falsehood is seldom forced. The attitude of sceptical balance is therefore the absolutely wise one if we would escape mistakes. What difference, indeed, does it make to most of us whether we have or have not a theory of the Röntgen rays, whether we

believe or not in mind-stuff, or have a conviction about the causality of conscious states? It makes no difference. Such options are not forced on us. On every account it is better not to make them, but still keep weighing reasons *pro et contra* with an indifferent hand.

[...]

The question next arises: Are there not somewhere forced options in our speculative questions, and can we (as men who may be interested at least as much in positively gaining truth as in merely escaping dupery) always wait with impunity till the coercive evidence shall have arrived? It seems *a priori* improbable that the truth should be so nicely adjusted to our needs and powers as that. In the great boarding-house of nature, the cakes and the butter and the syrup seldom come out so even and leave the plates so clean. Indeed, we should view them with scientific suspicion if they did.

IX.

Moral questions immediately present themselves as questions whose solution cannot wait for sensible proof. A moral question is a question not of what sensibly exists, but of what is good, or would be good if it did exist. Science can tell us what exists; but to compare the *worths*, both of what exists and of what does not exist, we must consult not science, but what Pascal calls our heart. Science herself consults her heart when she lays it down that the infinite ascertainment of fact and correction of false belief are the supreme goods for man. Challenge the statement, and science can only repeat it oracularly, or else prove it by showing that such ascertainment and correction bring man all sorts of other goods which man's heart in turn declares. The question of having moral beliefs at all or not having them is decided by our will. Are our moral preferences true or false, or are they only odd biological phenomena, making things good or bad for *us*, but in themselves indifferent? How can your pure intellect decide? If your heart does not *want* a world of moral reality, your head will assuredly never make you believe in one. [...] Moral scepticism can no more be refuted or proved by logic than intellectual scepticism can. When we stick to it that there *is* truth (be it of either kind), we do so with our whole nature, and resolve to stand or fall by the results. The sceptic with his whole nature adopts the doubting attitude; but which of us is the wiser, Omniscience only knows.

Turn now from these wide questions of good to a certain class of questions of fact, questions concerning personal relations, states of mind between one man and another. *Do you like me or not?* – for example. Whether you do or not depends, in countless instances, on whether I meet you half-way, am willing to assume that you must like me, and show you trust and expectation. The previous faith on my part in your liking's existence is in such cases what makes your liking come. But if I stand aloof, and refuse to budge an inch until I have objective evidence, until you shall have done something apt, as the absolutists say, *ad extorquendum assensum meum*, ten to one your liking never comes. How many women's hearts are vanquished by the mere sanguine insistence of some man that they *must* love him! he will not consent to the hypothesis that they cannot. The desire for a certain kind of truth here brings about that special truth's existence; and so it is in innumerable cases of other sorts. Who gains promotions, boons, appointments, but the man in whose life they are seen to play the part of live hypotheses, who discounts them, sacrifices other things for their sake before they have come, and takes risks for them in advance? His faith acts on the powers above him as a claim, and creates its own verification.

A social organism of any sort whatever, large or small, is what it is because each member proceeds to his own duty with a trust that the other members will simultaneously do theirs. Wherever a desired result is achieved by the co-operation of many independent persons, its existence as a fact is a pure consequence of the precursive faith in one another of those immediately concerned. A government, an army, a commercial system, a ship, a college, an athletic team, all exist on this condition, without which not only is nothing achieved, but nothing is even attempted. A whole train of passengers (individually brave enough) will be looted by a few highwaymen, simply because the latter can count on one another, while each passenger fears that if he makes a movement of resistance, he will be shot before any one else backs him up. If we believed that the whole car-full would rise at once with us, we should each severally rise, and train-robbing would never even be attempted. There are, then, cases where a fact cannot come at all unless a preliminary faith exists in its coming. *And where faith in a fact can help create the fact*, that would be an insane logic which should say that faith running ahead of scientific evidence is the "lowest kind of immorality" into which a thinking being can fall. Yet such is the logic by which our scientific absolutists pretend to regulate our lives!

X.

In truths dependent on our personal action, then, faith based on desire is certainly a lawful and possibly an indispensable thing.

But now, it will be said, these are all childish human cases, and have nothing to do with great cosmical matters, like the question of religious faith. Let us then pass on to that. Religions differ so much in their accidents that in discussing the religious question we must make it very generic and broad. What then do we now mean by the religious hypothesis? Science says things are; morality says some things are better than other things; and religion says essentially two things.

First, she says that the best things are the more eternal things, the overlapping things, the things in the universe that throw the last stone, so to speak, and say the final word. "Perfection is eternal," – this phrase of Charles Secrétan seems a good way of putting this first affirmation of religion, an affirmation which obviously cannot yet be verified scientifically at all.

The second affirmation of religion is that we are better off even now if we believe her first affirmation to be true.

Now, let us consider what the logical elements of this situation are *in case the religious hypothesis in both its branches be really true*. (Of course, we must admit that possibility at the outset. If we are to discuss the question at all, it must involve a living option. If for any of you religion be a hypothesis that cannot, by any living possibility be true, then you need go no farther. I speak to the "saving remnant" alone.) So proceeding, we see, first, that religion offers itself as a *momentous* option. We are supposed to gain, even now, by our belief, and to lose by our non-belief, a certain vital good. Secondly, religion is a *forced* option, so far as that good goes. We cannot escape the issue by remaining sceptical and waiting for more light, because, although we do avoid error in that way *if religion be untrue*, we lose the good, *if it be true*, just as certainly as if we positively chose to disbelieve. It is as if a man should hesitate indefinitely to ask a certain woman to marry him because he was not perfectly sure that she would prove an angel after he brought her home. Would he not cut himself off from that particular angel-possibility as decisively as if he went and married some one else? Scepticism, then, is not avoidance of option; it is option of a certain particular kind of risk. *Better risk loss of truth than chance of error,* – that is your faith-vetoer's exact position. He is actively playing his stake as much as the believer is; he is backing the field against the religious hypothesis, just as the believer is backing the religious hypothesis against the field. To preach scepticism to us as a duty until "sufficient evidence" for religion be found, is tantamount therefore to telling us, when in presence of the religious hypothesis, that to yield to our fear of its being error is wiser and better than to yield to our hope that it may be true. It is not intellect against all passions, then; it is only intellect with one passion laying down its law. And by what, forsooth, is the supreme wisdom of this passion warranted? Dupery for dupery, what proof is there that dupery through hope is so much worse than dupery through fear? I, for one, can see no proof; and I simply refuse obedience to the scientist's command to imitate his kind of option, in a case where my own stake is important enough to give me the right to choose my own form of risk. If religion be true and the evidence for it be still insufficient, I do not wish, by putting your extinguisher upon my nature (which feels to me as if it had after all some business in this matter), to forfeit my sole chance in life of getting upon the winning side, – that chance depending, of course, on my willingness to run the risk of acting as if my passional need of taking the world religiously might be prophetic and right.

All this is on the supposition that it really may be prophetic and right, and that, even to us who are discussing the matter, religion is a live hypothesis which may be true. Now, to most of us religion comes in a still further way that makes a veto on our active faith even more illogical. The more perfect and more eternal aspect of the universe is represented in our religions as having personal form. The universe is no longer a mere *It* to us, but a *Thou*, if we are religious; and any relation that may be possible from person to person might be possible here. For instance, although in one sense we are passive portions of the universe, in another we show a curious autonomy, as if we were small active centres on our own account. We feel, too, as if the appeal of religion to us were made to our own active good-will, as if evidence might be forever withheld from us unless we met the hypothesis half-way. To take a trivial illustration: just as a man who in a company of gentlemen made no advances, asked a warrant for every concession, and believed no one's word without proof, would cut himself off by such churlishness from all the social rewards that a more trusting spirit would earn, – so here, one who should shut himself up in snarling logicality and try to make the gods extort his recognition willy-nilly, or not get it at all, might cut himself off forever from his only opportunity of making the gods' acquaintance. This feeling, forced on us we know not whence, that by obstinately believing that there are gods (although not to do so would be so easy both for our logic and our life) we are doing the universe the deepest service we can, seems part of the living essence of the religious hypothesis. If the hypothesis *were* true in all its parts, including this one, then pure intellectualism, with its veto on our making willing advances, would be an absurdity; and some participation of our sympathetic nature would be logically required. I, therefore, for one, cannot see my way to accepting the agnostic rules for truth-seeking, or wilfully agree; to keep my willing nature out of the game. I cannot do so for this plain reason, that *a rule of thinking which would absolutely prevent me from acknowledging certain kinds of truth if those kinds of truth were really there, would be an irrational rule.* That for me is the long and short of the formal logic of the situation, no matter what the kinds of truth might materially be.

I confess I do not see how this logic can be escaped. But sad experience makes me fear that some of you may still shrink from radically saying with me, *in abstracto*, that we have the right to believe at our own risk any hypothesis that is live enough to tempt our will. I suspect, however, that if this is so, it is because you have got away from the abstract logical point of view altogether, and are thinking (perhaps without realizing it) of some particular religious hypothesis which for you is dead. The freedom to "believe what we will" you apply to the case of some patent superstition; and the faith you think of is the faith defined by the schoolboy when he said, "Faith is when you believe something that you know ain't true." I can only repeat that this is misapprehension. *In concrete*, the freedom to believe can only cover living options which the intellect of the individual cannot by itself resolve; and living options never seem absurdities to him who has them to consider. When I look at the religious question as it really puts itself to concrete men, and when I think of all the possibilities which both practically and theoretically it involves, then this command that we shall put a stopper on our heart, instincts, and courage, and *wait* – acting of course meanwhile more or less as if religion were *not* true[1] – till doomsday, or till such time as our intellect and senses working together may have raked in evidence enough, – this command, I say, seems to me the queerest idol ever manufactured in the philosophic cave. Were we scholastic absolutists, there might be more excuse. If we had an infallible intellect with its objective certitudes, we might feel ourselves disloyal to such a perfect organ of knowledge in not trusting to it exclusively, in not waiting for its releasing word. But if we are empiricists, if we believe that no bell in us tolls to let us know for certain when truth is in our grasp, then it seems a piece of idle fantasticality to preach so solemnly our duty of waiting for the bell. Indeed we *may* wait if we will, – I hope you do not think that I am denying that, – but if we do so, we do so at our peril as much as if we believed. In either case we *act*, taking our life in our hands. No one of us ought to issue vetoes to the other, nor should we bandy words of abuse. We ought, on the contrary, delicately and profoundly to respect one another's mental freedom: then only shall we bring about the intellectual republic; then only shall we have that spirit of inner tolerance without which all our outer tolerance is soulless, and which is empiricism's glory; then only shall we live and let live, in speculative as well as in practical things.

---

[1] Since belief is measured by action, he who forbids us to believe religion to be true, necessarily also forbids us to act as we should if we did believe it to be true. The whole defence of religious faith hinges upon action. If the action required or inspired by the religious hypothesis is in no way different from that dictated by the naturalistic hypothesis, then religious faith is a pure superfluity, better pruned away, and controversy about its legitimacy is a piece of idle trifling, unworthy of serious minds. I myself believe, of course, that the religious hypothesis gives to the world an expression which specifically determines our reactions, and makes them in a large part unlike what they might be on a purely naturalistic scheme of belief.

27

Is Belief in God Properly Basic?

Alvin Plantinga

Many philosophers have urged the *evidentialist* objection to theistic belief; they have argued that belief in God is irrational or unreasonable or not rationally acceptable or intellectually irresponsible or noetically substandard, because, as they say, there is insufficient evidence for it.[1] Many other philosophers and theologians – in particular, those in the great tradition of natural theology – have claimed that belief in God is intellectually acceptable, but only because the fact is there is sufficient evidence for it. These two groups unite in holding that theistic belief is rationally acceptable only if there is sufficient evidence for it. More exactly, they hold that a person is rational or reasonable in accepting theistic belief only if she has sufficient evidence for it – only if, that is, she knows or rationally believes some *other* propositions which support the one in question, and believes the latter on the basis of the former. In [4] I argued that the evidentialist objection is rooted in *classical foundationalism*, an enormously popular picture or total way of looking at faith, knowledge, justified belief, rationality and allied topics. This picture has been widely accepted ever since the days of Plato and Aristotle; its near relatives, perhaps, remain the dominant ways of thinking about these topics. We may

think of the classical foundationalist as beginning with the observation that some of one's beliefs may be *based upon* others; it may be that there are a pair of propositions A and B such that I believed A *on the basis of B*. Although this relation isn't easy to characterize in a revealing and non-trivial fashion, it is nonetheless familiar. I believe that the word "umbrageous" is spelled u-m-b-r-a-g-e-o-u-s: this belief is based on another belief of mine: the belief that that's how the dictionary says it's spelled. I believe that $72 \times 71 = 5112$. This belief is based upon several other beliefs I hold: that $1 \times 72 = 72$; $7 \times 2 = 14$; $7 \times 7 = 49$; $49 + 1 = 50$; and others. Some of my beliefs, however, I accept but don't accept on the basis of any other beliefs. Call these beliefs *basic*. I believe that $2 + 1 = 3$, for example, and don't believe it on the basis of other propositions. I also believe that I am seated at my desk, and that there is a mild pain in my right knee. These too are basic to me; I don't believe them on the basis of any other propositions. According to the classical foundationalist, some propositions are *properly* or *rightly* basic for a person and some are not. Those that are not, are rationally accepted only on the basis of *evidence*, where the evidence must trace back, ultimately, to what is properly basic. The existence

---

"Is Belief in God Properly Basic" by Alvin Plantinga, *Noûs* 15:1 (1981): 41–51.
[1] See, for example [1], pp. 400 ff., [2], pp. 345 ff., [3], p. 22, [6], pp. 3 ff. and [7], pp. 87 ff. In [4] I consider and reject the evidentialist objection to theistic belief.

of God, furthermore, is not among the propositions that are properly basic; hence a person is rational in accepting theistic belief only if he has evidence for it.

Now many Reformed thinkers and theologians[2] have rejected *natural theology* (thought of as the attempt to provide proofs or arguments for the existence of God). They have held not merely that the proffered arguments are unsuccessful, but that the whole enterprise is in some way radically misguided. In [5], I argue that the reformed rejection of natural theology is best construed as an inchoate and unfocused rejection of classical foundationalism. What these Reformed thinkers really mean to hold, I think, is that belief in God need not be based on argument or evidence from other propositions at all. They mean to hold that the believer is entirely within his intellectual rights in believing as he does even if he doesn't know of any good theistic argument (deductive or inductive), even if he doesn't believe that there is any such argument, and even if in fact no such argument exists. They hold that it is perfectly rational to accept belief in God without accepting it on the basis of any other beliefs or propositions at all. In a word, they hold that *belief in God is properly basic.* In this paper I shall try to develop and defend this position.

But first we must achieve a deeper understanding of the evidentialist objection. It is important to see that this contention is *normative* contention. The evidentialist objector holds that one who accepts theistic belief is in some way irrational or noetically substandard. Here "rational" and "irrational" are to be taken as normative or evaluative terms; according to the objector, the theist fails to measure up to a standard he ought to conform to. There is a right way and a wrong way with respect to belief as with respect to actions; we have duties, responsibilities, obligations with respect to the former just as with respect to the latter. So Professor Blanshard:

... everywhere and always belief has an ethical aspect. There is such a thing as a general ethics of the intellect. The main principle of that ethic I hold to be the same inside and outside religion.

This principle is simple and sweeping: Equate your assent to the evidence. [1] p. 401.

This "ethics of the intellect" can be construed variously; many fascinating issues – issues we must here forbear to enter – arise when we try to state more exactly the various options the evidentialist may mean to adopt. Initially it looks as if he holds that there is a duty or obligation of some sort not to accept without evidence such propositions as that God exists – a duty flouted by the theist who has no evidence. If he has no evidence, then it is his duty to cease believing. But there is an oft remarked difficulty: one's beliefs, for the most part, are not directly under one's control. Most of those who believe in God could not divest themselves of that belief just by trying to do so, just as they could not in that way rid themselves of the belief that the world has existed for a very long time. So perhaps the relevant obligation is not that of divesting myself of theistic belief if I have no evidence (that is beyond my power), but to try to cultivate the sorts of intellectual habits that will tend (we hope) to issue in my accepting as basic only propositions that are properly basic.

Perhaps this obligation is to be thought of *teleologically*: it is a moral obligation arising out of a connection between certain intrinsic goods and evils and the way in which our beliefs are formed and held. (This seems to be W. K. Clifford's way of construing the matter.) Perhaps it is to be thought of *aretetically*: there are valuable noetic or intellectual states (whether intrinsically or extrinsically valuable); there are also corresponding intellectual virtues, habits of acting so as to promote and enhance those valuable states. Among one's obligations, then, is the duty to try to foster and cultivate these virtues in oneself or others. Or perhaps it is to be thought of *deontologically*: this obligation attaches to us just by virtue of our having the sort of noetic equipment human beings do in fact display; it does not arise out of a connection with valuable states of affairs. Such an obligation, furthermore, could be a special sort of moral obligation; on the other hand, perhaps it is a *sui generis* non-moral obligation.

---

[2] A Reformed thinker or theologian is one whose intellectual sympathies lie with the Protestant tradition going back to John Calvin (not someone who was formerly a theologian and has since seen the light).

Still further, perhaps the evidentialist need not speak of duty or obligation here at all. Consider someone who believes that Venus is smaller than Mercury, not because he has evidence of any sort, but because he finds it amusing to hold a belief no one else does – or consider someone who holds this belief on the basis of some outrageously bad argument. Perhaps there isn't any obligation he has failed to meet. Nevertheless his intellectual condition is deficient in some way; or perhaps alternatively there is a commonly achieved excellence he fails to display. And the evidentialist objection to theistic belief, then, might be understood, as the claim, not that the theist without evidence has failed to meet an obligation, but that he suffers from a certain sort of intellectual deficiency (so that the proper attitude toward him would be sympathy rather than censure).

These are some of the ways, then, in which the evidentialist objection could be developed; and of course there are still other possibilities. For ease of exposition, let us take the claim deontologically; what I shall say will apply *mutatis mutandis* if we take it one of the other ways. The evidentialist objection, therefore, presupposes some view as to what sorts of propositions are correctly, or rightly, or justifiably taken as basic; it presupposes a view as to what is *properly* basic. And the minimally relevant claim for the evidentialist objector is that belief in God is *not* properly basic. Typically this objection has been rooted in some form of *classical foundationalism*, according to which a proposition *p* is properly basic for a person *S* if and only if *p* is either self-evident or incorrigible for *S* (modern foundationalism) or either self-evident or "evident to the senses" for *S* (ancient and medival foundationalism). In [4] I argued that both forms of foundationalism are self referentially incoherent and must therefore be rejected.

Insofar as the evidentialist objection is rooted in classical foundationalism, it is poorly rooted indeed: and so far as I know, no one has developed and articulated any other reason for supposing that belief in God is not properly basic. Of course it doesn't follow that it *is* properly basic; perhaps the class of properly basic propositions is broader than classical foundationalists think, but still not broad enough to admit belief in God. But why think so? What might be the objections to the Reformed view that belief in God is properly basic?

I've heard it argued that if I have no evidence for the existence of God, then if I accept that proposition, my belief will be groundless, or gratuitous, or arbitrary. I think this is an error; let me explain.

Suppose we consider perceptual beliefs, memory beliefs, and beliefs which ascribe mental states to other persons: such beliefs as

1   I see a tree,
2   I had breakfast this morning,

and

3   That person is angry.

Although beliefs of this sort are typically and properly taken as basic, it would be a mistake to describe them as *groundless*. Upon having experience of a certain sort, I believe that I am perceiving a tree. In the typical case I do not hold this belief on the basis of other beliefs; it is nonetheless not groundless. My having that characteristic sort of experience – to use Professor Chisholm's language, my being appeared treely to – plays a crucial role in the formation and justification of that belief. We might say this experience, together, perhaps, with other circumstances, is what *justifies* me in holding it; this is the *ground* of my justification, and, by extension, the ground of the belief itself.

If I see someone displaying typical pain behavior, I take it that he or she is in pain. Again, I don't take the displayed behavior as *evidence* for that belief; I don't infer that belief from others I hold; I don't accept it on the basis of other beliefs. Still, my perceiving the pain behavior plays a unique role in the formation and justification of that belief; as in the previous case, it forms the ground of my justification for the belief in question. The same holds for memory beliefs. I seem to remember having breakfast this morning; that is, I have an inclination to believe the proposition that I had breakfast, along with a certain past-tinged experience that is familiar to all but hard to describe. Perhaps we should say that I am appeared to pastly; but perhaps this insufficiently distinguishes the experience in question from that accompanying beliefs about the past not grounded in my own memory. The phenomonology of memory is a rich and unexplored realm; here I have no time to explore it. In this case as in the others, however, there is a justifying circumstance present, a condition that forms the ground of my justification for accepting the memory belief in question.

In each of these cases, a belief is taken as basic, and in each case properly taken as basic. In each case there is some circumstance or condition that confers justification; there is a circumstance that serves as the *ground* of justification. So in each case there will be some true proposition of the sort

4   In condition *C*, *S* is justified in taking *p* as basic.

Of course *C* will vary with *p*. For a perceptual judgment such as

5   I see a rose colored wall before me,

C will include my being appeared to in a certain fashion. No doubt *C* will include more. If I'm appeared to in the familiar fashion but know that I'm wearing rose colored glasses, or that I am suffering from a disease that causes me to be thus appeared to, no matter what the color of the nearby objects, then I'm not justified in taking (5) as basic. Similarly for memory. Suppose I know that my memory is unreliable; it often plays me tricks. In particular, when I seem to remember having breakfast, then, more often than not, I *haven't* had breakfast. Under these conditions I am not justified in taking it as basic that I had breakfast, even though I seem to remember that I did.

So being appropriately appeared to, in the perceptual case, is not sufficient for justification; some further condition – a condition hard to state in detail – is clearly necessary. The central point, here, however, is that a belief is properly basic only in certain conditions; these conditions are, we might say, the ground of its justification and, by extension, the ground of the belief itself. In this sense, basic beliefs are not, or are not necessarily, *groundless* beliefs.

Now similar things may be said about belief in God. When the Reformers claim that this belief is properly basic, they do not mean to say, of course, that there are no justifying circumstances for it, or that it is in that sense groundless or gratuitious. Quite the contrary. Calvin holds that God "reveals and daily discloses himself to the whole workmanship of the universe," and the divine art "reveals itself in the innumerable and yet distinct and well ordered variety of the heavenly host." God has so created us that we have a tendency or disposition to see his hand in the world about us. More precisely, there is in us a disposition to believe propositions of the sort *this flower was created by God* or *this vast and intricate universe was created by God* when we contemplate the flower or behold the starry heavens or think about the vast reaches of the universe.

Calvin recognizes, at least implicitly, that other sorts of conditions may trigger this disposition. Upon reading the Bible, one may be impressed with a deep sense that God is speaking to him. Upon having done what I know is cheap, or wrong, or wicked I may feel guilty in God's sight and form the belief *God disapproves of what I've done*. Upon confession and repentance, I may feel forgiven, forming the belief *God forgives me for what I've done*. A person in grave danger may turn to God, asking for his protection and help; and of course he or she then forms the belief that God is indeed able to hear and help if he sees fit. When life is sweet and satisfying, a spontaneous sense of gratitude may well up within the soul; someone in this condition may thank and praise the Lord for his goodness, and will of course form the accompanying belief that indeed the Lord is to be thanked and praised.

There are therefore many conditions and circumstances that call forth belief in God: guilt, gratitude, danger, a sense of God's presence, a sense that he speaks, perception of various parts of the universe. A complete job would explore the phenomenology of all these conditions and of more besides. This is a large and important topic; but here I can only point to the existence of these conditions.

Of course none of the beliefs I mentioned a moment ago is the simple belief that God exists. What we have instead are such beliefs as

6   God is speaking to me,
7   God has created all this,
8   God disapproves of what I have done,
9   God forgives me,

and

10   God is to be thanked and praised.

These propositions are properly basic in the right circumstances. But it is quite consistent with this to suppose that the proposition *there is such a person as God* is neither properly basic nor taken as basic by those who believe in God. Perhaps what they take as basic are such propositions as (6)–(10), believing in the existence of God on the basis of propositions such as those. From this point of view, it isn't exactly right to say that it is belief in God that is properly basic; more exactly, what are properly basic are such propositions as (6)–(10), each of which self-evidently entails that God exists. It isn't the relatively high level and general proposition *God exists* that is properly basic, but instead propositions detailing some of his attributes or actions.

Suppose we return to the analogy between belief in God and belief in the existence of perceptual objects, other persons, and the past. Here too it is relatively specific and concrete propositions rather than their more general and abstract colleagues that are properly basic. Perhaps such items are

11   There are trees,
12   There are other persons,

and

13   The world has existed for more than 5 minutes,

are not in fact properly basic; it is instead such propositions as

14   I see a tree,
15   that person is pleased,

and

16   I had breakfast more than an hour ago,

that deserve that accolade. Of course propositions of the latter sort immediately and self-evidently entail propositions of the former sort; and perhaps there is thus no harm in speaking of the former as properly basic, even though so to speak, is to speak a bit loosely.

The same must be said about belief in God. We may say, speaking loosely, that belief in God is properly basic; strictly speaking, however, it is probably not that proposition but such propositions

as (6)–(10) that enjoy that status. But the main point, here, is that belief in God or (6)–(10), are properly basic; to say so, however, is not to deny that there are justifying conditions for these beliefs, or conditions that confer justification on one who accepts them as basic. They are therefore not groundless or gratuitious.

A second objection I've often heard: if belief in God is properly basic, why can't *just any* belief be properly basic? Couldn't we say the same for any bizarre abberation we can think of? What about voodoo or astrology? What about the belief that the Great Pumpkin returns every Halloween? Could I properly take *that* as basic? And if I can't, why can I properly take belief in God as basic? Suppose I believe that if I flap my arms with sufficient vigor, I can take off and fly about the room; could I defend myself against the charge of irrationality by claiming this belief is basic? If we say that belief in God is properly basic, won't we be committed to holding that just anything, or nearly anything, can properly be taken as basic, thus throwing wide the gates to irrationalism and superstition?

Certainly not. What might lead one to think the Reformed epistemologist is in this kind of trouble? The fact that he rejects the criteria for proper basicality purveyed by classical foundationalism? But why should *that* be thought to commit him to such tolerance of irrationality? Consider an analogy. In the palmy days of positivism, the positivists went about confidently wielding their verifiability criterion and declaring meaningless much that was obviously meaningful. Now suppose someone rejected a formulation of that criterion – the one to be found in the second edition of A. J. Ayer's *Language, Truth and Logic*, for example. Would that mean she was committed to holding that

17   Twas brillig: and the slithy toves did gyre and gymble in the wabe

contrary to appearances, makes good sense? Of course not. But then the same goes for the Reformed epistemologist; the fact that he rejects the Classical Foundationalist's criterion of proper basicality does not mean that he is committed to supposing just anything is properly basic.

But what then is the problem? Is it that the Reformed epistemologist not only rejects those criteria for proper basicality, but seems in no hurry to produce what he takes to be a better substitute? If he has no such criterion, how can he fairly reject belief in the Great Pumpkin as properly basic?

This objection betrays an important misconception. How do we rightly arrive at or develop criteria for meaningfulness, or justified belief, or proper basicality? Where do they come from? Must one have such a criterion before one can sensibly make any judgments – positive or negative – about proper basicality? Surely not. Suppose I don't know of a satisfactory substitute for the criteria proposed by classical foundationalism; I am nevertheless entirely within my rights in holding that certain propositions are not properly basic in certain conditions. Some propositions seem self-evident when in fact they are not; that is the lesson of some of the Russell paradoxes. Nevertheless it would be irrational to take as basic the denial of a proposition that seems self-evident to you. Similarly, suppose it seems to you that you see a tree; you would then be irrational in taking as basic the proposition that you don't see a tree, or that there aren't any trees. In the same way, even if I don't know of some illuminating criterion of meaning, I can quite properly declare (17) meaningless.

And this raises an important question – one Roderick Chisholm has taught us to ask. What is the status of criteria for knowledge, or proper basicality, or justified belief? Typically, these are universal statements. The modern foundationalist's criterion for proper basicality, for example, is doubly universal:

18 For any proposition *A* and person *S*, *A* is properly basic for *S* if and only if *A* is incorrigible for *S* or self-evident to *S*.

But how could one know a thing like that? What are its credentials? Clearly enough, (18) isn't self-evident or just obviously true. But if it isn't, how does one arrive at it? What sorts of arguments would be appropriate? Of course a foundationalist might find (18) so appealing, he simply takes it to be true, neither offering argument for it, nor accepting it on the basis of other things he believes. If he does so, however, his noetic structure will be self-referentially incoherent. (18) itself is neither self-evident nor incorrigible; hence in

accepting (18) as basic, the modern foundationalist violates the condition of proper basicality he himself lays down in accepting it. On the other hand, perhaps the foundationalist will try to produce some argument for it from premises that are self-evident or incorrigible: it is exceedingly hard to see, however, what such an argument might be like. And until he has produced such arguments, what shall the rest of us do – we who do not find (18) at all obvious or compelling? How could he use (18) to show us that belief in God, for example, is not properly basic? Why should we believe (18), or pay it any attention?

The fact is, I think, that neither (18) nor any other revealing necessary and sufficient condition for proper basicality follows from clearly self-evident premises by clearly acceptable arguments. And hence the proper way to arrive at such a criterion is, broadly speaking, *inductive*. We must assemble examples of beliefs and conditions such that the former are obviously properly basic in the latter, and examples of beliefs and conditions such that the former are obviously *not* properly basic in the latter. We must then frame hypotheses as to the necessary and sufficient conditions of proper basicality and test these hypothesis by reference to those examples. Under the right conditions, for example, it is clearly rational to believe that you see a human person before you: a being who has thoughts and feelings, who knows and believes things, who makes decisions and acts. It is clear, furthermore, that you are under no obligation to reason to this belief from others you hold; under those conditions that belief is properly basic for you. But then (18) must be mistaken; the belief in question, under those circumstances, is properly basic, though neither self-evident nor incorrigible for you. Similarly, you may seem to remember that you had breakfast this morning, and perhaps you know of no reason to suppose your memory is playing you tricks. If so, you are entirely justified in taking that belief as basic. Of course it isn't properly basic on the criteria offered by classical foundationalists; but that fact counts not against you but against those criteria.

Accordingly, criteria for proper basicality must be reached from below rather than above; they should not be presented as *ex Cathedra*, but argued to and tested by a relevant set of examples. But there is no reason to assume, in advance, that everyone will agree on the examples. The Christian will of course suppose that belief in God is entirely proper and rational; if he doesn't accept this belief on the basis of other propositions, he will conclude that it is basic for him and quite properly so. Followers of Bertrand Russell and Madelyn Murray O'Hare may disagree, but how is that relevant? Must my criteria, or those of the Christian community, conform to their examples? Surely not. The Christian community is responsible to *its* set of examples, not to theirs.

Accordingly, the Reformed epistemologist can properly hold that belief in the Great Pumpkin is not properly basic, even though he holds that belief in God is properly basic and even if he has no full fledged criterion of proper basicality. Of course he is committed to supposing that there is a relevant *difference* between belief in God and belief in the Great Pumpkin, if he holds that the former but not the latter is properly basic. But this should prove no great embarrassment; there are plenty of candidates. These candidates are to be found in the neighborhood of the conditions I mentioned in the last section that justify and ground belief in God. Thus, for example, the Reformed epistemologist may concur with Calvin in holding that God has implanted in us a natural tendency to see his hand in the world around us; the same cannot be said for the Great Pumpkin, there being no Great Pumpkin and no natural tendency to accept beliefs about the Great Pumpkin.

By way of conclusion then: being self-evident, or incorrigible, or evident to the senses is not a necessary condition of proper basicality. Furthermore, one who holds that belief in God *is* properly basic is not thereby committed to the idea that belief in God is groundless or gratuitous or without justifying circumstances. And even if he lacks a general criterion of proper basicality, he is not obliged to suppose that just any or nearly any belief – belief in the Great Pumpkin, for example – is properly basic. Like everyone should, he begins with examples; and he may take belief in the Great Pumpkin as a paradigm of irrational basic belief.

References

[1]   Blanshard, Brand, *Reason and Belief* (London: Allen & Unwin, 1974).
[2]   Clifford, W. K., "The Ethics of Belief in *Lectures and Essays* (London: Macmillan, 1879).
[3]   Flew, A. G. N., *The Presumption of Atheism* (London: Pemberton Publishing Co., 1976).
[4]   Plantinga, A., "Is Belief in God Rational?" in *Rationality and Religious Belief*, ed. C. Delaney (Notre Dame: University of Notre Dame Press, 1979).
[5]   ———, "The Reformed Objection to Natural Theology," *Proceedings of the American Catholic Philosophical Association*, 1980.
[6]   Russell, Bertrand, "Why I am not a Christian," in *Why I am Not a Christian* (New York: Simon & Schuster, 1957).
[7]   Scrivin, Michael, *Primary Philosophy* (New York: McGraw-Hill, 1966).

28

Plantinga on Belief in God as Properly Basic

Michael Martin

Foundationalism was once a widely accepted view in epistemology and, although it has undergone modification, it still has many advocates. The motivation for the view seems compelling. All of our beliefs cannot be justified in terms of other beliefs without the justification generating an infinite regress or vicious circularity. Therefore, there must be some beliefs that do not need to be justified by other beliefs. Because they form the foundation of all knowledge, these are called basic and the statements expressing them are called basic statements.

Classical foundationalism considered only two types of basic statements: certain simple and true statements of mathematics, for example, "2 + 2 = 4," and logic, for example, "Either p or ~p," and those statements that are evident to the senses. Some foundationalists have included in the class of statements that are evident to the senses ones about observed physical objects, for example, "There is a blue bird in the tree." However, in modern times it has been more common to restrict statements that are evident to the senses to ones about the author's immediate sense impressions, for example, "I seem to see a blue bird in the tree," or "I am being appeared to bluely," or perhaps "Here now blue sense datum."

The most important representative of this point of view in contemporary philosophers of religion, Alvin Plantinga, has argued against classical foundationalism maintaining that belief in God should be considered a basic belief.[1] Although Plantinga has not to my knowledge held that all the fundamental doctrines of Christianity are basic beliefs this idea would certainly be in keeping with his general approach.

Following in a long line of Reformed thinkers, that is, thinkers influenced by the doctrines of John Calvin, Plantinga argues that traditional arguments for the existence of God are not needed for rational belief. He cites with approval Calvin's claim that God created humans in such a way that they have a strong tendency to believe in God. Although this natural tendency to believe in

"Plantinga on Belief in God as Properly Basic" from *The Case Against Christianity* by Michael Martin (Philadelphia: Temple University Press, 1991), pp. 27–32; 34. Used by permission of Temple University Press. © 1991 by Temple University. All Rights Reserved.

[1] See Alvin Plantinga, "Religious Belief Without Evidence," in *Philosophy of Religion: An Anthology*, 2nd edition, ed. Louis P. Pojman (Belmont, CA: Wadsworth Publishing Company, 1987), pp. 454–68; Alvin Plantinga, "Is Belief in God Properly Basic?" *Noûs* 15 (1981): 41–51 [see previous selection]; Alvin Plantinga, "Is Belief in God Rational?" *Rationality and Religious Belief*, ed. C. F. Delaney (Notre Dame, Ind.: University of Notre Dame Press, 1979), pp. 7–27. [. . .]

God may be partially suppressed, Plantinga argues that it is triggered by "a widely realizable condition"[2] such as "upon beholding the starry heavens, or the splendid majesty of the mountains, or the intricate, articulate beauty of a tiny flower."[3] This natural tendency to accept God in these circumstances is perfectly rational, he says. No argument is needed. He maintains that the best interpretation of Calvin's views, as well as of the other Reformed thinkers he cites, is that they rejected classical foundationalism and maintained that belief in God can itself be a properly basic belief.

Surprisingly, Plantinga insists that although belief in God and beliefs about God's attributes and actions are basic, for Reformed epistemologists this does not mean that there are no justifying circumstances or that they are without grounds. The circumstances that trigger the natural tendency to believe in God and to believe certain things about God provide the justifying circumstances for belief. So although beliefs about God are properly basic, they are not groundless.[4]

How are we to understand this claim that religious beliefs are basic but not groundless? This seems initially puzzling since one would normally suppose that basic beliefs by definition are groundless. Plantinga draws an analogy between basic statements of religion and basic statements of perception and memory. A perceptual belief, he says, is taken as properly basic only under certain circumstances. For example, if I know that I am wearing rose-tinted glasses, then I am not justified in taking the statement "I see a rose-colored wall before me" as properly basic; if I know that my memory is unreliable, I am not justified in taking the statement "I remember that I had breakfast" as properly basic. Although he admits that these conditions may be hard to specify, he maintains that their presence is necessary in order to claim that a perceptual or memory statement is basic. Similarly, he maintains that not every statement about God that is not based on argument or evidence should be considered properly basic. A statement is

properly basic only in the right circumstances. What circumstances are right? Plantinga gives no general account, but in addition to the triggering conditions mentioned above, the right circumstances include reading the Bible, having done something wrong, and being in grave danger. Thus if a person is reading the Bible and believes that God is speaking to him or her, his or her belief is properly basic.

Furthermore, Plantinga insists that although Reformed epistemologists allow belief in God to be a properly basic belief, this does not mean that they must allow that anything at all can be a basic belief. To be sure, he admits that he and other Reformed epistemologists have not supplied us with a criterion of what is properly basic. He argues, however, that this is not necessary. One can know that some beliefs in some circumstances are not properly basic without having an explicitly formulated criterion of basicness. Thus, Plantinga says that Reformed epistemologists can correctly maintain that belief in voodoo or astrology or the Great Pumpkin are not basic beliefs.

How is one to arrive at a criterion of being properly basic? According to Plantinga the route is "broadly speaking, *inductive*." "We must assemble examples of beliefs and conditions such that the former are obviously properly basic in the latter. . . . We must frame hypotheses as to the necessary and sufficient conditions of proper basicality and test these hypotheses by reference to those examples."[5] He argues that, using this procedure,

> The Christian will of course suppose that belief in God is entirely proper and rational; if he does not accept this belief on the basis of other propositions, he will conclude that it is basic for him and quite properly so. Followers of Russell and Madelyn Murray O'Hare [sic] may disagree; but how is that relevant? Must my criteria, or those of the Christian community, conform to their examples? Surely not. The Christian community is responsible to *its* set of examples, not to theirs.[6]

2   Plantinga, "Religious Belief Without Evidence," p. 464.
3   Ibid., p. 465.
4   Plantinga, "Is Belief in God Properly Basic?" p. 46 [see p. [175] above].
5   Plantinga, "Religious Belief Without Evidence," p. 468 [see also p. 177 above].
6   Ibid.

The problems with Plantinga's defense of the thesis that belief in God is basic can only be summarized here.[7] First, to consider belief in God as a basic belief seems completely out of keeping with the spirit and intention of foundationalism. Whatever else it was and whatever its problems, foundationalism was an attempt to provide critical tools for objectively appraising knowledge claims and to give knowledge a nonrelativistic basis. Paradoxically, Plantinga's foundationalism is radically relativistic and puts any belief beyond rational appraisal once it is declared basic.

Second, Plantinga's claim that his proposal would not allow any belief to become a basic belief is misleading. It is true that it would not allow any belief to become a basic belief *from the point of view of Reformed epistemologists.* However, it would seem to allow any belief at all to become basic from the point of view of *some* community.[8] Although Reformed epistemologists would not have to accept voodoo beliefs as rational, voodoo followers would be able to claim that insofar as they are basic in the voodoo community they are rational, and, moreover, that Reformed thought was irrational in this community.

Third, on this view the rationality of any belief is absurdly easy to obtain. The cherished belief that is held without reason by *any* group could be considered properly basic by the group's members. There would be no way to evaluate critically any beliefs so considered. The community's most cherished beliefs and the conditions that, according to the community, correctly triggered such beliefs would be accepted uncritically by the members of the community as just so many more examples of basic beliefs and justifying conditions.

Fourth, Plantinga seems to suppose that there is a consensus in the Christian community about what beliefs are basic and what conditions justify these. But this is not so for some Christians believe in God on the basis of the traditional arguments or on the basis of religious experiences; their belief in God is not basic. More important, there would be no agreement on whether certain doctrinal beliefs, for example, ones concerning the authority of the pope, the composition of the Trinity, the nature of Christ, or the means of salvation, were true, let alone basic.

Fifth, although there may not at present be any clear criterion for what can be a basic belief, belief in God seems peculiarly inappropriate for inclusion in the class since there are clear disanalogies between it and the basic beliefs allowable by classical foundationalism.[9] In his critique of classical foundationalism, Plantinga has suggested that belief in other minds and the external world should be considered basic. There are, however, many plausible alternatives to belief in an all-good, all-powerful, all-knowing God, but there are few, if any, plausible alternatives to belief in other minds and the external world. Although there are many skeptical arguments against belief in other minds and the external world, there are no arguments that are taken seriously that purport to show that there are no other minds or that there is no external world. In this world atheism and agnosticism are live options for many intelligent people; solipsism is an option only for the mentally ill.

Sixth, as we have seen, Plantinga, following Calvin, says that some conditions that trigger belief in God or particular beliefs about God also justify these beliefs so that although these beliefs concerning God are basic, they are not groundless. Although Plantinga gives no general account of what these justifying conditions are, he presents some examples of what he means and likens these justifying conditions to those of

[7] There are also problems with his critique of classical foundationalism. See Michael Martin, *Atheism: A Philosophical Justification* (Philadelphia: Temple University Press, 1990), chap. 10.

[8] Cf. Anthony Kenny, *Faith and Reason* (New York: Columbia University Press 1983), p. 16; William J. Abraham, *An Introduction to the Philosophy of Religion* (Englewood Cliffs, NJ: Prentice-Hall, 1985), pp. 93–6; Philip Quinn, "In Search of the Foundations of Theism," in *Philosophy of Religion*, ed. Pojman, p. 472; Louis Pojman, "Can Religious Belief Be Rational?" in *Philosophy of Religion*, ed. Pojman, p. 481; J. Wesley Robbins, "Is Belief in God Properly Basic?" *International Journal for the Philosophy of Religion* 14 (1983): 241–8.

[9] See Abraham, *An Introduction to the Philosophy of Religion*, p. 95.

properly basic perceptual and memory state-ments.[10] The problem here is, however, the weak-ness of the analogy. As Plantinga points out, before we take a perceptual or memory belief as properly basic we must have evidence that one's perception or memory is not faulty. Part of one's justification for believing that one's perception or memory is not faulty is that in general it agrees with the perception or memory of our epistemological peers; that is, our equals in intelligence, perspicacity, honesty, thorough-ness, and other relevant epistemic virtues[11] and also with one's other experiences.[12]

We have already seen that lack of agreement is commonplace in religious contexts. Different beliefs are triggered in different people when they behold the starry heavens or read the Bible. Beholding the starry heavens can trigger a pantheistic belief or a purely aesthetic response without any religious component; sometimes no particular response or belief at all is triggered. From what we know about the variations of religious belief, it is likely that people would not have the-istic beliefs when they behold the starry heavens if they had been raised in nontheistic environ-ments. In short, there is no consensus in the Christian community, let alone among Bible readers generally. So, unlike perception and memory, there are no grounds for claiming that a belief about God is properly basic since the conditions that trigger it yield widespread dis-agreement among epistemological peers.

[10] In his most recent writings Plantinga has begun to relate epistemic justification to proper cognitive function-ing and the latter to God's designing human beings in such a way that they tend to have true beliefs under certain circumstances. See Alvin Plantinga, "Epistemic Justification," *Noûs* 20 (1986): 15.
[11] Cf. Gary Gutting, *Religious Belief and Religious Skepticism* (Notre Dame, IN: University of Notre Dame Press, 1982), p. 83.
[12] See Richard Grigg, "Theism and Properly Basicality: A Response to Plantinga," *International Journal for the Philosophy of Religion* 14 (1983): 126.

29

Religious Experience Justifies Religious Belief

William P. Alston

1 Background

[T]he first job is to get straight about what *religious experience* is. In the widest sense, the term can be applied to any experiences one has in connection with one's religious life, including a sense of guilt or release, joys, longings, a sense of gratitude, etc. But here we are more specifically concerned with experiences taken by their possessor to be an awareness of God. As a way of focusing on this distinctive kind of "religious experience," I have called it *perception of God*.[1]

Two comments on this terminology. First, I use "perception" in a "phenomenological" sense. I will call anything a "perception of X" (a tree, God, or whatever) provided that is what it seems to the subject to be, provided the subject takes it to be a *presentation* of X to the subject's experience. It is then a further question whether X is really present to the subject, whether the subject *really* perceives X (in a stronger sense of "perceive"). When the supposed object of the perception is God, I will speak of *mystical perception*. Second, "God" may be used in a wider or narrower way. In the Judeo-Christian tradition and in Islam we think of God as a supreme personal being; but

in Buddhism the object of worship is often taken to be some sort of impersonal reality. To maximize coverage, I will let "God" range over any *supreme reality*, however construed.

What kinds of beliefs about God might possibly be supported by religious experience? It is difficult to draw sharp boundaries here, but for purposes of this discussion I will restrict myself to beliefs about what God is doing vis-à-vis the subject – comforting, guiding, strengthening, communicating a message – and about divine characteristics one might conceivably experience God as having – being powerful, loving, merciful. Let's call these *M-beliefs* ("M" for "manifestation").

It will make the topic more concrete to consider a particular case of mystical perception. Here is one taken from William James.

> [A]ll at once I . . . felt the presence of God – I tell of the thing just as I was conscious of it – as if his goodness and his power were penetrating me altogether. . . . I thanked God that in the course of my life he had taught me to know him, that he sustained my life and took pity both on the insignificant creature and on the sinner that I was. I begged him ardently that my life might

"Religious Experience Justifies Religious Belief" by William P. Alston, in *Contemporary Debates in Philosophy of Religion*, ed. Michael Peterson and Raymond J. Van Arragaon (Malden, MA: Blackwell Publishers, 2004), pp. 135–44. Reprinted by permission of the publishers, Blackwell Publishing.

[1]   William P. Alston, *Perceiving God* (Ithaca, NY: Cornell University Press, 1991).

be consecrated to the doing of his will. I felt his reply, which was that I should do his will from day to day, in humility and poverty, leaving him, The Almighty God, to judge of whether I should some time be called to bear witness more conspicuously. Then, slowly, the ecstasy left my heart; that is, I felt that God had withdrawn the communion which he had granted . . . I asked myself if it were possible that Moses on Sinai could have had a more intimate communication with God. I think it well to add that in this ecstasy of mine God had neither form, color, odor, nor taste; moreover, that the feeling of his presence was accompanied by no determinate localization . . . But the more I seek words to express this intimate intercourse, the more I feel the impossibility of describing the thing by any of our usual images. At bottom the expression most apt to render what I felt is this: God was present, though invisible; he fell under no one of my senses, yet my consciousness perceived him.[2]

This report is typical in several respects.

(1)   The awareness of God is *experiential*, as contrasted with *thinking* of God or *reasoning* about him. It seems to involve a *presentation* of God.

(2)   The experience is *direct*. One seems to be *immediately* aware of God rather than through being aware of something else. It is like seeing another human being in front of you, rather than like seeing that person on television. But there are more indirect experiences of God.

There was a mysterious presence in nature . . . which was my greatest delight, especially when as happened from time to time, *nature became lit up from inside* with something that came from beyond itself.[3]

(3)   The experience is a *non-sensory* presentation of God. But there are also experiences of God with sensory content.

I awoke and looking out of my window saw what I took to be a luminous star which

gradually came nearer, and appeared as a soft slightly blurred white light. I was seized with violent trembling, but had no fear. I knew that what I felt was great awe. This was followed by a sense of overwhelming love coming to me, and going out from me, then of great compassion from this Outer Presence.[4]

(4)   It is a *focal* experience, one in which the awareness of God is so intense as to blot out everything else. But there are also milder experiences that persist over long periods of time as a background to everyday experience.

God surrounds me like the physical atmosphere. He is closer to me than my own breath. In him literally I live and move and have my being.[5]

This discussion will be limited to *direct, non-sensory, focal* experiences, since they give rise to the strongest claims to be genuinely aware of God.

2   The Case for Experiential Support

The reporter of our first case (a French-speaking Swiss whom I will call "Bonnet") obviously supposes that he has learned something about God from his experience. In particular he supposes that he has perceived God to be loving and powerful, and perceived him to be telling him, Bonnet, to do his will from day to day. And since the perception was completely convincing to him, he has no more inclination to doubt it than he would have to doubt the veracity of a normal visual perception of an oak tree. But, of course, this confidence of his does not guarantee that the experience is, in fact, veridical. Even with sense perception one can be deceived. At dusk one can suppose that what one sees in the distance is a car when actually it is a cow. With both sense perception and mystical perception contradictions between reports prevent us from taking all of them to be veridical. Think of the divergent reports that witnesses give of automobile accidents. As

[2]   William James, *The Varieties of Religious Experience* (New York: Modern Library, 1902), pp. 67–8.
[3]   Timothy Beardsworth, *A Sense of Presence* (Oxford: Religious Experience Research Unit, 1977), p. 19.
[4]   Ibid., p. 30.
[5]   James, *Varieties of Religious Experience*, p. 71.

for mystical perception, some people think they perceive God telling them to murder as many Communists, postal workers, or schoolteachers as possible, while other people perceive God as supremely loving. They can't all be right. Hence in both areas we need some way of separating the sheep from the goats.

But though neither mystical experience nor sense experience is infallible, there are solid reasons for taking beliefs formed on the basis of either kind of experience to be, as we might say, *prima facie* rationally acceptable, rationally acceptable in the absence of sufficient reasons to the contrary (*overriders*). (Swinburne calls this "The Principle of Credulity."[6]) In other words, being formed on the basis of experience gives a belief an *initial credibility*, a *presumption* of truth. It is innocent until proved guilty. It is rationally acceptable (justified, warranted) so long as no one has sufficient reasons for taking it to be false (*rebutters*) or for taking the particular situation to be such that the experience does not have its usual force (*underminers*). Thus overriders come in two versions; rebutters and underminers. For a simple example concerning sense perception, suppose I think I see an elephant in my front yard. My belief that there is an elephant there would be justified unless there are strong reasons for thinking that there is no elephant in the area (rebutter) or that my vision is not working properly (underminer).

The main reason for accepting the Principle of Credulity is that it is the only alternative to complete skepticism about experience. Consider how we would show sense perception to be a generally reliable source of belief if we did *not* accord every perceptual belief an initial credibility. A survey of the most promising attempts to construct such an argument reveals that any otherwise strong candidate suffers from "epistemic circularity."[7] This consists of relying on the belief source whose credentials we seek to establish to provide us with premises for that establishment. Arguments for the reliability of sense perception that are not disqualified on other grounds (and many that are) depend on premises for which our only basis is sense perception. As a simple example, consider the popular line of thought that sense perception proves itself by its fruits, particularly by the way in which it puts us in a position to predict and thereby to control to some extent the course of events. It provides us with data on the basis of which we establish law-like generalizations, which we can then use as the basis for prediction and control. In this way we learn that milk sours more slowly when cold than when warm. This puts us in a position to predict that a refrigerated bottle of milk will last longer than an unrefrigerated one, and we can use this knowledge to control the condition of our milk. This is the humblest of examples, and the predictive power is greatly increased in scope and precision as we move further into the higher reaches of science; but the general point is the same. If sense perception weren't usually giving us the straight story about what is happening around us, how could we have so much success in anticipating the future course of events?

That sounds right. But how do we know that we are often successful in prediction? By induction from particular cases of success, obviously. But how do we know that we are successful in particular cases? By using our senses to determine whether what was predicted actually occurred. It is not as if an angel tells us this, or as if rational intuition does the job. But then the argument is tainted with epistemic circularity. We have to rely on sense perception for some of our crucial premises. The argument establishes the reliability of sense perception only if sense perception is in fact reliable. And that leaves us wondering whether that condition is satisfied.

If, on the other hand, we begin by assuming that perceptual beliefs are justifiably taken as true in the absence of sufficient overriders, we can use our empirical knowledge to support the claim that sense perception is reliable. For there will be many perceptual reports that we have no sufficient reasons *against*, and these can be used with impunity to pile up empirical evidence for the reliability of sense perception.

---

[6] Richard Swinburne, *The Existence of God* (Oxford: Clarendon Press, 1979).
[7] See William P. Alston, *The Reliability of Sense Perception* (Ithaca, NY: Cornell University Press, 1993).

But when the Principle of Credulity is applied to mystical perception, it will support the attribution of a significant degree of reliability only if there are no strong reasons for denying rational acceptability to all or most religious beliefs based on mystical experience. But many such reasons have been suggested. Most of these are based on dissimilarities – real or alleged – between sense perception and mystical perception. I will critically examine several of them in the next few sections.

3   Some Obvious Differences between Sense Experience and Mystical Experience

(1)   Sense experience is a common possession of mankind, while mystical experience is not. To be sure, several recent surveys have shown that many more people than is commonly supposed, even in our "secular" society, take themselves to have been directly aware of the presence of God. And the incidence in many other cultures is much higher. But still, by no means all people enjoy mystical experience, whereas no human being is totally without sense experience. And most of us have a rich variety of the latter.

(2)   Sense experience is continuously and unavoidably present during all our waking hours, while for most of those who are not wholly bereft of mystical experience, it is, at best, enjoyed only rarely. It is a very unusual person who, like Brother Lawrence of *The Practice of the Presence of God* fame, is blessed with a constant experiential awareness of God.

(3)   Sense experience, especially visual experience, is vivid and richly detailed, while mystical experience is meager and obscure. Though Bonnet's experience of God was deeply meaningful to him, and though he took it to show him something about God, still it could not begin to compare in richness and complexity of detail with a single glance out my study window at my front yard, crammed as that latter experience is with details of trees, flowers, passing cars in the street, neighbors' houses, etc.

Obvious differences like these make it difficult for some people to believe that mystical perception involves a genuine experience of objective reality. But on careful reflection we can see that this reaction lacks any basis worthy of the name.

We can usefully treat differences (1) and (2) together: (1) degree of dispersal in the general population and (2) frequency in the life of a given subject. Both have to do with the proportion of some relevant totality. So what does the extent of distribution in the population or the frequency within one subject have to do with the question of whether the experience contains important information? Why suppose that what happens only rarely cannot have cognitive value? We wouldn't dream of applying this principle to scientific or philosophical insight. That comes only rarely, and only to few people, but it is not denigrated for that reason. Would any reasonable person suggest that the kind of insight that led Einstein to the development of his Special and General Theory of Relativity is inferior in cognitive value to everyday visual awareness of one's surroundings, on the grounds that the latter is more widely shared and occurs more frequently? We can safely neglect frequency as an index to informational content.

As for (3), richness and detail of content, I can't see that it fares any better. Within sense perception there are large differences of this sort between sense modalities. Vision is miles ahead of the others in that regard, with touch and hearing placing a rather distant second, followed at a more considerable distance by taste and smell. One glance at a scene before me gives a much greater variety of information that one sniff or one taste. And the latter are severely restricted as to the kinds of information they provide. One glance at a scene can tell me that I am looking across a verdant valley at a green hillside on which are beautiful meadows, forests, barns, white farmhouses, and cows. How much more I learn from this than from a sniff that informs me that there is hot tar nearby or from a taste that tells me that the substance tasted has an acrid and rather smoky flavor. Yet this is no reason for denying that taste and smell can involve veridical perception of external realities and give us genuine information about them, albeit not as much. We cannot sensibly hold that less information is no information at all. That would be like maintaining that a simple folk melody, since it is much less complex than the Bach B Minor Mass, is not really music, or that since a crude map I draw for you of the route to my house gives much less geographical information than the Rand-McNally Atlas, it gives no information at all.

4   Attempted Naturalistic Explanations of Mystical Experience

A more serious argument for a general dismissal of epistemological claims for mystical perception is based on the general principle that one perceives an object X in having a certain experience only if X is among the causes of that experience, and only if X plays one causal role rather than others in the production of that experience. With vision, for example, one sees a dog only if light reflected from the dog produces the retinal stimulation that sets off the neural chain reaction that eventually leads to the excitations in the brain that are responsible for the visual experience in question. We get analogous stories for other modes of sense perception. Extrapolating this line of thought to mystical experience, such an experience can be a perception of God only if God plays a certain kind of causal role in the production of that experience. But it has frequently been claimed that mystical experience can be fully explained (its causes can be fully set out) in terms of processes within the natural world, without mentioning God at all. But if so, God does not figure anywhere among its causes and therefore has no claim to be perceived in a mystical experience. And if Bonnet was not perceiving God, as he supposed, then presumably the experience has nothing to tell him about God, at least directly.

Even if mystical experience can be adequately explained in terms of purely this-worldly factors (and I will have more to say about this below), it would be much too fast to conclude that God does not figure among the causes of mystical experience. Consider the point that though sense experience can be adequately explained by what goes on in the brain, we all take it that objects outside the brain are perceived in those experiences. How can this be? Obviously, it is because though brain processes are the *direct* cause of sensory experience, those processes themselves have causes, which in turn have causes . . . and if we trace that causal chain back

far enough, we come to the external objects that are perceived. Analogously, even if the direct causes of mystical experience are all within nature, it is still possible that God figures further back in the causal chain that leads to that experience. And, indeed, that is the case, according to theism and theistic religions, which hold that God is responsible for the existence and functioning of the world of nature.

But, it may be contended, even if that were the case, it would not follow that God figures in the causal chain in such a way as to be the object of perception. Going back to visual perception, many items figure in the causal chain leading to visual experience – neural transmission to the brain from the eye, retinal excitation, light reflected from an object striking the retina, etc. Most of this is not visually perceived. So to figure as a perceived object, it is not enough that an item figure in some way among the causes of the experience. It must figure in a certain way, one that enables it to be perceived. And why should we suppose that God figures in *that* way in the causal chain leading to mystical experience?

When we think hard about this issue, we come to a startling result. Going back to sense perception, notice first that the way a perceived object figures in the causal chain differs for different sense modalities. In vision it is something like *reflecting or generating light that then reaches the retina without additional reflection*; for audition it is something like *generating or reflecting sound waves that strike the eardrum*; and so on. For mystical perception it will be something different, the exact nature of which is obscure to us. Further, note that the causal contribution required for objecthood in each case is something we can learn only from experience, including the experience involved in that case and similar cases. We must have a number of cases of genuine perception of X in that modality before we are in a position to discover inductively what kind of causal contribution is required for being perceived in that modality. There is no a priori way of determining this. But notice where this leaves us. Since we are in no position to say what kind of causal contribution is required for objecthood until we have some genuine cases of perception to work from, we can't even embark on the project of specifying the necessary causal contribution until we recognize that there are authentic cases of perception in that modality. Hence one who denies that people ever perceive God in mystical experience has no basis for any supposition as to how God would have to be involved in causing mystical experience for God to be genuinely perceived in such an experience. Hence the critic could have no basis for arguing that God does not satisfy the requirement. She could, of course, point out that the advocate of divine perception has no idea of what is required either. But that still doesn't give her an *objection* to her opponent's position.

So we are left with the conclusion that even if there is an adequate naturalistic account of the proximate causes of mystical experience, that does not rule out the possibility that God plays a role in eliciting such experience that renders him perceived therein. But there are also reasons for questioning the claim that there is any such account. If we consider the most prominent candidates (and this is not a popular research field for social and behavioral scientists), we must judge them to be highly speculative and, at best, sketchily supported by the evidence. Mystical experience poses severe problems for empirical research. In addition to the difficulties in determining when we have a case thereof, it is something that cannot be induced at the will of the researcher and so is not amenable to experiment. Attempts to get around this by substituting drug-induced analogues are of little value, since it is an open question whether findings concerning the latter can be extrapolated to spontaneous cases. Since the states are usually short-lived, the researcher must rely on autobiographical reports; we can't expect a researcher to hang around a person on the off chance that he might happen to have a mystical experience. Hence the data are subject to all the well-known problems that attach to first-person reports. Moreover, the most prominent theories in the field invoke causal mechanisms that themselves pose unsolved problems of

identification and measurement: unconscious psychological processes like repression and mechanisms of defense, social influences on ideology and on belief and attitude formation. It is not surprising that theories like those of Freud, Marx, and Durkheim rest on a slender thread of evidential support and generalize irresponsibly from such evidence as they can muster.

5   Can Reports of Mystical Perception Be Checked?

It is not infrequently claimed by philosophers that the impossibility of effective public (intersubjective) tests of the accuracy of beliefs about God formed on the basis of mystical experience prevents that experience from being an awareness of any objective reality. Here are a couple of representative formulations.

> But why can't we have an argument based upon religious experiences for the existence of the apparent object of a given religious experience and its bearing the right sort of causal relation to the experience? There can be such an argument only if religious experiences count as cognitive. But they can count as cognitive only if they are subject to similar tests to those which sense experiences are.[8]
>
> But whereas questions about the existence of people can be answered by straightforward observational and other tests, not even those who claim to have enjoyed personal encounters with God would admit such tests to be appropriate here.[9]

The first thing to be said in reply is that there *are* tests for the accuracy of particular reports of mystical perception. Contemplative religious communities that, so to say, specialize in the perception of God have compiled systematic manuals of such tests; and many of them are used more informally by the laity. These include such things as (1) conformity with what would

[8]   Richard Gale, *On the Nature and Existence of God* (New York: Cambridge University Press, 1991), p. 302. [. . .]

[9]   Antony Flew, *God and Philosophy* (London: Hutchinson, 1966), pp. 138–9.

be expected on the basis of doctrines concerning the nature of God, (2) "fruits" of the experience as a stable inner peace and growth in spirituality, (3) a content of the experience that the person would not have developed on their own. The satisfaction of such conditions counts in favor of the veridicality of the experience, and their absence counts against it. Obviously these tests do not conclusively establish veridicality or the reverse, but that does not render them without value. Tests of the accuracy of sense perceptions don't always settle the matter definitively either.

It is certainly true that sense-perceptual reports can be checked in ways that mystical-perceptual reports cannot. Let's look for a moment at some of these ways. The most obvious ones involve the experiences of other persons. Suppose I claim to have seen a Russian plane flying over my house at a certain time. If we can find other people who were in the area at that time and looking up into the sky, we can determine whether they saw a Russian plane overhead. To be sure, if one or a few such people failed to notice a Russian plane, that would not decisively disconfirm my report. Perhaps they were inattentive, blinded by the sun, or preoccupied with other matters. But if a large number of people were in the area, were not especially preoccupied, were disposed to look up to determine the source of any loud noise, and none of them saw any such plane, my report would have been decisively disconfirmed. The general principle involved here is that if a visible object were present at a certain place and time, then any competent observer who was at that place and time and was looking in the right direction would (at least most probably) have seen it. If a large number of such observers did not see any such thing, we must conclude that the object wasn't there at that time. If, on the other hand, all or most such observers take themselves to have seen it, that confirms the original report. Thus sense-perceptual reports are often subject to a decisive test on the basis of the perceptions of other persons.

There are other kinds of public tests as well. The credentials of the reporter could be examined. Is his visual apparatus in order? Does he know how to distinguish a Russian plane from other kinds? Was he in a drugged or intoxicated condition? Did he have his wits about him at the time?

And so on. To change the example, suppose the report is that baking soda is sprinkled over my serving of rice. In addition to taste tests by others, the substance can be subjected to chemical analysis.

There is nothing comparable to this with mystical perception. God is always present everywhere, if present anywhere, and so the whereabouts of a subject has no bearing. If a mystical report were to be given a test by other observers in the sense-perceptual way, we would have to say that S really perceived God at time t only if every competent subject perceives God all the time. But no one would take this to be an appropriate test. "Why should we expect God to be perceivable by everyone all the time even if he is present everywhere all the time?" one might ask. To put the point more generally, there is no set of conditions such that if God is present to me at time t, then any other person satisfying those conditions would also perceive God at t. To be sure, we can say something about what is conducive to perceiving God. One must be sufficiently "receptive," sufficiently "spiritually attuned." It is only if one who possesses those characteristics fails to perceive God that this counts against the original report. But how can we tell whether a given subject qualifies? Again, something can be said. Those who address such matters typically lay down such characteristics as the possession of certain virtues (humility, compassion) and a loving, obedient attitude toward God as productive of openness to the presence of God. "Blessed are the pure in heart, for they shall see God" (Matt. 5:8, KJV). But there are two reasons why we still lack the kind of test we have for sense-perceptual reports. First, we are far from having reliable intersubjective tests for humility and a loving attitude toward God. And second, it can't seriously be claimed that any set of conditions we can list is such that one will perceive God *if and only if* those conditions are satisfied. The situation with respect to mystical perception is much more obscure and mysterious, much less tight than this. And so we are still a long way from being able to carry out the kind of *other observers* tests we have for sense perception. As for the other kinds of tests I mentioned above, what I have just said implies that we have no effective *state of observer* test to rely on here. And obviously nothing like chemical analysis is relevant.

But what epistemic relevance does this difference have? Why should we suppose that it prevents mystical reports from enjoying prima facie justification? Those who take this line make an unjustifiable assumption that reports of perception of God are properly treated by the same standards as reports of sense perception, so that if the former cannot be tested in the same way as the latter, they cannot provide a cognitive access to objective reality. But this assumption is no more than a kind of epistemic *imperialism*, subjecting the outputs of one belief-forming practice to the requirements of another. It can easily be seen that not all our standard belief-forming practices work like sense perception. Consider introspection. If I report feeling excited, there are no conditions under which my report is correct *if and only if* someone who satisfies those conditions also feels excited. Introspective reports can be publicly checked to a certain extent, but not in that way. Again, the fact that we can't use perceptual checks on mathematical reports has no tendency to show that rational intuition cannot yield objective truths. Different belief-forming practices work differently.

Thinkers like Gale and Flew will undoubtedly respond to this last example by saying that the availability of tests like those for sense perception are at least required for the epistemic efficacy of *experiential* sources of belief. But that no more goes beyond a mere prejudice than the more unqualified claim for belief sources generally. What basis do we have for the claim that the features of sense perception constitute *necessary* conditions for any effective experiential cognitive access to objective reality? I take it as uncontroversial that sense perception is *a* way of acquiring reliable beliefs of certain sorts about the world. Sense perception satisfies sufficient conditions for epistemic efficacy. But why suppose that this is the only set of sufficient conditions?

Experience amply attests that, in cognitive as well as in other matters, sharply different maneuvers can achieve a certain goal. Excellent dishes can be prepared by meticulously following well-tested recipes or, with experienced cooks, by inspired improvisation. Mathematical problems can be solved, in some cases, by following established algorithms, or, in some cases, by flashes of intuition. The picture of an ancient civilization can be built up from archeological remains or from extant documents or from some combination thereof. And so it goes. It would be the reverse of surprising if the purchase on objective reality attained by sense perception were only one of many experiential ways of achieving such a result. And the fact that the aspects of reality that mystical perception claims to put us in contact with are very different from those that are explored by sense perception reinforces the rejection of the idea that only what conforms to the latter can reveal anything about reality.

30

Do Mystics See God?

Evan Fales

And [the Lord] said, Thou canst not see my face [*panim*]: for there shall no man see my face and live

— Exod. 33:20

And Jacob called the name of the place Peniel: for I have seen God face [*panim*] to face, and my life is preserved

— Gen. 32:30

There's more than one way to skin a cat.

1 A Cautionary Tale

Theistic philosophers have perennially cited mystical experiences – experiences of God – as evidence for God's existence and for other truths about God. In recent years, the attractiveness of this line of thought has been reflected in its use by a significant number of philosophers. But both philosophers and mystics agree that not all mystical experiences can be relied upon; many are the stuff of delusion. So they have somehow to be checked out, their bona fides revealed. But can

they be? I will be arguing that (a) they must indeed be cross-checked to serve as good evidence; and that (b) they can't be – or not nearly well enough to permit pressing them into service as serious support for theism. The need for cross-checking, necessary in any case, is made acute by two facts: the extreme variability of mystical experiences and the doctrines they are recruited to support, and the fact that, especially in the face of this variability, mystical experiences are much more effectively explained naturalistically. Furthermore, our ability adequately to

"Do Mystics See God?" by Evan Fales, in *Contemporary Debates in Philosophy of Religion*, ed. Michael Peterson and Raymond J. Van Arragaon (Malden, MA: Blackwell Publishers, 2004), pp. 145–58. Reprinted by permission of the publishers, Blackwell Publishing.

cross-check mystical experiences (hereafter, MEs), in a way that would reveal the hand of God, is crippled by the fact that theists offer no hypothesis concerning the causal mechanism by means of which God shows himself to mystics.

Let's begin with my third epigraph. This insightful, if grisly, bit of folk wisdom tells much of our story. Permit me to spell out the dolorous tale. I am greeted by the sight of poor Sylvester, a heap of flayed flesh upon the lawn. I set out to reconstruct the crime. With but the denuded corpse as evidence, the possibilities are multiple. So I must locate other clues. A bloodied knife nearby might have secrets to reveal: suppose the hemoglobin tests out feline. Even better, perhaps I can find an eyewitness or two, discovering through further investigation that they are both sober and honest. I might find fingerprints on the knife. And so on.

In all this, I rely upon my senses to convey evidence of the deed. How is this managed? Why, through some causal sequence, a continuation of some of those sequences that converged upon the destruction of poor Sylvester, and that then diverged from there. Light waves bearing news of cat skin and flesh make their way from the *corpus delicti* to my "sensory surfaces," there to be processed in those still and possibly forever mysterious ways into cat-corpse-consciousness. Mysterious or not, what we do know is that cat and conscious episode are related as (partial) cause to (partial) effect. But for there being some suitable causal link between cat and experience, that experience, no matter its intrinsic characteristics, is not a perception of that cat.

But if the intrinsic content of my experience can be caused in multiple ways (the presence of an actual cat-corpse being but one of these), then how shall I ascertain that my senses do not deceive? The short answer to this importunate and persistent problem, the problem of perception, is: I must cross-check. But we cannot explore the substance of this remark without making two antecedent observations. First, no amount of cross-checking can produce evidence that will satisfy the radical skeptic. I can decide to pinch myself to check that I'm not just dreaming of cats; but of course I might just be dreaming that I've pinched myself. Second, because of this, and

because our project is to examine whether putative experiences of God must be cross-checked to carry evidential weight, not to respond to radical skepticism, we shall have to frame our discussion with some care. One could, of course, accept a counsel of despair: neither ordinary sense experience nor mystical experience can form the basis of justified beliefs about external matters. In that event, mystical theistic beliefs are in no worse shape, epistemically speaking, than ordinary perceptual beliefs. But that would be because neither set of beliefs could be in any worse shape, so far as justification goes. That sort of "pox on both your houses" skepticism is, however, not a very interesting position from the perspective of traditional debates about the warrant for theism. The interesting question is: If we suppose ordinary perceptual beliefs (and we may throw in scientific theory for good measure) to be warrantable by appeal to sense experience, then why shouldn't theistic beliefs be similarly warrantable by appeal to perceptual experience, whether sensory or mystical?

Here, in a nutshell, is what I shall argue. The problem of perception derives largely from the general truth that any effect – hence a perceptual experience – can be caused in more ways than one. Our strategy for removing this ambiguity is cross-checking. Ultimately, cross-checking involves just collecting more data, which are subject to the same ambiguity. Our implicit reasoning is that the total amount of ambiguity can nevertheless be progressively reduced in this way. The means by which science draws a bead on postulated "unobservable" entities (like electrons) is not in principle or in practice different in kind; it is just more systematic and careful than the humdrum of everyday perceptual judgments. In everyday contexts, cross-checking is informal, and it is so automatic, continuous, and pervasive that, except under duress (e.g., as we try to catch out a magician), it is scarcely noticed. I propose to show how cross-checking works; to argue that it is a mandatory feature of any recruitment of perceptual experience to epistemic ends; and that, therefore, it is a requirement that must be met in theistic appeals to mystical experience as evidence for theism. Finally, I shall argue that this requirement has not, and probably cannot, be met. So, I shall conclude, mystical experience provides hardly any useful support for theism.

2   Cross-Checking Explained

So, what is cross-checking? Why is it needed? And how does it work? Let "cross-checking" denote all those procedures and strategies we use to settle questions about the causes of something. These include, in particular, (1) using Mill's methods to pick out causally relevant antecedent conditions; (2) exploiting the fact that events have multiple effects, to "triangulate" the event in question, on the principle that qualitatively different causes will have *some* differences in their (potential) effects;[1] and (3) confirming the existence of causal mechanisms allegedly connecting a cause to its effects (when it is not a proximate cause). These strategies depend upon putting forward hypotheses and testing them by means of diagnostic experiments. I shall discuss mainly tests of type (3), but invoke strategy (2) when considering prophetic revelations as a test of MEs.

[. . .]

Let us make this anti-skeptical assumption. Evidence, in the face of which a hypothesis can be rescued only by revision of auxiliary assumptions, works to the disadvantage of that hypothesis – though perhaps not decisively so – in comparison with competitors which accommodate that evidence without revisions.

An obvious objection to all this will be that, plausible as it may be as a rational reconstruction of scientific reasoning, it does not at all capture the process by which we acquire warranted perceptual beliefs. Perceptual knowledge seems much more direct than this, even to those who concede the obvious fact that it is causally mediated. So I now want to argue that this is an illusion, that in fact warrant accrues to perceptual beliefs only insofar as, rationally reconstructed, their acquisition, too, requires inference to the best explanation.

3   The Pervasive Need for Cross-Checking

What, then, is it about cross-checking that establishes its essential and fundamental place as an epistemic method, even in the case of sense perception? This standing is a consequence of the fact that we are physical beings, situated within a spatiotemporal world in an environment with which we communicate via physical – that is, causal – processes. But the centrality of cross-checking is still more fundamental than this. It is demanded for knowledge of *any* causal process, in which causes are known *via* their effects. In particular, it is demanded in connection with any claim to have perceptual access to an extra-mental reality. It would be demanded, for example, if we were bodiless minds claiming perceptual contact with disembodied demons, evil or benign, with angels, or with a god. That is because the contact is perceptual, and because of the principle

P: If S perceives (has a perceptual experience of) X, then X is a suitable cause of S's experience.

First, three comments about P; and then, more on the connection between (P) and cross-checking:

1   When I say that X is *a* cause of S's experience, I mean just that it plays a role as one of the causal antecedents of S's experience.
2   Strictly speaking, it is events or states of affairs that are causes. If X is a particular, then it is not X *per se*, but X's having some property or undergoing some change which constitutes the cause in question.
3   When I say that this is a *suitable* cause of S's experience, I mean that it must cause the experience in the right sort of way for the experience to count as perception *of X*. Obviously, not all of the causal conditions of my now perceiving this pen are conditions I now perceive (those conditions include my eyes and brain working properly, the pen

---

[1]   See Evan Fales, *Causation and Universals* (London: Routledge, 1990), ch. 8.

being illuminated, and even God, if God caused the pen to exist and sustains me in existence). We cannot say *in general* what criteria distinguish the "right" sort of causal ancestry from the wrong sorts; but cross-checking has everything to do with how we justifiably identify the right items in particular cases.

Knowing what we are perceiving is a matter of knowing what is causing our experience in the right sort of way. But that is a matter of narrowing down the candidate causes of an experience so that – ideally – just one cause, situated in the right way, can explain our data. It is precisely here that cross-checking plays the crucial role, by enabling us to eliminate possible causes and to form a sufficiently precise conception of our environment and the causal processes that occur in it to "zero in" on the (or a) "suitable" cause.

William Alston misses the mark when he insists that a demand for similar cross-checking of the claims of mystics amounts to a kind of epistemic imperialism.[2] He insists that each epistemic practice, including mystical practice, gets to dictate its own standards and cross-checking criteria. But, as we shall see, those invoked by mystics are characteristically vacuous. Obviously, the sorts of evidence relevant to checking a perceptual claim will depend upon its modality and content. But determining what makes something *count* as evidence and justification is dictated by the causal structure of perception and cannot be commandeered by epistemic practices, so-called.

Many philosophers will reject this conception of perception and perceptual knowledge. They do so partly for dialectical reasons – that is, because they believe that the road so paved leads straight to skeptical perdition. They do so, further, for broadly phenomenological reasons – that is, because we do not ordinarily make perceptual knowledge claims on the basis of anything more than having the right sort of experience. We don't indulge in any cross-checking or inference in judging, for example, that there is someone in the seat next to us.

But these objections are, in the present context, misdirected. The phenomenological objection ignores what we might call "subliminal information processing," both past and occurrent, and the vital role that cross-checking plays in this processing. What sort of perceptual seemings a given environment can produce in one is a function not only of recent sensory stimulation, but of much else: of attention and motivational factors, of past experience and concepts thereby acquired, of expectations for which an inductive rationale could be supplied if required (but which ordinarily does not – and need not – enter into perceptual engagement with the world). We can look and just "see" that the refrigerator in the kitchen is white, in part because we have acquired an understanding of what refrigerators are and what they look like, readily expect such items to appear in kitchens, and know that white things look a certain way under the apparent conditions of illumination. An ability to "just see" directly that this refrigerator is white is a hard-won skill. Learning endows us with unconscious cognitive mechanisms that operate to apply concepts in forming a percept as if on the basis of various inductions.

Moreover, past learning and also the present cognitive processing incorporate cross-checking in fundamental ways. What our cognitive systems have learned is how "automatically" to make judgments that, were we rationally to reconstruct them, would involve *causal* reasoning to the best explanation for the multitude of sensory inputs with which we are provided. For example, the supposition that light travels in more or less straight lines, together with the hypotheses that there is a bulky, stationary, solid white object before us, and that we are in motion in a certain way relative to it, can help explain the sequence of our visual/tactile inputs. But any such reasoning (or unconscious surrogate for it) must invoke, implicitly, cross-checking. It is as if, for example, the various visual and tactile inputs serve to corroborate the judgment that there is a refrigerator, by eliminating alternative possibilities.

2   William P. Alston, *Perceiving God: The Epistemology of Religious Experience* (Ithaca, NY: Cornell University Press, 1991), pp. 209–22 [see also p. 190 above].

This kind of implicit cross-checking is absolutely pervasive; it comes to permeate all our perceptual "takings" as we mature and piece together our world. This feature of sense-perceptual processes explains a fundamental phenomenological feature of perceptual judgments: namely, how we can directly take ourselves to be *en rapport* with our physical surroundings, even though no single bit of sensory information could form an adequate basis for such a judgment (or even, I would add, for the formation of the *concepts* required to envision a three-dimensional space inhabited by physical continuants). It explains how it is that we do this without seeming to engage in any processes of inference from representations – of inference from effects to causes. That is why direct realist theories of perception can seem so plausible, even though in a *causal* sense, we are obviously *not* in direct contact with our physical surroundings.

4 Skepticism Bracketed

I have dwelt upon this point because I take it to be crucial to an assessment of the epistemic status of mystical experience, interpreted as perceptual contact with supernatural realities. But it also permits a response to the objection that conceding perception to involve an "indirect" (causal) contact with extra-mental reality, and perceptual judgment to require reasoning from effects to causes (or surrogates for that), gives the skeptic all he needs to undermine claims to have knowledge or justification.

Alston is particularly forceful and insightful in making this case with respect to sense perception (but of course it applies to mystical perception equally).[3] He argues that any attempt to justify a perceptual practice must fail on grounds of either unsoundness or circularity. Though Alston's argument is complex, we have seen why

this result is to be expected and, consequently, can specify the way in which I believe the issue concerning mystical perception ought to be framed.

So as not to beg any questions, I shall adopt Alston's view that there are distinguishable belief-forming practices, including different perceptual practices. Two such practices take as their inputs sense perception and mystical perception. If the possibility of mystical evidence for God is not automatically to be ruled out, we must find some way of deflecting skeptical objections as they apply to perceptual judgments generally. Seeing how this goes for sense perception will enable us to generalize to other perceptual practices, for the relevant similarities between them are more important than the differences. Alston, in spite of his insistence that each perceptual practice is beholden only to its own epistemic standards, recognizes this when he invokes, for all perceptual practices, what amounts to a kind of Principle of Credulity.[4] Alston takes it that, provided a perceptual practice meets certain conditions,[5] perceptual judgments formed in the normal ways provided for in that practice are prima facie justified. (They are only prima facie justified: every such practice must include what Alston calls an "overrider" system, and so a judgment can be overridden. Indeed, Alston's overrider systems reflect the importance of cross-checking, without properly recognizing its fundamentality.)

Any appeal to prima facie warrant – warrant occurring in the absence of even implicit or pre-conscious processes that could be rationally reconstructed in terms of inductive inference and cross-checking – is just the *wrong* way to bracket (radical) skepticism and frame our question. It is wrong because it short-circuits precisely the crucial justificatory procedures (or at least a crucial stage in their application), thereby begging, or at least certainly obscuring the bearing of, critical questions that the mystical theist must

---

[3]   See Alston, *Perceiving God*, ch. 3, and idem, *The Reliability of Sense Perception* (Ithaca, NY: Cornell University Press, 1993).
[4]   The term, and the principle itself, are due to Swinburne, though the idea can be traced back at least to Reid.
[5]   These conditions include being socially established, incorporating an overrider system, and being free of massive contradiction from within and from beliefs generated by other doxastic practices (see Alston, *Perceiving God*, ch. 4).

confront. They include the question whether cross-checking procedures must be, but are not, appropriately "built into," and cannot retrospectively be applied to, mystical experiences and the judgments they deliver. I shall argue that they are not, and that this flaw is fatal to mystical justifications of theism.

Cross-checking and cross-checkability must be integral parts of any perceptual epistemic practice because what a perceiver takes to be present on the basis of her experiences might not be what is in fact causally responsible for those experiences. Cross-checking "pins down" stages of the causal process, thereby eliminating alternative hypotheses as to how the input is produced.

What goes for sense perception goes for mystical experience as well. Theists who invoke such experiences as evidence may help themselves to the same inductive principles that our sensory practices evidently presuppose – in particular, those that vindicate cross-checking. However, if, granting those principles, mystical experiences fail to supply significant evidence for theism, an appeal to them will be of little help to theists.

I have been insisting that what we need to frame the debate productively is *not* some principle of credulity, but more general and fundamental inductive principles that will not short-circuit the issues. But even if I were to *grant* some form of credulity principle, it would avail the theist little. For the warrant it confers is only prima facie warrant, and, as it happens, there are good reasons to question that warrant in the mystical case. Since that is so, cross-checking can't be avoided, and its demands are made acute in proportion to the cogency of the cognitive challenges that mystical practices (MPs) confront.

5 Christian Mysticism: Challenges and Checks

There are a number of such challenges, in the form of alternative explanations for mystical experiences (MEs). One of these, which I shall not pursue, comes from within many MPs. It is the possibility that an ME is demonically caused. There are also naturalistic explanations. Here I shall mention two which complement one another and are jointly strong enough to outdistance any theistic explanation.[6] Fortunately (and *pace* Alston[7]), patterns of mystical encounter are so predictable and overtly manifested, in religious traditions ranging from Pentecostal worship to the ritual seances of Dinka and Tungus shamans, that it has been possible for anthropologists and psychologists to study the phenomenon in great detail in its natural settings.[8]

The first naturalistic explanation is due to the anthropologist I. M. Lewis, and derives from worldwide comparative studies which reveal certain general patterns among MPs.[9] In brief, Lewis shows that, at least where mystics "go public" and appeal to their experiences in the social arena, mysticism serves mundane interests either of the mystic him or herself, or of some group with which he or she identifies. Lewis discerns two types of mystics: socially marginalized mystics whose mysticism is a weapon in the struggle to achieve social justice for themselves and their group, and upwardly mobile mystics who use their mystical experiences as credentials to legitimate their claim on positions of social leadership. Lewis shows how the *descriptions* that mystics give of their experiences and the *behaviors* they exhibit prior to, during, and after mystical episodes serve these social ends in quite precise and predictable ways.

[6] So I argue with respect to Lewis's theory in Fales, "Scientific Explanations of Mystical Experience, Part I: The Case of St Teresa," and "Scientific Explanations of Mystical Experience, Part II: The Challenge to Theism," *Religious Studies*, 32 (1996), pp. 143–63 and 297–313 respectively. This can now be supplemented with the neurophysiological findings.

[7] Alston, *Perceiving God*, pp. 240–1.

[8] I have the report (private communication) of a Christian mystic trained in neurophysiology who has been able to record her own brain waves, and those of a colleague, during trance, who confirms the temporal lobe finding (see below). For a more detailed summary of the evidence and references, see Fales, "Scientific Explanations," Parts I and II, and *idem*, "Can Science Explain Mysticism?" *Religious Studies*, 35 (1999), pp. 213–27.

[9] I. M. Lewis, *Ecstatic Religion*, 2nd edn (London: Routledge, 1989).

One of the great strengths of Lewis's theory is that it cuts across the entire spectrum of MPs, providing a unity of explanation that the theist cannot hope to match.[10] Lewis's theory has, however, a significant lacuna. It says little about how the occurrence of favorable social circumstances gets translated into the incidence of mystical phenomenology. Moreover, Lewis gives no very adequate explanation for the apparent frequency of MEs which remain private. Many people, it seems, have occasional mystical experiences, but almost never disclose them.

But it looks now as if these gaps can be closed by the second naturalistic approach, which has begun to indicate the details of the neurophysiological mechanisms by means of which mystical experience is mediated. Such experiences, it turns out, are associated with micro-seizures of the temporal lobes of the brain. When these seizures are severe, they result in temporal lobe epilepsy. But mild seizures, which can even be artificially induced during brain surgery, can result in powerful mystical experiences.[11] A substantial portion of the general population has a disposition to such mild seizures, and there is some circumstantial evidence that they can be provoked by techniques traditionally used to induce mystical trance states.[12]

A theist may wish to reply here that God may well have a hand in these mechanisms, indeed employ them as his means for appearing to his worshippers.[13] But this is implausible on

a number of counts. For one thing, it is extraordinarily hard to explain why God would appear through the figure of Jesus to a Christian, as Allah to a Muslim, Brahman to a Hindu, the god Flesh to a Dinka, and as a variety of *loa* spirits to voodoo practitioners. And if a purely naturalistic explanation can be given for the non-theistic experiences, then why not also for the theistic ones?[14]

There are other problems. Suppose we take a naturalistic explanation of MEs and tack on the hypothesis that God is involved in some way. This is a God-of-the-gaps strategy. Given the lacunae in our understanding of even simple physical processes – to say nothing of the neurophysiology of the brain – this strategy is one a theist can deploy with some ease.

Indeed, it incurs the danger of being too easy. A theist could invoke divine intervention to explain why the radiator of my car cracked overnight. Our natural explanation is full of holes: we may not know exactly how cold the engine got last night, nor exactly how strong the walls of the radiator were at the rupture point, nor how to apply the known laws of nature to such a complex system. So, in principle, all the theist need do is find some gap in the posited causal etiology, and tack on the hypothesis that here the finger of God helped the process along – no doubt, to punish my sins.

Why do we (most of us!) not credit such an "explanation"? First, of course, because a long

[10]   See Fales, "Scientific Explanations of Mystical Experience, Part II."
[11]   The literature is substantial and growing. For a good bibliography, see Susan Blackmore, *Dying to Live: Near-Death Experiences* (Buffalo, NY: Prometheus Books, 1993), especially the citations for ch. 10.
[12]   See William Sargant, *The Mind Possessed: A Physiology of Possession, Mysticism, and Faith Healing* (Philadelphia: J. E. Lippincott, 1974).
[13]   Alston has suggested this possibility on a number of occasions – e.g., in "Psychoanalytic Theory and Theistic Belief," in John Hick (ed.), *Faith and the Philosophers* (New York: St Martin's Press, 1964), and in *Perceiving God*, pp. 230–3.
[14]   This argument is fleshed out in Fales, "Scientific Explanations of Mysticism, Part II." It is, moreover, very unclear just how, in principle, God would be able to communicate with human beings. If this is to occur via divine influence upon a person's brain states, and those states are macroscopic physical states, then any divine intervention will involve local violations of the highly confirmed laws of conservation of momentum and energy. If, one the other hand, we suppose that God intervenes at the quantum level, acting as a kind of "hidden variable" in determining the outcomes of indeterministic processes, as Nancey Murphy has recently proposed, then we can avoid the violation of physical laws, but only at the price of making in principle unknowable (since hidden by quantum uncertainties) the presence of divine intervention. On these issues see the articles by Murphy and Tracy in Robert J. Russell, Nancey Murphy, and Arthur R. Peacocke (eds), *Chaos and Complexity: Scientific Perspectives on Divine Action* (Vatican City: Vatican Observatory Publications, 1995).

history of experience teaches us that such gaps are often eventually filled by natural causes. But second, because the theistic explanation comes too cheaply: there are no constraints on when, how, and where God is likely to act, no attendant procedures for cross-checking or ferreting out the precise mode and locus of divine intervention, no positive suggestions about how the theistic account of theophysical interaction might be investigated, fleshed out, ramified – and virtually no concomitant predictive power. This theoretical poverty cripples cross-checking for divine influence.

Still, the presence of naturalistic competitors makes it imperative that we examine what sorts of cross-checking MP admits, and how successful such cross-checks have been. We run here into a number of obvious difficulties. Most prominent among them is the fact that mystical experiences are not public. Moreover, the sorts of checks typically invoked, by Christian mystics at least, are either epistemically irrelevant or question begging, absent quite strong auxiliary assumptions.

It is not that mystics are unconcerned about the veridicality of MEs. On the contrary, they often display a lively concern with this and offer multiple tests. But let us look at some of these tests, using Teresa of Ávila as a guide. Teresa exhibits a strong interest in the question of how veridical experiences are to be distinguished from those produced by what she calls "melancholy" and by Satan. (This interest is hardly surprising, given the regularity with which the Inquisition accused mystics – especially women – of nefarious motives, fraud, or demonic possession.) Teresa's list of tests includes: (1) the fruits of an experience – both in the actions and personality of the mystic and as producing an inner peace rather than a troubled state of mind, (2) the vividness of the memory of the experience, (3) conformity to Scripture, and (4) validation by the mystic's confessor.

It is not hard to see how these criteria might be designed to secure for the mystic immunity from Inquisitional prosecution, but not easy to see what epistemic force they could have. Test 3 looks straightforwardly question begging, inasmuch

as the authority of Scripture rests largely on the supposed authority of the revelations upon which it is based. Tests 1, 2, and 4 have no epistemic force except on the assumption that only God, and neither Satan's best deceptive efforts nor natural causes, can produce experiences that are memorable, convincing to confessors, or have good fruits. But what independent evidence is there for that? What cross-checks for these claims can theists supply? On this, Teresa is silent.

The final – and in principle the best – hope for cross-checking MEs lies with successful prophecy. Perhaps a theistic account *does* after all yield checkable predictions in a way that bears directly upon the evidential force of MEs. For, often enough, one of the fruits of a mystical encounter with God has been the revelation of a prophecy. Not only that, but prophecy has figured as a central component of Christian mystical practice (CMP) and many other MPs, and of the apologetical strategies associated with them. This is because prophecies permit, when certain conditions are satisfied, type-2 cross-checks of a fairly powerful and peculiarly direct sort. When the *content* of a ME contains some message, putatively from God or some supernatural source assumed to be in the know, concerning future events, the claim of genuineness can in principle be checked; ordinarily, the prophesied events will be of such a sort that it is within the purview of ordinary sense perception to determine their occurrence or nonoccurrence.

Yet, Alston tries to downplay the prophetic dimensions of MP.[15] Why? After all, the plain fact is that prophecy is a major and central feature of the MPs of many religious traditions; moreover, putatively successful prophecy is regularly appealed to precisely by way of confirming the genuineness of the prophet, the veridicality of his or her ecstatic visions, and the uniquely truth-connected status of the tradition that claims him or her as its own. Ecstatics who develop prophetic practice into a vocation are familiar figures in religious traditions – witness the oracle at Delphi, the Hebrew prophets, John on Patmos, and Jesus of Nazareth. Nor is this an aspect only of ancient MPs, long since superseded (within Jewish and Christian MPs). Far from it, as anyone who considers the claims of contemporary televangelists can confirm.

Prophecy, therefore, is a feature intrinsic to CMP, a feature by means of which the truth-claims produced by that practice can be quite directly checked. However, no such check will be very informative unless certain conditions are satisfied. Briefly, these include:

1 The prophecy must be of some event not intrinsically likely (not, e.g., "wars and rumors of wars" – Mark 24:6).
2 The prophecy must not be self-fulfilling, or of events the prophet or his or her followers can themselves bring about.
3 The prophecy must demonstrably have been made prior to the events which count as its fulfillment.
4 The prophecy must be sufficiently specific and unambiguous to preclude *ex post facto* reinterpretation to fit any of a wide range of possible "fulfillments."
5 The fulfillment of the prophecy must be verified independently of the say-so of the prophet or his or her partisans or tradition.

Here we have, at last, a cross-check which really *does* offer a test of mystical experience. The reasoning is straightforward: given 1–5, only the mystic's having received a message from a superhumanly prescient being (or, improbably, wild luck) can explain his or her prophetic success. (There are, to be sure, some added complications: for example, we must be careful to avoid the Jean Dixon fallacy. A clever prophet can issue hundreds of risky prophecies, in the hope of scoring a few memorable "hits," calculating that the "misses" will be forgotten. Our reasoning to the best explanation must take into account the prophet's entire track record.)

Now, just what is the record of Jewish and Christian MPs on this score? Rather than pursue this question at length, let me observe that I know of no recorded prophecy, either within the Jewish/Christian canon or outside it, that clearly satisfies criteria 1–5. (There are, however, a number of demonstrably *false* prophecies. Of these, perhaps the most decisive and poignant occurs at Matt. 16:27.)

Conclusion: Like any perceptual practice, CMP requires an elaborate system of cross-checks and cross-checking procedures. But, because of its theoretical poverty with respect to the causes of mystical experiences, no such system has been, or is likely to be, forthcoming. With respect to the one relatively strong cross-checking strategy that CMP has available (and has purported to use), its record is one of failure. Until these defects are remedied, mystical experience cannot hope to provide significant evidential support for theism.

Mystical Knowledge
Knowledge by Identity

Robert K. C. Forman

With little fanfare, and with even less justification, for the last half century or more a
single model has dominated academic thought
about mysticism. Put simply, the model is that
mystical experience is like ordinary intentional
experience: the mystic encounters some sort of
mystical "object." Inevitably, variations about
the particulars of this model abound, but the
underlying picture is unmistakable.

William Wainwright, for example, analyzes
mysticism as parallel to sensory experience
(Wainwright). Here the purported object is like
something touched or seen. Wainwright argues
that, just as one must actively construct a notion
of that pencil over there, so one must actively
construct a notion of the mystical object when
encountered. For Wayne Proudfoot the intentional
object is something like an emotion (Proudfoot).
Just as one labels any "visceral arousals" with
terms like "happiness," "fear," or "disgust," so the
mystic labels his or her visceral arousals with
terms like *samâdhi, Tao,* or *Christ.* W. T. Stace,
and Steven Katz, when he argues against Stace,
both take sensory objects as their model, notably
the purported differences (or lack thereof)
between sense experience and its description
(Stace; Katz 1978). When Katz uses the expression "experiences the mystic reality" at one

point, he intimates his underlying model (Katz
1978:27).

[. . .]

Using this model to think about mysticism
is initially plausible. First of all, mystics sometimes use intentional grammar to speak or think
about their experience. Eckhart speaks of the
encounter with "God's divine desert," for example,
which suggests that the experience is like an
experience of being in a desert. One can see,
feel, and walk through deserts; thus they can be
intentional objects. Shankara describes the mystical experience as "of" Brahman or "of" Atman;
again terms that look like objects of experience.
The Kabbalah mystic speaks of an experience
"of" *ayin,* the Sufi "of" *'fana.*

Second, it is plausible to employ this model
because this is the way we *always do* experience.
We always do because of the sorts of beings we
are. As human beings, we experience and perceive
"things" – be they feelings, thoughts, or sensory
objects.

Related to this is the Kantian argument: we
should apply this model because, were we to
experience in some other way, we would not be
able to integrate a non-intentional experience

"Mystical Knowledge: Knowledge by Identity" by Robert K. C. Forman, *Journal of the American Academy of Religion*
61:4 (Winter 1993): 705–32; 734–8. Reprinted by permission of the American Academy of Religion.

with the rest of our ordinary experiences, which come to us in the form subject–experiences–objects. It would come to us as unintelligible, for intelligibility is based on intentionality.

This model underlies what comes to be the received view on mysticism, which I have elsewhere called "constructivism."[1] To offer just one example, Jerry Gill points out that the notion that mysticism is like an experience of an intentional object is one of the most significant aspects of the constructivist approach:

Perhaps the most significant feature of Katz'[s] approach to this issue is discussion of the concept of intentionality at the close of his essay. He draws upon the work of early phenomenologists F. Brentano and E. Husserl by way of pointing out that human experience is vectorial in nature. (Gill 1984:113)

When he speaks of mystical experiences as intentional, i.e., vectorial in character, he communicates its nature like our experience of an intentional object. Referring to Brentano and Husserl, he maintains that, in general,

[O]ur awareness of the world is not that of passive observation, but is rather a function of the fact that we come into and at the world seeking meaning. Our consciousness is always *consciousness of* some concrete aspect of the world, of some particular aspect whose reality for us is constituted by our intentional activity in relation to it. This intentionality is clearly a mediational factor which undercuts the possibility of unmediated experience. The *vectorial character of consciousness* gives it a thrust or flow that provides the ever-present and necessary interpretive framework within which all experience is possible and understood. (Gill 1984:113; emphasis mine)

Gill clarified what he meant by the "vectorial" character of experience in his "Religous Experience as Mediated." There he notes that the basic character of mediated experience is what he calls its basic "from–to" structure:

Mediational awareness is always *of* something, *through* something else, or the prehender can be said to attend *from* certain factors *to* other factors. (Gill 1980:5; emphasis mine)

Because all experience is like an experience of an (intentional) object, Gill can say that all experience is mediated, or what amounts to the same thing, constructed. For in tending towards one factor or from one to another, the system of belief enters into the discrimination process. That is, any object of experience must be actively constituted and constructed as *that* object over against others as well as over against myself. Through such an active process of determining and constructing objects, we introduce relational terms, distinctions, and thereby the whole "set" in which these terms play their roles. Thus the model that mysticism is like my experience of an object is critical in forming the underpinning of Gill's constructivist picture of mysticism – and, I would suggest, it is critical for other constructivists as well. [...]

As Gill suggests, the application of this model to mysticism is critical for the mystical constructivists, for using such a model allows the constructivist to capitalize on the enormous theoretical and empirical research about the constructed character of ordinary experiences, thereby suggesting that mystical experiences are similarly shaped. If mysticism is parallel to my experience of a pencil, and if the pencil is in part "mediated" or "constructed" by my use of and understanding of pencils, then mysticism too must be liable to this sort of mediatory or constructive formation. It is because the constructivists work out of this model that they can *assume* certain epistemological verities.

My colleagues and I have argued in detail that constructivism as it has been formulated is vitiated by methodological failures, philosophical fallacies, textual misappropriation, and systematic vagueness (Forman 1988, 1990b; Perovich; Bernhardt; Rothberg; Franklin; Prigge and Kessler; Woodhouse). I will not repeat these criticisms. [...] It is now time to attempt the more difficult *con*structive work of developing a new model and position.

---

[1]   I have defined constructivism in 1990b. [...]

Before doing so, let me mention two points about our argument so far. First, our criticism of constructivism had focused on one common mystical experience, the pure consciousness event (PCE) (Forman 1990b; Bernhardt; Perovich; Prigge and Kessler; Franklin; Woodhouse). This phenomenon, which, we have argued, is found in virtually every major religious tradition, is defined as a transient phenomenon during which the subject remains conscious (wakeful, alert – not sleeping or unconscious) yet devoid of all mental content.

I define "mental content" broadly: it may include any or all of one's present thoughts and feelings – both emotions and sensations – not captured by a dispositional analysis. Thus abstract thoughts and concrete thoughts, indeterminate reveries or daydreams, pain and joy can all be content. In general, dispositions – intelligence, quickness, or the tendency towards depression – will become content only if I attend to them or think about them objectively. Similarly, merely knowing something or merely having a sensation does not necessarily make it content for consciousness; I must also attend to it consciously.

I would like to offer two reports of this state. In 1972 I was several months into a nine-month meditation retreat on a neo-Advaitan path. I had been meditating alone in my room all morning when someone knocked on my door. I heard the knock perfectly clearly, and upon hearing it I knew that, although there was no "waking up" before hearing the knock, for some indeterminate length of time prior to the knocking I had not been aware of anything in particular. I had been awake but with no content for my consciousness. Had no one knocked I doubt that I would ever have become aware that I had not been thinking or perceiving. The experience was so unremarkable, as it felt like, in retrospect, just regular me though utterly without content, that I simply would have begun at some point to recommence thinking and probably would never have taken note that I had been conscious yet devoid of mental content (Forman 1986; 1990b:28). Such states have been amply documented in many traditions (Forman 1990a; Matt; Griffiths; Chapple).

My second passage is an excerpt from an interview conducted with an advanced female practitioner of the Transcendental Meditation technique. She describes therein the decade-long development of her experience of the pure consciousness event. About her earliest experiences of the pure consciousness event, she said,

> I would only know afterwards that there had been something nice. It was a state that was different from my normal perception.... It was like if you have a blackboard filled with figures, and then somebody, without your knowing it, wipes it clean, and then you start writing on it again.[2]

Despite there being neither language employment nor perception during this event, both subjects state that they can remember that, for some indeterminate period, "I was awake," "the slate was clean," or "there was no content for consciousness."

While I and others have argued that the pure consciousness event may be found in many traditions, I have not argued for universality in the strong sense that pure consciousness events are undergone by every mystic in every age (1990b). I am maintaining, however, a weaker universalistic claim, that some mystics have undergone a pure consciousness event in more than one culture age and tradition, and that those experiences are identical in the sense of having indistinguishable subjective characteristics (Forman 1988, 1990b). Also, we make no claim that the PCE exhausts the range of mystical experiences. There are other, perhaps more complex and interesting ones.

My second point about our previous argument is that we have offered a new model for the relationship between the mystical experience of the pure consciousness event and the language system. Language does not construct this event because the very procedures used to bring it on require one temporarily to cease employing language and concept (Forman 1990b; Matt; Brown; Franklin). I take mystical texts seriously when they counsel their readers to "leave behind" or "forget" all concepts, language, beliefs, etc. (Forman 1990b:n94). If one truly forgets all

---

[2]   Alexander et al. (5–6). The passage is quoted in Forman (1990b:27–8).

concepts, beliefs, etc., for some period, then those beliefs, etc., cannot play a formative role in the etiology of the resultant conscious events. This "forgetting model," which was generated *from* mystical texts, does not impose on the mystical transformation process any theory developed to account for other, ordinary intentional experiences. Rather it analyzes the progression leading towards mysticism on its own terms. This model does the greatest justice not only to the relationship between language and mysticism, but to the peculiar physiological stamp of meditation and the pure consciousness event, hypoactivity.

The forgetting model shows how it might be possible that someone might cease using his or her concepts as s/he approaches the pure consciousness event. Yet it leaves many questions about mysticism unanswered. Some of the most obvious ones pointed out by critics and friends alike are: First, despite the fact that according to the forgetting model mystics temporarily cease thinking and hence "forget" to use language during the pure consciousness event, in both the above accounts, and in all other discussed accounts, people clearly claim to have *remembered* having undergone the PCE – at least enough to report that it has happened. Notice, it is not *content* which is reported – there is no claim that I remembered such and such. Rather one recalls merely that "I was awake" or "I didn't black out." The question remains: how can someone remember anything at all about the PCE if one experiences no objects and thinks no words or concepts?

A second issue which the forgetting model does not address is this: philosophers since Hume, Kant, Brentano, Sartre, and many others have maintained that consciousness is always *of* something. Hume, for example, wrote:

For my part, when I enter most intimately into what I call myself, I always stumble on some particular perception or other, of heat of cold, light or shade, love or hatred, pain or pleasure. I *never* can catch myself at any time without a perception, and *never* can observe anything but the perception. (Hume:252; emphasis mine)

Sartre called the claim that consciousness is always *of* something the very foundation of phenomenology.

Despite the claims of these eminent philosophers, here the claim is that consciousness *can* be empty and without an object. Thus our second question: Given what we know of consciousness, is it possible that consciousness can be empty? If so, how? This may be a semantic matter, given the way we use the term. Would the PCE actually qualify as an instance of "consciousness"?

These are the two major lacunae I would like to fill in this paper. I will propose a new model for "what" goes on in the pure consciousness event. This model will be developed from parallelisms observed in several accounts of mystics. I will then address several of the philosophical enigmas raised by this model. Finally, I will reflect on the model's strengths and weaknesses.

Mystics on "What" is Encountered

If there are no objects encountered in mysticism, then what is? Let us see what mystics themselves have said about "what" is encountered, for they more than anyone have tried to express faithfully the peculiar character of their experiences. I offer the following accounts, not because they emphasize this more than most, but because I happen to be familiar with them.

First, when Meister Eckhart ponders the experience of *gezucket* (rapture) and of the *Geburt* (birth) of the Word within the soul, he begins by discussing the "powers" within the soul:

Whatever the soul effects, she effects with her powers. What she understands, she understands with the intellect. What she remembers, she does with the memory; if she would love, she does that with the will, and thus she works with her powers and not with her essence. Every external act is linked with some means. The power of sight works only through the eyes; otherwise it can neither employ nor bestow vision, and so it is with all the other senses. The soul's every external act is effected by some means. (Walshe 1:3)

In addition to the five senses there are six powers: three lower (lower intellect, desire, and anger) and three higher (memory, higher intellect, and will). It is by their activity that the soul enters into and interacts with the external world (Walshe 1:4). We look at objects with our eyes, hear sounds with our ears, etc. (Walshe 1:4). The activity of the six higher powers generates thought and desire, that is, willing and cognitive or mental activity. So far, fairly standard scholastic psychology.

But, Eckhart continues, it is possible to "naught yourself for an instant . . ." (Walshe 1:144) in the state he calls *gezucket*, rapture, which is the pure consciousness event. In order to gain this state, one must stop the activities of the six powers and thereby come to "the soul's ground and innermost recess, into which no image ever shone nor (soul) power peeped" (Walshe 1:16). Because one has "forgotten" the powers, and gained "the summit of the soul," one reaches a realm "where time never entered, where no image ever shone in" (Walshe 1:148). This is the innermost level within the soul, the "innermost" man to which the powers have no access. To this realm Eckhart devotes his most enthralling language: within the soul there is a nameless place (Walshe 1:275), an "inmost man" (Clark and Skinner:183), a "silent middle." It is one's "being" or one's "essence." It is *in dem hochsten der sele*, the highest in the soul; *der sele geist*, the spirit of the soul; *das innigeist*, the inward spirit; *der grunt*, the ground; *das burgelin*, the little castle; etc. Most often, however, it is the *scintilla animae*, or *das funkelin der sele*, the spark of the soul.

It is here, to this "place" within, that man retires when he drops all external and internal works. When Eckhart continues the preceding passage, he describes this transcendent "place": "It is a strange and desert place, and is rather nameless than possessed of a name, and is more unknown than it is known" (Walshe 1:144). That is, despite the mystic going within, he or she will not arrive at a "place" which has any specific "objective" character: it is a "desert" and "nameless" place.

For Eckhart, then, the goal of the mystic's transformative journey is not an object at all, but is found within. It is found when one "forgets" images, that is, forgets cognitive and imaginative activities. Perhaps because it is beyond the powers, it cannot be named, it is a desert place, i.e., devoid of differentiating characteristics.

Finally, Eckhart emphasizes that it is the very highest realm within the soul, and it is connected with the ultimate.

The author of the *Cloud of Unknowing* argues for a similar idea. Although he, like Eckhart, advocates seeking God, in both *The Book of Privy Counselling* and in the *Cloud* he counsels his reader not to seek anything external. Rather one is to turn within, reducing all thoughts and affection (feeling) to naught: "Let your thought remain naked, your affection uninvolved, and remain nakedly as thou art" (Hodgson:76).[3] One is to hold oneself "whole and unscattered" in "naked blind being" (Hodgson:83). One is to eliminate all sense of externality: one is to remove all thoughts, for they scatter one's attention, and instead "hold thee before in the first part of thy spirit, which is thy being" (McCann:107); one is to hold the attention, "most substantially set in the naked sight and the blind feeling of thine own being" (McCann:109). Let the wits rest, let not the mind wander off to any "special beholding" (McCann:109) but rather remain at rest in the self. One is to remain within oneself at the deepest, quietest (McCann:105) point within. Most important, the practitioner is to move towards "that" which is at the "sovereign point of the spirit," i.e., move towards the very "highest" within the soul, beyond all the other powers and faculties. Hence when seeking that which is at the "sovereign point," it is not "to" somewhere or something "else" that one retires, but to the "highest" "place" within, indeed the very highest. Again we have an affirmation that the "goal" (a) is not "without" or an "object," but is found within the soul itself and (b) is found at "that" which is at the very highest within the soul, beyond the powers.

It is perhaps inevitable that two Christian mystics would assert something so similar. It may be more surprising that Eastern thinkers also assert that when one drops all thinking, perceiving, and imaging one gains access to that which is at once both sensory and thought transcendent, and also the very highest element within human life. For Shankara, the fundamental problematic to which he addresses himself is the conflation of the subject and the

---

[3] Translation mine in this and the next quotation.

object. When people superimpose (*adhyâsa*) the characteristics of the object "which has as its province the idea of the 'Thou,' and its qualities, to the pure spiritual subject, which has as its province the idea of the 'I' . . . so that they transfer the being and qualities of the one to the other, not separating object and subject," then ignorance (*avidyâ*) results (Deussen:52–4). When people take some feature of their personality or something they belong to or own to be that which is the self, then they have taken some object to be the subject. The soteriological aim of the Vedanta system is first to identify everything that is not the self, but which is transferred falsely to the self – all *upâdhi*s or individualizing personality features. These consist of all things and relations of the external world, the body, the *indriya*s, which are the five sense organs and five organs of action of the body, *manas*, or the inner organ *antaḥkaranam*, the central processing organ for both perception, thought and action, and the *mukhya prâṇa*, which provides nutrition to the body. Once identified, these can be seen as separate from the real Self or "I," which is present as spectator (*sâkṣin*) (Deussen:57–8). This true self consists only of consciousness (*caitanyam*). Thus, the goal of the mystic's journey is not some external object, as Brahman or Âtman is sometimes mistakenly described, but rather is inner, and indeed, the "highest" within the soul.

I had thought that Buddhism was an exception: although Yogâcârins and others speak of a hierarchical structure in the mind, with *sâmâdhi* being beyond all the powers, I had thought that when one retreats to that which is least "defiled" within the soul one gains not a something highest but a nothing. It was only when I read Gadjin Nagao's "'What remains' in *Śûnyatâ*" that I began to think that the pattern is again repeated here. In the highest meditative state, he notes, many texts have written that "something remains" (*avaśiṣṭa*). This sounds enigmatic, since *śûnyatâ* is generally accepted as negative in character. Nagao suggests that this is too simple a reading; rather, *śûnyatâ* has to do with the absence of the typical intentional relation between subject and object. As the *Madhyânta vibhāga* I:13 states this, "truly, the characteristic of emptiness is the nonexistence of the duality [of subject and object], and the existence of [that]

nonexistence" (Nagao:70). Whatever persists in the "highest" moments of meditation, then, is devoid of the usual intentional opposition between subject and object. [Nagao] goes on to document how this reading is found throughout much of the history of later Mahayana thought. Ninian Smart argues similarly (Smart:104). Thus that which is found, according to the Yogâcârins, in *samâdhi* transcends the ordinary subject–object structure of the ordinary perceptual thinking process, and is beyond the functions which lead to ordinary structures.

Now how can we best think about "what" is encountered during the mystic's experience? Most obviously, the mystic does not encounter anything like an external object. Rather it is found within. And indeed, "whatever" occurs there has nothing to do with the cognitive or affective powers. From my own experience I would affirm this. I knew, on coming out of the pure consciousness event, that I had been awake but was not thinking anything in particular. That is, in antique language, none of the intellectual powers had been functioning. And yet my persistence was not anything new, unusual, or "flashy." I was just the barest being present.

I propose the following model for this sort of experience: *what persisted in my meditative experience was consciousness itself*. I suggest that what is being spoken in different ways and with differing emphases by the above-quoted mystics as the highest within the soul *is the merest awareness itself*. It is not an object. It transcends the "powers." There is no distinction between subject and object in it, and it is the merest being present.

Towards a Definition of "Consciousness" as Used by Mystics

"Consciousness" is, of course, one of the most perniciously difficult terms to define. In part this is because it has such a multiplicity of uses and meanings. [. . .] Without denying the polyvalence of "consciousness," I will attempt to characterize its most fundamental meaning, for this is the sense of the term which is critical in mysticism. It is this sense of the term which is so difficult to define, principally because that to which it points resists clear and precise analysis or definition. As Sir William Hamilton observed:

Nothing has contributed more to spread obscurity over a very transparent matter, than the attempts of philosophers to define consciousness. Consciousness cannot be defined; we may be ourselves fully aware what consciousness is, but we cannot, without confusion, convey to others a definition of what we ourselves clearly apprehend. (Evans:45)

When John Dewey defined the "phenomenon of Self," he used the concept of consciousness in a similar way:

The self not only exists, but may know that it exists; psychical phenomena are not only facts, but they are facts of consciousness. . . . What distinguishes the facts of psychology from the facts of every other science is, accordingly, that they are conscious facts. . . . Consciousness can neither be defined nor described. We can define or describe anything only by the employment of consciousness. It is presupposed, accordingly, in all definitions and all attempts to define it must move in a circle.

When Dewey states that "we can define or describe anything only by the employment of consciousness," he points towards the sense of the term on which I wish to focus. "Consciousness" is that *for which* there are definitions, perceptions, etc. It is the knowing agent of any knowledge, and as such cannot (ordinarily) be known. Thus one cannot grasp hold of it enough to define it clearly. By its very nature it resists clear definition, since any definition is "for" consciousness.

Because this term so resists definition or analysis, I do not propose to define it, but rather, following John Wisdom, offer six "clues" to what I mean when I use this term. I am not trying to be coy, but instead as true as possible to the peculiar nature of consciousness. I believe that we know what it is to be conscious by virtue of our own experience of being conscious; I can only offer clues so that you know which aspect of your experience I mean.

(i) "Conscious" generally implies either "*feels*" or "*is aware*."

(ii) Wisdom wrote, "Consider the change which comes over a man as he comes round from chloroform or from dreamless sleep. You know quite well the kind of change I mean. That kind of change I call 'becoming conscious'." By this Wisdom did not mean the physiological changes, but rather "the kind of change which you immediately thought of when I spoke of the change from sleep or chloroform."

(iii) Wisdom notes that, while it may usually, "S is *conscious* need imply neither that (1) "S is conscious of his environment" nor (2) "S is conscious of himself." He points to dreams as an example of being conscious without an awareness of one's environment, and to a horse's or dog's consciousness as a being conscious devoid of self-awareness. A better example of a non-consciousness of one's environment is meditative experience, where the consciousness of one's physical positioning and environment rapidly fade away (Wisdom:12–15).

(iv) During meditation there is a difference between being awake without thoughts and being blacked out. There is a difference between being dead, asleep in dreamless sleep, being blacked out, and being conscious. The difference is more fundamental than that I perceive objects and think thoughts in one and not the other. The difference is that in one I am conscious and in the other I am not.

(v) There is no felt difference between being conscious during the thoughtless moments of meditation and being conscious during the rest of the day. Objects may fall off, but what it is to be conscious does not change. Another way of saying this is that at some level what it is like to be me does not change, whether or not I am perceiving objects.

(vi) If I am not conscious of a perception, I would say, "*I* did not perceive that." Even if I was in the room when something happened, but I was not conscious of it, I would say, "Oh, I didn't notice that." A perception must be for or by my consciousness to be mine. The difference between a perception and my perception is that I am conscious of the latter.

With my "clues" I am pointing to several interrelated aspects of our experience of being conscious. For me, being conscious is the critical feature in being awake, is what it is to be me at the most fundamental level, and is the subject of any knowing. Any thought or perception would not be mine and I would not be awake were I not conscious.

Typically consciousness carries an intentional tone; to be conscious is to be conscious of something. But with the pure consciousness event, mystics have added an unusual nuance to the ordinary intentional sense of "consciousness": human beings can persist though contentless. This leads towards the claim that a synonym of consciousness is not something like "awareness of anything at all" but rather "awareness *per se*."

Perhaps I can clarify what I mean by awareness *per se* by drawing an analogy with a radar receiver. In a radar system the transmitter sends out electro-magnetic waves of a certain frequency. If the waves reflect off of an object, say an airplane, the radar receiver "receives" and responds to those waves in various ways: it may send an electric signal to the monitor screen, it may set off a buzzer, whatever. While one might define a radar receiver as something which responds to the presence of airplanes, it seems to me it would be more accurate to say that a radar system is a mechanism which has the *capacity* to respond to the presence of airplanes in certain ways. For even if there are no airplanes within its range, if the machinery is turned on, the radar dish is "poised," as it were, to receive radar signals. It is "ready and able." It has the immediate capacity to receive and process appropriate incoming data without undergoing any structural changes in the way the electrons course through the wires or the radar dish spins.

Generally consciousness is thought to be intentional; that is, consciousness is thought to be analogous to the radar-dish-responding-to-airplanes. But this inappropriately includes the object in the definition of the subject or radar receiver. Consciousness should be defined more precisely as that which is *capable of* responding to certain phenomena, responding not to radar waves but, say, sound waves coming through our auditory faculty. Like the radar receiver, awareness *per se* undergoes no structural changes between being contentless and having

content. To be merely aware and to be aware of something need require no transformation in the continuity of awareness, but merely the addition of content.

I would point out that when we say that the radar dish is "on," we are pulling together several different notions. First is that it is poised to receive input. (This would be analogous to saying that to be conscious is to be awake and ready to perceive and/or act.) Second, when we say it is "on" we mean that if any airplanes fly across the radar's field, they will be noticed by this radar. That is, this radar will be the very same one which responds in certain ways to their presence. To be "on" is to be the agent of any responding, any "knowing." Similarly, when I assert I am conscious, I am asserting that I can be the subject of knowing, that I myself can become aware of anything at all. This is not to say that there are no mediating and/or constructive activities in any knowing. But it is to say that in order for there to be any knowing at all, someone must be aware of that knowing – in my case, *I* must be conscious of that knowing for it to be *my* knowledge.

One important implication here is that I am presenting consciousness as distinguishable from content. If consciousness was indistinguishable from its intentional objects, then it would be indistinguishable from some object. If so we could talk about objects but not about consciousness of those objects. That is, were consciousness not distinguishable from content, we could not conceive of the thesis of intentionality, which is, as Sartre put it, the notion that we are "confronted with a concrete and full presence *which is not consciousness*" (Sartre 1956:48; emphasis mine).

But even more compelling, the ability to tie together the beginning and end of any perception, or this pain with that perception or thought, requires a single enduring consciousness. To collapse the distinctions between content and consciousness would be to argue that successive perceptions belong to successive worlds of experience. This claim would force us to drop the possibility of both distinguishing successive mental states, and even make unintelligible the very notion of a single coherent stream of experience. That is, as Kant, Strawson, and others have argued, there must be some awareness which ties together temporally successive perceptions of content.[4]

Here then is my proposed model for what goes on in the pure consciousness event. The mystic persists being nothing other than, and nothing more than, the merest consciousness itself. If consciousness is defined as the persisting awareness itself, analogous to the persisting radar receiver itself, then conceiving of the pure consciousness event is unproblematic. In the pure consciousness event awareness itself persists, even though unaccompanied by intentional content. It is as if the radar dish were "switched on," but no airplanes happened to fly by.

Now that I have proposed a model for "what" is encountered in the pure consciousness event – an "experience" of awareness itself –, I would like address several possible objections to this proposed model. Primarily these objections center on a claim which seems, *prima facie,* incoherent.

Objections to the Model Considered

Objection 1: A number of philosophers state that all conscious experience must have content. Any claim that consciousness can be contentlessness is therefore a mistake. Consciousness is always and everywhere found with some content. "A person cannot be conscious without its being true that he is either perceiving, or having thoughts, emotions, etc." (Evans:49). "We can no more eliminate [conscious content] and be conscious without being conscious of something than we can separate a dog's bark from the dog" (Klein:36). After all, in any introspection all one ever comes across is the content or objects of consciousness, never consciousness itself. Hume, quoted above, stated this. So did G. E. Moore:

. . . the moment we try to fix our attention upon consciousness and to see what, distinctly, it is, it seems to vanish: it seems as if we had before us a mere emptiness. When we try to introspect the sensation of blue, all we can see is the blue: the other element is as if it were diaphanous. (Moore:17)

Because consciousness is always attending *to* some content, it cannot be directly encountered. As a result, when I try to introspect my own consciousness, what is doing the looking is gone by the time I look for it: now looking for the looker, as it were. It is like a dog trying to swallow its own tail: gone by the time that its head gets to where its tail was. Because consciousness is always found focused on some content, the search for itself is apparently doomed.

Response: Although these passages are taken from philosophical texts, they are actually making claims based on empirical observations. Hume makes the cogent and correct observation that whenever he enters into himself he stumbles on perceptions. When he says he *never can* catch himself without a perception, he is merely extrapolating from the empirical observation that he never *has*. Similarly Moore tries to fix his attention on consciousness but finds that it vanishes when he does so. When he tries to introspect the sensation of blue, his own consciousness seems to vanish into the perception. Both men are making empirical observations.

But on empirical matters, the statements of philosophers have absolutely no legislative force. No matter how many Humes, Moores, or Evanses claim that they cannot catch themselves devoid of perceptions, this tells us little about what a Sadhu, Carthusian monk, or Bhikku may be able to do after years of practice of certain mental or physical techniques. Indeed, many mystics do claim that they are undergoing something quite unusual and out of the ordinary. Hume may have tried to catch himself without a perception on two or three quiet, furtive attempts. Those attempts stood amidst a particular philosophical inquiry. Who is to say what he might have been able to accomplish in the way of achieving a silent consciousness after years of meditation, asceticism, and other practices whose "purpose" was (in part) to eliminate conscious content? Who is to say what a Moore might have seen in his sensation of blue after 20 years of Tantric visualizations of blue mandalas? These are *empirical* questions which deserve empirical – not logical – answers.

---

[4]   See Strawson (Part III, sect. 2). [. . .]

I am not saying that it is certain that a Hume would have achieved a pure consciousness event had he only had the right technique, but rather that the question of an empirical possibility is not something to which his empirical assertions about what he can or cannot sense in himself have finality or legislative force.

Objection 2: The claim that all states of consciousness have content is linguistic: we always and necessarily *mean* by "someone is conscious" that "someone is conscious of something." No state that is without content will count as a state of consciousness or awareness.

Response: According to this objection, the case against mine is approaching unfalsifiability. If anyone claims that they experience consciousness without objects, then it won't count as a "state of consciousness." What then would claims of pure consciousness events count for or against?

Furthermore, such a linguistic interpretation seems to reduce my critic's claims to a trivial exercise in semantics. Whether or not in general we use any particular term to signify awareness *per se* is beside the point. The mystic's claim is not semantic; rather it is that, to state it rather awkwardly, many people from a variety of ages and cultures claim to be sometimes non-sleeping, non-unconscious, and also without content. Perhaps we could invent a neologism or borrow a foreign term for consciousness in this new sense, e.g., *sakṣin, conscience, Bewusstsein sein,* etc. We should not eliminate the reports because they use language in a non-standard way, especially since part of the claim here is that there is a non-standard experience.

[...]

Knowledge of Consciousness by Acquaintance

I mentioned above that, as Wisdom suggested, I can only present "clues" to the meaning of consciousness. These are not ostensive or real definitions of consciousness, for logically they cannot be. Note that Wisdom said, "you know quite well the kind of change [from being under chloroform to being conscious] I mean," and that it is "the kind of change you immediately thought of." He is suggesting here what is

precisely correct about consciousness: we do not come to our acquaintance with consciousness by virtue of some analysis or ostensive definitions. Rather we know what it means to be conscious *by virtue of our being conscious.* That is, we take advantage of our *direct acquaintance* with being conscious.

This can be seen by thinking about how we might set about teaching what it means to be conscious to someone or something which was not conscious – say my Altima One computer. Even before beginning the attempt it is clear that this will be a hopeless enterprise, since what I mean by "conscious" seems available only to someone who knows what it is to be conscious by virtue of being conscious. No matter how many times my computer screen flashed the words "I know what it is to have a consciousness," I would not believe that it really did know what I meant. For like Wisdom, I can only define "consciousness" by referring the reader via clues or the equivalent towards that consciousness with which s/he has a direct acquaintance, the kind of direct acquaintance which comes from having a consciousness. Similarly, if someone proposes a theory of consciousness, I do not check it against some other theory of consciousness I know to be true; I check it against my own experience of being conscious.

There would be a temptation to interpret the acquaintance I have with my own awareness on the pattern of someone's being acquainted with another individual or with some information. But this would be decidedly wrong. Here there is no second party, no something *else* of which I have knowledge. The acquaintance which I have with being conscious is *sui generis.*

Language and the Knowledge of Consciousness

While it is true that we will have to identify "consciousness" for ourselves through a process of projection from "public" behavior and expressions like "you are conscious now, I see," that to which the term points is not a linguistically formulated entity. Just the reverse is true. This can be seen very simply. For a child to learn any language at all, he or she must be conscious. Being conscious, or having a consciousness, is presupposed by language acquisition, not the other way around. Awareness *per se* must be present not only before someone can learn the word "consciousness" and the concept "consciousness," but it must be present before one can learn or use any word at all. It makes no sense to say that someone can learn a language if they are not conscious, for one feature of being conscious is that they have the capacity to perceive, hear, or respond.

Hence consciousness itself is not constructed or formed by language, though an understanding *that* I am conscious is certainly so formed. Understanding that I am conscious and being conscious are not the same thing. When a child first learns the word "conscious" or "consciousness" s/he will ground that term on his/her own consciousness in exactly the same way as anyone else; i.e., s/he will capitalize on his/her own direct acquaintance with consciousness. Hence it is not the case that s/he will gain an acquaintance with consciousness by virtue of learning the term "consciousness," but vice versa. The acquaintance I have of what it means to be conscious cannot be *articulated* without knowledge of a language system, the term "consciousness," or a synonym. A non-speaking person's acquaintance with his/her own consciousness will remain mute; but in order for anyone to know what it is to be conscious s/he must be able to capitalize on that primary and direct acquaintance.

Consciousness as the Ability to Remember Anything at All

One function of awareness *per se* is that it is able to tie the beginning and end of a perception together. That is, entailed by the notion of consciousness is that we have the ability to *remember* anything at all. To be conscious is to be able to remember. This is not to assert that memory is a simple function. As philosophy of mind has shown, memory is a complex process which can involve comparison, deduction, inference, language, etc. But it is to say that the ability to tie two or more thoughts, percepts, feelings, etc., together requires a single consciousness which holds them together. To remember anything at all requires that I can tie

two thoughts or percepts together: and this is part of what it means to be conscious.

In the radar receiver analogy, we can say that to mark the presence of any airplane requires that its signal must be channelled to the very same radar dish and monitor that received signals from other airplanes. Otherwise we would not say that they were all seen by *this* radar receiver.

To remember anything at all also means that, in some sense, the awareness which perceived something in the past is the same awareness as the awareness which is remembering something now. That is to say that, as Strawson put this, there must be an unbroken continuity of awareness between past and present. And in order for both a past perception and a present one to be "my" perceptions, I must have been conscious of the past one and the present one. That is what I mean when I say I can remember something, i.e., that *I* was conscious of something in the past, and it is the same I as the I which is conscious in the present of the memory. Indeed, this is the basis of Kant's First Critique.

Being conscious in the sense of being able to remember anything at all is pre-required by learning a language. Language use is not entailed by memory (animals can remember), whereas the capacity to remember is entailed by language use. Part of remembering anything at all entails that there has been a continuity of awareness between past and present. This is part of what I mean when I say, "I am conscious."

Immediate Knowledge of Consciousness

I am certain that I have been awake for the last five minutes. Drawing this out, I am certain that I am conscious now and that I am tying together past with present in a single unbroken consciousness. I do not infer this. It is not based on observation or on evidence. I *just know* that I am awake now, that my consciousness is one and undivided (simple) with the consciousness I had five minutes ago.

There seems to be a *direct* form of knowledge at work here. With reference to most knowing, I would not disagree with Katz when he asserts that knowledge is generally available through a complex set of epistemological processes:

...all (sic) experience is processed through, organized by, and makes itself available to us in extremely complex epistemological ways. (Katz 1978:26)

And the kind of beings we are requires that experience be not only instantaneous and discontinuous, but that it also involve memory, apprehension, expectation, language, accumulation of prior experience, concepts, and expectations, with each experience being built on the back of all these elements and being shaped anew by each fresh experience. (Katz 1978:59)

However, the knowledge that I am and have been conscious does not seem to be "processed through" these "extremely complex epistemological ways." The knowledge that I am aware and have been aware for the last several minutes is not a matter of language and does not stand on the back of all prior experiences. I just know that I am and have been aware. It comes with being aware.

Of this continuity of consciousness I have, again, knowledge by direct acquaintance. This form of knowledge by direct acquaintance is at once simple yet ripe with possibilities: my awareness *per se* is a unity, but it can become aware of any thought or perception, any language, any possible concept, etc. Though it is required by any concept acquisition or application, this form of direct knowledge is not linguistic. It may be *expressed* in language, but it is pre-required by any speech or understanding. It is a direct "intuitive" knowing, if by intuitive we understand a non-analytical form of knowledge. The knowledge that I am aware is, in other words, not a knowledge like any other. It is direct, indubitable, and incorrigible.

It may be objected that sometimes certain facts or statements may be discerned which may cause me to question a judgment about a first-person experience statement, and therefore my first-person assertions are, at least in part, inferential. I may doubt, for instance, an experience of a reddish patch because I know that it could not have been one: I was looking, say, at a mountain bluebird (which has no red

areas) and my eyes are functioning normally. As Nelson Goodman says, "If a statement may be withdrawn in the interest of compatibility [with] other statements, it is not certain in any ordinary sense; for certainty consists of immunity to such withdrawal" (161). However, in the present case, I cannot imagine circumstances which might cause me to say, if awkwardly, "I thought I was conscious at what seemed to me to be a moment ago when I saw what I took to be a such and such (in either the waking or dreaming sense), but that does not make sense in the light of such and such a perception, thought, etc." One might object that I have been in a coma and what seemed to me to be a moment ago was really three days ago, or that I am on a spaceship travelling at nearly the speed of light and my sense of time is not that of an earthling's. But I am speaking here of a change in my sense of being conscious, not in my sense of time. My time sense is doubtable and therefore in part inferential, but my sense of being conscious is not.

Knowledge by Identity

Although I can say my sense of having an awareness *per se* is not inferential, I cannot say *how* I know this. I can never get "beyond" or "below" my own consciousness in order to trace any more fundamental principles on which to account for this knowing.

I would call the knowledge I have of my own consciousness a "knowledge by identity" and distinguish it from intentional knowledge.[5] In intentional knowledge three distinct elements must be involved: the knower, the object known, and the epistemological process(es) involved in that knowing. In the case of my knowledge of an external object, the object is clearly distinct from the subject. Here the sorts of complex mediating or constructing epistemological processes referred to by the constructivists are clearly involved. Even in the case of so-called self-knowledge, some aspect of the personality or ego, a disposition, or a concept

[5]   See Merrell-Wolff (93–7). [...]

of the self serves as the intentional object, and all the constructive activities of the mind come into play.

In knowledge by identity, on the other hand, the subject knows something by virtue of being it. In this case, I know what it is to be conscious, what it is to have "my" consciousness, because and only because I am or have that consciousness.[6] I am not acquainted with consciousness through a conceptual knowledge of something but because being something in this case carries within itself this odd self-referential form of knowledge. I know my consciousness simply because I am it.

It is hard to say much about the mechanics of this knowledge by identity. This is due in part to the fact that, by its nature, it is beyond what I *can* know. I cannot know anything about the mechanics of my ability to recall my own being awake, since my ability to recall anything at all is directly connected with this ability. I cannot know anything about the epistemological processes involved in tying perceptions and thoughts together, since, as stated, any epistemological processes are "for" this process, and knowing what it means to do this at all is part and parcel of the ability to do it, i.e., being conscious. Because this knowledge is *simple* in the sense of utterly without complexity or plurality, I cannot tease out its constituent parts and elements: parts and elements are known by consciousness.

I can say two things about this knowledge by identity, however: first, that being conscious and, related to this, each person's knowledge that "I am conscious," are one phenomenon which is utterly and precisely shared by all human beings. I stated above that I can't teach a computer what it means to be conscious. The knowledge of being conscious is available only to someone who knows this by virtue of being conscious, i.e., by a familiarity with consciousness by acquaintance. Indeed I would say that this acquaintance is part of, if not the principle element of, what it means to be human. No matter what our language and conceptual system may be, we are each as privy to this knowledge by identity as is anyone else. This knowledge by acquaintance is, by nature, available to anyone and everyone. And this acquaintance with our own consciousness is an acquaintance which is not pluralistic. We cannot in theory distinguish a thirteenth-century Dominican monk's having an awareness *per se* (or an acquaintance with having an awareness *per se)* from a twentieth-century practitioner of Siddha Yoga's having an awareness *per se.*

Second, knowledge by identity, because it is beyond the reach of all ordinary concepts and language, leaves it open to a virtually infinite range of theories, explanations, and modes of expression and descriptions. The reader will remember that I said above that I will check any theory of what it means to be conscious not against any other theory but against my own acquaintance with being conscious. Thus the only natural constraints on theories of consciousness are that they are enough in accord with our innate acquaintance with being conscious that they will stand up to that sort of check. Because that sort of check is so vague and ethereal, many theories can meet it. Hence theories of consciousness can be widely diverse. While I may speak of the acquaintance with the continuity of awareness *per se*, a Meister Eckhart may be referring to this element when he speaks of "*das funklein*" which is the highest "power." Consciousness is the highest "power," if we think of the cognitive capacities of the soul as hierarchically related. With the Advaitan we may speak of consciousness as separate from the *upâdhis* (individualizing personality features) and as a witness (*sâksin*). If so, then it is only consciousness (*caitanyam*). With the Buddhist we can say that the awareness *per se* is *śûnyatâ* in the sense of devoid of the subject/object distinction. With the *Cloud* author we may say that consciousness is at the level of my being, since what it is to *be* me is to have my consciousness.

---

[6] Here the terms "my," "I," etc. become problematic. Consciousness is at once the subject of any first-person appellation yet also unreatled to anything denoting personality, possession, etc. Some would have consciousness impersonal; some would have it personal. I note only it is problematic to say either.

Remembering in Meditation

In the pure consciousness event one "forgets" language but does not lose consciousness. As noted, I have argued elsewhere that meditation frequently involves a form of forgetting (1990b). Clearly, however, when the *Cloud* author instructs his readers to enter a cloud of forgetting, he is *not* suggesting that one should lose awareness *per se*. I said in one of my clues that I know there is a difference between being conscious and blacking out, and certainly these authors are not after utter blackout! Indeed, the reason that the pure consciousness event is so interesting is that consciousness itself does not go away when one ceases thinking. One stops thinking, not persisting.

It is striking that, although language, ordinary memory, etc. are laid aside, "something" remains to be "recalled." As Yogâcârins put this, "something remains." Once all language and constructed knowledge are laid aside, one reveals or comes to nothing but this innate capacity to be conscious, if you will, the capacity to hold together past and present. Generally this encounter with our own awareness *per se* is inaccessible due to the preoccupation with intentional content. To see anything at all is typically to be lost to our sense of being conscious. The above-quoted passage from G. E. Moore communicates this, as does McGinn:

> Consider your consciousness *of* some item – an external object, your own body, a sensation – and try to focus attention on that relation: as many philosophers have observed, this relation of consciousness to its objects is peculiarly impalpable and diaphanous – all you come across in introspection are the objects of consciousness, not consciousness itself. This feature of consciousness has induced some thinkers to describe consciousness as a kind of inner emptiness; it is nothing *per se* but a pure directedness on the things other than itself. (McGinn: 13)

However, if one has "forgotten" all content for consciousness in the pure consciousness event, he or she apparently has come to just that "impalpable and diaphanous" element which has been present all along.

I said above that in the pure consciousness event the mystic recalls being conscious in the ordinary way. Now I think we are ready to answer the quandary about how the mystic may remember that s/he has been conscious despite there being no content. It makes perfectly good sense to believe that in pure consciousness events the mystic is not having an experience which is linguistically formulated and/or constructed.

How is it possible that someone can remember that they have been awake during a PCE? To know this I would have to be able to say how someone could know that they were conscious a moment ago, that there was an unbroken continuity of awareness between then and now, and that they have an awareness at all. But I have said that, though I am as certain of this as I am of anything, *I cannot say how I know this*. I know that I do not infer it, for it is a fact more fundamental than any on which I might base my inference. Yet I have not the foggiest notion of how I do know this.

Malcolm quotes Wittgenstein as saying in a lecture that it is an important thing in philosophy to know when to *stop* (Malcolm:87). If ever there was an instance of knowing where to stop, it is in speculating about how we know that we are conscious and have been conscious and that the unbroken continuity between these two is a single consciousness.

In short, the answer to the seeming paradox of how someone can remember being awake without content is, quite frankly, *I do not know*. And this is because the mechanics of consciousness remembering itself are something we *cannot* know. This is not to say we cannot remember having been conscious a moment ago. We just do not know how we know this. And we are as in the dark for ordinary experiences as we are for mystical ones. There is no special problem in not knowing how I recall being awake in PCE. I just know I was awake, like always!

Objections Considered

Objection 1: "I know I was conscious a few moments ago by inference from the fact that I had certain content. Since there is no content in the pure consciousness event there is no basis for such an inference. Therefore it cannot be known."[7]

Response: To assert that I infer thus is incorrect. Making such an inference would be sufficient but not necessary. I do not always *infer* that I have been conscious for the last five minutes, for what could serve as conditions more fundamental to being conscious in terms of which I can make this inference? Rather any inference could, and probably sometimes does, go the other way. If someone said to me, "What was going on in your mind 5 minutes ago?" sometimes I remember what I was thinking about, and I could infer being conscious on its basis. But often I could say, "Let's see, I know I wasn't asleep, I'm sure I was conscious. Now what was I thinking about?" Very often you cannot remember your thoughts and would have to work to remember them. But you never have to work to remember that you were awake. You just know it. Having been conscious at what seemed to be 5 minutes ago is indubitable; knowing that I was thinking of such and such is highly doubtable.

I might also add that the objection begs the question. It *assumes* that we can remember only content. But this is just the point under debate: whether or not someone can remember being contentless.

Objection 2: I am asserting that we do not know *how* someone recalls being awake, yet that it makes sense *that* someone can plausibly remember this. This assertion of philosophical ignorance seems to justify neither the recall nor the non-recall of my consciousness.

Response: To this objection I respond that a plea of ignorance about how something takes place has no force concerning an empirical claim. That scientists do not understand how a bee can fly given the size of his wings doesn't hamper the bee one bit. I cannot say how I turn spaghetti into living tissue, yet I do it! That I cannot say *how* someone can remember being conscious does not mean that people cannot so remember. All the philosophical claim of ignorance accomplishes is to remove logical blocks from a claimed possibility. In this sense it is not neutral; it affects only one side, my

critics who say the claim of consciousness without objects is impossible.

Reflections on This Model

The model I have proposed in this paper is that, rather than encountering something like a pencil, a thought of a pencil, or a feeling about a pencil, the mystic in the pure consciousness event is encountering nothing other than his or her own consciousness. This model has several advantages. First, it makes sense of the non-linguistic character of the mystical experience suggested by the forgetting model. Just as consciousness itself is pre-required by any language acquisition and is therefore not linguistic, so, too, persisting in and through one's own consciousness is a persisting in and through perhaps our only non-linguistic feature.

Second, unlike the "object" model for mysticism, which is self-evidently based on non-mystical experiences, this model was developed out of a reading of mystical texts, mystical experiences, and interviews with people who have had such experiences. Thus it is a model which should fit the evidence more naturally.

And indeed, this model, though it is philosophically very obscure at points, does seem to cut at the joints. Our originating accounts suggest that there is something highly significant, indeed a touch of the ultimate, which the person carries within him- or herself "at the highest power" or at the level of their being. This, I propose, is consciousness itself, which is the highest "power" and which is essential to any knowing. In order to get to that highest power, we need to put the other powers behind a "cloud of forgetting" – i.e., "forget" to use the other intellectual and perceptual capacities. Consciousness is devoid of the distinction between subject and object. And consciousness is the "I" sought by Shankara.

But how are we to conceive of the mystic's recollection of this event? There are two major ways to conceptualize this, which may not be, at their heart, too different. On the one hand there are those who suggest that consciousness just has the capacity to remember itself: a self-referential

---

[7]   Such a critique was made by Wayne Proudfoot in a private conversation, November 1987.

capacity. It comes with being conscious, we might say. This is the vocabulary with which I am most comfortable. Part of being awake is not only tying together my consciousness at different times, but a direct knowledge, through a knowledge by identity, that I am and have been conscious. The other way to conceive of this was suggested to me by the Theravadin monk, Ven. Ananda Maitreya, which fits the Buddhist agenda more naturally: in the pure consciousness event subjectivity serves as its own "object." "What" I am aware of is my own consciousness-serving-as-object. Conceiving in this way he protected the intentional structure of the mind – not to mention intentional grammar – which is so important to Abhidamma thought.

The problems with this model, however, are not minor. First, it tends to affirm certain kinds of mysticism as paradigmatic. R. L. Franklin has observed that this model, as well as our interest in the pure consciousness event, tends to overemphasize this kind of experience and de-emphasize the intentional-sounding mystical experience of God, for example, or of Kṛṣṇa. Mine is, as Franklin and the anonymous reader of an earlier draft of this paper have rightly observed, an orientation which seems Advaitan. True, though perhaps some orientation is unavoidable given any language use. I like to think that I have at least gotten right the majority report. I do not think, however, that this accusation is entirely warranted. I have earlier suggested that awareness *per se*, which is encountered in meditation, may be construed as a "something" (not the sensory, not linguistic, not a thing, not characterized as an intentional object). For those mystics who seek a God at the highest power within, consciousness-as-a-something talk would suit best. For those seeking annihilation, a desert, or *śūnyatā*, then the pure consciousness event can best be spoken of with nothing-talk. This doesn't necessarily mean that because we have different language we have different entities: if any "thing" can be the same "thing" but conceived of differently, it is consciousness itself. Thus I would suggest that this model does allow for both pluralism of conception and a cross-cultural homogeneity of underlying structure and experience form. Mine may be viewed as a plea for the recognition of sameness *and* difference.

Philosophically there are several oddities about this model. It is odd to speak of anything without the ordinary subject–object distinction. Clearly grammatical problems abound. And, for those who haven't undergone such an experience, it is hard even to imagine it, though the readers who have undergone mystical experiences may not feel this.

But the extraordinary character of this claim may still, in this case, cut at the joints. Mystics do sometimes declare that, though we have always enjoyed something critical which makes such an event possible, the actual experiencing of this capacity is new. In this model, consciousness has always been present to itself, but the experiencing of consciousness *solo* is novel. This oddity seems the right oddity.

References

Alexander, Charles, Ken Chandler, and Robert Boyer n.d. "Experience and Understanding of Pure Consciousness in the Vedic Science of Maharishi Mahesh Yogi." Unpublished manuscript.

Bernhardt, Steven 1990 "Are Pure Consciousness Events Unmediated?" In *The Problem of Pure Consciousness*. Ed. by Robert K. C. Forman. New York: Oxford University Press.

Brown, Daniel 1986 "The Stages of Meditation in Cross-cultural Perspective." In *Transformations of Consciousness: Conventional and Contemplative Perspectives on Development*. Ed. by Ken Wilber, Jack Engler, and Daniel Brown. Boston: Shambhala.

Chapple, Christopher 1990 "The Unseen Seer and the Field: Consciousness in Samkhya and Yoga." In *The Problem of Pure Consciousness*. Ed. by Robert K. C. Forman. New York: Oxford University Press.

Clark, James M., and John V. Skinner, ed. and trans. 1958 *Meister Eckhart: Selected Treatises and Sermons*. London: Faber and Faber.

Deussen, Paul 1912 *The System of the Vedanta*. New York: Dover Publications.

Dewey, John   *Psychology*, third edition. New
1883   York: Harper.

Evans, C. O.   *The Subject of Consciousness.*
1970   London: George Allen and Unwin;
               New York: Humanities Press.

Forman,   "Pure Consciousness Events
Robert K. C.   and Mysticism." *Sophia* 251
1986   1:49–58.
1987   "Mystical Experience in the *Cloud*
               Literature." In *The Medieval
               Mystical Tradition in England:
               Exeter Symposium IV*. Ed. by
               Marion Glasscoe. Cambridge:
               D. S. Brewer.
1988   "A Construction of Mystical
               Experience." *Faith and Philosophy*
               5 3:254–68.
1990a   "Eckhart, *Gezucken* and the
               Ground of the Soul." In *The
               Problem of Pure Consciousness.*
               Ed. by Robert K. C. Forman.
               New York: Oxford University
               Press.
1990b   "Introduction: Mysticism, Con-
               structivism and Forgetting." In
               *The Problem of Pure Conscious-
               ness*. Ed. by Robert K. C. Forman.
               New York: Oxford University
               Press.

Franklin, R. L.   "Experience and Interpretation
1990   in Mysticism." In *The Problem
               of Pure Consciousness*. Ed. by
               Robert K. C. Forman. New York:
               Oxford University Press.

Gill, Jerry 1980   "Religious   Experience   as
               Mediated," Philosophy Section,
               American Academy of Religion,
               unpublished.
1984   "Mysticism   and   Mediation."
               Faith and Philosophy 1: 111–121.

Goodman, Nelson   "Sense and Certainty." *Philoso-
1952   phical Review* 61 2:160–7.

Griffiths, Paul J.   "Pure Consciousness and Indian
1990   Buddhism". In *The Problem
               of Pure Consciousness*. Ed. by
               Robert K. C. Forman. New York:
               Oxford University Press.

Hodgson, P.   *Deonise Hid Diuinite and Other
1955   Treatises on Contemplative Prayer
               Related to the Cloud of Unknow-
               ing*. London: Early English Text
               Society.

Hume, David   *A Treatise of Human Nature*. Ed.
1888   by L. A. Selby-Bigge. Oxford:
               Clarendon Press.

Katz, Steven T.   "Language, Epistemology and
1978   Mysticism." In *Mysticism and
               Philosophical Analysis*. Ed. by
               Steven Katz. New York: Oxford
               University Press.
1983   "The 'Conservative' Character of
               Mystical Experience." In *Mysticism
               and Religious Traditions*. Ed. by
               Steven Katz. New York: Oxford
               University Press.

Klein, David Ballin   *The Concept of Consciousness:
1984   A Survey*. Lincoln: University of
               Nebraska Press.

Malcolm, Norman   *Dreaming*. London: Routledge
1959   and Kegan Paul.

Matt, Daniel   "Ayin: The Concept of Nothing-
1990   ness in Jewish Mysticism." In
               *The Problem of Pure Conscious-
               ness*. Ed. by Robert K. C. Forman.
               New York: Oxford University
               Press.

McCann, Justin, ed.   *The Cloud of Unknowing and
1952   Other Treatises by an English
               Mystic of the Fourteenth Century*.
               London: Macmillan.

McGinn, Colin   *The Character of Mind*. Oxford:
1982   Oxford University Press.

Merrell-Wolff,   *Pathways   through   to   Space.*
Franklin   New York Warner Books.
1973

Moore, G. E.   *Philosophical Studies*. London:
1960   Routledge.

Nagao, Gadjin   " 'What Remains' in *Śunyatâ*:
1978   A Yogâcâra Interpretation of
               Emptiness." In *Mahâyâna Buddhist
               Meditation: Theory and Practice*.
               Ed. by Minoru Kiyota. Honolulu:
               University Press of Hawaii.

Perovich, Anthony,   "Does   the   Philosophy   of
Jr.   Mysticism Rest on a Mistake?"
1990   In *The Problem of Pure Con-
               sciousness*. Ed. by Robert K. C.
               Forman. New York: Oxford
               University Press.

Perry, Ralph Barton   "Conceptions and Misconcep-
1904   tions of Consciousness." *Psycho-
               logical Review* 11:282–96.

Prigge, Norman and Gary Kessler 1990 "Is Mystical Experience Everywhere the Same?" In *The Problem of Pure Consciousness*. Ed. by Robert K. C. Forman. New York: Oxford University Press.

Proudfoot, Wayne 1984 *Religious Experience*. Berkeley: University of California Press.

Rothberg, Donald 1990 "Contemporary Epistemology and the Study of Mysticism." In *The Problem of Pure Consciousness*. Ed. by Robert K. C. Forman. New York: Oxford University Press.

Sartre, Jean Paul n.d. *The Transcendence of the Ego*. Trans. by Forest Williams and Robert Kirkpatrick. New York: Farrar, Strauss and Giroux.

1956 *Being and Nothingness*. Trans. by Hazel Barnes. New York: The Philosophical Library.

Smart, Ninian 1976 *Doctrine and Argument in Indian Philosophy*. Atlantic Highlands: Humanities Press.

Stace, W. T. 1960 [1980] *Mysticism and Philosophy*. London: Macmillan.

Strawson, P. F. 1966 *The Bounds of Sense*. London: Methuen and Co., Ltd.

Wainwright, William 1981 *Mysticism: A Study of its Nature, Cognitive Value and Moral Implications*. Madison: University of Wisconsin Press.

Walshe, M. O'C. 1981 *Meister Eckhart: German Sermons and Treatises*. London: Watkins & Dulverton.

Wisdom, John 1934 *Problems of Mind and Matter*. Cambridge: Cambridge University Press.

Woodhouse, Mark 1990 "On the Possibility of Pure Consciousness." In *The Problem of Pure Consciousness*. Ed. by Robert K. C. Forman. New York: Oxford University Press.

The Difference between Union and Rapture

Teresa of Ávila

I. Union

While the soul is seeking God in this way, it feels with the most marvelous and gentlest delight that everything is almost fading away through a kind of swoon in which breathing and all the bodily energies gradually fail. This experience comes about in such a way that one cannot even stir the hands without a lot of effort. The eyes close without one's wanting them to close; or if these persons keep them open, they see hardly anything – nor do they read or succeed in pronouncing a letter, nor can they hardly even guess what the letter is. They see the letter; but since the intellect gives no help, they don't know how to read it even though they may desire to do so. They hear but don't understand what they hear. Thus they receive no benefit from the senses – unless it be that these latter do not take away their pleasure, since doing so would cause harm. In vain do they try to speak because they don't succeed in forming a word, nor if they do succeed is there the strength left to be able to pronounce it. All the external energy is lost, and that of the soul is increased so that it might better enjoy its glory. The exterior delight that is felt is great and very distinct.

This prayer causes no harm, no matter how long it lasts. At least it never caused me any, nor do I recall the Lord ever having granted me this favor that I didn't feel much better afterward no matter how ill I had been before. But what illness can produce so wonderful a blessing? The external effects are so apparent that one cannot doubt that a great event has taken place; these external powers are taken away with such delight in order to leave greater ones.

It is true that in the beginning this prayer passes so quickly – at least it happened this way to me – that neither these exterior signs nor the failure of the senses are very noticeable. But the soul well understands that the sun's brightness therein was powerful since it melted the soul away. It is noteworthy that the longest space of time, in my opinion, in which the soul remains in this suspension of all the faculties is very short; should it remain suspended for a half hour, this would be a very long time. I don't think I ever experienced this suspension for so long. It is true that since there is no sensory consciousness one finds it hard to know what is happening. But I am saying that in an occurrence of this prayer only a short time passes

"The Difference between Union and Rapture" by Teresa of Ávila, from *The Collected Works of St Teresa of Ávila*, Vol. 1, trans. Kieran Kavanaugh and Otilio Rodriguez (Washington, DC: ICS Publications, 1976), pp. 161–2; 172–5; 179–80. Reprinted by permission of ICS Publications.

without one of the faculties returning to itself. It is the will that holds high the banner; the other two faculties quickly go back to being a bother. Since the will remains quiet, the others are again suspended for a little while – then return again to life.

In this way a person can and in fact does spend several hours in prayer. Once the two faculties have begun to taste the divine wine and be inebriated by it, they easily lose themselves again so as to gain much more; and they accompany the will, and all three rejoice. But I say this loss of them all and suspension of the imagination – which as I understand it is also completely lost – lasts only a short while; yet these faculties don't return to themselves so completely that they are incapable of remaining for several hours as though bewildered while God gradually gathers them again to Himself.

[. . .]

II.   Rapture

I should like to know how to explain, with God's help, the difference there is between union and rapture, or, as they call it, elevation or flight of the spirit, or transport, which are all the same. I mean that these latter terms, though different, refer to the same thing; it is also called ecstasy. The advantage rapture has over union is great. The rapture produces much stronger effects and causes many other phenomena. Union seems the same at the beginning, in the middle, and at the end; and it takes place in the interior of the soul. But since these other phenomena are of a higher degree, they produce their effect both interiorly and exteriorly. May the Lord explain as He did for the other degrees. Certainly, if His Majesty had not given me an understanding of the manners and ways in which something could be said about them, I would not have known how to speak of them.

Let us consider now that the last water we spoke of is so plentiful that, if it were not for the fact that the earth doesn't allow it, we could believe that this cloud of His great Majesty is with us here on earth. But when we thank Him for this wonderful blessing, responding with works according to our strength, the Lord gathers up the

soul, let us say now, in the way the clouds gather up the earthly vapors and raises it completely out of itself. The cloud ascends to heaven and brings the soul along, and begins to show it the things of the kingdom that He prepared for it. I don't know if this comparison is holding together, but the truth of the matter is that this is what happens.

In these raptures it seems that the soul is not animating the body. Thus there is a very strong feeling that the natural bodily heat is failing it. The body gradually grows cold, although this happens with the greatest ease and delight. At this stage there is no remedy that can be used to resist. In the union, since we are upon our earth, there is a remedy; though it may take pain and effort one can almost always resist. But in these raptures most often there is no remedy; rather, without any forethought or any help there frequently comes a force so swift and powerful that one sees and feels this cloud or mighty eagle raise it up and carry it aloft on its wings.

I say that one understands and sees oneself carried away and does not know where. Although this experience is delightful, our natural weakness causes fear in the beginning. It is necessary that the soul be resolute and courageous – much more so than for the prayer already described – in order to risk all, come what may, and abandon itself into the hands of God and go willingly wherever it is brought since, like it or not, one is taken away. So forceful is this enrapturing that very many times I wanted to resist and used all my energy, especially sometimes when it happened in public or other times when in secret and I was afraid of being deceived. At times I was able to accomplish something, but with a great loss of energy, as when someone fights with a giant and afterward is worn out. At other times it was impossible for me to resist, but it carried off my soul and usually, too, my head along with it, without my being able to hold back – and sometimes the whole body until it was raised from the ground.

[. . .]

In those to whom this experience happens, the effects are remarkable. First, there is a manifestation of the tremendous power of the Lord and of how we are incapable, when His Majesty desires, of holding back the body any more than the soul, nor are we its master. Rather, whether or not we wish, we see that there is one who is superior, that these favors are given by Him, and that of ourselves we can do absolutely nothing; deep humility is impressed upon the soul. Yet I confess that the favor greatly frightened me; at first the fear is extreme. When one sees one's body so elevated from the ground that even though the spirit carries it along after itself, and does so very gently if one does not resist, one's feelings are not lost. At least I was conscious in such a way that I could understand I was being elevated. There is revealed a majesty about the One who can do this that makes a person's hair stand on edge, and there remains a strong fear of offending so awesome a God. Yet such fear is accompanied by a very great love for Him, which grows ever deeper upon considering what He does to so rotten a worm. It doesn't seem He is satisfied in truly bringing the soul to Himself, but it seems He desires the body even though it is mortal and, on account of the many offenses it has committed, made of such foul clay.

The experience also leaves a rare detachment, which I am unable to describe. It seems to me that I can say the prayer is in a certain way different. I mean that more than spiritual things alone are involved. For now that the spirit is completely detached from things, it seems in this prayer that the Lord wants to effect this detachment in the body itself, and there is brought about a new estrangement from earthly things that makes life much more arduous.

[. . .]

Now let us return to raptures and speak of what is more common in them. I say that often, it seemed to me, the body was left so light that all its weight was gone, and sometimes this feeling reached such a point that I almost didn't know how to put my feet on the ground. Now when the body is in rapture it is as though dead, frequently being unable to do anything of itself. It remains in the position it was when seized by the rapture, whether standing or sitting, or whether with the hands opened or closed. Although once in a while the senses fail (sometimes it happened to me that they failed completely), this occurs rarely and for only a short time. But ordinarily the soul is disoriented. Even though it can't do anything of itself with regard to exterior things, it doesn't fail to understand and hear as though it were listening to something coming from far off. I do not say that it hears and understands when it is at the height of the rapture (I say "height" to refer to the times when the faculties are lost to other things because of their intense union with God), for then, in my opinion, it neither sees, nor hears, nor feels. But as I said in speaking of the previous prayer of union, this complete transformation of the soul in God lasts only a short time; but while it lasts no faculty is felt, nor does the soul know what is happening in this prayer. Perhaps it doesn't know this because God doesn't want us to understand this while on earth; He knows we are incapable of doing so. I have seen this for myself.

Divine Intoxication

al-Ghazali (Abu Hamid)

The gnostics, after having ascended to the heaven of reality, agree that they see nothing in existence save the One, the Real. Some of them possess this state as a cognitive gnosis. Others, however, attain this through a state of lasting. Plurality is totally banished from them, and they become immersed in sheer singularity. Their rational faculties become so satiated that in this state they are, as it were, stunned. No room remains in them for the remembrance of any other than God, nor the remembrance of themselves. Nothing is with them but God. They become intoxicated with such an intoxication that the ruling authority of their rational faculty is overthrown. Hence, one of them says, "I am the Real!" another, "Glory be to me, how great is my station!" and still another, "There is nothing in my robe but God!"

The speech of lovers in the state of intoxication should be concealed and not spread about. When this intoxication subsides, the ruling authority of the rational faculty – which is God's balance in His earth – is given back to them. They come to know that what they experienced was not the reality of unification but that it was similar to unification. It was like the words of the lover during a state of extreme passionate love:

> I am He whom I love,
> and He whom I love is I!

It is not unlikely that a person could look into a mirror in an unexpected place and not see the mirror at all. He supposes that the form he sees is the mirror's form and that it is united with the mirror. Likewise, he could see wine in a glass and suppose that the wine is the glass's color. When the situation becomes familiar to him and his foot becomes firmly established within it, he asks for forgiveness from God and says:

> The glass is clear, the wine is clear,
> the two are similar, the affair confused,
> As if there is wine and no glass,
> or glass and no wine.

There is a difference between saying "The wine is the cup" and "It is *as if* the wine is the cup."

When this state gets the upper hand, it is called "extinction" in relation to the one who possesses it. Or, rather, it is called "extinction from extinction," since the possessor of the state is extinct from himself and from his own extinction. For he is conscious neither of himself in that state, nor of his own unconsciousness of himself. If

"Divine Intoxication" from *The Niche of Lights*, by al-Ghazali (Abu Hamid), trans. David Buchman (Provo, UT: Brigham Young University Press, 1998), pp. 17–18. Reprinted by permission of Brigham Young University.

he were conscious of his own unconsciousness, then he would [still] be conscious of himself. In relation to the one immersed in it, this state is called "unification," according to the language of metaphor, or is called "declaring God's unity," according to the language of reality. And behind these realities there are also mysteries, but it would take too long to delve into them.

34

Manifesting Suchness

Ehei Dogen

To learn the Buddha Way is to learn one's self. To learn one's self is to forget one's self. To forget one's self is to be confirmed by all dharmas. To be confirmed by all dharmas is to cast off one's body and mind and the bodies and minds of others as well. All trace of enlightenment disappears, and this traceless enlightenment continues on without end.

The moment you begin seeking the Dharma, you move far from its environs. The moment the Dharma has been rightly transmitted to you, you become the Person of your original part.

When a man is in a boat at sea and looks back at the shoreline, it may seem to him as though the shore is moving. But when he fixes his gaze closely on the boat, he realizes it is the boat that is moving. In like manner, when a person tries to discern and affirm things with a confused notion of his body and mind, he makes the mistake of thinking his own mind, his own nature, is permanent and unchanging. If he turns back within himself, making all his daily deeds immediately and directly his own, the reason all things have no selfhood becomes clear to him.

[. . .]

The attainment of enlightenment is like the moon reflected on the water. The moon does not get wet, and the surface of the water is not broken. For all the breadth and vastness of its light, the moon comes to rest in a small patch of water. The whole moon and the sky in its entirety come to rest in a single dewdrop on a grass tip – a mere pinpoint of water. Enlightenment does not destroy man any more than the moon makes a hole on the surface of the water. Man does not obstruct enlightenment any more than the drop of dew obstructs the moon or the heavens. The depth of the one will be the measure of the other's height. As for the time – the quickness or slowness – of enlightenment's coming, you must carefully scrutinise the quantity of the water, survey the extent of the moom and the sky.

[. . .] It is like boarding a boat and sailing into a broad and shoreless sea. You see nothing as you gaze about you but a wide circle of sea. Yet the great ocean is not circular. It is not square. It has other, inexhaustible virtues. It is like a glittering palace. It is like a necklace of precious jewels. Yet it appears for the moment to the range of your eyes simply as an encircling sea. It is the same with all things. The dusty world and the Buddha Way beyond may assume many different aspects, but

"Manifesting Suchness" by Ehei Dogen, in *The Heart of Dogen's Shobogenzo*, trans. Norman Waddell and Masao Abe (Albany, NY: SUNY Press, 2002), pp. 41–4.

we can see and understand them only to the extent that our eye is cultivated through practice. If we are to grasp the true and particular natures of all things, we must know that in addition to apparent circularity or angularity, there are inexhaustibly great virtues in the mountains and seas. We must realize that this inexhaustible store is present not only all around us, it is present right beneath out feet and within a single drop of water.

Fish swim the water and however much they swim, there is no end to the water. Birds fly the skies, and however much they fly, there is no end to the skies. Yet fish never once leave the water, birds never forsake the sky. When their need is great, there is great activity. When their need is small, there is small activity. In this way, none ever fails to exert itself to the full, and nowhere does any fail to move and turn freely. If a bird leaves the sky, it will soon die. If a fish leaves the water, it at once perishes. We should grasp that water means life [for the fish], and the sky means life [for the bird]. It must be that the bird means life [for the sky], and the fish means life [for the water]; that life is the bird, life is the fish. We could continue in this way even further, because practice and realization, and for all that is possessed of life, it is the same.

Even were there a bird or fish that desired to proceed further on after coming to the end of the sky or the water, it could make no way, could find no place, in either element. When that place is attained, when that way is achieved, all of one's everyday activities are immediately manifesting reality. Inasmuch as this way, this place, is neither large nor small, self nor other, does not exist from before, does not come into being now for the first time, *it is just as it is.*

Section V

Evil and the Rationality of Religious Belief

Introduction

A. General Introduction to the Section

We have now surveyed several evidentialist and non-evidentialist defenses of the rationality of belief in an Ultimate Sacred Reality. Note that on both approaches, counter-evidence cannot be ignored. On evidentialist approaches, counter-evidence must be weighed alongside supporting evidence. On non-evidentialist approaches, counter-evidence may undermine the *prima facie* rational warrant that religious beliefs would otherwise possess. Many have thought that the existence of evil is sufficient grounds for demonstrating the irrationality of religious belief. Does the existence of evil make religious belief unreasonable? Of course, in the end that will depend in large part upon the particular religious belief in question. As before, we will begin our examination within the context of Western theism and conclude with reflection on how evil has been addressed within some Eastern religious traditions.

That the experience of evil has raised critical questions for theistic belief is clear from scriptural texts and early philosophical work more than two thousand years ago in Greece (the work of Epicurus), the Near East (The Book of Job), and India (Buddhist and Jain[1] objections to theism). When Christian theology began to take more systematic form in conversation with Greek philosophy, the problems posed by evil became more sharply focused for Western theists. Augustine of Hippo (354–430) keenly felt the tension generated by affirming God's goodness and power in the face of evil, even while affirming both (see "Evil as a Privation of Good"): "For the Almighty God, who, as even the heathen acknowledge, has supreme power over all things, being Himself supremely good, would never permit the existence of anything evil among His works . . ." (p. 291). Later, David Hume (again through the mouth of his dialogue character, Philo) helpfully distinguished two versions of this general problem (see "The Argument from Evil," author's emphasis):

> [Even if] pain or misery in man is *compatible* with infinite power and goodness in the Deity . . . What are you advanced by all these concessions? A mere possible compatibility is not sufficient. You must *prove* these pure, unmixt, and uncontrollable attributes from the present mixed and confused phenomena. . . . (p. 295)

---

[1] Jainism is an influential minority religion in India that arose roughly contemporaneously with Buddhism in the sixth century BCE. Its adherents share a belief in *karma* and rebirth, as do most Hindus and Buddhists. However, unlike Hindus, they reject belief in God or Brahman; and unlike Buddhists, they believe that what is reborn are eternal soul-like selves.

On the one hand, there seems to be a problem of how God and any evil whatsoever could coexist, given the attributes traditionally ascribed to God (i.e., principally God's omnipotence and omnibenevolence). On the other hand, Hume contends that even if one could defend the strict logical compatibility of some evil and God's existence, there would remain the problem of reconciling God's existence with the types and great amount of evil one finds in the world. These have come to be known as the "logical" and "evidential" problems of evil for theistic belief.

B. Western Theism and the Logical Problem of Evil

B1. A Contemporary Presentation of the Logical Problem of Evil

In "Evil and Omnipotence," J. L. Mackie forcefully presents the logical problem of evil. After briefly introducing the problem, Mackie surveys and criticizes previous attempts by theists to escape what he regards as the only acceptable conclusions – namely, either that: (a) God does not exist; (b) God exists but lacks some perfection traditionally attributed to God; or (c) evil does not exist.

One aspect of Mackie's article that has been of special interest to subsequent writers is his discussion of what has come to be known as the "free will defense." According to this line of thought, evil is to be attributed to agents who have misused their God-given capacity to act freely. This strategy of responding to the logical problem of evil assumes that given the decision to create free agents (the existence of which is taken to be a great good), it was impossible for even God to guarantee that they would always act rightly. However, Mackie argues that this assumption is mistaken – that if there were a God, such a being could have created free agents who nevertheless always acted rightly.

B2. Diffusing the Logical Problem of Evil?

William Rowe is not convinced that the theist need worry about the logical problem of evil. In "The Logical Problem of Evil," the first of two selections by him in this section, he outlines two types of responses that one might make when presented with this version of the problem. First, one might pursue a limited negative strategy and argue that the skeptic has failed to establish that there is a logical inconsistency between the claims that God exists (and is omnipotent, omniscient, and wholly good) and that evil exists. Rowe carefully lays out the intermediary premises that someone like Mackie needs in order to establish such an inconsistency and argues that these intermediary premises are not necessarily true. Second, though Rowe himself does not attempt it, he explains that one might go further and try to positively show that there is no logical inconsistency in believing both that God exists (and is omnipotent, omniscient, and wholly good) and that evil exists. In other words, on this strategy, the theist does not rest content in pointing out that the skeptic has failed to show the irrationality of theism but instead proposes a logically possible scenario in which both God and evil exists. This, he points out, is the strategy that lies behind the free will defense.[2] This strategy is still less ambitious than that of defending a theodicy (described below), but if successful, it would demonstratively show that there is no irrationality – in the sense of logical inconsistency – in holding both that God exists and that evil exists.

C. Western Theism and the Evidential Problem of Evil

C1. A Theodicy of Moral and Spiritual Growth

Although some have held that the theist need do no more than defend the logically consistency

---

[2]   For the most influential contemporary formulation of the free will defense, see Alvin Plantinga's *God, Freedom, and Evil* (Grand Rapids, MI: William B. Eerdmans Publishing Co., 1977).

of his or her beliefs about God and evil, many have been convinced that the type and amount of evil in the world nevertheless threaten to undermine the reasonableness of theistic belief. In other words, even if the logical problem of evil is surmounted, the evidential problem remains.

John Hick takes up this challenge in "An Irenaean Theodicy." A theodicy, as Hick explains, is an attempt to explain not merely the existence but the types and extent of evil found in the world in a way that is logically consistent *and plausible*. Hick believes that Mackie has successfully demonstrated that it is logically possible that God could have created free agents who always acted rightly, so the task, as he sees it, is to explain what reason God might have had for not doing so. The explanatory hypothesis Hick offers suggests that the value of human freedom lies in the way that it allows morally and spiritually immature creatures increasingly to become remade in the likeness of God through their own free choices. Moreover, if this is the purpose for which they have been made, then they must be placed within a challenging environment and one in which the consequences of misusing one's freedom can be serious.

C2. Has the Evidential Challenge been Met?

As we saw earlier, William Rowe is not convinced that the theist need be concerned about the logical problem of evil. However, in this selection, "The Evidential Problem of Evil," Rowe argues that the type and profusion of evil do provide good reasons for thinking that there is no God who is omnipotent, omniscient, and wholly good. He begins by laying out the general pattern of reasoning behind the evidential problem, the pivotal first premise of which is that there are instances of intense suffering in the world that God could have prevented without thereby preventing the realization of some greater good. Rowe then entertains and rejects two possible responses to this reasoning. The first of these alleges that he has not provided sufficient reason to think that the pivotal premise in the argument is true. The second type of response is to provide a theodicy and thereby attempt to show that the pivotal premise in Rowe's argument is false. Hick's theodicy is just

such an attempt, but Rowe argues that it fails to accomplish its intended purpose.

Finally, though Rowe believes that his evidential argument has not been directly refuted, he sketches an indirect response to his argument that may remain open to the theist. This strategy involves appealing to some other independent grounds for thinking that God exists (e.g., perhaps an argument for God's existence or an appeal to religious experience). If there are such good independent grounds for belief in God, then Rowe acknowledges that perhaps the theist may yet have a good reason to reject the pivotal premise in the evidential argument from evil.

C3. The Holocaust and the Problem of Evil

Throughout human history, powerful aggressors have sometimes sought to target whole groups of people for elimination. Germany's Nazi regime (1933–45) stands out not only because of the unprecedented scale on which it engaged in such genocidal behavior, but also because of the way it institutionalized a host of means aimed at dehumanizing its victims on the way to their deaths. By the end of World War II approximately six million European Jews had died at their hands, along with perhaps another million non-Jewish Poles, ethnic Gypsies, homosexuals, and persons who were mentally ill or physically disabled.

Some have held that engaging in theodicy after the Holocaust is not only useless but immoral – that to attempt an explanation of such an event with the aim of salvaging some meaning in its wake involves a failure to appreciate its magnitude and thereby trivializes the suffering of its victims. As Hans Jonas acknowledges in "The Concept of God after Auschwitz: A Jewish Voice," the problem is especially acute for Jews, not only because they were the principal targets of the Nazi genocidal program, but also because part of the traditional Jewish religious self-understanding is that they are a people elected to be God's witnesses in the world.

Jonas responds with a philosophical myth, an "imaginative but credible conjecture" (p. 266). As he unpacks the implications of his myth, it becomes clear that he believes that some aspects of the classical theistic model of God should be abandoned in the wake of the Holocaust. In particular, Jonas holds that the traditional concept of omnipotence is inconsistent with our experience of such an evil.

D.   The Problem of Evil in India

D1.   Shankara (Samkara) on Evil, Creation, and Karma

It is the evidential problem of evil that seems to have been felt most keenly in India. As was the case with the author of the Book of Job, the principal problem for Indian thinkers was how to account for the apparently random – and thus seemingly unjust – distribution of suffering. Historically, the problem was most pointedly posed to Hindu theists, often by their non-theistic Buddhist and Jain counterparts. However, even the critics in this case – insofar as they sought to offer a religious alternative – were often interested in preserving an outlook in which justice is preserved. The doctrines of *karma* and rebirth (*samsara*) emerged as pivotal doctrines for meeting the challenge posed by evil in these three Indian traditions. The influence of these doctrines grew even further as Hinduism, Buddhism, and Jainism were later exported to other lands in East and Southeast Asia.

   According to Shankara (Samkara), the eighth-century Advaita Vedantan thinker, the nature of Brahman is ultimately non-dual and so beyond the category of personhood. Nevertheless, as we saw in section II, non-dual Brahman manifests itself to human agents as personal lord and creator. Thus, Shankara sometimes shares concerns with more straightforwardly theistic thinkers. Commenting on the *Brahmasutras* – an early Advaita Vedanta text summarizing the school's central teachings – Shankara pauses to respond to the objection that Brahman cannot be the cause of the world because this would entail that Brahman is unjust and cruel given the way suffering is distributed (see "Brahman, Creation, and Evil").

   As Bimal Matilal explains in "Ṣaṃkara's Theodicy," Shankara responds to this objection by appeal to two theses that are distinctive of how Indian thinkers have tended to respond to the problem of evil. The first of these is that the universe has existed in some form or another without beginning. Creation *ex nihilo* is rejected. Thus creation is an act of giving form to that which already exists. The second distinctive thesis is that creation is constrained by *karma*. That is, in this beginning-less universe there have always been creatures and their lives have always been governed by a principle of *karma*. The latter functions like a moral law of gravity – an impersonal feature of the universe that determines the consequences for a creature (often in a subsequent rebirth) based on the quality of its prior actions. It is *karma* then that guarantees that despite appearances, suffering is distributed justly.

D2.   Evaluating Theodicies Based on Karma and Rebirth

As Whitley Kaufman notes in "Karma, Rebirth, and the Problem of Evil," a number of contemporary Western thinkers have registered admiration for the way Indian thinkers have employed the dual doctrines of *karma* and rebirth to address the problem of evil and have claimed that such a theodicy is superior to those proposed in the West. Kaufman thus asks whether the doctrines – if true – would provide an adequate response to the problem of evil. (Grounds for thinking that the doctrines themselves are true or false are discussed further in the next section.) Kaufman raises five moral objections to the use of the doctrines as the basis of a theodicy and concludes that they fail to provide a solution to the problem of evil.

Suggestions for Further Reading

Adams, Marilyn, *Horrendous Evils and the Goodness of God* (Ithaca, NY: Cornell University Press, 2000).

Biderman, Shlomo, "A 'Constitutive' God – An Indian Suggestion," *Philosophy East and West*, 32 (1982): 425–37.

Clooney, Francis X., "Evil, Divine Omnipotence, and Human Freedom: Vedanta's Theology of Karma," *Journal of Religion*, 69 (1989): 530–48.

Farley, Wendy, *Tragic Vision and Divine Compassion: A Contemporary Theodicy* (Louisville, KY: Westminster/John Knox Press, 1990).

Filice, Carlo, "The Moral Case for Reincarnation," *Religious Studies*, 42 (2006): 45–61.

Griffin, David Ray, *God, Power, and Evil: A Process Theodicy* (Philadelphia: Westminster Press, 1976).

Griffin, David Ray, *Evil Revisited* (Albany, NY: State University of New York Press, 1991).

Hasker, William, "The Necessity of Gratuitous Evil," *Faith and Philosophy*, 9 (1992): 23–44.

Herman, Arthur L., *The Problem of Evil in Indian Thought*, 2nd edition (Delhi: Motilal Banarsidass Publishers, 1993).

Hick, John, *Evil and the God of Love*, revised edition (New York: Harper and Row, 1978).

Howard-Snyder, Daniel (ed.), *The Evidential Argument from Evil* (Indianapolis: Indiana University Press, 1996).

Leaman, Oliver, *Evil and Suffering in Jewish Philosophy* (New York: Cambridge University Press, 1995).

Martin, Michael, "Reichenbach on Natural Evil," *Religious Studies*, 24 (1988): 91–9.

O'Connor, David, *God and Inscrutable Evil* (Lanham, MD: Rowman and Littlefield, 1998).

Plantinga, Alvin, "The Probabilistic Argument from Evil," *Philosophical Studies*, 35 (1979): 1–53.

Reichenbach, Bruce R., *Evil and a Good God* (Grand Rapids, MI: William B. Eerdmans, 1977).

Rowe, William, "Friendly Atheism, Skeptical Theism, and the Problem of Evil," *International Journal for Philosophy of Religion*, 59 (2006): 79–92.

Sands, Kathleen M., *Escape from Paradise: Evil and Tragedy in Feminist Theology* (Minneapolis, MN: Fortress Press, 1994).

Stump, Eleonore, "Knowledge, Freedom and the Problem of Evil," *International Journal for Philosophy of Religion*, 14 (1983): 49–58.

Swinburne, Richard, *Providence and the Problem of Evil* (Oxford: Clarendon Press, 1998).

van Inwagen, Peter, "The Problem of Evil, the Problem of Air, and the Problem of Silence," in James Tomberlin (ed.), *Philosophical Perspectives, 5: Philosophy of Religion*, (1991): 135–65.

35

Evil and Omnipotence

J. L. Mackie

The traditional arguments for the existence of God have been fairly thoroughly criticised by philosophers. But the theologian can, if he wishes, accept this criticism. He can admit that no rational proof of God's existence is possible. And he can still retain all that is essential to his position, by holding that God's existence is known in some other, non-rational way. I think, however, that a more telling criticism can be made by way of the traditional problem of evil. Here it can be shown, not that religious beliefs lack rational support, but that they are positively irrational, that the several parts of the essential theological doctrine are inconsistent with one another, so that the theologian can maintain his position as a whole only by a much more extreme rejection of reason than in the former case. He must now be prepared to believe, not merely what cannot be proved, but what can be *disproved* from other beliefs that he also holds.

The problem of evil, in the sense in which I shall be using the phrase, is a problem only for someone who believes that there is a God who is both omnipotent and wholly good. And it is a logical problem, the problem of clarifying and reconciling a number of beliefs: it is not a scientific problem that might be solved by further observations, or a practical problem that might be solved by a decision or an action. These points

are obvious; I mention them only because they are sometimes ignored by theologians, who sometimes parry a statement of the problem with such remarks as "Well, can you solve the problem yourself?" or "This is a mystery which may be revealed to us later" or "Evil is something to be faced and overcome, not to be merely discussed".

In its simplest form the problem is this: God is omnipotent; God is wholly good; and yet evil exists. There seems to be some contradiction between these three propositions, so that if any two of them were true the third would be false. But at the same time all three are essential parts of most theological positions: the theologian, it seems, at once *must* adhere and *cannot consistently* adhere to all three. (The problem does not arise only for theists, but I shall discuss it in the form in which it presents itself for ordinary theism.)

However, the contradiction does not arise immediately; to show it we need some additional premises, or perhaps some quasi-logical rules connecting the terms "good", "evil", and "omnipotent". These additional principles are that good is opposed to evil, in such a way that a good thing always eliminates evil as far as it can, and that there are no limits to what an omnipotent thing can do. From these it follows that a good omnipotent thing eliminates evil

"Evil and Omnipotence" by J. L. Mackie, *Mind* 64 (1954): 200–12.

completely, and then the propositions that a good omnipotent thing exists, and that evil exists, are incompatible.

A. Adequate Solutions

Now once the problem is fully stated it is clear that it can be solved, in the sense that the problem will not arise if one gives up at least one of the propositions that constitute it. If you are prepared to say that God is not wholly good, or not quite omnipotent, or that evil does not exist, or that good is not opposed to the kind of evil that exists, or that there are limits to what an omnipotent thing can do, then the problem of evil will not arise for you.

There are, then, quite a number of adequate solutions of the problem of evil, and some of these have been adopted, or almost adopted, by various thinkers. For example, a few have been prepared to deny God's omnipotence, and rather more have been prepared to keep the term "omnipotence" but severely to restrict its meaning, recording quite a number of things that an omnipotent being cannot do. Some have said that evil is an illusion, perhaps because they held that the whole world of temporal, changing things is an illusion, and that what we call evil belongs only to this world, or perhaps because they held that although temporal things *are* much as we see them, those that we call evil are not really evil. Some have said that what we call evil is merely the privation of good, that evil in a positive sense, evil that would really be opposed to good, does not exist. Many have agreed with Pope that disorder is harmony not understood, and that partial evil is universal good. Whether any of these views is *true* is, of course, another question. But each of them gives an adequate solution of the problem of evil in the sense that if you accept it this problem does not arise for you, though you may, of course, have *other* problems to face.

But often enough these adequate solutions are only *almost* adopted. The thinkers who restrict God's power, but keep the term "omnipotence", may reasonably be suspected of thinking, in other contexts, that his power is really unlimited. Those who say that evil is an illusion may also be thinking, inconsistently, that this illusion is itself an evil. Those who say that "evil" is merely privation of good may also be thinking, inconsistently, that privation of good is an evil. [. . .]

In addition, therefore, to adequate solutions, we must recognise unsatisfactory inconsistent solutions, in which there is only a half-hearted or temporary rejection of one of the propositions which together constitute the problem. In these, one of the constituent propositions is explicitly rejected, but it is covertly re-asserted or assumed elsewhere in the system.

B. Fallacious Solutions

Besides these half-hearted solutions, which explicitly reject but implicitly assert one of the constituent propositions, there are definitely fallacious solutions which explicitly maintain all the constituent propositions, but implicitly reject at least one of them in the course of the argument that explains away the problem of evil.

There are, in fact, many so-called solutions which purport to remove the contradiction without abandoning any of its constituent propositions. These must be fallacious, as we can see from the very statement of the problem, but it is not so easy to see in each case precisely where the fallacy lies. I suggest that in all cases the fallacy has the general form suggested above: in order to solve the problem one (or perhaps more) of its constituent propositions is given up, but in such a way that it appears to have been retained, and can therefore be asserted without qualification in other contexts. Sometimes there is a further complication: the supposed solution moves to and fro between, say, two of the constituent propositions, at one point asserting the first of these but covertly abandoning the second, at another point asserting the second but covertly abandoning the first. These fallacious solutions often turn upon some equivocation with the words "good" and "evil", or upon some vagueness about the way in which good and evil are opposed to one another, or about how much is meant by "omnipotence". I propose to examine some of these so-called solutions, and to exhibit their fallacies in detail. Incidentally, I shall also be considering whether an adequate solution could be reached by a minor modification of one or more of the constituent propositions, which would, however, still satisfy all the essential requirements of ordinary theism.

1   "Good cannot exist without evil" or "Evil is necessary as a counterpart to good."

It is sometimes suggested that evil is necessary as a counterpart to good, that if there were no evil there could be no good either, and that this solves the problem of evil. It is true that it points to an answer to the question "Why should there be evil?" But it does so only by qualifying some of the propositions that constitute the problem.

First, it sets a limit to what God can do, saying that God *cannot* create good without simultaneously creating evil, and this means either that God is not omnipotent or that there are *some* limits to what an omnipotent thing can do. It may be replied that these limits are always presupposed, that omnipotence has never meant the power to do what is logically impossible, and on the present view the existence of good without evil would be a logical impossibility. This interpretation of omnipotence may, indeed, be accepted as a modification of our original account which does not reject anything that is essential to theism, and I shall in general assume it in the subsequent discussion. It is, perhaps, the most common theistic view, but I think that some theists at least have maintained that God can do what is logically impossible. Many theists, at any rate, have held that logic itself is created or laid down by God, that logic is the way in which God arbitrarily chooses to think. (This is, of course, parallel to the ethical view that morally right actions are those which God arbitrarily chooses to command, and the two views encounter similar difficulties.) And *this* account of logic is clearly inconsistent with the view that God is bound by logical necessities – unless it is possible for an omnipotent being to bind himself, an issue which we shall consider later, when we come to the Paradox of Omnipotence. This solution of the problem of evil cannot, therefore, be consistently adopted along with the view that logic is itself created by God.

But, secondly, this solution denies that evil is opposed to good in our original sense. If good and evil are counterparts, a good thing will not "eliminate evil as far as it can". Indeed, this view suggests that good and evil are not strictly qualities of things at all. Perhaps the suggestion is that good and evil are related in much the same way as great and small. Certainly, when the term "great" is used relatively as a condensation of "greater than so-and-so", and "small" is used correspondingly, greatness and smallness are counterparts and cannot exist without each other. But in this sense greatness is not a quality, not an intrinsic feature of anything; and it would be absurd to think of a movement in favour of greatness and against smallness in this sense. Such a movement would be self-defeating, since relative greatness can be promoted only by a simultaneous promotion of relative smallness. I feel sure that no theists would be content to regard God's goodness as analogous to this – as if what he supports were not the *good* but the *better*, and as if he had the paradoxical aim that all things should be better than other things.

[. . .]

It may be replied that good and evil are necessary counterparts in the same way as any quality and its logical opposite: redness can occur, it is suggested, only if non-redness also occurs. But unless evil is merely the privation of good, they are not logical opposites, and some further argument would be needed to show that they are counterparts in the same way as genuine logical opposites. Let us assume that this could be given. There is still doubt of the correctness of the metaphysical principle that a quality must have a real opposite: I suggest that it is not really impossible that everything should be, say, red, that the truth is merely that if everything were red we should not notice redness, and so we should have no word "red"; we observe and give names to qualities only if they have real opposites. If so, the principle that a term must have an opposite would belong only to our language or to our thought, and would not be an ontological principle, and, correspondingly, the rule that good cannot exist without evil would not state a logical necessity of a sort that God would just have to put up with. God might have made everything good, though *we* should not have noticed it if he had.

But, finally, even if we concede that this *is* an ontological principle, it will provide a solution for the problem of evil only if one is prepared to say, "Evil exists, but only just enough evil to serve as the counterpart of good". I doubt whether any theist will accept this. After all, the *ontological* requirement that non-redness should occur would be satisfied even if all the universe, except for a minute speck, were red, and, if there were a corresponding requirement for evil as a counterpart to good, a minute dose of evil would presumably do. But theists are not usually willing to say, in all contexts, that all the evil that occurs is a minute and necessary dose.

2   "Evil is necessary as a means to good."

It is sometimes suggested that evil is necessary for good not as a counterpart but as a means. In its simple form this has little plausibility as a solution of the problem of evil, since it obviously implies a severe restriction of God's power. It would be a *causal* law that you cannot have a certain end without a certain means, so that if God has to introduce evil as a means to good, he must be subject to at least some causal laws. This certainly conflicts with what a theist normally means by omnipotence. This view of God as limited by causal laws also conflicts with the view that causal laws are themselves made by God, which is more widely held than the corresponding view about the laws of logic. This conflict would, indeed, be resolved if it were possible for an omnipotent being to bind himself, and this possibility has still to be considered. Unless a favourable answer can be given to this question, the suggestion that evil is necessary as a means to good solves the problem of evil only by denying one of its constituent propositions, either that God is omnipotent or that "omnipotent" means what it says.

3   "The universe is better with some evil in it than it could be if there were no evil."

Much more important is a solution which at first seems to be a mere variant of the previous one, that evil may contribute to the goodness of a whole in which it is found, so that the universe as a whole is better as it is, with some evil in it, than it would be if there were no evil. This solution may be developed in either of two ways. It may be supported by an aesthetic analogy, by the fact that contrasts heighten beauty, that in a

musical work, for example, there may occur discords which somehow add to the beauty of the work as a whole. Alternatively, it may be worked out in connexion with the notion of progress, that the best possible organisation of the universe will not be static, but progressive, that the gradual overcoming of evil by good is really a finer thing than would be the eternal unchallenged supremacy of good.

In either case, this solution usually starts from the assumption that the evil whose existence gives rise to the problem of evil is primarily what is called physical evil, that is to say, pain. In Hume's rather half-hearted presentation of the problem of evil, the evils that he stresses are pain and disease, and those who reply to him argue that the existence of pain and disease makes possible the existence of sympathy, benevolence, heroism, and the gradually successful struggle of doctors and reformers to overcome these evils. In fact, theists often seize the opportunity to accuse those who stress the problem of evil of taking a low, materialistic view of good and evil, equating these with pleasure and pain, and of ignoring the more spiritual goods which can arise in the struggle against evils.

But let us see exactly what is being done here. Let us call pain and misery "first order evil" or "evil (1)". What contrasts with this, namely, pleasure and happiness, will be called "first order good" or "good (1)". Distinct from this is "second order good" or "good (2)" which somehow emerges in a complex situation in which evil (1) is a necessary component – logically, not merely causally, necessary. (Exactly *how* it emerges does not matter: in the crudest version of this solution good (2) is simply the heightening of happiness by the contrast with misery, in other versions it includes sympathy with suffering, heroism in facing danger, and the gradual decrease of first order evil and increase of first order good.) It is also being assumed that second order good is more important than first order good or evil, in particular that it more than outweighs the first order evil it involves.

Now this is a particularly subtle attempt to solve the problem of evil. It defends God's goodness and omnipotence on the ground that (on a sufficiently long view) this is the best of all logically possible worlds, because it includes the important second order goods, and yet it admits that real evils, namely first order evils, exist. But does it still hold that good and evil are opposed? Not, clearly, in the sense that we set out originally: good does not tend to eliminate evil in general. Instead, we have a modified, a more complex pattern. First order good (e.g. happiness) *contrasts with* first order evil (e.g. misery): these two are opposed in a fairly mechanical way; some second order goods (e.g. benevolence) try to maximise first order good and minimise first order evil; but God's goodness is not this, it is rather the will to maximise *second* order good. We might, therefore, call God's goodness an example of a third order goodness, or good (3). While this account is different from our original one, it might well be held to be an improvement on it, to give a more accurate description of the way in which good is opposed to evil, and to be consistent with the essential theist position.

There might, however, be several objections to this solution.

First, some might argue that such qualities as benevolence – and *a fortiori* the third order goodness which promotes benevolence – have a merely derivative value, that they are not higher sorts of good, but merely means to good (1), that is, to happiness, so that it would be absurd for God to keep misery in existence in order to make possible the virtues of benevolence, heroism, etc. The theist who adopts the present solution must, of course, deny this, but he can do so with some plausibility, so I should not press this objection.

Secondly, it follows from this solution that God is not in our sense benevolent or sympathetic: he is not concerned to minimise evil (1), but only to promote good (2); and this might be a disturbing conclusion for some theists.

But, thirdly, the fatal objection is this. Our analysis shows clearly the possibility of the existence of a *second* order evil, an evil (2) contrasting with good (2) as evil (1) contrasts with good (1). This would include malevolence, cruelty, callousness, cowardice, and states in which good (1) is decreasing and evil (1) increasing. And just as good (2) is held to be the important kind of good, the kind that God is concerned to promote, so evil (2) will, by analogy, be the important kind of evil, the kind which God, if he were wholly good and omnipotent, would eliminate. And yet evil (2) plainly exists, and

indeed most theists (in other contexts) stress its existence more than that of evil (1). We should, therefore, state the problem of evil in terms of second order evil, and against this form of the problem the present solution is useless.

An attempt might be made to use this solution again, at a higher level, to explain the occurrence of evil (2): indeed the next main solution that we shall examine does just this, with the help of some new notions. Without any fresh notions, such a solution would have little plausibility: for example, we could hardly say that the really important good was a good (3), such as the increase of benevolence in proportion to cruelty, which logically required for its occurrence the occurrence of some second order evil. But even if evil (2) could be explained in this way, it is fairly clear that there would be third order evils contrasting with this third order good: and we should be well on the way to an infinite regress, where the solution of a problem of evil, stated in terms of evil (n), indicated the existence of an evil ($n + 1$), and a further problem to be solved.

4   "Evil is due to human freewill."

Perhaps the most important proposed solution of the problem of evil is that evil is not to be ascribed to God at all, but to the independent actions of human beings, supposed to have been endowed by God with freedom of the will. This solution may be combined with the preceding one: first order evil (e.g. pain) may be justified as a logically necessary component in second order good (e.g. sympathy) while second order evil (e.g. cruelty) is not *justified*, but is so ascribed to human beings that God cannot be held responsible for it. This combination evades my third criticism of the preceding solution.

The freewill solution also involves the preceding solution at a higher level. To explain why a wholly good God gave men freewill although it would lead to some important evils, it must be argued that it is better on the whole that men should act freely, and sometimes err, than that they should be innocent automata, acting rightly in a wholly determined way. Freedom, that is to say, is now treated as a third order good, and as being more valuable than second order goods (such as sympathy and heroism) would be if they were deterministically produced, and it is being assumed that second order evils, such as cruelty, are logically necessary accompaniments of freedom, just as pain is a logically necessary pre-condition of sympathy.

I think that this solution is unsatisfactory primarily because of the incoherence of the notion of freedom of the will: but I cannot discuss this topic adequately here, although some of my criticisms will touch upon it.

First I should query the assumption that second order evils are logically necessary accompaniments of freedom. I should ask this: if God has made men such that in their free choices they sometimes prefer what is good and sometimes what is evil, why could he not have made men such that they always freely choose the good? If there is no logical impossibility in a man's freely choosing the good on one, or on several, occasions, there cannot be a logical impossibility in his freely choosing the good on every occasion. God was not, then, faced with a choice between making innocent automata and making beings who, in acting freely, would sometimes go wrong: there was open to him the obviously better possibility of making beings who would act freely but always go right. Clearly, his failure to avail himself of this possibility is inconsistent with his being both omnipotent and wholly good.

If it is replied that this objection is absurd, that the making of some wrong choices is logically necessary for freedom, it would seem that "freedom" must here mean complete randomness or indeterminacy, including randomness with regard to the alternatives good and evil, in other words that men's choices and consequent actions can be "free" only if they are not determined by their characters. Only on this assumption can God escape the responsibility for men's actions; for if he made them as they are, but did not determine their wrong choices, this can only be because the wrong choices are not determined by men as they are. But then if freedom is randomness, how can it be a characteristic of *will*? And, still more, how can it be the most important good? What value or merit would there be in free choices if these were random actions which were not determined by the nature of the agent?

I conclude that to make this solution plausible two different senses of "freedom" must be confused, one sense which will justify the view that

freedom is a third order good, more valuable than other goods would be without it, and another sense, sheer randomness, to prevent us from ascribing to God a decision to make men such that they sometimes go wrong when he might have made them such that they would always freely go right.

This criticism is sufficient to dispose of this solution. But besides this there is a fundamental difficulty in the notion of an omnipotent God creating men with free will, for if men's wills are really free this must mean that even God cannot control them, that is, that God is no longer omnipotent. It may be objected that God's gift of freedom to men does not mean that he *cannot* control their wills, but that he always *refrains* from controlling their wills. But why, we may ask, should God refrain from controlling evil wills? Why should he not leave men free to will rightly, but intervene when he sees them beginning to will wrongly? If God could do this, but does not, and if he is wholly good, the only explanation could be that even a wrong free act of will is not really evil, that its freedom is a value which outweighs its wrongness, so that there would be a loss of value if God took away the wrongness and the freedom together. But this is utterly opposed to what theists say about sin in other contexts. The present solution of the problem of evil, then, can be maintained only in the form that God has made men so free that he *cannot* control their wills.

This leads us to what I call the Paradox of Omnipotence: can an omnipotent being make things which he cannot subsequently control? Or, what is practically equivalent to this, can an omnipotent being make rules which then bind himself? (These are practically equivalent because any such rules could be regarded as setting certain things beyond his control, and *vice versa*.) The second of these formulations is relevant to the suggestions that we have already met, that an omnipotent God creates the rules of logic or causal laws, and is then bound by them.

It is clear that this is a paradox: the questions cannot be answered satisfactorily either in the affirmative or in the negative. If we answer "Yes", it follows that if God actually makes things which he cannot control, or makes rules which bind himself, he is not omnipotent once he has made them: there are *then* things which he cannot do. But if we answer "No", we are immediately asserting that there are things which he cannot do, that is to say that he is already not omnipotent.

It cannot be replied that the question which sets this paradox is not a proper question. It would make perfectly good sense to say that a human mechanic has made a machine which he cannot control: if there is any difficulty about the question it lies in the notion of omnipotence itself.

This, incidentally, shows that although we have approached this paradox from the free will theory, it is equally a problem for a theological determinist. No one thinks that machines have free will, yet they may well be beyond the control of their makers. The determinist might reply that anyone who makes anything determines its ways of acting, and so determines its subsequent behaviour: even the human mechanic does this by his *choice* of materials and structure for his machine, though he does not know all about either of these: the mechanic thus determines, though he may not foresee, his machine's actions. And since God is omniscient, and since his creation of things is total, he both determines and foresees the ways in which his creatures will act. We may grant this, but it is beside the point. The question is not whether God *originally* determined the future actions of his creatures, but whether he can *subsequently* control their actions, or whether he was able in his original creation to put things beyond his subsequent control. Even on determinist principles the answers "Yes" and "No" are equally irreconcilable with God's omnipotence.

Before suggesting a solution of this paradox, I would point out that there is a parallel Paradox of Sovereignty. Can a legal sovereign make a law restricting its own future legislative power? For example, could the British parliament make a law forbidding any future parliament to socialise banking, and also forbidding the future repeal of this law itself? Or could the British parliament, which was legally sovereign in Australia in, say, 1899, pass a valid law, or series of laws, which made it no longer sovereign in 1933? Again, neither the affirmative nor the negative answer is really satisfactory. If we were to answer "Yes", we should be admitting the validity of a law which, if it were actually made, would mean that parliament was

no longer sovereign. If we were to answer "No", we should be admitting that there is a law, not logically absurd, which parliament cannot validly make, that is, that parliament is not now a legal sovereign. This paradox can be solved in the following way. We should distinguish between first order laws, that is laws governing the actions of individuals and bodies other than the legislature, and second order laws, that is laws about laws, laws governing the actions of the legislature itself. Correspondingly, we should distinguish two orders of sovereignty, first order sovereignty (sovereignty (1)) which is unlimited authority to make first order laws, and second order sovereignty (sovereignty (2)) which is unlimited authority to make second order laws. If we say that parliament is sovereign we might mean that any parliament at any time has sovereignty (1), or we might mean that parliament has both sovereignty (1) and sovereignty (2) at present, but we cannot without contradiction mean both that the present parliament has sovereignty (2) and that every parliament at every time has sovereignty (1), for if the present parliament has sovereignty (2) it may use it to take away the sovereignty (1) of later parliaments. What the paradox shows is that we cannot ascribe to any continuing institution legal sovereignty in an inclusive sense.

The analogy between omnipotence and sovereignty shows that the paradox of omnipotence can be solved in a similar way. We must distinguish between first order omnipotence (omnipotence (1)), that is unlimited power to act, and second order omnipotence (omnipotence (2)), that is unlimited power to determine what powers to act things shall have. Then we could consistently say that God all the time has omnipotence (1), but if so no beings at any time have powers to act independently of God. Or we could say that God at one time had omnipotence (2), and used it to assign independent powers to act to certain things, so that God thereafter did not have omnipotence (1). But what the paradox shows is that we cannot consistently ascribe to any continuing being omnipotence in an inclusive sense.

An alternative solution of this paradox would be simply to deny that God is a continuing being, that any times can be assigned to his actions at all. But on this assumption (which also has difficulties of its own) no meaning can be given to the assertion that God made men with wills so free that he could not control them. The paradox of omnipotence can be avoided by putting God outside time, but the freewill solution of the problem of evil cannot be saved in this way, and equally it remains impossible to hold that an omnipotent God *binds himself* by causal or logical laws.

Conclusion

Of the proposed solutions of the problem of evil which we have examined, none has stood up to criticism. There may be other solutions which require examination, but this study strongly suggests that there is no valid solution of the problem which does not modify at least one of the constituent propositions in a way which would seriously affect the essential core of the theistic position.

Quite apart from the problem of evil, the paradox of omnipotence has shown that God's omnipotence must in any case be restricted in one way or another, that unqualified omnipotence cannot be ascribed to any being that continues through time. And if God and his actions are not in time, can omnipotence, or power of any sort, be meaningfully ascribed to him?

36

The Logical Problem of Evil

William Rowe

The existence of evil in the world has been felt for centuries to be a problem for theism. It seems difficult to believe that a world with such a vast amount of evil as our world contains could be the creation of, and under the sovereign control of, a supremely good, omnipotent, omniscient being. The problem has confronted the human intellect for centuries and every major theologian has attempted to offer a solution to it.

There are two important forms of the problem of evil which we must be careful to distinguish. I shall call these two forms the *logical* form of the problem of evil and the *evidential* form of the problem of evil. Although the important difference between these two forms of the problem will become fully clear only as they are discussed in detail, it will be useful to have a brief statement of each form of the problem set before us at the beginning of our enquiry. The logical form of the problem of evil is the view that the existence of evil in our world is *logically inconsistent* with the existence of the theistic God. The evidential form of the problem of evil is the view that the variety and profusion of evil in our world, although perhaps not logically inconsistent with the existence of the theistic God, provides, nevertheless, *rational support* for atheism, for the belief that the theistic God does not exist. [. . .]

The Logical Problem

The logical form of the problem implies that theism is internally inconsistent, for the theist accepts each of two statements which are logically inconsistent. The two statements in question are:

1 God exists and is omnipotent, omniscient, and wholly good.

and

2 Evil exists.

These two statements, so the logical form of the problem insists, are logically inconsistent in the same way as

3 This object is red.

is inconsistent with

"The Logical Problem of Evil" from *Philosophy of Religion: An Introduction*, 3rd edition, by William Rowe (Belmont, CA: Wadsworth, 2001), pp. 92–8; 109. Reprinted with permission of Wadsworth, a division of Thomson Learning.

4   This object is not colored.

Suppose, for the moment, that the proponent of the logical form of the problem of evil were to succeed in proving to us that statements 1 and 2 are logically inconsistent. We would then be in the position of having to reject either 1 or 2; for, if two statements are logically inconsistent, it is impossible for both of them to be true; if one of them is true then the other *must* be false. Moreover, since we could hardly deny the reality of evil in our world, it seems we would have to reject belief in the theistic God; we would be driven to the conclusion that atheism is true. Indeed, even if we should be tempted to reject 2, leaving us the option of believing 1, this temptation is not one to which most theists could easily yield. For most theists adhere to religious traditions which emphasize the reality of evil in our world. In the Judeo-Christian tradition, for example, murder is held to be an evil, sinful act, and it can hardly be denied that murder occurs in our world. So, since theists generally accept and emphasize the reality of evil in our world, it would be something of a disaster for theism if the central claim in the logical form of the problem of evil were established: that 1 is logically inconsistent with 2.

To Establish Inconsistency

How can we establish that two statements are inconsistent? Sometimes nothing needs to be established since the two statements are *explicitly contradictory*, as, for example, the statements "Elizabeth is over five feet tall" and "Elizabeth is not over five feet tall." Often, however, two inconsistent statements are not explicitly contradictory. In such cases we can establish that they are inconsistent by deriving from them two statements that are explicitly contradictory. Consider statements 3 and 4, for example. It's clear that these two statements are logically inconsistent, they cannot both be true. But they are not explicitly contradictory. If asked to prove that 3 and 4 are inconsistent, we can do this by deriving explicitly contradictory statements from them. To derive the explicitly contradictory statements we need to add another statement to 3 and 4.

5   Whatever is red is colored.

From 3, 4, and 5 we can then easily derive the explicitly contradictory pair of statements, "This object is colored" (from 3 and 5) and "This object is not colored" (repetition of 4). This, then, is the procedure we may follow if we are asked to establish our claim that two statements are logically inconsistent.

Before we consider whether the proponent of the logical form of the problem of evil can *establish* the claim that statements 1 and 2 are logically inconsistent, one very important point about the procedure for establishing that two statements are logically inconsistent needs to be clearly understood. When we have two statements which are not explicitly contradictory, and want to establish that they are logically inconsistent, we do this by adding some further statement or statements to them and then deriving from the entire group (the original pair and the additional statement or statements) a pair of statements that are explicitly contradictory. Now the point that needs very careful attention is this: in order for this procedure to work, the statement or statements we add must be not just true but *necessarily true*. Notice, for example, that the statement we added to 3 and 4 in order to establish that they are inconsistent is a necessary truth – it is logically impossible for something to be red but not colored. If, however, the additional statement or statements used in order to deduce the explicitly contradictory statements are true, but not necessarily true, then although we may succeed in deducing explicitly contradictory statements, we will *not* have succeeded in showing that the original pair of statements are logically inconsistent.

To see that this is so let's consider the following pair of statements:

6   The object in my right hand is a coin.

and

7   The object in my right hand is not a dime.

Clearly, 6 and 7 are *not* logically inconsistent, for both of them might be, or might have been, true. They aren't logically inconsistent because there is nothing logically impossible in the idea that the coin in my right hand should be a quarter or a nickel. (Contrast 6 and 7 with 3 and 4. Clearly there is something logically impossible in the idea that this object be red and yet not colored.) But notice that we can add a statement to 6 and 7 such that from the three of them explicitly contradictory statements can be derived.

8   Every coin in my right hand is a dime.

From 6, 7, and 8 we can derive the explicitly contradictory pair of statements, "The object in my right hand is a dime" (from 6 and 8) and "The object in my right hand is not a dime" (repetition of 7). Now suppose 8 is true, that in fact every coin in my right hand is a dime. We will have succeeded, then, in deducing explicitly contradictory statements from our original pair, 6 and 7, with the help of the *true* statement 8. But, of course, by this procedure we won't have established that 6 and 7 are logically inconsistent. Why not? Because 8 – the additional statement – although true, is not necessarily true. Statement 8 is not a necessary truth because I might (logically) have had a quarter or a nickel in my right hand. Statement 8 is in fact true, but since it logically could have been false, it is not a necessary truth. We must, then, keep clearly in mind that to *establish* two statements to be logically inconsistent by adding a statement and then deriving explicitly contradictory statements, the additional statement must be not just true, but necessarily true.

Application to the Logical Problem of Evil

Since (1) "God exists and is omnipotent, omniscient, and wholly good" and (2) "Evil exists" are not explicitly contradictory, those who hold that 1 and 2 are logically inconsistent need to make good this claim by adding a necessarily true statement to 1 and 2 and deducing explicitly contradictory statements. But what statement might we add? Suppose we begin with

9   An omnipotent, omniscient, good being will prevent the occurrence of any evil whatever.

From 1, 2, and 9 we can derive the explicitly contradictory statements, "No evil exists" (from

1 and 9) and "Evil exists" (repetition of 2). So if we can show that statement 9 is necessarily true we will have succeeded in establishing the thesis of the logical form of the problem of evil: that 1 and 2 are logically inconsistent. But is 9 necessarily true? Well, recalling our discussion of omnipotence, it would seem that God would have the power to prevent any evil whatever, for "preventing the occurrence of an evil" does not appear to be a logically contradictory task like "making a round square." But it is no easy matter to establish that 9 is necessarily true. For in our own experience we know that evil is sometimes connected with good in such a way that we are powerless to achieve the good without permitting the evil. Moreover, in such instances, the good sometimes outweighs the evil, so that a good being might intentionally permit the evil to occur in order to realize the good which outweighs it.

Gottfried Leibniz gives the example of a general who knows that in order to achieve the good of saving the town from being destroyed by an attacking army he must order his men to defend the town, with the result that some of his men will suffer and die. The good of saving the women and children of the town outweighs the evil of the suffering and death of a few of the town's defenders. Although he could have prevented their suffering and death by ordering a hasty retreat of his forces, the general cannot do so without losing the good of saving the town and its inhabitants. It certainly does not count against the general's goodness that he permits the evil to occur in order to achieve the good which outweighs it. Perhaps, then, some evils in our world are connected to goods which outweigh them in such a way that even God cannot achieve the goods in question without permitting the evils to occur that are connected to those goods. If this is so, statement 9 is not necessarily true.

Of course, unlike the general's, God's power is unlimited, and it might be thought that no matter how closely evil and good may be connected, God could always achieve the good and prevent the evil. But this overlooks the possibility that the occurrence of some evils in our world is *logically necessary* for the achievement of goods which outweigh them, so that the task of bringing about those goods to occur, without permitting the evils that are connected to them, is as impossible a task as making a round square.

If so, then, again, while being omnipotent God could prevent the evils in question from occurring; he could not, even though omnipotent, achieve the outweighing goods while preventing the evils from occurring. Therefore, since (i) omnipotence is not the power to do what is logically impossible, and (ii) it may be logically impossible to prevent the occurrence of certain evils in our world and yet achieve some very great goods that outweigh those evils, we cannot be sure that statement 9 is necessarily true, we can't be sure that an omnipotent, wholly good being will prevent the occurrence of any evil whatever.

What we have just seen is that the attempt to establish that 1 and 2 are inconsistent by deducing explicitly contradictory statements from 1, 2, and 9 is a failure. For although 1, 2, and 9 do yield explicitly contradictory statements, we are not in a position to know that 9 is necessarily true.

The suggestion that emerges from the preceding discussion is that we replace 9 with

10 A good, omnipotent, omniscient being prevents the occurrence of any evil that is not logically necessary for the occurrence of a good which outweighs it.

Statement 10, unlike 9, takes into account the possibility that certain evils might be so connected to goods which outweigh them that even God cannot realize those goods without permitting the evils to occur. Statement 10, then, appears to be not only true but necessarily true. The problem now, however, is that from 1, 2, and 10, explicitly contradictory statements cannot be derived. All that we can conclude from 1, 2, and 10 is that the evils which do exist in our world are logically necessary for the occurrence of goods which outweigh them, and that statement is not an explicit contradiction.

The general difficulty affecting attempts to establish that 1 and 2 are logically inconsistent is now apparent. When we add a statement, such as 9, which allows us to derive explicitly contradictory statements, we cannot be sure that the additional statement is necessarily true. On the other hand, when we add a statement, such as 10, which does seem to be necessarily true, it turns out that explicitly contradictory statements cannot be derived. No one has succeeded in producing a statement which is both known to be neces-

sarily true and, such that when added to 1 and 2, enables us to derive explicitly contradictory statements. In view of this, it is reasonable to conclude that the logical form of the problem of evil is not much of a problem for theism, for its central thesis, that 1 and 2 are logically inconsistent, is a thesis that no one has been able to establish by a convincing argument.

The "Free Will Defense"

Before turning to the evidential form of the problem of evil, it is important to understand the bearing of one traditional theistic defense on the logical form of the problem of evil. According to this defense – the "Free Will Defense" – God, even though omnipotent, *may not have been able* to create a world in which there are free human creatures without, thereby, permitting the occurrence of considerable evil. The basic assumption in this defense is that it is logically impossible for a person both *freely* to perform some act and to have been *caused* to perform that act. Without this assumption, the Free Will Defense collapses. For if it is possible for a person to be caused to do an act and yet to perform that act freely, then clearly God could have created a world in which there are free human creatures who only do what is right, who never do evil – for he, being omnipotent, could simply create the creatures and cause them to do only what is right.

Let's suppose that the basic assumption of the Free Will Defense is true, that it is logically impossible to be caused to do an act and yet to do that act freely. What this assumption means is that although God can cause there to be creatures and cause them to be free with respect to a certain act, he *cannot* cause them freely to perform the act, and he cannot cause them freely to refrain from performing the act – whether the person performs the act or refrains from performing it will be up to that person, and not up to God, if the performing or refraining is to be freely done. Now suppose God creates a world with free human creatures, creatures who are free to do various things, including good and evil. Whether the free human creatures he creates will exercise their freedom to do good or evil will be up to them. And it is logically possible that no matter what free creatures God causes to exist, each of them will use his freedom on some occasion to do evil. Since this is so, it is *possible* that God could not have created a world with free creatures who do only what is right; it is possible that any world that God can create containing creatures free to do good or evil is a world in which these creatures sometimes do evil.

What the above line of argument endeavors to establish is that it is logically possible that the following statement is true.

11 God, although omnipotent, cannot create a world in which there are free human creatures and no evil.

But if it is possible that 11 is true, and also possible that a world with free human creatures is a better world than a world without free human creatures, then it follows that 1 and 2 are not inconsistent at all. For consider the following group of statements:

1 God exists and is omnipotent, omniscient, and wholly good.
11 God, although omnipotent, cannot create a world in which there are free human creatures and no evil.
12 A world with free human creatures and some evil is a better world than a world with no free human creatures.
13 God creates the best world he can.

From 1, 11, 12, and 13 it follows that 2 "Evil exists." But if 1, 11, 12, and 13 imply 2 and there is no inconsistency in 1, 11, 12, and 13, then there can be no inconsistency between 1 and 2. If a group of statements is not inconsistent, then no statement that follows from that group can be inconsistent with any or all statements in the group.

We can now see the relevance of the Free Will Defense to the logical form of the problem of evil. We objected to the logical form of the problem of evil because no one has succeeded in establishing its central thesis, that (1) "God is omnipotent, omniscient, and wholly good" is inconsistent with (2) "Evil exists." But, of course, from the fact that no one has *proved* that 1 and 2 are inconsistent, it doesn't follow that they aren't inconsistent. What the Free Will Defense endeavors to do is to go the final step, to *prove* that 1 and 2 are really consistent. It does this by trying to establish that it is *possible* (logically) that both 11 and 12 are true and that there is no logical inconsistency in the group of statements, 1, 11, 12, and 13. Whether the Free Will Defense is successful in its aim of showing that 1 and 2 are logically consistent is a matter too complicated and controversial for us to pursue here.[1] Even if it is unsuccessful, however, the theist need not be unduly troubled by the logical form of the problem of evil, for, as we've seen, no one has established that 1 and 2 are inconsistent.

---

[1] A more elaborate account of the Free Will Defense can be found in Alvin Plantinga, *God, Freedom, and Evil* (New York: Harper & Row, Publishers, 1974).

37

An Irenaean Theodicy

John Hick

Can a world in which sadistic cruelty often has its way, in which selfish lovelessness is so rife, in which there are debilitating diseases, crippling accidents, bodily and mental decay, insanity, and all manner of natural disasters be regarded as the expression of infinite creative goodness? Certainly all this could never by itself lead anyone to believe in the existence of a limitlessly powerful God. And yet even in such a world, innumerable men and women have believed and do believe in the reality of an infinite creative goodness, which they call God. The theodicy project starts at this point – with an already operating belief in God, embodied in human living – and attempts to show that this belief is not rendered irrational by the fact of evil. It attempts to explain how the universe, assumed to be created and ultimately ruled by a limitlessly good and limitlessly powerful Being, is as it is, including all the pain, suffering, wickedness, and folly that we find around us and within us. The theodicy project is thus an exercise in metaphysical thinking, in the sense that it consists in the formation and criticism of large-scale hypotheses concerning the nature and process of the universe.

Since a theodicy both starts from and tests belief in the reality of God, it naturally takes different forms in relation to different concepts of God. In this paper I shall be discussing the project of a specifically Christian theodicy; I shall not be attempting the further and even more difficult work of comparative theodicy, leading in turn to the question of a global theodicy.

The two main demands upon a theodicy hypothesis are that it be (1) internally coherent, and (2) consistent with the data both of the religious tradition on which it is based, and of the world, in respect both of the latter's general character as revealed by scientific enquiry and of the specific facts of moral and natural evil. These two criteria demand, respectively, possibility and plausibility.

Traditionally, Christian theology has centered upon the concept of God as both limitlessly powerful and limitlessly good and loving; this concept of deity gives rise to the problem of evil as a threat to theistic faith. The threat was definitively expressed in Stendhal's bombshell, "The only excuse for God is that he does not exist!" The theodicy project is the attempt to offer a different view of the universe that is both possible and plausible and which does not ignite Stendhal's bombshell.

Christian thought has always included a certain range of variety, and in the area of theodicy it offers two broad types of approach. The Augustinian

"An Irenaean Theodicy" by John Hick from *Encountering Evil: Live Options in Theodicy*, new edition, ed. Stephen T. Davis (Atlanta: John Knox/Westminster, 2001), pp. 38–52; 213.

approach, representing until fairly recently the majority report of the Christian mind, hinges upon the idea of the fall as the origin of moral evil, which has in turn brought about the almost universal carnage of nature. The Irenaean approach, representing in the past a minority report, hinges upon the creation of humankind through the evolutionary process as an immature creature living in a challenging and therefore person-making world. I shall indicate very briefly why I do not find the first type of theodicy satisfactory, and then spend the remainder of this paper exploring the second type.

In recent years the free-will defense has dominated the philosophical discussion of the problem of evil. Alvin Plantinga and a number of other Christian philosophers have made a major effort to show that it is logically *possible* that a limitlessly powerful and limitlessly good God is responsible for the existence of this world and that all evil may ultimately result from misuses of creaturely freedom. But, they add, it may nevertheless be better for God to have created free than unfree beings; and it is logically possible that any and all free beings whom God might create would, as a matter of contingent fact, misuse their freedom by falling into sin. In that case it would be logically *impossible* for God to have created a world containing free beings and yet not containing sin and the suffering that sin brings with it. Thus it is logically possible, despite the fact of evil, that the existing universe is the work of a limitlessly good creator.

These writers are in effect arguing that the traditional Augustinian type of theodicy, based upon the fall from grace of free finite creatures – first angels and then human beings – and a consequent going wrong of the physical world, is not logically impossible. I am in fact doubtful whether their argument is sound, and I will return to the question later. But even if the Augustinian approach is sound, I suggest that their argument wins only a Pyrrhic victory, since the logical possibility that it would establish is one that, for very many people today, is fatally lacking in plausibility. Most educated inhabitants of the modern world regard the biblical story of Adam and Eve, and their temptation by the devil, as myth rather than as history; they believe further that far from having been created finitely perfect and then falling, humanity evolved out of lower forms of life, emerging in a morally, spiritually, and culturally primitive state. Further, they reject as incredible the idea that earthquake and flood, disease, decay, and death are consequences either of the human fall or of a prior fall of angelic beings who are now exerting an evil influence upon the earth. They see all this as part of a prescientific worldview, along with such stories as the world having been created in six days and of the sun standing still for twenty-four hours at Joshua's command. One cannot, strictly speaking, disprove any of these ancient biblical myths and sagas, or refute their elaboration in the medieval Christian picture of the universe. But people for whom the resulting theodicy, even if logically possible, is radically implausible, must look elsewhere for light on the problem of evil.

I believe that we find the light that we need in the main alternative strand of Christian thinking, which goes back to important constructive suggestions by the early Hellenistic Fathers of the church, particularly St Irenaeus (120–202 AD). Irenaeus himself did not develop a theodicy, but he did – together with other Greek-speaking Christian writers of that period, such as Clement of Alexandria – build a framework of thought within which a theodicy becomes possible that does not depend upon the idea of the fall, and which is consonant with modern knowledge concerning the origins of the human race. This theodicy cannot, as such, be attributed to Irenaeus. We should rather speak of a type of theodicy, presented in varying ways by different subsequent thinkers (the greatest of whom has been Friedrich Schleiermacher), of which Irenaeus can properly be regarded as the patron saint.

The central theme out of which this Irenaean type of theodicy has arisen is the two-stage conception of the creation of humankind, first in the "image" and then in the "likeness" of God. Re-expressing this concept in modern terms, the first stage was the gradual production of *homo sapiens*, through the long evolutionary process, as intelligent ethical and religious animals. The human being is one of the varied forms of earthly life and continuous as such with the whole realm of animal existence. But a human is uniquely intelligent, having evolved a large and immensely complex brain. Further, humans are ethical – that is, gregarious as well as intelligent animals, able to realize and respond to the complex demands of social life. They are also religious animals, with an innate tendency to experience the world in terms of the presence and activity of supernatural beings and powers. This portrayal, then, is early *homo sapiens*, the intelligent social animal capable of awareness of the divine. But early *homo sapiens* does not include the Adam and Eve of Augustinian theology, living in perfect harmony with self, with nature, and with God. On the contrary, the life of early *homo sapiens* must have been a constant struggle against a hostile environment, necessitating the capacity for savage violence against their fellow human beings, particularly outside their own immediate group. This being's concepts of the divine were primitive and often bloodthirsty. Existence "in the image of God" was thus a *potentiality* for knowledge of and relationship with one's Maker, rather than such knowledge and relationship as a fully realized state. In other words, people were created as spiritually and morally immature creatures, at the beginning of a long process of further growth and development, which constitutes the second stage of God's creative work.

In this second stage, of which we are a part, intelligent, ethical, and religious animals are being brought through their own free responses into what Irenaeus called the divine "likeness." Irenaeus's own terminology (*eikon, homoiosis; imago, similitudo*) has no particular merit, based as it is on a misunderstanding of the Hebrew parallelism in Genesis 1:26, but his conception of a two-stage creation of humanity, with perfection lying in the future rather than in the past, is of fundamental importance.

The notion of the Fall was not basic to this picture, although it later became basic to the great drama of salvation depicted by St Augustine and accepted within Western Christendom, including the churches stemming from the Reformation, until well into the nineteenth century. Irenaeus himself could not, however, in the historical knowledge of his time, question the fact of the Fall, though he treated it as a relatively minor lapse – a youthful error – rather than as the infinite crime and cosmic disaster that has ruined the whole creation. But today we can acknowledge that no evidence at all exists of a period in the distant past when humankind was in the ideal state of a fully realized "child of God." We can accept that, so far as actual events in time are concerned, a fall from an original righteousness and grace never occurred. If we want to continue to use the term "fall," because of its hallowed place in the Christian tradition, we must use it to refer to the immense gap between what we actually are and what in the divine intention we are eventually to become. But we must not blur our awareness that the ideal state is not something already enjoyed and lost, but is a future and as-yet-unrealized goal. The reality is not a perfect creation that has gone tragically wrong, but a still continuing creative process whose completion lies in the eschaton.

Let us now try to formulate a contemporary version of the Irenaean type of theodicy, based on this suggestion of the initial creation of humankind, not as finitely perfect, but as an immature creature at the beginning of a long process of further growth and development. We may begin by asking why humanity should have been created as an imperfect and developing creature rather than as the perfect being whom God is intending to create. The answer, I think, consists in two considerations that converge in their practical implications, one concerned with our relationship to God and the other with our relationship to other human beings. As to the first, we could have the picture of God creating finite beings, whether angels or humans, directly in the divine presence, so that in being conscious of that which is other than oneself the creature is automatically conscious of God, the limitless reality and power, goodness and love, knowledge and wisdom, towering above oneself. In such a situation the disproportion between Creator and creatures would be so great that the latter would have no freedom in relation to God; they would indeed not exist as independent autonomous persons. For what freedom could finite beings have in an immediate consciousness of the presence of the one who has created them, who knows them through and through, who is limitlessly powerful as well as limitlessly loving and good, and who claims their total obedience? In order to be a person, exercising some measure of genuine freedom, the creature must be brought into existence, not in the immediate divine presence, but at a "distance" from God. This "distance" cannot of course be spatial, for God is omnipresent. The distance must be epistemic, a distance in the cognitive dimension. And the Irenaean hypothesis is that this "distance" consists, in the case of humans, in their existence within and as part of a world that functions as an autonomous system and from within which God is not overwhelmingly evident. The world exists, in Bonhoeffer's phrase, *etsi deus non daretur*, as if there were no God. Or rather, the world is religiously ambiguous, capable of being seen either as a purely natural phenomenon or as God's creation and experienced as mediating his presence. In such a world one can exist as a person over against the Creator. One has space to exist as a finite being, a space created by this epistemic distance from God and protected by one's basic cognitive freedom, one's freedom to open or close oneself to the dawning awareness of God that is experienced naturally by a religious animal. This Irenaean picture corresponds, I suggest, to our actual human situation. Emerging within the evolutionary process as part of the continuum of animal life, in a universe that functions in accordance with its own laws and whose workings can be investigated and described without reference to a creator, the human being has a genuine, even awesome, freedom in relation to one's Maker. We are free to acknowledge and worship God, and free – particularly since the emergence of individuality and the beginnings of critical consciousness during the first millennium BC – to doubt the reality of God.

Within such a situation the possibility enters of human beings coming freely to know and love their Maker. Indeed, if the end-state that God is seeking to bring about is one in which finite persons have come in their own freedom to know and love him, this condition requires their initial creation in a state which is not that of already knowing and loving him (or her). To create beings already in a state of having come into that state by their own free choices is logically impossible. The other consideration, which converges with this in pointing to something like the human situation as we experience it, concerns our human moral nature. We can approach it by asking why humans should not have been created at this epistemic distance from God, and yet at the same time as morally perfect beings. That persons could have been created morally perfect and yet free, so that they would always in fact choose rightly, has been argued by such critics of

the free-will defense as Antony Flew and J. L. Mackie, and argued against by Alvin Plantinga and other upholders of that theodicy. On the specific issue defined in the debate between them, it appears to me that the criticism of the free-will defense stands, that a perfectly good being, although formally free to sin, would in fact never do so. If we imagine such beings in a morally frictionless environment, involving no stresses or temptation, then we must assume that they would exemplify the ethical equivalent of Newton's first law of motion, which states that a moving body will continue in uniform motion until interfered with by some outside force. By analogy, perfectly good beings would continue in the same moral course forever, with nothing in the environment to throw them off it. And even if we suppose morally perfect beings to exist in an imperfect world, in which they are subject to temptations, it still follows that, in virtue of their moral perfection, they will always overcome those temptations – as in the case, according to orthodox Christian belief, of Jesus Christ. It is, to be sure, logically possible, as Plantinga and others argue, that a free being, simply as such, may at any time contingently decide to sin. However, a responsible free being does not act randomly, but on the basis of a moral nature, and a free being whose nature is wholly and unqualifiedly good will accordingly never in fact sin.

But if God could, without logical contradiction, have created humans as wholly good, free beings, why did God not do so? Why was humanity not initially created in possession of all the virtues, instead of having to acquire them through the long, hard struggle of life as we know it? The answer, I suggest, appeals to the principle that virtues that have been formed within the agent as a hard-won deposit of right decisions in situations of challenge and temptation are intrinsically more valuable than ready-made virtues created within her without any effort on her own part. This principle expresses a basic value judgment that cannot be established by argument but which one can only present, in the hope that it will be as morally plausible, and indeed compelling, to others as to oneself. It is, to repeat, the judgment that a moral goodness that exists as the agent's initial given nature, without ever having been chosen in the face of temptations to the contrary, is intrinsically less valuable than a moral goodness that has been built up over time through the agent's own responsible choices in the face of alternative possibilities.

If, then, God's purpose was to create finite persons embodying the most valuable kind of moral goodness, he (or she) would have to create them, not as already perfect beings but rather as imperfect creatures, who can then attain to the more valuable kind of goodness through their own free choices. In the course of their personal and social history new responses would prompt new insights, opening up new moral possibilities and providing a milieu in which the most valuable kind of moral nature can be developed.

We have thus far, then, the hypothesis that humanity is created at an epistemic distance from God in order to come freely to know and love their Maker; and that they are at the same time created as morally immature and imperfect beings in order to attain through freedom the most valuable quality of goodness. The end sought, according to this hypothesis, is the full realization of human potential in a spiritual and moral perfection within the divine kingdom. The question we have to ask is whether humans as we know them, and the world as we know it, fit the hypothesis.

Clearly we cannot expect to be able to deduce our actual world in its concrete character, and our actual human nature as part of it, from the general concept of spiritually and morally immature creatures developing ethically in an appropriate environment. No doubt an immense range of worlds is possible, any one of which, if actualized, would exemplify this concept. All that we can hope to do is to show that our actual world is one of these. And when we look at our human situation as part of the evolving life on this planet we can, I think, see that it fits this specification. As animal organisms, integral to the whole ecology of life, we are programmed for survival. In pursuit of survival, primitives not only killed other animals for food but fought other humans when their vital interests conflicted. The life of prehistoric persons must often have been a constant struggle to stay alive, prolonging an existence that was, in Hobbes's phrase, "poor, nasty, brutish and short." And in his basic

animal self-regardingness, humankind was and is morally imperfect. In making this statement I am assuming that the essence of moral evil is selfishness, the sacrificing of others to one's own interests. It consists, in Kantian terminology, in treating others, not as ends in themselves, but as means to one's own ends, as the survival instinct demands. Yet we are also capable of love, of self-giving in a common cause, of a conscience that responds to others in their needs and dangers. And with the development of civilization we see the growth of moral insight, the glimpsing and gradual assimilation of higher ideals, and tension between our animality and our ethical values. But that the human being has a lower as well as a higher nature, that one is an animal as well as a potential child of God, and that one's moral goodness is won through a struggle with innate selfishness, are inevitable given our continuity with the other forms of animal life. Further, the human animal is not responsible for having come into existence as an animal. The ultimate responsibility for humankind's existence, as a morally imperfect creature, can only rest with the Creator. We do not, in our degree of freedom and responsibility, choose our origin, but rather our destiny.

In brief outline, then, this line of thought is the Irenaean theodicy's answer to the question of the origin of moral evil: the general fact of humankind's basic self-regarding animality is an aspect of our creation as part of the realm of organic life, and this basic self-regardingness has been expressed over the centuries both in sins of individual selfishness and in the much more massive sins of corporate selfishness, institutionalized in slavery, exploitation, and all the many and complex forms of social injustice.

But nevertheless our sinful nature in an often harsh world is the matrix within which God is gradually creating children out of human animals. For as men and women freely respond to the claim of God upon their lives, transmuting their animal nature into that of children of God, the creation of humanity is taking place. In its concrete character this response consists in every form of moral goodness, from unselfish love in individual personal relationships to the dedicated and selfless striving to end exploitation and to create justice within and between societies.

But one cannot discuss moral evil without at

the same time discussing the nonmoral evil of pain and suffering. (I propose to mean by "pain" physical pain, including the pains of hunger and thirst; and by "suffering" the mental and emotional pain of loneliness, anxiety, remorse, lack of love, fear, grief, envy, etc.) For what constitutes moral evil as evil is the fact that it causes pain and suffering. Conceiving of an instance of moral evil, or sin, that is not productive of pain or suffering to anyone at any time is impossible. But in addition to moral evil, another source of pain and suffering is present in the structure of the physical world, producing storms, earthquakes, and floods and afflicting the human body with diseases – cholera, epilepsy, cancer, malaria, arthritis, rickets, meningitis, AIDS, etc. – as well as with broken bones and other outcomes of physical accident. A great deal of both pain and suffering is humanly caused, not only by the inhumanity of man to man but also by the stresses of our individual and corporate lifestyles, causing many disorders – not only lung cancer and cirrhosis of the liver but many cases of heart disease, stomach and other ulcers, strokes, etc. But nevertheless, in the natural world itself, permanent causes of human pain and suffering remain. We have to ask why an unlimitedly good and unlimitedly powerful God should have created so dangerous a world, both in its purely natural hazards of earthquake and flood, for example, and in the liability of the human body to so many ills, both psychosomatic and purely somatic.

The answer offered by the Irenaean type of theodicy follows from and is indeed integrally bound up with its account of the origin of moral evil. We have the hypothesis of humankind being brought into being within the evolutionary process as a spiritually and morally immature creature, and then growing and developing through the exercise of freedom in this religiously ambiguous world. We can now ask what sort of a world would constitute an appropriate environment for this second stage of creation? The development of human personality – moral, spiritual, and intellectual – is a product of challenge and response that could not occur in a static situation demanding no exertion and no

choices. So far as intellectual development is concerned, this well-established principle underlies the whole modern educational process, from preschool nurseries designed to provide a rich and stimulating environment to all forms of higher education designed to challenge the intellect. At a basic level the essential part played by the learner's own active response to environment was strikingly demonstrated by the Held and Heim experiment with kittens.[1] Of two littermate kittens in the same artificial environment, one was free to exercise its own freedom and intelligence in exploring the environment, while the other was suspended in a kind of gondola that moved whenever and wherever the free kitten moved. Thus, the second kitten had a similar succession of visual experiences as the first, but did not exert itself or make any choices in obtaining them. And whereas the first kitten learned in the normal way to conduct itself safely within its environment, the second did not. With no interaction with a challenging environment its capacities did not develop. I think we can safely say that the intellectual development of humanity has been due to interaction with an objective environment functioning in accordance with its own laws, an environment that we have to explore actively and cooperate with actively in order to escape its perils and exploit its benefits. In a world devoid both of dangers to be avoided and rewards to be won, we may assume that virtually no development of the human intellect and imagination would have taken place, and hence no development of the sciences, the arts, human civilization, or culture.

The presence of an objective world – within which we have to learn to live on penalty of pain or death – is also basic to the development of our moral nature. For because the world is one in which men and women can suffer harm – by violence, disease, accident, starvation, etc. – our actions affecting one another have moral significance. A morally wrong act is, basically, one that harms some part of the human community, while a morally right action is, on the contrary, one that prevents or neutralizes harm or that preserves or increases human well-being.

[1]   R. Held and A. Heim, "Movement-Produced Stimulation in the Development of Visually Guided Behaviour," *Journal of Comparative and Physiological Psychology*, vol. 56 (1963), 872–76.

We can imagine a paradise in which no one can ever come to any harm. Instead of having its own fixed structure, the world would be plastic to human wishes. Or perhaps the world would have a fixed structure, and hence the possibility of damage and pain, but a structure that is whenever necessary suspended or adjusted by special divine action to avoid human pain. Thus, for example, in such a miraculously pain-free world, one who falls accidentally off a high building would presumably float unharmed to the ground; bullets would become insubstantial when fired at a human body; poisons would cease to poison; water to drown, and so on. We can at least begin to imagine such a world. A good deal of the older discussion of the problem of evil – for example, in Part XI of Hume's *Dialogues Concerning Natural Religion* – assumed that it must be the intention of a limitlessly good and powerful Creator to make a pain-free environment for human creatures, so that the very existence of pain is evidence against the existence of God. But such an assumption overlooks the fact that a world in which there can be no pain or suffering would also be one without moral choices and hence no possibility of moral growth and development. For in a situation in which no one can ever suffer injury or be liable to pain or suffering, no distinction would exist between right and wrong action. No action would be morally wrong, because no action could ever have harmful consequences; likewise, no action would be morally right in contrast to wrong. Whatever the values of such a world, its structure would not serve the purpose of allowing its inhabitants to develop from self-regarding animality to self-giving love.

Thus, the hypothesis of a divine purpose in which finite persons are created at an epistemic distance from God, in order that they may gradually become children of God through their own moral and spiritual choices, requires that their environment, instead of being a pain-free and stress-free paradise, be broadly the kind of world of which we find ourselves to be a part, a world that provokes the theological problem of evil. Such a world requires an environment that offers challenges to be met, problems to be solved, and dangers to be faced; and which accordingly involves real possibilities of hardship, disaster, failure, defeat, and misery as well as of delight and happiness, success, triumph, and achievement. By grappling with the real problems of a real environment – in which a person is one form of life among many, and which is not designed to minister exclusively to our well-being – people can develop in intelligence and in such qualities as courage and determination. In relationships with one another, in the context of this struggle to survive and flourish, humans can develop the higher values of mutual love and care, self-sacrifice for others, and commitment to a common good.

However, this condition will not apply to the rest of the animal kingdom, whose members are not undergoing moral and spiritual development. From our human point of view the teeming multitude of life-forms, each nourishing and nourished by others in a continuous recycling of life, constitutes the vast evolutionary process within which humanity has emerged; the fact that we are part of this ever-changing natural order is an aspect of our epistemic distance from God that we noted earlier. But if we ask why so many animals are carnivorous rather than vegetarian, killing and eating other species, no evident answer is available. We can note that the lower animals live almost entirely in the immediate present, unaware of their mortality, and without anxiety for the future or painful memories of the past – except, it would seem, for some individuals that have been in varying degrees adopted and domesticated by humans. But caution is in order. As the psychologists Eugene d'Aquili and Andrew Newberg say, "While it is difficult to determine with any certainty the emotions of animals, it seems that they must have some type of value response that tells them what to avoid and what to be drawn to. Whether these responses imply the emotions of fear and love as humans know them is, however, difficult to discern. . . . Suffice it to say that all animals must at least be able to derive an operational value from their experiences even if there is no emotional response similar in form to that of human beings."[2] Anthropomorphizing is easy here, and

[2] Eugene d'Aquili and Andrew Newberg, *The Mystical Mind: Probing the Biology of Mystical Experience* (Minneapolis: Fortress Press, 1999), 56–7.

yet on the other hand it seems safer to risk erring on that side rather than the other; in any case the question mark about emotion does not lessen the immediately felt physical pain that takes place all the time. One can only say that pain is an aspect of the process of biological evolution as it has actually occurred, and is to us part of the same mysterious totality as earthquakes, volcanic eruptions, storms, hurricanes, and tidal waves. The very fact that it is mysterious may, however, itself have value. We shall come presently to the positive role of mystery, according to the Irenaean theodicy.

To summarize thus far:

1   The divine intention in relation to humankind, according to our hypothesis, is to create perfect finite personal beings in filial relationship with their Maker.
2   For humans to be created already in this perfect state is logically impossible, because in its spiritual aspect it involves coming freely to an uncoerced consciousness of God from a situation of epistemic distance, and in its moral aspect, freely choosing the good.
3   Accordingly, the human being was initially created through the evolutionary process, as a spiritually and morally immature creature, and as part of a religiously ambiguous and ethically demanding world.
4   Thus, that one is morally imperfect (i.e., that there is moral evil), and that the world is a challenging and even dangerous environment (i.e., that there is natural evil), are necessary aspects of the present stage of the process through which God is gradually creating perfected finite persons.

In terms of this hypothesis, as we have developed it thus far, then, both the basic moral evil in the human heart and the natural evils of the world are compatible with the existence of a Creator who is unlimited in both goodness and power. But is the hypothesis plausible as well as possible? The principal threat to its plausibility comes, I think, from the sheer amount and intensity of both moral and natural evil. One can readily accept

the principle that in order to arrive at a freely chosen goodness one must start out in a state of moral immaturity and imperfection. But are the depths of demonic malice and cruelty that each generation has experienced necessary, such as we have seen above all in the twentieth century in the Nazi attempt to exterminate the Jewish population of Europe? Can any future fulfillment be worth such horrors? Consider Dostoyevsky's haunting question: "Imagine that you are creating a fabric of human destiny with the object of making men happy in the end, giving them peace and rest at last, but that it was essential and inevitable to torture to death only one tiny creature – that baby beating its breast with its fist, for instance – and to found that edifice on its unavenged tears, would you consent to be the architect on those conditions?"[3] The theistic answer is one that may be true but which takes so large a view that it baffles the imagination. Intellectually one may be able to see, but emotionally one cannot be expected to feel, its truth; and in that sense it cannot satisfy us. For the theistic answer is that if we take with full seriousness the value of human freedom and responsibility, as essential to the eventual creation of perfected children of God, then we cannot consistently want God to revoke that freedom when its wrong exercise becomes intolerable to us. From our vantage point within the historical process, we may indeed cry out to God to revoke his gift of freedom, or to overrule it by some secret or open intervention. Such a cry must have come from millions caught in the Jewish Holocaust, and in the more recent laying waste of Korea, Vietnam, Rwanda, and Kosovo, and from the victims of racism in many parts of the world. And the thought that humankind's moral freedom is indivisible and can lead eventually to a consummation of limitless value which could never be attained without that freedom, and which is worth any finite suffering in the course of its creation, can be of no comfort to those who are now in the midst of that suffering. But while fully acknowledging this, I nevertheless want to insist that this eschatological answer may well be true. Expressed in religious language it tells

---

[3]   Fyodor Dostoyevsky, *The Brothers Karamazov*, trans. Constance Garnett (New York: Modern Library, n.d.), bk V, chap. 4, 254.

us to trust in God even in the midst of deep suffering, for in the end we shall participate in the divine kingdom.

Again, we may grant that a world that is to be a person-making environment cannot be a pain-free paradise but must contain challenges and dangers, with real possibilities of many kinds of accident and disaster, and the pain and suffering which they bring. But need it contain the worst forms of disease and catastrophe? And need misfortune fall upon us with such heartbreaking indiscriminateness? Once again some answers may well be true, but truth in this area may nevertheless offer little in the way of pastoral balm.

We can see that a pain-free paradise would not constitute a person-making environment. But we cannot profess to see that the world's actual pains are just the amount needed and no more. However, at this point we meet the paradox that if we *could* see that, then the world would no longer serve a person-making purpose! For if we were right earlier in concluding that such a purpose requires a religiously ambiguous world, in which God is not evident, then God's purpose for the world must not be evident within it. That the world is as it is must be to us a mystery which, according to the Irenaean theodicy, is itself an essential aspect of its person-making character.

But one of the most daunting and even terrifying features of the world is that calamity strikes indiscriminately. In the incidence of disease, accident, disaster, and tragedy, no justice can be found. The righteous as well as the unrighteous are alike struck down by illness and afflicted by misfortune. There is no security in goodness, for the good are as likely as the wicked to suffer "the slings and arrows of outrageous fortune." From the time of Job this fact has set a glaring question mark against the goodness of God. But let us suppose that things were otherwise. Let us suppose that, misfortune came upon humankind, not haphazardly and therefore unjustly, but justly and therefore not haphazardly. Let us suppose that, instead of coming without regard to moral considerations, misfortune was proportioned to desert, so that the sinner was punished and the virtuous rewarded. Would such a dispensation serve a person-making purpose? Surely not. For wrong deeds would obviously bring disaster upon the agent while good deeds would bring health and prosperity. In such a world truly moral action, action done because it is right, would be impossible. The fact that natural evil is not morally directed, but is a hazard that comes by chance, is thus an intrinsic feature of a person-making world.

In other words, the very mystery of natural evil, the very fact that disasters afflict human beings in contingent, undirected and haphazard ways, is itself a necessary feature of a world that calls forth mutual aid and builds up mutual caring and love. Thus on the one hand to say that God sends misfortune upon individuals, so that their death, maiming, starvation, or ruin is God's will for them would be completely wrong. But on the other hand God has set us in a world containing unpredictable contingencies and dangers – in which unexpected and undeserved calamities may occur to anyone – because only in such a world can mutual caring and love be elicited. As an abstract philosophical hypothesis, this may offer little comfort. But translated into religious language it tells us that God's good purpose enfolds the entire process of this world, with all its good and bad contingencies, and that even amidst tragic calamity and suffering we are still within the sphere of God's love and are moving towards the divine kingdom.

But there is one further all-important aspect of the Irenaean type of theodicy, without which all the foregoing would lose its plausibility. This is the eschatological aspect. Our hypothesis depicts persons as still in the course of creation towards an end-state of perfected personal community in the divine kingdom. This end-state is conceived of as one in which individual egoity has been transcended in communal unity before God. In the present phase of that creative process the naturally self-centered human animal has the opportunity freely to respond to God's noncoercive self-disclosures, through the work of prophets and saints, through the resulting religious traditions, and through the individual's religious experience. Such response always has an ethical aspect; the growing awareness of God is at the same time a growing awareness of the moral claim that God's presence makes upon the way in which we live.

This person-making process, leading eventually to perfect human community, is obviously not completed on this earth. It is not completed in the life of the individual – or at best only in the few who have attained sanctification, or *moksha*, or nirvana on this earth. Clearly the enormous majority of men and women die without reaching such levels. As Eric Fromm has said, "The tragedy in the life of most of us is that we die before we are fully born."[4] Therefore if we are ever to reach the full realization of the potentialities of our human nature, this fulfillment can only come in a continuation of our lives in another sphere of existence after bodily death. The perfect all-embracing human community, in which self-regarding concern has been transcended in mutual love, not only has evidently not been realized in this world, but never can be, since hundreds of generations of human beings have already lived and died and accordingly could not be part of any ideal community established at some future moment of earthly history. Thus if the unity of humankind in God's presence is ever to be realized it will have to be in some sphere of existence other than our earth. In short, the fulfillment of the divine purpose, as it is postulated in the Irenaean type of theodicy, presupposes each person's survival, in some form, of bodily death, and further living and growing towards that end-state. Without such an eschatological fulfillment, this theodicy would collapse.

A theodicy that presupposes and requires an eschatology will thereby be rendered implausible in the minds of many people today. The belief, however, in the reality of a limitlessly loving and powerful deity must incorporate some kind of eschatology according to which God holds in being the creatures whom he has made for fellowship with God, beyond bodily death, and brings them into the eternal fellowship that he has intended for them. I have tried elsewhere to argue that such an eschatology is a necessary corollary of ethical monotheism; to argue for the realistic possibility of an after-life or lives, despite the philosophical and empirical arguments against this; and even to spell out some

of the general features that human life after death may possibly have.[5] Since this task is very large, far exceeding the bounds of this paper, I shall not attempt to repeat it here but must refer the reader to my existing discussion of it. That extended discussion constitutes my answer to the question of whether an Irenaean theodicy, with its eschatology, is not as implausible as an Augustinian theodicy, with its human or angelic fall. (If the Irenaean theodicy is implausible, then the latter is doubly implausible; for it also involves an eschatology!)

One particular aspect of eschatology, however, must receive some treatment here, however brief and inadequate: the issue of "universal salvation" versus "heaven and hell" (or perhaps "annihilation" instead of "hell"). If the justification of evil within the creative process lies in the limitless and eternal good of the end-state to which it leads, then the completeness of the justification must depend upon the completeness, or universality, of the salvation achieved. Only if it includes the entire human race can it justify the sins and sufferings of the entire human race throughout all history. But, having given us cognitive freedom, which in turn makes moral freedom possible, can the Creator bring it about that in the end all will freely turn to him in love and trust? The issue is very difficult, but I believe that reconciling a full affirmation of human freedom with a belief in the ultimate universal success of God's creative work is in fact possible. We have to accept that creaturely freedom always occurs within the limits of a basic nature that we did not ourselves choose, as is entailed by the fact of having been created. If a real though limited freedom does not preclude our being endowed with a certain nature, it also does not preclude our being endowed with a basic Godward bias, so that, quoting from another side of St Augustine's thought, "our hearts are restless until they find their rest in Thee."[6] If Augustine is correct, sooner or later, in our own time and in our own way, we shall all freely come to God; and universal salvation can be

[4]   Eric Fromm, "Values, Psychology, and Human Existence," in *New Knowledge of Human Values*, ed. A. H. Maslow (New York: Harper, 1959), 156.
[5]   John Hick, *Death and Eternal Life* (New York: Harper & Row, and London: Collins, 1976).
[6]   *The Confessions of St Augustine*, trans. F. J. Sheed (New York: Sheed and Ward, 1942), bk I, chap. 1, 3.

affirmed, not as a logical necessity but as the contingent but predictable outcome of the process of the universe, interpreted theistically. Once again, I have tried to present this argument more fully elsewhere, and to consider various objections to it.[7]

On this view the human, endowed with a real though limited freedom, is basically formed for relationship with God and destined ultimately to find the fulfillment of his or her nature in that relationship. This outlook does not seem to me excessively paradoxical. On the contrary, given the theistic postulate, this view seems to offer a very probable account of our human situation. If so, we can rejoice, for this situation gives meaning to our temporal existence as the long process through which we are being created, by our own free responses to life's mixture of good and evil, into "children of God" who "inherit eternal life."

---

[7] Hick, *Death and Eternal Life*, chap. 13.

38

The Evidential Problem of Evil

William Rowe

[The focus of this chapter is] the evidential form of the problem of evil: the form of the problem which holds that the variety and profusion of evil in our world, although perhaps not logically inconsistent with the existence of God, provides, nevertheless, *rational support* for the belief that the theistic God does not exist. In developing this form of the problem of evil, it will be useful to focus on some particular evil that our world contains in considerable abundance. Intense human and animal suffering, for example, occurs daily and in great plenitude in our world. Such intense suffering is a clear case of evil. Of course, if the intense suffering leads to some greater good, a good we could not have obtained without undergoing the suffering in question, we might conclude that the suffering is *justified*, but it remains an evil nevertheless. For we must not confuse the intense suffering in and of itself with the good things to which it sometimes leads or of which it may be a necessary part. Intense human or animal suffering is *in itself* bad, an evil, even though it may sometimes be justified by virtue of being a part of, or leading to, some good which is unobtainable without it. What is evil in itself may sometimes be good *as a means* because it leads to something which is good in itself. In such a case, while remaining an evil in itself, the intense human or animal suffering is, nevertheless, an evil which someone might be morally justified in permitting.

Taking human and animal suffering as a clear instance of evil which occurs with great frequency in our world, the evidential form of the problem of evil can be stated in terms of the following argument for atheism.

1 There exist instances of intense suffering which an omnipotent, omniscient being could have prevented without thereby preventing the occurrence of any greater good.
2 An omniscient, wholly good being would prevent the occurrence of any intense suffering it could, unless it could not do so without thereby losing some greater good.

Therefore,

3 There does not exist an omnipotent, omniscient, wholly good being.

What are we to say about this argument for atheism, an argument based on the profusion of one sort of evil in our world? The argument is valid; therefore, if we have rational grounds for accepting its premises, to that extent we have

---

"The Evidential Problem of Evil" from *Philosophy of Religion: An Introduction*, 3rd edition, by William Rowe (Belmont, CA: Wadsworth, 2001), pp. 98–110. Reprinted with permission of Wadsworth, a division of Thomson Learning.

rational grounds for accepting atheism. Do we, however, have rational grounds for accepting the premises of this argument?

The second premise of the argument expresses a belief about what a morally good being would do under certain circumstances. According to this belief, if a morally good being knew of some intense suffering that was about to occur and he was in a position to prevent its occurrence, he would prevent it *unless* he could not do so without thereby losing some greater good of which he was aware. This belief (or something very close to it) is, I think, held in common by theists and nontheists. Of course, there may be disagreement about whether something is good, and whether, if it is good, one would be morally justified in permitting some intense suffering to occur in order to obtain it. Someone might hold, for example, that no good is great enough to justify permitting an innocent child to suffer terribly. To hold such a view, however, is not to deny premise 2, which claims only that *if* an omniscient, wholly good being permits intense suffering *then* there must be some greater good (a good which outweighs the suffering in question) which the good being could not obtain without permitting the intense suffering. So stated, 2 seems to express a belief that accords with our basic moral principles, principles shared by both theists and nontheists. If we are to fault this argument, therefore, we must find some fault with its first premise.

Suppose in some distant forest lightning strikes a dead tree, resulting in a forest fire. In the fire a fawn is trapped, horribly burned, and lies in terrible agony for several days before death relieves its suffering. So far as we can see, the fawn's intense suffering is pointless, leading to no greater good. Could an omnipotent, omniscient being have prevented the fawn's apparently pointless suffering? The answer is obvious, as even the theist will insist. An omnipotent, omniscient being could easily have prevented the fawn from being horribly burned, or, given the burning, could have spared the fawn the intense suffering by quickly ending its life, rather than allowing the fawn to lie in terrible agony for several days. Since no greater good, so far as we can see, would have been lost had the fawn's intense suffering been prevented, doesn't it appear that premise 1 of the argument is true, that there

do exist instances of intense suffering which an omnipotent, omniscient being could have prevented without thereby preventing the occurrence of any greater good?

It must be acknowledged that the case of the fawn's apparently pointless suffering does not *prove* that premise 1 is true. For even though we cannot see how the fawn's suffering leads to any greater good, it hardly follows that it does not do so. After all, we are often surprised by how things we thought to be unconnected turn out to be intimately connected. Perhaps, then, there is some familiar good outweighing the fawn's suffering to which that suffering is connected in a way we do not see. Furthermore, there may well be unfamiliar goods, goods we haven't dreamed of, to which the fawn's suffering is inextricably connected. Indeed, it would seem to require something like omniscience on our part before we could lay claim to *knowing* that there is no greater good to which the fawn's suffering leads which an omnipotent, omniscient being could not have achieved without permitting that suffering. So the case of the fawn's suffering does not enable us to *establish* the truth of premise 1.

The truth is that we are not in a position to *prove* that 1 is true. We cannot *know* with certainty that instances of suffering of the sort described in 1 do occur in our world. But it is one thing to *know* or *prove* that 1 is true and quite another thing to have *rational grounds* for believing 1 to be true. We are often in the position where in the light of our experience and knowledge it is rational to believe that a certain statement is true, even though we are not in a position to prove or to know with certainty that the statement is true. In the light of our past experience and knowledge it is, for example, very reasonable to believe that wars between nations will continue to occur for some time to come, but we are scarcely in the position of knowing with certainty that this is so. So, too, with 1, although we cannot know with certainty that it is true, it perhaps can be rationally supported, shown to be a rational belief.

Consider again the case of the fawn's suffering. There are two distinct questions we need to raise: "Does the fawn's suffering lead to some greater good?" and "Is the greater good to which it might lead such that an omnipotent, omniscient being could not obtain it without permitting the fawn's suffering?" It may strike us as unlikely that the answer to the first question is yes. And it may strike us as quite a bit more unlikely that the answer to the second question is yes. But even if we should think it is reasonable to believe that the fawn's suffering leads to a greater good unobtainable without that suffering, we must then ask whether it is reasonable to believe that *all* the instances of profound, seemingly pointless human and animal suffering lead to greater goods. And, if they should somehow all lead to greater goods, is it reasonable to believe that an omnipotent, omniscient being *could not* have brought about *any* of those goods without permitting the instances of suffering which supposedly lead to them? When we consider these more general questions in the light of our experience and knowledge of the variety and profusion of human and animal suffering occurring daily in our world, it seems that the answer must be *no*. It seems quite unlikely that all the instances of intense human and animal suffering occurring daily in our world lead to greater goods, and even more unlikely that if they all do, an omnipotent, omniscient being could not have achieved at least some of those goods without permitting the instances of suffering that lead to them. In the light of our experience and knowledge of the variety and scale of human and animal suffering in our world, the idea that none of those instances of suffering could have been prevented by an omnipotent being without the loss of a greater good seems an extraordinary, absurd idea, quite beyond our belief. It seems then that although we cannot *prove* that premise 1 is true, it is, nevertheless, altogether *reasonable* to believe that 1 is true, that it is a *rational* belief.

Returning now to our argument for atheism, we've seen that the second premise expresses a basic belief common to theists and nontheists. We've also seen that our experience and knowledge of the variety and profusion of suffering in our world provides *rational support* for the first premise. Seeing that the conclusion, "There does not exist an omnipotent, omniscient, wholly good being" follows from these two premises, it does seem that we have *rational support* for

atheism, that it is reasonable for us to believe that the theistic God does not exist.

Responses to the Evidential Problem

Of the two forms of the problem of evil we've considered, the first (the *logical* form) was seen to be not a serious difficulty for theistic belief. The second form (the *evidential* form) has been seen to be a significant problem for theistic belief, for its basic thesis – that the variety and profusion of evil in our world provides rational support for atheism – has been shown to be plausible. It is time now to see how the theist might best respond to the evidential form of the problem of evil. The responses can best be explained in terms of the basic argument for atheism by means of which the evidential form of the problem of evil was presented. Indeed, the responses challenge either the first premise of that argument or the considerations advanced in support of it. We will consider two responses before looking at what is probably the best response open to the theist.

Fallacious Reasoning

The first response does not try to give any reasons for thinking that premise 1 is false. Instead, the theist here contends only that no good reasons have been given for thinking that premise 1 is true. Against the reasoning that was presented above in behalf of 1, the theist may endeavor to argue that the reasoning is fallacious, engaging in a faulty inference from "we don't know of any good that would justify an omnipotent being in permitting instances of suffering like the fawn's" to "there is no good that would justify an omnipotent being in permitting instances of suffering like the fawn's." Indeed, the theist might go on to argue that given the immense degree to which God's knowledge would exceed our own, it is somewhat likely that any good that would justify God in permitting instances of suffering like the fawn's would be beyond our ken, something that we shouldn't expect to comprehend.[1]

---

[1]   For some discussion of this first response see Stephen J. Wykstra, "The Humean Obstacle to Evidential Arguments From Suffering: On Avoid the Evils of 'Appearance,'" *International Journal for the Philosophy of Religion* 16 (1984), pp. 73–93.

Against this response, the proponent of the evidential argument may distinguish between goods we know about and goods beyond our ken, noting that no goods we know about could possibly justify God in permitting all the seemingly pointless evils that occur on a daily basis in our world. For the goods we know about either aren't good enough to justify God in permitting all these evils or could be achieved by God without his having to permit all these evils. But what of goods we don't know about, goods beyond our ken? Here the theist may suggest that God is like the good parent who may have to permit her child to suffer (perhaps through a painful surgical procedure) for a good the child cannot comprehend. And by analogy, won't the same be true of God in relation to us as his children? Indeed, since the disparity between his mind and ours may greatly exceed that of the good parent's mind to the mind of her child, isn't it likely that the goods that justify him in permitting us to suffer will often be beyond our comprehension? But against this argument from analogy, two points should be considered.

First, although arguments from analogy are rather weak, the analogy in question has some merit if drawn between a good parent and a good deity of considerable but nevertheless *finite* power and knowledge. For, like the good parent, a deity with great but *finite* powers may reasonably believe that he cannot realize some important future good for some of his creatures without permitting a present evil to befall them. And there may be occasions when, like the good parent, the finite deity is simply unable to prevent a dreadful evil befalling his creatures even though there is no good at all served by it. But the theistic God has unlimited power and knowledge. A good parent may be unable to prevent some suffering her child undergoes, or even prevent the child's death from some painful disease. Can we seriously think that an *infinitely* powerful, all-knowing deity was powerless to prevent the horror of Auschwitz? A good parent may see that she cannot realize some important future good for her child without permitting some present evil to befall the child. Can we seriously think that there is some far-off future good for the victims of Auschwitz, a good that a deity of *infinite* power and knowledge judged to be worth the horror of Auschwitz and

was powerless to achieve without permitting that horror? Perhaps we can if we turn from reason to faith. But the infinite distance between the God of traditional theism and the good mother with the sick child doesn't seem to provide human reason with solid grounds for thinking that such a being would be powerless to prevent many of the countless, seemingly pointless horrors in our world without losing some goods so distant from us that even the mere conception of these distant goods must elude our grasp.

Suppose we do reason from the good-parent analogy to the behavior of an all-powerful, all-knowing, infinitely good deity. We know that when a good, loving parent permits her child to suffer severely for some future outweighing good the child *cannot comprehend*, the loving parent then makes every effort to be consciously present to the child during his period of suffering, giving special assurances of her love, concern, and care. For the child may believe that the parent could prevent his present suffering. So, of course, the parent will be particularly careful to give her child special assurances of her love and concern during this period of permitted suffering for a distant good the child does not understand. And indeed, what we know about good, loving parents, especially when they permit their children to suffer intensely for goods the children cannot comprehend, is that the parents are almost always consciously present to their children during the period of their suffering, giving special assurances of their love and care. So, on the basis of the good-parent analogy, we should infer that it is likely that God, too, will almost always be consciously present to humans, if not other animals, when he permits them to suffer for goods they cannot comprehend, giving special assurances of his love for them. But since countless numbers of human beings undergo prolonged, horrendous suffering without being consciously aware of God's presence or any special assurances of his love and comfort, we can reasonably infer that the good-parent analogy is not helpful in enabling us to understand why God permits all the horrendous suffering that occurs daily in our world.

Of course, even here the theist may defend the good-parent analogy by suggesting that perhaps there is some further greater good that requires God not to be present to us with special assurances of his love and comfort, while he permits us to suffer severely for goods we cannot comprehend. The proponent of the evidential argument must admit that this suggestion cannot be ruled out. For since God's mind will most certainly comprehend goods we are incapable of understanding, then no matter how bad human life may become, no matter if we should suffer horrendously and continuously from earthly birth to earthly death, it would still be possible that there is some far-off good beyond our comprehension that justifies God in permitting us to suffer continuously from birth to death. But just as clearly, unless we have very convincing reasons to believe there is such a being as the God of traditional theism, in the event of our suffering continuously from birth to death it would be more rational to believe that the creator of our world, if there be such a being, is indifferent to us, not infinitely loving and leading us to the greatest good that he can as part of his divine plan.

Theodicies

The second sort of response consists in presenting a *theodicy*, an attempt to explain what God's purposes might be for permitting the profusion of evil in our world. Unlike the first response, a theodicy endeavors to provide some reasons for thinking that premise 1 may be false. Rather than providing very brief comments about various theodicies – evil is punishment for sin, evil is due to free will, evil is necessary for us to appreciate good, etc. – it will be more helpful for us to look in some depth at one of the more promising theodicies, one developed and defended by a prominent contemporary philosopher, John Hick, and referred to as a theodicy of "soul-making."[2]

Before giving a synopsis of the soul-making theodicy, it will be helpful to reflect on the general bearing of theodicies on the evidential problem of evil. Just what does a theodicy endeavor to do? Does it propose to tell us in some detail just what good it is that justifies God in permitting the fawn's suffering? No. Such an account would presume a knowledge of God's specific purposes, a knowledge that it would be unreasonable to expect we would have without some detailed revelation from God. What a theodicy does endeavor to do is to fasten on some good (real or imaginary) and argue that achieving it would justify an omnipotent being in permitting evils like the fawn's suffering. Whether obtaining the good in question is God's actual reason for permitting evils like the fawn's suffering is not really part of what a theodicy tries to establish. It only hopes to show that *if* obtaining the good in question were God's aim in permitting evils like the fawn's suffering, then (given what we know) it would be reasonable to believe that an omnipotent being would be justified in permitting such evils. In this way, then, a theodicy endeavors to cast doubt on premise 1 in our argument from evil.

The fawn's suffering is an instance of *natural* evil, evil that results from natural forces. When a person tortures and kills an innocent child, the suffering of the child is an instance of *moral* evil, evil that results from the conscious decision of some personal agent. What goods does Hick think are served by the profusion of natural and moral evil in our world? There are two goods that figure in Hick's theodicy. The first is the state in which all human beings develop themselves through their free choices into moral and spiritual beings. The second is the state in which such beings enter into an eternal life of bliss and joy in fellowship with God. Let's begin our synopsis by considering the first of these states, the state in which all human beings develop themselves through their free choices into moral and spiritual beings. How might the obtaining of such a good justify an omnipotent, omniscient being in permitting evils like the fawn's suffering and the suffering of the innocent child who is brutally tortured and killed?

Since the fawn's suffering and the child's suffering are instances of natural and moral evil, different answers may be required. Let's begin with horrendous moral evils like the child's suffering while being tortured. Hick's first step is to argue

2   See Hick's *Evil and the God of Love* (New York: Harper and Row, 1966), particularly chapter XVII of the revised edition, published in 1978, *God and the Universe of Faiths* (New York: St Martin's Press, 1973), and chapter 4 of *Philosophy of Religion*, 4th ed. (Englewood Cliffs, N.J.: Prentice-Hall, 1990).

that if moral and spiritual development through free choices is the good in question, then an environment in which there is no significant suffering, no occasion for significant moral choices, would not be one in which moral and spiritual growth would be possible. In particular, a world in which no one can harm another, in which no pain or suffering results from any action, would not be a world in which such moral and spiritual growth could occur.

I think we can concede to Hick that a pain-free paradise, a world in which no one could be injured and no one could do harm, would be a world devoid of significant moral and spiritual development. But what are we to make of the fact that the world we live in is so often inimical to such moral and spiritual development? For clearly, as Hick is careful to note, much of the pain and suffering in our world frustrates such development.

> The overall situation is thus that, so far as we can tell, suffering occurs haphazardly, uselessly, and therefore unjustly. It appears to be only randomly related either to past desert or to future soul-making. Instead of serving a constructive purpose, pain and misery seem to fall upon men patternlessly and meaninglessly, with the result that suffering is often underserved and often occurs in amounts exceeding anything that could have been morally planned.[3]

Hick's response to this point is to ask us what would happen were our world one in which suffering occurred "not haphazardly and therefore unjustly, but on the contrary justly and therefore non-haphazardly."[4] In such a world, Hick reasons that people would avoid wrongdoing out of fear rather than from a sense of duty. Moreover, once we saw that suffering was always for the good of the sufferer, human misery would no longer "evoke deep personal sympathy or call forth organized relief and sacrificial help and service. For it is presupposed in those compassionate reactions both that the suffering is not deserved and that it is *bad* for the sufferer."[5] Hick then concludes:

> It seems, then, that in a world that is to be the scene of compassionate love and self-giving for others, suffering must fall upon mankind with something of the haphazardness and inequity that we now experience. It must be apparently unmerited, pointless, and incapable of being morally rationalized. For it is precisely this feature of our common human lot that creates sympathy between man and man and evokes the unselfishness, kindness and goodwill which are among the highest values of personal life.[6]

Let's assume with Hick that an environment fit for human beings to develop the highest qualities of moral and spiritual life must be one that includes real suffering, hardships, disappointments, failure, and defeat. For moral and spiritual growth, presuppose these. Let's also assume that such an environment must operate, at least for the most part, according to general and dependable laws; for only on the basis of such general laws can a person engage in the purposeful decision-making essential to rational and moral life. And given these two assumptions it is, I think, understandable how an omniscient, omnipotent being may be morally justified in permitting the occurrence of evils, both moral and natural. Moreover, it is important, as Hick stresses, that it not be apparent to us that all the instances of suffering that occur are required for and result in the good of moral and spiritual growth. For then we would cease to strive to eliminate these evils and thereby diminish the very human struggles that so often bring about moral and spiritual development.

Our excursion into Hick's theodicy has shown us, perhaps, how a theodicy may succeed in justifying God's permission of both natural and moral evil. But so far we haven't been given any justification for the permission of the fawn's awful suffering, nor have we a justification for the intense suffering of the innocent child who is brutally tortured and killed by an adult human being. In the case of the fawn's suffering we can say that given the existence of the animals in our

3   Hick, *God and the Universe of Faiths*, p. 58.
4   Ibid.
5   Ibid., p. 60.
6   Ibid.

world and the operation of the world according to natural laws, it is unavoidable that instances of intense and prolonged animal suffering would occur. In the case of the suffering of that particular innocent child we can say that on their way toward moral and spiritual development, it is perhaps unavoidable that human beings will sometimes seriously harm others through a bad use of freedom. But neither of these points will morally justify an omnipotent, omniscient being in permitting the suffering of that particular fawn or the suffering of that particular innocent child. It is simply unreasonable to believe that if the adult acted freely in brutally beating and killing that innocent child, his moral and spiritual development would have been permanently frustrated had he been prevented from doing what he did. And it is also unreasonable to believe that permitting such an act is morally justified even if preventing it would somehow diminish the perpetrator's moral and spiritual odyssey. And in the case of the fawn, it is simply unreasonable to believe that preventing its being severely burned, or mercifully ending its life so that it does not suffer intensely for several days, would so shake our confidence in the orderliness of nature that we would forsake our moral and spiritual development. Hick seems not unaware of this limitation to his theodicy, at least with respect to natural evils. With respect to human pain due to sources independent of the human will, he remarks:

> In response to it, theodicy, if it is wisely conducted, follows a negative path. It is not possible to show positively that each item of human pain serves God's purpose of good; on the other hand, it does seem possible to show that the divine purpose, [. . .] could not be forwarded in a world that was designed as a permanent hedonistic paradise.[7]

What we've seen is that Hick's theodicy fails if it is intended to provide a good that would justify an omnipotent, omniscient being in permitting the fawn's intense suffering or the innocent child's intense suffering. The best that Hick can do is to argue that a world *utterly devoid* of natural and moral evil would preclude the realization of the goods he postulates as justifying an omnipotent, omniscient being in permitting evil. However, since the prevention of the fawn's suffering or the innocent child's suffering would not leave our world utterly devoid of natural or moral evil, his all-or-nothing argument provides no answer to our question. Nor will it do to say that if an omnipotent, omniscient being were to prevent the suffering of the fawn or the innocent child it would thereby be obligated to prevent all such evils. For were it to do so it may well be, as Hick has argued, that we would cease to engage in very significant soul-making. The problem Hick's theodicy leaves us is that it is altogether reasonable to believe that some of the evils that occur could have been prevented without either diminishing our moral and spiritual development or undermining our confidence that the world operates according to natural laws. Hick's theodicy, therefore, does not succeed in providing a reason to reject premise 1, that there exist instances of suffering that an omnipotent, omniscient being could have prevented without thereby preventing the occurrence of any greater good.

The "G. E. Moore Shift"

The best procedure for the theist to follow in rejecting premise 1 is an *indirect* procedure. This procedure I shall call the "G. E. Moore shift," so called in honor of the twentieth-century philosopher, G. E. Moore, who used it to great effect in dealing with the arguments of the skeptics. Skeptical philosophers such as David Hume have advanced ingenious arguments to prove that no one can know of the existence of any material object. The premises of their arguments employ plausible principles, principles which many philosophers have tried to reject directly, but only with questionable success. Moore's procedure was altogether different. Instead of arguing directly against the premises of the skeptic's arguments, he simply noted that the premises implied, for example, that he (Moore) did not know of the existence of a pencil. Moore then proceeded indirectly against the skeptic's premises by arguing:

---

[7]   Hick, *Philosophy of Religion*, p. 46.

I do know that this pencil exists.

If the skeptic's principles are correct I cannot know of the existence of this pencil.

Therefore,

The skeptic's principles (at least one) must be incorrect.

Moore then noted that his argument is just as valid as the skeptic's, that both of their arguments contain the premise "If the skeptic's principles are correct Moore cannot know of the existence of this pencil," and concluded that the only way to choose between the two arguments (Moore's and the skeptic's) is by deciding which of the first premises it is more rational to believe – Moore's premise "I do know that this pencil exists" or the skeptic's premise asserting that certain skeptical principles are correct. Moore concluded that his own first premise was the more rational of the two.[8]

Before we see how the theist may apply the G. E. Moore shift to the basic argument for atheism, we should note the general strategy of the shift. We're given an argument: p, q, therefore, r. Instead of arguing *directly* against p, another argument is constructed – not-r, q, therefore, not-p – which begins with the denial of the conclusion of the first argument, keeps its second premise, and ends with the denial of the first premise as its conclusion. Let's compare these two:

I. p II.   not-r
     q q
     r not-p

Now it is a truth of logic that if I is valid II must be valid as well. Since the arguments are the same so far as the second premise is concerned, any choice between them must concern their respective first premises. To argue against the first premise p by constructing the counterargument II is to employ the G. E. Moore shift.

Applying the G. E. Moore shift against the first premise of the basic argument for atheism, the theist can argue as follows:

not-3. There exists an omnipotent, omniscient, wholly good being.

2   An omniscient, wholly good being would prevent the occurrence of any intense suffering it could, unless it could not do so without thereby preventing the occurrence of some greater good.

Therefore,

not-1. It is not the case that there exist instances of intense suffering which an omnipotent, omniscient being could have prevented without thereby preventing the occurrence of any greater good.

We have now two arguments: the basic argument for atheism from 1 and 2 to 3, and the theist's best response, the argument from not-3 and 2 to not-1. What the theist then says about 1 is that she has rational grounds for believing in the existence of the theistic God, not-3, accepts 2 as true, and sees that not-1 follows from not-3 and 2. The theist concludes, therefore, that she has rational grounds for rejecting 1. Having rational grounds for rejecting 1, the theist concludes that the basic argument for atheism is mistaken.

Argument and Response: An Assessment

It is now time to assess the relative merits of the basic argument for atheism as well as the theist's best response to it. Suppose that someone is in the position of having no rational grounds for thinking that the theistic God exists. Either this person has not heard of the arguments for the existence of God or has considered them but finds them altogether unconvincing. Perhaps, too, he has not had any visions of God and is rationally convinced that the religious experiences of others fail to provide any good grounds for theistic belief. Contemplating the variety and scale of human and animal suffering in our world, however, this individual concludes that it is altogether reasonable to accept premise 1 as true. It must be admitted, I think, that such a

8   See, for example, the two chapters on Hume in G. E. Moore, *Some Main Problems of Philosophy* (London: George Allen & Unwin Ltd., 1953).

person is rationally justified in accepting atheism. Suppose, however, that another person has had religious experiences which justify him in believing that the theistic God exists. Perhaps, too, this person has carefully examined the Ontological Argument and found it rationally coercive. It must be admitted, I think, that such a person has some rational grounds for accepting theism. But what if this individual is aware of the basic argument for atheism and the considerations advanced in support of its first premise? In that case he will have some rational grounds for believing that theism is true and some rational grounds for believing that 1 is true, and, therefore, that theism is false. This person must then weigh the relative strength of his grounds for theism against his grounds for 1 and atheism. If the grounds for theism seem rationally stronger than the grounds for 1, this individual may reasonably reject 1, since its denial is implied by theism and 2. Of course, assessing the relative merit of competing rational grounds is no easy matter, but it seems clear that someone may be rationally justified in accepting theism and concluding that 1 and the basic argument for atheism are mistaken.

In terms of our own response to the basic argument for atheism and the theist's counterargument against 1, each of us must judge in the light of personal experience and knowledge whether our grounds for believing 1 are stronger or weaker than our grounds for believing that the theistic God exists. What we have seen is that since our experience and knowledge may differ it is possible, indeed likely, that some of us may be justified in accepting 1 and atheism, while others of us may be rationally justified in accepting theism and rejecting 1.

The conclusion to which we have come is that the evidential form of the problem of evil is a serious but not insurmountable problem for theism. To the extent that she has stronger grounds for believing that the theistic God exists than for accepting 1, the theist, on balance, may have more reason to reject 1 than she has for accepting it. However, in the absence of good reasons for believing that the theistic God exists, our study of the evidential form of the problem of evil has led us to the view that we rationally justified in accepting atheism.

We must not confuse the view that someone may be rationally justified in accepting theism, while someone else is rationally justified in accepting atheism, with the *incoherent* view that both theism and atheism may be true. Since theism (in the narrow sense) and atheism (in the narrow sense) express contradictory claims, one must be true and the other false. But since the evidence one possesses may justify one in believing a statement which, in the light of the total evidence, is a false statement, it is possible for different people to be rationally justified in believing statements which cannot both be true. Suppose, for example, a friend of yours takes a flight to Hawaii. Hours after takeoff you learn that the plane has gone down at sea. After a twenty-four-hour search, no survivors have been found. Under these circumstances it is rational for you to believe that your friend has perished. But it is hardly rational for your friend to believe that while she is bobbing up and down in a life vest and wondering why the search planes have failed to spot her. Theism and atheism cannot both be true. But because of differing experience and knowledge, someone may be rationally justified in accepting theism while someone else is rationally justified in believing atheism.

Earlier we characterized a theist as someone who believes that the theistic God exists, and an atheist as someone who believes that the theistic God does not exist. In the light of our study of the problem of evil, perhaps we should introduce further distinctions. A *friendly atheist* is an atheist who believes that someone may well be rationally justified in believing that the theistic God exists. An unfriendly atheist is an atheist who believes that no one is rationally justified in believing that the theistic God exists. Similar distinctions are to be made with respect to theism and agnosticism. An *unfriendly agnostic*, for example, is an agnostic who thinks that no one is rationally justified in believing that the theistic God exists and no one is rationally justified in believing that the theistic God does not exist. Again, we must note that the friendly atheist (theist) does not believe that the theist (atheist) has a *true* belief, only that he may well be rationally justified in holding that belief. Perhaps the final lesson to be drawn from our study of the problem of evil is that the *friendly* versions of theism, agnosticism, and atheism are each preferable to their respective unfriendly versions.

The Concept of God after Auschwitz
A Jewish Voice

Hans Jonas

What I have to offer is a piece of frankly speculative theology. Whether this behooves a philosopher is a question I leave open. Immanuel Kant has banished everything of the kind from the territory of theoretical reason and hence from the business of philosophy; and the logical positivism of our century, the entire dominant analytical creed, even denies to the linguistic expressions such reasonings employ for their purported subject matters this very object-significance itself, that is, any conceptual meaning at all, declaring already – prior to questions of truth and verification – the mere speech about them to be nonsensical. At this, to be sure, old Kant himself would have been utterly astounded. For he, to the contrary, held these alleged nonobjects to be the highest objects of all, about which reason can never cease to be concerned, although it cannot hope ever to obtain a knowledge of them and in their pursuit is necessarily doomed to failure by the impassable limits of human cognition. But this cognitive veto, given the yet justified concern, leaves another way open besides that of complete abstention: bowing to the decree that "knowledge" eludes us here, nay, even waiving this very goal from the outset, one may yet meditate on things of this nature in terms of sense and meaning. For the

contention – this fashionable contention – that not even sense and meaning pertain to them is easily disposed of as a circular, tautological inference from first having defined "sense" as that which in the end is verifiable by sense data or from generally equating "meaningful" with "knowable." To this axiomatic fiat by definition only he is bound who has first consented to it. He who has not is free, therefore, to work at the *concept* of God, even knowing that there is no *proof* of God, as a task of understanding, not of knowledge; and such working is philosophical when it keeps to the rigor of concept and its connection with the universe of concepts.

But of course, this epistemological laissez-passer is much too general and impersonal for the matter at hand. As Kant granted to the practical reason what he denied to the theoretical, so may *we* allow the force of a unique and shattering experience a voice in the question of what "is the matter" with God. And there, right away, arises the question, What did Auschwitz add to that which one could always have known about the extent of the terrible and horrendous things that humans can do to humans and from times immemorial have done? And what has it added in particular to what is familiar to us Jews from a millennial history of suffering and forms

"The Concept of God after Auschwitz: A Jewish Voice" by Hans Jonas, *The Journal of Religion* 67:1 (January 1987): 1–13. Reprinted by permission of the publisher, The University of Chicago Press.

so essential a part of our collective memory? The *question of Job* has always been the main question of theodicy – of general theodicy because of the existence of evil as such in the world, and of particular theodicy in its sharpening by the riddle of election, of the purported covenant between Israel and its God. As to this sharpening, under which our present question also falls, one could at first invoke – as the prophets did – the covenant itself for an explanation of what befell the human party to it: the "people of the covenant" had been unfaithful to it. In the long ages of faithfulness thereafter, guilt and retribution no longer furnished the explanation but the idea of "witness" did instead – this creation of the Maccabean age, which bequeathed to posterity the concept of the martyr. It is of its very meaning that precisely the innocent and the just suffer the worst. In deference to the idea of witness, whole communities in the Middle Ages met their death by sword and fire with the *Sh'ma Jisrael*, the avowal of God's Oneness, on their lips. The Hebrew name for this is *Kiddush hashem*, "sanctification of the Name," and the slaughtered were called "saints." Through their sacrifice shone the light of promise, of the final redemption by the Messiah to come.

Nothing of this is still of use in dealing with the event for which "Auschwitz" has become the symbol. Not fidelity or infidelity, belief or unbelief, not guilt and punishment, not trial, witness and messianic hope, nay, not even strength or weakness, heroism or cowardice, defiance or submission had a place there. Of all this, Auschwitz, which also devoured the infants and babes, knew nothing; to none of it (with rarest exceptions) did the factory-like working of its machine give room. Not for the *sake* of faith did the victims die (as did, after all, "Jehovah's Witnesses"), nor *because* of their faith or any self-affirmed bend of their being as persons were they murdered. Dehumanization by utter degradation and deprivation preceded their dying, no glimmer of dignity was left to the freights bound for the final solution, hardly a trace of it was found in the surviving skeleton specters of the liberated camps. And yet, paradox of paradoxes: it *was* the ancient people of the "covenant," no longer believed in by those involved, killers and victims alike, but nevertheless just this and no other people, which under

the fiction of race had been chosen for this wholesale annihilation – the most monstrous inversion of election into curse, which defied all possible endowment with meaning. There does, then, in spite of all, exist a connection – of a wholly perverse kind – with the god seekers and prophets of yore, whose descendants were thus collected out of the dispersion and gathered into the unity of joint death. And God let it happen. What God could let it happen?

Here we must note that on this question the Jew is in greater theoretical difficulty than the Christian. To the Christian (of the stern variety) the world is anyway largely of the devil and always an object of suspicion – the human world in particular because of original sin. But to the Jew, who sees in "this" world the locus of divine creation, justice, and redemption, God is eminently the Lord of *History*, and in this respect "Auschwitz" calls, even for the believer, the whole traditional concept of God into question. It has, indeed, as I have just tried to show, added to the Jewish historical experience something unprecedented and of a nature no longer assimilable by the old theological categories. Accordingly, one who will not thereupon just give up the concept of God altogether – and even the philosopher has a right to such an unwillingness – must rethink it so that it still remains thinkable; and that means seeking a new answer to the old question of (and about) Job. The Lord of History, we suspect, will have to go by the board in this quest. To repeat then, What God could let it happen?

For a possible, if groping, answer, I fall back on a speculative attempt with which I once ventured to meet the different question of immortality but in which also the specter of Auschwitz already played its part. On that occasion, I resorted to a *myth* of my own invention – that vehicle of imaginative but credible conjecture that Plato allowed for the sphere beyond the knowable. Allow me to repeat it here:

> In the beginning, for unknowable reasons, the ground of being, or the Divine, chose to give itself over to the chance and risk and endless variety of becoming. And wholly so: entering into the adventure of space and time, the deity held back nothing of itself: no uncommitted or unimpaired part remained to direct, correct, and

ultimately guarantee the devious working-out of its destiny in creation. On this unconditional immanence the modern temper insists. It is its courage or despair, in any case its bitter honesty, to take our being-in-the-world seriously: to view the world as left to itself, its laws as brooking no interference, and the rigor of our belonging to it as not softened by extramundane providence. The same our myth postulates for God's being in the world. Not, however, in the sense of pantheistic immanence: if world and God are simply the same, the world at each moment and in each state represents his fullness, and God can neither lose nor gain. Rather, in order that the world might be, and be for itself, God renounced his being, divesting himself of his deity – to receive it back from the Odyssey of time weighted with the chance harvest of unforeseeable temporal experience: transfigured or possibly even disfigured by it. In such self-forfeiture of divine integrity for the sake of unprejudiced becoming, no other foreknowledge can be admitted than that of *possibilities* which cosmic being offers in its own terms: to these, God committed his cause in effacing himself for the world.

And for aeons his cause is safe in the slow hands of cosmic chance and probability – while all the time we may surmise a patient memory of the gyrations of matter to accumulate into an ever more expectant accompaniment of eternity to the labors of time – a hesitant emergence of transcendence from the opaqueness of immanence.

And then the first stirring of life – a new language of the world: and with it a tremendous quickening of concern in the eternal realm and a sudden leap in its growth toward recovery of its plenitude. It is the world-accident for which becoming deity had waited and with which its prodigal stake begins to show signs of being redeemed. From the infinite swell of feeling, sensing, striving, and acting, which ever more varied and intense rises above the mute eddyings of matter, eternity gains strength, filling with content after content of self-affirmation, and the awakening God can first pronounce creation to be good.

But note that with life together came death, and that mortality is the price which the new possibility of being called "life" had to pay for itself. If permanence were the point, life should not have started out in the first place, for in no possible form can it match the durability of inorganic

bodies. It is essentially precarious and corruptible being, an adventure in mortality, obtaining from long-lasting matter on its terms – the short terms of metabolizing organism – the borrowed, finite careers of individual selves. Yet it is precisely through the briefly snatched self-feeling, doing, and suffering of *finite* individuals, with the pitch of awareness heightened by the very press of finitiude, that the divine landscape bursts into color and the deity comes to experience itself . . .

Note also this that with life's innocence before the advent of knowledge God's cause cannot go wrong. Whatever variety evolution brings forth adds to the possibilities of feeling and acting, and thus enriches the self-experiencing of the ground of being. Every new dimension of world-response opened up in its course means another modality for God's trying out his hidden essence and discovering himself through the surprises of the world-adventure. And all its harvest of anxious toil, whether bright or dark, swells the transcendent treasure of temporally lived eternity. If this is true for the broadening spectrum of diversity as such, it is even truer for the heightening pitch and passion of life that go with the twin rise of perception and motility in animals. The ever more sharpened keenness of appetite and fear, pleasure and pain, triumph and anguish, love and even cruelty – their very edge is the deity's gain. Their countless, yet never blunted incidence – hence the necessity of death and new birth – supplies the tempered essence from which the Godhead reconstitutes itself. All this, evolution provides in the mere lavishness of its play and the sternness of its spur. Its creatures, by merely fulfilling themselves in pursuit of their lives, vindicate the divine venture. Even their suffering deepens the fullness of the symphony. Thus, this side of good and evil, God cannot lose in the great evolutionary game.

Nor yet can he fully win in the shelter of its innocence, and a new expectancy grows in him in answer to the direction which the unconscious drift of immanence gradually takes.

And then he trembles as the thrust of evolution, carried by its own momentum, passes the threshold where innocence ceases and an entirely new criterion of success and failure takes hold of the divine stake. The advent of man means the advent of knowledge and freedom, and with this supremely double-edged gift the innocence of the mere subject of self-fulfilling life has given way to the charge of responsibility under the disjunction of good and evil. To the promise and risk of this agency the divine cause, revealed at last, henceforth finds itself committed; and its issue trembles in the balance. The image of God, haltingly begun by the universe, for so long worked upon – and left undecided – in the wide and then narrowing spirals of prehuman life, passes with this last twist, and with a dramatic quickening of the movement, into man's precarious trust, to be completed, saved, or spoiled by what he will do to himself and the world. And in this awesome impact of his deeds on God's destiny, on the very complexion of eternal being, lies the immortality of man.

With the appearance of man, transcendence awakened to itself and henceforth accompanies his doings with the bated breath of suspense, hoping and beckoning, rejoicing and grieving, approving and frowning – and, I daresay, making itself felt to him even while not intervening in the dynamics of his worldly scene: for can it not be that by the reflection of its own state as it wavers with the record of man, the transcendent casts light and shadow over the human landscape?[1]

Such is the tentative myth I once proposed for consideration in a different context. It has theological implications that only later unfolded to me. Of these I shall develop here some of the more obvious ones – hoping that this translation from image into concept will somehow connect what so far must seem a strange and rather willful private fantasy with the more responsible tradition of Jewish religious thought. In this manner I try to redeem the poetic liberties of my earlier, roving attempt.

First, and most obviously, I have been speaking of a *suffering God* – which immediately seems to clash with the biblical conception of divine majesty. There is, of course, a Christian connotation of the term "suffering God" with which my myth must not be confounded; it does not speak, as does the former, of a special act by which the deity at one time, and for the special purpose of saving man, sends part of itself into

a particular situation of suffering (the incarnation and crucifixion). If anything in what I said makes sense, then the sense is that the relation of God to the world *from the moment of creation*, and certainly from the creation of man on, involves suffering on the part of God. It involves, to be sure, suffering on the part of the creature too, but this truism has always been recognized in every theology. Not so the idea of God's suffering with creation, and of this I said that, prima facie, it clashes with the biblical conception of divine majesty. But does it really clash as extremely as it seems at first glance? Do not we also in the Bible encounter God as slighted and rejected by man and grieving over him? Do not we encounter him as ruing that he created man, and suffering from the disappointment he experiences with him – and with his chosen people in particular? We remember the prophet Hosea, and God's love lamenting over Israel, his unfaithful wife.

Then, second, the myth suggests the picture of a *becoming God*. It is a God emerging in time instead of possessing a completed being that remains identical with itself throughout eternity. Such an idea of divine becoming is surely at variance with the Greek, Platonic-Aristotelian tradition of philosophical theology that, since its incorporation into the Jewish and Christian theological tradition, has somehow usurped for itself an authority to which it is not at all entitled by authentic Jewish (and also Christian) standards. Transtemporality, impassibility, and immutability have been taken to be necessary attributes of God. And the ontological distinction that classical thought made between "being" and "becoming," with the latter characteristic of the lower, sensible world, excluded every shadow of becoming from the pure, absolute being of the Godhead. But this Hellenic concept has never accorded well with the spirit and language of the Bible, and the concept of divine becoming can actually be better reconciled with it.

For what does the becoming God mean? Even if we do not go so far as our myth suggests, that much at least we must concede of "becoming" in God as lies in the mere fact that he is affected

[1]   Hans Jonas, "Immortality and the Modern Temper," the 1961 Ingersoll Lecture at Harvard University, first printed in *Harvard Theological Review* 55 (1962): 1–20; now in H. Jonas, *The Phenomenon of Life* (Chicago and London: University of Chicago Press, 1982), pp. 262–81.

by what happens in the world, and "affected" means altered, made different. Even apart from the fact that creation as such – the act itself and the lasting result thereof – was after all a decisive change in God's own state, insofar as he is now no longer alone, his continual *relation* to the creation, once this exists and moves in the flux of becoming, means that he experiences something with the world, that his own being is affected by what goes on in it. This holds already for the mere relation of accompanying knowledge, let alone that of caring interest. Thus if God is in any relation to the world – which is the cardinal assumption of religion – then by that token alone the Eternal has "temporalized" himself and progressively becomes different through the actualizations of the world process.

One incidental consequence of the idea of the becoming God is that it destroys the idea of an eternal recurrence of the same. This was Nietzsche's alternative to Christian metaphysics, which in this case is the same as Jewish metaphysics. It is indeed the extreme symbol of the turn to unconditional temporality and of the complete negation of any transcendence that could keep a memory of what happens in time, to assume that, by the mere exhaustion of the possible combinations and recombinations of material elements, it must come to pass that an "initial" configuration recurs and the whole cycle starts over again, and if once, then innumerable times – Nietzsche's "ring of rings, the ring of eternal recurrence." However, if we assume that eternity is not unaffected by what happens in time, there can never be a recurrence of the same because God will not be the same after he has gone through the experience of a world process. Any new world coming after the end of one will carry, as it were, in its own heritage the memory of what has gone before; or, in other words, there will not be an indifferent and dead eternity but an eternity that grows with the accumulating harvest of time.

Bound up with the concepts of a suffering and a becoming God is that of a *caring God* – a God not remote and detached and self-contained but involved with what he cares for. Whatever the "primordial" condition of the Godhead, he ceased to be self-contained once he let himself in for the existence of a world by creating such a world or letting it come to be. God's caring

about his creatures is, of course, among the most familiar tenets of Jewish faith. But my myth stresses the less familiar aspect that this caring God is not a sorcerer who in the act of caring also provides the fulfillment of his concern: he has left something for other agents to do and thereby has made his care dependent on them. He is therefore also an endangered God, a God who runs a risk. Clearly that must be so, or else the world would be in a condition of permanent perfection. The fact that it is not bespeaks one of two things: that either the One God does not exist (though more than one may), or that the One has given to an agency other than himself, though created by him, a power and a right to act on its own and therewith a scope for at least codetermining that which is a concern of his. This is why I said that the caring God is not a sorcerer. Somehow he has, by an act of either inscrutable wisdom or love or whatever else the divine motive may have been, forgone the guaranteeing of his self-satisfaction by his own power, after he has first, by the act of creation itself, forgone being "all in all."

And therewith we come to what is perhaps the most critical point in our speculative, theological venture: this is not an omnipotent God. We argue indeed that, for the sake of our image of God and our whole relation to the divine, for the sake of any viable theology, we cannot uphold the time-honored (medieval) doctrine of absolute, unlimited divine power. Let me argue this first, on a purely logical plane, by pointing out the paradox in the idea of absolute power. The logical situation indeed is by no means that divine omnipotence is the rationally plausible and somehow self-recommending doctrine, while that of its limitation is wayward and in need of defense. Quite the opposite. From the very concept of power, it follows that omnipotence is a self-contradictory, self-destructive, indeed, senseless concept. The situation is similar to that of freedom in the human realm: far from beginning where necessity ends, freedom consists of and lives in pitting itself against necessity. Separated from it, freedom loses its object and becomes as void as force without resistance. Absolute freedom would be empty freedom that cancels itself out. So, too, does empty power, and absolute, exclusive power would be just that. Absolute, total power means power not limited by anything, not even by the mere existence of something other than the possessor of that power; for the very existence of such another would already constitute a limitation, and the one would have to annihilate it so as to save its absoluteness. Absolute power then, in its solitude, has no object on which to act. But as objectless power it is a powerless power, canceling itself out: "all" equals "zero" here. In order for it to act, there must be something else, and as soon as there is, the one is not all powerful anymore, even though in any comparison its power may be superior by any degree you please to imagine. The existence of another object limits the power of the most powerful agent at the same time that it allows it to be an agent. In brief, power as such is a *relational* concept and requires relation.

Again, power meeting no *resistance* in its relatum is equal to no power at all: power is exercised only in relation to something that itself has power. Power, unless otiose, consists in the capacity to overcome something; and something's existence as such is enough to provide this condition. For existence means resistance and thus opposing force. Just as, in physics, force without resistance – that is, counterforce – remains empty, so in metaphysics does power without counterpower, unequal as the latter may be. That, therefore, on which power acts must have a power of its own, even if that power derives from the first and was initially granted to it, as one with its existence, by a self-renunciation of limitless power – that is, in the act of creation.

In short, it cannot be that all power is on the side of one agent only. Power must be divided so that there be any power at all.

But besides this logical and ontological objection, there is a more theological, genuinely religious objection to the idea of absolute and unlimited divine omnipotence. We can have divine omnipotence together with divine goodness only at the price of complete divine inscrutability. Seeing the existence of evil in the world, we must sacrifice intelligibility in God to the combination of the other two attributes. Only a completely unintelligible God can be said to be absolutely good and absolutely powerful, yet tolerate the world as it is. Put more generally, the three attributes at stake – absolute goodness, absolute power, and intelligibility – stand in such a logical relation to one another that the

conjunction of any two of them excludes the third. The question then is, Which are truly integral to our concept of God, and which, being of lesser force, must give way to their superior claim? Now, surely, goodness is inalienable from the concept of God and not open to qualification. Intelligibility, conditional on both God's nature and man's capacity, is on the latter count indeed subject to qualification but on no account to complete elimination. The *Deus absconditus*, the hidden God (not to speak of an absurd God) is a profoundly un-Jewish conception. Our teaching, the Torah, rests on the premise and insists that we can understand God, not completely, to be sure, but something of him – of his will, intentions, and even nature – because he has told us. There has been revelation, we have his commandments and his law, and he has directly communicated with some – his prophets – as his mouth for all men in the language of men and their times: refracted thus in this limiting medium but not veiled in dark mystery. A completely hidden God is not an acceptable concept by Jewish norms.

But he would have to be precisely that if together with being good he were conceived as all powerful. After Auschwitz, we can assert with greater force than ever before that an omnipotent deity would have to be either not good or (in his world rule, in which alone we can "observe" him) totally unintelligible. But if God is to be intelligible in some manner and to some extent (and to this we must hold), then his goodness must be compatible with the existence of evil, and this it is only if he is not *all* powerful. Only then can we uphold that he is intelligible and good, and there is yet evil in the world. And since we have found the concept of omnipotence to be dubious anyway, it is this that has to give way.

So far, our argument about omnipotence has done no more than lay it down as a principle for any acceptable theology continuous with the Jewish heritage that God's power be seen as limited by something whose being in its own right and whose power to act on its own authority he himself acknowledges. Admittedly, we have the choice to interpret this as a voluntary concession on God's part, which he is free to revoke at will – that is, as the restraint of a power that he still and always possesses in full but, for the sake of creation's own autonomous right, chooses not fully to employ. To devout believers, this is probably the most palatable choice. But it will not suffice. For in view of the enormity of what, among the bearers of his image in creation, some of them time and again, and wholly unilaterally, inflict on innocent others, one would expect the good God at times to break his own, however stringent, rule of restraint and intervene with a saving miracle. But no saving miracle occurred. Through the years that "Auschwitz" raged God remained silent. The miracles that did occur came forth from man alone: the deeds of those solitary, mostly unknown "just of the nations" who did not shrink from utter sacrifice in order to help, to save, to mitigate – even, when nothing else was left, unto sharing Israel's lot. Of them I shall speak again. But God was silent. And there I say, or my myth says, Not because he chose not to, but because he *could* not intervene did he fail to intervene. For reasons decisively prompted by contemporary experience, I entertain the idea of a God who for a time – the time of the ongoing world process – has divested himself of any power to interfere with the physical course of things; and who responds to the impact on his being by worldly events, not "with a mighty hand and outstretched arm," as we Jews on every Passover recite in remembering the exodus from Egypt, but with the mutely insistent appeal of his unfulfilled goal.

In this, assuredly, my speculation strays far from oldest Judaic teaching. Several of Maimonides' Thirteen Articles of Faith, which we solemnly chant in our services, fall away with the "mighty hand": the assertions about God ruling the universe, his rewarding the good and punishing the wicked, even about the coming of the promised Messiah. Not, however, those about his call to the souls, his inspiration of the prophets and the Torah, thus also not the idea of election: for only to the physical realm does the impotence of God refer. Most of all, the *Oneness* of God stands unabated and with it the "Hear, O Israel!" No Manichaean dualism is enlisted to explain evil; from the hearts of men alone does it arise and gain power in the world. The mere permitting, indeed, of human freedom involved a renouncing of sole divine power henceforth. And our discussion of power as such has already led us to deny divine omnipotence, anyway.

The elimination of divine omnipotence leaves the theoretical choice between the alternatives of either some preexistent – theological or ontological – *dualism*, or of God's *self*-limitation through the creation from nothing. The dualistic alternative in turn might take the Manichaean form of an active force of evil forever opposing the divine purpose in the universal scheme of things: a two-god theology; or the Platonic form of a passive medium imposing, no less universally, imperfection on the embodiment of the ideal in the world: a form–matter dualism. The first is plainly unacceptable to Judaism. The second answers at best the problem of imperfection and natural necessity but not that of positive evil, which implies a freedom empowered by its own authority independent of that of God; and it is the fact and success of deliberate evil rather than the inflictions of blind, natural causality – the use of the latter in the hands of responsible agents (Auschwitz rather than the earthquake of Lisbon) – with which Jewish theology has to contend at this hour. Only with creation from nothing do we have the oneness of the divine principle combined with that self-limitation that then permits (gives "room" to) the existence and autonomy of a world. Creation was that act of absolute sovereignty with which it consented, for the sake of self-determined finitude, to be absolute no more – an act, therefore, of divine self-restriction.

[...]

My myth goes farther still. The contraction is total as far as power is concerned; as a whole has the Infinite ceded his power to the finite and thereby wholly delivered his cause into its hands. Does that still leave anything for a relation to God?

Let me answer this question with a last quotation from the earlier writing. By forgoing its own inviolateness, the eternal ground allowed the world to be. To this self-denial all creation owes its existence and with it has received all there is to receive from beyond. Having given himself whole to the becoming world, God has no more to give: it is man's now to give to him. And he may give by seeing to it in the ways of his life that it does not happen or happen too often, and not on his account, that it "repented the Lord" to have made the world.[2]

All this, let it be said at the end, is but stammering. Even the words of the great seers and adorers – the prophets and the psalmists – which stand beyond comparison, were stammers before the eternal mystery. Every mortal answer to Job's question, too, cannot be more than that. Mine is the opposite to the one given by the Book of Job: this, for an answer, invoked the plenitude of God's power; mine, his chosen voidance of it. And yet, strange to say, both are in praise.

For the divine renunciation was made so that we, the mortals, could be. This, too, so it seems to me, is an answer to Job: that in him God himself suffers. Which is true, if any, we can know of none of the answers ever tried. Of my poor word thereto I can only hope that it be not wholly excluded from what Goethe, in "Testament of Old-Persian Faith," thus put into Zarathustra's mouth:

All that ever stammers praising the Most High
Is in circles there assembled far and nigh.

---

[2]   The idea that it is we who can help God rather than God helping us I have since found movingly expressed by one of the Auschwitz victims themselves, a young Dutch Jewess, who validated it by acting on it unto death. It is found in *An Interrupted Life: The Diaries of Etty Hillesum, 1941–43* (New York: Pantheon Books, 1984). When the deportations in Holland began, in 1942, she came forward and volunteered for the Westerbork concentration camp, there to help in the hospital and to share in the fate of her people. In September 1943 she was shipped, in one of the usual mass transports, to Auschwitz and "died" there on November 30, 1943. Her diaries have survived but were only recently published. I quote from Neal Ascherson ("In Hell," *New York Review of Books* 31, no. 13 [July 19, 1984]: 8–12, esp. 9): "She does not exactly 'find God,' but rather constructs one for herself. The theme of the diaries becomes increasingly religious, and many of the entries are prayers. Her God is someone to whom she makes promises, but of whom she expects and asks nothing. 'I shall try to help you, God, to stop my strength ebbing away, though I cannot vouch for it in advance. But one thing is becoming increasingly clear to me: that You cannot help us, that we must help You to help ourselves. . . . Alas, there does not seem to be much You Yourself can do about our circumstances, about our lives. Neither do I hold You responsible. You cannot help us, but we must help You and defend Your dwelling place in us to the last.' " Reading this was to me a shattering confirmation, by a true witness, of my so much later and sheltered musings – and a consoling correction of my sweeping statement that we had no martyrs there.

40

Śaṃkara's Theodicy

Bimal K. Matilal

[...] It is believed that theodicy was not a problem for the Indians, specially for the Hindus, because evil was, according to them, an illusion. Particularly, it is urged, in Śaṃkara's Advaita Vedānta, the whole world is an illusion along with its evils, and hence the problem of evil is resolved. This belief is partly based upon a misconception. It is true, however, that the problem of evil did not dominate the field of Indian philosophy of religion, although the problem existed, that is, it was formulated and discussed. A resolution was suggested along a different line. Besides, the rather pervasive, but uncritical and unexamined assumption that in Śaṃkara's philosophy the world along with its evils is simply an illusion, leads to the misconception and false ideas about Indian philosophy in general and Śaṃkara's philosophy in particular.

Śaṃkara propounded a new cosmology by reconstructing or, to use a modern jargon, by "deconstructing" the old Scriptural texts on creation (sṛṣṭi-śruti). The world is identical with the Brahman, the so-called creation is identical with its creator, for the "creation" is, in a nut-shell, the imposition or superimposition of diverse names and forms on that one reality on account of what is called avidyā, the cosmic miscon-

ception, the congenital false belief of the creatures.[1] [...]

The author of the Brahmasūtra, however, has raised the problem of theodicy in unmistakable terms, and Śaṃkara explains the problem at that level too, without bringing in notions from his new cosmology. He does not say, for example, that since creation is nothing but superimposition of diversity through false belief, the question of the creators being unjust and cruel ([...] BS. 2.1.34) does not arise. On the other hand he finds it important and necessary to justify the realist's (or the popular) notion of creation and the Creator God. One may wonder why. I believe that he did not reject realism outright, but having a firm footing in the realist's world he argued that the ultimate truth transcends the realist's view of diversity and shows its ultimate unity with Brahman. Hence the defence of the ordinary notion of creation is also necessary. It is, perhaps, what he called sthūṇa-nikhanana-nyāya (BS 2.1.34 [p. 296 below]). When we dig a hole to plant or fix a flag-pole (sthūṇa = sacrificial post), we try the base of the hole at various points so that the pole may firmly be planted on the ground. The ordinary notion of creation is the base or the infra-structure

"Śaṃkara's Theodicy" by Bimal K. Matilal, *Journal of Indian Philosophy* 20 (1992): 363–76. With kind permission from Springer Science and Business Media.

[1] Śaṃkara, *Brahmasūtrabhāṣsya*, ed. J. Shastri, Delhi, Motilal Banarsidass, 1980, under 2.1.33.

upon which the edifice of Śaṃkara's new cosmology is built. So the digging of the base must be supervised as well.

I shall be concerned here with only the three sūtras, BS 2.1.34–6, and Śaṃkara's commentary upon them. 2.1.33 says that God, the creator, cannot be unjust or cruel, for He is *not* independent in his act of creation, and the Scriptures show His dependence upon other factors such as *karma* or the creatures' *dharma* and *adharma*. The word *karma* is not mentioned in this sūtra, but found in the next one. Śaṃkara supplements it and quotes in support from the *Kauśītakī-brāhmaṇa* and *Bṛhadāraṇyka Upaniṣad* as well as from the *Bhagavad-gītā*.

It seems that the problem of evil must have been a well-known and well-formulated issue at the time of the composition of the *Brahmasūtras*. The contemporary Buddhist and Jaina texts clearly raised the issue. It is said that even Nāgārjuna wrote a short tract to refute the idea that Lord Viṣṇu was the sole creator of the universe. In his *Twelve-Gate Treatise*, it is said:[2]

> If God is the maker of all things why did He not create all happy or all unhappy? Why did He make some happy and others unhappy?

This is a clear formulation of the *vaiṣamya* argument, i.e. the lack of equality, i.e. the injustice consisting of the lack of equal distribution of happiness and unhappiness. The *Mahāpurāṇa*, a Jaina text of probably 9th century AD says among other things:[3]

> And God commits great sin in slaying the children whom He Himself created. If you say that He slays only to destroy evil beings, why did He create such beings in the first place?

This is the *naighṛṇya* argument, i.e., the cruelty of the omnipotent creator. David Hume's oft-quoted lines have the same resonance[4]

> Is he [God] willing to prevent evil, but not able? then is he impotent. Is he able but not willing? then is he malevolent. Is he both able and willing? whence then is evil?

[...]

Turning to Śaṃkara, we must see what resolution he offers. If creation is *ex nihilo* and if the Creator is omnipotent, as it is generally emphasized in the Judeo-Christian tradition, then no satisfactory reconciliation can take place. The author of the Sūtras in Vedānta clearly repudiates the two antecedent conditions. First, creation is not *ex nihilo*, as BS 2.1.35 [p. 297 below] underlines. *Ex nihilo* presupposes a beginning, but here it is said that creation has no beginning [...]. Second, BS 2.1.34 [p. 296 below] emphasizes that [...] the Creator is not independent. He does not have free choice. Śaṃkara adds another dimension to the causality of God: [...]. Rainfall is the common cause for the production of rice, barley, etc. Rainfall does not show any favour or disfavour to the various seeds that are sown. God is likewise the common cause of the creation. The varieties and inequalities of the creatures are due to God's dependence upon the special factors in each case, the particular *nature* of the creature, which is usually determined by the destiny or the accumulated *karma* of the creature itself.

The next sūtra, 2.1.34, raises and answers the obvious objection to this position. In the very beginning of creation, no *karma* existed, so whence the diversity? Answer: there was no such beginning, just as time has no beginning. 2.1.36 [p. 297 below] tries to justify this notion of beginninglessness. First, the question is raised: if *karma* is the factor on which creation depends, then creation is also a factor on which *karma* depends, and so which one was first? This is ruled out as an idle question. For it is exactly like the chicken-and-egg (or in the Indian context, the seed-and-sprout) controversy. Second, had

---

[2]   See H. Cheng, *Nāgārjuna's Twelve Gate Treatise*, Dordrecht, Reidel, 1982, Ch. 8.

[3]   *The Mahāpurāṇa of Jinasena*, 4.16–31, 38–40. It is cited in *Sources of Indian Tradition* (Revised ed. Ainslie T. Embree), New York, Columbia University Press, 1988 (First ed. 1958), pp. 80–2.

[4]   D. Hume, *Dialogues Concerning Natural Religion*, Part X, in *A Treatise of Human Nature and Dialogues Concerning Natural Religion*, Vol. II, ed. T. H. Green and T. H. Grose, New York, Longmans, Green, and Co., 1898, p. 440 [see also p. 293 below].

there been a beginning of creation, it would have started by a pure accident or "causelessly" [. . .]. This seems to be reminiscent of the "why not sooner" argument, which is found to be tackled by the Greek and scholastic philosophers in the West (Sorabji).[5] Besides, creatures would have to suffer a lot for which they are not at all responsible [. . .], and varieties and inequalities of the creatures' happiness and unhappiness would be unaccounted for. To avoid such *absurd* consequences, one has to admit the beginninglessness of the creation. Śaṃkara adds: [. . .] "If beginninglessness is accepted, since it follows the process of seed-and-sprout regularity, no fault will arise." However, there seems to be a way out even without our conceding the "beginninglessness" hypothesis of the Hindus. If there was a beginning and the beginning was a happy one, but *free* creatures were created, and if through the exercise of *free* will they brought about inequalities etc. upon themselves, then the alleged absurdity vanishes. (See below.)

A number of important questions, however, arise for us, the moderners, and we may discuss only some of them here. [. . .] First it seems that the Hindu idea of a Creator God is decidedly different from the same in the Judeo-Christian tradition. The traditional view, which underlies Judaism, Christianity and Islam, regards, if we follow Spinoza, for example, God as independent of the world and makes the world dependent upon God. This means that the existence of God does not necessarily imply the existence of the world, for the world came into existence after it had not been in existence. This also implies that prior to its existence there was a God without a world and it is further believed that some day the world will end but God will continue, again, without a world. If this even remotely represents what is commonly believed by Judaism, Christianity and Islam, then the "beginninglessness" hypothesis of the Hindus is contradicted. However, the existence of time "prior" to the creation is not universally accepted by all Christians. Besides, as Sorabji points out (in a private correspondence) it was an important *Judeo-Christian view* that God would create "a new heaven and a new earth" (Isaiah 65.17). The idea of eternity or even pre-existence was, in some sense, present among the Greeks (cf. the conception of eternity of the world), although the Hindu idea of "beginninglessness" maintains its uniqueness. In fact some believers (in the revelation) maintain that any form of eternity of the world would be a restriction on the power of God. This is not, however, universally held – on the other hand we may note here another point. It may be pointed out in this connection that creation at a certain point of time and annihilation at a certain future date, minus the idea of a Creator God, is quite in keeping with the spirit of the modern natural science.

Second, in Judeo-Christian tradition, the Divine omnipotence has very seldom been compromised. In recognition of the problem of evil, both physical and moral evils, various explanations have been suggested since the days of Biblical scholarship. However, for the remaining problem, some sort of incomprehensibility of Providence has been appealed to. However, this has been the root of scepticism in the Western tradition. Spinoza called it "the asylum of ignorance" (*Ethics*, I, Appendix) and J. S. Mill described it as "an ignominious failure". (*Three Essays on Religion*, New York, 1878, p. 192). And yet those who have firm faith in revelation theology can hardly give up the Divine omnipotence. The old Philosophic way of understanding omnipotence is fourfold (I follow H. A. Wolfson's exposition): (1) God, if He willed, could have created a different world with different laws, and (2) if He wills, can undo this world and create a new one with a difference; but (3) He has created this world and implanted in it certain laws of nature by which it is run; and (4) He can, if He wills, override these laws and create miracles. Suprisingly, one notion of omnipotence in India is very similar. [. . .]

This seems to answer most of the problems of the notion of divine omnipotence. One problem is that there exists a clearly discernible distinction between what we call a logical truth or a logical law and what is a law of nature. Squaring a circle would represent violation of the former kind and while flying in the air like the Superman in the comic books or like Hanumān, the monkey chief in Indian mythology, would represent violation of the second kind. Most miracles' reports or God's reported interventions in many

---

5   R. Sorabji, *Time, Creation and Continuum,* London, Duckworth, 1983, pp. 232–8.

religious lores, fall in this latter category. Factual impossibilities lie within God's power, but he chooses not to exercise it. How about logical impossibilities? Can God square a circle? This has been discussed over centuries in the West. And usually it has been conceded that He can, but, chooses not to or he cannot, but such "cannot" does not detract from His omnipotence. The latter is also the view of modern writers on the subject, Plantinga, Kenny, Pike and others.

However, the [. . .] "dependence" thesis which BS 2.1.34 underlines and which Śaṃkara amplifies as God's dependence upon the *karma* of the creatures, seriously delimits, i.e., restricts God's omnipotence, which will not be shared by any of the Biblical religions, Judaism, Christianity or Islam.

Third, in Judeo-Christian tradition, God as creator, is either an artisan or a begetter. The Jewish conception is that of an omnipotent artisan who is in no need of material for any of his acts of making. St Thomas and the Christians in general chose the begetter model after the analogy of natural procreation. The begetter model may have some superficial similarity with popular Hinduism. There is also a more pronounced form of procreation analogy in the Śiva-Śakti model. As poet Kalidāsa says:

I bow down to the parents of the Universe, Śiva and Pārvatī.

The idea of a self-sufficient artisan has a distant resonance with the spider model of God which is well-known in the Upaniṣadic (Hindu) tradition. The spider weaves the net out of itself, much as God does.[. . .]

The Judaic artisan analogy is, however, very different from another Hindu "artisan" analogy. This is the analogy of a potter who makes pots with pre-existent clay. This model is favoured by the Nyāya-Vaiśeṣika and would be presumably favoured by Śaṃkara also when he explains the ordinary notion of creation [. . .]. Matter in the form of atoms pre-exists any creation. The pre-existence of matter is also a Platonic idea. A potter is an artisan who depends upon separate

and independent materials for creating whatever he creates. Here the Divine omnipotence is further curtailed, for God has to "depend upon" [. . .] both the atoms of the matter and the *karma* of the creatures. Since the eternity of creation is still maintained, for the beginninglessness thesis is not given up, "pre-existence" here means persistence between periodic (and partial) creation and dissolution. Such a position is diametrically opposed to the Biblical tradition of a unique and sudden creation through God's wilful intervention into history.

It is implied by most of what Plato says that matter existed beginninglessly, but in a chaotic state, until God formed it into the orderly universe we know. And it was also God who installed the celestial clock and created (measurable) time as we know it. This would mean that the ordering of matter had a beginning, while the existence of matter is beginningless. However, matter, according to Plato, is still not eternal in the fullest sense of being outside time in the way the Forms in Plato are eternal.[6]

Aristotle criticized Plato that the world could not have had a beginning (and some Platonists reinterpreted Plato's lines to answer that even the orderly world, according to Plato, existed beginninglessly). By eternity Aristotle meant endless time, not being outside time.[7]

[. . .]

In any case, the beginninglessness of the universe has been upheld by almost everybody in European antiquity outside the Judaeo-Christian tradition. [. . .]

This excursion in non-Indian philosophy has been made here simply to underline the point that beginninglessness is not a stupid or unintelligible notion. And there is no real logical difficulty in conceiving it, in the absence of any definite knowledge or even the possibility of such a knowledge about how the creation began. The second point is to question whether it is absolutely necessary to resort to the "beginninglessness" hypothesis in order to account for the inequalities and differences in suffering of the

[6] Ibid., I. Ch. 17.
[7] Ibid., pp. 125–7.

creatures. The Indian philosophies along with Śaṃkara seem to assume it. However, if with Plato we assume reincarnations, and if we assume further that the first incarnation was happy (I owe this point to Sorabji), inequalities and differences in happiness of the *free* creatures would not be unaccounted for.

Fourth, the *karma* doctrine has its own philosophical problems. The rational defence of *karma* seems to be based very much upon inadequate evidence and *a priori* assumption. Hence if one depends on *karma* to explain inequalities and presence of physical and moral evils rather than on the inscrutability of Providence, is one not flying from one "asylum of ignorance" to another? [...]

I have noted elsewhere how Max Weber thought of the *karma* doctrine, which was in his words "the most consistent theodicy" ever produced in history.[8] While I do not share Weber's enthusiasm about the *karma* doctrine, I believe the connection between *karma* and theodicy should not be lightly dismissed. [...] Indulging in a generalisation, which may not be an illicit one, we can say that the Hindus, the Buddhists and the Jainas – all try to uphold the idea of retributive justice in the creation, by making the existence of inequalities and differences dependent upon and conditioned by the *karma* doctrine, and the causal paradox (of *seeds* and *sprouts*) that is then generated is avoided by an appeal to the beginningless nature of the creation process.

Fifthly, *karma* is to be regarded as a hypothesis formulated to explain certain recalcitrant features in our conception of the creation of this universe. Hence the weakness or the strength of this hypothesis should be judged on the basis of its explanatory power. The doctrine of rebirth or transmigration is only an extension of the original hypothesis, and hence it is not impossible to uphold the *karma* hypothesis without the excess baggage of the rebirth hypothesis. The *Śvetāśvatara Upaniṣad* enumerated a number of rival hypotheses: nature, chance, destiny, Matter,

Time or human *karma*[9] [...]. Of these, *karma* is only one, and eventually this was thought to be more acceptable by the Indians.

[...]

Sixthly, [...] the hypothesis faces other formidable objections. Let us deal with only one. A significant objection from the point of view of a Westerner is that a sincerely held belief in the *karma* hypothesis confuses and conflates two very different domains sharply distinguished in modern Western philosophy: fact and value.

One may summarily reject the doctrine as unintelligible for it violates Hume's principle of distinguishing fact from value.[10] The separation is important and calls for significant methodological considerations in the pursuit of material science: causal explanation of factual events must be in terms of other factual events and their interconnections, not in terms of "subjective" values. The question, however, is much discussed today. As far as our present purpose is concerned, it does not matter a great deal whether or not evaluative statements or moral prescriptions can be derived from factual statements. I believe they can be derived within limits. The more pertinent question is how to justify the move to obliterate the distinction between a natural law like the law of Gravitation and a prescriptive law, a law involving the domain of value, which the law of *karma* inescapably implies. For the essence of this law, i.e., the *karma* doctrine, consists in actions being evaluated as morally good or bad, and justice, reward and punishment being distributed accordingly in automatic regularity. And to ask us to believe in it is in fact going against the current, that is, the acquired wisdom of the "scientific" Western civilization.

In plain language, how can we extend the law of natural causation of physical events to the domain of ethics and speak in dead seriousness about moral causation; unless the latter is only a

8   Max Weber, *The Religion of India*, tr. & ed. H. H. Gerth and D. Martindale, New York, Free Press, 1958 (original ed. 1920–1), p. 121.
9   *Śvetāśvatara Upaniṣad*, Ch. I, verse 2.
10   Terence Penelhum, "Critical Response", in *Karma and Rebirth* (ed. R. W. Neufeldt, Albany, SUNY, 1986), pp. 339–45.

metaphor? If I eat a lot one day I might have indigestion as a result, which may be my punishment, but it is by and large, physically accounted for. But if I am a compulsive liar and clever enough to cheat most people with impunity, there is very little factual ground on the basis of which one may say that I will receive my punishment no matter what unless of course it is presumed that nature has a teleology or there is retributive justice in the creation or the natural order has a purpose and a direction or, to use the Indian term, there is *Rta* in our cosmos. Even if we become hard-headed moral realists and treat moral qualities as objective as physical qualities, it would be too much to imagine that such qualities of my action would punish or reward me by sending me to hell or heaven. "Lying is wrong" may be true, but it cannot be true in the same sense as the Law of Gravitation or Heisenberg's uncertainty principle; at least, that is the received wisdom of our age. Natural law, one may contend, is nothing more than a given sequence, unless, of course, we imagine a divine mind who can be made responsible for the assumed teleology or we imagine such a teleology to be immanent in the natural universe.

It seems that the Greek Stoics believed in a similar teleology immanent in the natural universe: as materialists, they gave an entirely physical explanation of our unhappy states. Providence, then, was not clearly separable from the natural law, according to the Stoics. However, this was argued differently, and here we may have a contrast, and it may be philosophically fruitful to explain it.

The *karma* doctrine of the Indians masquerades as a factual proposition – as a natural law – which makes the moral qualities of the actions as potent as being able to produce reward and punishment for the agent on a future occasion. This defies the outlook which we have been accustomed to call "scientific" during the last two hundred years of human civilization.

In sum, I have focused upon two significant aspects of Śaṃkara's theodicy, which is also generalizable as an Indian version of theodicy. Whether this theodicy fails or not, its intelligibility depends upon these two aspects: the "beginning-lessness" argument and the dependence of creation upon *karma*. It has been shown that "beginning-lessness" is not at all an unintelligible concept. If creation had a beginning, the theist or religious people will have more problems to face and resolve. The *karma* doctrine is intelligible only if we assume that nature has a purpose and a direction. However, if we are unable to concede this, the *karma* principle may be taken to be a religious proposition, an article of faith. In fact, few arguments are given there in the vast philosophical literature of India. It is the *given* in Indian religion. It is not a fully worked out theory. It is given as the general guideline that is supposed to shape the Indian way of life, the social and moral behaviour of the Indians. [. . .]

41

Karma, Rebirth, and the Problem of Evil

Whitley R. P. Kaufman

According to the seed that's sown
So is the fruit ye reap therefrom.
Doer of good will gather good,
Doer of evil, evil reaps.
Sown is the seed, and thou shalt taste
The fruit thereof.

Samyutta Nikaya[1]

The doctrine of karma and rebirth represents perhaps the most striking difference between Western (Judeo-Christian and Islamic) religious thought and the great Indian religious traditions (Hindu, Buddhist, Jain). To be sure, Western theology also makes use of a retributive explanation of evil in which an individual's suffering is accounted for by his previous wrongdoing. But given the obviously imperfect correlation between sin and suffering in an individual's lifetime, Western religions have resorted to other explanations of suffering (including, notoriously, that of Original Sin). However, Indian thought boldly combines this retributionism with the idea of multiple human incarnations, so that all suffering in this life can be explained by each individual's prior wrongdoing, whether in this or in a prior life, and all wrongdoing in the present life will be punished in either this or a future life. In this way, Indian thought is able to endorse a complete and consistent retributive explanation of evil: all suffering can be explained by the wrongdoing of the sufferer himself. As Ananda Coomaraswamy declares, in answer to the question "Who did sin, this man or his parents, that he was born blind?": "The Indian theory replies without hesitation, *this man*."[2]

"Karma, Rebirth, and the Problem of Evil" by Whitley R. P. Kaufman, *Philosophy East & West* 59:1 (January 2005): 15–32. Reprinted by permission of the University of Hawaii Press.

[1]   Cited in Keyes, p. 262.

[2]   Coomaraswamy 1964, p. 108. The reference, of course, is to John 9:2, in which Jesus rejects the retributive explanation of a man's blindness.

It is frequently claimed that the doctrine of karma and rebirth provides Indian religion with a more emotionally and intellectually satisfying account of evil and suffering than do typical Western solutions to the problem of evil. Thus, for Max Weber, karma

> stands out by virtue of its consistency as well as by its extraordinary metaphysical achievement: It unites virtuoso-like self-redemption by man's own effort with universal accessibility of salvation, the strictest rejection of the world with organic social ethics, and contemplation as the paramount path to salvation with an inner-worldly vocational ethic.[3]

Arthur Herman, in his classic *The Problem of Evil and Indian Thought*, similarly asserts the superiority of karma to all Western theodicies: "Unlike the Western theories, . . . the doctrine of rebirth is capable of meeting the major objections against which those Western attempts all failed" (Herman 1976, p. 287).[4] Michael Stoeber also claims that the Indian idea of rebirth is "more plausible" than traditional Christian ideas such as purgatory (Stoeber 1992, p. 167). And the karma doctrine appears to be increasing in popularity in the West as well, perhaps because of these perceived advantages.

However, despite these and similar enthusiastic endorsements, karma as a theodicy has still received comparatively little critical analysis in comparison with the scrutiny to which dominant Western ideas such as Original Sin or free will have been subjected. Paul Edwards contrasts the "devastating critical examination" to which Christian and Jewish tenets have been subjected with the lack of any "similarly detailed critique of reincarnation and the related doctrine of Karma" by Western philosophers (Edwards 1996, p. 7). A bibliography of theodicy writings between 1960 and 1991 lists over four thousand entries, but only a half dozen or so of these

specifically address karma.[5] In this essay I would like to make a gesture toward filling in this gap. Whereas Edwards' work concentrates on the metaphysical and scientific critique of karma, I will limit my discussion to the specific question of whether a karma-and-rebirth theory, even if true, could solve the problem of evil. That is, can it provide a satisfactory explanation of the (apparent) unfairness, injustice, and innocent suffering in the world? I will argue here that the doctrine, in whatever form it is proposed, suffers from serious limitations that render it unlikely to provide a satisfactory solution to the problem of evil.

Preliminary Qualifications

Let me state at the outset my limited purposes in this essay. This is not an exercise in doctrinal exegesis or historical comparative anthropology; such issues are not my concern and are outside my competence in any case. Nor do I do intend to enter into the debate about the textual sources of the karmic doctrine (e.g., whether they first appear in the Upanishads, or whether there are precursors in the Brahmanas), or the question of the extent of the influence of the karma doctrine in contemporary Indian thought.[6] Rather, my method will be to examine a simplified, idealized version of the karma-and-rebirth doctrine, one abstracted as far as possible from particular historical or doctrinal questions.

Such an approach will not be without controversy. Many writers have, in fact, doubted whether karma is meant to function as a theodicy, or indeed whether Indian thought should be taken as recognizing a "problem of evil" in anything like its Western formulation. Wendy O'Flaherty points to the "widespread" belief that Indians do not recognize the problem of evil, or even that "there is no concept of evil at all in India" (O'Flaherty 1976, p. 4). Arthur Herman

---

[3]   Weber 1947, p. 359.

[4]   In the second edition, Herman backs off this claim, and says that he now thinks that the traditional problem of evil is "insolvable" (p. viii).

[5]   Whitney 1998.

[6]   On which there is enormous disagreement. See, for example, Creed 1986, p. 10 (karma is "not central to the modern Hindu philosophical curriculum"), and Walli 1977, p. 277 (the "entire structure of Indian culture" is "dominated" by the idea of karma).

makes the extraordinary claim that Indian thought is not much interested in the theodicy question precisely because the karma doctrine provides a fully satisfactory explanation of evil:

> since the rebirth solution is adequate for solving the theological problem of evil, this undoubtedly explains why the problem was never of much concern to the classical Indian, and why theodicy, as a philosophical way of life, was practically unknown to them. (p. 288)

However, O'Flaherty's *The Origins of Evil in Hindu Mythology* amply demonstrates the falsity of the claim that theodicy is solely a Western concern. She shows how Western scholars have "overlooked" the presence of the problem of evil in Indian thought by focusing on systematic philosophy and theology rather than mythology and folk tradition; in fact, "myths of theodicy are perennial in India" (p. 6).

Still, there remains the question of whether it is appropriate to use such doctrines as karma as solutions to the peculiarly Western formulation of the theodicy problem, structured as an inconsistent triad (God is omnipotent, God is good, and yet there is evil in the world). Thus, Charles Keyes points out that many writers have been uneasy with characterizing karma as a theodicy, because this presupposes the idea of a benevolent, omnipotent deity that is "uncharacteristic of South Asian religions" (Keyes 1983, p. 167). However, it would be a great mistake to insist on an unnecessarily narrow formulation of the problem of evil, in particular one that assumes an ethical monotheist religion. In fact, there is no reason to restrict the problem to monotheist religions, or to theist religions, or even to religions at all. As Susan Neiman points out, "nothing is easier than stating the problem of evil in non-theist terms" (Neiman 2002, p. 5); she cites, for example, Hegel's insistence that the real is identical to the rational. The problem of evil in its broadest question simply asks such universal human questions as "Why do the innocent suffer and the wicked flourish?" "Why is not the world better ordered and more just?" "Why is there suffering and death at all in the universe?" One might call this the "existential" problem of evil in contrast to the "theological" problem, and it is one that is shared by all people and all religions.

And to this broader existential problem of evil, karma clearly does function as a purported solution. As Keyes explains, karma is a "theory of causation that supplies reasons for human fortune, good or bad, and that can at least in theory provide convincing explanations for human misfortune" (p. 167).

There is yet one further question regarding my approach. Even granting that karma serves as a theodicy of some sort, is it appropriate to treat it as a rigorous and systematic theoretical explanation of all evil in the world? That is, does karma constitute a "theory" in the sense of a fully developed philosophical or theological account of the presence of evil? Scriptural references to the doctrine are notoriously vague and obscure and require substantial filling in (e.g., the epigraph given above).

[. . .]

However, the evidence that the theory can be treated as a self-contained theory on its own terms is precisely that modern defenders have done so. For the idea of karma is brilliant in its simplicity and straightforwardness. As Clooney characterizes it, the basic idea is simply that "people suffer because of their past deeds in this and previous lives, and likewise enjoy benefits based on past good deeds" (p. 530). The attraction of the idea is obvious: each person makes his own fate, and all suffering happens for a reason. There is no arbitrary or meaningless suffering in the world. Moreover, even if one is miserable in this life, one can look forward to happiness in future lives, if one does one's duty. The tremendous intellectual and emotional power of this theory no doubt accounts for its wide popularity over the ages.

Hence, my project here is to evaluate karma as a complete, systematic theory of the origins and explanation of human suffering. This view of karma is just what has attracted such Western thinkers as Max Weber, who praised the doctrine for its consistency, and Peter Berger, who characterizes the theory as the "most rational" type of theodicy: "every conceivable anomy is integrated within a thoroughly rational, all-embracing interpretation of the universe" (Berger 1967, p. 65). Arthur Herman singles out for praise the consistency and completeness of the theory (p. 288). Karl Potter is impressed by the "carefully worked-out theory concerning the mechanics of karma and rebirth" (Potter 1980, p. 248). And M. Hiriyanna equally defends karma as a systematic explanation of all events in the world: "the doctrine extends the principles of causation to the sphere of human conduct and teaches that, as every event in the physical world is determined by its antecedents, so everything that happens in the moral realm is preordained" (Hiriyanna 1995, p. 46).

It is this modern development of karma as systematic theodicy (whatever its historical antecedents) that I propose to examine and critique here. As Bruce Reichenbach argues, even if we have no way of knowing what historically was the problem that karma was originally intended to meet, the progressive development of the theory was no doubt motivated by a desire "rationally to account for the diversity of circumstances and situations into which sentient creatures were born, or for the natural events experienced during one's lifetime which affected one person propitiously and another adversely" (Reichenbach 1990, p. 63, see also p. 13). The attraction of the karma doctrine over time is, as Reichenbach says, "its alleged explanatory power in this regard which has gained for it adherents through the centuries" (ibid.). I propose, then, to examine the doctrine of karma as developed in the modern period into a complete and systematic explanation of human suffering. Hence, my focus will be on modern commentators and secondary sources rather than on scriptural origins, and I will analyze the doctrine of karma in its rationalized and simplified form; the particular details, or alternative formulations of the doctrine, will not be noted unless they appear relevant to the theodicy question.

I will restrict my analysis in particular to the issue of whether karma provides a morally satisfactory solution to the problem of evil. There are, of course, serious physical and metaphysical issues involved as well in evaluating karma, including the idea that there is a causal mechanism by which deeds in one's past life affect events in future lives, that the soul (or some entity independent of the physical body) is the bearer of individual identity, that the soul can inhabit different bodies at different times and does not die with the body's death, that it can act

wholly independent of the body, and that it is the bearer of moral responsibility (as well as personal identity) across time. Paul Edwards provides a careful critique of such issues in his *Reincarnation*. The present essay, in contrast, considers karma not as a metaphysics but solely as a theodicy: we will ask simply whether, even on these assumptions, the theory can explain the presence in the world of human suffering and misery. In the end, the purpose of this essay is not to evaluate the relative merits of one religion over another, but rather to explore one of the most intriguing conceptual possibilities in the theodicy debate: whether suffering can be wholly (or even mostly) explained and justified as the result of individual wrongdoing.

Karma as Systematic Theodicy: Five Moral Objections

The advantages of the karma theory are obvious and I will not dwell on them here. It is repeatedly pointed out, for example, that it can explain the suffering of innocent children, or congenital illnesses, with which Western thought has great difficulty. It is further argued that it is a more profoundly just doctrine, in that the fact of multiple existences gives the possibility of multiple possibilities for salvation – indeed, that in the end there can be universal salvation. This is again in contrast to the Western tradition, in which there is only one bite at the apple; those who fail in this life are doomed to eternal perdition. However, the doctrine as a whole is subject to a number of serious objections. Here I will present five distinct objections to the rebirth doctrine, all of which raise serious obstacles to the claim that rebirth can provide a convincing solution to the Problem of Evil. I do not claim this to be an exhaustive list, nor do I claim that everyone will agree with each of them. However, I think that they are serious enough as to require at the very least a fuller and more detailed defense of karma as theodicy than has so far been given.

The Memory Problem

An oft-raised objection to the claim of prior existences is the utter lack of any memory traces of previous lives. Both Paul Edwards and Bruce

Reichenbach point out the oddity that all of us have had long, complex past lives, yet none of us have any recollection of them at all. More often, this objection is raised to cast doubt on whether we did in fact have any past lives at all. But my concern here is the *moral* issue raised by this deficiency: justice demands that one who is being made to suffer for a past crime be made aware of his crime and understand why he is being punished for it. Thus, even Christmas Humphreys in his vigorous defense of karma concedes the "injustice of our suffering for the deeds of someone about whom we remember nothing" (Humphreys 1983, p. 84). A conscientious parent explains to his child just why he is being punished; our legal system treats criminal defendants in just the same way. Would not a compassionate deity or a just system make sure the guilty party knows what he has done wrong? It is true that one's belief that all crime is eventually punished might serve a disciplinary function even where one is not aware just what one is being punished for at the time. However, the fact that the sufferer can never know just what crime he is being punished for at a given time, that the system of meting out punishments is so random and unpredictable, constitutes a violation of a basic principle of justice.

Moreover, the memory problem renders the karmic process essentially useless as a means of moral education. Yet, strikingly, it is regularly claimed by adherents that one of the great virtues of karma and rebirth is precisely that "the doctrine presupposes the possibility of moral growth" and that rewards and punishments "constitute a discipline of natural consequences to educate man morally."[7] For example, suppose I am diagnosed with cancer: this must be a punishment for something I have done wrong – but I have no idea what I did to deserve this, or whether it occurred yesterday, last week, or infinitely many past lives ago. For that matter, I might be committing a sin right now – only I will not know it is a sin, because the punishment might occur next week, next year, or in the next life. Radakrishnan suggests that retaining

memory could be a hindrance to our moral development, since it would bring in memories of lower existences in the past (see Minor 1986, p. 32). But even if this is occasionally true, it is hardly plausible to say it is better *never* or even rarely to remember past deeds or lives; acknowledging past mistakes is in general an important (even essential) educating force in our lives. Yet none of us does remember such past events, nor is there definitive evidence that anyone has *ever* recalled a past life.

The memory problem is particularly serious for the karmic doctrine, since most wrongs will be punished in a later life, and most suffering is the result of wrongdoing in prior existences. (Recall that the theory is forced into this position in order to explain the obvious fact that most misdeeds do *not* get automatically punished in this world, and most suffering is not obviously correlated with wickedness.) How, then, can it be said that the doctrine promotes moral education? It is not an answer to say that our knowledge of moral duties can come from elsewhere, from religious scripture, for example. For the point is that the mechanism of karma itself is poorly designed for the purposes of moral education or progress, given the apparently random and arbitrary pattern of rewards and punishments. If moral education were truly the goal of karma and rebirth, then either punishment would be immediately consequent on sin, or at least one would have some way of knowing what one was being punished (or rewarded) for.

In fact, the difficulty is not merely one of moral education. It has been pointed out that the total lack of memory renders the theory more of a *revenge* theory than a retributive one – and hence morally unacceptable.[8] That is, it suggests that justice is satisfied merely because satisfaction has been taken on the perpetrator of the crime, ignoring completely a central moral element of punishment: that the offender where possible be made aware of his crime, that he acknowledge what he has done wrong and repent for it, that he attempt to atone for his crime, and so forth. As such the rebirth theory fails to respect the moral agency of the sinner in that it is apparently indifferent to whether or not he understands that what he has done is wrong. As Reichenbach rightly points out, the lack of memory prevents one from undergoing the moral process involved in repentance for one's crimes and even attempted rectification for them (p. 95). Further, as Francis Clooney recognizes, the lack of memory of prior lives undermines the pastoral effectiveness of karma as providing comfort to the sufferer: "little comfort is given to the suffering person who is usually thought not to remember anything of the culprit past deeds" (p. 535). A vague assurance that one must have done unremembered terrible deeds in the past is hardly satisfactory.

The Proportionality Problem

The rebirth solution to the Problem of Evil purports to explain every ill and benefit of this life by prior good or bad conduct. To be a morally adequate solution it must presuppose as well (although this is rarely stated explicitly) a proportionality principle – that the severity of suffering be appropriately proportioned to the severity of the wrong. But herein lies a problem: given the kinds and degrees of suffering we see in this life, it is hard to see what sort of sins the sufferers could have committed to deserve such horrible punishment. Think of those who slowly starve to death along with their family in a famine; those with severe depression or other mental illness; those who are tortured to death; young children who are rendered crippled for life in a car accident; those who die of incurable brain cancer; those burned to death in a house fire. It is difficult to believe that every bit of this kind of suffering was genuinely earned. One may grant that we as finite humans are not always in a position to judge what is just or unjust from God's perspective; nevertheless, the point of the rebirth theory is precisely to make suffering comprehensible to us as a form of justice. Indeed, belief in karma might make us tend to enact even more brutal and cruel penalties (e.g., torturing to death) if we try to model human justice on this conception of what apparently counts as divine justice.

The evidence from our own practices is that in fact we do not consider such punishments

morally justified. For example, capital punishment is considered excessive and inappropriate as punishment even for a crime as serious as rape. Yet according to the karma theory every one of us without exception is condemned to "capital punishment," that is, inevitable physical death, even apart from the various other sufferings we have to endure. An eye-for-an-eye version of the rebirth theory holds that if one is raped in this life it is because one must have been a rapist in a past life, and what could be fairer than that whatever harm one caused to others will be caused to you later? But it is hard to believe that we are all subject to death because we have all been murderers in a past life. Moreover, this answer simply will not work for most diseases (one cannot "cause" another to have Parkinson's or brain cancer). (It also leads to an infinite regress problem, on which see below). It is certainly hard to stomach the notion that the inmates of Auschwitz and Buchenwald did something so evil in the past that they merely got what was coming to them – but the rebirth theory is committed to just this position.

Nor does the idea of the "pool of karmic residues" solve this problem: it is equally hard to believe that even an enormous accumulation of past bad acts could justify the horrible suffering of this world, or indeed that fairness would allow all one's lesser wrongs to accumulate and generate a single, horrible punishment rather than smaller punishments over a longer period. Indeed, it raises the question of fairness of the mechanism: why would some people be punished separately for each individual wrong, while others are punished only all at once and horribly (further undermining the possibility of moral education, one might note)?

The Infinite Regress Problem

In order to explain an individual's circumstances in the present life, karma refers to the events of his prior life. But in order to explain the circumstances of that prior life, we need to invoke the events of his previous life – and so on, ad infinitum. The problem is quite general: how did the karmic process begin? What was the first wrong? Who was the original sufferer? This familiar objection points out that rebirth provides no solution at all, but simply pushes the problem back.[9] And the response typically given by defenders of rebirth is quite inadequate: they claim that the process is simply beginn-ingless (*anādi*), that the karmic process extends back infinitely in time.[10] But this is no answer at all; indeed, it violates a basic canon of ratio-nality, that the "explanation" not be equally as problematic as the problem being explained. Thus, explains Wendy O'Flaherty: "Karma 'solves' the problem of the origin of evil by say-ing that there *is* no origin. . . . But this ignores rather than solves the problem" (p. 17).

Roy Perrett has responded to this criticism by arguing that the doctrine of karma satisfactorily explains each individual instance of suffering, and it is unreasonable to demand that it give an "ultimate explanation" of the origin of suffering. After all, he says, "explanation has to come to an end somewhere" (Perrett 1985, p. 7). However, the fallacy in this argument can be illustrated by analogy. Consider the "theory" that the world is supported on the back of an elephant, which in turn rests on the back of a tortoise. Now if this is to be an explanatory account of what sup-ports the world, it only begs the question: what supports the tortoise? A famous (probably apoc-ryphal) exchange between Bertrand Russell and an anonymous woman goes as follows:

WOMAN: The world rests on the back of a giant
         turtle.
RUSSELL: What does the turtle rest on?
WOMAN: Another turtle.
RUSSELL: What does *it* rest on?
WOMAN: Another turtle.
RUSSELL: What does *it* rest on?

The discussion goes on this way for quite some time, until the woman becomes exasperated and blurts out: "Don't you see, Professor Russell, it's turtles *all the way down*!" It will hardly do for the woman to claim that, as her solution explains how the world is supported in each individual instance, she need not worry about the infinite regress. This solution is the equiva-lent of borrowing money in order to pay off a debt:

a solution that merely postpones the problem is no solution at all.

It is also noteworthy that the denial of a beginning to the process sidesteps the question of divine responsibility for the beginning of evil in the world. If there is a creator, then why is he not responsible for the misdeeds of his creations? There is no easy answer to this ques-tion, but neither can it be avoided altogether. Christianity has long been criticized for its doctrine of the Fall of Man and Original Sin for these same reasons. I do not claim here that the Christian solution succeeds, but only that the Indian solution does not evade these diffi-culties, either.

The Problem of Explaining Death

If rebirth is to account for all human suffering, it must, of course, explain the paradigmatic case of innocent suffering: death itself. But the prob-lem here is that in the typical rebirth theory death seems not to be presented as punishment for wrong, but rather is *presupposed* as the mech-anism by which karma operates. That is, it is through rebirth that one is rewarded or pun-ished for one's past wrongs (by being born in high or low station, healthy or sickly, etc.). But there can be no rebirth unless there is death. So even if one is moving up in the scale of karma to a very high birth for one's great virtue, one must still undergo death. This would appear to undermine the moral justification for (arguably) the greatest of evils, death itself. For in most versions of the theory death is not even taken as something that needs explaining, but is rather assumed as simply the causal process by which karma operates. Indeed, one might well ask why *everyone* is mortal; why are there not at least some who have been virtuous enough to live indefinitely? Did we all commit such terrible wrongs right away that we have always been subject to death? Typically, though, death and rebirth are not themselves morally justified but simply taken as the neutral mechanism of karma (see, e.g., Humphreys, p. 22).

---

[9]   See, for example, Watts 1964, p. 38; Hick 1976, pp. 309, 314; Hick 1990, p. 139; and O'Flaherty, p. 17.
[10] See Herman, p. 263, and Hiriyanna, pp. 47, 198. [. . .]

There are several ways one might try to get around this problem. Max Weber suggests that the finiteness of good deeds in our life accounts for the finiteness of our life span.[11] But this entails a quite different karmic system, one in which one is punished not for positive misdeeds, but for the lack of infinitely many good deeds. It also seems to suggest that we are morally required to be infinitely good to avoid death – a rather implausible moral demand on us and one that undermines the moral justification of karma to be a fair system of rewards and punishments (one might ask why we are not rewarded with infinitely long life for not committing "infinite evil"). Moreover, there is a troublesome hint of circularity in Weber's solution: it seems odd to say that the finiteness of our life span derives from the finiteness of our goodness; to do infinitely much good one apparently needs an infinitely long life.

Another possible solution is simply to deny that death is indeed an evil, since it is the means by which one reaches greater rewards in life. But this is hardly satisfying, for there is no reason at all that death needs to be the mechanism by which one attains one's rewards: why not simply reward the person with health, wealth, and long life, without having to undergo rebirth in the first place? Karma certainly does not need death and rebirth: as soon as one accumulates sufficient merit, one could be instantly transformed into a higher state of existence. Further, this solution simply resorts to denial of the commonsense fact that death usually involves a terrible and often physically painful disruption of one's existence, including the separation from all one's loved ones and from all that one holds dear.

A different strategy might be to say that the ultimate reward is indeed escape from death, the release from the cycle of *saṃsāra* or rebirth, as many Indians believe. The trouble with this solution is, to put it colloquially, that it throws out the baby with the bathwater. The problem of evil arises not because life itself is an unmitigated evil, but because it contains such a strange mixture of good and evil. Karma implies that all of

the good in life – health, wealth, happiness – is due to our good deeds. Why, then, is not perfect goodness rewarded with a perfectly good earthly life (one without death, pain, sickness, poverty, etc.)? If the idea that the ultimate goal is escape from life itself, it simply goes too far.[12] The idea of Nirvāṇa in Indian thought is often identified with release from not only the evil in life, but from all aspects of life, the good and the bad.[13] But to say that life itself (not just the bad aspects of it) is the problem cannot be a solution to the problem of evil, but rather an admission of failure to solve it. For why is life bad, full of suffering and misery, rather than good? It is also an implausible claim, since experience shows that life can be very good indeed, so why is it not good all the time?

The Free Will Problem

The karma solution is often presented as the ideal solution that respects free moral agency: one determines one's own future by one's present deeds. In fact, as is often pointed out, karma is paradoxically both a fatalist and a freewill theory. For Keyes, karma "manages to affirm and deny human responsibility at the same time" (p. 175); Walli tries to account for this peculiarity by interpreting karma in two stages: in the early stages of existence it is fatalistic, but later it becomes a "moral force" (Walli 1977, p. 328). It is often noted that, despite the promise of control over one's destiny, in practice the doctrine of karma can often result instead in an attitude of fatalistic pessimism in the believer. Thus, Berger argues that by legitimating the conditions of all social classes, karma "constitutes the most thoroughly conservative religious system devised in history" (p. 65).

Karma is also praised as a freewill theory on the grounds that it gives the individual multiple (infinitely many?) chances to reach salvation in future lives. However, it is not clear whether the multiple-life theory in fact constitutes an advantage over Christian doctrine. Since in Christianity the individual has but one life in

[11] Weber 1964, p. 145.
[12] See Hick 1976, pp. 321, 437.
[13] Hiriyanna, p. 69.

which to earn salvation, this entails a high degree of moral importance to one's life (especially given that death could come at any time). In contrast, for karma there is no such urgency, for all mistakes and misdeeds can be rectified in the fullness of future lives. The significance of a particular lifetime, let alone a particular action, is radically diminished if the "life of the individual is only an ephemeral link in a causal chain that extends infinitely into both past and future" (Berger, p. 65). Again, this could encourage fatalism, a sense that one's choice here and now does not matter much in the greater scheme of things.

But a deeper problem is whether the doctrine of karma can in fact be squared at all with the existence of free moral agency. The difficulty can be illustrated with the following example. Consider the potential terrorist, who is deciding whether to draw attention to his political cause by detonating a bomb in a civilian area. How are we to reconcile the automatic functioning of karma with the man's choice? The karma solution must face a dilemma here. There is either of the following possibilities:

(1) Karma functions in a determinate and mechanical fashion. Then, whomever the terrorist kills will not be innocent but deserving of their fate. From the terrorist's perspective, if he is the agent of karma his action is no more blameworthy than that of the executioner who delivers the lethal injection. Indeed, no matter what evils he does in the world, he can always justify them to himself by saying he is merely an agent for karma, carrying out the necessary punishments for these "wicked" people. Alternatively, it may be that his potential victims do not deserve to die this way, in which case the man must be determined not to kill them. In either case, freedom of the will (supposedly a virtue of the karma theory) is absent.

(2) The other possibility might be countenanced as a way to preserve freedom of the will. Perhaps it really is up to the terrorist to choose whether to kill his victims. Indeed, let us say that he has the potential to create genuine evil: to kill innocent, undeserving civilians. But now the problem is that a central, indeed crucial,

tenet of the karma theory has been abandoned: that *all suffering* is deserved and is justified by one's prior wrongful acts. For now we have admitted the genuine possibility of gratuitous evil, innocent suffering—just what the theory was designed to deny. One could, of course, suggest that such gratuitous suffering will eventually be fully compensated for in a future life. But this, as Arthur Herman recognizes, would be a theory very different from that of karma. It would be a doctrine that asserts that all suffering will be *compensated* for (eventually) rather than holding that all suffering is *justified* (i.e., by one's misdeeds). Herman rightly rejects this alternative version of the theory as a recompense, not a karma, theory (p. 213).[14]

This dilemma also undermines the idea of karma as a predictive, causal law (a status often asserted for it). Further, either horn of the dilemma undermines the moral-education function of karma as well (see Herman, p. 215). In (1) one cannot learn because one apparently cannot do wrong. In (2) if one suffers, one can never know if it is because one has done wrong or because of the gratuitous harm caused by the wrongdoing of others. Similarly, if one enjoys success one can never know if it is because of one's merits or because it is payback for the gratuitous evil one suffered earlier.

Reichenbach (p. 94) suggests a way in which some defenders of the doctrine of karma have tried to evade this difficulty and preserve the reality of free will: by asserting that karma explains only evil that is not caused by wrongful human choices (i.e., karma is a theory of "moral evil" rather than of "natural evil"). But this strategy is troublesome. First, there are innumerable cases where the categories of moral-versus-natural evil seem to break down: harm caused or contributed to by human negligence (negligent driving of a car, failing to make buildings earthquake proof); harm that was not directly caused but that was anticipated and could have been prevented (starvation in Africa); harm caused in cases of insanity or diminished mental capacity; harm caused while in a state of intoxication (drunk driving); and so forth. In such cases it is doubtful that we could draw a clear distinction

14 See also Reichenbach, p. 17.

between moral and natural evil, but the strategy fails if one cannot draw such a line. Moreover, the great comforting and consoling function of the karma doctrine is gone: one cannot be sure whether or not one's suffering is retribution for past wrong, and one cannot even know which of one's sufferings are punishments for one's prior wrongs and which are not. Even more importantly, this strategy represents not so much a solution to the difficulty as a whole-hearted concession to the radical limitations of the theory, an admission that enormous amounts of suffering cannot be explained or justified in terms of just punishment for past wrongs. One can no longer be sure whether the circumstances one is born into (e.g., poverty) are the result of one's previous sins or of someone else's wrong-doing. This revised explanation of moral evil presumes that suffering can be random, inexplicable, meaningless, freely chosen without regard to the victim's deserts, while the explanation of natural evil presumes that all suffering is explicable and justified. One might wonder whether the explanations of moral and natural evil are now so much at such cross-purposes that the rebirth theory as a whole loses its coherence.

Thus, the dilemma seems to show that karma is simply not consistent with the genuine possibility of free moral choice. The basic problem here is the deep tension (even incompatibility) between the causal determinism implicit in the karma doctrine and the ideal of free moral responsibility, which makes one fully responsible for one's actions. Most commentators never successfully reconcile the two, if indeed they can be reconciled. An example is Hiriyanna, who insists that "everything that happens in the moral realm is preordained;" but that this is fully consistent with human freedom, by which he means "being determined by oneself" (pp. 46–7 and n. 23). It is not clear how one can escape this contradiction. The more one insists on human freedom, the less are events in the world subject to karmic determination.

The difficulty is even worse for the interpretation of karma that extends the idea of causal determinism to one's character or disposition in

future lives. Thus, someone who does evil will inherit in the next life not only lowly circumstances but also a wicked, malevolent disposition; those who have a good disposition owe it to their good deeds in previous lives. Now even one's character and moral choice are influenced, even determined by, one's past lives; this threatens to do away with free moral choice altogether. And once one has a wicked disposition, it is a puzzle how one can escape spiraling down into further wrong-doing, or at best being permanently stuck at a given moral level, if karma has already determined one's moral character. (The problem is exaggerated even further if one accepts the view that particularly bad people become animals; how could one ever escape one's animal state, since animals do not appear to be capable of moral choice at all?)

There is in the end a fatalistic dilemma for the theory. Either the karma theory is a complete and closed causal account of evil and suffering or it is not. That is, either the present state of affairs is fully explained causally by reference to prior events (including human actions) or it is not. If it is fully explained, then there can be no progress or indeed no change at all in the world. Past evil will generate present evil, and present evil will in turn cause equivalent future evil. There is no escape from the process. Alternatively, if there is the possibility of change, then karma must no longer be a complete causal account. That is, it fails as a systematic theory and therefore cannot in fact solve the problem of evil, since there must be evil in the world for which it cannot account.

Karma and the Verifiability Problem

There is one final matter that I think has significant moral relevance in this debate: the charge that the rebirth (or preexistence) doctrine is objectionable because it is *unveritiable* (or unfalsifiable).[15] Whatever happens is consistent with the theory; no fact could apparently falsify it. Whatever the terrorist does is (as Humphreys insists) simply the determination of karma.

---

[15] A problem raised both by Paul Edwards (1996) and Bruce Reichenbach (1990).

Further, one has no capacity effectively to predict the future by this theory. Even if one has done wrong (assuming that there are precise guidelines for what counts as wrongdoing, a difficult assumption in a world of moral dilemmas), one has no way of knowing just what the punishment will be, or when it will occur, in this life or the next. A remarkable example of the willing endorsement of the advantages of unfalsifiability is made by Arthur Herman in defending karma:

> Thus no matter how terrible and awe-inspiring the suffering may be, the rebirth theorist can simply attribute the suffering to previous misdeeds done in previous lives, and the puzzle is over. Extraordinary evil is solved with no harm done to the majesty and holiness of deity.[16]

Another defender of karma and transmigration also unwittingly demonstrates the problem with such theories. He claims that the evidence for transmigration is provided by the law of karma itself (i.e., the law of moral cause and effect), since without the transmigration of souls, karma would be an inadequate solution to the Problem of Evil.[17] Such a justification is transparently circular: it presupposes that the karma solution is true in order to defend it.

Now, one might fairly doubt whether, in general, religious claims can meaningfully be held to the same standards of empirical verification as scientific claims. Nonetheless, the virtue of testability and falsifiability is that it provides a check against all of the familiar human biases: dogmatism, ethnocentrism, and so on. This is a particular problem for the karma theory, since the very unfalsifiability of the doctrine can be used to rationalize the status quo or justify oppression or unfairness on the grounds that their suffering is punishment for their prior wrongs (for they would simply have to pay their debt later). It is widely acknowledged that the repressive caste system in India lasted so long in large part because the doctrine of karma

encouraged Indians to accept social oppression as the mechanical workings of karma. Hiriyanna remarkably presents it as an *advantage* of the karma theory that in India sufferers cannot blame God or their neighbors for their troubles, but only themselves (even if their neighbors are indeed unjustly oppressing them).[18] Human fallibility being what it is, the idea that all suffering is due to a previous wrongful action provides a great temptation to rationalize the status quo with reference to unverifiable claims about one's past wrongs. This is surely too great a price to pay for whatever pastoral comfort such fatalistic reassurance provides.

Conclusion

I conclude that the doctrine of karma and rebirth, taken as a systematic rational account of human suffering by which all individual suffering is explained as a result of that individual's wrongdoing, is unsuccessful as a theodicy. Even if this conclusion is correct, however, it does not follow that the doctrine must be wholly discarded for purposes of theodicy. As I mentioned earlier, it is far from clear whether karma should be interpreted in the rationalistic manner of Max Weber and Peter Berger. Francis Clooney argues that the Vedānta rejects rationalism and "believes that reason working alone is eventually confronted with insoluble problems" (p. 545). Perhaps the doctrine of karma should not be taken in a literalistic sense as a system of "moral accounting," but rather be understood figuratively, as pointing to the higher mysteries of Indian religion such as the ultimate unity of *ātman* (the individual self) and *brahman* (the ground of being). In rejecting the rationalist account of karma as a theodicy, I leave it as an open and important question whether a mystical interpretation of the doctrine might be a better way to approach the profound mystery of human suffering.

---

[16] Herman, p. 287.
[17] Hiriyanna, p. 47.
[18] Ibid., p. 48 (although he does not specifically mention caste). See Humphreys, p. 55 (the condition of cripples and dwarfs can be justified by their sins).

References

Berger Peter. 1967. *The Sacred Canopy.* Garden City, NY: Doubleday.

Clooney, Francis. 1989. "Evil, Divine Omnipotence, and Human Freedom: Vedanta's Theology of Karma." *Journal of Religion* 69: 530–48.

Coomaraswamy, Ananda. 1964. *Buddha and the Gospel of Buddhism.* New York: Harper and Row.

Creed, Austin. 1986. "Contemporary Philosophical Treatments of Karma and Rebirth." In Ronald Neufeldt, ed., *Karma and Rebirth.* Albany: State University of New York Press.

Edwards, Paul. 1996. *Reincarnation: A Critical Examination.* New York: Prometheus Books.

Herman, Arthur. 1976. *The Problem of Evil in Indian Thought.* Delhi: Motilal Banarsidass.

Hick, John. 1976. *Death and Eternal Life.* New York: Harper and Row.

———. 1990. *Philosophy of Religion.* Englewood Cliffs, NJ: Prentice-Hall.

Hiriyanna, M. 1995. *The Essentials of Indian Philosophy.* Delhi: Motilal Banarsidass.

Humphreys, Christmas. 1983. *Karma and Rebirth.* London: Curzon Press.

Keyes, Charles. 1983. "Merit-Transference in the Kammic Theory of Popular Theravada Buddhism." In *Karma*, edited by Charles Keyes and Valentine Daniel. Berkeley: University of California Press.

Minor, Robert. 1986. "In Defense of Karma and Rebirth: Evolutionary Karma." In Ronald Neufeldt, ed., *Karma and Rebirth.* Albany: State University of New York Press.

Neiman, Susan. 2002. *Evil in Modern Thought.* Princeton: Princeton University Press.

O'Flaherty, Wendy Doniger. 1976. *The Origins of Evil in Hindu Mythology.* Berkeley: University of California Press.

Perrett, Roy. 1985. "Karma and the Problem of Suffering." *Sophia* 24: 4–10.

Potter, Karl H. 1980. "The Karma Theory and Its Interpretation in Some Indian Philosophical Systems." In Wendy O'Flaherty, ed., *Karma and Rebirth in Classical Indian Traditions.* Berkeley: University of California Press.

Reichenbach, Bruce. 1990. *The Law of Karma.* Honolulu: University of Hawai'i Press.

Stoeber, Michael. 1992. *Evil and the Mystics' Cod.* Toronto: University of Toronto Press.

Walli, Koshelya. 1977. *Theory of Karman in Indian Thought.* Bharata Mahisha.

Watts, Alan. 1964. *Beyond Theology.* New York: Vintage Books.

Weber, Max. 1947. *Essays in Sociology.* Translated by H. H. Certh and C. Wright Mills. London: K. Paul, Trench, Trubner.

———. 1964. *The Sociology of Religion.* Translated by Ephraim Fischoff. Boston: Beacon Press. (Original publication date in German: 1922).

Whitney, Barry, ed. 1998. *Theodicy: An Annotated Bibliography on the Problem of Evil, 1960–1991.* Bowling Green, OH: Philosophy Documentation Center.

42

Evil as a Privation of Good

Augustine of Hippo

By the Trinity, thus supremely and equally and unchangeably good, all things were created; and these are not supremely and equally and unchangeably good, but yet they are good, even taken separately. Taken as a whole, however, they are very good, because their *ensemble* constitutes the universe in all its wonderful order and beauty.

[. . .]

And in the universe, even that which is called evil, when it is regulated and put in its own place, only enhances our admiration of the good; for we enjoy and value the good more when we compare it with the evil. For the Almighty God, who, as even the heathen acknowledge, has supreme power over all things, being Himself supremely good, would never permit the existence of anything evil among His works, if He were not so omnipotent and good that He can bring good even out of evil. For what is that which we call evil but the absence of good? In the bodies of animals, disease and wounds mean nothing but the absence of health; for when a cure is effected, that does not mean that the evils which were present – namely, the diseases and wounds – go away from the body and dwell elsewhere: they altogether cease to exist; for the wound or disease is not a substance, but a defect in the fleshly substance, – the flesh itself being a substance, and therefore something good, of which those evils – that is, privations of the good which we call health – are accidents. Just in the same way, what are called vices in the soul are nothing but privations of natural good. And when they are cured, they are not transferred elsewhere: when they cease to exist in the healthy soul, they cannot exist anywhere else.

[. . .]

All things that exist, therefore, seeing that the Creator of them all is supremely good are themselves good. But because they are not, like their Creator, supremely and unchangeably good, their good may be diminished and increased. But for good to be diminished is an evil, although, however much it may be diminished, it is necessary, if the being is to continue, that some good should remain to constitute the being. For however small or of whatever kind the being may be, the good which makes it a being cannot be destroyed without destroying the being itself.

"Evil as a Privation of Good" from sections 10–13 of *The Enchiridion* by Aurelius Augustine, trans. S. D. Salmond, in *The Works of Aurelius Augustine, Bishop of Hippo*, ed. Marcus Dods (Edinburgh: T. & T. Clark, George Street, 1877), pp. 181–3.

An uncorrupted nature is justly held in esteem. But if, still further, it be incorruptible, it is undoubtedly considered of still higher value. When it is corrupted, however, its corruption is an evil, because it is deprived of some sort of good. For if it be deprived of no good, it receives no injury; but it does receive injury, therefore it is deprived of good. Therefore, so long as a being is in process of corruption, there is in it some good of which it is being deprived; and if a part of the being should remain which cannot be corrupted, this will certainly be an incorruptible being, and accordingly the process of corruption will result in the manifestation of this great good. But if it do not cease to be corrupted, neither can it cease to possess good of which corruption may deprive it. But if it should be thoroughly and completely consumed by corruption, there will then be no good left, because there will be no being. Wherefore corruption can consume the good only by consuming the being. Every being, therefore, is a good; a great good, if it cannot be corrupted; a little good, if it can: but in any case,

only the foolish or ignorant will deny that it is a good. And if it be wholly consumed by corruption, then the corruption itself must cease to exist, as there is no being left in which it can dwell.

[. . .]

Accordingly, there is nothing of what we call evil, if there be nothing good. But a good which is wholly without evil is a perfect good. A good, on the other hand, which contains evil is a faulty or imperfect good; and there can be no evil where there is no good. From all this we arrive at the curious result: that since every being, so far as it is a being, is good, when we say that a faulty being is an evil being, we just seem to say that what is good is evil, and that nothing but what is good can be evil, seeing that every being is good, and that no evil can exist except in a being. Nothing, then, can be evil except something which is good. And although this, when stated, seems to be a contradiction, yet the strictness of reasoning leaves us no escape from the conclusion.

The Argument from Evil

David Hume

And is it possible, CLEANTHES, said PHILO, that after all these reflections, and infinitely more, which might be suggested, you can still persevere in your Anthropomorphism, and assert the moral attributes of the Deity, his justice, benevolence, mercy, and rectitude, to be of the same nature with these virtues in human creatures? His power we allow infinite: whatever he wills is executed: but neither man nor any other animal are happy: therefore he does not will their happiness. His wisdom is infinite: he is never mistaken in chusing the means to any end: but the course of nature tends not to human or animal felicity: therefore it is not established for that purpose. Through the whole compass of human knowledge, there are no inferences more certain and infallible than these. In what respect, then, do his benevolence and mercy resemble the benevolence and mercy of men?

EPICURUS's old questions are yet unanswered.

Is he willing to prevent evil, but not able? then is he impotent. Is he able, but not willing? then is he malevolent. Is he both able and willing? whence then is evil?

You ascribe, CLEANTHES, (and I believe justly) a purpose and intention to Nature. But what, I beseech you, is the object of that curious artifice and machinery, which she has displayed in all animals? The preservation alone of individuals and propagation of the species. It seems enough for her purpose, if such a rank be barely upheld in the universe, without any care or concern for the happiness of the members that compose it. No resource for this purpose: no machinery, in order merely to give pleasure or ease: no fund of pure joy and contentment: no indulgence without some want or necessity accompanying it. At least, the few phenomena of this nature are overbalanced by opposite phenomena of still greater importance.

Our sense of music, harmony, and indeed beauty of all kinds gives satisfaction, without being absolutely necessary to the preservation and propagation of the species. But what racking pains, on the other hand, arise from gouts, gravels, megrims, tooth-aches, rheumatisms; where the injury to the animal-machinery is either small or incurable? Mirth, laughter, play, frolic, seems gratuitous satisfactions, which have no farther tendency: spleen, melancholy, discontent, superstition, are pains of the same nature. How then does the divine benevolence display itself, in the sense of you Anthropomorphites? None but we Mystics, as you were pleased to call

"The Argument from Evil" from Part X of *Dialogues Concerning Natural Religion* by David Hume, in *A Treatise of Human Nature and Dialogues Concerning Natural Religion*, Vol. II, ed. T. H. Green and T. H. Grose (New York: Longmans, Green, and Co., 1898), pp. 439–43.

us, can account for this strange mixture of phe-nomena, by deriving it from attributes, infinitely perfect, but incomprehensible.

And have you at last, said CLEANTHES smiling, betrayed your intentions, PHILO? Your long agree-ment with DEMEA did indeed a little surprise me; but I find you were all the while erecting a concealed battery against me. And I must confess, that you have now fallen upon a subject, worthy of your noble spirit of opposition and controversy. If you can make out the present point, and prove mankind to be unhappy or corrupted, there is an end at once of all religion. For to what pur-pose establish the natural attributes of the Deity, while the moral are still doubtful and uncertain?

You take umbrage very easily, replied DEMEA, at opinions the most innocent, and the most generally received even amongst the religious and devout themselves: and nothing can be more surprising than to find a topic like this, concerning the wickedness and misery of man, charged with no less than Atheism and profane-ness. Have not all pious divines and preachers, who have indulged their rhetoric on so fertile a subject; have they not easily, I say, given a solu-tion of any difficulties, which may attend it? This world is but a point in comparison of the universe: this life but a moment in comparison of eternity. The present evil phenomena, there-fore, are rectified in other regions, and in some future period of existence. And the eyes of men, being then opened to larger views of things, see the whole connection of general laws; and trace, with adoration, the benevolence and rectitude of the Deity, through all the mazes and intricacies of his providence.

No! replied CLEANTHES, No! These arbitrary suppositions can never be admitted, contrary to matter of fact, visible and uncontroverted. Whence can any cause be known but from its known effects? Whence can any hypothesis be proved but from the apparent phenomena? To establish one hypothesis upon another, is building entirely in the air; and the utmost we ever attain, by these conjectures and fictions, is to ascertain the bare possibility of our opinion; but never can we, upon such terms, establish its reality.

The only method of supporting divine bene-volence (and it is what I willingly embrace) is to deny absolutely the misery and wickedness of man. Your representations are exaggerated: Your melancholy views mostly fictitious: Your infer-ences contrary to fact and experience. Health is more common than sickness: Pleasure than pain: Happiness than misery. And for one vexa-tion, which we meet with, we attain, upon com-putation, a hundred enjoyments.

Admitting your position, replied PHILO, which yet is extremely doubtful, you must, at the same time, allow, that, if pain be less frequent than pleasure, it is infinitely more violent and durable. One hour of it is often able to outweigh a day, a week, a month of our common insipid enjoyments: And how many days, weeks, and months are passed by several in the most acute torments? Pleasure, scarcely in one instance, is ever able to reach ecstacy and rapture: And in no one instance can it continue for any time at its highest pitch and altitude. The spirits evaporate; the nerves relax; the fabric is disordered; and the enjoyment quickly degenerates into fatigue and uneasiness. But pain often, good God, how often! rises to torture and agony; and the longer it continues, it becomes still more genuine agony and torture. Patience is exhausted; courage lan-guishes; melancholy seizes us; and nothing termin-ates our misery but the removal of its cause, or another event, which is the sole cure of all evil, but which, from our natural folly, we regard with still greater horror and consternation.

But not to insist upon these topics, continued PHILO, though most obvious, certain, and import-ant; I must use the freedom to admonish you, CLEANTHES, that you have put the controversy upon a most dangerous issue, and are unawares introducing a total Scepticism, into the most essential articles of natural and revealed theology. What! no method of fixing a just foundation for religion, unless we allow the happiness of human life, and maintain a continued existence even in this world, with all our present pains, infirmities, vexations, and follies, to be eligible and desireable! But this is contrary to every one's feeling and experience: It is contrary to an authority so established as nothing can subvert: No decisive proofs can ever be produced against this authority; nor is it possible for you to com-pute, estimate, and compare all the pains and all the pleasures in the lives of all men and of all animals: And thus by your resting the whole system of religion on a point, which, from its very nature, must for ever be uncertain, you tacitly confess, that that system is equally uncertain.

But allowing you, what never will be believed; at least, what you never possibly can prove, that animal, or at least, human happiness, in this life, exceeds its misery; you have yet done nothing: For this is not, by any means, what we expect from infinite power, infinite wisdom, and infinite goodness. Why is there any misery at all in the world? Not by chance surely. From some cause then. Is it from the intention of the Deity? But he is perfectly benevolent. Is it contrary to his intention? But he is almighty. Nothing can shake the solidity of this reasoning, so short, so clear, so decisive; except we assert, that these subjects exceed all human capacity, and that our common measures of truth and falsehood are not applicable to them; a topic, which I have all along insisted on, but which you have, from the beginning, rejected with scorn and indignation.

But I will be contented to retire still from this intrenchment: For I deny that you can ever force me in it: I will allow, that pain or misery in man is *compatible* with infinite power and goodness in the Deity, even in your sense of these attributes: What are you advanced by all these concessions? A mere possible compatibility is not sufficient. You must *prove* these pure, unmixt, and uncontrollable attributes from the present mixed and confused phenomena, and from these alone. A hopeful undertaking! Were the phenomena ever so pure and unmixt, yet being finite, they would be insufficient for that purpose. How much more, where they are also so jarring and discordant!

Here, CLEANTHES, I find myself at ease in my argument. Here I triumph. Formerly, when we argued concerning the natural attributes of intelligence and design, I needed all my sceptical and metaphysical subtilty to elude your grasp. In many views of the universe, and of its parts, particularly the latter, the beauty and fitness of final causes strike us with such irresistible force, that all objections appear (what I believe they really are) mere cavils and sophisms; nor can we then imagine how it was ever possible for us to repose any weight on them. But there is no view of human life or of the condition of mankind, from which, without the greatest violence, we can infer the moral attributes, or learn that infinite benevolence, conjoined with infinite power and infinite wisdom, which we must discover by the eyes of faith alone. It is your turn now to tug the labouring oar, and to support your philosophical subtilties against the dictates of plain reason and experience.

44

Brahman, Creation, and Evil

Shankara (Samkara)

In order to strengthen the tenet which we are at present defending, we follow the procedure of him who shakes a pole planted in the ground (in order to test whether it is firmly planted), and raise another objection against the doctrine of the Lord being the cause of the world. – The Lord, it is said, cannot be the cause of the world, because, on that hypothesis, the reproach of inequality of dispensation and cruelty would attach to him. Some beings, viz. the gods and others, he renders eminently happy; others, as for instance the animals, eminently unhappy; to some again, as for instance men, he allots an intermediate position. To a Lord bringing about such an unequal condition of things, passion and malice would have to be ascribed, just as to any common person acting similarly; while attributes would be contrary to the essential goodness of the Lord affirmed by *śruti* and *smṛti*. Moreover, as the infliction of pain and the final destruction of all creatures would form part of his dispensation, he would have to be taxed with great cruelty, a quality abhorred by low people even. For these two reasons Brahman cannot be the cause of the world.

The Lord, we reply, cannot be reproached with inequality of dispensation and cruelty, "because he is bound by regards." If the Lord on his own account, without any extraneous regards, produced this unequal creation, he would expose himself to blame; but the fact is, that in creating he is bound by certain regards, i.e. he has to look to merit and demerit. Hence the circumstance of the creation being unequal is due to the merit and demerit of the living creatures created, and is not a fault for which the Lord is to blame. The position of the Lord is to be looked on as analogous to that of Parjanya, the Giver of rain. For as Parjanya is the common cause of the production of rice, barley, and other plants, while the difference between the various species is due to the various potentialities lying hidden in the respective seeds, so the Lord is the common cause of the creation of gods, men, &c., while the differences between these classes of beings are due to the different merit belonging to the individual souls. Hence the Lord, being bound by regards, cannot be reproached with inequality of dispensation and cruelty. . . . (II, 1, 34)

But – an objection is raised – the passage, "Being only this was in the beginning, one, without a second," affirms that before the creation there was no distinction and consequently no merit on

"Brahman, Creation, and Evil" by Shankara, *Brahmasutrabhasya*, II.1.34–6, *A Sourcebook of Advaita Vedenta*, ed. Eliot Deutsch and J. A. B. van Buitenen (Honolulu: University of Hawaii Press, 1971), pp. 191–2. Reprinted by permission of Professor Eliot Deutsch.

account of which the creation might have become unequal. And if we assume the Lord to have been guided in his dispensations by the actions of living beings subsequent to the creation, we involve ourselves in the circular reasoning that work depends on diversity of condition of life, and diversity of condition again on work. The Lord may be considered as acting with regard to religious merit after distinction had once arisen; but as before that the cause of inequality, viz. merit, did not exist, it follows that the first creation must have been free from inequalities.

This objection we meet by the remark, that the transmigratory world is without beginning. – The objection would be valid if the world had a beginning; but as it is without beginning, merit and inequality are, like seed and sprout, caused as well as causes, and there is therefore no logical objection to their operation.... (II, 1, 35)

The beginninglessness of the world recommends itself to reason. For if it had a beginning it would follow that, the world springing into existence without a cause, the released souls also would again enter into the circle of transmigratory existence; and further, as then there would exist no determining cause of the unequal dispensation of pleasure and pain, we should have to acquiesce in the doctrine of rewards and punishments being allotted, without reference to previous good or bad actions. That the Lord is not the cause of the inequality, has already been remarked. Nor can Nescience by itself be the cause, as it is of a uniform nature. On the other hand, Nescience may be the cause of inequality, if it be considered as having regard to merit accruing from action produced by the mental impressions of wrath, hatred, and other afflicting passions. Without merit and demerit nobody can enter into existence, and again, without a body merit and demerit cannot be formed; so that – on the doctrine of the world having a beginning – we are led into a logical see-saw. The opposite doctrine, on the other hand, explains all matters in a manner analogous to the case of the seed and sprout, so that no difficulty remains.... (II, 1, 36)

Section VI

Life after Death, Human Nature, and Personal Identity

Introduction

A. General Introduction to the Section

A deepening appreciation for the inevitability of one's own death can be a powerful motivation for philosophical and religious reflection. To give just two prominent examples: (1) in the traditional story of how the Buddha comes to embark upon his religious quest, he encounters four signs – the third of which is a corpse; and (2) according to a number of twentieth-century existentialist philosophers, living authentically requires that one confront one's impending death.[1]

Across human cultures, reflection on death has often generated the question of whether the demise of our present bodies is really equivalent to *our* demise. According to some, this question and the desire to answer it in the affirmative lie at the very heart of religion: "[T]the longing for the immortality of the soul, for the permanence, in some form or another, of our personal and individual consciousness, is as much of the essence of religion as is the longing that there may be a God."[2] Moreover, as we saw in the previous section, religious responses to the problem of evil often involve claims that evil is somehow overcome or redressed in an afterlife. Thus, much of religious significance might seem to hinge on the truth of claims that we survive the death of our present bodies.

Also, as we will soon see, reflection on the possibility of our continued survival beyond death leads us to more general and important philosophical questions. For example, what is the best account of the nature of a human being? Are we entirely physical beings, or is there some aspect of us – perhaps even the most important part of us – that is non-physical and to which we intend to refer with such words as "mind," "spirit," or "soul"? This latter question is taken up in the traditional so-called "mind–body" problem in philosophy. Further, what constitutes and preserves our personal identity over time despite the many changes we undergo (and would undergo in the future on the various afterlife scenarios)? Should we say that something about oneself must remain the same if one is going to be said to be the same person yesterday, today, and tomorrow?

Finally, a note about the kind of arguments one will and will not encounter in this section. In contemporary philosophy of religion, discussions of an afterlife have tended to focus more on whether various conceptions of an afterlife are possibly true than on whether there

---

[1] See, for example, Martin Heidegger, *Being and Time*, trans. John Macquarrie and Edward Robinson (New York: Haper and Row, 1962), p. 304.

[2] Miguel De Unamuno, *Tragic Sense of Life* (New York: Dover Publications, 1954), p. 221.

is evidence that persons do, in fact, survive their deaths. In other words, in response to skeptics, proponents of afterlife views often limit their defense to showing that such an afterlife is possible. Historically, this has not always been the case. Some philosophers – notably, Plato – pursued the more ambitious strategy of seeking to establish that an afterlife is not only possible but true. Many contemporary philosophers have also been wary of appealing to empirical considerations that others regard as relevant to establishing the reality of an afterlife. There are at least three main types of such data: (1) testimony from spiritual mediums who reportedly have communicated with dead individuals; (2) testimony from those who have undergone "near death experiences"; and (3) testimony from individuals who appear to remember having lived a previous life. In each of these cases, the crucial question is whether an afterlife hypothesis is the best means of explaining what is reported.[3]

B.   Some Western Conceptions of an Afterlife

B1.   Arguing for Extinction

In "A Naturalistic Case for Extinction," Linda Badham surveys three conceptions of an afterlife that have been popular with theists and argues that none are compatible with a contemporary worldview that takes reason and science seriously. The first and second of these views is that at some point after our deaths, we will be resurrected – i.e., brought back from death to exist again in a physically embodied form. The emphasis here on embodied survival parallels a similar emphasis in Indian conceptions of rebirth (discussed below). In the two versions of the resurrection view discussed by Badham,

a distinction is drawn between whether one's resurrected body is regarded as being the same as one's present body or a different body patterned upon one's former physical body. The third view she discusses is one that holds that we exist in an afterlife as an immaterial soul – either in a disembodied state or in conjunction with a physical body. Beginning around the onset of the Common Era, Western theists came to be increasingly influenced by Plato's account of such a soul (see "The Immortality of the Soul").

Badham's critical discussion of these afterlife views draws upon the two underlying and intertwining philosophical issues mentioned above. That is, many of Badham's objections to the afterlife views discussed are either: (a) that they presuppose a faulty view about our essential nature; and/or (b) that on such views our personal identities could not be preserved across lives.

B2.   Materialism and Life after Death

It is sometimes assumed that the possibility of an afterlife is ruled out if one holds a materialist view about our essential nature – that is, a view that we are wholly and only physical organisms. However, this assumption has been subjected to considerable critical scrutiny in recent years. In "'Brain Science and the Soul," Donald MacKay seeks to characterize a materialist view of the mind that would allow for the possibility of a resurrected existence (in the second sense discussed by Badham).

MacKay's strategy involves a distinction between different forms of materialism that associate the mind with the brain. On one sort of materialist view, one's mental states are strictly identical to – that is, not other than – states of one's brain. Thus, if those physical states of the human brain cease to exist at death, then we cease to exist as well, insofar as we are identified with those

---

[3]   The selection in this section by Joseph Prabhu is a notable exception to the generalizations made in this paragraph. He offers both a philosophical argument and arguments based on empirical considerations to support the claim that we have lived and will live additional lives. Also, for further discussion of the possible significance of empirical data of the sort cited in the text, see: Paul Edwards, *Reincarnation* (Amherst, NY: Prometheus Press, 1996); Gary R. Habermas, "Near Death Experiences and the Evidence – A Review Essay," *Christian Scholars Review* 26:1 (1996): 78–85; John Hick, *Philosophy of Religion*, 4th edition (Englewood Cliffs, NJ: Prentice Hall, 1990), pp. 125–30; Ian Stevenson, *Twenty Cases Suggestive of Reincarnation* (New York: American Society for Psychical Research, 1967); and William Rowe, *Philosophy of Religion*, 4th edition (Belmont, CA: Thompson Wadsworth, 2007), pp. 153–7.

mental states. MacKay argues that one need not think of the mind as strictly identical to the brain in this way but rather as a kind of activity that is "embodied" in the brain. Invoking an analogy with the operations of a computer, MacKay holds that while the mind's activity – like the computer's activity – is determined by the physical laws governing matter, neither activity is strictly identical to the material states of the object. In the case of the computer, this is illustrated by the fact that one can run the same program – and thus reproduce the same activity – on several different computers. Perhaps then, he suggests, the mind's activity – our mental life – could be reproduced in a different body in an afterlife, just as the activity of one computer can be reproduced on another computer.

B3.   Resurrection as Re-unification of Body and Soul

Though Stephen Davis thinks a materialist view like MacKay's is a viable option for theists, he seeks in "The Resurrection of the Dead" to defend a theory, which he calls, "temporary disembodiment," that he takes to be closer to the orthodox Christian view. According to this theory, human persons are essentially comprised of both a physical body and immaterial soul. Upon death, one's soul continues to exist but becomes temporarily separated from one's body. At some future time, Davis envisions God reconstituting our bodies, transforming them, and reuniting them with our souls, thereby rendering us whole persons once again.

After sketching the central aspects of the temporary embodiment theory, Davis seeks to address possible objections to his view, several of which have been raised in this section by Badham. For example, of particular importance for a view like his own is the objection that our personal identities could not be preserved across the sort of transitions entailed by the theory – namely, the transitions from: embodiment → disembodiment → embodiment. In other words, if I am essentially both my body and a soul, then how can "I" exist – even if only temporarily

– in a disembodied state? In response, Davis defends a version of the memory-based criterion of personal identity made famous by John Locke (1632–1704).[4] According to this criterion, one is the same person as another person earlier in time if one remembers things from that person's past and from the point of view of that former person.

C.   Some Eastern Conceptions of an Afterlife

C1.   Reincarnation

To become incarnate is to take on bodily form (literally, "enter into flesh"). Thus, a self is reincarnated when it is re-embodied. Though it is not typically referred to in this fashion, note that a theory of resurrection like that offered by Davis is a theory of reincarnation, for on his view one's soul is first united with a body, then temporarily disembodied, then re-embodied once again at a later date. The difference between this view and how reincarnation has traditionally been conceived in Eastern religious traditions like Hinduism and Buddhism lies in the cyclical nature of the latter. In the words of the Hindu classic *The Bhagavad-Gita*: "As a man discards worn-out clothes to put on new and different ones, so the embodied self discards its worn-out bodies to take on new ones."[5] Here, re-embodiment is conceived to occur in the cycle of *samsara* (literally, "wandering over"), which extends both backward into the remote past and forward in time. Also, the cycle is often thought to include not only human beings, but other forms of animal life, and celestial beings, as well. One's immediate aim in the process is to gain a higher-level rebirth, but ultimately, the goal is to be liberated from the cycle altogether (*moksha/nirvana*). Liberation requires that one escape the influence of *karma*, the causal principle that generates consequences on the basis of the moral worth of one's deeds – including how one will be reborn. It is important to realize that on most Indian views, *karma* operates independently of any divine control – as a

---

[4]   *An Inquiry Concerning Human Understanding* (New York: Oxford University Press, 1975), sec. 21.
[5]   *The Bhagavad-Gita*, trans. Barbara Stoler Miller (New York: Bantam Books, 1986), 2.22.

"moral law of gravity," so to speak – thus its consequences do not flow from divine judgment as on some theistic views.

In "The Idea of Reincarnation," Joseph Prabhu defends the coherence and plausibility of reincarnation. He first offers an argument inspired by Kant (1724–1804) that reincarnation is the best means of making sense of certain features of our moral experience. That is, Prabhu argues that if we possess a duty to work toward the completion of our moral and spiritual growth, then it must be possible for such completion to be realized, and since it is clearly not so realized in this life, then its possibility must lie in a future life. This line of argument is further supported by appeal to several empirical observations that, he argues, are best explained by the reincarnation thesis. Finally, Prabhu replies to three objections that have been raised against reincarnation models of an afterlife: (1) that it simply postpones rather than resolves questions raised by the existence of evil; (2) that it presupposes a deterministic model of human agency; and (3) that without memories of one's past lives, the process cannot serve the moral function it is proposed to serve (recall this objection by Kaufman from the previous section).

C2.   Rebirth without Self?

As discussed earlier (section II), the Buddha taught *anatman*, a teaching aimed at eradicating the tendency to view ourselves as independently existing changeless selves. Instead, the Buddhist view is that our selves are a bundle of causally integrated and constantly changing events. Acceptance of this view of the self raises an apparent puzzle in light of the fact that the Buddha seemed to accept the truth of *karma* and *samsara*. That is, these doctrines seem to presuppose a kind of self that the Buddhist teaching denies and so appear inconsistent. If there is no substance self, *what* is it that is reborn and is the recipient of karmic consequences for its earlier deeds? That this was an apparent tension

in Buddhist teachings was acknowledged in early Buddhist reflection (See "What is Reborn is Neither the Same nor Another"). Christopher Gowans explains how one might try to reconcile these strands of Buddhist teaching in "Not-Self, *Kamma*, and Rebirth."[6]

Gowans' strategy in responding to this apparent inconsistency first involves a distinction between two types of reality: independent and dependent reality. The first of these is a kind of reality that does not directly depend upon mental states – for example, the existence of the moon. The second type of reality is directly dependent upon mental states. Here Gowans uses the example of money. The value of a dollar directly depends on the mental states of human beings insofar as they agree to confer that value to pieces of paper printed in a certain fashion. Our selves, on his interpretation of the Buddhist *anatman* view, have no independent reality but only dependent reality. In other words, our selves exist only insofar as we hold a mistaken view that they are something other than dependently existing process selves. Gowan then argues that for such dependently existing process selves, a meaningful sense of identity can be preserved on the basis of causal continuities between earlier and later selves – a sense of identity he believes to be consistent with *karma* and *samsara*.

C3.   Non-dualism and Immortality

As we have seen, insofar as a model of rebirth rests on the notion of an individuated personal consciousness, it raises fundamental philosophical issues about human nature and personal identity that are similar to those that have arisen in reflection on the afterlife theories associated with Western brands of theism. However, some Eastern traditions – namely, Advaita Vedanta and Buddhism – have held not only that rebirth ceases for those who are enlightened and subsequently die, but also that individuated consciousness ceases upon their death. In "Nondualistic Problems of Immortality," Roy

---

[6]   In English texts, the Sanskrit form of Buddhist terms are typically used, and I have followed this convention. However, Gowans is drawing from the Pali Buddhist texts and so uses the Pali rendering of such terms. The central Pali terms in this selection and their Sanskrit equivalents are as follows: *dhamma = dharma*; *kamma = karma*; and *nibbana = nirvana*.

Perrett examines some distinctive issues that arise for such views – in particular as they arise within the context of Advaita Vedanta teachings.

As Perrett emphasizes, not all Hindu schools of thought agreed with Vedantists about the non-dual post-mortem existence of those who achieve *moksha*, or spiritual liberation. Some, like the eleventh-century Hindu philosopher Ramanuja, argued that the notion of consciousness itself presupposes individuated personal awareness and that the possibility of existing in a non-dual state after death could be of no religious concern to anyone because such an existence could not be an extension of one's own existence (see "The Conscious Subject Persists in the State of Release"). Perrett concludes by weighing the merits of Advaitin replies to these objections, the central line of which is to emphasize that on this view, the enlightened individual does not merge with a distinct non-dual reality upon death (and so make an ontological transition from an individuated self to a non-dual state) but rather comes to realize something that allegedly is already and always has been the case – that *atman* is *Brahman*.

Suggestions for Further Reading

Baker, Lynn Rudder, *Persons and Bodies: A Constitution View* (Cambridge: Cambridge University Press, 2000).

Clack, Beverley, "Feminism and Human Mortality," in *Feminist Philosophy of Religion: Critical Readings*, ed. Pamela Sue Anderson and Beverley Clack (New York: Routledge, 2004), pp. 183–96.

Collins, Steven, *Selfless Persons* (New York: Cambridge University Press, 1982).

Deutsch, Eliot S., "Karma as a 'Convenient Fiction' in the Advaita Vedanta," *Philosophy East & West* 15:1 (1965): 3–12.

Dilley, Frank B., "Taking Consciousness Seriously: A Defense of Cartesian Dualism," *International Journal for Philosophy of Religion* 55 (2004): 135–53.

Fleming, Jess, "Self and (In)Finitude: Embodiment and the Other," *Journal of Chinese Philosophy* 29:2 (2002): 171–91.

Flew, Anthony, *The Logic of Mortality* (Oxford: Basil Blackwell, 1987).

Forrest, Peter, "Reincarnation without Survival of Memory or Character," *Philosophy East & West* 28:1 (1978): 91–7.

Hasker, William, *The Emergent Self* (Ithaca, NY: Cornell University Press, 1999).

Hick, John, *Death and Eternal Life* (Louisville, KY: Westminster/John Knox, 1994).

Jantzen, Grace M., "Do We Need Immortality?" *Modern Theology* 1:1 (1984): 33–44.

Mavrodes, George I., "The Life Everlasting and the Bodily Criterion of Identity," *Noûs* 11:1 (1977): 27–39.

Murphy, Nancey, *Bodies and Souls, or Spirited Bodies?* (New York: Cambridge University Press, 2006).

Neufeldt, Ronald W., *Karma and Rebirth: Post Classical Developments* (Albany: State University of New York Press, 1986).

Parfit, Derek, *Reasons and Persons* (Oxford: Oxford University Press, 1986).

Perrett, Roy W., "Rebirth," *Religious Studies* 23 (1987): 41–57.

Price, H. H., "Survival and the Idea of 'Another World,'" *Proceedings of the Society for Psychical Research* 50 (1953): 1–25.

Reichenbach, Bruce, *The Law of Karma* (Honolulu: University of Hawaii Press, 1990).

Siderits, Mark, *Personal Identity and Buddhist Philosophy* (Burlington, VT: Ashgate Publishing, 2003).

Swinburne, Richard, *The Evolution of the Soul* (New York: Oxford University Press, 1986).

van Inwagen, Peter, "Dualism and Materialism: Athens and Jerusalem?" *Faith and Philosophy* 12 (1995): 475–88.

Zimmerman, Dean, "The Compatibility of Materialism and Survival: The 'Falling' Elevator Model," *Faith and Philosophy* 16 (1999): 194–212.

45

A Naturalistic Case for Extinction

Linda Badham

Introduction

It is a popularly held view that science and religion are antithetical. And this view is supported by the sociological fact that leading scholars and scientists are significantly less likely to be Christian than other groups in society.[1] Yet even so, there are a number of very eminent scientists, and particularly physicists, who claim that there is no real conflict between their scientific and religious beliefs.[2] And many Christian apologists have drawn comfort from such claims in an age where the tide of secularism threatens to engulf the ancient citadel of Christian belief. However, I have my doubts as to whether or not Christianity is secure from attack by science in general on some of its most crucial tenets. And, in particular, what I want to argue in this chapter is that the implications of modern science are far more damaging to doctrines of life after death than many Christian writers have supposed.

Resurrection of the Body (This Flesh)

Although many might think that belief in the resurrection of this flesh at the end of time is now unthinkable, it has to be recognized that this is the form that orthodox Christian belief took from at least the second century onwards. Thus the Apostles' Creed affirms belief in the resurrection of the flesh; the Nicene Creed looks for the "upstanding of the dead bodies"; and the Christian Fathers were utterly explicit that the resurrection was definitely a physical reconstitution.[3] Moreover, such belief is still Catholic orthodoxy: a recent *Catholic Catechism for Adults* declares that each one of us will rise one day "the same person he was, in the same flesh made living by the same spirit."[4] And Wolfhart Pannenberg, one of the most influential continental Protestant theologians of our day, also affirms belief in the traditional doctrine.[5] Hence it seems reasonable to suppose that this form of

"A Naturalistic Case for Extinction" by Linda Badham, in *Death and Immortality in the Religions of the World*, ed. Linda and Paul Badham (St Paul, MN: Paragon House Publishers, 1987), pp. 158–66; 168–9. Reprinted by permission of Paragon House Publishers.

[1] A sociological survey quoted by Daniel C. Batson and W. Larry Ventis in *The Religious Experience: A Social-Psychological Perspective* (Oxford: Oxford University Press, 1982), p. 225.

[2] See, for example, John Polkinghorne, *The Way the World Is* (London: SPCK, 1983); and Russel Stannard, *Science and the Renewal of Belief* (London: SCM, 1982).

[3] Paul Badham, *Christian Beliefs about Life after Death* (London: SPCK, 1978), pp. 47ff.

[4] R. Lawler, D. W. Whuerl and T. C. Lawler, *The Teaching of Christ: A Catholic Catechism for Adults* (Dublin: Veritas, 1976), p. 544.

[5] Cf. Wolfhart Pannenberg, *Jesus-God and Man* (London: SCM, 1968), pp. 82ff.

resurrection belief is still held among Christians. Yet a minimal knowledge of modern science seems sufficient to undermine it completely.

First, there is the problem that "this flesh" is only temporarily mine. I am not like a machine or artifact, which keeps its atoms and molecules intact throughout its existence, save for those lost by damage or replaced during repair. Rather, I am a biological system in dynamic equilibrium (more or less) with my environment, in that I exchange matter with that environment continually. As J. D. Bernal writes, "It is probable that none of us have more than a few atoms with which we started life, and that even as adults we probably change most of the material of our bodies in a matter of a few months."[6] Thus it might prove an extremely difficult business to resurrect "this" flesh at the end of time, for the atoms that will constitute me at the moment of death will return to the environment and will doubtless become part of innumerable other individuals. Augustine discussed the case of cannibals having to restore the flesh they had "borrowed" as an exception.[7] But in the light of our current knowledge, shared atoms would seem the rule rather than the exception.

Morever, there is the further problem that even if the exact atoms that constituted me at death could all be reassembled without leaving some other people bereft of vital parts, then the reconstituted body would promptly expire again. For whatever caused the systems failure in my body, which led to my death originally, would presumably still obtain if the body exactly as it was prior to death were remade. But perhaps we can overcome this problem with a fairly simple proviso: the resurrection body should be identical to the body that died, malfunctions apart. After all, it might be said, we have no difficulty in accepting our television set returned in good working order from the repair shop after a breakdown as one and the same television set that we took to be repaired, even though some or even several of its components have been replaced. But people are not television sets. What counts

as malfunction? Increasing age usually brings some diminution in physical and mental powers. Are all these to be mended too? How much change can a body take and still be the same person? Nor is it possible to suggest that the resurrection environment might be such as to reverse the effects of aging and disease. For this move implies such a great change in the properties of the matter that is "this flesh" as to make it dubious whether "this" flesh really had been resurrected. The more one actually fills out the vague notion of the resurrection of the same flesh that perished, the more problems arise.

And even if the problem of reconstituting each one of us to the same (healthy) flesh he was (or might have been) could be overcome, there would remain the question of where we could all be resurrected. There is a space problem. If the countless millions of human beings who have ever lived and may live in the future were all to be resurrected on this earth, then the overcrowding would be acute. Now there are at least two theological maneuvers that we could make to circumvent this embarrassment. If we want to retain resurrection on this earth, then we might say that only the chosen will be resurrected and thereby limit the numbers. But that solution raises insuperable problems about the morality of a God who would behave in such a way.[8] Alternatively, it might be argued that the resurrection will be to a new life in heaven and not to eternal life on earth. But in that case it has to be noted that resurrected bodies would need a biological environment markedly similar to the one we now live in. This leads to the implication that heaven would have to be a planet, or series of planets, all suitable for human life. The further one pushes this picture, the more bizarre and religiously unsatisfying it becomes.[9]

In sum, then, a little knowledge of the biochemistry of living organisms, together with a brief consideration of the physicochemical conditions that such organisms require if they are to live, ought to have rendered the traditional notion of literal bodily resurrection unthinkable.

[6] J. D. Bernal, *Science in History*, vol. 3 (Harmondsworth: Penguin, 1969), p. 902.
[7] Augustine, *City of God*, bk 22, chap. 20.
[8] Cf. Paul and Linda Badham, *Immortality or Extinction* (London: SPCK, 1984), pp. 58ff.
[9] Cf. Paul Badham, *Christian Beliefs about Life after Death*, chap. 4.

Resurrection of the Body (Transformed)

It might be argued, as John Polkinghorne claims, that all this is irrelevant: "We know that there is nothing significant about the material which at any one time constitutes our body. . . . It is the pattern they [the atoms] form which persists and evolves. We are liberated, therefore, from the quaint medieval picture of the reassembly of the body from its scattered components. In very general terms it is not difficult to imagine the pattern recreated (the body resurrected) in some other world."[10]

At this point we should note that the doctrine being proposed here has shifted in a very significant way. The old doctrine of resurrection of the flesh guaranteed personal survival because the resurrected body was physically identical with the one laid in the grave. Physical continuity supplied the link between the person who died and the one who was resurrected. But Polkinghorne's version of the resurrection envisages recreation of a *pattern* in some other world. This is open to a host of philosophical problems about the sense in which the recreation of a replica can count as the survival of the person who died.[11]

What would we say, for example, if the replica were created *before* my death? Would I then die happily knowing that someone was around to carry on, as it were, in my place? Would I think to myself that the replica really was me? Consider the possibility of cloning. Let us imagine that science reaches a stage where a whole adult human individual can be regenerated from a few cells of a person in such a way that the original – Jones I – and the copy – Jones II – are genetically identical, and that the clone knows everything that Jones I knows. We may imagine that the purpose of doing this is to give a healthy body to house the thoughts of the physically ailing, but brilliant Jones I. Now does Jones I die secure in the knowledge that he will live again? I would suggest that he might feel relieved to know that his life's work would carry on, and that his project would be entrusted to one incomparably suited to continue with it. He might also feel exceptionally close to Jones II and be deeply concerned for his welfare. But the other would not *be* him. In the end, Jones I would be dead and the other, Jones II, would carry on in his place. As far as Jones I was concerned, he himself would not live again, even though most other people would treat Jones II as if here were Jones I rejuvenated.

If these intuitions are correct, then they suggest that whatever it is that we count as essential for being one and the same person, it is not a "pattern." And I would suggest that all theories of resurrection that speak of our rising with new and transformed bodies fall foul of what I term the replica problem. For without some principle of continuity between the person who died and the one who was resurrected, then what was resurrected would only be something very similar to the one who died, a replica, and not a continuation of the dead person.

The Soul

Such considerations have led theologians at least from Aquinas onwards to argue that any tenable resurrection belief hinges on a concept of the soul. For even if we hold to a belief in the resurrection of some "new and glorious body," then we need the soul to avoid the replica problem. There has to be a principle of continuity between this world and the next if what is raised to new life really is one and the same person as the one who died. Moreover, this principle of continuity must encapsulate enough of the real "me" for both "old" and "new" versions to count as the same person. Might this requirement be fulfilled if we were to espouse a dualist concept of the person and say, with Descartes, that my essential personhood is to be identified with my mind, that is, with the subject of conscious experiencing?[12] However, I want to argue that not even this move is sufficient to rescue the Christian claim.

First, there are all the practical problems of which contemporary dualists are very much aware. Our personal experience and emotions are intimately linked to our body chemistry.

---

[10]   John Polkinghorne, *The Way the World Is*, p. 93.
[11]   Cf. Bernard Williams, *Problems of the Self* (Cambridge: Cambridge University Press, 1978).
[12]   Cf. René Descartes, *Discoures 4*. [. . .]

Indeed, the limits to what we are able to think at all are set by our genetic endowment; so that one man's physicochemical equipment enables him to be a brilliant mathematician, while another's lack condemns him to lifelong imbecility. If our diet is imbalanced and inadequate, or if certain of our organs are malfunctioning, then our bodies may be starved of essential nutrients or poisoned by the excessive production of some hormone. In such cases, the whole personality may be adversely affected. The "subject of my conscious experiences" would seem to be very much at the mercy of my physicochemical constitution.

A second difficulty lies in deciding which organisms count as having souls and which do not. And if God is to give eternal life to the former class and not to the latter, then even He has to be able to draw a line somewhere, and that non-arbitrarily. The problem occurs both in considering the evolution of the species Homo sapiens and the individual development of human beings. Even if we ignore the problem of nonhuman animals and restrict the possibility of possessing a soul to humans, there are still insuperable difficulties.

Consider first the evolutionary pathway that led from the early mammals to man. Somewhere along that line we would be fairly secure in denying that such and such a creature had any awareness of self. And it is also true to say that most normal adult humans possess such an awareness. But between these extremes lies a gray area. To have a nonarbitrary dividing line, it has to be possible for us to decide (at least in principle) where a sharp division can be drawn between the last generation of anthropoid apes and the first generation of true Homo sapiens. Are we to suppose that in one generation there were anthropoid apes who gave birth to the next generation of true Homo sapiens, and that the changes between one generation and the next were so great that the children counted in God's eyes as the bearers of immortality while their parents were "mere animals"? Yet unless dualists are prepared to fly in the face of evolutionary biology, how can they avoid this unpalatable conclusion?

[. . .]

There are, in addition, some further objections of a more purely philosophical nature, which I think need mentioning at this point. The subject of my conscious experiencing is singularly unconvincing as a principle of continuity that guarantees persistence of the "same" person through change. Moreover, defining the "real" me in this way actually misses a lot of what most of us would want to say is a part of the "real" me. I shall begin by discussing the question of a principle of continuity.

One great problem with my awareness of self is its lack of persistence, its transitoriness. My stream of consciousness is far from being a constant or even ever-present (though varying) flow. When I am unconscious, in a dreamless sleep, or even in a vacant mood, it just is not there. Yet I do not cease to exist whenever my conscious mind is, as it were, switched off temporarily. Secondly, we have to face the problem that this awareness of self is ever-changing. What I was as a child is very different from what I, as I am in myself, am today; and if I live to be an old lady, doubtless the subject of my conscious experiences will look back with a mixture of wry amusement and nostalgia at that other her of forty years ago. Now it might be thought that this problem of continual change is no greater a problem for the notion of same "self" than it is for the notion of same "body" since the body is also in a continual state of flux. But I would suggest that what supplies continuity through change is matter. It may be that all my constituent atoms will have changed in the next few months, but they will not have all changed simultaneously. Moreover, the physically-based blueprints from the chemistry that keeps my body going are passed on from one generation of cells to another in a direct physical line of succession. Thus, I would argue that what keeps the subject of my conscious experiencing belonging to one and the same person is this physical continuity.

The essential requirement of physical continuity can be illustrated if we return to the clone example. Let us modify the thought experiment a little, and makes Jones II a copy of a perfectly healthy Jones I. And let us also stipulate that the two Joneses emerge from the cloning laboratory not knowing who is the original and who the copy. In other words, Jones I and II are, seemingly, wholly similar. Neither they nor we can tell which is which, unless we trace the histories of the two bodies to ascertain which grew from a fertilized ovum and which developed as the result of cloning. Now if we apply the implications of this to the question of what might live again after death, we see that being "the subject of my conscious experiences" is not sufficient to guarantee that I am one and the same person as the one who died. For what the clone example shows is that both Jones I and Jones II may believe (or doubt) equally that he really is the same person as Jones I while he relies solely on his personal experience of himself as Jones. Only when he traces the path of physical continuity can he know whether he truly is Jones I or not. (Of course, we might want to say that where there had been one person, Jones, there were now two distinct individuals, both of whom were physically continuous with the original. But in that case the possibility of defining "same person" in terms of "same stream of consciousness" does not even arise.)

Thus I contend, a dualist definition of what I really am fails because it cannot provide adequate criteria for recognizing the "same" person through change. I can think of no other case where we would even be tempted to accept something as transitory and ever-changing as "consciousness of self" to be the essential criterion for defining what it is that an entity has to retain if it is to count as remaining the same individual through change.

I move on now to the problems that arise from the restrictedness of defining me as the subject of my conscious experiences. A great deal of what I am does not involve my conscious thoughts at all, even when I am fully awake. Take the familiar example of driving a car. When I was learning to drive, I certainly employed a great amount of conscious effort. But nowadays my conscious thoughts are fairly free to attend to other matters when I am driving, even though, of course, intense conscious attention instantly returns if danger threatens. I certainly do not want to say "my body" drove here. *I* drove here, even though most of the time the subject of my conscious experiences was not much involved.

Moreover, we cannot ignore the possibility that the conscious subject might actually fail to recognize a significant part of all that I really am. To exemplify the point: imagine someone who believes himself to be a great wit, when most of his colleagues find him a crashing bore. If he were to arrive in the resurrection world without his familiar characteristics – clumsiness of speech, repetitiveness, triviality, self-centeredness – would he really be the person who had died? Yet could he bring these characteristics with him if the subject of his conscious experiences, the "real" him, was wholly unaware of having been like this?

In sum, what I have been arguing against dualism is that this concept of the soul cannot bear the weight put on it. Yet it has to bear this weight if it is to be the sine qua non of my surviving bodily death. Considerations from the natural sciences and philosophy, and even religious implications, combine to render it far from convincing. [. . .]

Conclusion

When Christianity was originally formulated, man's entire world view was very different from our current beliefs. It was plausible to think in terms of a three-decker universe in which the center of God's interest was this Earth and its human population. The idea that God would raise man from the dead to an eternal life of bliss fitted neatly into this schema. However, the erosion of this picture, beginning from at least the time of Copernicus and Galileo, has cut the traditional Christian hope adrift from the framework of ideas in which it was originally formulated. What I have tried to show in this chapter is that various attempts, which have been made to try to accommodate some form of resurrection/immortality belief within our current world view, are inadequate and fail. I conclude, then, that a due consideration of man's place in nature leads us to the view that he belongs there and nowhere else.

46

Brain Science and the Soul

Donald MacKay

Mechanistic brain science proceeds on the working assumption that every bodily event has a physical cause in the prior state of the central nervous system. Traditional moral and religious thought, on the other hand, has always presupposed that some at least of our behaviour is determined by our thinking and deciding. This apparent conflict has given rise to suggestions that unless some parts of our nervous system are found to be open to non-physical influences, brain science will effectively debunk all talk of man as a spiritual being, and oblige us to accept a purely materialistic view of our nature. Many people seem to expect a battle to be fought between religion and the neurosciences like that waged by some theologians in the nineteenth century against evolutionary biology.

How justified is this impression? It is true that the seventeenth-century French philosopher–mathematician René Descartes held that the mind or soul would be powerless to influence bodily action unless some part of the brain could act as a transmitter–receiver for its controlling signals. He considered that the pineal gland, in the middle of the head, was ideally suited to the purpose. "In man", he says,

the brain is also acted on by the soul which has some power to change cerebral impressions just as those impressions in their turn have the power to arouse thoughts which do not depend on the will.... Only [figures of excitation] traced in spirits on the surface of [the pineal] gland, where the seat of imagination and common sense [the coming together of the senses] is ... should be taken to be ... the forms or images that the rational soul will consider directly when, being united to this machine, it will imagine or will sense any object.[1]

In recent years the neurophysiologist Sir John Eccles and the philosopher Sir Karl Popper have advanced theories of the "interaction" of mind and brain, which, though they differ in important respects from that of Descartes, agree with him that the brain must be open to non-physical influences if mental activity is to be effective.

At first sight this might indeed seem obvious common sense; but a simple counter-example throws some doubt on the logic of the argument. We are nowadays accustomed to the idea that a computer can be set up to solve a mathematical equation. The mathematician means by this that

"Brain Science and the Soul" by Donald MacKay in *The Oxford Companion to the Mind*, ed. Richard L. Gregory (New York: Oxford University Press, 1987), pp. 723–5.

[1]   R. Descartes, "The Treatise of Man," in *The Philosophical Writings of Descartes*, Vol. 1, ed. J. Cottingham, R. Stoothoff, and D. Murdoch (New York: Cambridge University Press, 1985), p. 106.

the behaviour of the computer is *determined* by the equation he wants to solve; were it not so, it would be of no interest to him. On the other hand, if we were to ask a computer engineer to explain what is happening in the computer, he could easily demonstrate that every physical event in it was fully *determined* (same word) by the laws of physics as applied to the physical components. Any appearance of conflict here would be quite illusory. There is no need for a computer to be "open to non-physical influences" in order that its behaviour may be determined by a (non-physical) equation *as well as* by the laws of physics. The two "claims to determination" here are not mutually exclusive; rather they are *complementary*.

The analogy is of course a limited one. We (unlike our computing machines) are conscious agents. The data of our conscious experience have first priority among the facts about our world, since it is only through our conscious experience that we learn about anything else. Our consciousness is thus not a matter of convention (like the mathematical significance of the computer's activity) but a matter of fact which we would be lying to deny. Nevertheless the logical point still holds. If we think of our mental activity as embodied in our brain activity, in the sense in which the solving of an equation can be embodied in the workings of a computer, then there is a clear parallel sense in which our behaviour can be determined by that mental activity, regardless of the extent to which our brain activity is determined by physical laws. The two explanations, in mental and in physical terms, are not rivals but complementary.

Note that we are here thinking of mental activity as *embodied in* brain activity rather than *identical with* brain activity. The latter is a notion favoured by what is called "materialist monism", at the opposite extreme from the "interactionism" of Eccles and Popper. This would simply identify "mind" and "brain", and would go so far as to attribute "thinking" and other mental activities to the matter of which the brain is composed. The objection to this extreme view can be

understood by once again considering the example of a computer. It is true that the solving of an equation is not a separate series of events, running in parallel with the physical happenings in the machine. It is rather the mathematical significance of one and the same series of events, whose physical aspect is well explained by the engineer. On the other hand it would be nonsensical on these grounds to identify equations with computers as physical objects, or to attribute mathematical properties (such as "convergence" or "being quadratic") to the physical matter in which the equation is embodied.

By the same token, even if we regard our thinking and deciding as a "mental" or "inner" aspect of one and the same (mysterious) activity that the neuroscientist can study from the outside as brain activity, this gives no rational grounds for taking the material aspect as more "real" than the mental, still less for identifying the two and speaking of thinking and deciding as attributes of matter. This would be a confusion of categories belonging to different logical levels, for which nothing in brain science offers any justification.

It might appear that thinking of our conscious experience as "embodied" in our brains would still be incompatible with the Christian concept of "life after death". What we have seen in the case of the computer, however, shows that there need be no conflict. The physical destruction of a computer is certainly the end of *that particular embodiment* of the equation it was solving. But it leaves entirely open the possibility that the same equation could be re-embodied, perhaps in a quite different medium, if the mathematician so desires. By the same logic, mechanistic brain science would seem to raise equally little objection to the hope of eternal life expressed in biblical Christian doctrine, with its characteristic emphasis on the "resurrection" (not to be confused with resuscitation) of the body. The destruction of our present embodiment sets no logical barrier to *our* being re-embodied, perhaps in a quite different medium, if our Creator so wishes.

47

The Resurrection of the Dead

Stephen T. Davis

I

One traditional Christian view of survival of death runs, in outline form, something like this: On some future day all the dead will be bodily raised, both the righteous and the unrighteous alike, to be judged by God; and the guarantee and model of the general resurrection (that is, the raising of the dead in the last days) is the already accomplished resurrection of Jesus Christ from the dead.

My aim in this paper is to explain and defend this basic view of resurrection. There are many ways it might be understood, of course, and perhaps more than one is coherent and, even from a Christian point of view, plausible. I shall defend one particular interpretation of the theory – an interpretation advocated by very many of the church fathers, especially second century fathers, as well as by Augustine and Aquinas.

It may help to clarify matters if I first provide a brief map of where we will be going in this paper. After introducing the topic I will discuss in turn what I take to be the three most important claims made by the version of the theory I wish to defend. Then I will consider one typical aspect of the traditional theory that has important philosophical as well as theological ramifications, namely, the notion that our resurrection bodies will consist of the same matter as do our present earthly bodies. Finally, since the version of the theory I wish to defend envisions a period of existence in a disembodied state, I will defend the theory against some of the arguments of those contemporary philosophers who find the notion of disembodied existence incoherent.

II

Now there are several ways in which the basic concept of resurrection sketched in the opening paragraph can be fleshed out. One option is to understand the nature of the human person, and hence the nature of resurrection, in a basically materialist or physicalist way. Perhaps human beings are essentially material objects, perhaps some vision of identity theory or functionalism is true. Now I am attracted to this option, and hold it to be a usable notion for Christians. But having defended elsewhere a physicalist conception of survival of death through resurrection, I will discuss it no further here.[1]

"The Resurrection of the Dead" by Stephen T. Davis in *Death and Afterlife*, ed. Stephen T. Davis (New York: St Martin's Press, 1989), pp. 119–44.
[1]   See Stephen T. Davis, "Is Personal Identity Retained in the Resurrection?" *Modern Theology*, 2(4)(1986).

Another option is to collapse talk of resurrection into talk of the immortality of the soul. A closely related move (and a popular one in recent theology) is to interpret resurrection in a spiritual rather than bodily sense (if this in the end differs significantly from immortality). Such a view will doubtless be based on some version of mind–body (or soul–body) dualism. Let us define dualism as the doctrine which says that (1) human beings consist of both material bodies and immaterial souls; and (2) the soul is the essence of the person (the real you is your soul, not your body). It then can be added that the body corrupts at death and eventually ceases to exist but the soul is essentially immortal.

It is surprising (to me at least) that so many twentieth century Christian thinkers are tempted toward some such notion as this. For it is quite clear, both in scripture and tradition, that classicial dualism is not the Christian position. For example, the biblical view is not that the soul is the essence of the person and is only temporarily housed or even imprisoned in a body; human beings seem rather to be understood in scripture as psycho-physical entities, that is, as unities of body and soul. And the notion that the body is essentially evil and must be escaped from (an idea often associated with versions of classical dualism) was condemned by virtually every orthodox Christian thinker who discussed death and resurrection in the first two hundred years after the apostolic age; the Christian idea is rather that the body was created by God and is good; the whole person, body and soul alike, is what is to be saved. Finally, the biblical notion is not that we survive death because immortality is simply a natural property of souls; if we survive death it is because God miraculously saves us; apart from God's intervention death would mean annihilation for us. Thus Irenaeus says: "Our survival forever comes from his greatness, not from our nature".[2]

It would be interesting to discuss this option further, and especially to ask why so many recent and contemporary Christian theologians are drawn toward it, how they might distinguish "spiritual resurrection" from immortality of the soul, and how they might defend the theory against criticisms such as those just noted. However, I will not do so in this paper. As noted above, my aim here is rather to explore and defend a third way of understanding the traditional Christian notion of resurrection, a theory virtually all (but not quite all) of the church fathers who discussed resurrection held in one form or another.[3] I will call this theory "temporary disembodiment".

This theory of resurrection is based on a view of human nature which says that human beings are essentially material bodies *and* immaterial souls; the soul is separable from the body, but neither body or soul alone (that is without the other) constitutes a complete human being. Thus Pseudo-Justin Martyr says:

> Is the soul by itself man? No; but the soul of man. Would the body be called man? No, but it is called the body of man. If, then, neither of these is by itself man, but that which is made up of the two together is called man, and God has called *man* to life and resurrection, He has called not a part, but the whole, which is the soul and the body.[4]

What this theory says, then, is that human beings are typically and normally psycho-physical beings, that the soul can exist for a time apart from the body and retain personal identity, but that this disembodied existence is only temporary and constitutes a radically attenuated and incomplete form of human existence.

I call the theory temporary disembodiment because it envisions the following scenario: We human beings are born, live for a time as psycho-physical beings, and then die; after death we exist in an incomplete state as immaterial souls;

[2] Cyril Richardson (ed.) *Early Christian Fathers* (Philadelphia: The Westminster Press, 1953), p. 389.
[3] See Harry A. Wolfson, "Immortality and Resurrection in the Philosophy of the Church Fathers", in Krister Stendahl (ed.) *Immortality and Resurrection* (New York: Macmillan, 1965), pp. 64–72. See also Lynn Boliek, *The Resurrection of the Flesh* (Grand Rapids, Michigan: Wm B. Eerdmans, 1962).
[4] Alexander Roberts and James Donaldson (eds) *The Ante-Nicene Fathers* (New York: Charles Scribner's Sons, 1899), pp. 297–8.

and some time later in the eschaton God miraculously raises our bodies from the ground, transforms them into "glorified bodies", and reunites them with our souls, thus making us complete and whole again.

[. . .]

[T]he problem of personal identity after death seems in one regard more manageable on this theory than on at least some others, for there is in this theory no temporal gap in the existence of persons (although there is a gap in their existence as complete, unified persons). There is no moment subsequent to our births in which you and I simply do not exist – we exist as soul-bodies or as mere souls at every moment till eternity.

III

There are three main aspects of temporary disembodiment that require discussion both from a philosophical and a theological perspective. Let me now consider them in turn. The first is the notion that after death the soul exists for a time, that is, until the resurrection, in an intermediate state without the body. The second is the notion that at the time of the parousia the body will be raised from the ground and reunited with the soul. And the third is the notion that the body will then be transformed into what is called a "glorified body".

The first main claim of temporary disembodiment, then, is that after death the soul temporarily exists without the body. This differs from physicalist concepts of resurrection on which the person does not exist at all in the period between death and resurrection. Temporary disembodiment need not be based on classical dualism as defined earlier, but is based on one tenet of classical dualism, namely, the claim that human beings consist (or in this case at least normally consist) of both material bodies and immaterial souls. (The soul is not said to be the essence of the person, however, and is said to survive death not because immortality is one

of its natural properties but because God causes it to survive death.)[5]

Now almost all Christians believe that there is some kind of interim state of the person between death and resurrection. But beyond this point there are very many theological differences. [. . .] I will argue [. . .] that the soul is conscious in the interim state. [. . .]

The state of being without a body is an abnormal state of the human person. This is one of the clear differences between temporary disembodiment and immortality of the soul, for the second doctrine (at least in versions of it influenced by Plato) entails that disembodiment is the true or proper or best state of the human person. On the theory we are considering, however, the claim is that a disembodied soul lacks many of the properties and abilities that are normal for and proper to human persons. Disembodied existence is a kind of minimal existence.

Which properties typical of embodied human persons will disembodied souls have and which will they lack? Clearly they will lack those properties that essentially involve corporeality. They will possess no spatial location, for example, at least not in the space-time manifold with which we are familiar. They will not be able to perceive their surroundings (using the spatial word "surroundings" in a stretched sense) – not at least in the ways in which we perceive our surroundings (that is, through the eyes, ears, and so on). They will not be able to experience bodily pains and pleasures. They will not be able to engage in bodily activities. Taking a walk, getting dressed, playing catch – these sorts of activities will be impossible.

But if by the word "soul" we mean in part the constellation of those human activities that would typically be classified as "mental", then the claim that our souls survive death entails the claim that our mental abilities and properties survive death. This means that human persons in the interim state can be spoken of as having experiences, beliefs, wishes, knowledge, memory, inner (rather than bodily) feelings, thoughts, language (assuming memory or earthly existence) – in short, just about everything that makes up what we call personality. H. H. Price, in his classic

---

5 Wolfson, op. cit., pp. 56–60, 63–4.

article "Survival and the Idea of 'Another World' ", argues convincingly that disembodied souls can also be aware of each other's existence, can communicate with each other telepathically, and can have dreamlike (rather than bodily) perceptions of their world.[6]

But Aquinas argues that the disembodied existence of the person in the interim state is so deficient that attainment of ultimate happiness is impossible. No one in whom some perfection is lacking is ultimately happy, for in such a state there will always be unfilfilled desires. It is contrary to the nature of the soul to be without the body, Aquinas says, and he takes this to mean both that the disembodied state must only be temporary, and that the true bliss of the human person is only attained after re-embodiment, that is, in the general resurrection. He says: "Man cannot achieve his ultimate happiness unless the soul be once again united to the body".[7]

IV

The second main claim of the theory that I am calling temporary disembodiment is that at the general resurrection the body will be raised from the ground and reunited with the soul. As the second century writer Athenagoras says:

There must certainly be a resurrection of bodies whether dead or even quite corrupted, and the same men as before must come to be again. The law of nature appoints an end . . . for those very same men who lived in a previous existence, and it is impossible for the same men to come together again if the same bodies are not given

back to the same souls. Now the same soul cannot recover the same body in any other way than by resurrection.[8]

As Athenagoras stresses, the idea is that each person's selfsame body will be raised; it will not be a different and brand new body but the old body. Aquinas (echoing the argument of very many of the fathers) notes the reason for this: "If the body of the man who rises is not to be composed of the flesh and bones which now compose it, the man who rises will not be numerically the same man".[9] Furthermore, in the resurrection there will be only one soul per body and only one body per soul. As Augustine says: "Each single soul shall possess its own body".[10] Otherwise (for example, if souls split and animate more than one body or if multiple identical copies of one body are animated by different souls) the problem of personal identity is unsolvable, and the Christian hope that we will live after death is incoherent.

The fathers and scholastics insisted, then, that both body and soul must be present or else the person does not exist. "A man cannot be said to exist as such when the body is dissolved or completely scattered, even though the soul remain by itself" – so says Athenagoras.[11] And Aquinas agrees: "My soul is not I, and if only souls are saved, I am not saved, nor is any man".[12] Thus the Christian hope of survival is not the hope that our souls will survive death (though on temporary disembodiment that is one important aspect of it), but rather the hope that one day God will miraculously raise our bodies and reunite them with our souls.

What is it, then, that guarantees personal identity in the resurrection? What is it that

[6]   H. H. Price, "Survival and the Idea of 'Another World'," in John Donnelly (ed.) *Language, Metaphysics, and Death* (New York: Fordham University Press, 1978), pp. 176–95. I do not wish to commit myself entirely to Price's theory; among others, John Hick has detected difficulties in it. See *Death and Eternal Life* (New York: Harper & Row 1976), pp. 265–77. But Price's main point – that disembodied survival of death is possible – seems to me correct.

[7]   Thomas Aquinas, *Summa Contra Gentiles*, trans. by Charles J. O'Neil; Book IV (Notre Dame, Indiana: The University of Notre Dame Press, 1975), IV, 79.

[8]   Athenagoras, *Embassy for Christians and the Resurrection of the Dead*, trans. Joseph H. Crehan, S. J. (London: Longmans, Green, 1956), pp. 115–16.

[9]   Aquinas, op. cit., IV, 84.

[10]   Augustine, *The Enchiridion on Faith, Hope, and Love* (Chicago: Henry Regnery, 1961), LXXXVII.

[11]   Athenagoras, op. cit., p. 115.

[12]   Cited in P. T. Geach, *God and the Soul* (London: Routledge & Kegan Paul, 1969), pp. 22, 40.

ensures that it will really be *us* in the kingdom of God and not, say, clever replicas of us? Aquinas argues as follows: since human beings consist of bodies and souls, and since both souls and the matter of which our bodies consist survive death, personal identity is secured when God collects the scattered matter, miraculously reconstitutes it a human body, and reunites it with the soul.[13] And this surely seems a powerful argument. If God one day succeeds in doing these very things, personal identity will be secure. It will be us and not our replicas who will be the denizens of the kingdom of God.

V

The third main claim of temporary disembodiment is that in the resurrection the old body will be transformed into a "glorified body" with certain quite new properties. This claim is based primarily on Paul's discussion of the resurrection in I Corinthians 15, and secondarily on the unusual properties the risen Jesus is depicted as having in some of the accounts of the resurrection appearances (for example, the apparent ability of the risen Jesus in John 20 to appear in a room despite the doors being locked). In the Pauline text just mentioned the apostle notes that some ask, "How are the dead raised? With what kind of body do they come?" His answer is an argument to the effect that the new "glorified" or "spiritual" body (*soma pneumatikon*) is a transformation of the old body rather than a *de novo* creation (much as a stalk of grain is a transformation of a seed of grain, that is, it exists because of changes that have occurred in the seed and can be considered a new state of the grain). Further, Paul argues, while the old or natural body is physical, perishable, mortal, and sown in weakness and dishonour, the glorified body is spiritual, imperishable, immortal, and sown in strength and honour. The first body is

in the image of the man of dust; the second body is in the image of the man of heaven.

The term "spiritual body" might be misleading; it should not be taken as a denial of corporeality or as a last-minute capitulation to some version of the immortality of the soul as opposed to bodily resurrection. By this term Paul means not a body whose stuff or matter is spiritual (whatever that might mean) or an immaterial existence of some sort; rather he means a body that is fully obedient to and dominant by the Holy Spirit. Paul says: "Flesh and blood cannot inherit the kingdom of God" (I Corinthians 15:50). What enters the kingdom of heaven, then, is not this present weak and mortal body of flesh and blood but the new glorified body. This new body is a physical body (Paul's use of the word *soma* implies as much),[14] and is materially related to the old body (taking seriously Paul's simile of the seed), but is a body transformed in such ways as make it fit to live in God's presence. If by the term "physical object" we mean an entity that has spatio-temporal location and is capable of being empirically measured, tested, or observed in some sense, then my argument is that the new body of which Paul speaks is a physical object.

Temporary disembodiment, then, entails that human souls can animate both normal earthly bodies and glorified resurrection bodies. Continuity between the two bodies is provided by the presence of both the same soul and the same matter in both bodies. Thus Augustine says:

Nor does the earthly material out of which men's mortal bodies are created ever perish; but though it may crumble into dust and ashes, or be dissolved into vapours and exhalations, though it may be transformed into the substance of other bodies, or dispersed into the elements, though it should become food for beasts or men, and be changed into their flesh, it returns in a moment of time to that human

---

[13] Aquinas, op. cit., IV 81.

[14] See Robert H. Gundry, *Soma in Biblical Theology. With Emphasis on Pauline Anthropology* (Cambridge: Cambridge University Press, 1976), pp. 164ff. For this and other points made in this paragraph, see C. F. D. Moule, "St Paul and Dualism: The Pauline Concept of Resurrection", *New Testament Studies*, 12 (2) (1966), and Ronald J. Sider, "The Pauline Conception of the Resurrection Body in I Corinthians XV. 35–54", *New Testament Studies*, 21 (3) (1975).

soul which animated it at the first and which caused it to become man, and to live and grow.[15]

The matter of our present bodies may be arranged differently in the resurrection, he says, but the matter will be restored.

Many of the theologians of the early church and of the medieval period stress also the perfection of the glorified body. It will be free of every bodily defect. It will be immune to evil because fully controlled by the spirit of God. It will not suffer. It will not grow old or die. It will have "agility" – which is presumably an ability like that of the risen Jesus to come and go at will, unimpeded by things like walls and doors. It will exist in a state of fulfilled desire. It will need no material food and drink, but will be nourished by the elements of the eucharist.[16]

VI

Is the picture of resurrection just presented coherent? Is it plausible? The main objections that have been raised against it in recent philosophy revolve around the problem of personal identity. Some philosophers argue that so far as disembodied existence is concerned this problem cannot be solved. That is, they argue that if some immaterial aspect of me survives death it will not be me that survives death. Since the view of survival of death I am defending essentially involves a period of disembodied existence, I had best try to defend the view against these sorts of objections. But a prior problem must be considered first – whether the fathers and scholastics were correct in their strong claim (I will call this claim "the Patristic theory") that if it is to be me in the kingdom of God the very matter of my original earthly body must be raised. Having discussed the point, I will then turn in section VII to the arguments of those philosophers who oppose the notion of disembodied existence because of the problem of personal identity.

Why did Aquinas and the fathers who influenced him insist that the same matter of my old body must be raised? Let us see if we can

construct an argument on their behalf. Like many arguments in the area of personal identity, it involves a puzzle case. Suppose that I own a defective personal computer which I rashly decide to try to repair myself. Having taken it apart (there are now, say, 60 separate computer components scattered on my work bench), I find that I am unable to repair it. I call the outlet that sold me the computer, and the manager suggests I simply bring all 60 components to that office for repair. I do so, but through a horrible series of misunderstandings and errors, the 60 pieces of the computer are then sent to 60 different addresses around the country. That constitutes the heart of my story, but there are two separate endings to it. *Ending number one*: it takes three years for everything to be sorted out, for the pieces to be located and collected in one place, for the repairs to be made, and for the parts to be reassembled and restored, in full working order, to my desk. *Ending number two*: After three years of trying in vain to locate and collect the scattered pieces, the manager gives up, collects 60 similar parts, assembles them, and the resulting computer ends up on my desk.

Now I do not wish to raise the interesting question whether my computer *existed* during the three-year period. I am interested in the related question whether the computer now located on my desk is *the same* computer as the one that was there three years ago. And so far as ending number one is concerned, it seems most natural to affirm that the computer I now possess is indeed the same computer as the one that I possessed before. The computer may or may not have had a gap in its existence, that is, a period when it did not exist, but it seems clear that identity has here been preserved. And so far as ending number two is concerned, it seems most natural to deny that the computer I now possess is the same computer as the one that I possessed before. Furthermore, we would doubtless insist on this denial even if each of the 60 components the manager used to construct the computer I now possess was qualitatively identical to the 60 old components. What I now have is a qualitatively similar but numerically different computer.

[15]   Augustine, op. cit., LXXXVIII.
[16]   See Irenaeus, in Richardson, op. cit., p. 388; Augustine, op. cit., XCI; Aquinas, op. cit., IV 83–7.

Now I doubt that the church fathers often pondered personal identity test cases involving computers, and it is obvious that personal computers are different from human beings in many striking ways. But it was perhaps *the sort* of insight arrived at above that led them to take the strong stand they took on the resurrection. Only if God reassembles the very particles of which my body once consisted will it be me who is raised. Otherwise, that is, if other particles are used, the result will be what we would call a replica of me rather than me.

But despite the above argument, does it still not seem that Aquinas and the fathers in their strong stand have made the solution to the problem of personal identity more difficult than it need be? Even granting the point that some of the particles of the matter of which our bodies consist will endure for the requisite number of years, why insist that God must re-collect it, that is, that very matter, in the resurrection? For surely in the interim state it will be us (and not soul-like replicas of us) who will exist without any body at all; surely the fathers and scholastics insist on this much. Thus the soul alone must guarantee personal identity; what philosophers call the memory criterion (which is typically taken to include not just memory but all one's "mental" characteristics and properties) must suffice by itself. Identity of memory, personality, and other "mental" aspects of the person are sufficient conditions of personal identity. To admit this much is not necessarily to go back on the traditional notion that the soul is not the whole person and that the whole person must be raised. It is merely to insist that the existence of my soul entails *my* existence. Otherwise talk of my existence in the interim state is meaningless.

Now I do not claim that the Patristic theory is logically inconsistent. It is possible to hold that when I die my soul will be me during the interim period but that it will no longer be me if my soul in the eschaton animates a body consisting of totally new matter, even if the new body is qualitatively identical to the old one. (Perhaps an essential property of my soul is that it can only animate *this* body – where "this body" means in part a body consisting of *these* particles. So if *per impossible* my soul were to animate a different body the result would not be me. Or perhaps every configuration of particles that can possibly constitute a human body has it as one of its essential properties that it can be animated by one and only one soul.) But while logically consistent, this view seems to me exceedingly difficult to defend; it is hard to see how the suggested theses could be argued for.

Thus so far as the problem of personal identity is concerned, it is not easy to see why a defender of temporary disembodiment cannot dispense with all talk of God one day re-collecting the atoms, quarks, or whatever of our bodies. Perhaps human beings in this regard are unlike computers. Why not say God can award us brand new bodies materially quite unrelated to (although qualitatively similar to) the old ones? If the existence of the soul is sufficient for personal identity, and if the human soul never at any moment subsequent to its creation fails to exist, it will be us who exist after the resurrection in the kingdom of God whether or not our old bodies are reconstituted.

Furthermore, it needs to be noted here that identity of particles of bodily matter does not seem necessary to preserve the identity of an ordinary human person even during the course of a lifetime. As Frank Dilley says:

> We constantly replace our atoms over time and there is no reason to think that any eighty year old person has even a single atom in common with the newborn babe. If a person maintains personal identity over a process of total atom-by-atom replacement, it is difficult to see why such identity would not be preserved through a sudden replacement of all the atoms at once.[17]

Dilley's argument seems plausible, but we should notice that it does not necessarily follow. Perhaps gradual replacement of all the individual atoms of a human body is consistent with personal identity while all-at-once replacement of them is not. Perhaps some strong sort of material continuity is needed. One of the difficulties encountered by philosophers who discuss personal identity is that different persons' intuitions run

[17] Frank Dilley, "Resurrection and the 'Replica Objection'", *Religious Studies*, 19 (4) (1983), p. 462.

in different directions. For example, in a slightly different connection, Peter Van Inwagen argues that sameness of person requires both (1) sameness of atoms and (2) regular and natural causal relationships between those atoms. So if God were now to try to raise Napoleon Bonaparte from the dead by omnisciently locating the atoms of which his body once consisted and miraculously reassembling them, the result would not be Napoleon.[18] Now I do not agree with Van Inwagen here; I see no reason for his second stipulation. I raise his argument merely to show that his intuitions run in a different direction than do Dilley's. Since Dilley's case of sudden-replacement-of-all-the-atoms-at-once seems to constitute something *un*natural and *ir*regular, Van Inwagen would doubtless deny that in such cases personal identity would be preserved.

What if there were, so to speak, some natural way of reassembling persons out of totally new matter? Derek Parfit considers in detail a series of test cases involving an imagined Teletransporter.[19] This is a machine that is designed to send a person to distant places like Mars by (1) recording the exact state of all the body's cells (including those of the brain); (2) destroying the body and brain; (3) transmitting the information at the speed of light to Mars; where (4) a Replicator creates out of new matter a body and brain exactly like the old one. Suppose Parfit enters the machine and is "teletransported to Mars". Would the resulting Parfit-like person on Mars *be* Parfit? Here again our intuitions might differ, even in this relatively simple case (that is, apart from complications like the original Parfit somehow surviving on earth or 15 Parfit-like persons appearing on Mars). Those (like the church fathers and Aquinas) who hold to some strong requirement about bodily continuity will deny it is Parfit. Those who stress the memory criterion are free to affirm that Parfit is now on Mars. So are those, (for example, John Hick) who believe that identity is exact similarity plus uniqueness. Those who think that identity is exact similarity plus the right kind of causal

origin or causal ancestry might go either way, depending on whether they think the operation of a Teletransporter constitutes an appropriate sort of causal origin for the Parfit-like person on Mars.

The moral of the story thus far, I think, is that the fathers and Aquinas may be right in what they say about resurrection, but it is not clear that they are right. Their position may be consistent, but it does seem implausible to hold both (1) that it will be me in the interim period without any body at all (that is, the presence of my soul is sufficient for personal identity), and (2) that it will not be me in the eschaton, despite the presence of my soul, if the body which my soul then animates consists of new matter. There may be other (perhaps theological) reasons why we should hold that it is the very matter of our old bodies that is raised, but so far as the problem of personal identity is concerned, a strong case can be made that it will not matter.

Recent and contemporary Christian theologians who discuss resurrection seem for the most part to have departed from the Patristic theory. The more common thesis is that our glorified bodies will be wholly different bodies, not necessarily consisting of any of the old matter at all. As John Hick, an articulate spokesperson for this new point of view, says:

> What has become a widely accepted view in modern times holds that the resurrection body is a new and different body given by God, but expressing the personality within its new environment as the physical body expressed it in the earthly environment. The physical frame decays or is burned, disintegrating and being dispersed into the ground or the air, but God re-embodies the personality elsewhere.[20]

[...]

It is not hard to see why such a view has come to be widely adopted. (1) As noted above, personal identity does not seem to require the

[18] Peter Van Inwagen, "The Possibility of Resurrection", *International Journal for Philosophy of Religion*, IX (2) (1978), p. 119.
[19] Derek Parfit, *Reasons and Persons* (Oxford: Oxford University Press, 1986), pp. 199f. [...]
[20] Hick, op. cit., p. 186.

resurrection of the old body. (2) The Patristic theory seems to many contemporary Christians to be scientifically outmoded and difficult to believe; the idea that in order to raise me God must one day cast about, locate, and collect the atoms of which my earthly body once consisted seems to many people absurd. (3) Many such theologians want to hold in any case that the kingdom of God is not spatially related to our present world. It exists in a space all its own, and so can contain no material from this spatio-temporal manifold.

I am unable to locate any philosophical or logical difficulties in the "modern" theory. It seems to me a possible Christian view of resurrection, and can fit smoothly with the other aspects of the traditional notion I am calling temporary disembodiment. Are there any theological reasons, then, for a Christian to retain the old theory, that is, to believe that our old bodies will be raised? Two points should be made here. The first is that the most natural reading of Paul in I Corinthian 15 is along the lines of the Patristic theory. That is, Paul seems to be suggesting there that the old body *becomes* or *changes into* the new body, just as a seed becomes or changes into a plant. Thus, just as there is material continuity between the seed and the plant, so there will be material continuity between the old body and the new; the plant is *a new form of* the seed. [. . .]

The second point has to do with the difficulty of God one day collecting the atoms, quarks, or whatever fundamental particles human bodies consist of. This may well be the oldest philosophical objection ever raised against the Christian notion of resurrection. Virtually every one of the fathers who discussed resurrection tried to answer it, as did Aquinas. Such scenarios as this were suggested: What if a Christian dies at sea and his body is eaten by various fishes who then scatter to the seven seas? How can God later resurrect that body? Or what if another Christian is eaten by cannibals, so that the material of her body becomes the material of their bodies? And suppose God later wants to raise all of them from the dead, cannibals and Christians alike. Who gets what particles? How does God decide?

The move made by virtually all of the fathers in response to this objection is to appeal to omnipotence. You and I might not be able to locate and reconstitute the relevant atoms of someone's body, not surely after many years or even centuries have passed, but God can do this very thing. And as long as (1) the basic constituents of matter (for example, atoms) endure through time (as contemporary physical theory says they normally do); and (2) it is merely a matter of God locating and collecting the relevant constituents, I believe the fathers were right. An omnipotent being could do that.

But with the cannibalism case and other imaginable cases where God must decide which constituent parts shared at different times by two (or even two thousand) separate persons go where, the matter is more serious. The problem does not seem insoluble, but much more needs to be said. Perhaps some constituent parts of human bodies are essential to those bodies and some are not. That is, perhaps God will only need to collect the essential parts of our bodies and use them, so to speak, as building blocks around which to reconstruct our new bodies. And perhaps omnipotence must accordingly guarantee that no essential part of one person's earthly body is ever a constituent part, or an essential constituent part, of someone else's body. If these stipulations or ones like them are followed [. . .] it still seems that the fathers were correct – an omnipotent being will be able to raise us from the ground.

Reacting against these and similar patristic appeals to omnipotence in order to rationalise resurrection, Paul Badham argues as follows:[21]

Given belief in a once-for-all act of creation on the pattern of Genesis 1, then the act of resurrection cannot be difficult for an all-powerful God. Given that God made the first man by direct action, the restoration of a decomposed man becomes an easy task. Given that man consists of particles, it is easy to believe that omnipotence could reassemble these particles. But today each of these premises has lost its validity, and hence the conclusions drawn from them cannot stand. That man as a species is part of a slowly

21 Paul Badham, *Christian Beliefs About Life After Death* (London: Macmillan Press, 1976), p. 50. [. . .]

evolving process of life and in every respect continuous with the processes of nature from which he has emerged does not provide a congenial background for the idea of resurrection. Further, our increasing knowledge of the incredible complexity and constant changing of our physical components makes it difficult to see the resurrection as simply involving the re-collection of our physical particles. We are not composed of building bricks but of constantly changing living matter.

It is not easy to see exactly what the arguments here are meant to be. For one thing, Badham is right that nature is incredibly complex, as are human bodies; our bodies surely do consist of constantly changing living matter. But does any of this deny – or indeed does contemporary physics deny – the idea that our bodies consist of particles? I think not. Furthermore, it is hard to see how a commitment to evolutionary theory (a commitment I make) undercuts the ability of an omnipotent being to raise us from the dead. [...]

VII

Several philosophers have argued in recent years that the concept of disembodied existence is incoherent or at least that no disembodied thing can be identified with some previously existing human person. [...] [L]et me [...] focus on the case John Perry makes in his excellent little book, *A Dialogue on Personal Identity and Immortality*.[22]

Perry seems, in this dialogue, to speak primarily through the character of Gretchen Weirob, a mortally injured but still lucid philosopher who does not believe in life after death. And Weirob seems to present three main arguments against the conceivability or possibility of survival of death. All are versions of arguments we find elsewhere in the literature, but the virtue of Perry's work is that they are presented with great clarity and forcefulness. Perry's first argument has to do with the soul and personal identity; the second concerns memory and personality identity; and

the third is an argument about the possibility of duplication of persons.

The first argument says that immaterial and thus unobservable souls can have nothing to do with establishing personal identity. Personal identity does not consist in sameness of soul, for if it did, we would never know who we are or who others are. Since souls are not observable, no thesis having to do with souls is testable (not even the thesis, "My soul is me"). So I cannot know whether other human beings have souls, or even whether I have a soul; I have no idea whether I have one soul or several, or whether I have one soul for a time and then later a different soul. Thus there are no criteria for, and hence no way to make informed judgements about, "the same soul". It is possible simply on faith to assume criteria like, "Same body, same soul", or "Same mental traits, same soul", but since we never independently observe souls, there is no way to test these principles, and thus no reason to think they hold. But since we evidently are able to make correct personal identity judgements about persons, it follows that personal identity has nothing to do with souls. Personal identity must instead be based upon bodily criteria. Thus, concludes Perry, no thesis about my survival of death via the survival of my soul is coherent.

Perry's second argument is that the memory criterion of personal identity, which those who believe in immortality must rely on, is never sufficient to establish personal identity. This is because of the obvious fact that memory is fallible. Without some further criterion, we will never be able to distinguish between apparent memories and genuine memories. In fact, believers in immortality are committed to a kind of circularity – they claim that genuine memory explains personal identity (that is, a purported Jones in the afterlife really is Jones just in case the purported Jones genuinely remembers from Jones's point of view events in Jones's past), and they claim that identity marks the difference between apparent and genuine memories (the purported Jones can have genuine memories of events in Jones's past just in case the purported Jones *is* Jones – otherwise the memories are merely apparent memories). Thus again, the thesis that our souls

---

[22] John Perry, *A Dialogue on Personal Identity and Immortality* (Indianapolis, Indiana: Hackett, 1978).

survive death, which must rely on the memory criterion of personal identity, is incoherent.

Finally, Perry argues that the thesis of survival of death through immortality is rendered incoherent by the possibility of multiple qualitatively identical persons in the afterlife. Weirob says:[23]

> So either God, by creating a Heavenly person with a brain modeled after mine, does not really create someone identical with me but merely someone similar to me, or God is somehow limited to making only one such being. I can see no reason why, if there were a God, He should be so limited. So I take the first option. He would create someone similar to me, but not someone who would *be* me. Either your analysis of memory is wrong, and such a being does not, after all, remember what I am doing or saying, or memory is not sufficient for personal identity. Your theory has gone wrong somewhere, for it leads to absurdity.

When told by one of the discussants that God may well refrain from creating multiple qualitatively identical persons in the afterlife and that if God does so refrain the immortality thesis is coherent, Weirob replies that a new criterion has now been added. What suffices for personal identity (that is, what makes it such that the purported Jones in the afterlife *is* Jones) is not just memory but rather memory plus lack of competition. An odd way for someone to be killed in the afterlife, she remarks – all God has to do is create, so to speak, an identical twin to Jones, and then *neither* is Jones; Jones has not survived death. Identity is now made oddly to depend on something entirely extrinsic to the person involved. Thus if memory does not secure personal identity where there are two or more Jones's in the afterlife, it does not secure personal identity at all. Weirob concludes it is best simply to abandon any thought of survival of death – when my body dies, I die.

Perry's first argument in favour of the notion that survival of death is incoherent is based on an element of truth, but is used by him in an erroneous way. Throughout his book he seems illicitly to jump back and forth between talk about criteria of personal identity and talk about

evidence for personal identity. It is surely true that the soul is not observable, and that the presence or absence of a soul or of a certain soul is not something for which we can successfully test. What this shows, as I suppose, is that the soul is not *evidence for* personal identity. We cannot, for example, prove that a given person really is our long-lost friend by proving that this person really has our long-lost friend's soul. But it still might be true that the soul is *a criterion of* personal identity. That is, it still might be the case that the person really is our long-lost friend just in case this person and our long-lost friend have the same soul. It might even be true to say that a purported Jones in the afterlife is the same person as the Jones who once lived on earth just in case the purported Jones has Jones's soul. How we might test for or come to know this is another matter. Maybe only God knows for sure who has what soul. Maybe the rest of us will never know – not apart from divine revelation anyway – whether the purported Jones has Jones's soul. But it can still be true that if they have the same soul, they are two different temporal episodes of the same one person.

And the claim that personal identity consists in or amounts to the presence of the soul does not rule out the possibility of our making reliable personal identity judgements on other grounds, as Weirob seems to claim it does. Those who believe in the possibility of disembodied existence need not deny that there are other criteria of personal identity (for example, if the person before me has the same body as my long-lost friend, this person *is* my long-lost friend) and other ways of producing evidence in favour of or against personal identity claims.

Perry's second argument is also based on an element of truth – memory certainly is fallible; we do have to distinguish between apparent memories and genuine memories. So unless I have access to some infallible way of making this distinction, the mere fact that the purported Jones seems to remember events in Jones's life from Jones's point of view will not establish beyond conceivable doubt that the purported Jones is Jones (though it might count as evidence for it). As above, however, this does not rule out the

23   Ibid., p. 3.

possibility that memory is a criterion of personal identity – if the purported Jones does indeed remember events in Jones's life from Jones's point of view, then the purported Jones is Jones.

It is sometimes claimed that the memory criterion is parasitic on the bodily criterion and that use of the memory criterion never suffices by itself to establish identity. But such claims are surely false. We sometimes do make secure identity claims based on the memory criterion alone – for example, when we receive a typed letter from a friend. We hold that it is our friend who wrote the letter solely on the basis of memories and personality traits apparently had by the letter's author that seem to be memories and personality traits our friend has or ought to have. Of course if doubts were to arise we would try to verify or falsify the claim that our friend wrote the letter by the use of any evidence or criterion that might seem promising. We might check the letter for finger prints; we might try to see if it was written on our friend's typewriter; we might even telephone our friend. What this shows is not that we must always rely on the bodily criterion; there are equally cases where we might try to verify an identity claim originally based on the bodily criterion by means of memories. What it shows is that in cases of doubt we will look at both criteria.

But in the cases where the bodily criterion cannot be used – for example, during the interim period postulated in temporary disembodiment – can identity claims rationally be made? Can we ever be sure that a disembodied putative Stephen Davis *is* Stephen Davis? The problem is especially acute since memory is notoriously fallible; without recourse to the bodily criterion, how can we distinguish between actual memories and purported memories? I would argue that secure identity claims can be made without use of the bodily criterion, and that this can be achieved in cases where there are very many memories from very many different people that cohere together well. The context would make all the difference. If there are, say, 100 disembodied souls all wondering whether everyone in fact is who he or she claims to be, it would be irrational to deny that their memories are genuine if they all fit together, confirm each other, and form a coherent picture. Doubt would still be conceivable, but not rational. And something like this

is precisely what defenders of temporary disembodiment claim will occur during the interim period.

The third or duplication argument is one that critics of disembodied existence frequently appeal to, but is is one of the advantages of Perry's *Dialogue* that he grasps the defender's proper reply to it, and then moves to deepen the objection. After the comment from Weirob quoted above, Perry has Dave Cohen, a former student of hers, say: "But wait. Why can't Sam simply say that if God makes one such creature, she is you, while if he makes more, none of them is you? It's possible that he makes only one. So it's possible that you survive". This seems to me the correct response. Of course immortality or resurrection would be difficult to believe in if there were, say, 14 qualitatively identical Weirobs in the afterlife, each with equal apparent sincerity claiming to be Gretchen Weirob. But surely you can't refute a thesis, or the possible truth of a thesis, by imagining possible worlds where the thesis would be exceedingly hard to believe. Survival of death theses might well make good sense if in the afterlife there is never more than one person who claims to be some pre-mortem person. And since it is possible there will be but one Gretchen Weirob in the afterlife, survival of death is possible.

In response to this point Perry deepens the objection with Weirob's points about there now being two criteria of personal identity (memory and lack of competition) and about the oddness of God's ability to prevent someone's surviving death by creating a second qualitatively identical person. Both points seem to me correct, but do not render the survival thesis incoherent or even, as Weirob claims, absurd. What exactly is wrong with saying (in the light of God's evident ability to create multiple qualitatively identical persons) that memory plus lack of competition are criteria of personal identity? Lack of competition is a criterion that technically applies in this life as well as the next – we never bother to mention it because it rarely occurs to us that God has the ability to create multiple qualitatively identical persons here as well. And I suppose it *is* odd that God can prevent someone's survival in the way envisioned, and that personal identity is here made in part to depend on something entirely extrinsic to the person. These facts are odd, but they do not seem to me to impugn the possibility of the survival thesis.

Christians strongly deny that there will be multiple qualitatively identical persons in the eschaton. They would hold, however, that God has the ability to create such persons, so it is perfectly fair for critics to ask: How would it affect your advocacy of resurrection if God were to exercise this power? Now I prefer to hold that the existence of multiple qualitatively identical Joneses in the eschaton would place far too great a strain on our concept of a human person for us to affirm that Jones has survived death. Our concept of a person, I believe, includes a notion of uniqueness – there is and can be only one instance of each "person". Uniqueness or "lack of competition" (as Weirob puts it) is a criterion of personal identity. So I would argue at the very least that we would not know what to say if there were more than one Jones in the afterlife (perhaps our concept of a human person would have to be radically revised to include amoeba-like divisions, or something of the sort). More strongly, I would argue that Jones (the unique person we knew on earth) has not survived death.

[...]

My overall conclusion is that the theory of resurrection I have been considering (which can be interpreted in either the Patristic or the "modern" way) is a viable notion for Christians. Temporary disembodiment seems eminently defensible, both philosophically and theologically. I do not claim it is the only viable option for Christian belief about life after death; I do claim it is an acceptable way for Christians to understand those words from the Apostles' Creed that say, "I believe in ... the resurrection of the body".

Much contemporary philosophy tends, in its understanding of human nature, in a behaviourist or even materialist direction. No believer in temporary disembodiment can embrace philosophical materialism, but such believers can have great sympathy with any view which says that a disembodied person would hardly be a human person, not surely in the full sense of the word. They too embrace the notion that a disembodied person is only a minimal person, a mere shadow of a true human person – not completely unlike a person who is horribly disabled from birth or from some accident but who continues to live.

Such Christians will accordingly embrace the notion that full and true and complete human life is bodily life. That is why they look forward to "the resurrection of the body". As Pseudo-Justin says:[24] "In the resurrection the flesh shall rise entire. For if on earth He healed the sickness of the flesh, and made the body whole, much more will He do this in the resurrection, so that the flesh shall rise perfect and entire".

---

[24] Roberts and Donaldson, op. cit., p. 295.

48

The Idea of Reincarnation

Joseph Prabhu

I should like in this paper to explore the idea of reincarnation as a metaphysical and moral notion shedding interpretive light on our experience. I shall argue that it provides a plausible and coherent account of our moral and spiritual life. Being concerned with its appeal at a general philosophical level, I shall not go into an exegesis of the idea as articulated in different philosophical and religious systems. Rather, I will borrow freely from these contexts to construct a version of it, that in its generality seems to me worth considering as a view about the nature and destiny of human life, and specifically about the evolution of consciousness.

I shall begin first with an argument defending the probability of survival of consciousness beyond physical death as against the extinction of all life at death. Next I shall argue that there are good reasons why survival should take an embodied rather than disembodied form. I shall contend further that these reasons are pointed to by the character of our moral experience, and provide in turn a perspective from which to look at our lives. Then I shall take up the question of empirical evidence. Finally, I shall address some of the objections made against the idea and attempt to show that they are not decisive. The overall result of these investiga-

tions is to suggest the plausibility of a different view of life from that which seems to hold in our empirical-scientific culture.

Let me begin with the argument for survival. The fact of our moral consciousness, argues Kant, is the guarantee of personal immortality. The highest good must consist in the union of virtue and happiness. The orientation of the ethical will is towards virtue, while that of the sensuous will is towards happiness. But between virtue and happiness no causal relation exists empirically, while ethically no teleological relation can be permitted either. And yet our fundamental moral conception is one of ultimate justice, expressed in the thought that virtue alone is, in the final analysis, worthy of happiness. While we cannot, of course, use this eudaemonistic conception as a basis of morality, it still serves as a high-order, "transcendental" postulate, if morality is to be meaningful at all. This demand of our moral consciousness is not satisfied by the experience of empirical life, where virtue often requires renunciation of worldly happiness and where vice often goes along with success and the temporary happiness therefrom. If, therefore, moral consciousness requires such ultimate justice, without which it lacks completeness, and if such justice is not to be found in empirical life, it follows

"The Idea of Reincarnation" by Joseph Prabhu, in *Death and Afterlife*, ed. Stephen T. Davis (New York: St Martin's Press, 1989), pp. 65–80.

that we have to go beyond the limits of such life and postulate another order of existence, which Kant called "immortal life", in order to make such a union of virtue and happiness both final and permanent. What is important about this argument for our purposes is that it is the demand of morality itself, as Kant conceives it, that points to the conceptual necessity of a life beyond death.

My argument for survival has the same form as Kant's, though a more phenomenological content, which I maintain points towards both post-existence and pre-existence. It is not just the abstract requirement of moral faith that entails an extension beyond empirical life. Rather it is the concrete texture of our moral lives that suggests the need to go beyond the parameters of a single earthly life. The seriousness of our endeavour to shape our lives according to ideals of truth, wisdom, love and compassion, and all that they entail in terms of the development of virtue, together with the sense of inadequacy in our actual achievement, warrant the presumption that a single life cannot be all that we are destined to have. To grant that would make a mockery of our moral experience. It would mean that the very real possibilities of moral purification that we discern on the path from ego-centredness to reality-centredness, to use Hick's expression, would for most of us, who do not achieve full enlightenment in this life, be forever unfulfilled. But these moral and spiritual possibilities are not imaginative fantasies; they are real, both as regulative guides without which our moral lives would lack direction, and as ideals that we, to vary-ing degrees, fulfil.

I am emphasising more phenomenological and developmental aspects of morality by con-ceiving it in terms of the education of moral consciousness oriented to complete and trans-parent self-knowledge. In doing so I take a different view of morality, and specifically of its relation to religion, than Kant. Whereas he in some sense reduces religion to morality by basing his analysis on the primacy of duty, I, by contrast, wish to see morality in terms of the demands of spirituality and of spiritual self-knowledge. The movement from ego- to Reality-centredness is primarily a movement of self-consciousness and freedom, in the sense of *moksa*, ultimate spiritual liberation. Till such

time as there is misidentification of who we really are, we are destined to remain bound to the world of *samsāra*, which in Sanskrit means "passing through intensely", where the passing through refers to the embodiment of spiritual consciousness in a series of bodies. By contrast, when self-consciousness does not tie itself to its empirical masks or personae, but is able to see through them and use them for its self-education till it recognises its true spiritual nature, it is free of the samsāric realm and of reincarnation.

It is obvious that this view, which I have sketched very briefly in order to provide a con-text within which to locate the idea of reincar-nation, is dependent on a certain conception of Ultimate Reality and of the human spirit's participation in it. Again I am forced to be brief in order to focus on the question of reincarna-tion itself. *Saccidananda* is how much of Indian philosophy describes Ultimate Reality, being (*sat*), consciousness (*cit*), and bliss (*ananda*). It is beyond the scope of this essay – and indeed of most human lifetimes – to unpack the full con-tent of this notion. Let me just say that reality is seen as being completely and thoroughly spiritual, with all its modes and appearances being, in the final analysis, good. The funda-mental assumption of an empirical-scientific mentality that the world is morally neutral, is thought in this perspective to be limited. Within this limited context, explanation of the world in purely empirical terms has a relative truth and appropriateness. It is certainly proper to explain mechanical, chemical, and biological realities in respectively mechanical, chemical, and biological terms, without invoking moral or spiritual categories. But when one wants to see the world as a whole, or when one wants to investigate realities of a different order, these categories are no longer appropriate. Kant recog-nised this in his attempt to keep theoretical and practical and teleological reason apart, and to recognise the primacy of practical reason. He does so, however, in the thrall of Newtonian physics, which he thinks provides the true expla-nation of the natural world. It is because of this that he is forced to shrink morality to a narrow deontological conception of duty derived from the rational will alone. But Kant cedes too much to Newtonian physics and to the epistemologies and philosophy of mind built on it. The Indian view is different from Kant's in thinking that questions of the meaning and purpose of the universe, which Kant with his epistemological strictures felt he had banished from the realm of pure reason, are in fact perfectly intelligible questions, but intelligible in terms of moral-spiritual rather than physical categories. Physical causation itself is placed within a larger and more comprehensive spiritual causation.

What are the alternatives? A naturalist may say that these speculations are baseless, when the facts of natural science establish that everything that we can plausibly call personality ceases at the time of physical death. If one ignores the results of psychical research, or at least suspends judgement about them as being problematical, one is compelled to say that in the nature of the case natural science cannot pronounce on what is clearly beyond its domain. It is a strange step from this recognition to argue that just because natural science, as presently constituted, cannot in principle give an answer to the question of life after death, that the very question ought to be dismissed. The price of this dismissal, however, is greater than just the nullity of its speculation about a possible afterlife; what is more damaging is that it leaves unexplained the deeper moral impulses of this life. We may grant that there is for both the naturalist and the believer in an afterlife, the incentive to achieve as much moral goodness as one can within the span of a lifetime. The difference is, however, that the very attempt to do this brings into sharp focus the vaster reaches of goodness, that for most of us cannot be attained in a single life-span. It is this inner, dynamic aspect of goodness which is part of the experience of a great many people, that is simply denied, implicitly or explicitly in the naturalist's position.

Suppose we grant that our moral consciousness establishes a strong presumption of post-existence. We still have to argue that pre-existence is intelligible and probable. I have dealt above with moral aspiration and what it points to prospectively. But it is a fact that moral aspirations themselves differ greatly between people. It is also a fact that hindrances to the fulfilment of such aspirations, rooted in the character of people, differ significantly. In truth, these hindrances determine the nature and extent of moral response. So, how can we explain the patent inequalities

of people in this matter, not to mention inequalities in other sorts of ability, in circumstances and opportunities? One line of explanation may be that these inequalities are the result of the agents' own actions in this life. But in many cases, this will not do, because people have not lived long enough to have naturally achieved such abilities or disabilities. How, for example, can one account for the advanced spiritual evolution of a Krishnamurti, while still in his early twenties, and at the other end of the scale the depravity of a Richard Ramirez, the California criminal, at the same age?

To this question believers in reincarnation provide a thoroughly causal answer: those of unequal abilities are such only by virtue of their own actions – the principle of *karma*, or the moral law of cause and effect. Therefore, since their actions in this life are insufficient to account for their abilities, the latter are due to actions in a prior life. This is, of course, a completely different answer from the orthodox Christian view that God creates each human soul *ab initio*, which saddles God with the responsibility for inequalities. But the implications of this ascription are at the very least problematical for a traditional conception of God as all-good and all-powerful. The Indian view makes each agent herself responsible via her *karma*. This may not solve "the problem of evil" in any ultimate sense, but I shall argue later that it sees the problem quite differently from the Judaeo-Christian perspective.

While, of course, the notion of *karma* is logically distinct from that of rebirth, the two ideas are run together, because in combination they provide a more powerful explanation for the inequalities that plague existence. It is worth examining both the principle of *karma* and the associated notion of rebirth, in order to get clearer about what precisely is being asserted and what the rationale for it is.

In maintaining that one's moral nature is entirely determined by one's own actions, rather than the adventitious operations of fate, chance, or divine grace, the *karma* theory provides a thoroughgoing application of causation to the moral and spiritual world and with it the notion of complete personal responsibility for one's present character and dispositions. As for the operation of *karma* itself, it is important to define what seems to me to be the important insight, and separate it from various accretions that have grown around the notion, which have given rise to many misunderstandings, some of which I will consider later. I have consistently emphasised that the workings of *karma* apply to the moral and psychological realms, to the interior life of a person, where her basic dispositions and attitudes are an exact product of what she has wanted and done in the past. This is not at all to deny that these dispositions are also acquired as a result of contingent choices made in this life and that these choices were in part influenced by heredity and environment. There is no claim made that *karma* is the exclusive cause of all that happens to us. The theory does not deny the role of both heredity and environment in explaining the moral and psychological traits of an individual, but if it is to have any punch, it has to claim, as indeed it does, that *karma* is the critical factor in explaining a person's moral make-up. How can this arguement be made? The idea is that these other factors serve as instrumentalities for the operation of *karma* in a manner that permits a great deal of flexibility, such that there is no rigid one to one correlation between certain kinds of acts and their consequences. Karmic laws state tendencies rather than inevitable consequences. The general principle is that morally good acts tend to produce suitably good consequences, while morally evil acts do the opposite.

[...]

It may be claimed that all this is vague and far-fetched and that heredity and environment and present life choices are sufficient to explain psychological and, perhaps, moral traits. Against this is the patent evidence of similarity in hereditary and environmental influences producing different psychological traits. Thus, H. H. Newman, who has made a special study of twinning and of identical twins in particular, observes:

> In describing several pairs of these strange twins, writers have commented upon their lack of close similarity. Such twins have been regarded as the only kind of twins that are beyond question derived from a single egg and therefore surely identical in their hereditary make-up. One would expect such twins, since they have not only a common heredity but a common environment (for they must be in the same environment all the time), to be even more strikingly similar than pairs of separate twins that are not so intimately associated. The fact is, however, that Siamese twins are almost without exception more different in various ways than any but a very few pairs of separate one-egg twins. One of the most difficult problems faced by the twinning specialist is that of accounting for this unexpected dissimilarity of the components of Siamese twin pairs.[1]

This difference is surely due to a third factor other than heredity and environment, and while this by itself does not establish the presence of a karmic factor, it may possibly point in that direction. So, too, do the cases of geniuses or child prodigies, whose accomplishments cannot be accounted for in terms of heredity or environment.

In the second place I think it is important to reiterate that what the *karma* theory is designed to explain is the spiritual status and evolution of an individual, and while these are undoubtedly conditioned by the above-mentioned factors, they are so, neither exhaustively nor even primarily. The claim is that spiritual forces are indeed shaped and moulded by the empirical, but that they have a degree of autonomy, expressed in dispositions which are only analysable by laws that are *sui generis*.

Granted that rebirth may be a possibility, does this appear more reasonable than disembodied survivors? In answer to that question I wish to make clear the rationale behind the idea of reincarnation and show its plausibility. Here, too, I shall abstract from the variety of justifications offered in different systems and come up with a general one.

There are two main reasons for embodiment, one metaphysical and the other ethical and they are closely related. The metaphysical thesis is that human life, and more generally the life of

1 Quoted in K. N. Jayatillike, *Karma and Survival in Buddhist Perspective* (Kandy: Buddhist Publication Society, 1969), pp. 55–6.

the soul in the samsāric realm, must be seen as a psycho-physical unity, so that both pre- and post-existence must be in a body and a body which expresses the inner character of an individual. In contrast to the Greek notion of the immortality of the soul in a disembodied state, Indian and Christian eschatologies affirm the essential role of the body, though in different ways.

In the Indian scheme an evolutionary movement is postulated beginning at the most elemental level, where the *jīva* or soul passes through a series of increasingly complex bodies, until at last a human one is attained. Up to this point, the soul's evolution is straightforward and automatic in its upward ascent. This automaticity ceases, when chemical, biological and organic life reaches the human level where, depending on the actions performed, the soul can either ascend or descend in the evolutionary scale. This set of alternatives betokens the reaching of self-consciousness and with it responsibility for one's choices. But even though at the human level one may retrogress, the nisus and dynamic of the whole movement are upwards towards self-conscious identification with the Absolute. The moment this identification is complete, the whole samsāric realm is transcended and karma and rebirth are finally overcome.

This metaphysical doctrine points to its ethical counterpart. The body can be conceived as the soul's necessary self-externalisation, and externalisation necessary for self-consciousness and its intentional nature. Thus, as self-consciousness becomes more spiritual in terms of its deepening identification with the Absolute, the conception of the body changes from a gross, materialistic one, where the primary modality is absorption in sense-gratification, to a centre of pure energy radiating the energy of the Divine, as Jesus did at his transfiguration on the mountain and the Buddha at his enlightenment under the Bodhi tree. Once this enlightenment is complete, however, the whole realm of *samsāra* and bodies is transcended in a state of Pure Consciousness, which is not intentional at all, and is not conscious "of" anything including itself.

The body, then, serves as the stage on which the ethical and spiritual drama is played out, with the action being controlled by the director, the *ātman* or true self, to varying degrees depending on the co-operation of the actors, the moral and psychological traits of the individual. Sometimes the actors can become egotistical and wilful, in which case the vision of the director is obscured. At other times, they can serve as living instruments of his design and express his purpose transparently. If the *jīva* provides the thread of "inner" continuity, the body is the arena in which its psychic life is acted out, and it is only in the acting out and the articulation through the body that self-awareness is attained. Prior to that the soul exists as a bundle of potentialities, some of which are actualised in a particular manner. We can make the point clearer by a change of image. A novelist may start out with only the faintest glimmer of the eventual book, a scene, a character, a mood perhaps. What these amount to only become clear in and through the writing, in the process of which she may become aware of what she really wants to say. In a similar fashion the body serves as a self-articulation of the soul. Sometimes the expression may not be appropriate to the inner state, as in [the] example of the person identifying the desire for happiness with the greedy acquisition of wealth. Gradually through trials and errors made visible in the body, the soul is educated to identify true happiness with the Absolute and not with any partial or limited instantiation of it.

If the purpose of embodiment, then, is to enable the soul to educate itself and thus evolve, the mode in which this education proceeds is through justice in a law-abiding moral universe. As you sow, so shall you reap, if not in this life, then in some future one. But [...] it is a justice that is not simply retributive but rather a discipline of natural consequences designed to impart moral knowledge. And for this purpose too, bodily experience is necessary, as the place where such consequences are made visible. When misfortunes befall us, which we feel we in no way deserve, because of no wrongdoing on our part in this life, which we can detect, or "when bad things happen to good people", to use the title of Rabbi Kushner's book, it is not God, or our neighbour, or some cruel fate that is to be blamed. They (that is, misfortunes) may serve as a reminder of some wrongdoing or weakness that we may well have forgotten, or may have been too insensitive even to recognise. Or, if that is not the case, as for example, in children or infants stricken with illnesses or handicaps, the belief is that this is the consequence of some crime committed in a previous life. This belief is neither fanciful nor vacuous, as is often alleged. I think it is a common part of our experience to encounter within ourselves some weakness or temperamental flaw or alternatively, some skill or facility that we cannot satisfactorily account for by the pattern of our present lives. We cannot, of course, know for sure that the actions of a previous life are responsible for this, but the belief is a reasonable one, especially when placed in the context of a more comprehensive belief in a moral universe. There is then no bitterness about life, but rather a calm acceptance of what it has to offer, of joy or of sorrow, aware that both are given us to draw the soul upwards toward God.

It may be argued that the viability of the argument from justice requires a certain memory of our past lives, without which it seems to lose its point. I shall tackle that particular objection later, but at this stage let me say that the argument requires only that one's own actions have consequences on one's life and that one's present actions do not satisfactorily explain one's present condition.

With these explanations I come now to the question of empirical evidence. What evidence, you may ask, is there that any of these speculations are true? There is now a considerable amount of scientific data garnered according to the strictest standards. Ian Stevenson's investigations are the best known. Five volumes of his case histories have thus far been published, while the number of reincarnation-type cases now in his files totals over two thousand. His research has revealed a number of instances where the details people, usually small children, give of their past lives could not possibly have been done in their present lives, details whose accuracy was largely verified, when investigated. Nor is it true, as some have suggested, that these cases are mainly to be found in cultures, where the belief in reincarnation is prevalent. In July 1974 Stevenson's colleague at the University of Virginia, J. G. Pratt, carried out a census of Stevenson's cases and found that of the 1,339 cases then in Stevenson's file, "the United States has the most, with 324 cases

(not counting American Indian and Eskimo) and the next five countries in descending order are Burma (139 cases), India (135), Turkey (114), and Great Britain (111)."[2]

Most of the time Stevenson has gathered his information from children between the ages of two and four, though occasionally older, who spontaneously offered information about their previous lives and personae in the course of conversation. He prefers children to adults as subjects because of the obviously greater difficulty in controlling subconscious influences from information adults have been exposed to, as also the more pronounced tendency to indulge in fantasies, imaginative inventions and other forms of psychological projection.

Among the most frequently observed characteristics in these cases are the possession of a skill not taught or learned, including knowledge of a foreign language to which the person has not been exposed in this life; names of people whom they claim to have known previously, places where they lived and incidents in these lives, all of which Stevenson found to be about 90 per cent accurate; a phobia for objects and circumstances associated with their previous deaths; and an ability to detect changes in people and surroundings in the places of their former lives.

Now Stevenson is most scrupulous in asserting that he has uncovered possible evidence for reincarnation and not definitive proof. He himself has explored a number of alternative hypotheses to explain his data, from fraud and fantasising to clairvoyance, telepathy and mediumistic possession. Again it is beyond my scope to go into the plausibility or otherwise of these hypotheses, because I would have to examine each individual case in detail. Suffice it to say that Stevenson, who does not explicitly profess a personal belief in reincarnation, said in an interview in 1974, looking back on his own research,

what I do believe is that, of the cases we now know, reincarnation – at least for some – is the best explanation that we have been able to come up with. There is an impressive body of evidence and it is getting stronger all the time. I think

2 J. Gunther Pratt and Naomi Hintze, *The Psychic Realm: What Can You Believe?* (New York: Random House, 1975), quoted in Sylvia Cranston and Carey Williams, *Reincarnation: A New Horizon in Science, Religion and Society* (New York: Julian Press, 1984), pp. 49–69, from which a good deal of the information in the paragraph is taken.

a rational person, if he wants, can believe in reincarnation on the basis of evidence.[3]

Needless to say, in spite of the fact that his research is respected by his peers, his findings and conclusions can hardly be said to be accepted by the scientific establishment at large. This is only to be expected, because a reincarnation hypothesis goes against the beliefs of many reared in a materialist or physicalist culture. Within these assumptions, the scope of observation, experiment and reality-testing is going to be restricted, while the limited data uncovered by these methods in turn reinforces these narrow assumptions. This problem of the theory-ladeness of all data and of what counts as evidence is well known from discussions in contemporary philosophy and history of science. Data alone will not dislodge a set of theoretical assumptions, because data that does not fit a theory will usually be explained away in some fashion or another.

That, however, is not my problem. I have not offered the idea of reincarnation as an empirical hypothesis though given my openess to it, I am impressed by the evidence. My tack in this paper has been different, concerned more with the significance of reincarnation than with its empirical status. I have tried to argue that it makes sense of our moral experience, as part of the evolution of consciousness towards complete and transparent self-knowledge. Within this framework the notion of *karma* expresses the internal law of our moral life according to which actions produce consequences which are strictly proportional to their moral nature. Thus, it is our actions alone that are responsible for our fate. This notion, in turn, requires the idea of rebirth, because the consequences of action may spread over many lifetimes and conversely, starting at the other end, our present status may not be explainable in terms of the actions of this life combined with the forces of heredity and environment. The particular form in which I have tried to couch my argument for rebirth has been as a kind of

transcendental deduction based on a phenomenological analysis of our moral experience.

I want to proceed now to three objections which are often made against the notion of reincarnation:

1 that it does not really offer a solution to the inequalities and natural evils that pervade existence;
2 that a belief in reincarnation is likely to produce a fatalism or at least passivity; and, finally,
3 that the claim of evolution in moral education is undercut, if in fact we lack memories of our previous lives, which most of us do.

Let me begin with the first objection, which is that the theory does not really tackle the problem of inequalities, but instead simply pushes it back to an indeterminate stage of existence. Hick puts it this way:

> For we are no nearer to an ultimate explanation of the circumstances of our present birth when we are told that they are consequences of a previous life if that previous life has in turn to be explained by reference to a yet previous life, and that by reference to another, and so on in an infinite regress. One can affirm the beginningless character of the soul's existence in this way; but one cannot then claim that it renders either intelligible or morally acceptable the inequalities of our present lot. The solution has not been produced but only postponed to infinity.[4]

Now, much depends on how exactly we define the problem that we are attempting to solve. The assumptions behind Hick's argument are taken from a western and predominantly Christian perspective, where the problem of natural evil is thrown back on God and we are faced with the conundrum of how an all-good and all-powerful divine creator can escape responsibility for his creation. Many streams of Indian philosophy see things differently. The Ultimate Reality, *Saccidananda*, is seen more as an impersonal

[3] Ibid., p. 68. The original source of the quote is Alton Slagle, "Reincarnation: A Doctor Looks Beyond Death", *Sunday News*, New York, 4 August 1974.
[4] John Hick, *Death and Eternal Life* (New York: Harper & Row, 1980), p. 309.

process, an eternal moral order that comes into its own in and through the realm of *samsāra*, which too is eternal. Why the Ultimate Reality goes through this process is a mystery, at least to those in the samsāric realm. But the evolution of consciousness gives us some clues.

Goodness is to be conceived primarily in terms of spiritual knowledge, while evil is seen essentially as ignorance. Knowledge in the dynamic sense of knowing, or coming to know, can be construed as the overcoming of such ignorance. Just as it is not possible to talk about knowledge without also talking about ignorance, so also "good" and "evil" are seen as correlative terms. Indian philosophy in general is far more accepting of evil seen in gnostic terms than western thought, which sees it in largely moral terms, tends to be. It is relativised as a phase that is constantly being overcome, rather than being absolutised as a thing in itself. There is no expectation, therefore, of God's creating a perfectly good world. The Divine is conceived much more as a immanent process of progressively more transparent self-consciousness. Human beings participate in and partially constitute that divine process, so that when it comes to evil, there is no external agency to be blamed.

It is true, to return to Hick's argument, that by saying the soul always and eternally has a character and a set of dispositions, we are in fact not offering a solution to the precise set of concerns that Hick has in mind. But the Indian is satisfied with the thought that if he pushes back far enough he will be able to see how his own choices, from among the possibilities presented, alone produced his present situation. No doubt some were disposed to make better choices at that stage, but the inequity of the conditions that produced the different choices, some better and some worse, matters less in an infinite time framework than the conviction that one alone is responsible for one's present state. After all, everyone has a chance to learn from their mistakes and the difficult situations they find themselves in; the fact that it may take longer for some than for others matters little in an infinite time span. And so, if "the solution has only been postponed to infinity", the Indian is not as worried about it as Hick is.

These last remarks set the stage for the second objection, namely, that if what we are is conditioned by our past actions, then we are fated to bear their consequences, good or bad, and there is nothing we can do to change our lot. And, indeed, this is how it is often understood. But this is false. To say that one is conditioned, is not to say that one is determined, even by the consequences of one's own actions. This becomes clearer when we attempt to analyse an action and its fruits. Every act of ours has a double result, which we may term its direct and indirect results. The direct result is the pain or pleasure, which follows upon the act depending upon its nature. The indirect result is the tendency that is created to repeat the act again if it was pleasant and to avoid it in the future if painful (which is a negative way of expressing the first proposition, to the extent that the act of avoiding something painful can itself be conceived as a pleasurable act). The "necessity" inherent in the law of *karma* applies only to the direct result – there is no way of avoiding the immediate consequences of what we do. Where the indirect result is concerned, we may grant that we are predisposed to perform the act again, but we have a measure of freedom in succumbing to that predisposition or resisting it.

Wherein does this freedom consist? Not in trying merely to repress this tendency, but rather by understanding its operation and the circumstances in which it comes to fruition, and then by initiating a different set of circumstances. Let us consider the example of a cigarette smoker trying to give up the habit. Nothing will erase the direct result of smoking – the physiological consequences. But the tendency to continue smoking can be checked both by not giving in to the tendency and by producing circumstances in which that tendency simply cannot be expressed, till such time as it withers away from neglect.

This psychological point has moral significance. While our tendencies do indeed predispose us to act in certain ways, to give in to them is not to be truly self-determining, but in fact to be determined. Self-determination consists in directing and regulating our tendencies as they tend to express themselves in action. Thus, far from being fatalistic in its implications, the *karma* theory is optimistic: our past actions may have produced our present state, but in the measure of freedom that we enjoy, we can direct our present actions towards the betterment of our moral nature in the future. The attitude is expressed in a much quoted Sanskrit saying:

> Fortune comes to a person, who is as energetic as a lion, but cowards think that it is the gift of Fate. Let us overcome this Fate by our power and make all possible personal endeavours; no blame will attach to us, if our best efforts do not succeed.[5]

By thus orienting our actions towards moral progress, one may grow indifferent to what happens in the present, as the inevitable consequence of past karma which is behind us now as we face the future.

This point leads to the third objection: the question whether we can benefit from the just retribution involved in *karma*, if we have no memory of our previous lives. Leibniz, in discussing this with one of his correspondents, writes, "What good would it do you, sir, to become king of China on condition of forgetting what you have been? Would it not be the same thing as if God at the same time he destroyed you, created a king in China?"[6] But it depends what we mean here by "memory". If we mean by that the preservation of a comprehensive span of memories describing our situation, then surely that condition is too strong for establishing identity. None of us finds his sense of identity weakened by the fact that he has no memories of the first years of childhood. That our conscious identity in that case is established by spatio-temporal continuity is true, and, of course, that distinguishes a previous life that we cannot remember from circumstances of our present life that we have forgotten. But we may point to a weaker but still intelligible sense of "memory", where continuity of memory is established through the persistence of dispositions and tendencies. The fact that the circumstances of our present life may not satisfactorily explain our skills, traits or weaknesses, forces us back, if we accept the principle of *karma*, to a consideration of previous lives. That we may have no conscious memory of them is not fatal, because all that the *karma* theory asserts is that past lives will have an effect on the present. If this is so, we may grant that we are in fact different persons in different lives, while still holding on to dispositional continuity carried in the soul. "Personality", after all, is a mask, and what matters is the continuity of the spiritual consciousness underlying it, rather than the identity of the masks it assumes at various times. Huston Smith expresses it well; his words can serve as a fitting conclusion to this essay:

> Our word "personality" comes from the Latin *persona*, which originally meant the mask an actor donned as he stepped onto the stage to play his role ... This mask is precisely what our personalities are ... The disturbing fact, however, is that we have lost sight of the distinction between our true selves and the veil of personality that is its present costume ... We have come completely under the fascination of our present lines, unable to remember previous roles or to anticipate future ones. The task is to correct this false identification. Turning his awareness inward, [man] must pierce and dissolve the innumerable layers of the manifest personality until, all strata of the mask at length cut through, he arrives finally at the anonymous actor who stands beneath.[7]

---

[5]   Yajnavalaya-Smrti, I, pp. 349–51, quoted in S. Chatterjee *The Fundamentals of Hinduism: A Philosophical Study* (Calcutta: Dasgupta, 1960), p. 87.
[6]   G. W. Leibniz, *Die philosophische Schriften*, 7 vols, edited C. I. Gerhardt (Berlin: Weidmann, 1875–80), IV, p. 300.
[7]   Huston Smith, *The Religions of Man* (New York: Mentor Books, 1959), chapter 2.

49

Not-Self, *Kamma*, and Rebirth

Christopher Gowans

Two Conceptions of the Self: Substance and Process

A view prominent at the time of the Buddha held that each person's true self was identical with the ultimate ground of reality (*brahman*). It might be suspected that the Buddha's not-self doctrine is nothing more than a rejection of this distinctive understanding of the self. If this were the case, then most Western observers might have little or no disagreement with the Buddha's teaching about the absence of self (since they are unlikely to understand their selves as identical with the ground of reality). However, though the Buddha does deny views about the self that were prominent in his culture, his not-self doctrine has implications that go beyond the denial of these local views. In particular, he rejects a conception of the self that is probably accepted by many people and has been widely endorsed in the Western philosophical tradition. I will call this the substance conception of the self.[1] On the other hand, there is another conception of the self that the Buddha implicitly appears to affirm, albeit in a significantly qualified form. I will call this the process conception of the self. Let us first

describe these two conceptions and then consider what the Buddha says about them.

According to the *substance conception*, a self is a single, unified substance (we might also say it is a being, entity, or thing). In this respect, a self is like other substances in the world such as ordinary physical objects. A substance is something that is *ontologically distinct* from other substances – that is, though a substance has properties, it is not itself the property of another substance. Moreover, though one substance may causally depend on other substances, each substance remains a distinct or separate entity. For example, the sun might cause a plant to live, but the sun is one thing and the plant is another. In addition, a substance is something that has *identity* – that is, in some respects it persists through time unchanged so long as it exists. A substance may change, but it cannot change in every respect and remain the substance it is. Hence, some properties of a substance may change over time. For instance, a planet might gradually change from bright red to reddish-brown. The color of a planet is an accidental property. But a substance also has essential properties, properties that cannot change without the substance ceasing to be

"Not-Self, *Kamma*, and Rebirth," from *Philosophy of the Buddha* by Christopher Gowans (New York: Routledge, 2003), pp. xi; 69–74; 104–8. Copyright © 2003, Routledge. Reproduced by permission of Taylor & Francis Books UK.

This is an interpretation of the teaching of the Buddha Sakyamuni as represented in the Sutta *Pṭaki* of the Pali Canon.

[1] It was briefly discussed in *Philosophy of the Buddha* (New York: Routledge, 2003), chapter 3, section 3.

what it is. These properties are necessary to the identity of the substance. An essential property of planets is that they orbit a star such as the sun. If Pluto ceased to orbit the sun and moved unendingly away from it, it would no longer be a planet. Hence, as long as a particular planet exists, it has the property of orbiting a sun.

On this account, then, a self is a substance in the sense of being ontologically distinct from other substances and having a set of essential, unchanging properties that are necessary for its identity as a self. The properties that are distinctive of a self, in contrast to substances such as plants and planets, are that it has capacities that enable it to regularly experience, remember, imagine, feel, desire, think, decide, act, and so on. A self is a substance that has all or most of these attributes as essential properties (hence, we say a self is a subject who experiences and an agent who acts). In some cases, a self *undergoes* these things. For example, we might think of an experience or feeling as something that happens to us. But in other cases, a self *does* these things. For example, thinking, deciding, and acting are usually considered things a self does rather than undergoes. Sometimes, as in a daydream, it may be unclear whether an attribute of a self is something it undergoes or does. But that a self is a substance that undergoes some things and does others is essential to what it means to be a self. Moreover, a self *controls* those things it does in a sense that it does not control those things it undergoes. For example, I cannot change the fact that when I look at the book in front of me I have an experience of something rectangular, but I can determine whether or not to pick up the book. Finally, on this account, a self has a reflexive property: it is capable of being *aware of itself as a substance-self*. A self not only experiences and decides, it can be and often is aware of the fact that it is a self that experiences and decides. A self has the capacity for self-awareness or self-consciousness.

To sum up, according to the substance conception, a self is a substance-self, a substance that is ontologically distinct from other substances (*distinctness*) and has essential properties that do not change (*identity*); these properties include

the regularly exercised capacities to experience, remember, imagine, feel, desire, think, decide, act, and the like (*attributes of undergoing and doing*); the substance-self controls those things it does (*self-control*); and it has the capacity to be aware of itself as a substance-self (*self-awareness*). This conception of the self is familiar in Western traditions. For example, Descartes appeared to have such a conception in mind when he declared that he was "a thing that thinks" – that is, "a thing that doubts, understands, affirms, denies, is willing, is unwilling, and also imagines and has sensory perceptions".[2] Each aspect of the substance conception of the self may invite controversy and would require a more detailed formulation to be fully adequate. But this account should be sufficient for our present purpose. It is important to recognize that this description is neutral with respect to several important philosophical controversies concerning the self. For instance, it does not specify whether or not the self is immortal, is distinct from the body, is found in human beings but not other animals, or possesses a free will. (Descartes affirmed all of these points, but they are not part of the substance conception of the self as defined here.) Nonetheless, for many persons, an essential part of the reason human beings have the value they have – for example, that they are worthy of love or respect – is the fact that they are substance-selves.

Let us now turn to the *process conception* of the self. On this account, there are no substance-selves. Rather, the phenomena the previous account described as substances-selves are in fact process-selves. The key difference between the two accounts is that the process conception rejects what the substance conception regards as fundamental: that the world is made up of substances that are ontologically distinct and have identity through time. Instead, according to the process conception, the world should be understood as consisting solely of processes. Whereas the substance conception takes (apparently) discrete and stable objects such as moons and monoliths as its paradigms of what is real, the process conception suggests that the proper paradigms are occurrences such as whirlpools and wind storms

---

[2]   R. Descartes, "Meditations on First Philosophy," in *The Philosophical Writings of Descartes*, ed. J. Cottingham, R. Stoothoff, and D. Murdoch, Vol. II (Cambridge: Cambridge University Press, 1984), p. 19

that are obviously interdependent on their environment and ever-changing. On this account, a process is not a thing, entity, or being, but an event, activity, or becoming: it is a specific movement within the world, interconnected with other movements and in constant change in every respect. A particular process is not a thing that has necessary properties and is distinct from other things. It is an aspect of the overall movement that constitutes the world. As a movement, a process has an important temporal character: it involves a continuous passage of becoming from past to present to future. But ordinarily a process is not random: it manifests an ordered, lawful causal development. Moreover, on account of interconnection, processes involve other processes: a given process typically contains smaller-scale processes and is contained within larger-scale processes.

Now, according to the process conception, a self is not a substance, but an integrated set of processes. Specifically, a process-self is a structured nexus of continuous, interacting processes that are not ontologically distinct from other processes and that are in constant change in every respect. The specific processes that constitute the process-self are typically the aforementioned undergoings and doings of the self. But instead of describing these as necessary properties of a substance, the process conception says a self is nothing but a nexus of processes such as experiencing, remembering, imagining, feeling, desiring, thinking, acting, and so on. Moreover, since a process-self is not ontologically distinct from other processes, both what it does and what it undergoes are conditioned by other processes. (However, a distinction between doing and undergoing is still affirmed.) Finally, a process-self has false self-awareness: it mistakenly believes it is aware of itself as a substance-self (this feature may distinguish this account of the self from other process accounts; we will see momentarily why it is an important aspect of the Buddha's position).

In short, according to the process conception, a self is a process-self, a nexus of processes such as experiencing, acting and the like that is not ontologically distinct from other processes, that is in constant change in every respect, that is conditioned in what it does as well as what it

undergoes, and that falsely believes it is aware of itself as a substance-self. On this account, a self is not a distinct substance with identity through time. Rather, it is an integrated set of ever-changing processes enmeshed in a world of other processes. Process understandings of reality are not predominant in Western philosophical traditions, but they have been accepted by a minority of philosophers from Heraclitus in the sixth century BCE to Whitehead in the twentieth century. Among persons in the West, the substance conception of the person is probably closer to the "common sense" view than the process conception is, but it is a large question as to which conception is philosophically more adequate. Each account has its share of perplexities.[3]

A Coherent Interpretation of the Buddha

We may now return to the teaching of the Buddha. A problem of interpretation arises because the Buddha speaks a great deal about the absence of any self and yet sometimes seems to refer to or presuppose a self. In my view, the resolution of this problem – the best overall interpretation of his teaching – is that he believed that substance-selves have no reality and that process-selves have no independent reality but do have a form of dependent reality. There are no substance-selves because reality does not consist of substances. When the Buddha speaks of the absence of any self he should be understood as meaning (in part) the absence of any substance-self. On the other hand, when he appears to presuppose selves in the doctrines of *kamma* and rebirth, and more generally when he seems to refer to selves, he should be understood as referring to the dependent reality of process-selves. However, process-selves have no independent reality. Hence, in independent reality there are no selves at all. This is the Buddha's not-self doctrine.

In order to understand this interpretation, we need to consider the distinction between dependent and independent reality. The reality or existence of some things directly depends on mental states such as beliefs, desires, or attitudes (understood here as processes). For example, the

---

[3] See *Philosophy of the Buddha*, chapter 8.

value of a monetary currency such as the dollar directly depends on the belief that it has value. If people stopped believing this (as tends to happen in times of severe inflation), then the dollar would lose its value. In one sense, the value of the dollar is obviously a real feature of the world. People make important decisions in their lives based on this assumption. But in another sense it is not real. For example, ordinarily we suppose that the existence of the moon does not directly depend on mental states such as what we think about it. In this sense, the moon has independent reality. The value of the dollar, by contrast, does not have independent reality the way the moon does.

Let us say that something has *dependent reality* if its reality directly depends on mental states, and that something has *independent reality* if its reality does not directly depend on mental states. According to the Buddha's teaching of dependent origination, ultimately everything is interdependent and thus nothing is completely independent. Nonetheless, only some things are directly dependent on mental states. By comparison, other things may be said to be independent, meaning not directly dependent on mental states. Hence, the distinction between dependent and independent reality as defined here is consistent with dependent origination.

The distinctive idea of the Buddha is that the dependent reality of process-selves is the only reality of selves there is. Substance-selves have no reality. On the other hand, process-selves have no independent reality, but they do have dependent reality: they exist only insofar as there are certain beliefs, desires, feelings, attitudes, and so on. Specifically, a person's process-self exists only insofar as the person falsely believes it is a substance-self and hence is attached to its desires and feelings as properties of its substance-self, as features of the world it regards as "mine." The delusion that I am a substance-self maintains the dependent reality of my being a process-self. As long as this delusion and the consequent attachments to desires and feelings continues, the process-self referred to by "me" will continue to exist (and suffer and be reborn and suffer again, and so on). But once the belief that

I am a substance-self ceases along with the attachments to specific desires and feelings as "mine," the process-self that was me ceases – and *Nibbāna* is attained. Like the value of a monetary currency, a process-self exists because of what is believed. However, there is an important disanalogy in this comparison. Belief in the value of the dollar need not involve a mistake on our part (we might be correct in thinking it is worth a certain amount), but the belief that one is a substance-self is a mistake for the Buddha. In fact, it is the most fundamental error we make: it is what preserves the existence of process-selves and brings about suffering.

It is important to remember that the not-self doctrine is only part of the Buddha's teaching about the nature of human persons. His full teaching may be summarized as follows.

1   We are not substance-selves in any sense.
2   We are process-selves in a dependent sense and hence have better or worse, but always unsatisfactory, rebirths in accord with the morality of our actions.
3   We are that which has the opportunity to escape the cycle of rebirth and attain *Nibbāna*.

We are dependently process-selves because we mistakenly think we are substance-selves. As a result, we suffer through repeated rebirths. Completely liberated from this delusion, we attain *Nibbāna*, the highest form of happiness, provisionally during life and fully after death. Our most fundamental reality gives us a genuine hope of this attainment; if not in this lifetime, then in lives to come. Emphasis on (1) and (2) alone may seem a depressing prospect. But this misses (3), and (3) is what really matters from the Buddha's standpoint. Our highest fulfillment is found in literally living selflessly.

The idea of *Nibbāna* raises its own perplexities.[4] For now, we need to consider the validity of (1) and (2) as an interpretation of the Buddha's not-self doctrine. An interpretation of this doctrine should strive to make consistent sense of everything the Buddha says or assumes concerning both the absence of self and the presence of self,

[4]   These are discussed in ibid., chapters 12 and 13.

and it should try to show how the doctrine could be thought to provide a cogent account of our lives. [. . .], A key issue will be whether or not the ideas of *kamma* and rebirth can be understood solely in terms of the dependent reality of process-selves. Does it make sense to say, with reference to a process-self, that its morally good (bad) actions cause its future happiness (unhappiness) and that it has existed before this life and may exist again after this life? We will discuss this issue in the next section.[5]

[. . .]

The Nature of *Kamma* and Rebirth

A central teaching of the Buddha is that each person lives a series of lives extending indefinitely into both the past and the future (until *Nibbāna* is attained), and that the moral quality of a particular life of a person causally influences the happiness of the lives of that person that follow. These are the basic notions of rebirth and *kamma* respectively. In a representative statement, the Buddha says: "It is by reason of conduct not in accordance with the *Dhamma*, by reason of unrighteous conduct that some beings here, on the dissolution of the body, after death, reappear in states of deprivation, in an unhappy destination, in perdition, even in hell." On the other hand, "it is by reason of conduct in accordance with the *Dhamma*, by reason of righteous conduct that some beings here, on the dissolution of the body, after death, reappear in a happy destination, even in the heavenly world" (M 380). As examples of the kinds of unrighteous conduct that will lead to an unhappy destination, the Buddha refers to killing living beings, stealing, engaging in sexual misconduct, speaking falsely, maliciously, harshly, and uselessly, being covetous, and having wrong views. Forms of conduct contrary to these are righteous and lead to a happy destination. In general, the roots of unrighteous conduct are "greed, hatred, and delusion," while the roots of righteous conduct are the opposite of these (N 49).

The importance *of kamma* and rebirth is indicated by the fact that they are said to be an essential part of the three forms of knowledge the Buddha attained at the time of his enlightenment. The last was the Four Noble Truths. The first two were "knowledge of the recollection of past lives" and "knowledge of the passing away and reappearance of beings" in which those who were ill-conducted "have reappeared in a state of deprivation" while those who were well-conducted "have reappeared in a good destination" (M 105–6).

The doctrine of *kamma* concerns the effects of our actions (the word "*kamma*" means action). At first glance, the idea is straightforward conceptually: insofar as a person's actions are morally wholesome (*kusala*) they will improve the person's well-being in the future, and insofar as a person's actions are morally unwholesome (*akusala*) they will diminish the person's well-being in the future. The future effects of our actions may be in this life or in future lives. The most important factor in determining the moral quality of actions is the person's intention. For example, it is intentional honesty that brings about happiness and intentional theft that results in unhappiness. It is tempting to see this idea as a form of the common belief that morally good persons deserve to be happy while morally bad persons deserve to be unhappy – with the important addition that the universe is causally constructed to ensure that desert is always correctly allocated. However, the Buddha does not present *kamma* as a doctrine of desert per se, much less as a theory of cosmic reward and punishment. Rather, *kamma* is a central instance of dependent origination: it is understood as a law of nature, similar to the principle of gravity, that dictates the causal effects produced by morally good and bad actions. Sometimes the moral quality of an action is compared to a seed that will naturally grow in a happy or unhappy direction. *Kamma* is not administered by an agent such as God. It is an impersonal feature of the causal relationships in the world, and there is no prospect of deviation from the causal effects of *kamma* on the ground of mercy.

---

[5] The Buddha's rationale for the not-self teaching is discussed in ibid., chapters 7 and 8.

Kamma is not a form of determinism about actions. Though a person's current state of well-being is always a causal function of his or her past actions, what a person does at a given time is not determined by past actions. As we have seen, the Buddha thinks we are always free to choose the morally better or worse course. Since these choices affect our future well-being, it is always in our power to improve or diminish our future happiness, and to achieve ultimate happiness through enlightenment. To some extent our character may be determined by past actions, but our character never fully determines our actions.

The cycle of rebirth is described by the Buddha in vast cosmological terms. The universe is said to be arranged in a hierarchy of thirty-one planes of existence, understood to involve higher and lower degrees of well-being. The human level is found among eleven planes of the sense-sphere realm. Below us stand the progressively worse levels of titans, ghosts, animals, and hell; above us are the six levels of the lower gods (*devas*). Above the sense-sphere realm are the sixteen planes of the form realm in which the higher gods dwell, and above these are the four planes of the formless realm: infinite space, infinite consciousness, nothingness, and neither-perception-nor-non-perception. Hence, each human being may be reborn at a lower level (for example, as an animal) or at a higher level (for example, as a god). Animals, humans, and gods belong to a single cosmic framework of rebirth. Depending on the moral quality of our lives, each of us may be reborn above or below our current human level, or at the human level in better or worse circumstances. But no rebirth is a final destination. We are all involved in an ongoing process of rebirth called *saṃsāra* ("perpetual wondering"). This process extends indefinitely into the past and will extend indefinitely into the future until one escapes the cycle of rebirth altogether and attains *Nibbāna* (understood as a state beyond the thirty-one planes from which no return is possible).

No account of the ultimate purpose of this cosmic scheme is offered, but it is obviously intended to show that our well-being will be improved as we move to higher levels of existence and ultimately attain *Nibbāna*. For our purpose, the details of this cosmology are not important. We are interested in the basic rationale for the ideas of *kamma* and rebirth.

The Consistency Objection

Among the oldest quandaries in the teaching of the Buddha is the question of whether or not the notions of *kamma* and rebirth are consistent with the not-self doctrine. If I am not a self, then in what sense can my morally good actions now increase my happiness later? And if there are no selves, then what does it mean to say we will be reborn? On my interpretation, the basic answer to these questions is that the dependent reality of process-selves is sufficient to render the ideas of *kamma* and rebirth intelligible. In fact, one of the main reasons for accepting this interpretation – that the Buddha denies any reality to substance-selves, but grants dependent reality to process-selves – is that it reconciles these ideas and his not-self teaching.

A process-self is a unified nexus of continuous, interacting processes (the aggregates) that are in constant change in every respect and are not ontologically distinct from other processes in the world. [...] In order to account for our ordinary understanding of one another as selves, the process view needs to be able to explain the appearance of identity and distinctness: that I am the same person as the person who married my wife several years ago, and that I am a distinct person from my neighbor.[6] The heart of the solution is that this appearance may be explained in terms of the causal continuity and consequent similarity of the processes constituting the person over time, and the internal integration of these processes at a given time. Let us suppose for the sake of argument that this solution is adequate. If it is, then it is relatively unproblematic for the process view also to make sense of *kamma* and rebirth.

Consider *kamma* first. The issue here may be understood by thinking about a single life in which I perform a morally good action now and this results in greater happiness for me next year.

[6]   See ibid., chapter 8.

The objection is that this makes sense only if I am a substance-self, a distinct entity with identity that both performs the action now and gains the benefit later. The response is that this also makes sense if I am a process-self. As long as there is sufficient causal continuity and similarity between my process-self now and my process-self later, the idea of *kamma* is coherent. [. . .] If the process view can make sense of ordinary cases in which we speak of identity over time, then it can also make sense *of kamma.* Of course, it is another question whether *kamma* is true.

A related objection is that process-selves are not adequate to explain our beliefs concerning moral responsibility – for example, that we hold persons accountable, and praise and blame them, for what they have done. We should remember that *kamma* is not put forth as a doctrine of moral responsibility. It is an account of the causal relationships between the moral quality of our actions and our subsequent well-being, and it does not refer to our practices of holding people accountable. Nonetheless, we might reasonably think that, in order to be adequate, the process view should be able to make sense of these practices. According to the process view, it does make sense of them. Once again, all we need is causal continuity and similarity, not identity. As long as my process-self now stands in the right causal relationships to my process-self in the past, it is reasonable to hold my current process-self accountable for the actions of my past process-self.

Let us now consider the consistency of the idea of rebirth and the not-self doctrine. The objection is that I could be reborn only if the substance-self that is now me were to exist in a later life. The response is that rebirth would also make sense if I were a process-self and not a substance-self. A dialogue with the *bhikkhu* Sāti suggests that the Buddha accepted this view. Sāti wonders whether "it is this same consciousness that runs and wanders through the round of rebirths, not another." The Buddha replies: "Misguided man, to whom have you ever known me to teach the *Dhamma* in that way? Misguided man, in many discourses have I not stated consciousness to be dependency arisen, since without a condition there is no origination of consciousness?" (M 350). The Buddha rejects the claim that "this same consciousness" is

reborn. That is a version of the substance view. Instead, the Buddha says we should think of consciousness in terms of dependent origination. This refers to the process view, and it suggests that rebirth should be understood in terms of a causal continuity between a process-self in one life and in another life that is its rebirth.

There is an obvious complication here. Suppose I die and am reborn as a person in a subsequent life. There is no *physical* continuity between me and this later person. At death my body disintegrates, and there is no evident causal connection between that disintegrating body and the physical beginning of the life of the later person. But on this account there has to be some causal continuity between me and the later person if he or she is to be the rebirth of me. Hence, the causal continuity must concern my *mental* attributes, and this mental continuity must be understood as not depending on physical continuity. In short, the Buddha thought that in rebirth my mental process-self now stands in a relationship of causal continuity, and presumably consequent similarity, with the later mental process-self that is my rebirth (this would obviously have to be the case if I were reborn as a god). He assigned consciousness (*viññāṇa*) the role of conveying this continuity (see L 226). In this way, the process view can make sense of rebirth. Moreover, as long as there is mental continuity, the effects of the morality of my actions in this life can be felt in the experiences of a successor life. Hence, both *kamma* and rebirth may be reconciled with the not-self doctrine.

This reconciliation presupposes that the physical world is not the whole of reality. But it is obvious for many reasons that the Buddha accepted this presupposition. The distinction between mentality (*nāma*) and materiality (*rūpa*) is pervasive. Moreover, any account of rebirth would need to accept it as well, since it is difficult to render rebirth intelligible in a strictly physical framework (given what we know of the physical world). Hence, this presupposition is not problematic in showing the consistency of the idea of rebirth and the not-self teaching. Of course, it is a further question as to whether this idea is correct.

A final word about the consistency objection is in order. Early in the history of Buddhism a distinction was drawn between "ultimate truth" (*paramattha sacca*) and "conventional truth" (*sammuti sacca*). It is sometimes said that this distinction may be employed to answer the consistency objection as follows. When the Buddha says there are no selves, he should be understood as expressing ultimate truth, and when he speaks as if there are selves, as in the doctrines of *kamma* and rebirth, he should be interpreted as referring to conventional truth. The distinction between ultimate and conventional truth is not explicitly drawn in the *Sutta Piṭaka*, but it has such a long history that it is commonly regarded as an implicit feature of the Buddha's teaching.[7] However, despite its long lineage, the use of the distinction in the response to the consistency objection is misleading. The problem is not merely that the Buddha speaks as if there are selves. It is that the ideas of *kamma* and rebirth require that there be some intelligible notion of a self that has some kind of reality. Hence, the consistency problem can be resolved only by supposing there are process-selves that have dependent reality (or selves in some sense). We might express this by saying that, though in ultimate truth there are no selves in any sense, in conventional truth there are process-selves. However, this is misleading at least insofar as the English phrase "conventional truth" implies conventions people have agreed to for the sake of convenience, such as the division of the week into seven days. The reality of process-selves is more fundamental and stubborn than a mere convention: though it does depend on what we believe, it is deeply rooted in our entire way of living, and it can be overcome only by the rigorous program of the Eightfold Path.

Abbreviations

References are to page numbers, preceded by volume number in roman numerals when appropriate. Translations are sometimes altered slightly for the sake of uniformity.

L   *The Long Discourses of the Buddha*, translated by M. Walshe, Boston: Wisdom Publications, 1987.

M   *The Middle Length Discourses of the Buddha*, translated by Bhikkhu Ñāṇamoli and Bhikkhu Bodhi, Boston: Wisdom Publications, 1995.

N   *Numerical Discourses of the Buddha: An Anthology of Suttas from the Aṅguttara Nikāya*, translated by N. Thera and Bhikkhu Bodhi, Walnut Creek, CA: AltaMira Press, 1999.

---

[7] "These are merely names, expressions, turns of speech, designations in common use in the world, which the *Tathāgata* uses without misapprehending them" (L 169). For discussion of this distinction, see K. N. Jayatilleke, *Early Buddhist Theory of Knowledge* (London: George Allen & Unwin, 1963), pp. 361–8.

50

Nondualistic Problems of Immortality

Roy W. Perrett

[...] In order to understand properly the Hindu eschatology that is presented in Advaita Vedānta, a couple of preliminary points are necessary. Firstly, that the monistic picture under discussion is a particular Hindu *eschatology*, rather than a "pareschatology."[1] That is, it is a picture of the ultimate post-mortem state (*mokṣa*), rather than a picture of what happens between death and that ultimate state. In Advaita Vedānta (as in all Hindu thought) it is held that ordinary beings after death are reincarnated again. Only those who have freed themselves of binding ignorance (*avidyā*) will achieve the final state of release (*mokṣa*) wherein human individuality has been left behind.

Secondly, although this monistic picture is evident in various of the *Upaniṣads* (and hence scripturally based), Advaita Vedānta is only *one* Hindu philosophical system. It has been (and remains) one of the most important and influential Hindu views, but it would nevertheless be an error to mistake it for *the* Hindu position. Within Vedānta alone there are rival schools like Visiṣṭādvaita and Dvaita that oppose Advaitin monism in the cause of theism. Similarly, both Vaiṣṇava theologians (like Nimbārka and the followers of Caitanya) and the school of Śaiva Siddhānta insist on a dualism between God and his creation. Finally, within the orthodox six schools of Hindu philosophy (*ṣaḍdarśana*) Nyāya, Vaiśeṣika, Sāṃkhya, Yoga, and Mīmāṃsā all affirm that *mokṣa* involves the existence of innumerable, monadic disembodied selves.

A good example of this latter view can be found in what is probably the oldest of the Indian dualist schools: namely, Sāṃkhya, classically expounded in Īśvarakṛṣṇa's *Sāṃkhyakārikā*.[2] Indeed, in order to understand the Advaitin position better it will be helpful, first, to say a little about the Sāṃkhya system and, secondly, to indicate how Advaita can be seen as developing some of its characteristic theses in relation to difficulties implicit in the Sāṃkhya view.

Sāṃkhya is clearly a dualistic system in that it espouses a radical division of reality into two categories: *puruṣa* ("spirit," "soul") and *prakṛti* ("nature," "matter"). Suffering is caused by our confusion of *puruṣa* with *prakṛti*, and emancipation follows from correct understanding of the real nature of *puruṣa* and its difference from *prakṛti*.

"Nondualistic Problems of Immortality," a selection from "Dualistic and Nondualistic Problems of Immortality" by Roy W. Perrett, in *Philosophy East and West* 35:4 (October 1985): 341–50. Reprinted by permission of the University of Hawai'i Press.

[1] This useful terminology was coined by John Hick in his *Death and Eternal Life* (London: Collins, 1976), p. 12.

[2] For translations of this and other Sāṃkhya texts see Sarvepalli Radhakrishnan and Charles A. Moore, eds, *A Sourcebook in Indian Philosophy* (Princeton, New Jersey: Princeton University Press, 1957), pp. 426–52. A [...]

In keeping with its intellectualistic conception of liberation, Sāṃkhya attempts to present rational *arguments* for its major theses. Thus the existence of *puruṣa* is argued for (*Kārikā* XVII) on the grounds that consciousness exists and distinctions in the world are *for* this consciousness, which is itself apart from the world. If it were not so apart, *puruṣa* would be determined by the world and liberation would be impossible. Moreover there must be a plurality of *puruṣas* because otherwise whatever happens to one consciousness will happen at the same time to every consciousness, which is contrary to the perceived diversity of births, deaths, and faculties (XVIII).

Prakṛti, on the other hand, is a unitary material substance which evolves into the world we perceive through our senses. The proximity of *puruṣa* acts as a catalyst in releasing the causal transformation of primordial nature (*mūlaprakṛti*) into the whole of the perceptible world (XX). It is important to note, however, that while Sāṃkhya insists on a dualism of *puruṣa* and *prakṛti*, the intellect (*buddhi*) is itself considered to be a highly refined type of matter. Hence there is no mind–body dualism here as in Western metaphysics, for while *puruṣa* is individual consciousness, it is itself inactive. The active, personal self-consciousness in Sāṃkhya is associated with the notions of *buddhi*, *ahaṃkāra*, and *manas*, that is, the first evolutes of *prakṛti*.

Now Sāṃkhya maintains that the association of *puruṣa* and *prakṛti* is the cause of suffering. Thus it is held to be crucial to recognize that *puruṣa* and *prakṛti* are absolutely separate. *Puruṣa* is not in fact bound to the world, but merely appears so to the undiscriminating. Rather only *prakṛti* in its various forms transmigrates, is bound and is released (LXII). Even though *puruṣa* and *prakṛti* are in proximity to and in association with each other and this proximity activates the evolution of *prakṛti*, they remain nonetheless entirely separate realities. The soteriological goal is *kaivalya* (literally "isolation"), wherein the true nature of the *puruṣa* as "pure consciousness" is rediscovered. Sāṃkhya eschatology offers a picture of innumerable monadic *puruṣas* in *kaivalya*.

Two points are especially worth noting about this picture. Firstly, the "pure consciousness" gambit might be seen as an attempt to meet the difficulties [...] that attend the ascription of feelings and sensations to disembodied souls. The *puruṣa* is just pure, contentless consciousness; its condition in *kaivalya* is a condition in which consciousness is no longer consciousness of something. However, this leads us to the second point. Even if *puruṣas* are not personal, they are supposed to be individual, and a plurality of them is supposed to exist. But, as the Advaitins were quick to point out, there is no sense in talking of a plurality of pure, contentless consciousness. What distinguishes one consciousness from another? Thus, while Advaita accepts the intelligibility of the notion of a pure, contentless consciousness, it insists that there can only be *one* such consciousness, that is, *Brahman*. The crux of Advaita is the assertion of nonduality between the Self (*ātman*) and the Absolute (*Brahman*). Advaita interprets the Upaniṣadic "*tat tvam asi*" ("Thou art That") to mean that *Brahman* and *ātman* are in reality one. The highest truth (*paramārtha*) is that there exists only one supreme contentless consciousness, although in terms of our ordinary (*vyāvahārika*) knowledge it is proper to talk of individual transmigrating selves (*jīvas*).

This position is by no means free of difficulties. Some of these centre around the notion of a pure, contentless consciousness. In his *Śrībhāṣya* (I.1.1) the Viśiṣṭādvaitin philosopher Rāmānuja puts forward some trenchant criticisms of this notion. Firstly, Rāmānuja argues that consciousness is irreducibly intentional: it is always *someone's* consciousness of *something*. Here he appeals to ordinary usage:

> ...as appears from ordinary judgments such as "I know the jar", "I understand this matter", "I am conscious of (the presence of) this piece of cloth."[3]

The standard Advaitin reply to this criticism, drawing upon the four-level analysis of consciousness in the *Māṇḍūkya Upaniṣad*, is that in

---

[3] *The Vedānta-Sūtras with the Commentary by Rāmānuja*, trans. George Thibaut (Delhi: Motilal Banarsidass, 1962), p. 56.

the state of deep dreamless sleep (*suṣupti*) we do have a glimpse of this consciousness without a content. Rāmānuja rejects this analysis of the deep sleep state. When content is lost from consciousness, as when the individual passes from the waking or dreaming state into the state of deep dreamless sleep, what we say is not that he is now aware of contentless consciousness but that he is *unconscious*. As evidence, Rāmānuja draws our attention to the manner in which we express the state of deep, dreamless sleep to ourselves and to others. This is "by the thought presenting itself to the person risen from sleep, 'For so long a time I was not conscious of anything.'"[4] Furthermore, Rāmānuja argues that there can be no proof of a substance devoid of difference nor any meaningful talk of such a thing since all our means of valid knowledge (the *pramāṇas* of Indian philosophy) and the very language in which we express this knowledge are dependent on difference and distinction.

Thus a "pure consciousness" is indistinguishable from unconsciousness. As David Hume was later to remark about a similar conception of a divine mind:

A mind, whose acts and sentiments and ideas are not distinct and successive; one, that is wholly simple, and totally immutable; is a mind, which has no thought, no reason, no will, no sentiment, no love, no hatred; or in a word, is no mind at all. It is an abuse of terms to give it that appellation; and we may as well speak of limited extension without figure, or of number without composition.[5]

Moreover, "survival" of death conceived in terms of the continued existence of a pure contentless consciousness can apparently have no real personal relevance to an *individual*. The Advaitin eschatology seems to offer only the uninteresting promise that it is the pure-contentless consciousness that persists in the state of *mokṣa*. It is these sorts of considerations that motivate Rāmānuja's second major line of attack upon the Advaitin position:

To maintain that the consciousness of the "I" does not persist in the state of final release is again altogether inappropriate. It, in fact, amounts to the doctrine – only expressed in somewhat different words – that final release is the annihilation of the self. . . . Moreover, a man who, suffering pain, mental or of other kind, . . . puts himself in relation to pain – "I am suffering pain" – naturally begins to reflect how he may once for all free himself from all these manifold afflictions and enjoy a state of untroubled ease; the desire of final release thus having arisen in him he at once sets to work to accomplish it. If, on the other hand, he were to realise that the effect of such activity would be the loss of personal existence, he surely would turn away as soon as somebody began to tell him about "release". . . . Nor must you maintain against this that even in the state of release there persists pure consciousness; for this by no means improves your case. No sensible person exerts himself under the influence of the idea that after he himself has perished there will remain some entity termed "pure light"![6]

What can the Advaitin say in reply to these charges? Let us take Rāmānuja's second objection first. The claim is that the "survival" involved in final release (*mokṣa*) is such a bleak and empty prospect that no reasonable person would be motivated to attempt to achieve such a goal. One sort of reply to this involves an appeal to the primacy of the elimination of suffering (*duḥkha*) as an intrinsic value. Thus, given that life is *duḥkha* and that *mokṣa* involves freedom from *duḥkha*, *mokṣa* is worth pursuing. This is the sort of reply offered by Nyāya-Vaiśeṣika and Sāṃkhya-Yoga. In these schools it is not claimed that the liberated soul enjoys any special happiness over and above the absence of suffering. But the Advaitins reject this minimal account of *mokṣa* and assert that the liberated soul experiences a positive bliss over and above the mere cessation of suffering. Contrary to what the Naiyāyikas claim, mere cessation of suffering cannot be sufficient for the bliss of liberation promised in the scriptures. The classic Advaitin counterexample here is Maṇḍana Miśra's in the *Brahmasiddhi* (I,2).

[4]   Ibid., p. 53.
[5]   *Dialogues Concerning Natural Religion*, IV, in Richard Wollheim, ed., *Hume on Religion* (London: Fontana, 1963), p. 133.
[6]   *The Vedānta-Sūtras with the Commentary by Rāmānuja*, pp. 69–70 [see also p. 353 below].

Consider the case of a man half immersed in a cool pond in the heat of the day. The pain due to the heat over half his body has been removed, but he is not happy because of the heat over his upper body that still exists. Hence bliss cannot be merely the absence of suffering.

This counterexample is uncompelling since it can easily be squared with the minimal account of *mokṣa* by insisting that "elimination of suffering" means "*complete* elimination of suffering." Nevertheless, it must be conceded that the Hindu scriptures do often seem to allude to the bliss of *mokṣa* in a way that it seems forced to be construed as meaning merely absence of suffering.

However, the advocates of the minimal interpretation of *mokṣa* also offer a second argument for their view. If *mokṣa* is thought to be worth seeking only because it is pleasant, then it will become an object of desire. But such a desire will be counterproductive, for the desire for a permanent state of bliss is as binding as any other desire and thus a hindrance to achievement of the goal desired. The Advaitins resist this argument. Not every motivation to action involves an attachment to an object of desire. As Maṇḍana puts it (*Brahmasiddhi* I,4), not every wish (*icchā*) is passion (*rāga*), and so actions directed towards the bliss of *Brahman* are not based on passion. True, if the activity of escaping from the suffering of *saṃsāra* and reaching the bliss of *Brahman* were passion, then the achievement of *mokṣa* would be impossible. But the desire for *mokṣa* need not be so motivated. Indeed the advocate of the minimal interpretation of *mokṣa* is himself committed to the possibility of such nonattached desires, for otherwise the desire to eliminate suffering will be just as counterproductive as the desire for the bliss of *mokṣa*. In both cases the appropriate attitude towards the object of desire is one of quiet nonattachment (*vairāgya*).

In fact this debate conflates two separate questions.[7] One question is a metaphysical question: Does an individual in the state of final release really experience some sort of eternal positive pleasure? The other question is a question in ethics or moral psychology: Should someone

intent on liberation wish to attain a final state of permanent positive pleasure? Now the Advaitins respond affirmatively to both questions; the Naiyāyikas (and Sāṃkhyas) respond negatively to both questions. In both cases the answer to the second question is based upon the answer to the first. However, if we insist on distinguishing these two questions, we can offer a resolution of the dispute here. That is, we can remain agnostic about the truth of the competing answers to the metaphysical question, but still insist that the most reasonable answer to the psycho-ethical question is the minimal one. Given that the elimination of suffering is a basic intrinsic value, then the goal of the cessation of suffering ought to be pursued for its own sake. Whether liberation also brings with it an eternal positive happiness is a separate question that need not be answered by the aspirant to *mokṣa* (and very likely cannot be answered anyway). This position has a certain resemblance (which must not, however, be overemphasized) to Kant's view about the relation between virtue and happiness. The Kantian moral agent pursues virtue for its own sake; the coincidence of virtue and happiness may be a metaphysical truth, but it ought not to be a motive to moral action.

What, however, of Rāmānuja's other line of attack? Even if we concede the highly problematic existence of a pure contentless consciousness, Rāmānuja wants to insist that this consciousness would not be *me*, and thus the post-mortem existence of such a disembodied consciousness could not represent *my* survival. This, of course, is the same identity problem [. . .] attending the notion of disembodied survival. The monistic suggestion offered by Advaita claims that there exists only one disembodied being, hence evading the problem of individuating multiple disembodied souls. However, this might seem to amount to the suggestion that if I die and achieve *mokṣa* I will be merged with the Absolute. But then the identity claim involved in maintaining a deceased person to be now one with *Brahman* is to rest upon what criterion of identity? After all, presumably all liberated souls are one with

---

[7] On the importance of distinguishing these two questions and the possibility of a "Kantian" resolution of the dispute see A. Chakrabarti, "Is Liberation (*Mokṣa*) Pleasant?" *Philosophy East and West* 33, no. 2 (April 1983): 167–82.

Brahman. But if A and B, both deceased, are one with *Brahman*, then how can both A and B survive as distinct individuals? And if they do not survive as individuals, then what content can be given to the "survival" promised here?

The Advaitin reply here begins by insisting that the identity of the Self (*ātman*) with *Brahman* does not involve a merging of the individual with the Absolute, nor a union with God, nor the achievement of a unitive state. This *ātman/Brahman* identity already obtains, whether or not it is recognized. Properly speaking, I cannot *attain mokṣa*, nor *become Brahman*. *Mokṣa* is realizing what has always been one's innate character, but has been temporarily forgotten. The classic Advaitin illustration is the case of a king's son who, brought up as a hunter from infancy, discovers he is of royal blood.[8] This discovery involves no ontological change, for he remains what he has always been: a prince. However, now he feels or realizes that he is one. Similarly, liberation is just the removal of the ignorance (*avidyā*) which hides our true nature from us.

This reply, then, involves a very bold way with the identity problem. The original problem was how to justify the claim that the liberated soul "survives" as identical with *Brahman* – in other words, what preserves identity in a process of change from life to death to *mokṣa*. Even if the claim that there exists only one disembodied Self is intelligible, what prevents my identity with it at *mokṣa* from being equivalent to the annihilation of *me* (that is, the annihilation of my personal individuality)? The Advaitin answer is extremely radical. Firstly, *mokṣa* involves no ontological change in the Self and hence involves no problem about specifying what preserves identity through change. Secondly, Advaita presses home the logic of monism and denies that the individual self ceases to exist in *mokṣa*, for the individual self was never real in the first place! Or more precisely, the individual human person (the *jīva*) is a combination of reality and appearance. It is real insofar as *ātman* is its ground;

but it is unreal insofar as it is identified as finite, conditioned, relative.

Of course, the Advaitin reply here is by no means the end of the matter. Rather it just shifts the ground of the dispute. For example, there remains a cluster of problems about the nature of the *jīva* and its relation to *ātman/Brahman*. Two influential models are offered. The first is "reflectionism" (*pratibimbavāda*), whereby the *jīva* is said to "reflect" the *ātman*. It is thus (like a reflection in a mirror) not entirely distinct from the prototype, but neither is it to be identified with the prototype. The second is "limitationism" (*avacchedavāda*), whereby *ātman* is said to be like space and the individual *jīvas* like space in jars. When the jars are destroyed, the space which they enclosed remains part of space. Two important subschools of Advaita divide in particular upon which model to prefer: the Vivaraṇa school favors "reflectionism" and the Bhāmatī school favors "limitationism." The discussion of the merits and demerits of each model is one of the major concerns of post-Śaṃkara Advaitin dialectics.[9] However, I do not wish to pursue the intricacies of the Advaitin system any further here. Suffice it for our purposes to say that Advaita has resources for dealing with the identity problem as originally posed. To do so, of course, it has to construct a whole system of monistic metaphysics and epistemology, the details of which we cannot enter into here. The characteristic tenets of the system may well turn out to be false, but the developed system is too sophisticated for a charge of incoherence to be easily proven. Nevertheless, it must be admitted that the possibility of disembodied immortality it offers requires a radically different conception of the nature and value of the individual self than that familiar to us from, for instance, the Judeo-Christian tradition.

To sum up, then: The doctrine of immortality, when conceived of in the form of disembodied survival of death, faces a number of problems – problems, for instance, about the relation of the

[8]   Compare Śaṃkara's *Bṛhadāraṇyakopaniṣad-bhāṣya*, II.1.20. The illustration is not unique to Advaita: compare *Saṃkhyasūtra*, 4.1.
[9]   For an interesting review of some of this argumentation see Karl H. Potter, *Presuppositions of India's Philosophies* (Englewood Cliffs, NJ: Prentice-Hall, 1963), pp. 157–182.

doctrine to dualism, and about the intelligibility of ascribing typical person-predicates to disembodied beings. These, however, do not seem insuperable. But the identity problem remains far more recalcitrant. One way to try to meet this problem is the monistic eschatology offered in Advaita Vedānta. Although apparently coherent, this scenario requires a fully developed monism and a correspondingly radical appraisal of the notion of the individual human person.

There is, however, a further consideration that may make the Advaitin eschatology seem less strange than it might appear at first sight. This is to do with the *value* of immortality. Many religious traditions recognize that the religious significance of immortality cannot consist simply in endless duration; a transformed quality of post-mortem life is required. Recall also in this connection Wittgenstein's remarks about the temporal immortality of the human soul in the *Tractatus* (6.4312):

> . . . but, in any case, this assumption completely fails to accomplish the purpose for which it has always been intended. Or is some riddle solved by my surviving forever? Is not this eternal life itself as much of a riddle as our present life?

But then the problem of immortality becomes twofold. On the one hand we have the *intelligibility* problem; and on the other hand, we have the *value* problem. Now in this paper we have been basically concerned with the intelligibility question. The identity difficulty that bedevils the notion of disembodied existence is a problem about the intelligibility of one version of the doctrine of immortality. Advaita meets this difficulty at a cost, for it involves radically reconstruing the nature and value of ordinary empirical life and the individual human person.

However, it does seem that if immortality is to have any real value it must involve a transformation of ordinary mortal life. Consider, for instance, John Hick's widely discussed defence of the notion of resurrection.[10] Hick posits a

doctrine of resurrection to assist with two outstanding problems: (i) to provide for the meaningfulness of religious assertions via the possibility of eschatological falsification; and (ii) to solve the problem of evil by allowing for post-mortem restitution. But in both cases the attempt to meet the attendant identity problem involves insisting on the close similarities between the ante-mortem and post-mortem lives. However, if the lives are *that* similar, then the desired resolution of the ante-mortem difficulties that the doctrine of resurrection was supposed to offer will presumably be just as unsatisfactorily inconclusive in the afterlife as it is in this life.[11] Price's scenario of disembodied existence, on the other hand, attempts to provide a genuinely *different* sort of afterlife; and hence faces the identity problem. There seems, then, a kind of "dilemma of immortality" here. If immortality is construed as being very like this life, we can perhaps make better sense of the identity claim involved; but the value question remains unresolved. However, if we insist on a very sharp difference between ordinary life and immortality, we can perhaps meet the value problem; but we then face the recalcitrant identity problem.

Insofar as the doctrine of immortality is supposed to have religious significance, the value problem will be felt by adherents of the doctrine to be particularly pressing. Now Advaita Vedānta is clearly a religious philosophy. Hence it is not surprising to see it giving prominence to the value difficulty, which it tries to meet by an insistence on the essential divinity of the *ātman* and its identity with the Absolute. The eschatological picture offered, then, is one distinct from ordinary, worldly existence. This move, of course, sharpens the other horn of the dilemma in the form of the identity problem attending the notion of disembodied "survival." The Advaitin solution is radical, but apparently coherent. Its initial strangeness may be less likely to put us off if we realise how it tries to enable its adherents to evade the "dilemma of immortality" in a consistent and religiously satisfactory way.

---

[10]   See especially his *Faith and Knowledge*, 2d ed. (London: Macmillan, 1967), chap. 8; *Evil and the God of Love* (London: Fontana, 1968), chap. 17; and *Death and Eternal Life*, particularly chaps 8, 15.

[11]   To be fair to Hick it should be noted that his most recent position is that resurrection is only a possible *paraeschatology*. Ultimately the value question will have to be resolved on the level of a possible *eschatology*: compare *Death and Eternal Life*, chap. 22.

51

The Immortality of the Soul

Plato

Do we believe that there is such a thing as death?

To be sure, replied Simmias.

And is this anything but the separation of soul and body? And being dead is the attainment of this separation when the soul exists in herself, and is parted from the body and the body is parted from the soul – that is death?

Exactly: that and nothing else, he replied.

And what do you say of another question, my friend, about which I should like to have your opinion, and the answer to which will probably throw light on our present inquiry: Do you think that the philosopher ought to care about the pleasures – if they are to be called pleasures – of eating and drinking?

Certainly not, answered Simmias.

And what do you say of the pleasures of love – should he care about them?

By no means.

And will he think much of the other ways of indulging the body, – for example, the acquisition of costly raiment, or sandals, or other adornments of the body? Instead of caring about them, does he not rather despise anything more than nature needs? What do you say?

I should say that the true philosopher would despise them.

Would you not say that he is entirely concerned with the soul and not with the body? He would

like, as far as he can, to be quit of the body and turn to the soul.

That is true.

In matters of this sort philosophers, above all other men, may be observed in every sort of way to dissever the soul from the body.

That is true.

Whereas, Simmias, the rest of the world are of opinion that a life which has no bodily pleasures and no part in them is not worth having; but that he who thinks nothing of bodily pleasures is almost as though he were dead.

That is quite true.

What again shall we say of the actual acquirement of knowledge? – is the body, if invited to share in the inquiry, a hinderer or a helper? I mean to say, have sight and hearing any truth in them? Are they not, as the poets are always telling us, inaccurate witnesses? and yet, if even they are inaccurate and indistinct, what is to be said of the other senses? – for you will allow that they are the best of them?

Certainly, he replied.

Then when does the soul attain truth? – for in attempting to consider anything in company with the body she is obviously deceived.

Yes, that is true.

Then must not existence be revealed to her in thought, if at all?

"The Immortality of the Soul" from the *Phaedo* by Plato, in *Dialogues of Plato*, trans. Benjamin Jowett (New York: D. Appleton and Co., 1898), pp. 414–16; 421; 432–5.

Yes.

And thought is best when the mind is gathered into herself and none of these things trouble her, – neither sounds nor sights nor pain nor any pleasure, – when she has as little as possible to do with the body, and has no bodily sense or feeling, but is aspiring after being?

That is true.

And in this the philosopher dishonors the body; his soul runs away from the body and desires to be alone and by herself?

That is true.

[...]

And now, Simmias and Cebes, I have answered those who charge me with not grieving or repining at parting from you and my masters in this world; and I am right in not repining, for I believe that I shall find other masters and friends who are as good in the world below. But all men cannot receive this, and I shall be glad if my words have any more success with you than with the judges of Athenians.

Cebes answered: I agree, Socrates, in the greater part of what you say. But in what relates to the soul, men are apt to be incredulous; they fear that when she leaves the body her place may be nowhere, and that on the very day of death she may be destroyed and perish, – immediately on her release from the body, issuing forth like smoke or air and vanishing away into nothingness. For if she could only hold together and be herself after she was released from the evils of the body, there would be good reason to hope, Socrates, that what you say is true. But much persuasion and many arguments are required in order to prove that when the man is dead the soul yet exists, and has any force or intelligence.

True, Cebes, said Socrates; and shall I suggest that we talk a little of the probabilities of these things?

I am sure, said Cebes, that I should greatly like to know your opinion about them.

[...]

Must we not, said Socrates, ask ourselves some question of this sort? – What is that which, as we imagine, is liable to be scattered away, and about which we fear? and what again is that about which we have no fear? And then we may

proceed to inquire whether that which suffers dispersion is or is not of the nature of soul – our hopes and fears as to our own souls will turn upon that.

That is true, he said.

Now the compound or composite may be supposed to be naturally capable of being dissolved in like manner as of being compounded; but that which is uncompounded, and that only, must be, if anything is, indissoluble.

Yes; that is what I should imagine, said Cebes.

And the uncompounded may be assumed to be the same and unchanging, whereas the compound is always changing and never the same?

That I also think, he said.

Then now let us return to the previous discussion. Is that idea or essence, which in the dialectical process we define as essence or true existence – whether essence of equality, beauty, or anything else: are these essences, I say, liable at times to some degree of change? or are they each of them always what they are, having the same simple self-existent and unchanging forms, and not admitting of variation at all, or in any way, or at any time?

They must be always the same, Socrates, replied Cebes.

And what would you say of the many beautiful, – whether men or horses or garments or any other things which may be called equal or beautiful, – are they all unchanging and the same always, or quite the reverse? May they not rather be described as almost always changing and hardly ever the same, either with themselves or with one another?

The latter, replied Cebes; they are always in a state of change.

And these you can touch and see and perceive with the senses, but the unchanging things you can only perceive with the mind – they are invisible and are not seen?

That is very true, he said.

Well, then, he added, let us suppose that there are two sorts of existences, one seen, the other unseen.

Let us suppose them.

The seen is the changing, and the unseen is the unchanging?

That may be also supposed.

And, further, is not one part of us body, and the rest of us soul?

To be sure.

And to which class may we say that the body is more alike and akin?

Clearly to the seen: no one can doubt that.

And is the soul seen or not seen?

Not by man, Socrates.

And by "seen" and "not seen" is meant by us that which is or is not visible to the eye of man?

Yes, to the eye of man.

And what do we say of the soul? is that seen or not seen?

Not seen.

Unseen then?

Yes.

Then the soul is more like to the unseen, and the body to the seen?

That is most certain, Socrates.

And were we not saying long ago that the soul when using the body as an instrument of perception, that is to say, when using the sense of sight or hearing or some other sense (for the meaning of perceiving through the body is perceiving through the senses), – were we not saying that the soul too is then dragged by the body into the region of the changeable, and wanders and is confused; the world spins round her, and she is like a drunkard when under their influence?

Very true.

But when returning into herself she reflects; then she passes into the realm of purity, and eternity, and immortality, and unchangeableness, which are her kindred, and with them she ever lives, when she is by herself and is not let or hindered; then she ceases from her erring ways, and being in communion with the unchanging is unchanging. And this state of the soul is called wisdom?

That is well and truly said, Socrates, he replied.

And to which class is the soul more nearly alike and akin, as far as may be inferred from this argument, as well as from the preceding one?

I think, Socrates, that, in the opinion of every one who follows the argument, the soul will be infinitely more like the unchangeable, – even the most stupid person will not deny that.

And the body is more like the changing?

Yes.

Yet once more consider the matter in this light: When the soul and the body are united, then nature orders the soul to rule and govern, and the body to obey and serve. Now which of these two functions is akin to the divine? and which to the mortal? Does not the divine appear to you to be that which naturally orders and rules, and the mortal that which is subject and servant?

True.

And which does the soul resemble?

The soul resembles the divine, and the body the mortal, – there can be no doubt of that, Socrates.

Then reflect, Cebes : is not the conclusion of the whole matter this, – that the soul is in the very likeness of the divine, and immortal, and intelligible, and uniform, and indissoluble, and unchangeable; and the body is in the very likeness of the human, and mortal, and unintelligible, and multiform, and dissoluble, and changeable. Can this, my dear Cebes, be denied?

No, indeed.

But if this is true, then is not the body liable to speedy dissolution? and is not the soul almost or altogether indissoluble?

Certainly.

And do you further observe, that after a man is dead, the body, which is the visible part of man, and has a visible framework, which is called a corpse, and which would naturally be dissolved and decomposed and dissipated, is not dissolved or decomposed at once, but may remain for a good while, if the constitution be sound at the time of death, and the season of the year favorable? For the body when shrunk and embalmed, as is the custom in Egypt, may remain almost entire through infinite ages; and even in decay, still there are some portions, such as the bones and ligaments, which are practically indestructible. You allow that?

Yes.

And are we to suppose that the soul, which is invisible, in passing to the true Hades, which like her is invisible, and pure, and noble, and on her way to the good and wise God, whither, if God will, my soul is also soon to go, – that the soul, I repeat, if this be her nature and origin, is blown away and perishes immediately on quitting the body, as the many say? That can never be, my dear Simmias and Cebes. The truth rather is that the soul which is pure at departing draws after her no bodily taint, having never voluntarily had connection with the body, which she is ever avoiding, herself gathered into herself (for such abstraction has been the study of her life). And what does this mean but that she has been a true disciple of philosophy, and has practised how to die easily? And is not philosophy the practise of death?

Certainly.

That soul, I say, herself invisible, departs to the invisible world, – to the divine and immortal and rational: thither arriving, she lives in bliss and is released from the error and folly of men, their fears and wild passions and all other human ills, and forever dwells, as they say of the initiated, in company with the gods. Is not this true, Cebes?

Yes, said Cebes, beyond a doubt.

52

The Conscious Subject Persists in the State of Release

Ramanuja

To maintain that the consciousness of the "I" does not persist in the state of final release is again altogether inappropriate. It, in fact, amounts to the doctrine – only expressed in somewhat different words – that final release is the annihilation of the self. The "I" is not a mere attribute of the self so that even after its destruction the essential nature of the self might persist – as it persists on the cessation of ignorance; but it constitutes the very nature of the self. Such judgments as "I know," "Knowledge has arisen in me," show, on the other hand, that we are conscious of knowledge as a mere attribute of the self. – Moreover, a man who, suffering pain, mental or of other kind – whether such pain be real or due to error only – puts himself in relation to pain – "I am suffering pain" – naturally begins to reflect how he may once for all free himself from all these manifold afflictions and enjoy a state of untroubled ease; the desire of final release thus having arisen in him he at once sets to work to accomplish it. If, on the other hand, he were to realise that the effect of such activity would be the loss of personal existence, he surely would turn away as soon as somebody began to tell him about "release." . . . Nor must you maintain against this that even in the state of release there persists pure consciousness; . . . No sensible person exerts himself under the influence of the idea that after he himself has perished there will remain some entity termed "pure light"! – What constitutes the "inward" self thus is the "I," the knowing subject.

This "inward" self shines forth in the state of final release also as an "I," for it appears to itself. The general principle is that whatever being appears to itself appears as an "I"; both parties in the present dispute establish the existence of the transmigrating self on such appearance. On the contrary, whatever does not appear as an "I," does not appear to itself, as jars and the like. Now, the emancipated self does thus appear to itself, and therefore it appears as an "I." Nor does this appearance as an "I" imply in any way that the released self is subject to ignorance and implicated in the *saṃsāra* [cycle of existence]; for this would contradict the nature of final release, and, moreover, the consciousness of the "I" cannot be the cause of ignorance and so on. Ignorance is either ignorance as to essential nature, or the cognition of something under an aspect different from the real one (as when a person suffering from

"The Conscious Subject Persists in the State of Release" by Ramanuja, in *A Sourcebook in Indian Philosophy*, ed. Sarvepalli Radhakrishnan and Charles A. Moore (Princeton, NJ: Princeton University Press, 1957), pp. 547–8. © 1957 Princeton University Press, 1985 renewed PUP. Reprinted by permission of Princeton University Press.

jaundice sees all things yellow), or cognition of what is altogether opposite in nature (as when mother of pearl is mistaken for silver). Now the "I" constitutes the essential nature of the self; how, then, can the consciousness of the "I," i.e., the consciousness of its own true nature, implicate the released self in ignorance, or, in the *saṁsāra*? The fact, rather, is that such consciousness destroys ignorance, and so on, because it is essentially opposed to them. . . .

53

What is Reborn is Neither the Same Nor Another

Anonymous (Translator T. W. Rhys Davids)

The king said: "He who is born, Nâgasena, does he remain the same or become another?"

"Neither the same nor another."

"Give me an illustration."

"Now what do you think, O king? You were once a baby, a tender thing, and small in size, lying flat on your back. Was that the same as you who are now grown up?"

"No. That child was one, I am another."

"If you are not that child, it will follow that you have had neither mother nor father, no! nor teacher. You cannot have been taught either learning, or behaviour, or wisdom. What, great king! is the mother of the embryo in the first stage different from the mother of the embryo in the second stage, or the third, or the fourth? Is the mother of the baby a different person from the mother of the grown-up man? Is the person who goes to school one, and the same when he has finished his schooling another? Is it one who commits a crime, another who is punished by having his hands or feet cut off?"

"Certainly not. But what would you, Sir, say to that?"

The Elder replied: "I should say that I am the same person, now I am grown up, as I was when I was a tender tiny baby, flat on my back. For all these states are included in one by means of this body."

"Give me an illustration."

"Suppose a man, O king, were to light a lamp, would it burn the night through?"

"Yes, it might do so."

"Now, is it the same flame that burns in the first watch of the night, Sir, and in the second?"

"No."

"Or the same that burns in the second watch and in the third?"

"No."

"Then is there one lamp in the first watch, and another in the second, and another in the third?"

"No. The light comes from the same lamp all the night through."

"Just so, O king, is the continuity of a person or thing maintained. One comes into being, another passes away; and the rebirth is, as it were, simultaneous. Thus neither as the same nor as another does a man go on to the last phase of his self-consciousness."

[...]

The king said: "What is it, Nâgasena, that is reborn?"

"What is Reborn is Neither the Same Nor Another" from the *Questions of King Milinda*, trans. T. W. Rhys Davids (Delhi: Motilal Banarsidass Publishers, 1890/1992), pp. 63–4; 71–4. Reprinted by permission of Motilal Banarsidass Publishers (P) Ltd.

"Name-and-form is reborn."

"What, is it this same name-and-form that is reborn?"

"No: but by this name-and-form deeds are done, good or evil, and by these deeds (this Karma) another name-and-form is reborn."

"If that be so, Sir, would not the new being be released from its evil Karma?"

The Elder replied: "Yes, if it were not reborn. But just because it is reborn, O king, it is therefore not released from its evil Karma."

"Give me an illustration."

"Suppose, O king, some man were to steal a mango from another man, and the owner of the mango were to seize him and bring him before the king, and charge him with the crime. And the thief were to say: 'Your Majesty! I have not taken away this man's mangoes. Those that he put in the ground are different from the ones I took. I do not deserve to be punished.' How then? would he be guilty?"

"Certainly, Sir. He would deserve to be punished."

"But on what ground?"

"Because, in spite of whatever he may say, he would be guilty in respect of the last mango which resulted from the first one (the owner set in the ground)."

"Just so, great king, deeds good or evil are done by this name-and-form and another is reborn. But that other is not thereby released from its deeds (its Karma)."

"Give me a further illustration."

[...]

"Suppose, O king, a man were to take a lamp and go up into the top storey of his house, and there eat his meal. And the lamp blazing up were to set the thatch on fire, and from that the house should catch fire, and that house having caught fire the whole village should be burnt. And they should seize him and ask: 'What, you fellow, did you set our village on fire for?' And he should reply: 'I've not set your village on fire! The flame of the lamp, by the light of which I was eating, was one thing; the fire which burnt your village was another thing.' Now if they, thus disputing, should go to law before you, O king, in whose favour would you decide the case?"

"In the villagers' favour."

"But why?"

"Because, Sir, in spite of whatever the man might say, the one fire was produced from the other."

"Just so, great king, it is one name-and-form which has its end in death, and another name-and-form which is reborn. But the second is the result of the first, and is therefore not set free from its evil deeds."

Section VII

Making Sense of Conflicting Religious Truth Claims

Introduction

A. General Introduction to the Section

The long history of diversity in religious belief and practice is well documented. Thus, in one sense religious diversity is itself nothing new. However, for most of that history, members of one religious tradition often lived their lives with only a dim appreciation for the genuine breadth and depth of religious diversity. As cross-cultural exchange and then cross-cultural immigration began to increase rapidly, so did our understanding of differences in religious outlook. This growing appreciation for religious diversity has motivated philosophical reflection on how best to characterize the nature and significance of the apparent conflict between religious claims. The focus here, then, is that it often seems as though the claims made by those in one religious tradition cannot be true if the claims made by those of another are true. For example, note that it does not seem as though the claims in the left column can be true at the same time as those in the right.

Ultimate Sacred Reality is a personal God.	Ultimate Sacred Reality is non-personal.
God created the universe *ex nihilo* at a particular moment in time.	The universe has always existed in some form or another.
We live one and only one embodied life on earth.	We have lived and (most) will live many future embodied lives on earth.

While writing on the topic of whether one could ever justifiably believe that a miracle had occurred, David Hume articulated one way to respond to such conflicting testimony from religious persons – namely, reject all of it. Drawing on a legal analogy, he argued that when the testimony of witnesses conflicts (none of whose testimony one has special reason to privilege), it is reasonable to dismiss all of it.[1] Even if we set aside questions about whether Hume's legal analogy is an appropriate one in this context, one might wonder about what is reasonable to believe for the witnesses themselves once confronted by the fact that someone else has offered

---

[1] "Of Miracles," in *Enquires Concerning Human Understanding and Concerning the Principles of Morals*, 3rd ed., ed. P. H. Nidditch (New York: Oxford University Press, 1975), pp. 121–2.

contradicting testimony and that they too seem sincerely committed to the pursuit of truth. Would it be reasonable for each of the witnesses to continue to privilege their own testimony – that is, believe that their own perspective is correct and that of others wholly mistaken? The selections in this section seek to address the parallel question of whether it is reasonable, upon becoming aware of the extent and nature of the world's religious diversity, for members of one religious tradition to believe that members of other traditions are mistaken insofar as they make conflicting truth claims.

In recent discussions of this issue, reference is often made to three broad types of responses to the awareness of religious diversity (though these do not exhaust the possibilities). First, one may adopt an exclusivist stance, according to which one's own religious perspective on Ultimate Sacred Reality is regarded as correct and those conflicting with it are incorrect. Second, one may adopt an inclusivist stance. On this view, one grants that those in other traditions may have grasped some religious truths but holds that what is of central religious importance is still most accurately and completely apprehended in one's own tradition. Those who achieve at least a partial grasp of religious truth are thought on this view to be in some sense included in one's own tradition as "anonymous" members.[2] Third, one may adopt the pluralist stance. The pluralist holds that many (if not all) of the world religions are authentic responses to one Ultimate Sacred Reality and thus that each of their religious perspectives is roughly equally true.

B. One Ultimate Sacred Reality Apprehended Diversely or Apprehended Exclusively?

B1. *Plural Responses to the Real?*

In "A Religious Understanding of Religion: A Model of the Relationship between Traditions," John Hick argues that the most reasonable of the three positions sketched above is the pluralist view. One of the main reasons he cites for thinking so is that it seems that the world's major religious traditions each – in their own way – offer a similar path of spiritual/moral development aimed at transforming individuals away from ego-centeredness, and that they each also appear to be roughly equally successful in helping individuals achieve this goal. The best means of explaining these similarities, Hick argues, is to embrace the hypothesis that each tradition is, in fact, responding to the same Ultimate Sacred Reality, what Hick calls the Transcendent, or the Real.

A pluralist view like Hick's faces an important difficulty – namely, that the way members of each tradition characterize their Ultimate Sacred Reality often appears to be inconsistent with the characterizations offered in other traditions. The most stark of these differences was noted above – that of characterizing Ultimate Sacred Reality as a personal God vs a non-personal Absolute. How, given these very different characterizations, could members of different traditions be referring to the same thing? In order to meet this difficulty, Hick notes two distinctions: (1) a distinction often drawn within religious traditions themselves between how Ultimate Sacred Reality is characterized in words vs how it really is; and (2) a Kant-inspired distinction between how a thing is experienced through the cognitive filters of the human mind vs how it exists in-itself. Drawing on these, Hick argues that we should regard competing characterizations of Ultimate Sacred Reality as products or projections of our socially and historically conditioned contexts yet also conclude that they are nevertheless a response to a reality – the Transcendent, or the Real – that exists apart from those humanly constructed portraits.

B2. *Justifed Exclusion?*

Hick's argument suggests that once a religious person becomes aware of the genuine breadth and depth of religious diversity, it is no longer

---

[2] The phrase "anonymous Christians" was coined by theologian Karl Rahner to capture this sense in which he believed that members of other religions could nevertheless be members of his own without realizing it. See *Theological Investigations*, Vol. 5 (London: Darton, Longman, & Todd, 1966), p. 131.

reasonable for her to remain an exclusivist about religious truth. In contrast, Jerome Gellman argues "In Defence of a Contented Religious Exclusivism" that one who takes the exclusivist stance in the face of religious diversity need not be unreasonable in doing so. For Gellman, a "contented" exclusivist is one who may be aware of religious diversity but for whom that diversity has not been experienced as a problem that demands critical scrutiny. Initially, it may not be experienced as a problem because, as he notes, a religious upbringing in one's "home religion" typically supplies one with ready-made explanations for why members of other traditions have failed to recognize the truth.

So the question now becomes: Is one being unreasonable if one allows one's religious beliefs to remain unreflective by deliberately forgoing opportunities to critically reflect on them that may be generated by increased awareness of religious diversity? "Perhaps, but not necessarily," replies Gellman. We are, he says, only rationally obligated to scrutinize our beliefs when they "squeak" – that is, when something challenges our confidence in that belief – and awareness of religious diversity need not cause one's "home" beliefs to squeak. In support of this claim, he first points out that religious beliefs are typically part of a larger interpretative framework. If this framework is allowing one to successfully navigate life, including one's encounters with religious diversity, then those encounters need not cause one's exclusivist beliefs to squeak. Second, Gellman argues that theists have a special reason to be cautious about engaging in too much critical reflection – namely, that excessive critical reflection may risk undermining the personal relationship they believe themselves to enjoy with God.

B3. Is the Real Still Real?

In "John Hick and the Question of Truth" Brian Hebblethwaite traces the development of Hick's view in order to highlight an alleged instability. As he notes, much of Hick's work over the years has been aimed at defending a "realist" account of religious statements. There are three components to the realist view. First, to say that a particular religious use of language is "realist" is to say that it is asserting something to be true or false – as opposed to serving merely to express emotions or a value commitment.[3] Second, to be a realist about the use of religious language is to maintain that those assertions are referring to the existence of a transcendent Ultimate Sacred Reality – as opposed to being veiled attempts to refer only to truths about human beings.[4] Third, the realist holds that at least some of those assertions affirming the existence of an Ultimate Sacred Reality are true.

Hick refers to his own view as a "critical realist" view. On this view, religious statements reflect the fact that all human experience, including religious experience, involves an interpretative element. This is to say that all experience is influenced by the concepts one brings to that experience, concepts that in turn have been shaped by one's socio-historical circumstances. Though this is in part inspired by Kant's epistemological view, it broadens and magnifies the influence of the interpretative element in human experience. According to Hebblethwaite, it is this element that destabilizes Hick's commitment to religious realism. He argues that the human contribution to the content of religious claims is so great now on Hick's view that it is hardly recognizable as a religious perspective at all, differing very little from the naturalist's view that religion is entirely a human artifact.

---

[3] For example, Richard Schacht denies this aspect of the realist view in maintaining that "[r]eligions . . . are fundamentally a matter of the expression, affirmation, elaboration, and promotion of certain sets of values. . . . To ask whether they are true or false is to make a kind of category mistake, akin to that which one would be making if one asked the same question with respect to operas or symphonies" ("After Transcendence," in *Religion without Transcendence*, ed. D. Z. Phillips and Timothy Tessin [New York: St Martin's Press, 1997], pp. 85–6.)

[4] For example, New Testament scholar and theologian Rudolph Bultmann denies this aspect of realism in saying, "I *am* trying to substitute anthropology for theology, for I am interpreting theological affirmations as assertions about human life" (*Kerygma and Myth*, Vol. 1 [New York: Harper & Row, 1961], p. 107.)

C.   Multiple Ultimate Sacred Realities?

C1.   Plural Responses to Plural Ultimate Sacred Realities

Recall from our earlier discussion (section II) that process philosophers and theologians – similar to Buddhist thinkers – hold that a proper take on reality requires that we give metaphysical pride of place to the notion of an event, or process, rather than to that of a substance, or thing. Working from this perspective, John B. Cobb, Jr, attempts in "A Process Approach to Pluralism" to articulate a version of religious pluralism that is importantly different from that proposed by Hick.

Like Hick, Cobb grants that the mind plays an active and constructive role in human experience, including religious experience. However, Cobb emphasizes that this constructive role depends upon our capacity to discern – to varying degrees of accuracy – real features and patterns in the vast matrix of interrelated events that make up the world. On his view, religious claims about the nature of Ultimate Sacred Reality can be plausibly regarded as constructions based on *different* aspects of reality that have been discerned. In other words, members of different traditions may be referring to different Ultimate Sacred Realities, and each might be correct in their discernment. Cobb sketches three possible complementary Ultimates around which the world religions have seemed to gravitate: Formless Creativity, a Realm of Possibilities, and the World Itself. The virtues of this form of pluralism are twofold, according to Cobb. First, one can grant that individuals making conflicting claims might nevertheless each be speaking the truth, without insisting that they are, at some level, talking about the same thing. Second, one can resist the slide to sheer relativism by maintaining that reality is not wholly constructed by the human mind – that underneath the constructions is a genuine discernment of what-is.

C2.   A Dynamic Unifying of Plurality

In "A Dynamic Unity in Religious Pluralism: A Proposal from the Buddhist Point of View," Masao Abe finds much to appreciate in Cobb's respect for the differences between religions and resistance to the view that members of different religions are all, in effect, talking about the same thing. Abe finds this aspect of Cobb's view congenial to the Mahayana Buddhist emphasis on the emptiness of all views. No view, from this perspective, can claim to be genuinely ultimate, yet each can be respected as distinctive and contextually ultimate. However, Abe questions a second aspect of Cobb's view – namely, his claim that the multiple Ultimate Sacred Realities are complementary rather than in tension with one another. According to Abe, one could assert this complementarity only from some higher, more unified, perspective, yet Cobb seems to want to resist making claims from such an overarching standpoint.

Abe then argues that one can make sense of the complementary nature of the various Ultimates by invoking an analogy with the *tri-kaya*, or "three bodies," doctrine in Mahayana Buddhism. According to this doctrine, Buddha Nature is made manifest in three ways: (a) as physical and historical figures (*nirmana-kaya*), e.g., Gautama Buddha; (b) as cosmic trans-historical personal beings to whom one may direct devotional practice (*sambogha-kaya*), e.g., the figure Amida Buddha in Japan; and at the most fundamental level (c) as Emptiness itself, or "Boundless Openness" (*dharma-kaya*). Utilizing this doctrine as a unifying framework, Abe suggests that the world's leading religious figures correspond to *nirmana-kaya* – that is, they are the realization in physical form of the highest religious truth. At the next level, the various conceptions of God and god-like beings correspond to *sambogha-kaya*. Finally, they, in turn, are manifestations of *dharma-kaya*, or "Boundless Openness" – a dynamic process of self-emptying – which is the ultimate ground of all. According to Abe, it is this unifying ground of all ultimates that ensures their complementary nature.

Suggestions for Further Reading

Alston, William, "Religious Diversity and the Perceptual Knowledge of God," *Faith and Philosophy* 5 (1988): 433–48.

Basinger, David, *Religious Diversity: A Philosophical Assessment* (Burlington, VT: Ashgate Publishing Company, 2002).

Chittick, William, "A Sufi Approach to Religious Diversity," in *Religion of the Heart*, ed. Seyyed Hossein Nasr and William Stoddart (Washington, DC: Foundation for Traditional Studies, 1991).

D'Costa, Gavin, "Whose Objectivity? Which Neutrality? The Doomed Quest for a Neutral Vantage Point from which to Judge Religions" *Religious Studies* 29 (1993): 79–95.

Doniger, Wendy, "Pluralism and Intolerance in Hinduism," in *Radical Pluralism and Truth*, ed. Werner G. Jeanrond and Jennifer L. Rike (New York: Crossroad Publishing, 1991), pp. 215–33.

Eddy, Paul R., "Religious Pluralism and the Divine: Another Look at John Hick's Neo-Kantian Proposal," *Religious Studies* 30 (1994): 467–78.

Griffin, David (ed.), *Deep Religious Pluralism* (Louisville, KY: Westminster John Knox Press, 2005).

Griffiths, Paul, *Problems of Religious Diversity* (Malden, MA: Blackwell Publishers, 2001).

Heim, Mark, *Salvation: Truth and Difference in Religion* (Maryknoll, NY: Orbis Books, 1995).

Kaufman, Gordon, *God-Mystery-Diversity: Christian Theology in a Pluralistic World* (Minneapolis, MN: Fortress Press, 1996).

McKim, Robert, *Religious Ambiguity and Religious Diversity* (New York: Oxford Press, 2001).

Quinn, Phillip, and Meeker, Kevin (eds), *The Philosophical Challenge of Religious Diversity* (New York: Oxford University Press, 2000).

Rowe, William, "Religious Pluralism," *Religious Studies* 35 (1999): 139–50.

Runzo, Joseph, "God, Commitment, and Other Faiths: Pluralism vs. Relativism," *Faith and Philosophy* 5 (1988): 343–64.

Senor, Thomas (ed.), *The Rationality of Belief and the Plurality of Faith* (Ithaca, NY: Cornell University Press, 1995).

Twiss, Sumner B., "The Philosophy of Religious Pluralism: A Critical Appraisal of Hick and His Critics," *The Journal of Religion* 70 (1990): 533–67.

Ward, Keith, *Religion and Revelation: A Theology of Revelation in the World's Religions* (Oxford: Clarendon Press, 1994).

A Religious Understanding of Religion
A Model of the Relationship between Traditions

John Hick

A large part of the academic study of religion consists in its objective investigation of a range of forms of human thought and behavior. This deals with the history of religions; with the interactions between religions, societies and cultures in the past and present; with the historical and literary analyses of religious texts; with the sociology of religious practices and organizations; with the psychology of religious experience and belief. And all such study is, in principle, entirely independent of the question whether or not there is any transcendent Reality of limitless value such as religious people affirm when they speak of God, *Brahman*, the *dharmakāya*, the Tao, and so on.

The objective study of religion is thus a branch of anthropology in the broadest sense of that term, and is as such of profound interest and importance as a contribution to the study of humankind.

But distinctively religious ideas and practices differ from others in referring intentionally beyond humankind and beyond our natural environment. There is accordingly a fundamental difference between non-religious understandings of religion as a human phenomenon, and religious understandings of it as our response to the Transcendent. The relationship between these two points of view is asymmetrical. A non-religious study of the religious aspects of human life cannot refer to the Transcendent, although it must of course refer to human ideas of and beliefs in a transcendent Reality. On the other hand, a religious understanding of religion must, as part of its essential discourse, refer to the Transcendent, although it can also, and indeed certainly should, be interested in the human character and material conditions of the response, in its varying forms, to the supposed transcendent Reality itself – or herself or himself.

If we set aside any naturalistic prejudice, we must acknowledge that religious understandings are intrinsically as legitimate as non-religious understandings of religion. They are also of course of particular interest to that large number of men and women who are religious practitioners or believers or – to use a truly horrid word – religionists. In the past, religious interpretations of religion have normally been restricted in their scope to a single tradition. There has been Christian discourse concerning the Holy Trinity and the history of human response to the Trinity. There has been Buddhist discourse about *nirvāṇa*, the *dharmakāya*, *śūnyatā*, and the history of human awakening to this Reality. And there has been Jewish, Muslim, Hindu,

"A Religious Understanding of Religion: A Model of the Relationship between Traditions" by John Hick, in *Inter-Religious Models and Criteria*, ed. James Kellenberger (New York: St Martins Press, 1993), pp. 21–36.

Taoist discourse, and so on. Each of these constitutes a religious (as distinguished from a non-religious or a naturalistic) account of one particular stream of religion, but not of religion around the world and across centuries.

There is of course no such thing as religion in general: religion exists only in its many concrete forms. But because there is a plurality of such concrete forms, a religious interpretation of religion over this wide range will inevitably differ from the particular self-understanding developed within any single tradition. The latter will see religion as a response specifically to the Christian Trinity, or to the Qur'ānic *Allāh*, or to *Brahman*, or the *dharmakāya*, and so on, whereas a global religious understanding of religion will see it as the range of forms taken by our human response to the Transcendent. We must not, then, expect a comprehensive religious understanding of religion to be identical with a Christian, or a Buddhist, or a Muslim, or any other one confessional interpretation of it. [. . .]

Because religion is concretely plural, a global religious interpretation of religion has to be approached through one or other of its particular concrete forms. We start from within one of the religious traditions – which in my case is Christianity. From within any one of them the believer is committed to the fundamental faith that this stream of religious experience is not purely a human projection but is at the same time a response to the presence of a transcendent Reality. But a believer must today be aware that in addition to her own religion there are also other great world faiths, as well as many smaller religious movements both old and new, all likewise seeing themselves as responses to the Transcendent. At this point she may opt for the exclusivist claim that her own religion is an authentic response to the Divine but that all others are fundamentally different in nature, as products of the human imagination, in other words follow Karl Barth in accepting Feuerbach's projection theory as applying to all forms of religion except one's own. But this is, naturally enough, a position that will only appeal to other members of the same tradition. It is thus arbitrary in a way that must worry any reasonable person. Suppose, then, that instead we follow an analogue of the Golden Rule by granting to others the same basic faith assumption

that we have made for ourselves, namely that religious experience within one's own tradition is an authentic response to the Transcendent. At this point a further choice opens up. One option is the inclusivist position that whilst other traditions are also responses to the Transcendent, our own is the purest or fullest or most direct such response, including but exceeding all that is valuable in the others. However this is only a modified version of the absolutist claim, and suffers from the same arbitrariness. The more radical alternative is the pluralist view that the great world religions all seem, so far as unbiased human observation can tell, to be more or less on a par as salvific responses to the Transcendent. Of course no comparative judgment in this area is capable of being proved. There can be endless debate between, on the one hand a Christian version, or a Buddhist version, or a Muslim or any other version of inclusivism and, on the other hand, a pluralism that acknowledges the rough parity of the great traditions as human responses to the Transcendent. However, I am not going to stage those debates here. For my concern at the moment is only to see how these traditions, despite their immense differences, may nevertheless constitute alternative responses to the same ultimate transcendent Reality; and whether or not they constitute more or less equally full and authentic responses is a further question that could only be settled – if indeed it could ever be settled – by extensive historical research into the religions of the world, studied both synchronically and diachronically. I have argued elsewhere that the historical data are so complex that one can at present only come to the negative conclusion that no one tradition stands out as soteriologically supreme: but I am not going to argue that here.

Our present question, then, is whether the great religious systems of the world can all have been formed in response to the same divine Reality. And it must be admitted that the initial appearances are against this. For the intentional objects of the different traditions are so clearly different. Phenomenologically (i.e. as describable) the Holy Trinity of Christianity is obviously not identical with the *Allāh* of Islam or with the Jahweh of biblical Judaism or the Vishnu or Shiva of theistic Hinduism. Jahweh, for example, is depicted in the Hebrew scriptures as living in close interaction with the children of Israel, but not as showing any interest in the life of India; whilst Krishna, as the incarnation of Vishnu, is depicted in the *Bhagavad Gita* as living in close interaction with some of the tribes of India but not as showing any interest in ancient Middle Eastern history. Further, the religious ideas and assumptions expressed by Krishna reflect a distinctly Indian background whilst those expressed by Jahweh are distinctly Hebraic in character. And neither these nor any other of the Gods is depicted as being at all like the non-personal *Brahman* of advaitic Hinduism, or the Tao, or the *nirvāṇa* of the Theravāda, or the *dharmakāya* or *śūnyatā* of the Mahāyāna.

Should we then opt, as regards the theistic religions, for polytheism, and as regards the non-theistic traditions, for what we shall have to call polyabsolutism? We should then be saying that *Allāh* is a real divine being who is strictly unitary and who has never become incarnate; and that the Holy Trinity is another, more complex divine being, one aspect of whom became incarnate as Jesus of Nazareth; and that Jahweh, or Adonai, is yet another divine being, specially related to the Hebrew people; and Vishnu yet another; and Shiva another; and so on. And also that *Brahman* exists, as the unlimited consciousness, *sat-chit-ānanda*, which in the depths of our own being we all are; and that in addition to this there exists the universal Buddha nature, which is the ultimate *dharmakāya*, embodied in the interdependent flow of existence when one selflessly participates in it; and that there is also the ineffable state of *nirvāṇa* which manifests itself in human spiritual enlightenment.

However, such a plurality of ultimates would reduce itself to a plurality of penultimates. For the monotheistic concept of God is that of the creator and ruler of everything that exists other than God; and clearly there can only be one such being. If there are two or more, then none of them is God, conceived as the truly ultimate Reality. The Adonai of Judaism, the Heavenly Father of Christianity, the *Allāh* of Islam, and the Vishnu of the *Bhagavad Gita* is each said to be the ground and lord of the entire universe; and clearly not more than one of them can be this. Further, none of these monotheisms is compatible with the ultimacy of a non-personal Absolute. Again, if the ultimately Real is the immutable universal consciousness of *Brahman*, it cannot also be the *dharmakāya*, which is not a consciousness; and nor again can the unchanging *Brahman* be identified with the ceaselessly changing process of *pratītya samutpāda*. Thus if the God-figures of the great monotheisms, and the Absolutes of the great non-theistic religions, are all of them real, no one of them can be the sole ultimate reality which it is said to be. The reality of any of them must reduce any other of them to a co-ultimacy or a penultimacy which its tradition firmly denies. I believe that we therefore have to consider attributing to each of them a status which is different from that attributed to them within their own religion.

But before taking such a radical step let us ask if we could instead see them as different names and descriptions of the same referent – as, for example, the names "Morning Star" and "Evening Star", which were once thought to refer to two different heavenly bodies, are now known both to refer to the planet that today we call Venus? On reflection this does not seem to be a viable move. For in order for different descriptions to have the same referent they must, although different, not be excessively incompatible. But the descriptions of the Holy Trinity, one aspect of whom became incarnate as Jesus of Nazareth, is not compatible with the description of the Qur'ānic *Allāh*, who has emphatically never become incarnate as a human being. And neither of these is compatible with the description of *Brahman* or the *dharmakāya* or *śūnyatā* or the Tao. And indeed, although there are certain limited compatibilities within the total range, the general picture is clearly one of differing descriptions which cannot all, as they stand, reasonably be regarded as referring to the same reality.

Could these differently identified realities, however, perhaps be different aspects of one larger and more complex Reality? Again, on reflection, No, not as they are currently described within their respective traditions. For in each case their descriptions do not allow them to be regarded as aspects of something greater than themselves. The God of developed monotheism is conceived, in Anselm's famous phrase, as that than which no greater can be conceived, and thus by definition not as an aspect of anything greater. And the non-personal Absolutes are likewise each presented within their own tradition as truly ultimate and thus not as an aspect of some yet larger reality. Nor for the same reason can they, as they are described within their respective traditions, be regarded as different *parts* of a greater reality, as in the ancient allegory of the elephant and the blind men.

We are driven, then, to the conclusion that if the Gods and Absolutes of the great traditions are not purely products of the human imagination, neither on the other hand can they all be simply identical with the transcendent Reality itself.

Where can a religious understanding of religion go from this apparent impasse? I suggest that the way forward involves some kind of distinction between, on the one hand, the Gods and Absolutes of the different traditions and, on the other hand, a postulated ultimate transcendent Reality in which they all are somehow grounded and of which they are all somehow expressions. For we want to say that in responding to the Gods and Absolutes, men and women are indeed responding to the ultimately Real, and yet that these experienced God-figures and non-personal Absolutes are not themselves the Ultimate as it is in itself but are nevertheless genuine manifestations of it to human awareness. We thus need a distinction such as is suggested by Joseph Campbell's phrase, "the masks of God". This implies a transcendent Ultimate, which as Westerners we call God, and a plurality of masks, or faces, or manifestations, or appearances of that reality as Jahweh, as God the Father, as the Qur'ānic *Allāh*, as *Brahmān*, as the *dharmakāya*, and so on.

In further considering such a distinction we can begin by noting that some form of it is already familiar within the thought of each of the great traditions, though occurring with varying degrees of prominence. In advaitic Hinduism it is the distinction between *nirguna Brahman*, *Brahman* without attributes because beyond the entire network of human concepts, and *saguna Brahman*, *Brahman* as humanly thought and experienced as a personal deity known under many aspects and names as the gods of the different strands of Hindu devotional life. In Mahāyāna Buddhism it is the distinction between

the *dharmakāya* as it is in itself, which is śūnyatā, emptiness – empty of everything that the human mind projects in its acts of awareness – and on the other hand that emptiness as given form within human awareness. As one classical Buddhist thinker, T'an-luan, put it, "Among Buddhas and bodhisattvas there are two aspects of *dharmakāya*: *dharmakāya*-as-suchness and *dharmakāya*-as-compassion. *Dharmakāya*-as compassion arises out of *dharmakāya*-as-suchness, and *dharmakāya*-as-suchness emerges into [human consciousness through] *dharmakāya*-as-compassion. These two aspects of *dharmakāya* differ but are not separate; they are one but not identical".[1] In Christianity the distinction is between God in God's eternal self-existent being, "before" and independently of creation, and God in relation to and as known from within the created realm – God *a se* and God *pro nobis*. In mystical Judaism and in Sufi Islam the distinction is between *En Soph*, the Infinite, or *al-haqq*, the Real, and the self-revealing God of the scriptures. And, again, the *Tao Te Ching* begins by saying that "The Tao that can be expressed is not the eternal Tao".

This distinction, between the ultimate divine Reality as it is in itself and as manifested within human thought and experience, is in line with the distinction familiar within Western epistemology between an object – say a wooden table – as it is in itself, unobserved, and that same table as it appears to different observers situated at different places or with different perceptual equipment. What is to us, at our particular point on the macro–micro scale, a table must be something very different to the fly which alights on it or the woodworm that burrows within it, or to a dog, who perhaps experiences it as much in terms of odor as of color. Further, the same entity may be differently perceived and responded to in terms of different conceptual systems. Thus stone age persons suddenly transported into the twentieth century would not see the table as a table, because they would not have the concept of a table, or the wider system of sortal and practical concepts that surrounds it and in terms of which we ourselves inhabit the world as our life environment. This distinction between things as they are

---

[1] Quoted by Shinran, *Notes on "Essentials of Faith Alone"* (Kyoto: Hongwanji International Centre, 1979), p. 5.

in themselves and as they are for different perceivers, although first introduced into western thought by the philosophers, has been confirmed more recently by cognitive psychology and further enlarged within the sociology of knowledge. Again, we are familiar from contemporary physics with the idea of a dynamic field of quanta of discharging energy in incessant motion, which is experienced by us as a single solid static colored object; and, more fundamentally, with the idea that the perceived world is relative to the location of the observer, and that the act of observation makes an important difference to what is observed. Indeed it is today virtually universally agreed that the mind is not passive in awareness but is always active, being conscious of the environment, not only as it has been heavily filtered by the limitations of our perceptual machinery, but also as it is endowed by us with meaning in terms of the system of concepts embodied in our language.

It is this conceptual contribution of the human mind that is most relevant to religious awareness. It requires the distinction between reality as it is in itself and as it comes to consciousness in terms of different systems of human concepts. I want to suggest that this distinction may provide a clue to a religious interpretation of religion in its many diverse forms. I am still restricting what I say here to the "great world faiths", because these have proved themselves as responses to the Transcendent over many centuries and in millions of lives; and when we go beyond them new issues arise which are extremely important and interesting but which I do not have time to tackle here. My suggestion, then, is that the great world religions should be seen, from a religious point of view, as having come about at the interface between the Transcendent and different human communities with their different sets of religious concepts. These concepts have made possible different modes of experience of the Transcendent, which have in turn given rise to different concrete forms of religious response. One could put this in terms borrowed from Kant's first *Critique*, as a distinction between the noumenal Transcendent or Real or Ultimate, and its plurality of phenomenal manifestations within human consciousness. In other words, something partially analogous to Kant's account of sensory experience

may apply to religious experience. Kant held that the human mind actively contributes to the experienced world by fitting it into a categorical system that brings it within the scope of a unitary finite consciousness. Thus we never observe the world as it is in itself, unobserved, but only as humanly observed; and such observation is always both selective and creative. And the religious person's awareness of the Divine is likewise not of the Divine as it is in itself but always as thought and experienced within the framework of a particular human system of religious concepts and spiritual practices.

Our human contribution to the awareness of the Transcendent is in fact both conceptual and practical. Conceptually, our sense of the Transcendent comes to consciousness in terms of one or other of the two basic notions of deity, through which the Transcendent is experienced as personal, and of the absolute, through which it is experienced as non-personal. The former is much the more widespread form of awareness, though it is not on that account to be regarded as superior. But of course religious experience is never of deity as such or of absoluteness as such, but always of a particular God figure or a particularly conceived Absolute. In Kantian terminology again, the general concept of deity or of the absolute is schematized or made more concrete, in actual experience in terms, not of abstract time, as in Kant's system, but of filled time, the time of human history and culture, including the rich particularities of the religious traditions. Accordingly the Ultimate, in being thought and experienced as a divine Thou, takes the form of a specifically male or female deity, living in relationship with this tribe or people or that, actively involved in this or in that strand of history, speaking through this or that prophet or guru. Thus the Divine is known as the Jahweh of Israel, or as the *Allāh* of the Qur'ānic revelation, or as the heavenly Father or Holy Trinity of the Christian church, or as the Vishnu or Shiva of Vaishnavite or of Shaivite Hinduism, and so on. And the parallel concept of the non-personal Absolute is likewise schematized, though with a much lesser degree of concreteness, in terms of different philosophical conceptualities (which however may well also have their own historical and cultural roots) as the eternal unchanging *Brahman*, or as the Emptiness of *śūnyatā*, or again as the ineffable *dharmakāya* or *nirvāṇa*, or the Tao, and so on.

The associated practical aspect of our human contribution to the formation of the experienced Gods and Absolutes comes through the distinctive spiritual practices that have developed within the different traditions. Thus the conception of the Transcendent as personal is both elicited and reinforced by the practice of prayer. And correlated with conceptions of the Transcendent as non-personal are different forms of meditation, leading to illumination, awakening, or becoming one with the Infinite, whether in the depths of our own being or as the immanent ground of the incessant life of the universe.

Thus a religious conceptuality and its associated spiritual practice jointly make possible the particular form of religious experience that lies at the heart of each living religion. And together with the other aspects of a tradition – its sacred scriptures and its other classical writings; its myths, legends, creeds and confessions of faith; its history and sagas and its whole treasury of stories; its saints and community leaders; its music, architecture, sculpture and painting; its life-style and its ethics – it constitutes a complex living "lens" through which those within that faith community are aware of the Divine. The particular "lens" formed by each tradition is different and unique. But they are all human products, shaping and coloring in their own way what is perceived. Thus the "lens" metaphor captures the idea of a variety of historically contingent modes of awareness of the ultimate divine Reality. That Reality is perceived as having different concrete characteristics which are joint products of the universal presence of the Divine and a particular set of human concepts and religious practices.

What does this picture imply concerning the status of the particular Gods and Absolutes – Jahweh and Vishnu, *Brahman* and the *dharmakāya*, and so on? Let us take the Jewish experience of the Divine as an example, and then proceed to generalize it. The Jahweh who was experienced in the theophanies described in the Torah, who inspired a succession of prophets to declare his will, who was experienced as acting again and again within Hebrew history, and who is known today as an unseen presence on the high holy days and in the daily life of pious Jews – this distinctive divine figure, the Adonai of Judaism, exists at the interface between the ultimate transcendent Reality and the Hebrew people. He is the Transcendent as seen through Hebrew eyes and as given form by the Hebraic religious imagination. And his laws are the particular way in which the practical difference that the presence of the Transcendent makes for human life has come to consciousness in Hebrew experience. But this particular concrete divine *persona* did not exist prior to and independently of the strand of history of which he is an integral part. What existed prior to and independently of that history is the transcendent Reality itself, whose impact upon the stream of Hebrew consciousness has taken this particular experienceable shape. The concrete figure of Jahweh is thus not identical with the ultimate divine Reality as it is in itself but is an authentic face or mask or persona of the Transcendent in relation to one particular human community.

This is, of course, the point at which a global religious understanding of religion inevitably differs from an exclusively Jewish one or, to an equal extent, from the particular understanding exclusive to any other tradition. But on the other hand such a global interpretation will add that in responding in life to the God of Abraham, Isaac and Jacob the Jewish people have been and are making their own authentic response to the Transcendent. Thus on this view Judaism is emphatically a "true religion". But it is not the one and only true religion, and its distinctive awareness of the Ultimate as Adonai is one of a plurality of awareness of different divine *personae*. For precisely the same has to be said of the heavenly Father of Christianity, of the *Allāh* of Islam, of Vishnu, of Shiva and so on.

If we now ask the same question about one of the non-personal Absolutes, or (to coin a term) the *impersonae* of the Real, the answer will be essentially similar and yet also appropriately different. In the advaitic Hindu tradition, for example, the Transcendent is experienced as the *ātman* which is also *Brahman*, the universal non-personal consciousness which we become aware of being when we totally transcend individual egoity. For a global religious understanding of religion this universal mind, which we all are in the final depths of our own being, is a manifestation of the ultimate ground of the universe, transcending the grasp of the finite intellect. But as in the case of Jahweh, the universal *ātman* did not exist prior to and independently of human life, but is a manifestation of the Ultimate to purified human consciousness. Thus, on the one hand, a pluralistic interpretation of advaitic Hinduism will deny that the *ātman* is simply identical with the transcendent Reality in itself; and this is to deny something that advaitic Hinduism affirms in its identification of *ātman* with *Brahman*. But on the other hand it will want emphatically to affirm that in relinquishing egoity to become one with the *ātman*, men and women are making an authentically salvific response to the Transcendent. Thus advaitic Hinduism is a "true" religion; but it, too, is not the one and only "true" religion. And the same has to be said in turn of each of the other non-theistic streams within the great religious traditions.

When we say that in transcending egoity to become one with the universal *ātman*, or that in living faithfully in accordance with the Torah, or that in being filled with the spirit of Christ, one is making an authentic response to the Transcendent, what is meant by "authentic"? An answer occurs only within the circle of faith which affirms that (within the great traditions at least) religious experience is not only a product of the human religious imagination but constitutes at the same time our human response to the universal presence of the Transcendent. For a religious understanding of religion, then, the great world faiths are differing human responses to the Ultimate. However they are never perfect responses, but always human, all-too-human phenomena, with the ugly marks upon them of blindness, greed, cruelty and prejudice. As historical realities each is its own unique mixture of good and evil. And so we have to look within their varied life to see, amidst this mixture, what kind of human change they centrally value as constituting a right relationship to, or within, the Transcendent. They all aim at a radical human transformation, which is variously known as salvation, redemption, peace with God, *mokṣa*, *satori*, *nirvāṇa*, awakening. I suggest that this change consists at its core in a turning from self-centredness to a new orientation centered in the Divine. The "saved" or "submitted" or "enlightened" or "awakened" person has been liberated from ego-centered concerns and has become to some significant degree "transparent" to the Transcendent. Such a one is a servant of God who,

in the words of the *Theologia Germanica*, is to the eternal Goodness what one's own hand is to a human being; or again is an enlightened or awakened one in whom the eternal reality of *Brahman*, or the universal Buddha nature, has been realized. And so when we speak of a religious tradition as constituting an authentic response to the Transcendent we mean that that tradition is an effective context of this salvific transformation. Its religious authenticity consists in its soteriological power, its capacity to mediate the transforming presence of the Transcendent to human life.

I think it is a striking fact that those whom most people within each tradition spontaneously revere as being much closer than themselves to the ideal of humanity in true relationship to the Transcendent – the saints, gurus, jivanmuktas, awakened ones – exhibit a common basic profile as unselfcentered servants or channels or realizations of the Transcendent. The fact that the systems of ideas and the images in their minds are so different, and that they have arrived in this state by such different spiritual paths, does not seem to negate what they have in common in a radical turning from ego to participate in the universal reality of the Transcendent. I cannot help thinking that if, *per impossibile*, we could bring together across the differences of time and space and language such persons as St Francis or Mother Julian, and Kabir or Ramakrishna, and al-'Arabī or Rūmī, and Shinran or the present Dalai Lama, and enable them to interact with one another, they would arrive at a profound mutual recognition and respect. Thus, if we prescind from the metaphysical theories and the historical contingencies that distinguish the people of different traditions, and look at the actual human transformation that occurs within those traditions, we find that essentially the same salvific change is taking place within all of them, even though taking such different forms as the contemplative life of a Julian of Norwich and the political activism of a Mahatma Gandhi. This is indeed the main reason for preferring the assumption of a single universal Ultimate to that of a plurality of co-penultimates. Neither possibility is compatible with the claims of the different traditions as they stand; for as they stand each tradition holds that its own object of worship or focus of meditation is truly and uniquely ultimate. But whereas the polytheism and the polyabsolutism of the plural-ultimates theory has no compensating advantage, the single-ultimate theory is supported by the consideration that since the Gods and Absolutes all seem to produce essentially the same salvific human transformation, they are probably different manifestations of the same ultimate divine Reality.

But let us look further at this idea of a single ultimate Reality underlying the plurality of divine *personae* and metaphysical *impersonae* – the Gods and the Absolutes – which are the intentional objects of worship and the foci of meditation within the great world faiths. What the metaphor of "lying behind" is meant to indicate is the relationship (in Kantian language) between an ultimate noumenal reality-in-itself which lies outside the network of human concepts, and is accordingly not experienceable by us as it is in itself; and on the other hand the phenomenal appearances of that Reality within human religious consciousness.

It follows that we cannot ascribe to the Ultimate in itself the characteristics of its concrete manifestations. The Real *an sich* is not subject to the conceptual schemas in terms of which it takes form and color within our human experience. These schemas include the distinctions of personal/non-personal, purposive/non-purposive, good/evil, substance/process, even one/many. (We speak of "the Real" only because the English language requires us to refer to the Real either as singular or as plural, and it seems less misleading to use the singular.) We cannot, then, apply any of these concrete characterizations to the ineffable Reality in itself.

This does not however mean that the proposition "The Real is personal" should, without further explanation, be declared false, for its falsity would imply that "The Real is non-personal" is true; and these two statements would jointly negate the radical ineffability claim that the personal/non-personal distinction does not apply to the Real. Consider as an analogy another case of a range of characteristics which does not apply to a given thing. Color is a mass effect of millions of molecules, and color terms apply to these aggregates but not to individual molecules. This being so, we can if we want insist on saying that a molecule is not red. And as an atomic proposition this is true. But as part of discourse about molecules it is misleading. For normally to say that

X is not red carries with it the implication that X is the sort of thing that has color but that its color is not red. To avoid this false implication, and to indicate that color words do not apply to it at all, it seems (to me) best to reject both "A molecule is red" and "A molecule is not red" and to say instead that rather than being true or false these statements do not apply to molecules. The situation is like a questionnaire that asks inappropriate questions; or like "Have you stopped beating your wife?", when Yes and No both carry false implications and the better answer is that the question does not apply. Likewise, to say that the Real is not personal would be true but misleading, since it implies that the Real is the sort of referent that could be personal, but isn't; whereas I want to say that the personal/non-personal distinction does not apply to it.

It does not follow however that we cannot say anything at all about it. We can make purely formal statements, as for example when we say that it is ineffable. For it is logically impossible to refer to something that does not even have the attribute of being incapable of being referred to! And beyond such purely formal attributions we can make the positive statement that it is that which is humanly thought and experienced in the range of ways to which the history of religions bears witness. Thus it is known, in the mode of I–Thou encounter, as a loving or demanding, sustaining or challenging, personal presence; and in the unitive mode, as the Buddha nature of all things, or as the limitless consciousness that opens up when we transcend the boundaries of the separate ego. However in itself the ultimate transcendent Reality is not identical with any or all of these, but is that which is manifested in these different ways to different human mentalities forming and formed by different spiritual paths.

However, may not some forms of mystical experience constitute an exception to the principle that we cannot experience the ultimate Reality in a direct and unmediated way but only in forms that are shaped by our own human concepts? This is today a much debated issue. Steven Katz and others, for example in *Mysticism and Philosophical Analysis*, argue that mystical experience is always shaped by the distinctive concepts of a particular tradition; whilst Ninian Smart and others argue for a core mystical experience that occurs within all the great traditions; and again Robert Forman and others, in *The Problem of Pure Consciousness*, argue that a pure content-less consciousness occurs within all of them. I do not want to argue these questions here, because the basic hypothesis that the world religions constitute different human responses to an ultimate transcendent Reality is capable of being developed in alternative ways that can accommodate either of these divergent under-standings of mysticism. However, my opinion, in brief, is this: Granting the logical possibility of a rare and exceptional form of religious awareness constituting a direct and unmediated cognition of the Real in itself, I nevertheless doubt whether we have good reason to think that this possibility is in fact realized. For the mystics who claim such a direct cognition of the Ultimate produce incompatible accounts of it as personal or as non-personal, as unchanging or as in ceaseless process. It thus looks as though their experiences have been influenced by the basic concepts of their tradition, and are accord-ingly not experiences of the Ultimate as it is in itself but rather as experienced from a particular human standpoint. Again, the pure contentless consciousness for which some contend may very well occur; but I am doubtful whether it can properly be said to be an experience of the Ultimate, or indeed properly speaking an experience of anything. It rather seems to be a moment of blank consciousness. However I am aware that I may be mistaken about this, and so I want to stress that the basic pluralistic hypothesis that I have been outlining does not in principle exclude such a possibility.

Let us now turn, finally, to the challenge that an unexperienceable Ultimate is vacuous and otiose. Why postulate a Reality that is not in itself humanly experienceable? Is it not a mere non-entity, such that it makes no difference whether it be there or not?

Let me first remind you that all of the great traditions have held that the divine Reality is ultimately beyond the grasp of human thought. The final mystery of God, of *Brahman*, the Tao, the *dharmakāya* has always been affirmed by the deeper religious minds. For example, within Christianity, St Augustine said that "God tran-scends even the mind",[2] and St Thomas declared that "by its immensity, the divine substance sur-passes every form that our intellect reaches",[3] and that "The first cause surpasses human understanding and speech".[4] And many of the Christian mystics have said similar things. St John of the Cross, for example, wrote that God "is incomprehensible and transcends all things".[5] The great Jewish thinker, Moses Maimonides, distinguished between the unknowable divine essence and the various attributes which God has in relation to us.[6] The Qur'ān declares that God is "beyond what they describe".[7] The same theme is widespread within Hinduism. The Upanishads declare that *Brahman* is that "before which words recoil, and to which no under-standing has ever attained",[8] and that "There the eye goes not, speech goes not, nor the mind".[9] And within the Buddhist tradition there has always been a strong insistence upon the radical in-ability of human thought to grasp the Ultimate: all human teachings are instances of *upaya*, "skilful means" to help the hearer towards the experience of awakening. However, this insistence upon the ineffability of the ultimate Real has always been accompanied by an equal insistence upon the religious authenticity of the concrete ways in which the Real impinges upon us in the form of revelation, enlightenment, or an experience of the divine presence in history and in individual lives. This dual affirmation of the final tran-scending mystery of the Divine in itself, and of its genuine manifestations within human experi-ence, is of course precisely the picture that I am

---

[2] *De Vera Religione*, 36:67.
[3] *Summa contra Gentiles*, I, 14, 3.
[4] *In librum De Causis*, 6.
[5] *Ascent of Mount Carmel*, [16th century], trans. E. Allison Peers (Garden City, NY: Image Books), p. 310.
[6] *Guide to the Perplexed*, I, 58.
[7] *Qur'ān* 21:22; 37:180.
[8] *Taittiriya Upanishad*, II, 4, 1.
[9] *Kena Upanishad*, I, 3.

advocating and am seeking to generalize across the entire field of the religions.

We can now directly face the question, Why postulate an ineffable and unexperienceable divine Reality "behind" the experienced Gods and Absolutes? The answer lies in the difference between a religious and a naturalistic understanding of religion. We have to recognize today that there is a considerable human element in religion in all of its many forms. It has been evident and undeniable at least since the work of Max Weber, Emile Durkheim, and Sigmund Freud that geographical, climatic, economic, political, sociological and psychological factors have always influenced the development of religious ideas, beliefs, practices and modes of experience. The question is whether this is all that there is to religion or whether in ways shaped by these mundane circumstances religion constitutes our human response to the Transcendent. Is religious projection a purely gratuitous or a genuinely responsive projection?

To affirm that it is responsive is to affirm the transcendent Reality to which it is a response. But because of the plurality of religions, this cannot be simply identified with the distinctively Christian or the distinctively Buddhist or the distinctively Muslim or any other one particular conception of it. And to affirm the Ultimate beyond these divine *personae* and metaphysical *impersonae* is to insist that they are not purely human projections but are the forms taken by our human awareness of the transcendent Reality.

So far, then, from it making no difference whether we postulate an ineffable divine Reality behind the experienced God-figures and the experienced non-personal Absolutes, it makes the greatest possible difference – the difference between a religious and a non-religious understanding of religion. Putting it another way, the central issue between a realist – not of course a naive but a critical realist – interpretation of religious language, and a non-realist and therefore naturalistic interpretation of it, hinges upon the affirmation or denial of an ultimate divine Reality beyond the immediate objects of worship and foci of religious meditation. For since the fact that there is a plurality of these intentional objects and foci means that they cannot each be simply identified with the Ultimate in itself, the faith that they are not purely creations of the human imagination requires the affirmation of a transcendent Reality that underlies them and is manifested to us through them.

55

In Defence of a Contented Religious Exclusivism

Jerome Gellman

My topic is the epistemology of religious plural-ism. I want to defend the possibility that what I call a "contented religious exclusivist" will be fully rational and not neglectful of any of her epi-stemic duties in holding to her exclusivism.

A "religious exclusivist" or just plain "exclu-sivist" shall be a person who, in recognition of the diversity of the world's religions, believes that her religion is true, and that other religions are false insofar as they contradict her home religion. The "contented" exclusivist does not consider adjudicating the differences between her home religion and other religions. She does not raise the question of whether her home religion really is superior to others. She does not reflect on the issue. She is, in short, a "contented exclusivist".

In what follows, I do not intend to endorse con-tentedness as a rational policy for all exclusivists. My argument is with the philosophical view that contented exclusivism must always fall short of full rationality. I hope to produce at least one white crow, by describing a contented exclusivist who is fully rational with his exclusivism and in his contentment. A contented exclusivist need not be derelict in any epistemic obligations.

Who Can Be a Contented Exclusivist?

Most people, as John Hick is fond of pointing out, adhere to the religious tradition in which they were raised. Let me add that this is so if they remain religious at all. Thus, a Jew raised in a traditional Jewish home will generally be a believer in the Jewish religion, if he remains reli-gious at all. One raised in the Catholic church is likely to remain a Catholic, or at least a Christian, if she remains religious at all. The religion one's parents raised one in will almost always be exclusivist. (There are exceptions.) The home religion will teach that it is true and that other religions are false to the extent that the latter clash with the home religion.

One's home religion will include as a matter of course a ready explanation for the failures of other religions to recognize the truth. For example, Christians in medieval Europe were familiar with cathedral statues of two women, "Church" and "Synagogue", side by side, with Synagogue's eyes covered by a blindfold. This taught Christian worshippers of the blindness of the Jews to the "Christ event". Medieval Jews learned from the uncensored version of the

"In Defence of a Contented Religious Exclusivism" by Jerome Gellman, *Religious Studies* 36 (2000): 401–10; 414–17.

Talmud that Jesus did miracles through surreptitious, magical means. Christianity, then, was founded on gullibility. And devout Moslems are taught that the Jews falsified the biblical record to make it cohere with the Jews' perverted, beliefs about God and God's prophets. These are all beliefs that come with the territory of the home religion.

In more contemporary times, the home religion may recognize some truth and some salvific value in other religions, but will interpret that in terms of the home religion. For example, if the religion is Christianity, it might teach that genuinely spiritual adherents of other religions are "anonymous Christians" who live in Jesus, without knowing it. If Jewish, they might receive the traditional teaching that Christianity and Islam have benefited from what has remained in them from Judaism, and that descendants of Abraham brought some echoes of religious truth to the East. In virtue of following their home religion, then, believers will typically have built-in explanations for the failures and successes of other religions.

In acquiring their overall religious outlook, such believers are depending on testimony, accepting what others tell them. Believers accept what they are told by their elders, teachers, and their religious culture at large. There is no alternative to starting with the testimony of others. In so doing they are acting rationally. As a result, they acquire an elaborate network of religious beliefs. From within this network of beliefs they confront their world.

Let us say that a belief, any belief, is "unreflective", to the degree a person has not subjected it to critical scrutiny. Plausibly, it is better that a belief be reflective rather than unreflective, better, that is, for a person to subject her beliefs to critical scrutiny rather than not. Subjecting her belief to critical scrutiny enhances a person's chances of achieving truth rather than chancing error. The deliberate avoidance of critical scrutiny of a belief seems a clear violation of one's epistemic duty.

Now, religious belief acquired by way of absorbing the testimony of one's culture, starts out as an unreflective belief. A person simply goes along with what she is taught. So it might seem plausible to think it would be better for this belief to be reflective rather than unreflective,

that the believer should subject this belief to critical scrutiny. And it might seem plausible that holding this belief unreflectively is less than fully rational, and deliberately refraining from subjecting it to critical scrutiny a violation of one's epistemic duties. So some might think that failing to engage in an attempt to adjudicate between rival religious traditions, failing to scrutinize one's epistemic situation in one's home belief, when faced with countering religious traditions, is less than fully rational.

My thesis is that, on the contrary, a person's religious beliefs acquired as described earlier can legitimately, and without impugning full rationality, serve for assessing other religions or religious claims outside one's own religious circle. An exclusivist need not necessarily reflect on the rival claims of religions other than her own. She need not try to adjudicate between the home and the "visiting" religious traditions.

The defence of my position rests on the claim that religious beliefs may stay rationally unreflective for the religious believer in the face of other religions. A believer may rationally invoke her unreflective religious belief to defeat opposing religious claims, without having to consider the question any further.

I begin by noting that a person cannot subject all of his beliefs to critical scrutiny. In order to begin to engage in reflective scrutiny a person must leave some beliefs as unreflective. We have already noted that to begin with it is rational for a person to accept the testimony of others. After acquiring one's initial stock of beliefs, how is one rationally to proceed to subject them to scrutiny? I propose an epistemic strategy growing out of my grandmother's supremely rational advice. My grandmother used to say: "If the wheel does not squeak, don't oil it". Only a wheel that squeaks requires attention. So the epistemic strategy should be to let the beliefs that do not "squeak" be the unreflective base for considering the beliefs that do "squeak". A belief, B, "squeaks" when one's confidence in B is challenged (1) by others of one's beliefs more firmly held than B, or (2) by an epistemic tension between B and others of one's other beliefs held perhaps equally firmly, causing one to at least consider giving B up to restore epistemic peace, or (3) by a new belief-candidate that one perceives to threaten one's belief in B or its justification (including a belief-candidate to the effect that one's home group is not to be trusted). As long as a person's home belief does not squeak for her, she will be rationally entitled to reflect on her other beliefs and on new belief-candidates by its lights, not having subjected it itself to reflective scrutiny.

This entitlement may become rationally strengthened in the course of a believer's judging other beliefs in the light of her home beliefs. This would happen when one's starting convictions do a good job of sorting out belief-candidates in a way that seems intuitively plausible to the person in question. In that case, the home beliefs will be well oiled, and quite far from squeaking.

So, I contend, when confronted with other religions and their apparent spiritual successes, a religious believer may rationally treat his home religion non-reflectively and judge other religions by its lights, so long as his confidence in his home religion has not been challenged in any of the ways enumerated above. This entitlement would be stronger the more success the believer had experienced in the past proceeding in this way.

This should not yet be convincing, however, since I must show that a religious believer could be rational in not losing confidence in his home religion when confronted with the pervasiveness of religious diversity. I now proceed to offer an argument for that conclusion.

My argument points to two characteristic features of religious belief. The first has to do with the fact that religious belief constitutes a pervasive *interpretive framework* for a believer. Religious belief is far more than a matter of assenting to propositions, though it includes that. A religious adherent understands and interprets her world with the categories provided by her religious belief. Through it she understands God, history, the nature of the self, human suffering, human cognition, values, the future, the afterlife, metaphysics, art, and, finally, other religions. As such she can be rationally justified in interpreting the religious claims of others in her own terms, as long as she rationally possesses the requisite confidence in her beliefs.

Now in saying this I do not mean to endorse a Wittgensteinian or neo-Wittgensteinian view of the matter. In *On Certainty*, Wittgenstein seems to deny any intellectual space from within which we could discuss clashing interpretive frameworks. That's because he seems to think that concepts such as "good reason" and "evidence" are relative to interpretive frameworks. That is a claim I reject. I see no reason to think there could not be a common framework in which the matter could be discussed. I claim only that a religious believer may not be rationally obliged to enter that common intellectual space to try to adjudicate matters, in order to preserve her rationality. She will not be rationally obliged to do so, if her home religion provides her with all she rationally needs to interpret her world satisfactorily. The very existence of other religions, with their somewhat limited spiritual successes, which the home religion, in any case, has a thing or two to say about, does not require a religious person to raise the truth-question for the given interpretive framework in which she lives and thrives.

In saying all of this, I also do not mean to assimilate religious belief to what some Wittgensteinian philosophers call "framework propositions". Such propositions are supposed to provide justification for other beliefs but are themselves not in need of justification. Propositions are supposed to have the status of framework propositions for a person in virtue of their role for a socio-cultural complex of which she is a member. My position is different. A person can very well lose confidence in religious beliefs absorbed from her sociocultural setting by being challenged by other beliefs, including religious beliefs of outside religions. Another person may be strengthened in her aboriginal religious convictions by her satisfaction with the way they interpret her world. Her religious beliefs simply may not squeak. Whether original religious beliefs do or do not squeak for a person will depend, at least in part, on the epistemic situation of each *individual* believer, including what life brings them as well as the weights he or she rationally gives to competing belief-candidates, and not on the a priori status of those beliefs in one's religious grouping.

Of course, a believer can be dishonest with himself or otherwise insincere in assessing his beliefs, failing to properly disown a belief that really has become irrational for her. I intend my defence to apply only to human beings sincere about the epistemic status of their religious beliefs. In any case, I am not at all interested in providing a religious believer with a defence of exclusivism to be trotted out for the consumption of critics. I am interested only in whether a person can *be* a contented exclusivist.

There is a second reason why religious belief can remain rationally unreflective. This reason applies specifically to some forms of theistic belief. In some forms of theistic belief the believer sees herself as standing in a personal relationship to God. For example, she believes God sent her God's only Son to atone for her sins. She feels God's presence in her life, most strongly when in church, or when reading the Bible with openness and seriousness. She feels herself close to God and feels God close to her. It would be a serious violation of her relationship to God for her to consider for a moment that some other religion might be true rather than the one God encourages her in daily. Doing so would be a disturbing violation of her closeness to God, God who is closest to her in moments of prayer in her church, God who has provided her with eternal salvation by sending God's only Son to forgive her sins. She owes it to God and to the relationship they have to refrain from entering into such a relationship-harming activity. In short, her religious belief requires from her what is called in Hebrew: "*tmimut*". This is a word hard to translate into English. It has all of the following components: being simple, uncomplicated, innocent, trusting, faithful, loyal, being whole, perfect without blemish, being devoted. The concept of *tmimut* is meant to apply to personal relationships. As stated in Deuteronomy 18.13, "You shall be *tamim* with the Lord your God", "*tamim*" being the adjectival form of "*tmimut*".

So here we have a second reason why a person can be a contented exclusivist. It is because her relationship to God may preclude her from entering into the epistemic issue of religious diversity. As Augustine once wrote, "I will rather not be inquisitive than be separated from God".[1]

Tmimut, however, is not just an interpersonal virtue. For the believer, *tmimut* can be an epistemic virtue as well. A believer might take her close relationship with God to afford her insights to truth she would not have and would likely lose were she to lose that relationship. God, for her,

is a source of truth. Her past successes in judging truth from within her home theistic religion supports that assumption. Hence, to weaken her relationship to God would have the effect of weakening her epistemic access to truth. So, if trying to adjudicate the differences between religions might hurt one's relationship to God, then our believer has a good epistemic reason not to engage in such an enterprise.

Consider this analogy: the police present a mother with evidence that her son has committed a serious crime. She is certain he did not do it. She displays *tmimut* with regard to her son's innocence. Granted, this can be an irrational attitude for her to take with regard to her son's guilt. However, there will be cases where she will be perfectly rational in her belief that her son did not commit the crime, in spite of the contrary evidence. These will be cases where she is rationally convinced that her loving relationship with her son gives her an advantage over others in knowing deeply what he is like, and knowing, therefore, that it is extremely unlikely that he could ever find the power within him to do such a heinous act. Her sensitivity to his soul gives her a privileged understanding of what her son could and could not do. For this reason, she alone may possess a plausible way of interpreting the evidence so that it no longer points to his guilt. This, of course, will not always be the case, but it can be the case sometimes. In such cases, the mother's *tmimut* can grant her an epistemic advantage over others. My point is that *tmimut* can be an epistemic virtue in that it affords an insight into the truth of the matter lacking to those devoid of *tmimut*.

So, an exclusivist can be rationally justified in her contentment if she perceives that her *tmimut* in her relationship to God affords her an epistemic advantage over others. As long as she cleaves to God through the true religion in which she knows God, her capacities of judgement will be clear and true. If she diverges from clinging to God, she may cloud her critical judgement. She may be perfectly rational to think that if she were to attempt to scrutinize her religion in the face of opposing religions this would expose her to the

[1] Augustine, "On the morals of the Catholic Church", in Philip Schaff (ed.) *A Select Library of the Nicene and Post-Nicene Fathers of the Christian Church*, vol. 4 (Grand Rapids, MI: Eerdmans, 1956), 47.

dangers of error and confusion, which might just cause her to lose her most precious truth. Under such circumstances, she would be rational to refuse to even try to adjudicate the differences between the home and the visiting religions.

This is all well and good, I hope you will say. Yet, it does not give us a way of dealing with Hick's ubiquitous observation that it is a pure accident of birth that, for example, someone was born a Jew, rather than a Gentile Christian, or Buddhist. If so, realizing this should obligate a Jewish believer to reflect on whether his commitment to his home religion may be due to nothing more than that he so happens to have been born into it. So does he not have an epistemic duty to see to it that this specific belief, his exclusivist religious one, be subject to rational reflection, be accepted anew by him as a *reflective belief*?

Well, is it rational for our Jewish believer to believe he could have been born a Gentile rather than a Jew? The answer will depend on his religious beliefs. If he believes, for example, that the essence of a person is his soul, and that souls are uniform across the Jewish–Gentile divide, then he will have reason to believe that a person who is born a Jew, could have been born a Gentile instead. Suppose, however, he believes, as part of the complex of religious beliefs he rationally holds unreflectively, that while one's soul is indeed one's essence, Jewish souls are essentially different from Gentiles' souls. (Such teachings exist in some strands of Jewish tradition.) Then he may rationally believe that he, a Jew, could not have been born a Gentile. So it was no accident that he was born a Jew. He has good reason to think that Hick's observation is false, in his case at least.

This response does not neutralize Hick's observation entirely. For it allows that a Jewish person raised as a traditional Jew could have been a Jew but raised as an atheist, and in all likelihood would have turned out an atheist. So it remains an accident of birth that he believes in Judaism. So he has an epistemic responsibility to reflect on his belief, and not leave it at the unreflective level.

Whether this is so or not, will, once again, depend on one's religious beliefs. Our Jewish believer may rationally believe, for example, that while in a sense he could have been born to an atheist Jewish family and have turned out an atheist himself, still it was no accident that he was placed into conditions fortuitous for his becoming a traditional Jew. This is to be explained by God's decreeing that he be given an excellent opportunity to know the one true religion. Our believer may feel deep gratitude to God for the love God has shown him. In short, whether one believes it really was an accident of history that he was born into his home religion, rather than another, may depend on what religious beliefs he brings to the issue. Since a believer is rationally justified to start with what he is taught by his elders and since he is rationally justified not to oil the wheels of his religious beliefs if they don't squeak, he can be rationally justified in believing that his devotion to his home religion is no accident. So Hick's observation lacks compelling consequences for the rationality of contented exclusivism.

David Basinger's Argument

David Basinger has been a skilful and persevering critic of the idea that, in the face of religious diversity, an exclusivist belief can be "properly basic", in the technical sense of that term. I am not addressing precisely that issue here. Nonetheless, some of Basinger's arguments seem to have the consequence that my "contented exclusivist" would stand in violation of some prima facie epistemic duty. In my terminology, that would make the contented exclusivist less than fully rational. So I now turn to discuss an argument of Basinger's, one directly relevant to the position I am taking here. I will try to convince, naturally, that Basinger's argument is inadequate to show that the contented exclusivist is not fully rational. The discussion will also help clarify my defence of the contented exclusivist.

Basinger observes that an exclusivist cannot demonstrate on epistemic grounds that "are (or should be) accepted by all rational people that her perspective actually is a more accurate description of reality than those descriptions offered by proponents of divergent perspectives".[2]

To this observation, Basinger adds an epistemic principle he takes to be valid, let's call it "EP":

---

[2]   David Basinger, "The challenge of religious diversity: a middle ground", *Sophia*, 38 (1999), 41–53.

When significant numbers of seemingly know-
ledgeable, sincere individuals differ on an issue,
the fact that the superiority of a given perspective cannot be demonstrated on grounds that are
(or should be) accepted by all (or at least most)
rational participants is a prima facie reason not
to believe that this perspective is actually superior to all others.

From the observation and (EP), Basinger infers that:

Since a significant number of seemingly know-
ledgeable, sincere individuals affirm differing
religious perspectives, the fact that the proponent of a specific religious perspective cannot
demonstrate on grounds that are (or should be)
accepted by all (or most) rational people that
her perspective is superior to all others is a
prima facie reason for her not to believe that this
perspective is actually superior to all others.

According to Basinger, therefore, an exclusivist has
a prima facie reason not to believe that her perspective is superior to others, including its being
closer to the truth than they are. She then must
have an epistemic justification for remaining an
exclusivist, a reason that will override the prima
facie reason for her not to believe that her perspective is superior. Basinger believes such reasons
may be available to the exclusivist, but that she
must at least attend to the issue if she is not
to violate any epistemic duties in holding to
her exclusivism.

My contented exclusivist does not recognize
a duty to reflect upon the superiority of her
religious perspective. So, if Basinger is right, my
contented exclusivist fails to fulfil an "everything
else being equal" epistemic duty and is less
than fully rational.

Suppose Basinger is right that the exclusivist
cannot demonstrate on the basis of any set of commonly accepted epistemic criteria that her religious
perspective is superior. In contrast to Basinger, I
doubt EP is a valid epistemic principle. It seems
far too optimistic about the presumption of general consensus for rational thinking. I suppose
deduction, induction, scientific method, and the
like, are commonly accepted epistemic criteria
for justifying beliefs. However, beyond that, in the
very first place rationality underdetermines what

one's set of epistemically valid criteria is to be. So,
in the very first place there is no reason to accept
a presumption in favour of commonly accepted
epistemic criteria. Let me explain.

Robert Nozick has observed: "Philosophers
traditionally have sought to formulate rules
for rational belief. . . . They seek rules with an
appealing face, which recommend themselves
to reason by their content and also yield the
inferences and beliefs we are most confident
of".[3] The initial attractiveness of both rules *and*
beliefs is to be taken into account when aiming
for acceptable epistemic criteria for rational
belief. Nozick points out that discordance can
arise between the attractiveness of candidates for
rational rules and the confidence we have in our
most cherished beliefs. Rules that help preserve
our most cherished beliefs may themselves not
be so highly convincing on their face. And rules
for proceeding rationally that appear most attractive on their face may fail to preserve our most
confident beliefs, or may lead to their rejection.
When that happens, we have to reach an epistemic
equilibrium between the intrinsic plausibility
of the rules and the degree to which we are
confident about the beliefs. In the end, a rule
may be so strongly convincing on its face that
it will overweigh the lesser impressiveness of a
favoured belief. And the opposite can happen as
well: some beliefs may be so dear as to override
a rule with less plausibility.

The very concept of rationality *underdetermines*
the outcome. Rational persons can disagree here.
That is because rationality is, sometimes at least,
silent about what weights to assign to our starting stock of epistemic criteria and to our beliefs.

To illustrate, consider how philosophers have
differed about how to weigh up the attractiveness of rules against the attractiveness of initial
beliefs. David Hume, for example, was more
impressed by his rules for rational enquiry than
he was by his belief that physical objects exist.
So Hume was willing to urge his favourite rules
for rational enquiry to the point of ending up
with no rational justification for his belief in
an external world. G. E. Moore, on the other
hand, in his "proof of an external world", contended that his belief in the existence of his
own hands had greater epistemic weight than

---

[3] Robert Nozik, *The Nature of Rationality* (Princeton, NJ: Princeton University Press, 1993), 75.

rules of rational reasoning that would deny him that conviction. So, Moore argued, we should reject those rules of reasoning that would yield the wrong results. And Roderick Chisholm once endorsed the recognition of any rules of rational enquiry that would yield the "right results", although I imagine he required some minimum degree of plausibility for those rules.

So, I repeat, the very concept of rationality underdetermines what our final total set of epistemic criteria are going to be. At best, rationality can sagely direct us to find the "best" equilibrium between principles and beliefs. Rationality fails to dictate just what that equilibrium will be, however.

Now of course each of Hume, Moore, and Chisholm may have been convinced that every rational person *should* agree with his way of balancing rules and beliefs. That, though, is an empty expectation, reflecting only each one's conviction that he was right. There is no way to bring consensus here in the name of rationality.

So it is doubtful that just because a believer cannot demonstrate the superiority of her religious perspective on any set of commonly accepted epistemic criteria she then has a (prima facie) reason not to accept her exclusivism. There is no large-scale presumption in favour of generally accepted epistemic criteria. To put it differently: there is no expectation that valid epistemic criteria for rational reasoning, save for a basic few, will be commonly accepted. So why should it count against the exclusivist that the set of epistemic criteria favoured by her or by her and her co-religionists are not accepted by all or most rational people or that she has no way of showing that they *should* accept her grounds? I do not see that it does.

Similar remarks apply to the charge that might be made that the contented exclusivist has a "bias" that contaminates his rational assessment of the situation. However, we cannot determine what is a bias, independently of how our favoured beliefs and epistemic criteria combine into epistemic equilibrium. What interferes with getting the "right results" is a bias, what does not, is not. Hence, a criteria-belief complex powerful enough to deal with the issues of life, including that of religious diversity, might be expected to

have a way of judging what constitutes a "bias", in part indebted to its particular criteria-belief equilibrium. The charge of bias, then, cannot always be made to stick, and in some cases the charge is no more than a statement of one's own position, rather than a reflection upon the "nature of rationality".

I would like to make a second point here. It is an Enlightenment dream that rationality would determine a consensus on belief and courses of action. "It was a central aspiration of the Enlightenment", writes Aliasdair MacIntyre, "to provide for debate in the public realm, standards and methods of rational justification by which alternative courses of action in every sphere of life could be adjudged just or unjust, rational or irrational, enlightened or unenlightened".[4] The same is true for beliefs. The standards and methods were to be "in the public realm", accessible to all, applicable by all, and leading to general consensus. What is rational could be shown to be so publicly and consensually. This consensus excluded only those "corrupted" by their institutional and cultural environment.

Now a contented exclusivist may have a good religious reason to reject the Enlightenment conception. As he may see it, the Enlightenment conception is not simply a result of "seeing" what rationality demands, but is motivated, among other things, precisely by a perverse resolve to reject justified belief in any traditional religion, including his own. As we know, Enlightenment figures standardly perceived traditional religions to be part of the corrupting power of one's environment, to be set aside by a "Man of Reason".

A traditional theistic, contented exclusivist may then perceive this stance as providing part of the motivation driving an uncompromising commitment to Enlightenment styles of reasoning. He would then have good religious reasons to reject the Enlightenment requirement that standards and methods of rational justification be restricted to the "public realm". This requirement, he might believe, was designed in the very first place to disqualify his own religious perspective, and proceeded from desires invalid from his religious perspective. The Enlightenment stance, he may be convinced, was undertaken precisely to throw off the kingdom of God, the very

---

[4] Alasdair Macintyre, *Whose Justice? Which Rationality?* (London: Duckworth, 1988).

God who became revealed in the way the believer's own religion teaches. In the name of his religion he denies the Enlightenment preference for "a set of commonly accepted epistemic criteria".

So, I think there is reason to doubt Basinger's epistemic principle, and reason to think that it is not decisive against the contented exclusivist.

[. . .]

A Different Sort of Exclusivist

I maintain that, whether or not a particular exclusivist is rational in being contented depends upon further facts about him. If he has worked out a satisfactory equilibrium in a criteria-belief complex, is true to the weights he perceives to be appropriately assigned to beliefs in this complex, finds that his religious beliefs simply do not squeak in the face of religious diversity, and otherwise sticks to rational procedures of reasoning such as deduction and induction, then he is fully rational to be a contented exclusivist if that is what his epistemic situation yields. So, a contented exclusivist can be fully rational.

That having been said, I want now to describe a type of religious exclusivist who may very well not be rational, if a contented exclusivist in the face of religious diversity. The type of case I have in mind is when, independently of the issue of religious diversity, a believer's hold on her religion has been weakened, but not to the point of needing to abandon it rationally.

A person's conviction of the truth of her home religion can be weakened in various ways, chief among them by the challenge of scientific findings and by the challenge of changing values. Since she lives in an age of great scientific accomplishment she may be especially impressed by what science has to say. In addition, since she lives in an age in which new constellations of values are emerging, sometimes involving a radical break with the past, she may be influenced by new possibilities of valuation. Scientific findings may weaken or undo her belief in the factual claims made by her religion. She may come to believe that important historical claims made by her religion are doubtful or even false. As a result she may look for fallback positions that will keep her in the religion, in a way that makes all of her beliefs consistent and coherent. This may turn out to be

less than successful, creating epistemic tension in her belief structure.

Also, she may be acutely affected by a new way of seeing values for herself and society. For example, she may come to believe that her religion has been profoundly injurious to women over its history, that this is due to a structural defect, and that therefore she no longer can accept her religion as is. Here, too, she may look for a fallback position that allows her to stay at home in her religion, introducing modifications to bring her belief structure into a consistent and coherent whole. Again, the accommodation may turn out to be less than totally successful, creating epistemic tension in her belief structure.

Now, let's suppose, our "epistemically challenged" believer comes face to face with other religions, both traditional and contemporary, liberal versions of them. Or, suppose she meets other versions of her home religious tradition, especially more liberal versions than her own. She comes to know and to have some appreciation of the teachings and the way of life the alternatives offer to their adherents. Given the epistemically challenged hold she has on her home religion, the claim that she has a prima facie obligation to the truth to at least try to adjudicate the conflict between her own religious belief and the alternatives begins to look more promising. Then it seems, one may indeed have at least a prima facie obligation to the truth to try at least to consider, weigh, and reflect on whether an alternative religious understanding might not fare better than hers. This is especially true for other versions of her own religious tradition. Such a person is in a very different situation from the exclusivist I portrayed earlier, who has no such doubts or leaks in her religious belief. Our believer may simply no longer be able to hold positions that would render her exclusivism rational. My defence of a rational exclusivism, therefore, cannot rationally be invoked as a protective strategy by just any want-to-be exclusivist.

Some Final Objections

I close by considering two objections to my position. The first is that if I am right, then just any exclusivist religious position can be rational, if the person just satisfies my requirements. If so, a Jonestown suicider could have been rational if he fulfilled all of my requirements. Isn't this obviously unacceptable?

My reply is that in principle a person could be perfectly rational to hold a Jonestown theology. If this sounds outrageous that may be because we tend to place too much importance on rationality. Rationality is only one of the categories for the evaluation of the goodness or worthiness of belief. There are others. A belief may be rational and false, or rational and immoral. Finally, a belief can be rational and just plain crazy. It will be crazy because of its content. Admittedly I do not have an epistemology for craziness, but do believe a belief can be rational and at the same time crazy. It will be rational if the holder of the belief has worked out a satisfactory equilibrium in a criteria-belief complex, is true to the weights he perceives to be appropriately assigned to beliefs in this complex, finds that his religious beliefs simply do not squeak, and otherwise sticks to rational procedures of reasoning such as deduction and induction. All that being said, the belief may be outright crazy. Conceding rationality is not saying the final word about the worthiness or goodness of a belief. So the fact that any religious belief might turn out to be rational by my lights is not yet giving it a stamp of approval.

The second objection is this. Suppose someone knows others have brainwashed her to accept a religion that she otherwise would not now believe. Is it not obvious that she could not possibly be rational in just agreeing with what she has been brainwashed to believe? If so, though, how is the ordinary religious case different? If a person knows that she believes in her religion only because it was inculcated by her surroundings, how could she be rational to just agree with it? Does she not have an obligation to independently assess what she has thus acquired?

My reply is that there are clear cases of brainwashing and clear cases of non-brainwashing, and cases in between in which we must judge whether they are "sufficiently like" the clear cases or not. For the in-between cases, our attitude toward the results will influence our judgement. If we endorse the results we will be inclined to say it is not brainwashing. It is more like "education" or "granting an optimal opportunity" to gain the truth. If we do not care for the results we will be quicker to see the similarities to brainwashing. It will be "like" brainwashing, or perhaps will be "sheer indoctrination". For this reason, none of us is likely to see the inculcation of moral values to our children, like the prohibition of murder, as akin to brainwashing or sheer indoctrination.

Now, rational people can differ over whether a present case is sufficiently similar to brainwashing to be condemned or otherwise rejected. The religious case is surely not a clear case of brainwashing, if we think of the paradigms of brainwashing from the Korean War, say. Hence, a religious person can be perfectly rational to think she has not undergone anything remotely akin to brainwashing when she was "educated into" or granted the gift of "glimpsing from close-up" the religious life of her religious group. This judgement will be strengthened by the perceived success of the religious outlook in interpreting the world for the believer. Others might differ, but that is their judgement to which rationality does not obligate her.

Finally, I acknowledge a potential danger in the contented religious exclusivist position I have defended. Such a stance is open to abuse as an insincere protective strategy, enabling an exclusivist who does not fit my requirements simply to refuse to engage in a search for truth. It can also lead to thinking that one need never try to empathically understand other religious positions. Worse yet, the position I am defending might result in a lack of tolerance for the religious beliefs of others. None of this, of course, must follow in any way from my position. True enough, my contented exclusivist may rationally believe that all religions other than the home religion are works of the devil, and that the devil tricks others into believing them. However, just as well, my contented exclusivist can recognize that adherents of other religions may be fully rational in their beliefs, holding them in a nonculpable manner. He can also appreciate the sincerity and integrity of believers in religions other than his, and may admire spiritually uplifting aspects of their religions. Yet I realize that the contented exclusivist position might be unjustifiably used to slide into positions I would want to reject. Hence, I close with an appeal that philosophical defences of contented religious exclusivism always be accompanied by declarations of religious tolerance.

56

John Hick and the Question of Truth in Religion

Brian Hebblethwaite

John Hick's writings on the philosophy of religion reveal an increasing tension between his commitment to critical realism regarding the cognitive fact-asserting nature of religious language, on the one hand, and the key devices which he employs in order to work out and defend a philosophy of religious pluralism, on the other. In this essay I shall argue that it is the Kantian element in Hick's epistemology that both enables him to hold these two basic positions together at one and the same time, notwithstanding the tension, and also accounts for the threat which Hick's religious pluralism now poses to his critical realism.

Hick's commitment to critical realism is evident from his inaugural lecture at Birmingham in 1967[1] to his contribution to the Realism/Anti-Realism conference in Claremont in 1988.[2] These two pieces reflect decades of polemic against the so-called "Wittgensteinian fideism" of D. Z. Phillips, as well as against earlier "non-cognitivists", such as A. J. Ayer, R. B. Braithwaite, and J. H. Randall. Hick has, of course, been more concerned with religiously sympathetic figures such as Braithwaite, Randall and Phillips (and,

latterly, Don Cupitt) than with the anti-religious logical positivists such as Ayer. And indeed it is the former who represent the greater threat to Christian self-understanding: for they challenge a cognitive or realist conception of the faith not from outside but from within. This issue – whether or not Christian God-talk is referential, conveying truth about transcendent matters of ultimate concern – was spoken of by Hick in 1967 as "theology's central problem",[3] and it has continued to preoccupy him to the present day. Hick still holds that religion, whatever else it is, is "fact-asserting", including, that is, truth-claims in the sense of putative articulations of how things really or ultimately are. Thus, in the Claremont paper, he argues that the cosmic optimism of the great world faiths depends upon a realist interpretation of their language. Only if it is *true* that the world has a transcendent meaning and a future goal that will indeed be realised in the end, have they genuine hope to extend to suffering humanity.

That this commitment to critical realism remains, despite Hick's more recent espousal and defence of a philosophy of religious pluralism is

"John Hick and the Question of Truth in Religion" by Brian Hebblethwaite, in *God, Truth, and Reality: Essays in Honour of John Hick*, ed. Arvind Sharma (New York: St Martins Press, 1993), pp. 124–34.

[1] John Hick, *God and the Universe of Faiths* (London: Macmillan, 1973), Chapter 1.
[2] John Hick, "Religious Realism and Non-Realism", in Joseph Runzo (ed.), *Is God Real?* (New York: St Martin's Press, 1993), pp. 3–16.
[3] *God and the Universe of Faiths*, loc. cit.

clear from the way in which this pluralism is expressed. Each major "post-axial"[4] world faith constitutes a possible salvific path from self-centredness to Reality-centredness.[5] The vehicle of each such path is religious experience; but it is the testimony of (nearly) all forms of religious experience that they are experience *of* transcendent, ultimate Reality – albeit under various guises. Salvific experience, therefore, in its many forms, points to a transcendent Real as its source and goal.[6] There are thus implicit truth-claims about the transcendent embedded in (nearly) all the practical life-transforming and life-reorientating religious traditions in the post-axial history of humankind.

But if an underlying cognitive realism is retained throughout the corpus of his writings, Hick's understanding of the truth-content of such implicit claims has undergone a sea-change. Whereas in early books the cognitive aspect of religious experience was articulated in the language of biblical faith in a personal God revealed in Christ,[7] in later writings Hick speaks of an Ultimate, or a Real, manifested now in the personal representations of the theistic faiths, now in the impersonal representations of Theravāda Buddhism or monistic Vedantic Hinduism.[8] What enables continuity, in Hick's overall view, despite this pretty drastic change, is a basically Kantian epistemology concerning both the nature of truth and human access to truth.

As is well known, for Hick, religious truth is grasped, in faith, through a particular way of interpreting experience.[9] Faith is defined as the interpretative element within religious experience. This involves the application to the religious case of a more general epistemology of interpretation. All experience is experiencing-as. Raw experience is indefinite or ambiguous until interpreted as significant in some specific way. This occurs at every level of our experience – natural, moral and religious. Even at the level of our experience of the natural world, the mind is active in applying a range of concepts to what is given, so that we construe ourselves as living in a material world of interacting objects. The ambiguity, at this level, is minimal. Ordinary everyday experience presupposes a basic realist interpretation, even though our everyday world-view involves a selection of practically-relevant features of the given. Moral experience is less immediate. It involves seeing the sphere of inter-personal life as imposing certain demands and obligations upon us. It is quite possible to miss or turn a blind eye to such significance. Religious experience, in its Christian mode, involves experiencing the whole world as God's creation and the sphere of God's providence. Our whole lives become a response to the immanent presence of this transcendent Spirit, and we look, in faith, for an eschatological consummation, beyond death, when all ambiguity will be resolved. For ambiguity is at its greatest in the case of religious experience. Our whole world and our own lives *can* be experienced naturalistically. On Hick's view, this would be a systematic error, but it is quite rational. Equally rational is the decision of faith, whereby the religious interpretation is allowed to structure our whole life-world. Such a faith perspective, Hick believes, is true and will be confirmed as true in the end.

The Kantian element in all this is the stress on the contribution of the knowing mind to the interpretation of experience as naturally, morally, or religiously significant. This contribution is not arbitrary. There are less and more appropriate ways of so structuring our experience as to gain access to reality; but since at each level reality is apprehended through our own interpretative concepts, we only know it as it appears to creatures endowed with sensible, moral, and spiritual faculties such as ours. Kant is not in fact mentioned in Hick's earlier writings on "experiencing-as", except in respect of our experience of a categorical

[4] This phrase goes back to Karl Jaspers. See John Hick, *An Interpretation of Religion* (London: Macmillan, 1989), pp. 29ff.
[5] John Hick, *Problems of Religious Pluralism* (London: Macmillan, 1985), p. 44.
[6] *An Interpretation of Religion*, Chapter 11.
[7] *God and the Universe of Faiths*, Chapter 3.
[8] *An Interpretation of Religion*, Chapters 15 and 16.
[9] John Hick, *Faith and Knowledge*, 2nd edn (Ithaca, NY: Cornell University Press, 1966), Chapter 5.

moral demand; but that Hick's whole epistemo-logy is fundamentally Kantian is confirmed by the Gifford Lectures, where Kant's seminal distinction between noumenon and phenomenon, between the thing in itself and how it appears to beings such as ourselves, is explicitly transferred from the basic case of our knowledge of our perceived environment to the more controversial case of the epistemology of religion.[10]

By this time, of course, the religious interpretation is not restricted to its Christian mode. There is an intriguing parallel with the story of post-Kantian general epistemology here. For Kant the world appears to beings endowed with faculties of sense and understanding such as ours in only one, shared, way. Even though we do not have access to the world as it is in itself, the world as it appears, the phenomenal world, is a uniform, public world that we all experience similarly and that Newtonian science explores and describes systematically. Post-Kantian philosophy has lost this confidence. The possibility of many different, perhaps systematically incommensurable, ways of interpreting the data of experience has been explored by writers such as Quine.[11] Hick now sees a comparable plurality in ways of interpreting the world religiously. Whereas in the early writings, religious faith was spoken of solely in Christian terms – as experience of a personal God of creation, providence, and eventual redemption – now, in the more recent writings, this is seen as only one of a range of phenomenal representations of the ultimate noumenal reality that are not only possible but actual in the history of religions. Hick's so-called "Copernican revolution", like Kant's, transfers much of what used, pre-critically (or even critically, in Hick's case) to be ascribed to the object of religious experience to one way in which that unknown noumenal object appears to those of us nurtured in a particular religious tradition. Hick now employs a neutral term, "the Real", for the ultimate transcendent, noumenal, religious object, and re-locates the God of Judaeo-Christian theism among the various "personae"

of the Real, that is, the set of ways in which, for certain traditions, notably those of Semitic origin – but also for devotional Hinduism and other Eastern and African faiths – the Real is represented as a divine Thou, evocative of worship, and sustaining human beings in a variety of life-transforming ways. In these personal modes, the spiritual resources of the transcendent are experienced as grace and love. But there are other traditions – equally resourceful in spiritual, life-transforming, power – which represent the Real, phenomenally, through various "impersonae" – that is, interpretations of the Real as a non-personal Absolute, as Brahman, in Vedantic Hinduism, for example, or Nirvāṇa or Śūnyatā in the various Buddhist schools.[12] In these traditions of interpretation, union with the absolute yields peace, bliss, and unlimited compassion. The ethical and salvific effectiveness of all these ways of religiously "experiencing-as" forbids our attempting to "grade" them from some allegedly neutral standpoint.[13]

Let us now ask how the question of truth in religion fares in this newer pluralistic context. Previously, as we have seen, it was the concepts supplied by the Christian tradition that enabled Hick to interpret his religious experience, cognitively, as experience of an ultimate, personal, source of grace and love, to be encountered unambiguously, though still mediated through the (now-risen) Christ, in the eschaton. These were basic religious truths, both disclosed in and evocative of Christian salvific experience. Despite the interpretative processing involved, Christian faith gave cognitive access to the noumenally real as actually being personal and gracious. But now, in the pluralist context, nearly all these alleged truths are transferred to the phenomenal level. They cease to be true of ultimate reality as it is in itself. One might still say that they remain true of that reality *as it appears* in one of its personalist manifestations. But Hick himself is more inclined to speak of them now as *myths*, expressive of religiously appropriate attitudes, namely attitudes conducive

---

[10]   *An Interpretation of Religion*, pp. 240ff.
[11]   W. V. O. Quine, *Ontological Relativity and Other Essays* (New York: Columbia University Press, 1969).
[12]   *An Interpretation of Religion*, Chapter 16 [see also Hick's "A Religious Understanding of Religion" above].
[13]   *Problems of Religious Pluralism*, Chapter 5.

to ethical and spiritual transformation – from self-centredness to Reality-centredness.

We encounter this shift regarding the truth-content of religious beliefs at what might be termed its half-way stage in the book *Truth and Dialogue*,[14] which came out of a 1970 conference in Birmingham on the apparently conflicting truth-claims of the world religions. The conference was dominated by the contribution of Wilfred Cantwell Smith and reactions to it. For Cantwell Smith, religious truth is not propositional, cognitive, or fact-asserting, but rather personal – a life-transforming quality of sincerity and commitment – as persons inwardly appropriate their faith's spiritual power and vision. In his own essay in that book, Hick endorses the practical orientation of Cantwell Smith's view, but points out that a religion can only become true in the latter's existential, personalistic sense if it is already true in a more universal and objective sense. Neither Christianity nor Islam could become true if there were no God. Hick, therefore, retains his critical realistic account, even when endorsing the practical, personalist approach. (It is clear that the same must in fact be said of Cantwell Smith himself, as later work has shown.[15]) The problem of conflicting truth-claims therefore remains. Hick goes on to consider the hypothesis that all the great religions are in contact with the same ultimate divine reality, but that their differing experiences of that reality, shaped over centuries in different historical and cultural contexts, have received different conceptualisations in their respective theologies. It is this basically Kantian distinction between experience and interpretation that enables Hick to graft his emerging pluralism on to his longstanding critical realism. At this stage the suggestion is of complementary rather than of rival truths.[16] Hick is optimistic here about the possibility of convergence and the discovery of common ground, even between the personal and non-personal experience of what he still

calls the divine. At the doctrinal level, however, he is already resorting to the language of myth, as one way of dealing with a disputed doctrine such as that of reincarnation.

"Myth" becomes an increasingly important category in Hick's writings during the 1970s and 1980s, most notably and notoriously in connection with *The Myth of God Incarnate*.[17] There "myth" is defined as "a story which is told but which is not literally true, or an idea or image which is applied to someone or something but which does not literally apply, but which invites a particular attitude in its hearers",[18] and it is used particularly of the Incarnation, which must, indeed, be "demythologised" if the pluralistic hypothesis is to be sustained. This definition of myth, not surprisingly, has been attacked as being purely subjectivist and expressivist; but, of course, that does not do justice to Hick's intention. The "myth" of God incarnate may express an attitude to Jesus, but the attitude in question is still one of reverence for and commitment to one who has enabled and whose memory still sustains the Christian form of salvific encounter with God. So there are still underlying truth-claims about God involved in mythical talk about Jesus. The situation is very similar to that of Hick's own reply to Cantwell Smith.

In subsequent writings, this notion of the mythological is greatly extended. Indeed, in the Gifford Lectures, it is suggested that talk of God (as of Nirvāṇa) functions mythologically *vis-à-vis* the transcendent Real.[19] Hick is clearer now about the implicit reference to the Real – we might call this the residual truth-claim in the pluralist hypothesis – that underlies the attitudinal definition of myth. Myths express appropriate attitudes and responses that enable salvific realignments with the Real. I notice, however, a certain residual tension between what Hick says at this point about the mythological function of religious language and what he says at the end of the book when explicitly

---

[14]   John Hick (ed.), *Truth and Dialogue* (London: Sheldon Press, 1974).
[15]   W. Cantwell Smith, *Toward a World Theology* (London: Macmillan, 1981).
[16]   *Truth and Dialogue*, p. 152.
[17]   John Hick (ed.), *The Myth of God Incarnate* (London: SCM Press, 1977).
[18]   Ibid., p. 178.
[19]   *An Interpretation of Religion*, p. 351.

addressing the problem of conflicting truth-claims. In the penultimate chapter it seems that all the doctrines of all the religions refer at the phenomenal level only to personae or impersonae of the Real. In so far as they refer beyond the phenomenal to the noumenal Real, they function mythologically. But in the final chapter, the category of myth appears to be restricted to specific narratives like those of creation, incarnation, or eternal life, while the primary underlying affirmations may yet be discovered to be complementary.[20] It must be said that the bulk of the Gifford Lectures favours the former rather than the latter view. The final chapter seems to revert to what I called the half-way stage where complementarity still remains a possibility. The main thrust of the Gifford Lectures lies in the direction of extending the category of myth to cover all aspects of phenomenal manifestations of the Real. Personae and impersonae alike are phenomenal, and everything we say about them is therefore mythological vis-à-vis the Real. In other words, Hick has become less optimistic about cognitive complementarity, and tends to fall back on comparable salvific efficacy.

This means that the ultimate referent of religious language – the noumenal Real, lying behind all phenomenal representations – becomes more and more vague and unknown as Hick's Copernican revolution gets further developed. As with Kant's noumenon, virtually nothing can be said about it. We have no cognitive access to it. Only a practical faith – the aforementioned salvific transformation from self-centredness – bears witness to the unknown Real responsible for such effects in all the different (indeed incommensurable) forms of spiritual life.

But it may well be asked whether it is necessary to retain such a vague transcendent reference point. Just as post-Kantian phenomenalists and constructivists accept Kant's analysis of the contribution of the knowing mind to what it knows but drop all reference to an inaccessible noumenon lying behind the phenomena, so Don Cupitt now suggests[21] that Hick's religious "personae" and "impersonae" can be appropriated as human social constructs without

the postulation of a transcendent Real behind them. They may still be spiritually effective in the lives of different communities of faith even if there is no ultimate object of faith at all. On Cupitt's view, Hick's ever-receding noumenal object has become so vague as to be entirely redundant. It is in this sense that the Kantian element in Hick's epistemology, developed and deployed in defence of religious pluralism, has become a threat to his critical realism. And, of course, if the single noumenal Real is dropped, the variety of salvific life-ways becomes unproblematic.

It is worth pondering the reasons why Hick wishes, against Cupitt and all non-cognitivists, to retain a transcendent noumenal Real, even though we have no access to it as it is in itself. There is no doubt that Hick believes that religious myths do express experiences and attitudes that are not self-supporting. In the context of both personalist and impersonalist faiths they are responses to, evoked by, and sustained in relation to, something from beyond both the natural and the human worlds. Intriguingly, Hick's well-known notion of eschatological verification still provides the litmus test of the fact-asserting nature of religious language. For it is an implication of all the great faiths that human beings are not snuffed-out at death but caught up into a further purifying process which will demonstrate, less and less ambiguously, that their beliefs about an ultimate resource of spiritual transformation were true. Once again there has been a pretty drastic change in Hick's assessment of the details of this eschatological hope. No single heavenly scenario will now perform this role. The ultimate will continue to be manifested, albeit less ambiguously, in a variety of phenomenal forms – but the fact that this process continues beyond death will verify the critically realistic claim that the personae and impersonae of the Real are indeed of the Real and not purely human constructions. For purely human constructions are bound to end for all of us at death.

A footnote in the Gifford Lectures bears this out.[22] In his book, Theology and Religious

[20]   Ibid., p. 374.
[21]   In seminar discussion.
[22]   An Interpretation of Religion, p. 361.

Pluralism,[23] Gavin D'Costa had argued that eschatological verification would require the prediction of a single ultimate future state, which would thus refute the pluralistic hypothesis. Hick replies that "the cosmic optimism of post-axial religion expects a limitlessly good fulfilment of the project of human existence. But this fulfilment could take many forms". So even in respect of eschatological verification our predictions, and perhaps our post-mortem experiences themselves, retain the character of mythical representations. The only residual truth-claim in the cognitively realist sense is that there will be some such limitless good fulfilment beyond death.

It is worth attempting to list the residual, underlying, noumenal truth-claims to which Hick remains committed, despite the increasing weight he places on different phenomenal manifestations in the religions of the world. They are:

1   There is an ultimate transcendent Reality, to which all human religions, in their very different modes, are historically and culturally shaped responses.
2   Salvific religious experience, leading to transformation from self-centredness to Reality-centredness, is not a purely human possibility. Religion, in all its different forms, involves spiritual resources from beyond.
3   Human life will be extended, beyond death, towards some form of perfected consummation in the end.

It is difficult to see that there are any further assertions of transcendent fact which Hick could now endorse in the light of his pluralistic hypothesis. All other religious assertions function mythologically, expressing attitudes evoked either by historical figures or merely phenomenal representations.

Two questions may be posed regarding Hick's now minimal critical realism. In the first place, can these three residual truth-claims resist the threat of collapse into redundancy in the light of purely expressivistic, constructivist, alternatives? And, secondly, can religious believers be expected to accept that these three residual

truth-claims represent the cognitive heart of their traditions' central doctrines? The first question is a question for philosophers of religion, the second for the respective members of each community of faith.

Both questions seem to call for answers in the negative. It is highly dubious that religious experience alone can be thought to carry the weight of sustaining such minimal and vague claims concerning the transcendent. Even if it is conceded that all the world faiths may be construed in this way, that they *must* be so construed seems very implausible in the light of the alternative accounts (by no means all hostile or reductive in any pejorative sense) that are now available. The second question can only be answered from within a particular faith community; but it seems that Buddhists as well as Christians, Hindus as well as Muslims, will resist the relegation of their most characteristic doctrines to the level of appearance, functioning only mythologically *vis-à-vis* the Real.

Any challenge to Hick from the realist side of this debate must go right back to the Kantian epistemology which has allowed this gradual process of erosion towards the affirmation of an increasingly minimal set of truth-claims about the transcendent, in the interests of the pluralistic hypothesis. Kant greatly overestimated the contribution of the knowing mind to how what is known appears. This is most obviously true of space and time, which must surely be admitted to be relational dimensions of the world as it is discovered to be in itself – and to have been long before human minds evolved. But it is also true of the categories and concepts in terms of which we process the data of sense and understand ourselves and our world. Our basic categories are required by and evoked by the very nature of what we encounter all the time, and our concepts, though partial and selective, are likewise determined by the given nature of things as we discover them to be. Similarly our moral experience is of objective demands and claims that impose themselves upon us in the dictates of conscience, irrespective of and sometimes despite social conditioning. And if we admit the force of reason and

[23]   Oxford: Basil Blackwell, 1986.

revelation as well as that of experience in the sphere of religion, we will, at least in the context of the religions of Semitic origin, find ourselves constrained to affirm that ultimate reality is personal and not impersonal, graciously active and not inert, and to hope realistically for a consummation beyond death that will take the form of a perfected communion of love and not absorption into a featureless Absolute. Christians will go further than this in claiming that God's personality and love have been definitively revealed in the Incarnation, whose truth they therefore maintain.

The upshot of this discussion is that, when we have firmly rejected, as we must, Kantian epistemology in all its forms, we will find ourselves able to make many more discriminating truth-claims in religion than Hick's pluralistic hypothesis can allow. Among them will be a different hypothesis concerning the relation between the truths contained in the Christian tradition and the truths contained in other religions.[24]

---

[24] See now G. D'Costa (ed.), *Christian Uniqueness Reconsidered* (Maryknoll, NY: Orbis Books, 1990).

A Process Approach to Pluralism

John B. Cobb, Jr

[...] Process metaphysics speculates that the world is composed of a vast plenum of events of all sorts. Each event is an inexhaustible creative synthesis of antecedent events. No two are identical. The patterns of relationship among the events are also inexhaustible. Human events are enmeshed inextricably in this total matrix.

Confronting this infinite complexity, the human mind has primarily the task of discerning and establishing structures that are important to practical life. It also functions to find answers to questions that express curiosity. We all know that in the end many answers found in this primarily theoretical quest have also turned out to have practical importance in both religion and science.

Although in all cultures reason has had both these functions, their respective importance has varied. Further, diverse cultural practices and languages have selected differing features of the inexhaustible matrix for attention and emphasis. Each in this sense constructs its own world. Yet *constructs* is misleading when used alone. The construction is always based on discernment.

Discernment is necessarily of some features of the inexhaustible complexity in which we are all immersed. It is necessarily highly selective. The ideal of discerning everything at once is utterly remote from any human possibility. The question is not whether discernment abstracts from the whole – it does – but whether the abstractions are useful, relevant, and illuminating.

Construction introduces interpretation and relates what is discerned in ways that may resemble or differ widely from the relations of the events in which the elements are discerned. Interpretation and patterning may also be more or less useful, relevant, and illuminating. In any case, they build up a world of human meaning and direct human activities. The events embodying these meanings become an important part of the total matrix of events in which we are enmeshed.

Discernment and construction are not in fact separated from one another. What is discerned of the given reality depends on prior construction, just as what is constructed is affected by what is discerned. In addition there is a secondary discernment into features of what has been constructed. The effort to distinguish the elements of primary discernment from the constructions in which they are enmeshed is a difficult one, of whose success one can never be sure.

Given this metaphysical speculation, how shall we understand the plurality of religious traditions, especially when their claims about

"A Process Approach to Pluralism," a selection from "Metaphysical Pluralism" by John B. Cobb, Jr in *The Intercultural Challenge of Raimon Panikkar*, ed. Joseph Prabhu (Maryknoll, NY: Orbis Books, 1996), pp. 49–54. Reprinted by permission of Orbis Books.

truth and goodness clash? First, we will see that these claims arise from their respective constructions. Since these have developed from different discernments, and since there is no assurance that the interpretations and the patterns established among them are accurate, we will not be surprised that there is conflict. We will encourage adherents of all traditions to recognize that they have constructed worlds of meaning that are of great value to themselves but should not be treated as universal truths.

Second, however, we will also expect that adherents of each tradition decline to be fully relativized. Some may be prepared to agree that much of the theory and practice they prize is relative to the specifics of their histories and cultures, but most will insist that in and through the culturally specific there is also an apprehension of what is universal and universally important. We will expect that they are right, because we believe that there are elements of primary discernment as well as of construction in all tradition, and we will accordingly support the conviction that sheer relativity is not the last word.

Third, the fact that there are elements of discernment in all religious traditions will not lead us to assume that what is discerned in all is the same. That the same or at least similar aspects of the inexhaustible matrix of events have been discerned independently in several cultures is certainly possible, but it should be asserted only when it can be shown by careful examination. The fact that all cultures have religious aspects does not in itself entail that all have discerned the same or even similar things. There is no assurance, for example, that what is experienced as sacred in one culture will also be what is experienced as sacred in another. On the contrary, we will be equally open to discovering that what have been discerned are quite different features of the total matrix. Especially since what is discerned is so deeply influenced by construction, we will expect that differences are important at this level as well.

This is a highly abstract statement. Let me offer some more concrete judgments about diverse foci of attention and resultant discernment derived from the foregoing understanding of the relation of thought to reality. Consider first what happens in cultures whose constructions lead them to discern that they are indeed constructions. Buddhism is the example par excellence. Some very influential people, beginning with Gautama, concluded that the constructed world of meaning led to suffering and that this suffering could be escaped as persons became free from the influence of all construction. Such freedom would lead to a life of pure discernment in the terms I have proposed.

Sometimes Buddhists claim that this discernment is wholly non-selective and exhaustive. In terms of the metaphysics here proposed, this is impossible. The constructs in which we find meaning are a major factor of selectivity in discernment, so that when their influence is removed, more can be discerned. But the human organism is already a system of selection and amplification. The inexhaustible complexity of reality is far beyond the human capacity to appropriate, even the capacity of the enlightened Buddhist.

Others who recognize that there is a large constructive element in their cultural world of meaning draw differing conclusions. They, too, recognize that the received construction distorts and falsifies in at least some respects, but this does not lead them to try to overcome the process of construction altogether. Instead, it leads to the goal of improving the construction to make it more functional, or more correspondent to reality, or some combination of the two. The Greek religio-philosophical movements were of this sort. In modern times religious energies were poured into the scientific enterprise. At times the social and psychological sciences have been looked to for salvation. The features of reality discerned and conformed to have been quite diverse in these various movements.

In other instances this distinction of construction and discernment has not been thematically considered. What has seemed important has been righteousness. What is discerned in human experience is the distinction between what occurs and what might have occurred, a purpose partly realized, partly missed. This leads further to discernment of the causes of missing the mark as well as of a source of the mark. It leads also to attention to ways of assuaging the guilt that is intensified through this emphasis. Needless to say, I have in mind the Abrahamic traditions.

In recent times in the West there have been those who have held that there is no discernment at all – only construction. They advocate deconstruction, and some suggest that seeing through the constructional character of our worlds will be our ultimate liberation. The seeing through is itself discernment of the character of our worlds of meaning, hence it is an exaggeration to say that they deny all discernment. What they deny is primary discernment into features of a world that is not humanly constructed.

Still other traditions have grown out of and encouraged discernment of patterns in the natural and social worlds. In China Taoism represents the former, Confucianism, the latter. Taoists discerned the patterns of reciprocity, balance, and harmony in natural events. Confucianists discerned patterns of human behavior and social order that led to stable and harmonious political life.

At a highly abstract level generalizations can be made about all of these movements. All see something wrong and propose ways of righting it. But to go beyond that in identifying commonalities is quite dubious. It would have to be shown that what the Buddhist experiences in pure discernment is what the Abrahamic religions have discerned as the source and call for righteousness in human life. It would have to be shown that the patterns of order discerned in nature by the Taoist are the same patterns as those discerned by Greek philosophers and modern natural scientists.

If these commonalities cannot be shown, that does not indicate that one is right and the others wrong. It indicates only that in the inconceivably complex totality of events, different features have been discerned and diversely interpreted and ordered. On the other hand, that does not entail a stance of neutrality. All religious traditions tend to exaggerate the importance of their own achievements. All neglect the degree of abstraction involved in their discernments and the simplifications and distortions involved in their constructions. All thereby damage their own adherents as well as benefit them, and none opens itself as willingly to the potential contributions of others as one could wish. Judgments about the extent of these failures are warranted by the perspective here offered.

Today, as religious traditions are forced to deal with one another, many adherents revert defensively to absolutes that carry little conviction. The result is fanaticism. But others find increasingly in the heart of their own discernments reason to believe that others may have discerned something, too. This leads to a willingness to give and take, to teach and receive.

Whiteheadian Speculations for the Ordering of the Plurality

Although the vision of myriads of complexly interrelated events is the foundational feature of process metaphysics, there are additional levels of speculation by individual process thinkers that provide further ways of ordering religious diversity. These further speculations may prove wrong without invalidating the most fundamental aspects of the metaphysics, but I share an example taken from Whitehead because, thus far, it has seemed illuminating to me in my efforts to correlate some of the major religious traditions. I share it also to show that process thought can develop a plurality of typologies of religious systems. Pluralism is important at this level as well.

Whitehead discerns in every event a conjunction of the disjunctive many, that is, of other events. He speculates that the ultimate truth about the world is that "the many become one and are increased by one."[1] The new "one" is itself one of many new events that participate in the disjunctive that become conjunctively the next new events. So the process continues, on and on. This ultimate reality that characterizes every matter of fact Whitehead calls "creativity." Creativity is not a thing or a process or an event or an activity. But one could identify it as "process itself" or "activity itself," quite analogous to "being itself" in those philosophies that think of the world as made up of beings rather than events. Creativity in itself, like being in itself,

---

[1]   Alfred North Whitehead, *Process and Reality*, corrected ed., David Ray Griffin and Donald W. Sherburne, eds (New York: The Free Press, 1978), p. 21.

has no form or character of its own. Although it is not an actual entity, it is not abstract either; for it is that by virtue of which actual entities are actual.

The form of each event, each instantiation of creativity, is largely derived from the forms of the events that make up the many out of which it constitutes itself. But this is not, by itself, an adequate account. If it were, the present would be the wholly determined outcome of the past. Of course, many philosophies accept this conclusion; but Whitehead discerns – especially, but not only, in human experience – an element of decision, a cutting off of some possibilities in favor of others. For him, what is genuinely possible for each event is more varied than what becomes actual in it. This means that in the constitution of the one out of the many, there is not the causal efficacy of the past but also the effective relevance of possible ways of interpreting, ordering, and supplementing what is received from the past and, thereby, of responding to the past creatively instead of only conformally. Thus the realm of possibility, of what Whitehead calls "eternal objects" is a second ultimate factor in the metaphysical situation alongside formless creativity.

There is a third factor as well, one that I have already mentioned. It is the world itself in all its everchanging particularity and actuality. At any given moment this is the entire past relative to whatever locus in the space-time continuum is taken as the present.

These three factors found in the analysis of any event are all, in an important sense, *ultimate.* That is, they are not hierarchically arranged, and none is merely derivative from the others. Indeed, the relation of any pair is better thought of as non-dual, for they mutually require one another. There can be no creativity apart from the eternal objects, and there can be no creativity or eternal objects apart from the actual world. Equally, there can be no actual world apart from creativity and the eternal objects, and no eternal objects apart from creativity and the actual world.

This metaphysical triad turns out to be useful in the interpretation of the diversity of religious traditions. One of [Raimon] Panikkar's illustrations of differences between India and the West can illustrate part of this. He points out that, especially in India, one image of final destiny is

the falling of a drop of water into the ocean. To Western ears this often appears profoundly unacceptable, since Westerners identify themselves with the *drop* of water in its distinction from other drops of water. The particularity of the drop (hence, personal identity as understood in the West) is lost as the drop merges with the ocean. To Indians, on the other hand, the true self is not lost, for the true self is the water of which the drop is but a passing form.

The water here represents Ātman, or Brahman, or Being, which resembles what in Whitehead's language is "creativity." To realize that one is nothing but an instance of this external, indestructible, ultimate, releases one from all anxieties attendant on identifying oneself in one's difference from others.

The image of the drop of water leads more to the Hindu vision than to the Buddhist. It suggests a common substance underlying all things or of which all things are composed. Buddhism resembles process thought in denying that there are things composed of substances and affirming instead that there are events which are instantiations of dependent origination. This corresponds closely with Whitehead's doctrine of creativity.

But whether the term is *Ātman* or *dependent origination*, the aspect of reality which is discerned and toward which attention is directed is much the same. The question is: Of what am I, and of what are all others, ultimately composed? What am I when all transient forms are stripped away? The Vedantist Hindu answers Ātman, or Nirguna Brahman, Brahman without attributes. The Buddhist says dependent origination or emptiness. There is nothing left when all particularity is stripped away, for the event is nothing but an instance of dependent origination.

This line of questioning has not preoccupied the West, although it has appeared from time to time. On the contrary, the West has attended to form. This is particularly apparent in the Platonic tradition. But the Hebrews also understood creation and redemption as forming and reforming and transforming. They concentrated attention on the contrast between what is and what might be and upon the choices made by human beings among real options. The goal is a new heaven and a new earth – not the realization of what has always been and what always will be.

In those traditions that seek the realization of what is beneath the particularizing forms or in and through all particularization by forms, the sacred connects itself with this realization, or with that which is realized in and through it. In the Abrahamic traditions, the sacred connects itself with the Creator, the One who forms all things and who then promises new forms, provides alternatives, and calls for the realization of some of these and the rejection of others. In a quite different way, the Platonic tradition also associates the sacred with the highest forms or with the One who is pure form or who knows all forms.

There have been others for whom the natural world itself is sacred. To live rightly is to live according to nature, to accord with its rhythms, to embody its harmonies. For them, it is a mistake to concentrate either upon underlying reality or upon the forms that particularize, whether in their function as particularizing or in their character as atemporal universals. It is unity of form and matter in concrete actuality that elicits wonder and provides value. Taoism represents this style of religious life, but in this it is continuous with much of primal and contemporary religiousness as well.

Viewed thus, these three ways of being religious are all valid and conformal to what-is. What each discerns is real, and as its constructions encourage further penetration into the facet of reality, each has gained a deeper wisdom. However different the discernments may be in the three ways, they cannot contradict one another. They are, like all discernments, complementary.

The situation with respect to the constructions associated with these discernments is quite different. Almost inevitably each is so formulated as to belittle the others if not so as to contradict them. The goal of dialogue is to work through these constructions to the discernments they express and defend, so that their complementary character can become visible and the possibility arises for appropriation by each of insights gained by the other. Whitehead's speculations can facilitate some aspects of this process. [. . .]

A Dynamic Unity in Religious Pluralism
A Proposal from the Buddhist Point of View

Masao Abe

[. . .]

I

The primary reason that the pluralistic situation of religion is such a problem to the adherents of various religions is the fear that it will threaten each religion's claim to absoluteness. People fear that an affirmation of religious pluralism will lead to a vicious relativism and finally to a selfdefeating skepticism. They see it as a viewpoint that will undermine their religious commitment. The major reactions to religious pluralism may be classified as the following three attitudes:

First, a person may view religions other than his/or her own as rivals or enemies and simply reject them or try to convert their adherents to his/or her own faith. This attitude has prevailed in the Semitic religions until recent times and, to a greater or lesser extent, has been present in all religions.

Second, a person may attempt to find parallels between his/or her own religion and other religious traditions and to evaluate the religious significance of the beliefs of others without prejudging or rejecting them. In contemporary Christianity, Richard Niebuhr and R. C. Zaehner may be mentioned as examples of this sympathetic approach. Niebuhr emphasizes the need for Christians to be open and responsive to the criticisms by other religious believers of the Christian confession of Jesus as the Christ. He argues that through openminded dialogue, believers in different traditions can deepen and enrich their own grasp of religious truth. Such a fair recognition and positive esteem of parallel truths among different religions are clearly evident in the writings of Niebuhr. But, at the same time, we must recognize that he is much less concerned with Eastern religions than with nonChristian Western movements such as Marxism, Freudianism and Existentialism. On the other hand, Zaehner is deeply involved in the study of Hinduism and Buddhism, as well as Islam and Zoroastrianism. In his writings he has emphasized the urgent need to understand these religions from within. However, while finding parallels between Christianity and other religious traditions, he finally asserts Christianity as the fulfillment or consummation of all other religions, thereby rendering doubtful his own intended openness and objectivity toward nonChristian (and nonCatholic) religions.[1]

"A Dynamic Unity in Religious Pluralism: A Proposal from the Buddhist Point of View" by Masao Abe, in *The Experience of Religious Diversity*, ed. John Hick and Hasan Askari (Brookfield, VT: Gower Publishing Co., 1985), pp. 167–80; 182–90; 225–7.

[1] R. C. Zaehner, *Christianity and Other Religions* (New York, 1964), p. 8.

Third, a person may, with even greater openness, recognize a common Reality underlying the different religious traditions and claim that they are different manifestations of this common Reality. Such an attitude is most evident in Indian religions such as Hinduism, but is not difficult to uncover in contemporary Christian thinkers. William Ernest Hocking and Wilfred Cantwell Smith are two illustrious examples. Emphasizing that religion is universal and inherent in all humankind, Hocking takes the essence of all religions as "a passion for righteousness, ...conceived as a cosmic demand."[2] Although he rightly recognizes particular and separative aspects of religion, especially in terms of communication of religious truth, he talks much about "the same God" and the "need for a common symbol."[3] On the other hand, clearly denying that all religions are the same, Cantwell Smith talks about "the unity or coherence of humankind's religious history."[4] By saying that "the evident variety of their religious life is real, yet is contained within an historical continuum,"[5] Smith emphasizes the interrelatedness and continuity of the history of religions as the possible basis for the common term "faith."

The history of man's religious life, which for some centuries was divided into self-conscious parts, is beginning to include also a developing history of diverse instances of of selfconsciousness of the whole, open to each other.[6]

The attitude that all religions partake of one and the same Reality at their depth has been taken repeatedly, *mutatis mutandis*, in the West as well as in the East, though predominately in the East. In Japan, this attitude has been expressed in a poem as follows:

Though paths for climbing a mountain
From its foot differ,
We look up at the same moon
Above a lofty peak.

In the contemporary context of religious pluralism, such an attitude seems to be getting rather widely accepted.

John Cobb challenges this widespread attitude. [...] Cobb emphasizes that "the insistence of a given identity among the several religious Ways continues to block the urgently important task of learning from one another."[7] To make this point clear, he describes the features of his own firsthand experience of dialogue with Japanese Zen Buddhists. In this connection, he remarks that "they (Buddhists) have experienced *Emptiness* and what they have experienced is not describable as most Christians want to describe God."[8] He also examines the writings of Catholic fathers who have been involved practically in Zen disciplines and refers to Father William Johnston's view by saying that "he has increasingly seen that Zen and Christian mysticism are different throughout, regardless of the parallels that may be found."[9] Cobb concludes as follows:

This strongly suggests that to insist as Christians that Emptiness is a Buddhist name for what we call God is dangerous and misleading. It cuts us off from our Biblical heritage, forcing us to take as normative the Neo-Platonic mystical stream in our tradition. Even then it demands of us changes in this tradition which break its last ties to the Bible. The result is to reinterpret "God" in terms of Emptiness. We can no longer understand God in terms of Yahweh or the Father of Jesus Christ.[10]

[2] William Ernest Hocking, *Living Religions and A World Faith* (New York, 1940), p. 26.
[3] Ibid., pp. 265–6.
[4] Wilfred Cantwell Smith's *Towards A World Theology* (London and Philadelphia, 1981), Chapter 1.
[5] Ibid.
[6] Ibid., Chapter VIII.
[7] "Christian Witness is a Plural World," in *The Experience of Religious Diversity*, ed. John Hick and Hasan Askari: (Brookfield, VT: Gower, 1985).
[8] Ibid., p. 156.
[9] Ibid., p. 156.
[10] Ibid., pp. 156–7.

This conclusion which John Cobb has recently reached through his own experience and observation of ongoing Buddhist–Christian dialogue is important and justifiable. On its basis he proposes as a working hypothesis that "What is named by 'Yahweh' and 'the father of Jesus Christ' is not the same as what is named by 'Emptiness'."[11] On the basis of this hypothesis, rather than rejecting one of them as unreal, "We could allow parallels and similarities to appear, but we would have no need to obscure differences at the most fundamental level."[12] He continues in this vein:

If we do not need to find some common denominator in all religious movements, then we can listen carefully to the important nuances of difference in all of them and learn from each without imposing common categories. Similarly, the distinction between religious and secular loses importance.[13]

In this connection, Cobb further suggests that:

there is a very deep asumption that when two traditions both claim to deal with what is transcendent and ultimate, they must be understood as relating to the same reality. What is ultimate, it is assumed, is truly ultimate, and therefore must be ultimate for all.[14]

Clearly rejecting this deep assumption, Cobb tries to establish his own dialogical standpoint on the understanding that there is no common denominator in all religious traditions.

So far, I have no objection at all to John Cobb's position. Rather I find in him a standpoint which is congenial with the Buddhist one. As is well known, the Buddha answered with silence any metaphysical question concerning "ultimate Reality," such as whether the world is eternal or not. His silence, however, does not indicate agnosticism but rather a thoroughgoing criticism of all possible metaphysical propositions implied in various philosophical schools of his day. Hence his teachings of *Anatman* (no-self)

and *madhyama pratipad* (the Middle Way). The Middle Way should not be construed as a position in the sense of a third position lying at a middle point between the two extremes, but as a no-position or no-standpoint which supersedes both of the other opposed views. It is a positionless position or a standpoint which is free from any standpoint. *Pratitya-samutpada* (dependent co-origination) is no less than another term for this Middle Way. This positionless position unique to the Buddha is more clearly and definitely grasped by Nagarjuna in terms of "eightfold negation" and *Sunyata* (*Emptiness*). The positionless position together with "eightfold negation" and "Emptiness" can be properly realized only *existentially*, not merely logically or conceptually. This Mahayanist position established by Nagarjuna rejects any view or theory of the "ultimate Reality" as a thought-construction and does not admit any notion of "common denominator" or "ultimate unity" in all philosophical or religious traditions. Instead, by taking a positionless position represented by "dependent co-origination" and "Emptiness" he freely recognizes the distinctiveness and the relative or contextual ultimacy of other philosophical positions. On the one hand, the Mahayana positionless position does not at all admit one absolute, ultimate Reality because it realizes Emptiness or the nonsubstantiality of everything; but, on the other, it freely recognizes the relative or contextual ultimacy of various philosophic-religious traditions without eliminating their distinctiveness. Herein, the plurality of various spiritual traditions is given a positive significance without falling into a mere relativism or skepticism. For, in the positionless position made possible by the realization of "Emptiness" or the nonsubstantiality of everything, the relative is ultimate and the ultimate is relative. In other words, the relativity of various religions and the ultimacy of each religion are dynamically nondual and identical. This dynamic position is possible only through the denial of "common denominator" or "ultimate

---

[11] Ibid., p. 157.
[12] Ibid.
[13] Ibid., p. 158.
[14] Ibid.

unity" in various spiritual traditions. In the sense that Cobb also rejects a "common denominator," I find in his writings a standpoint which is congenial with Buddhism.

We must, however, raise a question as to whether Cobb's position can really afford to affirm the dynamism which freely recognizes the relative ultimacy of plural religious traditions without eliminating their distinctivenes, such as is done by Buddhism with its positionless position. Let us examine Cobb's position more closely.

Emphasizing the complementary rather than contradictory character of Buddhism and Christianity, Cobb says:

> Instead of speaking of ultimacy in general, it is better to examine more exactly what Mahayana Buddhists would mean by the ultimacy of Emptiness, should they employ such terminology. Similarly, we should investigate what the Biblical writers would mean by the ultimacy of Yahweh or of the heavenly Father, should they use this language. I am convinced that the respective claims of the Buddhist and Christian scriptures are profoundly different and that finally they are complementary rather than contradictory.[15]

He then elucidates the different nature of the ultimacy of Buddhist "Emptiness" and Christian "God" by saying that:

> It [Emptiness] is the ultimate answer to the question *what* one is and *what* all thing are. It is not the answer to the question *how* and *why* things have the particular character or form they have. The study of forms and why and how they inform our experience and our world was pursued far more intensively in the eastern Mediterranean (in terms of the Biblical God) than in the sphere of Buddhist influence.[16]

Consequently, Cobb argues:

> There is no reason in principle to assume that the Buddhist and Christian claims exclude each

other. The fact that all things are empty does not directly contradict the claims that I should place my ultimate trust in God.[17]

This, then, is how John Cobb understands the complementary relationship between Buddhist and Christian claims of ultimacy. It seems to me, however, that the *ground* or *reason* for such a complementarity is not as clear as it might be. Even if we admit with Cobb that the Buddhist and Christian claims do not exclude or directly contradict each other, such an admission is only a negative, not a positive, basis for the complementarity. Again, even if we acknowledge that Buddhist "Emptiness" is the ultimate answer to the question of *what* things are and that the Christian "God" is the answer to questions of *how* and *why* things are, the very relationship between the questions *what* and *how–why* and between their respective answers, is quite unclear. Cobb seems to distinguish Buddhist and Christian ultimacy and just to juxtapose them. As stated before, he clearly denies the existence of a "common denominator" or "ultimate unity" underlying the various religious ways, and instead proposes as a working hypothesis for Buddhism and Christianity the complementarity of their two different forms of ultimacy. However, the complementarity between the two religions is asserted without revealing its positive ground. The question should be asked: Whenever Cobb emphasizes the complementary relation between the ultimacy of "Emptiness" and the ultimacy of "Yahweh," where is he taking his own stand? Is he taking the ultimacy of "Emptiness," the ultimacy of "Yahweh," or some third position as his own stand? Since it is impossible to *properly* talk about *complementarity* between two items by merely taking *one of them* as one's own position, we must assume that Cobb is consciously or unconsciously taking some *third* position as his own. If this is the case, what is that third position? Isn't his position that of a speculative metaphysics? Isn't he emphasizing the complementary nature of the relationship between Buddhist and Christian ultimacy on a

15 Ibid.
16 Ibid., p. 159.
17 Ibid., p. 160.

conceptually established ground? These questions lead me to suggest that Cobb's working hypothesis lacks a dynamism through which the plurality of religious traditions can be truly given positive significance, and the relativity of various religions and the ultimacy of each religion can be realized as dynamically nondual. The positionless position realized by Mahayana Buddhism, on the other hand, possesses just such a dynamism.

II

In this connection, I would like to make a concrete proposal from the Buddhist point of view. In order to do so the three-body (*tri-kaya*) doctrine may be introduced herein.

The three-body doctrine concerns the Buddha-body (buddha-kaya) or the forms in which the Buddha is manifested. After the Buddha's death, his disciples and followers gradually began to idealize his historical existence and various forms of the Buddha-body doctrine have been widely and profoundly developed, particularly in Mahayana tradition. The three-body doctrine, that is, the doctrine of the threefold Buddha-body: *nirmana-kaya*, *sambhoga-kaya* and *dharma-kaya*, is the most representative form of the Buddha-body doctrine and has been predominant for centuries in Mahayana Buddhism. *Nirmana-kaya*, which means assumed-body, apparitional-body or transformation-body, is no less than the historical Buddha in the person of Gautama. The historical Buddha who was believed in and reverenced by his disciples and followers as the Enlightened One or the One who awakened to Dharma, lived, preached and passed away. Through the great shock of confronting the death of Gautama Buddha, his disciples eventually came to believe that, behind the appearance of the historical Buddha, there is a suprahistorical or nonhistorical Buddha. Gautama was a realizer of Dharma but, having a physical body, was limited by time and space. According to this doctrine, however, he was the transformation-body of the suprahistorical Buddha who is beyond time and space, and who thus is the formless, colorless, unlimited, eternal Buddha. In other words, the historical existence of Gautama Buddha is understood and believed to be an acccommodated body through which the suprahistorical

Buddha revealed himself to the earthly disciples because of his great compassion. This suprahistorical Buddha is, in turn, divided into two different bodies, that is *sambhoga-kaya* and *dharma-kaya*. *Sambhoga-kaya*, which means bliss-body, reward-body, or enjoyment-body, is the suprahistorical Buddha who has fulfilled Dharma and is enjoying various virtues because of the merit he has attained. While *sambhoga-kaya* is suprahistorical or nonhistorical, freed from time and space, and in this sense is formless and colorless, it may nevertheless be said to have a particular form, though invisible, according to the kinds of virtue which it is enjoying as the merit of its fulfillment. *Dharma-kaya* is the truth-body without any personal character. (Therefore, the term "body" is here rather misleading.) It is Dharma (Truth) itself which is to be fulfilled and enjoyed by *sambhoga-kaya*. As Dharma itself, *dharma-kaya* is beyond time and space, is universal and eternal, and is completely formless and colorless.

I explained the three-body doctrine above in order of *nirmana-kaya*, *sambhogan-kaya* and *dharma-kaya*. Essentially speaking, however, this order should be reversed. Without *dharma-kaya* as their foundation, *sambhoga-kaya* and *nirmana-kaya* cannot appear. Again, without *sambhoga-kaya* as its basis *nirmana-kaya*, that is transformation-body, is inconceivable. At the same time, in essence, the threefold body of Buddha is not divided. The Awakened One in his transformation body, of which Gautama was the first instance, is still one with the formless dharma-body and invisible reward-body. All three bodies, although different, are in actuality one living, acting Reality.

In Mahayana Buddhism, *dharma-kaya* is identified with *sunyata* or Emptiness. As Dharma or Truth itself, which is the ultimate ground of both reward-body and transformation-body, *dharma-kaya* is in itself. More strictly speaking, *dharma-kaya* neither *is* in itself, nor *is not* in itself. It is neither *existent* nor *not existent*, neither *fulfilled* nor *unfulfilled*. It is empty and entirely formless. It is, however, not "emptiness" nor "formlessness" in the static mode, rather it is always emptying itself. Constant activity of emptying everything including itself is no less than the reality of Dharma itself which is termed *dharma-kaya* in the three-body doctrine. Again, *dharma-kaya*, negating any form, constantly negates its own formlessness and takes various forms freely without hindrance. This is the reason that as the ultimate ground *dharma-kaya* takes a form of invisible *sambhoga-kaya* (reward-body) and a form of visible *nirmana-kaya* (transformation-body) freely without losing its own formlessness. *Dharma-kaya* is not less than dynamic activity as the ground of everything and is nonobjectifiable and inconceivable.

In contrast to this, *sambhoga-kaya*, as the reward-body which is attained as the virtue of the fulfillment of Dharma, is the suprahistorical embodiment of the formless *dharma-kaya*. Use of the term "fulfillment" raises a question about the fulfillment of *what* and *for what*. "Of what," in this case, is "of Dharma." "For what" is "for itself and all other creatures." Therefore, *sambhoga-kaya* bears a kind of form and a kind of subject-object dichotomy. Although suprahistorical, *sambhoga-kaya* stands for others as well as for itself. Thus, it may well be said to be *personal*. *Sambhoga-kaya*, however, is different from *nirmana-kaya*, i.e., the historical Buddha who appeared with visible form and color among man in this world. By means of its virtue, *sambhoga-kaya* never remains in the self-enjoyment of its own fulfillment of Dharma. It necessarily takes an historical form of Buddha-body, *nirmana-kaya*, as its own transformation in order to share its fulfillment with all fellow beings.

In short, *sambhoga-kaya*, unlike *nirmana-kaya*, is beyond time and space and thus formless, colorless, unlimited and eternal, and yet, unlike *dharma-kaya*, has a kind of form as a Buddha who was fulfilled Dharma, and thus in some sense stands facing others. It is the reality of *fulfilled* Dharma *for itself*, and at the same time, is the reality of *unfulfilled* Dharma, which is to be fulfilled *for all others*.

In Mahayana Buddhism both *sambhoga-kaya* and *nirmana-kaya* are plural, not singular. This is because *dharma-kaya* as the ultimate ground for both is not One God nor One Substance, but formless Emptiness or boundless Openness which, emptying itself, takes forms freely. [...] This is quite different from the case of Yahweh in the Judeo-Christian tradition, "Whose name is jealous and is a jealous God" (Exod. 34:14). In Mahayana Buddhism, in additon to Amida and Mahavairocana, there are many *sambhogan-kaya*

in the form of Buddhas and Bodhisattvas. They are all reward-bodies with a particular name and form who have fulfilled Dharma and are enjoying various virtues for themselves and at the same time are encouraging all others to attain the same fulfillment.

As for *nirmana-kaya*, that is assumed-body or transformation-body, Gautama Buddha is not the one and only instance. There are innumerable forms of the transformation-body throughout Buddhist history. Gautama Buddha is simply the first instance. For Buddha as *nirmana-kaya* is no less than the one who, if any, awakened to Dharma. Accordingly, Indian masters such as Nagarjuna (around 150–250 AD) and Vasubandu (420–500), Chinese masters such as T'ien-t'ai Chih-i (531–597) and Shan-tao (613–681), all have been revered alongside Gautama Buddha and, according to the three-body doctrine, may be said to have been regarded as *nirmana-kaya*. In Japanese Buddhism, this is more conspicuous. The founders of powerful Japanese Buddhist sects such as Kukai (774–835), Honen (1133–1212), Shinran (1173–1262), Dogen (1200–53), Nichiren (1222–82) have been worshipped by their respective followers almost in place of Gautama Buddha. Again, according to the three-body doctrine, these figures can be properly regarded as *nirmana-kaya*. In Christianity, however great and important St Thomas Aquinas and Martin Luther may be to Catholic and Protestant churches respectively, they are not revered alongside Jesus. Even St Paul cannot be an exception. This is simply because Jesus is the only incarnation of the Godhead – the transformation-body of God. This great difference stems from the fact that while Jesus Christ is believed to be the only son of Father God Yahweh, Gautama Buddha and other great Buddhist figures are understood to be, in essence, equally representative of the transformation-body of one and the same Dharma which is entirely empty, open and formless. Accordingly, however crucial Gautama Buddha may be, and however important the founders of various sects may be to the adherents of these sects, there has been little conflict between Gautama and these founders, or between founders themselves. [...] This fact stems almost exclusively from the notion of Dharma (or Dharma-kaya) as the ultimate ground which is dynamically formless.

Because Gautama and the founders of various sects are regarded as various forms of the transformation-body of the nonsubstantial, open and formless Dharma, there is little possibility for serious conflict.

[. . .]

III

Is it not possible that the Buddhist doctrine of the threefold body may contribute to the establishment of a dynamic unity in religious pluralism? In this connection as a working hypothesis, the following threefold reality may be offered: "Lord," "God," and "Boundless Openness." "Lord" roughly stands for *nirmana-kaya*, an historical religious figure that is the center of faith; "God" approximately represents *sambhoga-kaya*, a personal God who is supra-historical but has a particular name and virtue(s); "Boundless Openness" or "Formless Emptiness" generally expresses *dharma-kaya*, Truth itself, which is also supra-historical and is the ultimate ground for both a personal "God" and a central historical religious figure as "Lord." "Lord," "God" and "Boundless Openness" are three different realities which nevertheless have a dynamic identity with "Boundless Openness" as its ultimate ground.

In the Judeo-Christian tradition, the term "Lord" is often used to refer to Yahweh. As Paul said (I Cor. 8:6), however, for Christians it may be said that there is only "one God, the Father," and only "one Lord, Jesus Christ." In the present proposal, in clear distinction from the term "God," the term "Lord" is used to refer to someone like Jesus Christ or Gautama Buddha – an historical transformation or embodiment of the formless Reality which appeared in a particular form of religion. Further, the term "Lord" here is used in a still wider sense by applying its connotation of "master." In this wider sense the term may include such religious figures as Moses and Muhammad. However crucial he may be to Judaism, Moses is not a transformation-body of Yahweh. In the Jewish tradition, however, Moses

is regarded as the "founder" of Hebraic religion and as the unique law-giver of Israel. Further, the Christian tradition has always considered Moses as the forerunner and "type" of Christ. Moses delivered the Old Israel, Christ the New.[18] Again, however important he may be to Islam, Muhammad is not more than a prophet, is never regarded as a transformation-body of Allah. In this sense he cannot be identified with Jesus Christ. As the central figure of Islamic history, however, the role of Muhammad is so indispensable and crucial to Islamic faith that he may be here included, together with Moses, under the term "Lord" (or Master). Such a free and flexible usage of the term "Lord" is not, I hope, arbitrary because in the present proposal the term is understood basically as an historical embodiment of the "Boundless Openness," not simply as an historical incarnation of One God.

The term "God" is also here used somewhat flexibly although it always indicates a personal God with a particular name and virtue(s). This refers to Yahweh, Allah, Isvara (Siva, Visnu, etc.), Amida and so forth. Most of these Gods are believed by their adherents to be the one absolute deity and as the very center and focus of their faiths. These Gods are also believed to have as virtues, love, justice, eternal life, wisdom, compassion and the like. Although in a majority of cases, these Gods are regarded as ultimate Reality, in the present proposal they are to be regarded as reward-bodies (*sambhoga-kaya*), i.e., the deity who attained the fulfillment of ultimate Reality – Boundless Openness or Formless Emptiness – in terms of virtue with a particular name and form (though invisible) through which they can be distinguished from each other.

In the present proposal, Ultimate Reality for all religions is understood as formless, colorless, nameless, unlimited, impersonal "Openness" or "Emptiness," which stands for *dharma-kaya*. As stated earlier, this Emptiness is not a static state of emptiness, but rather a dynamic activity constantly emptying everything including itself. It is formless by negating every form, and yet, without remaining in formlessness, takes various forms freely by negating its own formlessness. This is the reason that "Formless Emptiness" or

[18]   Alan Richardson, ed., *A Theological Word Book of The Bible* (New York, 1953), p. 156.

"Boundless Openness" is here regarded as the ultimate ground which dynamically reveals itself both in terms of personal "Gods" and in terms of "Lords" that are historical religious figures.

In Christianity, Father God Yahweh is believed to have begotten the son of God, Christ, who gave up the form of God and "emptied himself, taking the form of servant, being made in the likeness of men" (Phil. 2:7). This *kenosis* is a great self-negation of Father God to reveal himself in the form of Jesus Christ in this historical world. Even so Yahweh still remains as Father God and his Self-negation is not thoroughgoing. It was Christian mystics such as Meister Eckhart and St John of the Cross who went beyond Father God and became united with the Godhead. For them, the Godhead is impersonal, formless and nameless "Nothing." Herein, God's *kenosis* is fully realized.

In Hinduism, Isvara is regarded by his devotees as a central manifestation of Brahman, the impersonal, highest principle of the creation of the universe. Accordingly, Brahman should not be identified with a personal God such as Yahweh, Allah or Amida, but rather with the source of personal Gods. In the present proposal, however, Brahman is not taken as "Boundless Openness." For although *neti neti* ("not this, not this") is necessary for the acknowledgment of Brahman, Brahman, which is identified with Atman (eternal Self), is strictly speaking still somewhat substantial and not completely formless or empty. This is the reason Gautama Buddha did not accept Brahman as the ultimate Reality and instead emphasized Anatman (no-self) and dependent co-orignation which is no less than another term for "Emptiness."

Space limitation does not allow a detailed discussion of Amida Buddha in Pure Land Buddhism. It may only be mentioned that, though suprahistorical, Amida has a personal form with a particular name and is thus well regarded as "God" in the above sense, but not as "Boundless Openness." In order, however, to find a positive significance in the present situation of religious diversity and to establish a dynamic unit in religious pluralism, it is not appropriate to take "God" (as understood in the present proposal) as the ultimate Reality. Going beyond "God," one should return to and take one's stand on the rootsource from which various

"Gods" are understood to emerge. For Gods, with particular names and particular virtues, however universal the nature of their virtue may be, are by nature not truly compatible with, but rather exclusive of, each other because each of them is believed by their adherents to be the positive center and focus for their religious faiths. Only when one goes beyond "God" and takes "Boundless Openness" as the ultimate Ground can a dynamic unity in religious pluralism be established without eliminating each religion's claim to absoluteness. "Boundless Openness" or "Formless Emptiness," here offered as the ultimate ground, is certainly the basic principle which integrates all religions dynamically, but is not a common denominator or an underlying given identity among the various religious traditions. Unlike Brahman, which is regarded in Hinduism as the underlying principle of the identity of everything in the universe, "Boundless Openness" or "Formless Emptiness" is entirely nonsubstantial and self-emptying or self-negating without a claim to a particular form of absoluteness. Accordingly, while it is working as the dynamic, self-negating principle of unity for all religions, "Boundless Openness" does not eliminate but rather allows or guarantees each religion's claim to absoluteness in terms of "God" and centeredness in terms of "Lord," This is because the various forms of "God" and the various instances of "Lord" in the various religious ways are equally and respectively grasped as manifestations of the dynamic "Boundless Openness" as the ultimate ground.

In World Religions

Lord (*nirmana-kaya*)	Jesus	Muhammad	Krsna(?)	Gautama
God (*sambhoga-kaya*)	Yahweh	Allah	Isvara (Siva, Visnu) (Brahman)	Amida

Boundless Openness – Formless and boundless Reality of Emptiness (Openness) – (*dharma-kaya*)

The key point of the present proposal lies in its emphasis of the necessity for the clear realization of dynamic "Boundless Openness" or "Formless Emptiness" as the ultimate ground for all religions and as the basis for a dynamic unity in religious pluralism. In order, however, to open up a dynamic unity in religious pluralism, which is an urgent task for all religions today, each religion, especially religions based on the notion of "God," must break through their traditional form of personal-God-centeredness, and return to and take their stand on the realization of dynamic "Boundless Openness" as the ultimate Reality. Likewise, a religion which is not based on a personal "God" but on the underlying absolute unitary principle, such as Brahman, must go beyond its substantial, self-identical principle and awaken to the dynamic, self-negating "Boundless Openness" as the ultimate Ground.

This means that although "Boundless Openness" embraces various forms of "God" and "Lord" as their ultimate ground, this is not a blind acceptance but a critical acknowledgment of them. While "Boundless Openness" is all-embracing and thus able to accept various religions without eliminating the distinctiveness of their Gods and Lords, it is at the same time constantly emptying them – even asking them to abnegate themselves and return to itself ("Boundless Openness") as their ultimate ground. The *dynamic* nature of "Boundless Openness" in regard to various religions indicates no less than this dynamic identity of the all-embracing acceptance and the critical approach of constant emptying.

Every religion must be involved in a cultural and social milieu in order to actualize its spirit and life. However, when this historical-cultural involvement creates an institutionalization and fixation of doctrine, ritual, religious order and so forth, it stereotypes that religion and leads to unnecessary conflicts with other religions. This possiblity is especially serious in our time in which religious pluralism is so evident.

It is thus extremely important and necessary for each religion today to break through its traditional forms of doctrine and practice and to realize the dynamic ground, "Boundless Openness," as its own basis. This is necessary not only in order to develop real mutual understanding among religions, but also to encourage learning from each other in the interfaith dialogue. Such a breakthrough is also urgently necessary if each religion is to grapple with the challenge posed by contemporary anti-religious ideologies. As stated earlier, all religions are now exposed to the attack of various religion-negating forces prevailing in our time. The *raison d'être* of religion is now questioned on numerous fronts. To cope with this situation, all religions must reexamine themselves radically and grasp the quintessence of their own faiths. It is here suggested, standing at the intersection of the two forms of challenge, the challenge of pluralism within religion and the challenge by antireligious ideologies, that the realization of "Boundless Openness" may serve as the ultimate ground to meet the double challenge.

John Cobb is right when he says, "[W]hat is named by 'Yahweh' and 'the Father of Jesus Christ' is not the same as what is named by 'Emptiness' [in Buddhism]."[19] For in my understanding, "God Yahweh" and "Emptiness" are standing on two different levels of religious realization and thus are not comparable. Cobb is, however, unclear in what sense or on what basis "Yahweh" and "Emptiness" must be said to be not the same. Accordingly, Cobb is , not justified in insisting on the complementarity of the ultimacy of Yahweh and the ultimacy of Emptiness. This is the reason I earlier raised the questions: "From what standpoint is he talking about the complementarity of these two ultimacies?" "Is he not, consciously or unconsciously, taking a third position in regard to the two ultimacies, a position which is constructed conceptually?" "What is, after all, the ground of that complementarity?" To use the term complementarity, an answer to the last question should be this – the ground of "complementarity" between the ultimacy of God, Yahweh and the ultimacy of Emptiness lies in Emptiness itself. This is because the positionless position, which is constantly self-emptying and self-negating, Emptiness, can negate its own ultimacy and give the foundation to the ultimacy of God Yahweh. They are "complementary," not *immediately* but in the sense that God Yahweh is a manifestation of "Formless Emptiness" or "Boundless Openness" through its dynamic activity of self-emptying or self-negation. Through complete *kenosis*, *God* Yahweh abnegates his name and himself and returns to the Godhead which is now realized as "Boundless *Openness*" or "Formless Emptiness." The ultimacy of Yahweh is an affirmative and positive ultimacy whereas

[19] Cobb, "Christian Witness," p. 156.

the ultimacy of Emptiness is a negative and self-negating ultimacy. Since the ultimacy of Emptiness is a self-negating one, it can give the foundation to, and is complementary with, the ultimacy of God Yahweh.

One may say that such a proposal of threefold reality, that is, "Lord," "God" and "Boundless Openness" as the basis for a dynamic unity in religious pluralism is nothing but a form of Buddhist imperialism because it is based on the Buddhist notion of Emptiness. It is true that the proposal is suggested by the Buddhist *tri-kaya* doctrine and that "Boundless Openness," as the ultimate ground in the present proposal, stands

for the Buddhist notion of *dharma-kaya*. However, only if "Boundless Openness" or "Formless Emptiness" is substantial, not self-negating, and represents *a position affirmatively insisting its ultimacy*, must the present proposal, which is based on it, be said to be a form of Buddhist imperialism. Since to the contrary, as repeatedly emphasized, "Boundless Openness" or "Formless Emptiness" is a dynamic activity of ever-self-emptying and thus is a positionless position which makes other positions possible and alive in a dynamic harmony, it cannot be imperialistic. Rather, it is this "Boundless Openness" that opens up a dynamic unity in religious pluralism in our time.

Section VIII

Questioning the Foundations of Inquiry and Mapping New Territory

Introduction

A. General Introduction to the Section

In the foregoing, questions occasionally have arisen about the limits of human language and reason when utilized in relation to Ultimate Sacred Reality. Moreover, in some cases – for example, according to some Eastern non-dual perspectives – these limitations have been regarded as a pervasive feature of all human experience. Here at the conclusion of our study we will focus more closely on how general concerns about the limitations of language and reason have generated criticisms of the way inquiry is typically conducted in Anglo-American philosophy of religion. Accompanying these criticisms are some proposals concerning the new direction to be taken. Finally, we will also see how some Eastern perspectives appear sympathetic to these criticisms and proposals.

A number of the authors in this section are critical of one or more of these broad theses as well as much of the work done in contemporary philosophy of religion insofar as it seems to presuppose them:

- **Mind-Independent Reality:** There exists a reality, the existence and character of which is not determined by human minds.

- **Concepts and Truth:** The meaning of concepts expressed in human languages can be rendered clear. Once their meanings are sufficiently clarified, concepts can be used in statements about mind-independent reality that are objectively true or false.
- **The Power of Reason:** When used properly, reason can free itself of distorting influences and provide rational confidence in some objective truths about mind-independent reality.[1]

Although the intellectual heritage of these claims extends much further into the past, they are sometimes described as characteristic of the modern period in Western thought (beginning circa the seventeenth century). Those who believe that one or more of these theoretical presuppositions are no longer tenable (or at least that they have been seriously thrown into doubt) often contend that we have now entered a "post-modern" period of philosophy. The use of the word "postmodern" and its cognates has proliferated in recent decades in many different contexts both within and outside of philosophy, making it difficult – if not impossible – to provide a unifying characterization.[2] Nevertheless, it is common for proponents of views labeled

---

[1] Note that these are broader versions of the claims described as constitutive of religious realism in the introduction to the previous section.
[2] For an overview of some varieties of postmodernism, see Kevin Hart, *Postmodernism: A Beginner's Guide* (Oxford: Oneworld Publications, 2004).

"post-modern" in philosophy to be suspicious of one or more of the above claims. A central reason often cited for such suspicion is that such claims reflect a failure to recognize the existence (or degree of influence) of a number of important factors that govern our use of language, concepts, and the pursuit of rational inquiry – for example, that our language, concepts, and reasoning are inescapably shaped by such things as our desires, gender, and socio-historical context.

As we saw in the previous section's discussion of religious pluralism, acknowledging a strong interpretative element in human experience generates tension within a realist account of religious language – the view that it is possible to make objectively true statements about the existence and character of a mind-independent Ultimate Sacred Reality. According to some, it is time to abandon religious realism. We thus begin this section with an examination of one post-modern variety of religious non-realism.

B.   Postmodernism and Western Philosophy of Religion

B1.   Non-Realist (or Anti-Realist) Philosophy of Religion

In "Anti-Realist Faith," Don Cupitt embraces Nietzsche's (1844–1900) proclamation that there are no facts – "only interpretations."[3] On Cupitt's reading, this means that one must recognize that reality is constituted by our constantly shifting perspectives, perspectives that are defined by our historical and cultural settings and encoded in our languages. Thus, in contrast to a proponent of the claims sketched above, Cupitt holds that it makes sense neither to speak of a reality that exists independently of human minds, nor to think that words and concepts can be employed to state objective truths about the existence and character of such a reality. As a consequence, there are no objective truths on this view. Rather, truth is relative, defined by

broad consensus formed within various communal perspectives, which also determine the rules by which reason must play in that context.

Given this general outlook, Cupitt urges us to rethink our approach to philosophy of religion. Some might think that if God can no longer be referred to in the realist sense that religion should be abandoned, but Cupitt disagrees. Although religious language should no longer be viewed as an attempt to mirror another mind-independent realm, it can and should continue to be used as a tool for governing our lives. The word, "God," on Cupitt's version of religious non-realism, refers no longer to a supernatural being but instead to a guiding human ideal. Moreover, he urges others to realize that since religion is thoroughly a humanly constructed artifact, its future form is firmly in our hands.

B2.   Non-Realism and Theistic Religiousness

Paul Badham acknowledges a trend toward offering non-realist re-interpretations of some doctrines in liberal forms of Christianity, but he maintains in "The Religious Necessity of Realism" that theists cannot abandon certain core realist beliefs about God without losing the basis of their distinctive form of religiousness. In other words, all that is important in theistic religion cannot be re-interpreted in non-realist fashion, as he takes Cupitt to be suggesting. According to Badham, at the heart of theistic religion lies the possibility of entering into a personal relationship with a transcendent divine presence. Thus, if God does not exist in the realist sense, then the emotive attitudes of love and devotion that constitute the transforming experience of that relationship cannot be sustained, along with the ritual practices (e.g., prayer) designed to evince and express them.

B3.   The Power of Negative Thinking

In "Postmodernism and Religious Reflection," Merold Westphal articulates some further post-

---

[3]   *The Will to Power*, trans. Walter Kaufman and R. J. Hollingdale (New York: Random House, 1968), p. 267. Amongst Nietzsche scholars, there is dispute about whether this passage – published posthumously on the basis of notes Nietzsche had made – is an accurate expression of his view, and if so, whether it is best interpreted in the non-realist fashion that Cupitt endorses. For helpful discussion of Nietzsche's view of truth, see Richard Schacht, "Nietzsche on Philosophy, Interpretation, and Truth," *Noûs* 18:1 (1984): 75–85.

modern themes in the context of philosophy of religion, though in a way that does not entail a wholesale slide into the non-realism and relativism characteristic of Cupitt's view. Like Cupitt, Westphal emphasizes the way that our concepts and the thinking that employs them are always embedded in a socio-historical context. This entails that our encounter with reality is always heavily mediated and "muddied" in a way that the second "modernist" thesis above fails to reflect. Borrowing a phrase made famous by Jacques Derrida (1930–2004), he wishes to deny a "metaphysics of presence" – i.e., the view that mind can achieve (via reason or mystical experience) an unmediated and thus absolutely undistorted and certain grasp of reality.

Westphal also draws on Martin Heidegger's (1889–1976) critique of "ontotheology." For Heidegger, this term refers to an unfortunate failure in the history of Western thought to preserve the distinctive aims of two realms of inquiry – ontology and theology. Ontology is an area of metaphysics devoted to the study of existence, or being itself – that which rationally unifies and serves as the ground of all things that exist. According to Heidegger, this philosophical project became wedded to theology in ancient Greece when it was illegitimately assumed that what unifies all that exists and thereby makes all things rationally intelligible must at the same time be their divine creative source. Heidegger's original worry about this marriage seems to have been that it distorted metaphysical inquiry, but Westphal is more concerned about its consequences for theology. That is, he believes that when philosophers of religion treat theological claims about God as if their purpose is to serve the aims of metaphysical investigation, they transform the God revealed in scripture into a mere explanatory hypothesis in order serve the all too human demand that the universe be thoroughly intelligible, an aspiration he critiques as a form of "logocentrism."

According to Westphal, what these strands of postmodern thought have to offer philosophers of religion is "the power of negative thinking" – a means of curbing a distorting impulse to make metaphysical judgments with greater confidence than that to which one is entitled and to remake God so as to remove a mystery at the heart of the universe. This emphasis on negation, he argues, need not lead to atheism or relativism, for like other forms of anti-rationalism encountered earlier in this book (see section III), they may be regarded as a means of pointing toward something that is not adequately grasped by reason alone.

B4. Objectivity as a Legitimate Aspiration

Though not directly focused on philosophy of religion, Robert Kane seeks to address an important aspect of the postmodern critique in his article "The Ends of Metaphysics." Kane accepts much of the postmodernist emphasis on the way in which our thinking is inescapably influenced by a conceptual scheme, which is in turn shaped by our socio-historical context. Nevertheless, he argues that we need not give up on a central aspiration within traditional metaphysics – the aspiration to objectivity – as many postmodernists have maintained This aspiration takes two forms: (a) an aspiration to give objective and comprehensive explanations of what exists and why; and (b) an aspiration to specify what is objectively valuable and so worthy of our striving. The way forward in thinking about both objective explanation and objective worth, according to Kane, lies in prying ourselves away from the tendency to assume that the goal is to arrive at *the* way a thing is in itself (or *the way* that is good/excellent). If instead we seek a summation of "the *ways* a thing is" (or the *ways* of being good/excellent) and acknowledge the fallible nature of this practice, he believes we can salvage a working notion of objectivity.

B5. New Feminist Forays

Earlier in the text (section II), we encountered feminist reflection on the nature of Ultimate Sacred Reality. In "Feminism and Analytic Philosophy of Religion," Sarah Coakley summarizes and evaluates some of the new work being done by feminists that has been critical of the "analytic" approach to doing philosophy of religion. The phrase "analytic philosophy" refers loosely to a widely practiced way of doing philosophy in the English-speaking world that begins with an attempt to get clear on the meaning of some central philosophical concepts and then seeks to evaluate the truth of claims employing those concepts. For example, notice how this methodological approach is reflected in much of the philosophical reflection on theism in this anthology. The first task on this approach to doing philosophy of religion is to get clear on the meaning of "God." Once that meaning is clarified, one proceeds to evaluate the truth of claims concerning such a God.

Coakley discusses the recent work of two other feminist philosophers: Grace Jantzen and Pamela Sue Anderson. Both authors draw on varieties of postmodern philosophy in contending that analytic philosophy is blind to its masculinist bias. That is, they charge that while analytic philosophers conceive of their approach and methods as a neutral means of pursuing truth, they are, in fact, distorted by interests that are characteristically those of men and thereby contribute to the subordination of the interests of women. Both authors also express an interest in bridging the current divide between postmodernist forms of feminism and analytic philosophy of religion, but Coakley argues that the resources for such a dialogue are largely lacking on Jantzen's view because of her allegation that all appeals to truth and rationality are tainted by male bias, which entails a rejection of realism about truth in general as well as religious realism in particular. Moreover, given these rejections, Coakley argues that it is no longer clear that a view like Jantzen's can provide a basis for the liberation aims of feminism.

Coakley is more sympathetic to Anderson's approach, which seeks a "renegotiation" of the sort of rationality prized in analytic philosophy of religion rather than its outright rejection. For her, this renegotiation involves embracing standpoint epistemology. Like Kane's view, this theory emphasizes the importance of gathering multiple perspectives on reality – here, especially the perspectives of those on society's margins – in order to work toward a more adequate account. Applying this in philosophy of religion, the view holds that no one has full access to the truth about Ultimate Sacred Reality but all have some access, and those at society's margins may have the strongest claim to truth. According to Anderson, it is through the imaginative exercise of entering into the perspectives of others that one may achieve a less biased perspective.

C. Parallels in the East

C1. Authenticity and Enlightenment

Above, Merold Westphal drew on Martin Heidegger's critique of ontotheology to caution fellow philosophers against thinking of God in a way that subordinates the Divine to the aims of philosophy. In "Heidegger and Buddhism," Michael Zimmerman focuses on another aspect of Heidegger's thought in order to highlight a parallel between his philosophy and that of Mahayana Buddhism. Both, he maintains, diagnose that the fundamental source of human suffering is an inauthentic self-conception – a way of viewing oneself as an isolated independent ego that exists over against other independently existing objects. Both also contend, according to Zimmerman, that the solution – the path to authenticity – lies in recognizing the "nothingness" of all things.

As discussed earlier (section II), the use of words like "nothingness" and "emptiness" in contexts like these is intended to refer not to a complete lack of anything at all but rather to the absence of a particular kind of existence: no-thingness. As Zimmerman sketches, Heidegger's early thought on these topics was influenced by Christian mystics like Meister Eckhart, who spoke of God as "Divine Nothingness" in order to emphasize that God is not to be regarded as simply a being that is distinguished from others by supernatural characteristics and a heavenly address. Heidegger borrows and applies this conceptual device to illuminate the nature of human existence (and, later, Being itself). The human self, like Eckhart's God, is not simply a thing that exists apart from other things, but instead a locus in which the process of being, or constant unfolding of reality, takes place. In Heidegger's terminology, human existence is *Dasein*, literally, "here presencing." As Zimmerman notes (and as should be clear from our earlier discussion of the Buddhist view in sections II and VI), this Heideggerian conception of human existence resembles the Buddhist teaching that the self is *anatman*, or empty (*sunyata*) of independent existence – that it exists instead as a collection of events coming to be and passing away in accordance with dependent co-origination (*pratitya-samutpada*).

For Heidegger, anxiety is a mood of great significance, for it indicates a latent awareness of the groundlessness of one's self (note the parallel with *dukkha*). The goal is to submit to what anxiety prompts us to see and thereby live an authentic existence, marked by a willingness to "let things be" on their own terms rather than insisting that they conform to one's ego-driven (or, more broadly, human-driven) interests. In this way, according to Zimmerman, authentic existence for Heidegger closely resembles the kind of freedom and compassion that are said to derive from enlightened self-understanding in Mahayana Buddhism.

C2. Confucianism as Religious Humanism

In the opening section of this book, it was proposed that religion aims to provide an appropriate way of being related to that which is conceived to be Ultimate Sacred Reality. In "*Li* and the A-theistic Religiousness of Classical Confucianism," Robert Ames argues that this Ultimate Sacred Reality need not be a transcendent reality but instead can be a wholly immanent aspect of the human community. In this way, his characterization of the religiousness of Confucianism suggests a parallel with the sort of non-realist religious humanism envisaged by Don Cupitt above.

Ames begins by emphasizing that the Chinese philosophical sensibility has always been to regard all creation as co-creation and to regard relations as intrinsic to an individual's identity. Thus, the nature of what exists is to be understood by a narrative mapping of those particular relationships that cooperatively constitute a thing's identity. For example, on the Confucian view, the proper way to understand my nature is not to seek an account of internal characteristics that set me apart from others, but rather to map the relationships with others that define me: son of Mildred and Arthur, brother to George, husband of Martha, father of A. J., teacher of these students, etc. In other words, my identity is co-created through my roles and relationships.

As Ames explains, human flourishing on this model of human nature involves learning how to continually adapt one's attitude and behavior appropriately in accordance with ritualized

social roles and relationships, or *li*. Through the process of investing oneself wholly in *li*, one both continually refines oneself and contributes to the development of others in ever-widening circles of relationships. The spirituality of Confucianism is understood in reference to an awareness that accompanies the extension and growth of one's influence. According to Ames, this process of growth yields religious experience in the form of both a deep acceptance of things as they are and a focused appreciation for the unique co-creative role one plays in determining what will be.

Suggestions for Further Reading

Anderson, Pamela Sue, *A Feminist Philosophy of Religion: The Rationality and Myths of Religious Belief* (Malden, MA: Blackwell Publishers, 1998).

Anderson, Pamela Sue and Beverley Clack (eds), *Feminist Philosophy of Religion: Critical Readings* (New York: Routledge, 2004).

Bynum, Caroline Walker, Stevan Harrell, and Paula Richman (eds), *Gender and Religion: On the Complexity of Symbols* (Boston: Beacon Press, 1986).

Byrne, Peter, *God and Realism* (Burlington, VT: Ashgate Publishing, 2003).

Caputo, John D., *The Prayers and Tears of Jacques Derrida: Religion without Religion* (Bloomington, IN: Indiana University Press, 1997).

Caputo, John D. (ed.), *The Religious* (Malden, MA: Blackwell Publishers, 2002).

Derrida, Jacques and Gianni Vattimo (eds), *Religion* (Stanford, CA: Stanford University Press, 1998).

Dewey, John, *A Common Faith* (New Haven, CT: Yale University Press, 1934).

Eshleman, Andrew, "Can an Atheist Believe in God?" *Religious Studies* 41:2 (2005): 183–99.

Feuerbach, Ludwig, *The Essence of Christianity*, trans. George Eliot (New York: Harper Torchbooks, 1841/1957).

Frankenberry, Nancy, *Religion and Radical Empiricism* (Albany, NY: State University of New York Press, 1987).

Groenhout, Ruth E. and Marya Bower (eds), *Philosophy, Feminism, and Faith* (Indianapolis, IN: Indiana University Press, 2003).

Harding, Sandra and M. B. Hintikka (eds), *Discovering Reality: Feminist Perspectives on Epistemology, Metaphysics, Methodology, and Philosophy of Science* (Dordrecht: Reidel, 1983).

Heidegger, Martin, *Being in Time*, trans. John Macquairre and Edward Robinson (New York: Harper & Row, 1962).

Heisig, James W., *Philosophers of Nothingness* (Honolulu: University of Hawaii Press, 2001).

Irigaray, Luce, *Sexes and Genealogies*, trans. Gillian C. Gill (New York: Columbia University Press, 1993).

Irigaray, Luce, *Between East and West: From Singularity to Community*, trans. S. Pluhacek (New York: Columbia University Press, 2002).

Jantzen, Grace M., *Becoming Divine: Towards a Feminist Philosophy of Religion* (Bloomington, IN: Indiana University Press, 1999).

Joy, Morny, Kathleen O'Grady and Judith L. Poxon (eds), *Religion in French Feminist Thought: Critical Perspectives* (London, New York: Routledge, 2003).

Kearney, Richard, *The God Who May BE: A Hermeneutics of Religion* (Indiana University Press 2001).

King, Richard, "Philosophy in a Post-Colonial World," in *Indian Philosophy: An Introduction to Hindu and Buddhist Thought* (Washington, DC: Georgetown University Press, 1999), pp. 230–45.

Parks, Graham (ed.), *Heidegger and Asian Thought* (Honolulu: University of Hawaii Pres, 1987).

Rorty, Richard, "Pragmatism as Romantic Polytheism," in *The Revival of Pragmatism*, ed. Morris Dickstein (Durham, NC: Duke University Press, 1998).

Rosenbaum, Stuart (ed.), *Pragmatism and Religion* (Urbana, IL: University of Illinois Press, 2003).

Runzo, Joseph (ed.), *Is God Real?* (New York: St Martin's Press, 1993).

Wettstein, Howard K., "Awe and the Religious Life," in *Midwest Studies in Philosophy*, vol. XXXI, ed. Peter A. French, Theodore E. Uehling, Jr, and Howard K. Wettstein (Notre Dame, IN: University of Notre Dame Press, 1997), pp. 257–80.

59

Anti-Realist Faith

Don Cupitt

Around two hundred years ago a change came over Western thought. It became much more aware of itself and of its own interpretative and constructive activity than it had been before. Slowly, thinking shifted from being dogmatic to being critical. A whole new realm came into view, as people became conscious of the hitherto hidden apparatus by which we put a construction upon our experience. At first, the rationalists and Kant tried to prove that there was nothing very alarming about the new discovery, because (they said) this thinking machinery of ours is timeless and necessary. They argued that the world *must* be thought in the way that it is thought, so that for these first critical thinkers reality still held firm. But later, as it became obvious that people do in fact see the world and think of the world very differently in different societies and historical periods, it came to be recognised that all our thinking is historically conditioned. Whereas the older dogmatic type of thinking had always tended to go straight from the mind to the cosmos, critical thinking became preoccupied with the variable cultural apparatus that guides the way we perceive and interpret what's out there.

Philosophy did not give up. As before, it fought a determined rear-guard action in favour of necessary truth. Like Kant, Hegel also believed that the difference between science and philosophy is

that science is concerned with what merely happens to be so, whereas philosophy is concerned with what must be so. Accordingly he tried to prove that there remains a sort of rational necessity in the way that, living just where and when I do, I must perceive the world as I do. That is, Hegel tried to show that there is philosophical necessity in the process of historical development and in the succession of human cultural forms. As everyone knows, Karl Marx and other historicist thinkers held the same view; but eventually it broke down, leaving a doctrine which has been called perspectivism.

The main doctrines of perspectivism are as follows. There isn't any pure or quite neutral experience or knowledge of reality. In order to have any experience or knowledge at all, you must have a practical slant, an interest, an angle or a perspective which, so to say, makes certain things stand out and become noticeable. To take the simplest possible example, acute hunger may give you an interest in dividing up the world in such a way that the edible stands out from its inedible background. There are indefinitely many such perspectives or angles upon the world – and they are all of them historically occasioned, human and contingent. Some, like certain branches of our natural sciences, are very highly refined. But even the most advanced scientific

"Anti-Realist Faith" by Don Cupitt, in *Is God Real?*, ed. Joseph Runzo (New York: St Martin's Press, 1993), pp. 45–55.

theories are still human, perspectival, historically evolved and subject to future revision. None of them can claim the sort of dogmatic absoluteness that people thought they had in pre-critical times, when all the most important knowledge was unchanging and came down to us from the past and from above.

So reality has now become a mere bunch of disparate and changing interpretations, a shifting loosely held coalition of points of view in continual debate with each other. Politics is like that nowadays, and so is every faculty in a modern university. So is human reality generally, which is why in modern culture we represent reality to ourselves predominantly through an endless proliferation of perspectival fictions, in the novel, drama and the cinema. We are all of us non-realists nowadays.

The position just described was reached by Nietzsche during the 1880s. He used the slogan, "There are no facts, only interpretations", and he coined the term "anti-realism" to describe his doctrine. At the same time, critical thinking was preparing to advance yet another stage as it became aware of language. The new development appears in the United States in C. S. Peirce's doctrine of thought-signs, in Austria in Fritz Mauthner's philosophy of language, and in Switzerland in Ferdinand de Saussure's structural linguistics, but it achieved really wide currency only as the work of Wittgenstein and the French structuralists became known in the 1950s.

Most of the key new ideas about language are by now very familiar. People seem to start by thinking that language is a more or less unsatisfactory dress in which we clothe our thoughts, and that the meaning of a word is an object outside language, as if a word were a label. Because we think there has to be something for a word to stand for, we suppose that the great words of philosophy, religion, ethics and so forth, must stand for unchanging and invisible essences, like the Platonic Ideas. Thus laws, standards, values, concepts and the rest are thought of as being rather like spirits, but impersonal; they are seen as ghostly things that control events. So the popular view of language makes us realists in philosophy and in theology.

The linguist's vision of language is, however, quite different. To him, it is a very large, historically evolving and living system. In effect it coincides with culture, seen as a system of signs. There is no need to go outside language in order to explain it. We are always already within language, and the dictionary is well able to explain every printed mark simply in terms of its relations with other printed marks. A word's meaning cannot be anything external to language because any and every meaning is just a presently held position within a vast dynamic and evolving system of relativities. Since there cannot be any unchanging meaning, there cannot be any timeless truths. The whole world of meaning, which is the true starting point for philosophy, is by its very nature shifting all the time like the prices in a stock market, as human power relations shift.

Like the prices in a stock market, the meanings of words are essentially publicly determined, for a meaning is the resultant of an interplay of forces in the public domain. The philosophers who first saw this, such as C. S. Peirce, quickly grasped that it meant the end of the individualistic approach to philosophy that had dominated the West since the Reformers and Descartes. I cannot determine any meanings all by myself, so I cannot begin my philosophy from myself. Society and the public domain come first. Culture is a system of symbols, and society is a busy communications network. Messages in the various codes are flying back and forth all the time, and we all contribute to the humming activity of the whole.

Concerning the meanings of the symbols used in society's communication code, there is an amazingly high level of agreement. Each one of us is phenomenally sensitive to just what is and is not currently being done with each individual word in present-day idiomatic English, and we are all the time minutely adjusting our own usage in response to social change and new things that we've heard being said. Our desire for mutual understanding and sympathy must be very strong for it to have produced such a refined unanimity as there is among any local group of native speakers on their own home ground.

The comparison that I am drawing between our continual public debate about everything and a market brings out a striking difference between meaning and truth. On the one hand, through our ceaseless chatter we achieve a very high degree of consensus about the meanings of words. On the other hand, in our modern large-scale and highly communicative societies there is no single grand overarching dogmatic truth any longer. All truths, beliefs, theories, faiths, perspectives become just individual stocks in the market. They rise and fall relative to each other as conditions change.

Now comes the point that is hard to grasp: just as there is no sense in asking for the absolute price of something, so there is no sense in trying to step outside the changing human debate and fix realities, meanings and truths absolutely. We have to live and act without absolutes. To take just one example, I personally am prepared to fight tooth and nail for modern evolutionary biology against creationism. But I cannot claim that current evolutionary theory is, in any part of it, objectively, dogmatically and perennially just true. On the contrary, over the generations to come I expect that every bit of current evolutionary theory will be replaced by something different. In this shifting relativistic world of ours, we can still choose our values and fight for them, but our beliefs won't have the old kind of permanent anchorage in an unchanging ideal order.

The point here is hard to express without paradox, but let's try: our modern experience is that there isn't any objective, fixed, intelligible reality out there, such as many be replicated in our language and invoked to check our theories. We now live wholly *inside* our own history, our language and the flux of cultural change. We find that our world isn't made of Being any more, but of symbols and of conflicting arguments. The long-term effect of the critical revolution in our thinking has been to make us so much aware of our own theories, viewpoints and ways of thinking that objective reality has melted away. We haven't got a proper cosmos any longer, only a bunch of chronic disagreements.

Let us now by contrast briefly evoke the traditional religious and philosophical outlook of medieval Christianity. It was Platonic, making a sharp contrast between this changing and corruptible material world below and the eternal controlling intelligible world above. It was pre-critical, so that people made no very clear distinction between culture and nature. They blithely supposed that their own cultural conceptions were part of the natural order of things.

It was pre-scientific, and many events were ascribed to supernatural causes. It was also pre-historical, and people's vision of the past was short and very hazy. Life was governed by tradition, a fixed body of knowledge that had come down from the Fathers and from above. Faith was therefore dogmatic, binding you to a body of truths and a form of life that would remain immutable from the primitive era until the end of historical time.

In such a context both philosophy and theology were oriented towards necessity, changelessness and ideal perfection. For both traditions the goal of human life was to attain absolute knowledge of absolute reality. In that timeless contemplation of absolute necessity and perfection, which religion called the Vision of God, you would find perfect fulfilment and happiness. Thus the old Christian culture was highly realistic in being centred around objective, eternal, necessary, intelligible and perfect Being. Faith was dogma-guided longing for Heaven, and the monk whose way of life anticipated Heaven was the highest human type. The body, time, culture, language, disagreement, history and biological life were all relatively neglected or disparaged.

Now consider how completely we have reversed the traditional outlook of Christian Platonism. The world above and all the absolutes are gone. The whole of our life and all our standards are now inside language and culture. For good or ill *we* make our own history, *we* have shaped our own world, *we* have together evolved all norms to which our life is subject. Religion for us must inevitably be something very different from what it was in the heyday of Platonic realism. Indeed, it is plain that if I am right, then Christianity must be revolutionised to survive.

There are people who still hope that the old order can be restored. For them, there is no intermediate position; the end of dogmatism is the beginning of nihilism. They are terrified by the thought of a world without certainties. They yearn for a society constrained by one absolute truth determined by one absolute power. But anti-realists like me reject their view, and claim that Christianity can and should be modernised. We invoke the symbol of the Day of Pentecost, when God scattered Himself and was distributed as spirit to each individual believer. Just as Truth has come down from heaven and is now immanent within the movement of our various human conversations; just as political sovereignty is no longer wholly vested in a super-person above society but is dispersed throughout the body politic; just as, indeed, the whole of the former world above is now resolved down into the life of this world – so God also is now in each of us.

This discussion has I hope made a little clearer what we mean by a non-realist philosophy of religion. Realists think our religious language tells of beings, events and forces that belong to a higher world, an invisible second world beyond this world of ours. But I believe that there is only one world and it is this world, the world we made, the human life-world, the world of language. To think of language as replicating the structure of some extra-linguistic reality, some world beyond the world of our language, is I believe a mistaken way of thinking of language *anyway*. Every word is more like a tool for doing a job than like a xerox copy of something that is not a word. The only language we can know is wholly human, completely adapted to its job of being the medium in which human life is lived in the only world we have. So we should see religious language in terms of the part it can play in our lives, rather than see it in a mythological way as conjuring up a picture of a second world. For us, there is only *one* world, and it is *this* world, the manifest world, the world of language, the world of everyday life, of politics and economics. And this world has no outside. It doesn't depend in any way on anything higher, and there is no meaning in the suggestion that our cultural beliefs and practices need to be set on any external foundation.

Thus I believe in only one continuous but multi-perspectival common world. In it language and experience, meaning and feeling, nature and culture are fully interwoven. This one world is human, cultural and historically changing. Religion is wholly inside it, and it has no outside. I don't take a realistic view of *any* non-manifest entity. The Word has become flesh, say Christians: that is, the intelligible world must now be resolved back into its manifest basis.

This fully secularised and incarnational vision of things became dominant about two centuries ago. Among the historical events that marked its emergence were the industrial revolution, the democratic revolutions, the Romantic movement, German Idealist philosophy and the rise of the novel. It is emergent in David Hume, but is stated most grandiosely by Hegel. More recently its implications have been spelt out in one way by American pragmatists like Richard Rorty who follow John Dewey, and in another way by Nietzsche and the modern French philosophers who admire him.

These may seem a disparate group of thinkers, but what they have in common is a desire to escape from the legacy of Plato. They are all naturalistic. They reject two-worlds dualism, and in particular they see our life as being so profoundly historical that there can be no sense in the idea that we are subject to the controlling influence of a timeless order. Our language, our knowledge and our morality are human and ever-changing, not cosmic. There's no point in trying to assess them in terms of their relation to just one set of timeless, superhuman intellectual and moral standards.

An example: conservatives sometimes complain that moral or academic standards are lower than they used to be. But the world of two or three generations ago was a different world, with different standards. In their world they measured things by their standards; in our world we measure them by ours. We have no more reason to absolutise their standards than we have to absolutise our own. In fact, we shouldn't absolutise *either* set of standards: instead we should simply recognise that historical change happens and that it demands a continuous reinterpreting and recreating of our standards.

In this way we come to see that our standards and all our supposed "absolutes" are themselves historical, immanent within language and subject to continual remaking. This has in turn the effect of making certain old ways of thinking no longer possible to us. Consider, for example, "the Word of God". Our understanding of what language is has become so fully human, cultural and historical that we now cannot conceive a solitary non-human and extra historical language user. At one time people naively saw God as a member of their own language group. He spoke to them in the tongue of their own place and time. But how shall we put it now? To what language community does God belong? In what dialect and of what period is God's speech, and how in terms of modern linguistic theory do His words have meaning for Him? What instinctual drives power His utterance, and what body has He to vibrate as He produces it?

Just to raise these questions is to realise that a realistic view of God as a language user has long been impossible to us. And as we turn now to the philosophy of religion, I must repeat that I am merely describing the world as it has been this past two centuries. It is the world as ordinary people experience it in their political and economic life and represent it to themselves in the novel, the newspapers and the cinema. It is the way the world is for students of language, the social sciences and history. I cannot say that it is the metaphysical truth of the human condition, because it is how things look after the end of metaphysical truth. No one vision of things can any longer be compulsory. The philosopher cannot claim the authority to act as culture-policeman. Instead he'll have to be something more like an interpreter of the times, who seeks to show *both* the diversity of the possibilities at present before us *and* the family resemblance among all the perspectives and forms of life that are available in some one period, such as our own. So I am not telling you how things are absolutely, but only offering you an interpretation of the way they seem, just now.

It is in that undogmatic and post-authoritarian spirit that we return to the question of realism and anti-realism in the philosophy of religion.

First, we must obviously acknowledge that the majority report of tradition comes down in favour of theological realism. Most believers have thought that supernatural beings and influences really exist, independently of us. They have thought that there is a real God out there controlling world events, who may intervene, assist us by His Grace, answer our prayers and so on; and they have thought that there is a real supernatural world wherein we may go on living after we have died. That surely is how most people have seen matters.

There are, however, two massive exceptions to this generalisation. First, the ancient tradition of Christian Platonism clearly recognised that our words are only human words, and accordingly stressed the descriptive inadequacy of all our talk about divine things so strongly as to be agnostic. Between the third-century and the Reformation, most of the great theologians stood in this tradition. Secondly, the Hebraic and Protestant tradition always saw religious language as being imperative rather than indicative. It tells us how we must think and live, rather than how things are. Its purpose is to govern rather than to inform. These two themes, the negative theology and voluntarism, have between them ensured that throughout the Christian tradition the intellectuals have been much less realistic in their belief than ordinary people.

This has continued to be true in the modern period. The great founders of modern religious thought, Kant, Hegel and Schleiermacher, were all in their different ways anti-realists about God, two centuries ago. Their influence has ensured that most of the long line of Continental theologians since have been anti-realists also, but they used slightly veiled language and their English readers have not understood what has been happening. This was true, for example, of Schweitzer, Bultmann, Neibuhr, Bonhoeffer and Tillich in our own century. The case of church history is also very notable, for fully non-supernaturalist church history began to be written in the Prussian universities in the 1740s, and nobody today complains that it leaves out anything. We seem to accept that purely secular church history tells the whole story.

Furthermore, we habitually put forward an anti-realist interpretation of *other people*'s religious beliefs. Thus, I have at home several small bronze images of Shiva. Ask me, and I can, in principle if not in fact, tell you all there is to know about Shiva and how he is worshipped, and I don't have to leave anything out. I need miss nothing, I can sympathetically explain everything, and I can even join in if I wish. The anti-realism consists in the recognition that Shiva is real only to his followers and within their perspective. If Hinduism vanished from the earth, there'd be nobody left to whom Shiva was real. But, for the present, Shiva lives. The anti-realist can in principle see all there is to see and say all there is to say. Since we have given up ideas of absolute truth and error, we can look down other perspectives without prejudice.

The anti-realist viewpoint has already made it possible for us to view other people's faiths more sympathetically, and to enter into them more deeply, than in the past. How much more then will we profit if we move over to an anti-realist view of *our own* faith!

The reason why we would gain so much is that realism in religion acts as an ideological defence of the *status quo*. It discourages us from attempting to carry through much needed reforms, and even prevents us from seeing their necessity. By suggesting that our religious beliefs were revealed to us by an eternal and objective God, realism makes us afraid to question them. And realism brings with it two other ideas that also inhibit us from thinking. *Essentialism* suggests that Christianity is a timeless, coherent system of thought no part of which can be altered without weakening the whole, and *primitivism* maintains that faith was purest near its point of origin so that we have to keep going back to the past for correction and for legitimation.

All these ideas are surely wrong. To the historian's eye Christianity is not a timeless and coherent system of thought, but a product of history and in continual change. It is a rather loose aggregate or miscellany of ideas from different times and places, many of which are at odds with each other. There is no reason to think that just being old makes an idea more likely to be right. On the contrary, we usually find that very old ideas are now very bad, and need to be replaced. And since critical study shows that despite the myth of immutable truth Christianity has in fact been evolving throughout its long history, there is no reason why we should not now do openly and consciously what our forerunners did unknowingly.

So, indeed, we *are* now doing, for we are increasingly aware of our responsibility for modernising Christianity and getting it up to date. We set about bending the tradition and rewriting history. We seek to purge the cruelty and sexism from Christian symbolism, and we begin to ordain women. By doing all this we now admit that it was we who made our religious beliefs, it is we who are responsible for them, and it is up to us to put them right. In short, our religious beliefs and practices are an integral part of the evolving totality of culture, and must change with it. So we acknowledge that religion is human, historical and cultural all the way through. It could not have been otherwise. Nor does this matter, because if we remember our Bibles we'll recall that the religious system was never *intended* to be an end in itself. It is only a means: eventually it should make itself redundant, because the goal of the religious life is a spiritual state that is beyond all the symbols. So you have to have the ladder to climb, and you have to know when to kick it away. Often, religion fails to liberate people spiritually because they take its teachings too literally and don't know when and how to pass beyond them. In Asian religion it was a well-accepted principle that a particular name of God, or a particular set of worship-guiding images, should be used only for so long as they are helpful, and should then be left behind. People were encouraged to treat their own religious ideas lightly. In the West, unfortunately, our religious outlook has usually been heavy, crude, gloomy and terroristic. The anti-realist point of view offers the prospect of Western religion's becoming a little more sophisticated than it has been in the past. It's about time this happened, because Christianity as we have known it so far has been, frankly, barbarous compared with what it should be. We have been locked into truly frightful excesses of power and guilt, cruelty and sentimentality. We need a clean-up urgently.

Again, anti-realism helps, because now for the first time the believer no longer claims any special cosmic privilege. I am a priest, I practise Christianity in full, and I try to tread the spiritual path. I have found joy in loss, for now there is no remaining respect in which I think that I am in the light and some other human being is in darkness. I have no old-style supernatural or Plato-type metaphysical beliefs. I am as ignorant as everyone else, and I shall die like everyone else. Having no cosmic advantage, I can claim no spiritual authority or power over other human beings, and I have no moral standing for making them feel guilty. As I follow Christ I am now as naked as he is. By the standards of earlier centuries, my views are certainly radically sceptical. God is a guiding spiritual ideal, eternal life is holiness now. We must become radically emptied out and free. And in this state we can learn to practise Christianity a great deal better than in the past. The end of theological realism will at last make possible a Christian ethics which is more than mere obedience, an ethic of productive, world-changing and value-realising Christian action.

We can thus become creative, for the first time in Christian history. In the old scheme of things God did all the creating. God stood on the far side of the world, everything was ready-made for us, and nothing much could be altered. Human beings were not in fact spoken of as creative before the eighteenth-century. Today, by contrast, human creativity confronts the flux. God has moved round to our side, and looks through our eyes. Christian action is now at last liberated. The believer is like an artist. The material we have to work on is our world and our own lives.

60

The Religious Necessity of Realism

Paul Badham

Don Cupitt is undoubtedly right that ever since the enlightenment there has been a steady ebbing of the Sea of Faith,[1] and that Christian thinkers who are sensitive to the thought of their own day find themselves increasingly forced to abandon or reinterpret the claims of historic Christianity. Compared with their ancestors in the faith, almost all contemporary Christians are to a greater or lesser extent non-realist in their understanding of at least some elements in Christian doctrine. For example, a Christian speaking of the divine inspiration of the Bible will not usually claim that God literally dictated the text to the human scribes. Nor are Christians usually happy to spell out any clear or coherent presentation of how God can be thought of as acting in history, or providentially determining what happens to each one of us. Liberal Christians have felt uneasy at the notion of Christ's death literally bringing at-one-ment with God by changing God's attitude to the human race, and few can be found to defend a full-blooded account of hell or judgment. More controversially, it has been common for radical Christian thinkers to remove any biological content to the concept of the virgin birth, or any objective content to belief in the resurrection of Jesus, his

second coming, or a life after death. In proposing that Christians should take leave of the notion of an objective God, Cupitt is taking the final step on a road along which many Christians have been walking.

Cupitt believes that modern European thought has decisively undermined the historic claims of Christianity. Yet he thinks that some religious values have been an inspiration for good, and that it would be a tragedy if these values were to be lost to humanity simply because the thought-forms which nourished them in the past seem on the verge of perishing forever. Ostensibly therefore Don Cupitt claims that non-realism enables religious values to be preserved, while untenable propositional claims are abandoned.[2]

In one sense therefore Cupitt might be thought to be doing what liberal Protestants claimed to be doing, that is, to liberate the kernel of true faith from the husk of outmoded thought. But there is a difference between pruning over-luxuriant growth, and pulling up all the flowers by the roots. Liberals characteristically affirmed all the old beliefs but suggested they be reinterpreted in the light of modern knowledge. Thus, for example, liberals abandoned belief in a six-day creation in favour of belief in God

"The Religious Necessity of Realism" by Paul Badham, in *Is God Real?*, ed. Joseph Runzo (New York: St Martin's Press, 1993), pp. 183–92.

[1]   Don Cupitt, *The Sea of Faith* (London: BBC, 1984).
[2]   Don Cupitt, *Taking Leave of God* (London: SCM Press, 1980), p. 82.

creating through evolution; a degree-Christology replaced an ontological Christology; and exemplarist theories of the atonement replaced objective ones. But in all cases the heart of the belief system remained in place. This is not the case with non-realism, which proposes that the heart be removed. And though it is essential to Cupitt's case that "religious values" can be preserved, there are major difficulties in giving content to this notion for the values to which theistic religions have given most importance depend on a realist view of God.

At the heart of all theistic faith is the belief that through prayer, worship, religious or mystical experience or vision it is possible to enter into a relationship with God. This belief in a divine encounter is utterly undermined by the claim that such experiences do not have any transcendent source, but arise solely from the subjectivity of the believer. Hence the unknown author of the Epistle to the Hebrews was expressing an important psychological truth about belief when he said that whoever would draw to God must believe both that he exists and that he rewards those who seek him.[3] Throughout the centuries countless deeply religious men and women have been haunted by the fear that their faith might be based on a delusion. This was indeed Muhammad's first response to his sense of a divine call, that it might be nothing more than the product of his own deranged imagination.[4] Four centuries later, shortly after the completion of his elegant Platonic argument for God's existence, St Anselm found himself tortured by the thought that perhaps the all-perfect God of his beautifully constructed thought-system was precisely that, and no more. For Anselm this undercut the whole of his religious life. He found himself unable to sleep, eat, pray or fulfil his duties as prior, such was "the agony and conflict of his thoughts".[5] For if God exists in the mind alone, and not in reality also, he could not be that perfect being who alone could be worthy of human devotion. As we know Anselm ultimately

underwent an overwhelming religious experience which he described thus:

> I have found a fulness of joy that is more than full. It is a joy that fills the whole heart, mind, and soul. Indeed it fills the whole of a man, and yet joy beyond measure remains.[6]

On the basis of this experience St Anselm was led to what might be, for the believer personally, a legitimate conclusion: "This *is* so truly that it is not possible to think of it as not existing."[7] And this fact about what is necessary for the personal faith of the devout believer is not affected by the falsity of St Anselm's subsequent application of this as an argument for others concerning God's necessary existence. The most that can be legitimately claimed is that belief in God's reality is a necessary condition for believing that one has entered into a living relationship with him.

What is significant is that both Muhammad and Anselm took for granted that if their religious experience *had been* auto-induced, and not inspired by a transcendent source, it would thereby have been falsified. Hitherto this has been the all but unanimous view of all Jews, Christians and Muslims, as well as of scholars opposed to these traditions. This is why over the past two centuries, psychological or sociological theories, such as those of Feuerbach, Marx or Freud, which have offered alternative explanations for religious feelings have been felt to provide the most damaging critiques of religion. I suggest that they remain so, for if one starts from within the Judaeo-Christian tradition it is clear that the supreme religious value, as summarised by the Torah, and as endorsed by Jesus, is that God be loved with the whole heart, soul (mind) and strength.[8] And God cannot be truly loved if we believe him to be only a non-real concept of our own choosing. Moreover, if we explore what loving God means by reference to the Psalms of the Old Testament or the Epistles of the New, it is clear that the love of God has two components:

[3] Hebrews 11:6.
[4] W. Montgomery Watt, *Muhammad* (Oxford: Oxford University Press, 1961), pp. 21–2.
[5] R. W. Church, *St Anselm* (London: Macmillan, 1899), p. 85.
[6] St Anselm, *Prayers and Meditations* (Harmondsworth: Penguin Classics, 1973), p. 265.
[7] Ibid., p. 245.
[8] Deuteronomy 6:4; Mark 12:30.

personal emotional commitment and devotion, and the thought that such devotion will naturally lead to a wish to keep God's commandments.[9] Comparable claims can be made for Islam and Sikhism, where what is of supreme religious value is the attitude of adoring submission to God and of obedience to his holy will. In all these theistic traditions, as well as in Bhakti Hinduism, loving devotion to, or humble adoration of, God as a transcendent reality is seen as the supreme religious value. And hence any account of "religious values" which ignores these dimensions ignores aspects which seem to be at the heart of the religious quest of most of the human race.

From the perspective of the one who prays, religious experience cannot be classified as non-real. When prayer is experienced in terms of encounter, or personal relationship, or of communion, it cannot, without contradiction, be thought by the believer to be subjective. Only a realist understanding of theism can allow for the genuine possibility of this type of religious experiencing, and if this is thought to be of value then a non-realist understanding of theology cannot be religiously satisfying.

Don Cupitt recognises this. Consequently although he wishes "formal" modes of worship to continue, he denies that the ecstatic, personal or mystical forms of worship have any authentic place in Christianity. He believes that mystical experience is "pagan rather than Christian", and derives from "thwarted eroticism". In fact this kind of religion "just is sublimated and purified eroticism".[10] Cupitt believes that "modern anthropomorphic theism with its demand for a *felt* relation to a personal God has become a different religion from the more austere faith of the ancient and medieval periods".[11] He thinks that modern piety with its idea of "an intimate one-to-one rapport with a vividly experienced guiding and loving fatherly presence" is very different from ancient and medieval prayer, which "was relatively formal, distant and highly ritualised."[12] Hence Cupitt thinks that the idea of a felt relationship to God, so far from being the essence of faith, is simply a heterodox and modern[13] distortion of it, which has gained power in contemporary Christianity for reasons which Freudian psychology can help us to understand.[14] "Faith in a personal God" is for Cupitt a "state of erotic fixation or enslavement" from which we need deliverance.[15]

At this point the issue hinges on what one believes is important in the Christian religion. If one accepts a basically Freudian explanation of theistic religious experience, and if one also accepts Cupitt's historical judgment that belief in a relationship with a personal God represents a modern deviation from authentic Christian spirituality, then the fact that this kind of piety would not be available to a person who accepted non-realism is of no significance. On the other hand, if one thinks that not all mystical experience can be categorised as "sublimated eroticism", and that many mature and happily married Christians have a strong sense of communion with God, and if one thinks that from the psalmists onwards a personal relationship with God has been part and parcel of the Judaeo-Christian tradition, then one would come to a very different conclusion. My own reading of the historical data is that the prophets and psalmists in ancient Israel had a very profound sense of closeness to God, and that this understanding was greatly developed in New Testament Christianity. Within the historic tradition I would see the Confessions of St Augustine, the writings of the Cappadocian Fathers, the prayers of St Anselm, the hymns of St Bernard and the poems of the Medieval Mystics of England as testifying through the ages to the experience of intimate, immediate and close relationship with God as the living heart and fount of Christian spirituality.[16]

---

[9]   Psalm 119, 41–8, 1 John 5:3.
[10] Don Cupitt, *Life Lines* (London: SCM Press, 1986), p. 49.
[11] Ibid., p. 55.
[12] Ibid., p. 56.
[13] Ibid.
[14] Ibid., p. 110.
[15] Ibid., p. 109.
[16] John Burnaby, *Amor Dei* (London: Hodder, 1938).

Hence I would argue that theological realism is a religious necessity.

Turning from personal and mystical prayer to the liturgical worship of which Don Cupitt approves, I fail to see why he feels that participation in such worship is sensible for a person with a non-realist faith. He makes a reasoned case for believing that worship could be justified for both an atheist and non-realist Christian for the effect it could have on the inwardness of the worshipper, and he believes that since "the aim of worship is to declare one's complete and *disinterested* commitment to religious values,"[17] there is no need to postulate the existence of a divine being to validate such worship. His discussion is in many ways reminiscent of Kant's justification for worship in his *Religion within the Limits of Reason Alone*. Kant believed that godliness should "merely serve as a means of strengthening that which in itself goes to make a better man, to wit, the virtuous disposition" and consequently the only authentic purpose of prayer or worship is to establish goodness *in ourselves*, and to spread abroad such goodness within the ethical community.[18] However, Kant recognised that this was all completely theoretical since that worship actually on offer in the Christian Churches was not appropriate for the purposes he had in mind, and indeed unhelpful to it. Hence he never actually attended public worship, and even made a point of leaving university processions at the church door.[19]

The point is that worship in all the Christian Churches is thoroughly realist, and increasingly under the influence of the ecumenical and liturgical movements is becoming more and more uniform focusing on the Eucharist, and therein rehearsing a constant succession of propositional claims about God and his saving activity in the life and work of Christ. Liberal Christians often find their worshipping marred by the pre-critical way these claims are presented, but by a process of internal reinterpretation they are enabled to continue in their participation. For liberals characteristically believe themselves not to be abandoning, but to be reappropriating, essential truths contained in outmoded forms. It is much harder to see why a non-realist should worship, because for the non-realist there is no inner core of truth to be discovered.

Don Cupitt has sought to meet this objection by pointing out that much of Christian worship consists of Old Testament material which reflects a religion, society and culture utterly removed from the thought-world of the contemporary Christian.[20] If for two thousand years Christians have used in their worship the hymn book of the second Jewish Temple without endorsing the belief system assumed by it, why cannot the contemporary non-realist celebrate a Christian Eucharist with just as much ease? But this analogy will not do. Christians have not used the Old Testament in its own right. In pre-critical days a tradition of reinterpretation led the Old Testament to be read through Christian spectacles, and reinterpreted to illustrate Christian themes. Since the rise of criticism the Old Testament has been less and less used and, at least in the main Sunday worship, only such carefully selected extracts as accord with Christian ideals continue to be read. In particular the Psalms have been used, not as alien literature, but because they articulate what Christians wish to say. Hence I reject the analogy and suggest that only for a realist faith does Christian worship remain a sensible activity.

It should be noted that the arguments I have hitherto used in associating worship with realism apply even more strongly in other religious contexts. Since celibacy is regarded as sinful in Zoroastrianism, and is not valued in Islam, Freudian interpretations of their worship are much less plausible. In the case of Islamic worship the prayer is wholly centred on the adoration and praise of God and would become a nonsensical activity if God were thought to be unreal. The same also applies to Sikhism and to Hindu worship in the Bhakti tradition.

It might be thought that I have laid too much weight on religious "feeling". But I have done so

---

[17]   Cupitt, *Taking Leave of God*, op. cit., p. 69.

[18]   Immanuel Kant, *Religion within the Limits of Reason Alone* (New York: Harper & Row, Harper Torchbooks, 1960), pp. 171 and 181.

[19]   Ibid., p. xxix.

[20]   Cupitt, *Taking Leave of God*, op. cit., pp. 134–5.

because the possibility of a personal relationship with God is of crucial importance to a realist account of faith today. The strength of the non-realist case is that many professed theists have an entirely secular world-view in that their expectations of life are not affected by their belief in God. For most Christians, belief in particular providence perished with the rise of actuarial statistics, the indiscriminate slaughter of the First World War, and the holocaust of European Jewry in the Second. And though some may continue to believe in special divine intervention or answered prayer, the problems of fitting such alleged instances into any coherent theodicy seem insuperable. So what difference does belief in God make? Unless some answer can be given to this question the non-realist case is established.

Only two answers seem possible: first that through the existence of a personal relationship with God human situations can be transformed from within; second that in the light of the quality of the personal relationship with God it may seem for the believer plausible to hope that God will wish to sustain the relationship through death. Are these answers intelligible? First, at least some believers do claim that their consciousness of God's presence has utterly transformed otherwise intolerable situations. Bishop Leonard Wilson of Birmingham, who ordained me, affirmed that he had never been so conscious of God's sustaining and redeeming love than when he was being tortured in Changi prisoner-of-war camp. In external terms God did precisely nothing. No particular providence rescued him from his torturers, and yet his sense of the presence of God suffering with him in his distress, not merely transformed the situation for him then, but subsequently sustained him in his faith for the rest of his life. This is no isolated case, but is typical of the record of countless Christian martyrs and sufferers through the ages. Now of course there are problems with such claims. No doubt a psychological theory of compensatory projection can be constructed, and cases can be raised, as in the instance of Jesus's cry of dereliction from the cross, when God seems wholly to abandon the sufferer at precisely the time when he was most

needed. Nevertheless it is significant that belief in divine grace can make a difference to the human experience of events in the world, both in some cases of suffering, and also through conversion experiences. It may be impossible to demonstrate to others that such experiences arise from anything other than the human subconscious. But it is essential for the believer to suppose that they come from a transcendent source. The experience has its transforming power because it is believed to come from a real God.

Belief in a life after death is another case where a difference between realist and non-realist interpretations of faith becomes apparent. For Christians who interpret life after death as a factual claim, their belief stems from their trust in the constancy of God, his power and his love. I believe it can be shown that throughout the history of Christian thought belief in a future life was of supreme importance, that it was understood in a thoroughly realist sense, and that it significantly affected the way Christians looked at life.

Don Cupitt however, believes that "it is spiritually important that one should not believe in life after death but should instead strive to attain the goal of the spiritual life in history."[21] He believes that faith in a future life should be rejected on religious grounds because it conflicts with his understanding of *disinterestedness* as the supreme spiritual value. To love God for the sake of benefits whether in this life or the next would be spiritually corrupting. Hence in prayer we should learn to expect no benefits whether earthly or heavenly, but follow St John of the Cross in the purgative way up the Ascent of Mount Carmel.[22] In this context Cupitt (but not St John of the Cross!) believes that "it is a great help to be a religious person who does not believe in life after death." For realising the finality of our death helps to liberate us from self-concern. Hence on religious grounds we should reject realist claims about a future life, quite apart from the fact that there is "no chance" of them being realised since we are "quite certain to die and be annihilated".[23]

On one point I fully agree with Don Cupitt: virtue is its own reward and ought to be done for

[21]   Ibid., p. 10.
[22]   Ibid., p. 138.
[23]   Ibid., p. 161.

its own sake irrespective of any notion of subsequent reward or punishment in a future life. However, on the substantive issue, I think that a Christian realist must call into question Cupitt's interpretation of *disinterestedness* as an absolute value. The doctrine is not Biblical, but entered Christian thought from Cicero's work, *On Friendship*. Peter Abélard was the first Christian writer to argue that our love for God should be wholly disinterested, and Etienne Gilson has shown that Abélard came to this view, not simply from reading Cicero, but because he felt that the selfless and enduring love of Héloïse for him throughout the calamities of his life represented the highest form of human love.[24] Though I would agree that Héloïse's fidelity was indeed commendable, it would seem better for all concerned when love is able to be mutually fulfilling. And though God should be loved simply because he is love, I do not think Abélard was being necessarily inconsistent when he also looked forward to the joys of heaven in his great hymn "O Quanta Qualia". To love God for the sake of heaven would indeed be akin to using friendship as a means of place-seeking. But to find joy in religious experience, and to look forward to the beatific vision is not a distortion, but a fulfilment of what a relationship with God can be. As Austin Farrer put it: "Heaven is not a payment for walking with God; its where the road goes."[25]

It is not surprising that Don Cupitt should highlight those elements in earlier Christian tradition which have spoken of the unknowability of God, of the importance of a disinterested approach to him, and of the Dark Night of the Soul in which prayer seems to go dead. He sees a non-realist account of theology as the natural successor to such teachings. And it is indeed true that many of the greatest thinkers of the Christian past would have been dismayed by the

confident anthromorphism of much contemporary preaching, and the auto-induced religious euphoria of some charismatic developments. Christian apologetic can be too realist, and may present a too easily conceptualised idol in place of the one who transcends all that we can imagine or describe.

Nevertheless the fact remains that though the greatest fathers of the Church were conscious of the ambiguity of human language, and the limitations of human thought, nevertheless, they were in the end theological realists. They believed that in the darkness they had indeed encountered the holy and living God in whom they lived and moved and had their being.[26] Of none was this more true than St John of the Cross. Cupitt encourages his readers and his students to suppose that this great Doctor of the Church arrived at the same concept of the *nihil* as himself.[27] He is able to do this only by consciously deciding to disregard all the Saint's poems. For the poems speak at length of "the sense of God living constantly in the soul, of the warmth of reciprocal love, and of God's goodness in all things" and they clearly emerge from the Saint's "direct and joyful experience of God".[28] Any similarity between the *via negativa* of the mystical tradition and the non-realism of contemporary Christian philosophy is very much a matter of the surface only and does not extend to the depths of historic faith.

What is valued most in the Christian tradition is a sense of the presence of God. This supreme value is contingently dependent on the believer remaining convinced that God exists in reality as well as in our minds. It may be that our whole culture is passing through a Dark Night of the Soul, and that a genuine recovery of faith may be a future possibility. This possibility will be realised if, and only if, Christians can defend the objective reality of the being of God.

[24] Burnaby, op. cit., p. 257.
[25] Austin Farrer, *Saving Belief* (London: Hodder, 1964), p. 140.
[26] Cf. Vladimir Lossky, *The Mystical Theology of the Eastern Church* (London: James Clarke, 1957), Chapter 2.
[27] Cupitt, *Taking Leave of God*, op. cit., p. 139.
[28] Rowan Williams, *The Wound of Knowledge* (London: Darton, Longman & Todd, 1979), p. 175.

61

Postmodernism and Religious Reflection

Merold Westphal

The French philosophers who come most readily to mind when the term "postmodernism" is mentioned are not conspicuously pious. By this I do not mean that they follow the admonition of Jesus to do their praying behind closed doors (Matt, 6:5–6). They are a pretty secular lot and seem to be the spiritual grandchildren of Sartre and Camus, whose atheism they presuppose, often without bothering even to assert it, much less argue for it.

But it does not follow that they are only of negative significance for religious faith, for theology, and for the philosophy of religion. If Sartre's analysis of the Look and of love as the demand to be loved, developed against the background of his account of bad faith and the desire to be God, is one of the great treatises on original sin in the history of theology, it is possible that the writings of Derrida, Foucault, Lyotard, Lacan, Baudrillard, Deleuze, and others will also turn out to have more to contribute to the life of faith and to reflection on it than we might at first suspect. In fact, I shall argue that postmodern philosophical theology can serve the life of faith as theology in general aspires to do when it understands itself as faith seeking understanding (which is not the same as faith seeking security by going beyond itself to absolute knowledge).

This is not to deny the negative thrust of a thinking that sees itself as standing with Nietzsche in the twilight of the idols, has deep roots in Heidegger's destruction of the history of ontology, and in perhaps its most widely influential form goes under the name of deconstruction. What postmodernism rejects about modernity is its dalliance with the quest for absolute clarity (meaning) and certainty (truth) that, since Plato, has often been seen as the very heart of philosophy itself; more specifically, it is the rejection of the two dominant modern strategies for achieving absolute knowledge, Cartesian immediacy and Hegelian totality.

If we understand by immediacy the mutually naked presence of thought and its object to each other, the paradigm will be the Platonic rendezvous of the soul with the forms in which we approach each object "as far as possible, with the unaided intellect ... applying [our] pure and unadulterated thought to the pure and unadulterated object". In this way we "contemplate things by themselves with the soul by itself".[1] Neither inference nor interpretation separates us from immaculate, infallible intuition. Meister Eckhart reaffirms this mystical mission for philosophy when he says it is the intellect that "pulls

"Postmodernism and Religious Reflection" by Merold Westphal, *International Journal for Philosophy of Religion* 38 (1995): 127–37; 140–2. With kind permission from Springer Science and Business Media. Reprinted by permission of Merold Westphal.

[1]   *Phaedo*, 65e–66e.

off the coat from God and perceives him bare, as he is stripped of goodness and being and of all names". When we free ourselves from images "then the soul's naked being finds the naked, form-less being of the divine unity, which is there a being above being ... how noble is that acceptance, when the soul's being can accept nothing else than the naked unity of God!"[2]

This beatific vision (or is it voyeurism?) is pure presence, spatial and temporal. The object is totally here and at no distance that might dim or distort our view of it; and that view occurs in a now that needs no reference to a past to which it is essentially indebted or to a future in which it will be completed. This view, in its many variations, is what Derrida calls the metaphysics of presence.

Since French postmodernism is also post-structuralism, it often speaks the language of signifier and signified. This requires us to be a bit more specific by taking into account Frege's distinction between *Sinn* and *Bedeutung*. If we think of the signified, these "unadulterated objects" or "things by themselves" as the referents of our thoughts, postmodernism is the Nietzschean perspectivism that says "there are no facts, only interpretations".[3] If we think of them as the meanings with whose help we refer, postmodernism is the denial that we have any clear and distinct ideas; it becomes the move from the Russell/Whitehead/(early) Wittgenstein dream of a totally unambiguous, univocal language to the later Wittgenstein's claim that our meanings are always muddy, mediated by usages embedded in language games that express whole forms of life, themselves in constant flux.

As the denial of unmediated presence to either meanings or facts postmodernism is a critique of the metaphysics of presence. Classical foundationalism, as an epistemological strategy, is a paradigm of

this posture. It is not just the simple claim that some beliefs rest upon or are derived from other beliefs, while other, foundational beliefs, do not have this dependence. It is the stronger claim that (at least some of) our foundational beliefs must be and can be a *fundamentum inconcussum*, must and can stand on their own in absolute, self-supporting certainty, whether this be by being self-evident, by being evident to the senses, or by being incorrigible.[4] (Unfortunately, for most of us it is our kids or our colleagues who are incorrigible, not our beliefs.) Each of these three kinds of belief or judgment is held by those who give it a foundational role to be epistemically immediate, standing alone in a clarity and certainty dependent upon no other.

While classical foundationalism has premodern versions and, in the modern period, empiricist as well as rationalist versions, it seems to be Descartes who is most often the target of anti-foundationalist critiques. As such a critique, postmodernism is a vigorous rejection of Cartesian immediacy and all its cousins.

But it is equally opposed to Hegelian totality. Hegel recognizes that Cartesian immediacies regularly turn out to be mediated. Unlike Spinozistic substances, they are not able to exist by themselves or to be conceived through themselves. Meanings and things occur only in contexts, as parts of larger wholes. The only exception to this rule is the whole of wholes (which already for Spinoza had replaced the Holy of Holies). The only true immediacy, then, is the mediated immediacy of the totality, for which there is, indeed, no other.

But just as there is for postmodernism no Alpha in human knowledge, so there is also no Omega. If we are always too late to stand at the pure origin of any thought, which always turns out already to presuppose something prior, we are also always too early to stand at the culmination

[2] Sermon 9, *Quasi stella matutina*, in *Meister Eckhart: Teacher and Preacher*, ed. Bernard McGinn (New York: Paulist Press, 1986), p. 258; and Sermon 83, *Renovamini spiritu*, in *Meister Eckhart: The Essential Sermons, Commentaries, Treatises, and Defense*, trans. Edmund Colledge, O.S.A., and Bernard McGinn (New York: Paulist Press, 1981), p. 206.
[3] For Nietzsche's statement of this position, see *The Will to Power*, trans. Walter Kaufmann and R. J. Hollingdale (New York: Random House, 1968), p. 267. [...]
[4] I take this very helpful account of classical foundationalism from Nick Wolterstorff. See his "Can belief in God be rational if it has no foundations?", in *Faith and Rationality*, ed. Alvin Plantinga and Nicholas Wolterstorff (Notre Dame, IN: University of Notre Dame Press, 1983).

of all the mediations in which our meanings and our truths are embedded and entangled so as to be able to produce the philosophical version of unified field theory or what Hegel calls, simply, The Idea or The System. We always find ourselves, to use a phrase theologians used to like, *zwischen den Zeiten*.

French postmodernism is not anti-Hegelian in the style of Marx, a modernist who accepts the Hegelian totality as a realistic epistemic and social ideal that could be but unfortunately (and therefore not essentially) hasn't yet been realized. It is anti-Hegelian in the style of Kierkegaard and Nietzsche, post-moderns who find it preposterous to think that we could enact any intellectual or social revolution that would generate the realized eschatology assumed by Hegel's theories of cognition and community.

As the denial of Hegelian totality postmodernism is a critique of onto-theo-logy. This is Heidegger's term for a feature of Aristotle's metaphysics that he finds at the heart of a tradition that includes Hegel as a major representative. [. . .] Aristotle says that "all men suppose what is called wisdom to deal with the first causes and principles of things" (981b27). The science of being qua being will therefore seek "the principles and causes of the things that are" (1025b3), and it will do so differently from the special sciences, "because none of these deals generally with being as being. They cut off a part of being and investigate the attributes of this part . . ." (1003a24). Metaphysics is thus, to use Heidegger's phrase, "the question about beings as such *and* as a whole".[5]

What is the relation of this science to theology, "the first science [which, in contrast to natural science and mathematics] deals with things which are both separable and immovable [i.e., unchangeable]"? "We answer that . . . if there is an immovable substance, the science of this must be prior and must be first philosophy, and universal in this way, because it is first. And it will belong to this to consider being qua being – both

what it is and the attributes which belong to it *qua* being" (1026a16, 27ff., my emphasis).

Heidegger comments: "Western metaphysics, however, since its beginning with the Greeks has eminently been both ontology and theology . . . The wholeness of the whole is the unity of all beings that unifies as the generative ground. To those who can read, this means: metaphysics is onto-theo-logy".[6] Metaphysics is ontology because it thinks of the Being of beings "in the ground-giving unity of what is most general, what is indifferently valid everywhere", and it is theology because it also thinks the Being of beings "in the unity of the all that accounts for the ground, that is, of the All-Highest . . . The essential constitution of metaphysics is based on the unity of beings as such in the universal and that which is highest".[7]

To understand how metaphysics is onto-theo-logy it is not sufficient to notice, Heidegger tells us, that "the deity enters into philosophy". We must ask the more specific question, "How does the deity enter into philosophy . . ."? Referring to philosophy's aspiration for autonomy (which, incidentally, might be achieved either through immediacy or totality), he answers that "the deity can come into philosophy only insofar as philosophy, of its own accord and by its own nature, requires and determines that and how the deity enters into it".[8]

If philosophy requires that and determines how the deity becomes its partner (or should we say its servant, since we are dealing with a command and not an invitation?), to what end does it issue this subpoena and what stipulations does it place upon the appearance of the deity? The answer is clear. Because philosophy is ontology, the science of being *qua* being, the question about "beings as such *and* as a whole" and not one of the special sciences that "cut off a part of being and investigate the attributes of this part",[9] it calls upon the deity to play a decisive role in its project of gathering the whole of being into an intelligible totality. God enters philosophy as

---

[5]   "The onto-theo-logical constitution of metaphysics" (1957), in *Identity and Difference*, trans. Joan Stambaugh (New York: Harper & Row, 1969), p. 54; cf. p. 51. Henceforth OTL. [. . .]
[6]   Heidegger, OTL, 54; cf. 59 and 61. [. . .]
[7]   Heidegger, OTL, 58, 61.
[8]   Heidegger, OTL, 55–6.
[9]   See the paragraph above that ends with note 5.

the πρώτη ἀρχή, *causa prima, ultima ratio*, or *causa sui*[10] rather than, say, the cuckolded husband of Hosea or the hen whose chicks refuse to be gathered (Matt. 23:37), because philosophy has a task for the deity to perform in its service. Philosophy can stand at the Alpha and Omega points of Being and Truth only with the help of a deity who is presented as Being Itself and Truth Itself but who turns out to be a means to a human, all too human end, the totalizing project of metaphysics as onto-theo-logy.

Being can render itself accessible to human thought's demand for total intelligibility from start (Alpha) to finish (Omega) only if "Being manifests itself as thought", and according to Heidegger it is the Λόγος tradition in western metaphysics, culminating in Hegel's *Science of Logic*, where this announcement of the identity of thought and being most explicitly occurs.[11] As the denial of the identity of (human) thought and being, postmodernism is a critique of logocentrism. Postmodernism sees logocentrism as the distinctive hubris of western philosophy, whether this occurs as the appeal to an immdiacy prior to language (Husserl) or as the claim to a total mediation after history (Hegel).

These three terms, the metaphysics of presence, onto-theo-logy, and logocentrism are bandied about rather loosely in postmodern contexts, often with less attention to their meaning than to their usefulness as Shibboleths for flaunting one's ideo-political correctness and as clubs for bashing "the tradition". But they can be given reasonably precise meanings, and when they are they turn out to be more or less interchangeable because, while the sense is different in each case, the reference is pretty much the same. They point, in different ways, to the perennial tendency of western philosophy to overvalue its conceptual currency.

Moreover, these three tendencies of the tradition are mutually implicative in a fairly strong sense. Once the logocentric subpoena has been issued, compelling reality to adequate itself to human thought, it is all but inevitable that various forms of the metaphysics of presence will emerge and that, when these fail, the onto-theo-logical ploy will be employed. When

postmodernism is described as the critique of metaphysics, the latter term signifies, rather precisely, the confluence of logocentric aspirations with these intuitionist and holistic strategies.

Postmodernism is convinced of the power of negative thinking; and its critique of metaphysics has negative implications for the philosophy of religion. These constraints are not totally new because postmodernism is not as nearly unique as either its proponents or its critics sometimes suppose. Its vocabulary, its rhetorical style, and even at least some of its arguments (yes, postmodern philosophy offers arguments) may well be distinctive. But very similar challenges to philosophical hubris can be found in the writings of such thinkers as Hume and Kant, Marx and Freud, Peirce and Dewey, Quine and Kuhn, Gadamer and Ricœur, Merleau-Ponty, and Wittgenstein.

This is not to deny, of course, that among these critiques of the claim to absolute knowledge there are important differences. For example, there is the important difference between the hermeneutics of finitude and the hermeneutics of suspicion. The former emphasizes the embeddedness of our concepts and our judgments in the sensible, temporal, linguistic, historico-cultural milieux from which we can never fully extract ourselves by reflection; the latter emphasizes the role of interests and desires, often disreputable enough to require repression and denial, in the work of the mind that would like to call itself "Reason".

Furthermore, Wittgenstein's analysis of finitude differs from Merleau-Ponty's, just as Marx's suspicion differ's from Freud's. So the inclusion of postmodernism in this wider circle of thought should not be construed as the claim that there are no interesting differences among these thinkers, including the postmodernists themselves. For example, Derrida's strongest affinities are with the hermeneutics of finitude, while Foucault's are with the hermeneutics of suspicion.

Pointing to these affinities may seem to take all the steam out of postmodernism. "What's the big deal?" one might ask. "In this post-foundationalist era doesn't everyone concede the

---

10 Heidegger, OTL, 60.
11 Heidegger, OTL, 57–60.

hermeneutical point, the situated character of human thought? Aren't we all fallibilists, now, anyway?" But that may be a little like saying, "Why should we bother to read Peirce, since we already have Kant?" or "What can Dewey add to what Peirce has already said?" If God is in the details, so is the force of the argument, and a thinker need not be utterly unique in order to be illuminating.

In this case, fallibilism may be too weak a concession. It is possible to acknowledge that confirmation is never final while denying other important parts of the critique postmodernism shares with other philosophies. For example, if one abstracts from speech acts (and their psychological and historical conditioning) and from sentences (in a particular language) in order to focus attention on propositions, which are thought to have a kind of timeless, extralinguistic status, one can easily think that at least at the level of meaning, if not of truth, one has transcended the human condition and is able to speak *sub specie aeternitatis*. The critique of the metaphysics of presence is a powerful resistance to this flight from concreteness and the fallacy of misplaced concreteness that inevitably results.

There is a second sense in which fallibilism may be too weak a concession. If we focus exclusively on its question of truth, we ignore important questions, not only about meaning but also about use. We implicitly deny that our motives as well as our meanings are muddy. A philosophy of religion that situates itself immediately in the heavenly world of propositions immunizes itself all but completely thereby from any concern for the uses to which those propositions are put in the earthly world of daily life. In other words, it isolates itself from the awkward questions raised by the hermeneutics of suspicion.

Usually the hermeneutics of suspicion focuses on ways in which Truth is put in the service of the will to power of human groups or individuals. The critique of onto-theo-logy requires us to think in terms of an intellectual will to power. The ontological project of rendering the world fully intelligible to human thought takes on a

theological character when God is assigned the role of making this possible. The use of theological discourse that is put in question here is its explanatory use.

In reply to the critiques of Heidegger and Derrida, Kevin Hart explores the possibility of a postmetaphysical theology, one that would break with "all discourses which presuppose a ground". It would "show that metaphysics obliges us to take God as a ground; it would uncover a sense in which God could be apprehended as a non-ground; and it would show that the conceptions are systematically related".[12]

To give up speaking of God as creator of the world would be unthinkable for any theist. But that is not what Hart's proposal requires. It rather requires us to give up the assumption that when we say "In the beginning God created the heavens and the earth", we have thereby explained the world. If we had an adequate knowledge of who God is and what it means to create, such a statement could count as an explanation; but we could have such knowledge only if we had seen God naked and had been present in eternity when God created the world, i.e., only if we had radically transcended the human condition. The kind of postmodern theology Hart envisages permits us to say that God is the explanation of the world, but it forbids us to count this as an explanation, a satisfaction of the philosophical demand for intelligibility. The explanans is, if anything, more mysterious than the explanandum. God does not enter into philosophy on the latter's terms. Statements about God as creator will have to find employment elsewhere than at Onto-Theo-Logy Inc.

Walter Lowe applies the onto-theological label to "any effort or tendency to think of God and the finite order in univocal terms. That would seem simple enough, until one pauses over 'tendency'. It might well be that a theology which had spoken solemnly and at length about how our language about God is never more than analogical would nevertheless, in practice, *tend* to use the language univocally".[13] It would do so, for example, when it treated its statements about

---

[12]   Kevin Hart, *The Trespass of the Sign: Deconstruction, Theology and Philosophy* (Cambridge: Cambridge University Press, 1989), pp. 75, 104. [. . .]

[13]   Walter Lowe, *Theology and Difference: The Wound of Reason* (Bloomington: Indiana University Press, 1993), p. 79.

God as creator as explanations of the world, as articulations of its intelligibility. From our own experience we understand the teleological causality of the artisan in relation to the artifact (as distinct from the mechanical causality of billiard balls). But we face this dilemma: to treat God as the cosmic artisan is to tend toward univocity, to make God fit our human conceptions, while to acknowledge that we do not know how an artisan can produce something, much less everything but itself, from nothing is to acknowledge that our creation talk does not explain. It points to mystery rather than to intelligibility.

If the postmodern critique of religious discourse challenged its truth, it might be hard to see how it could have positive import for religious reflection. We have just seen, however, that on the question of truth it only requires fallibilism while focusing its attention on questions of meaning and use. The possibility of a constructive use, beyond these constraints, emerges the moment we add the names of Kierkegaard and Nietzsche to our list of kindred spirits. They were omitted from the earlier list because their affinity for postmodernism is sufficiently strong and evident that in the eyes of many they have become proto-po-mos. They have graduated from being the founding fathers of existentialism to being the unfounding fathers of a postmodernism that is nervous about all father imagery.

The mention of their names together can serve as a useful reminder that the sophisticated and many layered postmodern critique of the excesses of the tradition is not essentially secular. Kierkegaard can develop it in the attempt to rescue Jerusalem from Athens just as easily as Nietzsche can employ it in the attempt to bury them both on the grounds that "Christianity is Platonism for 'the people'."[14]

Heidegger is especially clear about this. He insists that "the onto-theological character of metaphysics has become questionable for thinking, not because of any kind of atheism, but from the experience of a thinking which has discerned in onto-theo-logy the still *unthought* unity of the essential nature of metaphysics". As if to prove his point, he proceeds to make an essentially Pascalian claim. With reference to the god of the philosophers, he writes,

> Man can neither pray nor sacrifice to this god. Before the *causa sui*, man can neither fall to his knees in awe nor can he play music and dance before this god.
> The god-less thinking which must abandon the god of philosophy, god as *causa sui*, is thus perhaps closer to the divine God. Here this means only: god-less thinking is more open to Him than onto-theo-logic would like to admit.[15]
> ...a confrontation with Christendom is absolutely not in any way an attack against what is Christian, any more than a critique of theology is necessarily a critique of faith.[16]

Heidegger's point is clear. Logocentrism has demanded that God enter into philosophy as its guarantor or co-signer, a kind of cosmic collateral for its otherwise unsecured borrowings of such cosmic (or are they comic?) titles as Alpha and Omega. Jerusalem has every right and reason to protest this Athenian ploy. What is endangered by postmodernism is not faith, nor even theology, but a certain concordat between Jerusalem and Athens, between the life of faith, including its search for understanding, and a very specific, very ambitious philosophical project that would claim an exclusive copyright on "Logos" as its logo.

We might think here of Job. He subpoenaed Yahweh to appear on his terms, to answer his questions and silence his critics. In this earliest of postmodern narratives, Yahweh surprises us by answering the subpoena rather than seeking to get it quashed, but only to deconstruct both Job's questions and the whole frame of reference they presuppose. The blinding light of the divine presence ("now my eye sees you" – Job 42:5) shatters the metaphysics of presence; it results in an enlightened blindness that differs from Job's previous condition in that he now understands that he does not understand.

[14]   *Beyond Good and Evil*, trans. Walter Kaufman (New York: Random House, 1966), Preface.
[15]   Heidegger, OTL, 55, 72.
[16]   "The word of Nietzsche: 'God is Dead'," in *The Question Concerning Technology and Other Essays*, trans. William Lovitt (New York: Harper & Row, 1977), p. 64.

The religious traditions that preserve this story in their scriptures have a deep affinity with the learned ignorance of Socrates, as Kierkegaard reminds us constantly, and with contemporary attempts, however secular their motivation, to resist the Platonizing *Aufhebung* of Socratic ignorance into speculative gnosticism.

Looked at closely, what postmodern arguments can most accurately be summarized as seeking to show is that we are not God (which is fairly easy) rather than that God is not there (which is considerably harder). If some writers slip back and forth without notice between saying that we are not the Alpha and Omega and saying that there is no Alpha and Omega, they avoid making this an explicit inference, since the *non sequitur* would be too obvious even for those whose enthusiasm for logic has been cooled down by their suspicions of logocentrism.

But wherever postmodern writers slide into this fallacy, however obliquely, they show, without noticing the irony, how deeply Hegelian they remain. As I have put it elsewhere, the Hegelian assumption is that if the perfection of absolute knowing is real we must be its embodiment, while the postmodern assumption, when it is logically careless, is that since we are not the embodiment of such a perfection it must not be real.[17] The common ground between postmodernism in this mode and Hegel is that neither is able to take seriously the possibility of a real difference between the human and the divine. If one is sufficiently unhegelian to entertain this possibility seriously, as Kant and Kierkegaard were, one will have opened the door to religious appropriations of postmodern insights.

[. . .] I must consider and reply to a potentially fatal objection. "You want to say that postmodern negativity can be put to positive uses, that the critique of the (logocentric) gods of the philosophers opens a space for renewed reflection on the (biblical) God of Abraham, Isaac, and Jacob. But postmodernism is utterly fatal to ethics, so it cannot possibly be open to religion. Whatever had

to die so that everything would be permitted has died, whether it be God, or the Subject, or Truth, or the System, or the Transcendental Signified, or all of the above. Now postmodernists feel free to play without rules, to make up the world as they go along. No beliefs or practices are better than any others. Postmodernism is nihilism pure and simple."

Put in the language of Kierkegaard's Judge William, postmodernists "march around existence seven times, blow the trumpet, and then let the whole thing collapse".[18] The charge is that postmodernism is a form of the aesthetic stage so cynical as to be cut off from all contact with the ethical and, a fortiori, with the religious. A standard reply is to call this portrayal a caricature and to insist that only college sophomores, and they only in philosophy classes, maintain that all beliefs and practices are equally acceptable. But what if this portrayal is the kind of caricature that makes for good political cartoons, exaggerated, to be sure, and not to be taken literally, but nevertheless recognizable and with a (rather sharp) point?

I believe it is important to distinguish two types of postmodernism, or perhaps two tendencies within it. The above description is a good caricature of one of these but not of the other. Kierkegaard's distinction between Socratic irony and sophistry is helpful here. Both embody an infinite negativity disruptive of the finite status quo. But "sophistry is the everlasting duel of knowledge with the phenomenon in the service of egotism", while Socratic irony is in the service of the Idea, without becoming the speculative claim to possess the Idea.[19]

Different aspirations can motivate one to become a gadfly, a disturber of the metaphysical peace. Essentially the same "what" is differentiated, in each case, by the "how" with which it keeps company. Kierkegaard puts it this way. "Irony [as infinite negativity] is a healthiness insofar as it rescues the soul from the snares of relativity; it is a sickness insofar as it cannot bear the

---

[17]   "Onto-theo-logical straw: Reflections on presence and absence," in *Postmodernism and Christian Philosophy*, ed. Roman T. Ciapalo (Mishawaka, IN: American Maritain Association, 1997), pp. 258–67.
[18]   Søren Kierkegaard, *Either/Or*, trans. Howard V. and Edna H. Hong (Princeton: Princeton University Press, 1987), II, 161.
[19]   Søren Kierkegaard, *The Concept of Irony*, trans. Howard V. and Edna H. Hong (Princeton: Princeton University Press, 1989), pp. 25, 17, and 131. [. . .]

absolute except in the form of nothing ...".[20] This sickness, whether we call it nihilism or cynicism, is a recognizable tendency in some forms of postmodernism. But other forms exhibit the healthy negativity, and it is important not to identify these as relativism. To seek to rescue a soul or a culture "from the snares of relativity" is to render the relativity of its beliefs and practices as conspicuous as possible and to protest as strongly as possible against the idolatry that takes them to be absolute. But it is not necessarily to claim, much less to show, that such relativities are all there is. The angry/frightened labelling of any exposure of relativity as relativism or, in other words, the conflation of Socrates with the sophists, is a defense mechanism of those too deeply wedded to their own absoluteness to be open to self-examination.

Or to the recognition that those who expose human relativity sometimes point to something beyond. Socrates points to the Idea; Kierkegaard's Climacus claims that reality is a system for God even if not for us;[21] and Derrida says, "Justice in itself, if such a thing exists, outside or beyond law, is not deconstructible. ... Deconstruction is justice".[22] Philosophy as critique is both possible and necessary because the deconstruction of positive laws is the work of a justice that is not a human construction, any more than it is a human possession. If this is the case, the postmodern death of the metaphysically overextended subject may be linked to the rebirth of a metaphysically modest Socratic subject, ignorant by speculative standards, but infinitely responsible. Could this be part of what Jesus meant when he said, "Those who want to save their life will lose it, and those who lose their life for my sake will find it" (Matt. 10:39)? Could Derrida have shown us this without intending to?

Just as the rejection of onto-theo-logy is not necessarily the rejection of God or even of every theology, so the critique of philosophical ethics is not necessarily the denial of moral responsibility. Autonomy can be just as much an idol as intelligibility. We can say of postmodernism what Ricoeur says of psychoanalysis. In relation to religion both are iconoclastic, but it is possible that "this 'destruction' of religion can be the couterpart of a faith purified of all idolatry. ... The question remains open for every man whether the destruction of idols is without remainder ...".[23] [...]

[20] *The Concept of Irony*, p. 77.
[21] *Concluding Unscientific Postscript*, trans. Howard V. and Edna H. Hong (Princeton: Princeton University Press, 1989), I. 118.
[22] Jacques Derrida, "Force of law: The 'Mystical Foundation of Authority'", in *Deconstruction and the Possibility of Justice*, ed. Drucilla Cornell, Michel Rosenfeld, and David Gray Carlson (New York: Routledge, 1992), pp. 14–15. [...]
[23] Paul Ricœur, *Freud and Philosophy: An Essay on Inetrpretation*, trans. Denis Savage (New Haven: Yale University Press, 1970), pp. 230, 235. [...]

62

The Ends of Metaphysics

Robert Kane

I. Introduction

Metaphysics has been under attack in the West since the end of the Enlightenment, when Hume advocated consigning its writings to the flames and Kant insisted that its claims went beyond the bounds of possible experience. It was prophetic that these attacks came toward the end of the Enlightenment period, whose optimistic assessment of the powers of human reason was beginning to be questioned. For we now live in a "post-Enlightenment" age in which metaphysics is again under attack from a variety of new perspectives that go by such names as "postmodernism," "poststructuralism," "deconstruction," and a host of others, which have generated a heated debate about the possible end of metaphysics.

The purpose of this paper is to enter into this debate by asking whether and how the traditional "ends" of metaphysics themselves might be rethought to meet these new challenges. Much of what I say is provisional, as befits such weighty matters, and is meant only to add another voice to the debate. (As St Augustine rightly said, the way of seeking wisdom is a manifestation of humility.) Metaphysics is not without its defenders, but I will argue that

there are neglected and important themes in the current debate about metaphysics that need to be given more attention.

Recent attacks on metaphysics are not the first of the twentieth century, to be sure. Logical positivists, influenced by the early Wittgenstein and the Vienna Circle, dismissed metaphysical claims as meaningless, while followers of Nietzsche and Heidegger announced a fateful end to the metaphysical traditions of the West; and ordinary language philosophers traced metaphysical problems to confusions in the use of language. But the new postmodernist challenges to metaphysics are at once more powerful and more pervasive. Positivist challenges to metaphysics eventually failed because they were based on a faulty and too narrow understanding of language and meaning – a flaw which Wittgenstein himself diagnosed in his later writings. Positivist views about verifiability and meaning were comparatively easy targets for defenders of traditional metaphysics.

By contrast, current postmodernist challenges to metaphysics are heir to all the sophisticated developments of the philosophy of language and logic, theory of meaning, and philosophy of science, since the 1950s. Figures like Lyotard and Rorty[1] have made use of Wittgenstein's later

"The Ends of Metaphysics" by Robert Kane, *International Philosophical Quarterly* 33:4 (December 1993): 413–28. Reprinted by permission of Philosophy Documentation Center, on behalf of *International Philosophical Quarterly*.

[1] Jean-François Lyotard, *The Postmodern Condition* (Minneapolis: Univ. of Minnesota Press, 1984); Richard Rorty, *Philosophy and the Mirror of Nature* (Princeton: Princeton Univ. Press, 1979).

notions of "language games" and "forms of life," of Quine's critique of the analytic – synthetic distinction, and of postempiricist philosophies of science inspired by Kuhn, Lakatos, and others. They have learned from ordinary language philosophy without buying into its limiting assumptions about the powers of language; and they have appropriated the most powerful arguments of Nietzsche, Heidegger, and others against the metaphysical tradition.

The resulting postmodernist critique of metaphysics has been much discussed. What lies behind it is the idea that all knowing and understanding involve interpretation in terms of some conceptual scheme or linguistic framework, some language game or form of life, which is local and particular to the knower or inquirer. The claim is that human inquirers are inevitably embedded in historical traditions and cultural frameworks from which they cannot escape to make the transhistorical, transcultural assertions to which traditional metaphysics aspired. As some put it, there can be no "neutral" or "absolute" perspective, no "God's eye point of view" (to use Hilary Putnam's expression) from which claims can be made about the True, the Real, and the Good that are valid for all persons and from every point of view.

Lyotard expresses this theme by defining postmodernism as the "rejection of all metanarratives," meaning by "metanarrative" any grand theory of God or the Absolute, Eternal Forms, Universal History, or Being in Itself, which is supposed to be true for all times and from all points of view. In a similar vein, Rorty says that we can talk if we wish about what is true or real or good (with small letters), so long as we realize that these terms signify only what is warrantedly assertible from our point of view, within our language game, tradition, or form of life. Interpretation in terms of a point of view, as he puts it, "goes all the way down" to the most elementary facts and "all the way up" to the most general principles. On the one hand, all observation is "theory-laden," as the philosophers of science say. There can be no uninterpreted "given" which is objectively there for all knowers. On the other hand, even the most general principles of logic and meaning are not immune to revision in the light of further experience. Any attempt to show that one point of view is

objectively right and all others wrong would have to appeal to the presuppositions and standards of rationality of one among other points of view and could not therefore claim either certainty or objective truth.

This critique is by now well known. The fact is that, while it is often called postmodernist or poststructuralist, its presuppositions are shared by modern thinkers of many stripes, not only those who would label themselves postmodernists or poststructuralists. The image of human inquirers embedded in historical and cultural traditions, which they cannot transcend in order to attain a neutral or objective point of view, is a pervasive image (perhaps *the* dominant image) of the modern intellectual landscape. My purpose is to ask how the traditional ends of metaphysics fare in the light of it.

II.   Metaphysical Ends

As we know, in the first book ever to be called "Metaphysics," Aristotle referred to its subject matter as *prōtē philosophia*, or first philosophy, and also simply as *sophia*, or wisdom. In fact, the whole of philosophy was said to be the love of this first philosophy, or the love of wisdom. We should read into this, not that metaphysics is the whole of philosophy, but that all of philosophy should be inspired by the love of wisdom or first philosophy, that is, by the love of metaphysics. So it is not surprising that those who claim we have entered a postmetaphysical age, should also call it postphilosophical. If a culture is not inspired by the love of wisdom, i.e., metaphysics, it is either prephilosophical or postphilosophical, but not philosophical.

What, then, is this first philosophy or wisdom of which Aristotle speaks, the love of which should inspire all of philosophy? Like other human enterprises it is defined by its ends or purposes. And the "ends of metaphysics," I suggest, are two in number (here I begin to climb out on a limb). The first is explanation of a basic and general kind which, for lack of a better term, I am going to call "Objective Explanation" or "Explanation of Being qua Being." The second end I call "Objective Worth."

(1) Objective Explanation as an end of metaphysics is the goal of understanding, in

Aristotle's terms, the principles or reasons, the *archai kai aitiai* of things, which will account objectively and comprehensively for what is, and why. Since to explain is to give *reasons* (*aitiai*), this end may also be described as understanding what is *reasonable to believe* about the nature of things and why.

The term "objective" is pivotal to this definition in the light of the modern critique of metaphysics and I mean to make sense of it in due time. Meanwhile, few would deny that some such explanatory goal is part of the metaphysical tradition, though there is plenty of room for debate about its interpretation and attainability. Wisdom seeks answers to the questions "What is?" and "Why?" But more than that, it seeks to know why it is reasonable to believe or accept any answers proffered. In this respect the lover of wisdom – the *philosophos* – is more demanding than the lover of myth – the *philomythos* – though they are kindred spirits, as Aristotle says. Of this first metaphysical end, my theme will be that it must be transformed in the light of modern criticisms, but not given up.

The second metaphysical end is, if anything, more controversial: (2) To seek Objective Worth as an end of metaphysics is to seek to understand what is *objectively valuable and worth striving for*. To parallel the description of the first end, which concerns what is objectively *reasonable to believe* about the nature of things, this end may be described as understanding what is objectively *reasonable to strive for* in the nature of things.

If metaphysics is in fact defined by this second end, then its task is always in part self-referential because *its* objective worth is also in question, and objective worth generally is one of its ends. Are its ends worth striving for? If one should think them unattainable or not worth attaining, then the conversation of mankind might continue, but it will not be philosophical in the traditional sense. I take it that this is what the end-of-metaphysics debate is all about.

Why *two* ends? Do they not really come to the same thing? Do we not attain one in attaining the other? This was certainly the classical

ideal. Objective explanation of the nature of things would tell us what was ultimately worth striving for. One had only to search out the *archai* or explaining principles and in the process would find out what was objectively worthy. We know how this worked for the ancient and medieval philosophers. Aristotle held that among the *archai* are the final causes or ends which tell us for each thing what is worth striving for. For Plato, the unity of the ends is embodied in the dual meaning of the notion of an ideal. "Ideal" may mean "abstract," as in the case of mathematical forms, or it may mean "perfect," as in the case of evaluative forms, like "Justice" or "Beauty." In this duality of ideality lie concealed the two ends of metaphysics. The unity of the ends is also evident in the Platonic notion that the intelligible world is illumined by the Form of the Good. As we might put it, no objective explanation without objective worth: to know what is reasonable to believe about what is, is to know what is reasonable to strive for in the nature of things.

But I speak of two ends rather than one, despite the fact that the two have been thought of as a unity down through much of the Western tradition. And I do so for the following reasons. In the modern age, beginning in the aftermath of the Renaissance, there has been a slow and fitful, but unmistakeable, tendency to pry them apart, to separate objective explanation from objective worth. This is, in fact, one of the major themes of the continuing story of what has come to be called "modernity," a story told in many illuminating ways, most recently by Hans Blumenberg, Jürgen Habermas, and Charles Taylor.[2] Hegel was the first to bring our attention to the sunderings (*Entzweiungen*) that characterize the modern age as it reached its apogee in the Enlightenment – the sunderings of subject and object, individual and community, and so on. To this list, we should add the sundering of the two ends of metaphysics – explanation and worth.

The rise of modern Western science and consequent eclipse of Aristotelian final causes undoubtedly played a role in this development. After the seventeenth century it could seem to

---

[2] Blumenberg, *The Legitimacy of the Modern Age*, trans. R. Wallace (Cambridge, MA: MIT Press, 1983); Habermas, *The Philosophical Discourse of Modernity* (Cambridge: MIT Press, 1987); Taylor, *Sources of the Self* (Cambridge, MA: Harvard Univ. Press, 1989).

many that the task of explaining "what is" might gradually be taken over by the empirical sciences, leaving objective worth to dangle in the wind. Kant is a pivotal figure who both participated in this development and reacted against it. He saw that the classical unity of theoretical explanation and objective worth was shattered, but could not let go of objective worth, bringing it in the back door as a presupposition of practical, but not theoretical, reason. This attempt to have it both ways is one of the characteristics of a modernity that shattered the unity of explanation and worth, yet was unwilling to accept the consequence that objective worth was entirely without rational grounding and was perhaps a matter of arbitrary will. The rescue attempts have been many, beginning with Kant and Hegel, but none has been deemed successful. Nietzsche is thought to be a pivotal figure because he is the prophet of failure.

It should be noted for further reference that this sundering of the ends of metaphysics – objective explanation and objective worth – involves, but does not reduce to, some other well known sunderings of modernity, e.g., those between fact and value and theory and practice. The fact/value division, for instance, is only a part of the problem of the sundering of metaphysical ends. There are many ways to show that the division between fact and value is not as sharp as once thought. The two merge in everyday experience, in ordinary language, in explanations of human action, and so on. As Spinoza pointed out, terms like "joy" and "gladness" not only describe experiences, but evaluate them as prima facie good (just as terms like "sadness" and "loneliness" evaluate experiences as prima facie bad). For it is by having such experiences that we first learn what the terms "good" and "bad" mean.[3] From the very start, then, descriptions of human experience are value-laden and this value-ladenness continues as human purposes and goals become more sophisticated. It is a commonplace to say that science itself, which is supposed merely to describe facts, presupposes explanatory values (accuracy, comprehensiveness, simplicity, etc.) by virtue of its being a purposeful human activity.

But it would be a mistake to suppose that this merging of fact and value in human experience and language overcomes the modern sundering of the metaphysical ends of objective explanation and objective worth. This is one of those too easy triumphs we must beware of. Where fact and value do merge – in experience, in language, in action or practice – the value involved is always relative to experiencers, language users, and agents or societies of agents. It is a good (or bad) *for* the experiencer (who is glad or sad) or for the agent (who seeks to fulfill his or her purposes) or a community of inquirers (who seek accurate and simple explanations). In sum, where fact and value merge in everyday experience and action it is *relative* value that we are given. By contrast, *objective* worth cuts deeper. The traditional search for it was a search for absolute or non-relative value, for what was worthy *in the nature of things*. Overcoming the fact/value distinction by noting that descriptions of human experience and action are often both factual and evaluative does not necessarily mean overcoming the sundering of the metaphysical ends of objective explanation and objective worth.

III. The End of Metaphysics Critique

If the sundering of the ends of metaphysics is a problem of modernity, by contrast postmodernist critics of metaphysics have doubts about *both* metaphysical ends – objective explanation and objective worth. The sunderings of modernity, according to its postmodernist critics, were but symptoms of modernity's inevitable demise. For, the claim that human inquirers are embedded in historical traditions and cultural frameworks from which they cannot escape to a "neutral" or "absolute" perspective eventually threatens the ideal of objective explanation as well as that of objective worth. In such manner, the modernist predicament leads to the postmodernist critique. Can the ends of metaphysics survive both?

In an attempt to respond, let us focus first on objective explanation and come back to objective worth later. The force of the term "objective" in "objective explanation" was usually taken to

[3] I have discussed this Spinozist theme about the value-ladenness of experiential terms at length in "Prima Facie Good: *Freude schöne Götterfunken . . .*," *The Journal of Value Inquiry* 22 (1988), 279–97.

be this: as the subject matter of metaphysics, reality or being was to be understood *as it is in itself*, and not merely as it is known or as it appears to us. This is at least one meaning of that elusive Aristotelian requirement that wisdom seeks to know "being qua being" – though surely not the only meaning. And here the postmodernist critique creates problems. If all understanding is dependent on conceptual scheme or linguistic framework, how can we grasp an objective Reality in the sense of the way things are in themselves, rather than merely as they appear to us? The very ideas of objective Truth, objective Reality, and objective Worth – seemingly required by the traditional metaphysical ends – are apparent casualties of the critique. The rejected absolute perspective, or God's eye point of view, is just the perspective from which such reality or worth would be described.

These charges have become so familiar that it is hard to think clearly about them. What needs to be said first in response is something that a number of recent philosophers have been saying: that the central theme of the postmodernist critique – the scheme dependence of all understanding – does not of itself imply that we relinquish notions of objective truth and reality. Donald Davidson puts this point nicely when he says, "In giving up dependence on the concept of uninterpreted reality, something outside all schemes and science, we do not relinquish the notion of objective truth."[4] Why not? The answer to be given here is not exactly Davidson's, though there are some overlapping themes. It does owe something to other recent thinkers, e.g., to Elliott Sober, Hilary Putnam, and, especially, John Post.[5]

When it is said that "if all understanding is scheme dependent, we cannot grasp an objective Reality in the sense of the way things are in themselves," trouble is already brewing with the expression "the way things are in themselves." It assumes that there is such a thing as *the* way things

are, when it is likely that there are different ways things are, described in different vocabularies for different purposes. Think of the history of a city over a twenty-four hour period as told by a society columnist, an economist, a weatherman, a political reporter, a social historian, etc. Or think of the cube described by astronomer Philip Morrison: the chemist tells us it is made up of very thin alternating strips of several different metals and gives us a full physical analysis of it; but he fails to say that it tells the story of Huckleberry Finn (the thin layers of metal form a code), for chemistry lacks the vocabulary to do that. Or think of reciting the history of chess to someone who understands English but has never heard of chess.

The point is that "the *ways* the world is" may be accessible to us only with the proper language games. This much supports the postmodernist and poststructuralist critics. But does it rule out objective explanation? Not necessarily. For the way the world is may simply be all the different ways the world is, described in the different vocabularies. The history of the city may be the *summation* of what the weatherman, the economist, the social historian, and others correctly say. To describe fully the way the world is would require learning and using many vocabularies. To learn about particle physics these days one has to learn about vector spaces; and to do this is not only to learn a new vocabulary, but a new way of thinking. Yet human beings can learn new ways of thinking and speaking, adding them to the ones they already have. If some of these ways are incommensurable with, or irreducible to, others (if they cannot be wholly translated into, or reduced to, some one level of description), so be it. It is not an entirely new thought we are expressing if we say that such incommensurability or irreducibility of perspectives is compatible with objectivity.[6] But it is an important thought. And one key to seeing how it can be the case is to note that objective truth may be the logical

[4]   "On the Very Idea of a Conceptual Scheme," *Proceedings of the American Philosophical Association* 47 (1973–4), 5–20.
[5]   Sober, "Realism and Independence," *Noûs* 16 (1982), 369–86; Putnam, *The Many Faces of Realism* (Lasalle, IL: Open Court, 1987); Post, *The Faces of Existence* (Ithaca, NY: Cornell Univ. Press. 1987). I am especially indebted in the next few paragraphs of the paper to Post's groundbreaking work on this subject.
[6]   Post and Putnam (n. 5 above) make this point, as do Richard Bernstein, in *Beyond Objectivism and Relativism* (Philadelphia: Univ. of Pennsylvania Press, 1983), and Ernest Sosa, in "Serious Philosophy and Freedom of Spirit," *The Journal of Philosophy* 84 (1987), 707–26.

sum of truths from different perspectives, not their logical product.

Compare the ancient Buddhist tale of the blind men describing different parts of the elephant. The point of the tale is that each blind man has it wrong if he claims to be describing what the elephant really is. Yet, for all that, the real elephant need not be some unknowable thing-in-itself. It may be what is correctly described (but only partially) by each of the blind men and by others from other perspectives, just as the city may be the sum of what is described by the weatherman, the society columnist, the economist, etc. Each goes wrong only in claiming to have the *whole* truth about it. This is not the notion of the absolute or God's eye view that we are accustomed to, i.e., it is not a "neutral" perspective, but the summation of different non-neutral perspectives. Yet it is a notion we should take seriously.

But there is a catch. To believe that these vocabularies, or any perspectives, are telling us about ways that the city or the world really are, there have to be standards for determining objective truth and falsity from each perspective, standards for assessing evidence or establishing warranted assertibility; and there would have to be ways to be wrong as well as be right by these standards.

This points to a second reason why the central theme of the postmodernist critique – the scheme dependence of all understanding – does not imply that we relinquish notions of objective truth and reality. To say that sentences like "Black holes exist" or "The cube tells the story of Huckleberry Finn" are *objectively* true or false is to say that their truth or falsity is in some sense independent of the properties of potential knowers or inquirers who might assert them. Their truth or falsity depends on the way the world is, or one of the ways the world is, independent of its being known. The problem of understanding objective truth and objective explanation is to spell out this independence from inquirers or potential knowers. And the problem is complicated if the postmodernist critique is correct, for then all inquiry takes place within the context of some language game with its own conventions for determining when propositions are true or false, what constitutes evidence for them, etc. Let us call beings who must go about understanding the world by collecting evidence in this way, and

who are neither omniscient nor infallible, "finite inquirers." Finite inquirers – such as we humans are – are not mere spectators viewing the world from outside, but beings immersed in the world, whose knowing is a kind of practice.

Here we clearly have a dependence on scheme. But does this dependence rule out notions of objective truth and reality? Again, not necessarily. For it is one thing to say that the conventions for determining the truth or falsity, and therefore also the meaning, of sentences are determined by the language games or schemes of such inquirers, and another to say that the truth or falsity itself of the sentences is determined by the language games. To explain the point for contingent truth and falsity (necessary truths would require special treatment), we can follow the lead of John Post and deploy a technical notion of determination which turns out to be the converse of one relation of supervenience: X *determines* Y in the relevant sense just in case, given the way that X is, there is one and only one way that Y can be. In terms of this idea, we can say that sentences are objectively true or false if their truth or falsity is not "determined" in this sense solely by the satisfaction of the conditions of belief and evidence which make them warrantedly assertible, in other words, not determined by our procedures of inquiry. The truth or falsity of "Black holes exist" or "The cube tells the story of Huckleberry Finn" is not determined by these procedures alone but also by something beyond the language game, i.e., the way the world is (in this case, by the way the world is regarding black holes or the structure of the cube, the purpose for which it was made, and so on). This does not mean that our procedures for warranting assertions cannot attain truth. But it does mean that we cannot be *absolutely certain* they do because reality always outstrips our modes of inquiry.

It is worth noting that the certainty being rejected here is an absolute, or Cartesian, certainty – the logical impossibility of being in error. What is certainly known in this absolute sense is such that in no logically possible world in which you had this belief and this evidence would the belief be false (i.e., evidence guarantees truth). To reject such absolute certainty is not necessarily to reject the possibility of knowledge in modest senses which are preferred by many contemporary epistemologists. Knowledge in these modest senses requires only that what you believe is in fact true in the actual world, plus certain further conditions about how your evidence is related to (or "tracks") the truth in similar possible worlds. One might even claim for such modest knowledge a more humble "existential certainty," which does not require that the opposite of what is believed be logically impossible, given the evidence, but only that *as a matter of fact* one is not now deceived and has sufficient evidence to assert it. The key is that any kind of knowledge or certainty that would survive the critique would be de facto, or contingent, not necessary, and would not rule out the logical possibility of error. It would involve giving up the impossible Cartesian dream of absolute certainty, without giving up the possibility of knowing an objective reality.[7]

To sum up, the postmodernist critique does not invalidate notions of objective truth and reality, but does undermine the idea that objective truth about contingent realities can be known with absolute certainty. It is not an argument against the attainability in principle of objective truth and hence objective explanation, but rather an argument for the *radical contingency* of any such attainment. Attainment and absolute certainty of attainment are two different things. This is what the fallibilist aspect of the critique comes to: there is always the possibility of learning that one's scheme is wrong or incomplete in certain ways, that it might be superseded by something better.

IV. Aspiration and Realism

Such a result may lead us to alter our attitude toward the traditional ends of metaphysics, but not to give them up. Let us say that if an end of inquiry is attainable in principle, but its attainment is radically contingent in the sense just described, it can be an object of *aspiration*. Kant said that if we are fully to understand the human condition there are three questions we must answer: "What can we know?" "What should we do?" and "What can we aspire to?" The third question has received comparatively little attention, but I think its centrality for metaphysics needs to be taken seriously. The ends of metaphysics (objective explanation and objective worth), I want to say, are legitimate objects of aspiration, even if they cannot be objects of absolutely certain knowledge. The metaphysical quest is radically contingent, as is the questor.

"Aspiration" is a good word for this idea of a radically contingent seeking. Literally, it means "going out from the spirit," and the "going out" in the case of metaphysics is a going out toward objective reality and objective value. It has something to do with what Kenneth Schmitz has called "noetic discourse," discourse carried on in a condition of "openness to the ontological truth relation" without assuming that one has a completed or certain grasp of the truth. The love of wisdom, we might say, is manifested in this kind of "outflowing" or aspiration toward objective reality and objective worth, but we must keep in mind, as a consequence of what we have just said, that what is sought – objective reality – is always partly revealed and partly concealed, for we lack certain knowledge of it. Relevant also to this kind of aspiration or outflowing of the spirit is Whitehead's well-known statement that "philosophy is the self correction by consciousness of its own initial excess of subjectivity."[8] Such aspiration, unlike absolutely certain knowledge, is consistent with the idea that, for any explanatory scheme we have, we must accept the possibility

---

[7]   I am much indebted to Norris Clarke, S.J. for the thoughts on certitude in this paragraph. He says (in unpublished comments on this paper): "I think all too many Western philosophers have allowed themselves to get trapped into a Cartesian notion of certitude as though it were the only one. i.e.. only that proposition is certain the opposite of which is logically impossible." And to this effect he quotes C. S. Peirce (from "The Fixation of Belief," in *Classic American Philosophers*, ed. M. Fisch [New York: Appleton Century Croft, 1951], p. 143): "It is not necessary to have premises that cannot be doubted; all we need are premises that are free from all actual doubt." The notion of de facto or existential certitude mentioned in the paragraph, and supported by Clarke, is developed in an excellent article published earlier in this journal by Merrill Ring, "Infallibility, Knowledge and the Epistemological Tradition," *International Philosophical Quarterly* 23 (1983), 367–81, which spells out these themes as well as anyone has done.

[8]   *Process and Reality*, trans. D. Griffin and D. Sherburne (New York: Free Press, 1978), p. 22.

that it might be incorrect or incomplete and superseded by a better alternative.

A related point of some importance is that the kind of objective explanation we have been discussing has connections with realism as well as fallibilism. "Realism" is an elusive word with many meanings in the history of philosophy. But one common way of defining it today is to say it is the view that truth is radically non-epistemic, that truth is not determined solely by consciousness, linguistic conventions, conditions of evidence, verifiability, or warranted assertibility, even in the long run. It is determined by the way the world is and this is independent in some sense of our ways of knowing that world. An interesting feature of preceding arguments is the implication that realism in this sense is intimately related to fallibilism – the very fallibilism argued for by the critique of metaphysics. Objective truth is so defined that it is underdetermined by the conditions of belief and evidence of knowing subjects. That such fallibilism entails a realist view is not a new idea. It was presciently seen by C. S. Peirce, who deserves to be called its progenitor. The idea that no scheme can demonstrate of itself or any other that it has the objective truth is tied up with the idea that what accounts for such truth is something – namely, objective reality – that is not just another scheme. Truth transcends texts. That is why it can be aspired to, and even possessed, but not known with certainty. To say this is also to express the great truth that Yeats claimed to have reached at the end of his life, and which he put thus: "man can embody the truth, but he cannot know it."[9]

[. . .]

V. Objective Worth

I turn now to the second metaphysical end – objective worth. Understanding objective worth – what is worth striving for in the nature of things – might be a consequence of objective explanation, as the ancients believed. But then again it might not. Physicists and biologists might learn more and more about how the physical universe began, how it will end, and how it evolves, only to conclude that the whole process seems humanly pointless. This is, in fact, the ultimate nightmare of modernity – the final sundering of objective explanation and objective worth.

One could object that this might be the outcome if we were to consider only the physical sciences. If, however, we were to add the human sciences, hermeneutics, and history to our understanding, it would not be so, for we would get objective worth as well. But, while the problem of objective worth for the physical or natural sciences is an absence of value in the world described by them, the problem of objective worth for the social sciences is just the opposite, *too much value* – too many cultures, forms of life, language games, too many competing systems of value, and no way to tell which is the right one. Thus, for different reasons, natural sciences and social sciences might come up short in telling us what is "objectively worthy" in the nature of things. The physical sciences would give us value neutrality and the social sciences value relativism. Either way, objective worth, or non-relative value, would be lost. The end-of-metaphysics critics, of course, think there is no such thing as objective worth in the non-relative sense, just as they think there is no such thing as objective explanation.

So we must take a closer look at the notion of objective worth, which has more complexity than one might think. The following examples illustrate this notion. Consider, first, a fellow we will call Alan the artist. Alan has been very ill and depressed, so much so that a rich friend concocts a scheme whereby he arranges to have Alan's paintings bought at the local gallery under assumed names for $10,000 apiece. Alan's spirits are thereby lifted because he thinks, mistakenly let us assume, that his paintings have great artistic merit and are being duly recognized. Now imagine two possible worlds, one of which involves Alan in the circumstances just described where he thinks he is a great artist, but is not, and as similar a world as possible in which Alan has as many of the same experiences and thoughts, including thinking he is a great artist, but in which he really *is* a great artist. In both worlds,

9 From a letter from Yeats to Lady Elizabeth Pelham written four weeks before Yeats' death, quoted in John Unterecker. *A Reader's Guide to William Butler Yeats* (New York: Noonday Press, 1959). p. 6.

Alan dies a happy man, knowing the truth in one world but not in the other.[10]

We begin to understand what objective worth is all about when we ask whether it makes any difference *to Alan* which of these worlds he lives in, given that he believes he is a great artist in both and is not less happy in one than in the other. Knowing how his spirits were lifted by his friend's ploy, we expect he would answer the question "Which of the worlds would you rather live in?" by opting for the world in which he is not deceived but really is a great artist. If he does so, Alan endorses a notion of objective worth. Like most of us, he would find it demeaning to be told: "Your painting (or music, or scientific work or whatever) is objectively worthless, but so what? You are having fun doing it, and that is what counts." One of the consequences of such an endorsement is that subjective happiness is not regarded as the final measure of value, since subjectively one is equally happy in both worlds. And this shows in part why objective worth is such a problematic notion for modernity, which, having sundered objective explanation and worth, has left worth wholly on the subjective side.

Now the postmodernist critic will surely respond that there is something odd and problematic about the choice we have given Alan. For Alan to make the judgment that one of these worlds is better, he must view the worlds objectively, from outside both. From inside both worlds, that is, subjectively (which is the only view he really can have, according to these critics), one world will not appear to him to be better than the other since he is equally happy in both. Of course, there is a third possibility: he might find out he is deceived and his self-esteem might consequently be horribly deflated. That would clearly be the worst of the three worlds, even subjectively for Alan. But since this possibility is not realized, the critic might ask why it should matter to Alan if he is deceived and never knows it.

In other words, the postmodernist is questioning the relevance of the objective view, outside

the worlds. What do other possible worlds matter if they are never realized? But I suggest that if one takes metaphysics seriously unrealized worlds do matter, and Alan is right to say that "the undeceived world would be better for me, even if in the other world I would never know I had been deceived." Let it be granted that the third world (in which he is deceived and finds out) is the worst of the three. Still, it is reasonable for Alan to say that the second (undeceived) world is better than the first (in which he is deceived and never finds out). And this is to acknowledge the importance of objective worth.

A second example of how objective worth enters into our thinking involves a traditional metaphysical issue of some importance. Hobbes, Jonathan Edwards, and others held that the so-called conflict between free will and divine predestination is a pseudo-problem. As Hobbes put it, even if God predestined our every move, what difference would that fact make to us? Since in our everyday experience we would not know, and could not know, what it was that God had predestined us to do, we would have to go on deliberating about the best way to act *in exactly the same way* we would have to do if God were not predestining us. There would be no practical difference for us between a world in which our acts were predestined by God and another in which they were not. In recent years writers on free will, like Daniel Dennett, have revived this Hobbesian line of thought without its theological trappings to show that determinism would not make any difference for human freedom.

It is not difficult to see a connection here with Alan the artist. Those who would choose to live in a non-predestined world rather than a predestined one (even if they would never know the latter was predestined), make this choice because they believe the difference in worlds reflects upon their objective worth in the scheme of things. In the predestined world, the ultimate explanation of what they do – the *archē* or *aitia* of their action – lies outside of their own wills in

---

[10]   In this thought experiment one will recognize some connections to Robert Nozick's well-known example of the "experience machine" in *Anarchy, State and Utopia* (New York: Basic Books, 1974). This is not accidental because Nozick's example is another attempt to get at the idea of objective worth. I choose different examples because I want to bring out the complexity of the idea which is not made clear by Nozick's example – e.g., the fact that the idea of objective worth has a number of different dimensions, as well as its connection to various traditional metaphysical issues, to ideas of the self, and to traditional notions of desert, love, etc.

something else, and they are not therefore ultimately responsible for their choices. It is not merely a matter of what they may know in subjective circumstances of decision-making, but a matter of what they *are* in general – the ultimate creators of their own destinies – just as for Alan it is not a matter just of what he subjectively feels in a deceived world, but of what he *is* as an artist. In the tradition that runs from Hobbes to other modern thinkers who believe that living in a determined world would not matter insofar as human freedom is concerned, we see not only a position on a well-known philosophical issue, but a negative modern attitude toward modes of thought that sustain metaphysical thinking about objective worth.

One final example shows yet another important dimension of objective worth. The Polish writer Stanislaw Lem has written a fascinating novel about a planet called "Solaris," covered by an ocean with astonishing powers.[11] Among the things this living ocean can conjure up are what seem to be real figures of its human visitors from the past, in the case of the hero, his long-dead ex-wife. He believes she is resurrected and they renew their love affair, trying to change some of the traits that pushed them apart. But then a fearful thought begins to dawn on him. The wife-image is not a real person conjured up by the ocean, but a simulacrum reconstructed by the ocean out of his own unconscious mind and memories. It is a far more elaborate dream than he himself could conjure, but a dream nonetheless. Now this realization is crushing, as it would be to any of us. Why? Because, among other things, he realizes his ex-wife is not *really* resurrected. Their relationship had not really been renewed at all. And it is not just that this is a sad thing for him, as when Kierkegaard says that one always despairs over the loss of oneself. No, it is not just that. He loved the woman and he wanted her to be *for her sake*. Augustine says somewhere that "to love me is to want me to *be*." I have always thought this was one of the most profound of metaphysical utterances because it connects objective reality and objective worth: to love something, anything, is to want it to be – real.

This example also shows the importance of the inner life for objective worth. If the hero of Solaris were a functionalist or eliminativist about the mind, he might think that the phantom wife was, for all intents and purposes, as good as the real wife if she could do everything the real wife could do. But of course, the phantom wife is not the real wife from the inside. This is what he sadly realizes. What we want to be real when we love in this way are the others in their subjectivity, from their point of view – that they have a phenomenology, an inner life, what Gerard Manley Hopkins wonderfully calls an "inscape." Otherwise it is not the person, but a mere simulacrum. Without a phenomenology of the inner life, objective worth in this dimension – worthiness for love – cannot get a full grip in the real world.

I have explored worth from different directions, showing how it is tied up with questions about what is really the case from various objective perspectives – and thus the manner in which it propels us toward asking questions about what is objectively real. Now the critique of metaphysics says that objective worth, like objective explanation, is not worth striving for because it is unattainable. And it is unattainable because it requires an absolute or neutral perspective from which all true value judgments are correctly made, and this is a perspective which, according to the critique, cannot be attained. In fact, the very idea of it is supposed to be incoherent.

But the answer here must parallel our answer to the critique of objective explanation. Just as there need not be one and only one "way the world is," so there need not be one and only one way to be good or excellent. Bach, for example, is excellent in one way, Einstein in another, Michelangelo in a third. To appreciate these differences requires different modes of understanding, or initiations into what some would call different practices, or traditions, or forms of life. But this is no more an argument against the existence of objective Good than the appeal to scheme dependence of understanding was an argument against objective Truth. For the objective good in one of its dimensions might be the *summation* of all that was excellent in diverse

---

[11] *Solaris* (New York: Berkeley Medallion Books, 1971).

practices or forms of life, just as the objective truth about the city or the cube was the summation of what was truly said about it in the various vocabularies by the chemist, the weatherman, the economist, the social historian, etc.

Nor need these vocabularies be commensurable in each case, as they surely are not for Bach or Einstein or Michelangelo. They may represent incomparably different kinds of value. Nor need the different kinds of value be understandable and appreciable by everyone. It is no argument against the objective truth of "Black holes exist" that some Hottentot somewhere cannot believe it because he cannot even express it in his language (and no argument against the truth of what the weatherman says about New York City if some people cannot understand his jargon). Similarly, it is no argument against Bach's excellence that a tone deaf person hears his music only as noise. A poem by Jack Gilbert relevant to this theme begins, "What if Orpheus should go down into hell . . . and there, surrounded by the closing beasts, and readying his lyre, should find . . . they had no ears."[12] This unfortunate situation would certainly tell against Orpheus' retrieving his fair Eurydice, but it would not tell against the objective excellence of his music.

In sum, objective worth, like objective explanation, does not require that its excellence be universally recognized. Objective worth is rather a kind of desert – it is existence or excellence *deserving* of acknowledgment (in the form of recognition, respect or love) by all, even by those who cannot at present recognize it. (This, of course, is what Alan wanted for his paintings.) The idea is that it *adds to the total sum of good in the universe* even if it can at present be appreciated only by certain persons, or in and through a certain form of life. And this is meant to parallel the claim made earlier that objective truths may add to the sum total accounting of reality, even if they can be understood at present only by certain persons or in and through a certain vocabulary, explanatory scheme, or language game.

The postmodernist critique does not show that objective worth in this sense cannot exist or cannot be attained. What it does show is that we can never be absolutely certain of attainment

because we can never be certain of our place and that of our form of life in the overall scheme of things. Attainment, then, is radically contingent as in the case objective explanation, so that objective worth, like objective explanation, belongs to the realm of aspiration, not absolutely certain knowledge. It is something we can aspire to and even attain, but cannot be certain of. This induces a kind of humility which, as we said earlier, Augustine associated with the love of wisdom.

VI.   Conclusion

Rorty says that the ultimate question regarding the debate about the end of metaphysics is a pragmatic question – whether a postmetaphysical, and hence postphilosophical, culture is something "worth trying for," or "worth *striving* for."[13] This is indeed a pragmatic issue, and since I have argued that metaphysics, through its two ends, is tied to the domain of striving or aspiration, the pragmatic question must have its day. The question *is* how we want to live, or what we want to strive for.

But there seems to me to be an ambivalence in the way in which this question is posed by Rorty and other postmodernists. On the one hand, it seems as if we have a rational choice before us: do we wish to live in a post-metaphysical or a metaphysical culture? On the other hand, it seems as if, for Rorty, there is no choice after all between the two options, for it is suggested that there is only one rational option open to the enlightened person. The choice for a metaphysical culture is really no longer reasonable because its guiding ends (objective explanation and objective worth) have been shown by the critique to be unattainable and incoherent. So it seems that we are not given a pragmatic choice at all, but are being told to prepare ourselves to live in a postmetaphysical culture. If the flood is coming, then learn to live under water.

But if, by contrast, we are faced with a real pragmatic choice between a postmetaphysical and a metaphysical culture, where both are genuine options, the parameters of choice seem clear to

12   *Poems*, Yale Series of Younger Poets (New Haven: Yale Univ. Press, 1962).
13   *Philosophy and the Mirror of Nature.*

me. I have argued that the ends of metaphysics are not unattainable and not incoherent, though we can never be absolutely certain of their attainment. And since I believe they are worth striving for, I have a pretty clear idea of where to go if faced with such a choice. It seems to me that belief in the notions of an objective Truth and Goodness which underlie the metaphysical ends, and the striving to attain them, vivify human efforts and give meaning to life. By contrast, a postmetaphysical culture seems a cold thing to me, suitable only for aesthetes, on Rorty's version, or for power seekers, on the Foucault version.

Interestingly enough, Rorty's and Foucault's versions of a postmetaphysical culture correspond to the two faces of Nietzsche's Overman. Some see in the Overman the face of the creative artist. Others see the power seeker. They may both be right, because these are two kinds of beings that might flourish when metaphysics dies. Unfortunately, in a world of artists and power seekers, the artists will not last for long. There would seem to be no grounding for non-conventional goodness in such a society as over against power, as has often been said of postmodernism. Against this charge, Rorty proposes a "philosophy of solidarity" to fend off barbarism.[14] As I understand this, philosophers of solidarity are huddled masses of intellectuals yearning to be creative. But will cultural solidarity alone keep the power seekers at bay, if no one any longer believes in objective worth? I think not. Yet it is to the credit of the postmodernist critics, and especially Rorty, that they have forced us to face this issue.

Let me conclude with a personal story. I knew a philosopher, a colleague of some distinction in his time, who was a postmetaphysical thinker before Rorty, Lyotard, Derrida, Foucault, and the rest. This philosopher, Outs Bouwsma, was not only an admirer of the later Wittgenstein who was his teacher, but, interestingly enough, also was a devotee of Nietzsche's work. He used to say to me with a characteristic twinkle in his eye: "Citizen Kane" (his usual appellation for me) "when you die they are going to find a sled in your basement called 'Metaphysics.'" Despite his distrust of metaphysics, the interesting difference between Bouwsma and contemporary postmetaphysicians was that his attack upon metaphysics was motivated by a religious streak. He was a religious man who once said with measured irony that what interested him about Nietzsche was "the religious dimension." One got the impression of metaphysics dying to make room for faith – though an ironical faith to be sure. Whereas for contemporary postmetaphysicians, one gets the impression that religion will survive, if at all, only as an art form.

The lesson here is striking: beware of killing off or overcoming metaphysics in the service of religion. For it will not be religious people who will dance at the funeral, but aesthetes and tyrants – and the aesthetes not for long. And if you are prone to respond, as postmodernists surely will, by saying that tyrants and power seekers of the past have been propped up by dogmatic metaphysics and by philosophers of objectivity, who believed they had the certain truth, your point will be well taken. But its lesson should be that metaphysics can no longer be dogmatic or totalitarian in the sense of claiming to have the final or whole truth, not that it should not exist at all. For I think Plato was right to believe that the only lasting safeguard against tyranny is the love of wisdom.

[14] "Solidarity and Objectivity," in *Contingency, Irony and Solidarity* (Cambridge: Cambridge Univ. Press, 1989).

63

Feminism and Analytic
Philosophy of Religion

Sarah Coakley

The relation between analytic philosophy of religion and feminist thought has to date been a strained one. To the extent that most analytic philosophers of religion have attended to feminist theory or feminist theology at all, their acknowledgment has generally gone no further than a belated concession to the use of gender-inclusive language. More substantial issues raised by feminist philosophy or theology have in large part been ignored in the standard literature. Although there have been certain notable exceptions to this "rule," it is undeniable that analytic philosophy of religion remains predominantly "gender blind" in its thinking, and thus, no doubt unsurprisingly, when feminist thinkers have troubled to comment on the discipline, their criticisms have tended to be severe.

The primary purpose of this chapter, then, is to probe the reasons for the mutual incomprehension between the disciplines of analytic philosophy of religion and feminist thought, and to chart – and assess – the feminist criticisms leveled against analytic philosophy of religion for

what is claimed to be its covert "masculinist" bias.[1] Although there is now a burgeoning literature in the genre of "feminist philosophy of religion," most of the woman scholars involved have no truck with analytic philosophy of religion at all, and are primarily engaged with French feminist thought, or American pragmatism, or both. But as the focus of this chapter is the potential interchange between feminist thought and analytic philosophy of religion, I shall concentrate on the two feminist thinkers who have recently devoted book-length accounts to a critique of analytic philosophy of religion: Pamela Sue Anderson (1998) and Grace Jantzen (1998). Some of their criticisms overlap, but they are by no means in agreement about what, if anything, can be salvaged from the project of analytic philosophy of religion as far as future feminist work is concerned. A critical comparison of their views will thus prove instructive in highlighting what the prospects are for a rapprochement between feminist thought and analytic philosophy of religion. As we shall see, much depends here on whether analytic

---

"Feminism and Analytic Philosophy of Religion" by Sarah Coakley in *The Oxford Handbook of Philosophy of Religion*, ed. William J. Wainwright (New York: Oxford University Press, 2005), pp. 494–525. Reprinted by permission of Oxford University Press Inc.

[1] Jantzen (1998) uses the term "masculinist" to denote that which covertly privileges men's position of privilege; I follow her in this usage throughout this chapter. Other cognate terms used by both Jantzen and Anderson (1998) are "sexist," "patriarchal," "phallocentric" (with specifically Lacanian psychoanalytic overtones, discussed intra), and (in Anderson) "male-neutral": a view or philosophical position posing as universal in its validity, but actually assuming male privilege. My own term for the latter is "the generic male."

philosophers of religion are already prejudiced from the outset against post-Kantian continental traditions of philosophy, psycholinguistics, and social theory. A complete refusal to learn from these traditions will certainly also prevent fruitful interaction with feminist thought.

The second, and much shorter, purpose of this chapter is more speculative. It is to suggest some ways in which future philosophy of religion in the analytic tradition might usefully – and indeed, creatively – take up the task of responding to the challenges of such feminist critique *without* altogether abandoning its own most cherished goals. Because such qualities as clarity, logical incisiveness, generalizable philosophical persuasiveness, and a commitment to a realist theory of truth are commonly deemed prime desiderata by analytic philosophers of religion, it will be clear following our discussion below that feminists who are *unreservedly* committed to French psycholinguistic feminist theory are unlikely to be persuaded of a possible accord between the disciplines. For Jantzen, especially, such highly vaunted characteristics of analytic philosophy of religion as clarity and rational persuasiveness are themselves prime manifestations of "phallocentric" thought (of the "male," "symbolic" realm, in Jacques Lacan's terms), and hence intrinsically demeaning to the project of feminist revision. That there is nonetheless a remaining possibility of mutual enrichment between feminist thought and analytic philosophy of religion, on rather different theoretical presumptions, it will be the purpose of the final part of this chapter to suggest. Anderson also suggests some possibility of positive mediation, which we shall duly note; my own suggestions will probe a little further. In short, I show that imprecise judgments on the possible positive interactions between analytic philosophy of religion and feminism are to be avoided: it is the *particular* form of feminist theoretical or theological commitment that is the crucial variable, along with the willingness of analytic philosophy of religion to broaden its consideration about what could "count" as relevant to its task.

Let us now turn, first, to an analysis and comparative critique of the work of Jantzen and Anderson.

[. . .]

Jantzen's Critique of Analytic Philosophy of Religion

A simple account of Jantzen's book is not easy, since she discusses a great deal of diverse literature and her central themes only emerge, cumulatively, throughout the book. Nonetheless, a brief résumé of her core thesis might go as follows. At the outset she claims to be writing her book to "find [her] own [sc. feminist] voice in the philosophy of religion" (Jantzen 1998, 1), and simultaneously to build a "bridge" between analytic and continental traditions in philosophy of religion (4). But the reader rapidly begins to wonder whether the "bridge" metaphor is somewhat disingenuous. Once the key categories of French psycholinguistics have been introduced, it becomes clear that Jantzen sees modern Western thought in general, and analytic philosophy of religion in particular, as hopelessly in thrall to a "masculinist imaginary" – a "symbolic" order (to use the terminology of Lacan) that is obsessed with death and incapable of delivering the liberative vision of God that would allow women to "flourish." This large-scale thesis undergirds Jantzen's whole book and imparts to it a deep pessimism about the cramping restrictions of the existing status quo in Anglo-American philosophy. Right from the start, it is hard to see how Jantzen actually *could* build a "bridge" between her position and that of analytic philosophy of religion, for the latter, according to her, hides under its "cool, guarded, ostensibly neutral" approach a "modern," "Protestant," and "scientific" obsession with "truth" and "belief" that can lead only to "patriarchal necrophilia" (18, 20–3). The only solution to this state of affairs is for women to construct for themselves (with explicit debt to Feuerbach and to the French feminist Luce Irigaray) a new so-called feminine imaginary. This must be a vision of the divine that will sustain women's interests and *release* them from the "masculine symbolic," which, from the moment of their very entry into language, has enslaved them in "masculinist" modes of thinking.

Why exactly is the interest in "truth" in analytic philosophy of religion associated with "masculinism," and especially with death? And why is any language system thought of as intrinsically tainted by such "masculinism"? The answer lies in the theoretical underpinnings provided by French post-Freudian psycholinguistics, especially in Luce Irigaray's feminist adjustment of Lacan's contrast of the so-called symbolic and semiotic realms. As Jantzen explains (1998, ch. 1), Lacan's understanding of the "symbolic" realm explains the child's entry into language (and thence into civilization and culture), and the achievement thereby of a conscious "subjectivity"; in the case of the male child, this is associated, according to Lacan, with a crucial repression of his desire for the mother and a more or less unconscious identification with "phallocentric" goals: order, control, "system," and "truth." The "semiotic" realm, in contrast, is that which disturbingly *interrupts* the "male" or "phallocentric" thought-forms of the "symbolic" and brings a disruptive reminiscence of identification with the maternal. (It is often expressed in poetry, art, or music that defies "order," or it may be theorized in psychoanalytic or cultural theory.)

Once this basic psycholinguistic gender binary between symbolic and semiotic is taken as given, it takes a feminist critique, provided most notably by Irigaray (1985a, 1985b), to point out that "feminine subjectivity" is fatally occluded by the dominance of the "symbolic" in this theory. For as in Freud, so also in Lacan, woman is fundamentally defined as "lack" (of the penis in Freud, of "phallocentric" consciousness in Lacan). And if the *normative* entry into independent personhood is conceived of as "male," and the repression of the maternal presumed to be a necessity of such growth, how could the theory possibly accommodate an adequate account of "feminine" personhood? If a young woman follows the directives of the "symbolic," she can at best achieve a false "equality" with men on their own terms; her own distinctive subjectivity will remain undeveloped and unacknowledged. For Irigaray, Lacan's "Law (or Name) of the Father" is assumed to be so deeply inscribed into Western culture that, despite pervasive secularism, it still summons the authoritative power of a *male* "God." Jantzen adds to this insight her insistence that the "Law of the Father" is also

death-obsessed: "necrophilia" is intrinsically bound in with the "Law of the Father," since it ceaselessly seeks to conquer, master and subdue the "other". The same goes, mutatis mutandis, for the quest for "truth," which, for Jantzen, equally assumes this competitive and destructive attitude. Only a different, "feminine imaginary" can provide a God who does not repress, but sustains, women's "flourishing."

It is Jantzen's claim from early on in her book that analytic philosophy of religion, specifically, is incapable of acknowledging the existence of the "Rule of the Father" to which it is nonetheless enslaved (1998, 24). Even when an analytic philosopher of religion occasionally mentions the significance of the "unconscious" (a rare enough event in itself),[2] there is a "deafening silence," she says, about the relation of this realm to questions of gender and the problem of women's subjectivity. Jantzen applies at this point the pragmatist criterion of what is "helpful" to further women's goals. Women must rejoice in their "natality" rather than becoming absorbed in questions of death, judgment, and afterlife. They must develop what Irigaray has called a "sensible transcendental," that is, a new vision of the divine which does not abstract from the earthly and physical but rejoices in them. Indeed, the ultimate solution for Jantzen is for women to see *themselves* as "becoming divine," a projective and imaginative task that she links (at the end of her book) with process thought and a pantheistic metaphysics (ch. 11).

These are the central themes in Jantzen's work, and together form what we might call the "bookends" of *Becoming Divine* (1998, chs 1 and 11). As Jantzen herself recapitulates the core thesis of the book in chapter 11 (254): "The central contention . . . has been that it is urgently necessary for feminists to work towards a new religious symbolic focused on natality and flourishing rather than death, a symbolic which will lovingly enable natals, women and men, to become subjects, and the earth on which we live to bloom." But the intervening chapters of the book greatly complexify the picture and allow Jantzen to draw on a wide range of continental heroes and

[2]   See Jantzen (1998, 23–4; compare 32–40) [. . .].

heroines from post-Kantian philosophy, social theory, and feminist thought. Interestingly, Jantzen has little time for the work of the pioneering feminist theologians (Rosemary Radford Ruether, Elisabeth Schüssler Fiorenza, Daphne Hampson, for instance), whom she regards as making philosophically naïve appeals to "women's experience" as privatized and generically female, and as failing to acknowledge the "irreducibly diverse" nature of the many variables in women's lives (race, class, sexual orientation, and so on; see Jantzen 1998, ch. 5). Indeed, besides the French feminists Luce Irigaray and Julia Kristeva, and the German American ethicist Hannah Arendt, it is noteworthy that Jantzen's main intellectual heroes are all *male*: Martin Heidegger, Jacques Derrida, Emmanuel Levinas, and Michel Foucault, while the "enemy" is represented repeatedly as analytic philosophy of religion and its major male exponents (Richard Swinburne, Paul Helm, Alvin Plantinga, Brian Davies, Vincent Brümmer, D. Z. Phillips, and John Hick are all singled out for trenchant criticism, despite their own many differences of opinion). Because much of the force of Jantzen's book depends on how one reads *this* further disjunctive binary (between male continental social theory/philosophy and male analytic philosophy of religion), we need to examine it in a little more detail in order to assess the success and consistency of Jantzen's proposal. What we shall find here is that the occasional calls made by Jantzen – in the spirit of Derrida – to overcome *all* disjunctive binaries (Jantzen 1998, 62, chs 3 and 11), are seemingly rendered merely rhetorical by the relentless force of her dismissal of the analytic school. Likewise, the more eirenic moments when Jantzen calls for some kind of "fusion or healing of the rift between semiotic and symbolic" (203) ring rather hollow given the repetitive fury commonly manifested by her against the "symbolic" realm tout court. Let us now scrutinize these paradoxical dimensions of the book a little further, and in so doing relate a number of important subthemes in Jantzen that have bearing on our assessment of the possibility of any future fruitful interaction between feminism and analytic philosophy of religion.

[...]

First, Jantzen's appeal (1998, 205) to Thomas Nagel's (1986) celebrated dictum about the "God's-eye view" being nothing but the "view from nowhere" indicates her strong commitment to dissolving the realism–antirealism binary and replacing it with criteria of "justice" and "trustworthiness" (Jantzen 1998, ch. 9). Likewise (ch. 10), "ontotheology," as critiqued by Heidegger, must be replaced by primary ethical concerns for the "other"; yet Levinas' ethical "first philosophy" also must be adjusted – with the help of Arendt's stress on action and community – to acknowledge how *gendered* "otherness" can easily be forgotten. This pragmatist and ethical "turn" supposedly rebuts the epistemological realism of most analytic philosophy of religion by a quick rejoinder of false consciousness: *any* claim to such privileged access to the "real" must be playing "God" from the platform of the "male symbolic" – "the phallus as universal signifier" (Jantzen 1998, 204). It would appear, then, that "Any claim to objective (let alone universal) truth ... would have to be abandoned in favour of a respectful pluralism" (214). But here Jantzen wavers; she has to acknowledge that not all epistemological "standpoints" are equally valid (else we would have to be "respectful," likewise, to the perspectives "that slavery is acceptable" or "that lesbians should be killed"). Yet Jantzen refuses – and here is an important contrast with Anderson, which we shall explore later – to adopt the well-known feminist "standpoint epistemology" of Nancy Hartsock (1983) and Sandra Harding (1993), and claim a *greater* "objectivity" for the perspectives of the oppressed (Jantzen 1998, 121–7; 215). Because, for Jantzen, *any* claim to "truth" or "objectivity" is tainted by "phallocentrism," it can thus only serve the deathly agonistics of "male" power. This leaves her in a sticky position epistemologically, which she seeks to alleviate by appeal to the intrinsic pragmatic worth of "struggle" (215), the admission of an irreducible plurality of "perspectives," and the need for discernment on the basis of the criteria of "justice" and communal "trustworthiness." Whether Jantzen can ultimately avoid *all* appeals to "truth," metaphysical or otherwise, is a question to which we shall return. But certainly, it is her avowal, in the spirit of Foucault, that such claims invariably hide devious attempts at power-mastery.

Notable, too, is Jantzen's complete disdain for the strategies of apophatic discourse, which one might have expected her to employ as a feminist riposte to "literal" truth claims about the divine from some analytic philosophers. But as she has discussed more extensively in previous work (Jantzen 1995), so here again: she denounces "darkness mysticism" in the tradition of Pseudo-Dionysius as yet another elitist "male" ploy to establish the hegemony of the intellect and to prevent women's voices being heard at the apex of the "ecclesiastical hierarchy" (1998, 174–5).

The remaining cluster of objections to analytic philosophy of religion [. . .] are wielded by Jantzen as other parts of her argument unfold. The penchant among some philosophers of religion (but by no means all) toward "evidentialism" is discussed by Jantzen (1998, ch. 4) as a foil to her thesis that "desire" is repressed in the discourses of analytic philosophy. To seek to "justify" religious beliefs by "evidences," she argues, is ostensibly a quest for objective "rationality" but actually hides a *desire* to project one's own image into the divine: "A deconstructive reading of this . . . discourse . . . reveals that although the insistence on evidence is meant as a denial or repression of desire and projection, these elements are always already operative" *(77)*. Richard Swinburne (1979) and Paul Helm (1994), especially, receive harsh criticism for failing to note the lessons of Nietzsche and Feuerbach on power and projection; Swinburne's and Helm's concern about the weighing of "evidences" ignores their *own* projective desire for divine power and fatally "constructs desire as rationality's other" (Jantzen 1998, 81). Jantzen, in contrast, marshalls the aid of Feuerbach and Irigaray to insist that the "path of desire" is a necessary means to women "becoming divine" and to ousting the "male symbolic" in favor of a new "feminine imaginary." As we have already seen, however, a naïve appeal to (female) "religious experience" is to be avoided here, according to Jantzen, since it can already be part of a false objectification and privatization of religious piety, which merely plays back into the hands of the "male symbolic."

Unsurprisingly, we find Jantzen also launching an attack on analytic philosophy of religion's presumed tendency to a mind–body dualism, and its failure to acknowledge gendered difference, as part of her theory about the discipline's

occlusion of "desire" (1998, 31–4). Once again, as elsewhere in this book, Jantzen does not stop to comment on the great variety of views within analytic philosophy of religion on the mind–body issue and other matters, and her wide sweeps of judgment about the Christian tradition's views of the "self" (from Augustine to Descartes) also do not recount the internal complexity of this history. She admits (31) that "The intensity with which embodiment, gender and the unconscious are wilfully ignored and repressed in much Anglo-American philosophy of religion, and the anxiety such repression bespeaks, would be a significant study in itself," which she cannot here explore in detail. Her discussion (in the same chapter) of the purported identification of the "male" philosophical subject with God in analytic philosophy of religion is equally brief: three very different scholars (Richard Swinburne, Keith Ward, and Vincent Brümmer) are taken to task for an "unproblematic" assumption that "God is . . . a relatively straightforward analogate of a human person" (29). The criticism has a point, especially in the case of Swinburne's earlier work, but, as we shall see, Jantzen will not have recourse to a sliding scale of "analogy" to help either her or those whom she accuses off the hook of the "literal" identification between the human and the divine.

It is in fact somewhat later in Jantzen's book, in connection with her critique of the apophatic, that she launches her attack on "analogical" speech for God (1998, 173–7). Again, one cannot help wondering whether this ploy is in her own best feminist interests; for might one not think that a nuanced account of how God profoundly *differs* from humans – ontologically, and thus also in our mode of linguistic apprehension – would help the deconstruction of "male" idolatry? But in fact, for Jantzen, the appeal to "analogical" speech can only be subject to the same hermeneutic of suspicion that attended her dismissal of "negative theology." Her (frankly, eccentric) reading of "analogy" in Thomas Aquinas and his various modern followers starts with the assertion that "the doctrine of analogy . . . [shows] how the masculinist imaginary . . . [forecloses] the divine horizon by trying to *pin down* the sense and reference of words about God" (175, my emphasis). She goes on to assert, even more oddly, that "philosophers of religion who appeal to analogy" fail to notice Thomas's "debt to Pseudo-Dionysius." Whether or not this is true, it would not help them, according to Jantzen, if they did notice the debt, since she has already claimed to reveal the fatal "masculinism" in Dionysius's own valorization of "men's minds" (177).

Jantzen's final criticisms of analytic philosophers of religion circle back, more explicitly, to the question of necrophilia. In her discussion of "salvation" in philosophy of religion, Jantzen claims that the doctrine is central to Christian, especially Protestant, thought, precisely because it is "embedded in an imaginary of death" (1998, 159). "Patriarchal" interests in "salvific" individual rewards and punishments repress the material and the maternal, she claims, and should be contrasted with a feminist focus on natality. Her attack here on John Hick (1973, 1976) for his well-known interests in "salvation" in the context of world religions seems a little strained granted Hick's own "liberal" reduction of metaphysical belief structures to ethical or pragmatist alternatives, a ploy that Jantzen herself endorses (see 1998, 168–9). More predictable, doubtless, are Jantzen's objections to the way that the problem of evil has classically been handled in analytic philosophy of religion. As we might expect, she finds the emphasis on the "free will defence," and especially the "higher order goods theory," morally repugnant as strategies of theodicy; the "conundrum" of the problem of evil "does not arise," she avers, "unless the attributes of omnipotence, omniscience, and goodness are explicitly accepted as those of the God of the western onto-theological tradition" (260). Only, in other words, if "God" looks suspiciously like the male moral agent of the "symbolic" consciousness will the arguments fall out as they do: "By making [the problem of evil] an intellectual problem to be solved, concentration on the adequacy . . . of the preferred solution can take up all the time and energy that could otherwise be devoted to doing something about the suffering itself" (260).

Once again denouncing such purportedly "masculinist" presumptions, Jantzen feels free to move on at the end of her book to enunciate her own explicitly "pantheistic" projection of the "feminine divine." Although she has drawn heavily on the thought of Feuerbach, Heidegger, Derrida, and Levinas in the course of her book, she finally finds all these – her male "pantheon" of continental heroes – inadequate when it comes to the "Western" masculinist "dread of death" (Jantzen 1998, 129), in which, she claims, even these scholars share. Some help, however, is provided by the French feminist Julia Kristeva, whose analysis of the transgressive potential of the "semiotic" – expressed in poetry, music, childbirth, or Mariology – suggests ways of escaping the dominating power of the "male imaginary" and the "change of Gestalt to an imaginary of natality" (Jantzen 1998, 200). Finally, Jantzen hangs her hope on the possibility of such a redefinition of the divine.

This detailed account of Jantzen's argument has indicated how complex and rich is her network of appeals to continental philosophy and feminist theory, but also how deep is her resistance to the discourses of analytic philosophy of religion. Can that discipline represent anything but a whipping boy for Jantzen? That is the question we must face as we now attempt a brief assessment of her book. In doing this, we shall point forward to those themes that Pamela Sue Anderson will treat rather differently, themes that will have crucial implications for our interest in a possible future rapprochement between analytic philosophy of religion and feminist theory.

Perhaps the most puzzling aspect of Jantzen's book, first, is the ambivalence one detects in her adherence to the Lacanian theory of the male symbolic and to Irigaray's and Kristeva's critical enunciation of the same theme. There are times when Jantzen announces the Rule of the Father as if there were no hope of shifting its influence, at one point (1998, 217) declaring it impossible even for good-hearted feminist women to escape its power and linguistic constraints altogether: "We speak in our fathers' tongue." Because the pessimistic theory of language as intrinsically phallocentric is so general as to fall foul of the Popperian principle of empirical nonfalsifiability, Jantzen rests her whole case on a dangerously fragile fundament. Yet her own blanket dismissal of "empiricism" would presumably disallow any investigation of this matter according to *evidences*. But what if we were to *challenge* the theory of the repressive masculinism of all systems of language? Would we not merely underline or reinscribe the mutual incomprehension of discourses that currently exists between analytic philosophy of religion and French feminist psycholinguistics? But it is precisely that incomprehension that we seek to overcome, and Jantzen, ironically, does little to help us here. Indeed, she herself shows considerable indecision about the extent to which even the tactics of French feminism can indicate a liberating escape route from Lacan's binaries of the regnant symbolic and the marginalized semiotic. At times, as we noted above, she speaks of a hope for a "fusion" – some sort of sublation of the linguistic (and gender) binary that so exercises and afflicts Western culture; when following Kristeva's leads on the creativity of semiotic expression, she will voice a hope that "women can and do become speaking subjects" (Jantzen 1998, 203). At other times, she writes as if the heavy hand of masculinism is a cultural given that is simply immovable.

The same indecision affects Jantzen's attitudes to binaries in general. Following Derrida (Jantzen 1998, ch. 11), she would ostensibly seek to upend and subvert the binaries of symbolic/semiotic, male/female, or death/life. Yet her own argument is curiously ambiguous on this front, at times generalizing incautiously about the male symbolic, while simultaneously insisting on a *deconstruction* of generalizing claims about women; at times accusing the entire Western religious tradition of an obsession with death, while also refusing the possibility that life and death might need to be considered *together* in a religion committed to the doctrines of incarnation and resurrection (life through death). If only natality is acceptable for Jantzen, and death suppressed, has she not precisely recapitulated the binary she is seeking to overcome?

In sum, if the Lacanian view of language is as repressive as Jantzen would have it, and Irigaray's and Kristeva's solutions for adjustment are inadequate, then a more confident, mediating, and robust strategy for cultural escape from the symbolic is needed than Jantzen appears to provide. This, indeed, is the final irony of her poststructuralist commitment: if the symbolic is as pervasive and as powerful as she avers, there is seemingly little hope for feminism except to withdraw into an alternative sectarian world. Jantzen's last chapter on process thought, and the world as "God's body," represents views she came to hold long ago (see Jantzen 1984), before her interest in deconstruction and French feminism developed; it is somewhat hard to see how these older interests cohere with the new theoretical perspective: how exactly does process thought relate to the semiotic, or indeed escape the taint of making realist claims? Jantzen brushes this objection away by claiming that the realism/nonrealism debate is a stale and unproductive one. Yet her new commitment (with Irigaray) to a Feuerbacherian form of "projectionism," in which women themselves "become divine," *disposes* of a transcendent divinity and of realist truth-claims in a way that is unlikely to satisfy many Christian believers spiritually and may cause them to worry about new forms of "feminine" idolatry. Her answer to such critics can only be that they are suffering from the delusions of masculinism – and so the circularity of the argument repeats itself.

Jantzen's further claim that *all* appeals to truth or rationality smack of feminist false consciousness and necrophilic obsession seems self-defeating granted that she herself makes many "truth" claims, en passant, in her book. For instance, as we have already noted, her commitment to pantheistic process thought is definitely recommendatory and "realist" in tone, and her view that women are universally marginalized and repressed is not, surely, expressed as a mere relativistic "perspective." Further, her insistence that there *is no* God's-eye view (even for "God"?) has all the paradoxically of a passionate conviction voiced by one who has ostensibly disclaimed all truths. But even Jantzen admits at one point that the claims of truth cannot be evaded altogether (1998, 127); it is to be doubted whether her substitution of "justice" can altogether escape continuing (if somewhat covert) "truth" claims as well. Similarly, it is hard to see how her ethical commitments to natality and flourishing can ultimately evade the taint of some sort of *belief*; Jantzen's attempt to overcome "intellect" with ethics thus looks suspiciously like another unsublated binary. This is why, finally, her position on feminist "standpoint epistemology," already discussed, also seems open to question: if *all* perspectives are "partial" (126–7), how can one appropriately reckon one more partial than another? Does not the Foucauldian charge of self-interest merely boomerang back on the feminist critic? To this crucial point we shall return in our discussion of Anderson's work, whose position on standpoint epistemology is importantly different from Jantzen's.

Finally, we must mention the awkwardness of the part played by the "enemy" – analytic philosophy of religion – in Jantzen's work. As we mentioned at the outset, Jantzen is ostensibly set on a mediating exercise to bring analytic philosophy of religion to its senses, as it were, and to instruct it in the insights of continental and feminist philosophy. But in fact, for the most part, the discipline does indeed play the part of whipping boy in Jantzen's text, and, being larded with blame, is therefore hardly able to contribute anything to the future way forward in philosophy of religion that Jantzen announces.

One of the effects of this scapegoating ploy is that Jantzen finds it difficult to acknowledge that "analytic philosophy of religion" is by now itself a highly diverse discourse; her "identikit" caricature of the disembodied "man of reason," repressive of feeling, anxiety, and gender consciousness, may well fit *some* authors in the field, but really cannot any longer be applied to all. Indeed, there is an increasing consciousness of post-Kantian continental philosophy in the guild of Anglo-American analytic philosophy of religion, which one would expect Jantzen to applaud. Moreover, her vehemence against Protestant thought, more generally, only occasionally stops to acknowledge that "Reformed epistemology" has of late disavowed itself of many of the features of evidentialism and foundationalism that Jantzen particularly abhors. And as for the varieties of Thomism that are now represented in the field, Jantzen has little to say of them at all. Her own rejection of analogy and apophaticism tends to make her read Thomists, negatively, as covert evidentialists or honorary Protestants, and her irritation at the discipline of philosophy of religion as a whole allows only grudging acknowledgment that Wittgensteinians like D. Z. Phillips, liberals like John Hick, or scholars like William Wainwright, who have investigated the significance of "affectivity" for rational judgment, might occasionally be saying something rather akin to her own pronouncements. In sum, Jantzen's rhetorical strategy of "castigation by lumping" where analytic philosophy of religion is concerned makes her occasional suggestions that the way forward lies in an *expansion* of

rationality, rather than its rejection (1998, 69), look half-hearted and undeveloped. More commonly, one senses that Jantzen wants no more truck with the "male" discipline at all, and may thereby have permanently relegated herself to the semiotic margins of the currently constituted academic discussion.

However, it is precisely at this point of strategic, political decision vis-à-vis the academic status quo that Pamela Sue Anderson's work is of relevance and interest. Sharing, as we shall see, many of the same feminist interests and bibliographical sources as Jantzen, she nonetheless sketches a more hopeful path of possible interchange between the disciplines than Jantzen is able to envisage. To Anderson's alternative proposals we shall now turn, before moving to our own final assessments and positive suggestions.

Anderson's Vision of Feminist Philosophy of Religion

[. . .]

Like Jantzen, Anderson draws deeply, first, on the resources of contemporary continental philosophy, especially on the insights of the post-Lacanian French feminists Luce Irigaray and Julia Kristeva. Likewise, "desire" is also a key category for Anderson, and a theme that she sees largely repressed in current analytic philosophy of religion. Like Jantzen, she traces that repression to a latent mind–body split in the thought of many in the guild, as well as to an unacknowledged epistemological normativity given to the male self (as falsely "male-neutral," in her terms), and to an accompanying modeling of "God" on the same idolatrous male self. Like Jantzen, Anderson is particularly scathing of the discipline's classic investment in *empirical* and probabilistic demonstrations of God's existence – a Lockean endeavor which Anderson takes in any case to be defunct since Kant's first *Critique*, but especially tinged with "masculinist" repression of feminist interests. Why she makes this charge of *empiricism*, in particular, we shall have reason to probe and query later. She is scathing, too, of the metaphysical "realism" that commonly accompanies such an endeavor, since she assumes (again summoning Nagel), that such claims can arise only from blinkered male attempts at epistemological privilege. A moral disgust, similar to Jantzen's, with the way that the problem of evil has been discussed in the discipline again appears in Anderson's book, though here with more attention to distinctive recent contributions by female analytic scholars. The Foucauldian question of whose *interests* are served by the discourses, of analytic philosophy of religion attends Anderson's whole exercise, as it does Jantzen's, and the commitment to reconceive the divine, and along with it the entire enterprise of philosophy of religion, drives the whole project. The goal of this undertaking, finally, again as in Jantzen, is to allow women, and themes stereotypically associated with them (desire, birth, death, excess, the unconscious, any despised or subordinated "other"), to be fully accommodated into the discussion.

[. . .]

Probably the most decisive difference between the two women's projects arises in the area of their fundamental *epistemological* commitments. Early on in her book (1998, 42–7, and ch. 2) Anderson helpfully spells out three broad epistemological options that feminist philosophers have at their disposal. The first, and least radical, is an extension of the empiricist project for feminist ends: on this view, what is needed to liberate women in the sphere of philosophy is simply the *taking into account* of empirical factors (about women, their lives, their concerns, etc.) which have been falsely occluded in traditional "male-neutral" philosophy. Anderson declares herself less than fully satisfied with this first option, on the grounds that it cannot take sufficiently critical account of the all-encompassing epistemological *perspective* of male privilege from which women's issues have classically been marginalized. And she has, in any case, as we have seen, already expressed her reservation about covert sexisms in empiricist approaches. Hence, the second, and somewhat more radical, epistemological option appeals to her more: that of so-called standpoint epistemology. We have already mentioned Jantzen's (rather hasty) dismissal of this approach, above; Anderson spends much more time and trouble (ch. 2), explicating its possibilities. Following Sandra Harding's (1993) important

development of this option, Anderson takes the view that differing epistemological "standpoints" are capable of revealing *perspectives* on truth, and indeed that perspectives from the "margins" (whether from women, or blacks, or other oppressed people) are intrinsically *more* likely to be revelatory of truth than those that are bolstered by the prejudice and delusions of male privilege (Anderson 1998, 73). Thus, as Harding suggests, this approach can ironically claim a *stronger* "objectivity," epistemologically speaking, than standard "male-neutral" theories of knowledge, whose blindnesses ironically "weaken" their presumed objectivity, and whose implicit claim to occupy the God's-eye view actually results in an epistemic *disadvantage*. (This argument, as Harding explains, has its origins in Hegel's master/slave parable and in Marxist interpretation of it.) But what primarily commends the standpoint approach to Anderson is that, like the empiricist option, it does not give up on a shared domain of "truth" seeking alongside the male-neutral. But, unlike the straightforward empiricist alternative, it attends to the specificity of the standpoint of feminism(s), not simply to an additional collection of *facts* to be accounted for. The crucial point is that objectivity and perspective can thereby be seen as *coincident*: purported "perspectivelessness" (the "view from nowhere") is, by contrast, a chimera (78).

Anderson, however, is not entirely confident about the success of Harding's argument for "strong objectivity," chiding her at one point with a slippage into relativism that would undermine that possibility (1998, 77); yet she also seeks, as we shall see, to set her own standpoint epistemology in a more strongly Kantian framework than does Harding, thereby appearing to *weaken* the possibility of an achieved "realism" from any one particular standpoint (even a "marginalized" one). Frankly, these two divergent strands in Anderson's thesis on standpoint do not find a satisfactory resolution in her book. The first causes her to announce that her ultimate epistemological aim is to learn to "think from the lives of *others*" (78, my emphasis) in order to offset the necessary restrictions even of her own, feminist perspective; at this juncture the notion of standpoint seems to start to dissolve in the cause of a more universal perspective. The second strand, however, presses Anderson in the opposite direction, even to the point of admitting that standpoint epistemology must embrace "incoherence," given the apparent incommensurability to be found between widely differing perspectives (86). To this core problem of coherence in Anderson's position we shall return shortly, but what she nonetheless helpfully clarifies, in detailing her remaining commitment to standpoint epistemology, is its important *difference* from the poststructuralist, psycholinguistic epistemology of the French feminists and of Jantzen. For whereas this *third* feminist epistemological option, as we have described at length above, invites one into the magic epistemological circle of those who *see* the repressive power of the male symbolic realm, it appears to provide no clear way of persuading the skeptical male-neutral philosopher that he is suffering from its baleful influence in the first place. But nor, equally worryingly, does it present the post-Lacanian feminist with any obvious mode of epistemological reform for *all*; she is seemingly consigned to the margins, fated to resort to minor, destabilizing semiotic interruptions, or at best, as Jantzen espouses, called to reimagine a feminine divine to which only some, liberated natals will be drawn.

Having opted for standpoint epistemology as the most promising way to revitalize the scope of philosophy of religion, and having retained thereby a specifically feminist commitment to truth and objectivity (duly redefined), Anderson also spells out other reasons why she is unwilling to abandon the modern Western project of "rationality" (which is for Jantzen, of course, intrinsically and hopelessly tainted by sexism). For a start, Kant figures largely in Anderson's appreciative feminist reappraisal of certain Enlightenment strands of thought. Not only, as we have already mentioned, does Anderson consider Kant's critique of the traditional arguments for the existence of God to be definitive and successful (thus undermining, she believes, the attempts to revive them in analytic philosophy of religion), but, along with many post-Kantians, she also interprets Kant's epistemology as demonstrating a "*lack of correspondence* between rationality and reality for any individual embodiment of reason" (1998, 11, my emphasis), and she happily embraces this view as an aid to her critique of what see dubs the "naïve realism"

endemic to analytic philosophy of religion. In other words, Anderson reads Kant's epistemology as one that first and foremost *distances* the knower from the known, even though it also allows, as she proposes later, a form of "perspectival" realism (76–94). Anderson is equally insistent that some of the classical Enlightenment enunciations of personal and political goals – justice, universal love, liberty, rights – are abandoned at the contemporary feminist's peril; so, although each of these key terms is necessarily subject to feminist rethinking, she conceives of her project as a feminist *renegotiation* of rationality, not as a tolling of its death knell.

That this defense of rationality is held (contra Jantzen's more extreme pessimism about the phallocentric taint of all claims to rationality and truth), is in large part explained by Anderson's different mixture of philosophical and feminist influences. As we now see, it is a form of Kantianism that undergirds her standpoint epistemology (no one has privileged or complete access to reality, but we all have *some* access), and she conjoins that view with an important appeal to W. V. O. Quine's (1953) famous image of the Neurathian ship, on which mariner-epistemologists – now to be joined by their feisty feminist counterparts! – continuously pull up planks and renegotiate the seaworthiness of the epistemological ship as it ploughs on its continuing way through the watery darkness of the unknown. As Anderson puts it, "Once recognized as philosophers, women could seek to rebuild the ship's planks of mistaken belief" (1998, 12). It is with the aid of this adjusted Quinean image that Anderson is willing to enunciate the possibility of a future creative accord between feminist epistemology and analytic philosophy of religion. For if the standpoint approach is promising for the claims to incorporate feminist insights into the human world, why not also apply it to divine states of affairs?

But a final, and crucial, feminist influence on Anderson also impinges on her chosen epistemology, and here we note the distinctiveness of a French feminist voice not discussed by Jantzen. Unlike Irigaray and Kristeva (whom Anderson will also utilize, but rather differently from Jantzen), Michèle Le Doeuff (1989, 1990, 1991) argues convincingly, on rather different grounds, for an *expanded* feminist notion of rationality, rather than for its displacement. Her analysis of what she calls the "Héloise complex" (1991) is particularly telling in this regard. Taking the famous medieval love story of Abelard and Héloise as her paradigm, Le Doeuff suggests that even the few women philosophers of the modern era who have achieved eminence have tended to shelter under the guardianship of their male mentors (Beauvoir's relation to Sartre is a notable instance). As Anderson puts it (1998, 50), citing Le Doeuff, "A woman's admiration for her male mentor, which as a philosopher he genuinely needs, prevents her from seeing the value of her own thinking. This prevents the faithful woman from scrutinizing the rationality of her own beliefs, emotions or feelings, and desires." Once freed from this vicious circle of male narcissism, however, the woman philosopher is intellectually fully equipped to develop her own authentic insights and intuitions. The rationality she took for granted in her mentor she now sees to be narrow and deficient, but the male "philosophical imaginary," she also sees, was all along feeding off the unacknowledged power of her "feminine" contribution – the "other of reason," as Le Doeuff calls it.

However, there is a crucial difference in Le Doeuff's understanding of the philosophical imaginary from the Lacanian parsing of the male symbolic that we have seen in both Irigaray and Jantzen. In Le Doeuff's distinctive usage, as Anderson explains (1998, 25 n. 26), the category of the imaginary is not primarily psychoanalytic, and thus not *intrinsically* male, as in Lacan's usage; rather, it bespeaks the mythological and imagistic subtext that laps at the base of the philosophical discourse and actually sustains the power of its argument (Le Doeuff 1989, 4–20). As such, this material is not inexorably destined to remain as the marginalized feminine/semiotic, but in principle is capable of transformation and conscious integration into an expanded feminist rationality. However, as we shall shortly chart, this task of integration involves the subtle unearthing and recasting of moods of "desire" and "mimesis" latent in the texts of philosophy. As such, an element of psychoanalytic assessment, it would seem, still hangs over the enterprise; we are dealing here with materials more latent in the text than overt (the "often unrecognized use of figures and imagery"; Anderson 1998, 25), and thus pre-

sumably always subject to a response of blanket denial by the male-neutral author. To this issue we must return, when we examine Anderson's revealingly "suspicious" reading of some of the influential texts of analytic philosophy of religion.

By now we have spelled out in some detail the first, and central, *epistemological* divergence of Anderson's views from those of Jantzen. Anderson is a standpoint epistemologist rather than a poststructuralist; thus, we are not surprised that, en passant, she can remark that her views clearly diverge "from the extremes of postmodernism" and that she does not "give up completely the modern, Enlightenment project of epistemology and its claims concerning the autonomous reason" (1998, 53). In the same breath she forecasts the *second* way her project differs most obviously from Jantzen's; this lies in the fact that she does not "assume that an essential *female desire* exists which should be valued more highly than an essential male reason" (53, my emphasis). In other words, more clearly and consistently than Jantzen, Anderson seeks to find a way of integrating desire and reason. It is to Anderson's particular construal of desire, then, that we now turn, for in it is encapsulated much of what she proposes in the latter part of her book for a renewed, feminist philosophy of religion. Anderson's understanding of the category is different not only in substance from Jantzen's, but also in range of application. While Anderson, too, draws extensively on Irigaray and Kristeva at this point in her book, she not only reads them rather differently from Jantzen, but supplements and adjusts their views by superimposing insights from Le Doeuff's concept of the philosophical imaginary.

The arguments in this second major portion of Anderson's book (1998, chs 3–5) are somewhat diffuse and unfinished, by Anderson's own admission, but perhaps the central theses can be summed up in the following way. First, Anderson utilizes her own reading of Irigaray and Kristeva to argue that "feminist poststructuralism does not *necessarily* privilege desire over reason, irrationality over rationality" (246, my emphasis). Anderson realizes that she is apparently backtracking here on what she has said critically about feminist poststructuralism in her previous chapter on standpoint. But her point now is that we can still learn from the psycholinguistics of the poststructuralist school, without subscribing to its apparently fatal epistemological binary; for "it offers feminist epistemologists the psycholinguistic tools to begin to unearth what has been buried by patriarchal structures of belief and myth" (246). Accordingly, she uses Irigaray's work, first, to illustrate how male "scientific" rationality may draw on the erotic power of female desire while also repressing it out of sight: "In [the male's] quest for God," as Irigaray puts it, "he takes her light to illuminate his path . . . He [has] stolen her gaze" (1993, 209–10; see Anderson 1998, 99). Anderson's use of Kristeva's writing is rather different (and indeed, she is more careful than Jantzen not to elide the views of the two thinkers, or to subsume one in the other). Thus, whereas Anderson reads Irigaray as conjoining the quest for God with repressed *female desire* in the unconscious motivation of the male subject, Kristeva, in contrast, is seen as focusing more on the "repressed maternal" in patriarchal culture, and its link back to the divine through the figure of Mary, the "mother of God." And whereas Irigaray hypothesizes the absolute need for a projected "feminine divine" in order for women to claim their full ("feminine") identity, Kristeva looks more subtly to the saving irruptions of the semiotic for the location of divine power. Here, according to Kristeva, the evocations of the "maternal" break through the gaps of male, symbolic discourse and return us to the unspeakable sense of original union with the mother. Anderson thinks we can draw richly on these poststructuralist and psychoanalytic insights to demonstrate that the discourses of analytic philosophy of religion, too, occlude female desire and the maternal in their quest for God; but she does not thereby recommend a straightforward acceptance of Irigaray's or Kristeva's thought as "theology" (Anderson 1998, 117); nor, as we have seen, does she embrace the problematic, dualistic epistemology that accompanies their insights.

Hence, what remains for Anderson to indicate in the final sections of her book (1998, chs 4–5) is that desire and reason are capable of some new alignment, which in turn could transform the shape of philosophy of religion in creative and liberating ways. To demonstrate this possibility, Anderson argues that only "mythology" has the power to be the medium of this realignment, and that "mimesis" (understood by Irigaray as a creative reconfiguration of the hierarchy of gender) must be the means by which that power is enacted to disrupt male-neutral distortions and to bring forth the impassioned "woman of reason" (135–47). We note in this exposition of mythology and mimesis that Anderson's (1993) earlier work on the philosophy of Paul Ricoeur strongly influences her view that radical changes in philosophical thinking cannot be effected without the mediation of these (apparently more subliminal) forms of expression and practice. For it is also Le Doeuff's philosophical imaginary that is at stake here, with all its previously unacknowledged cargo from the male unconscious; the mere taking of thought is insufficient to shift the key of the discourse. For similar reasons, another category that becomes important for Anderson's exposition of the transformation of female desire at this point is bell hooks's (1990) notion of "yearning." Anderson adopts this term as a means of rethinking the notion of female desire as a desire precisely to *transform* rationality through passion. Later she can speak of the "substantive form" of reason as *consisting in* yearning (1998, 213).

A final twist in Anderson's argument at the end of her book links to this attempt to mediate between passion and intellect, and presents a fascinating contrast with Jantzen's attack on necrophilia and the patriarchal culture of death. Rather than avoiding the subject of death, or simply identifying it with male obsession, Anderson sees the acknowledgment of death as a sign of embodiment accepted, of "death's intimate connection with yearning for love between fully embodied men and women" (1998, 247). Perhaps this may stand as the final, and most revealing, contrast between Anderson's and Jantzen's construal of the philosophical significance of the French feminists. For Jantzen, the feminine imaginary should flee from death and embrace natality, whereas for Anderson, the presence of death in the philosophic discourse is, at worst, a reminder that embodiment cannot be denied and, at best, a signal of the necessary presence of desire in the discourses of reason.

As we have seen from the start of this exposition of A *Feminist Philosophy of Religion*, Anderson, unlike Jantzen, does not reject analytic philosophy of religion tout court; instead, she seeks to build feminist bridges toward it, and so to transform its thought-forms, goals, and interests. But it must be said that her final proposals for change in the subject, drawing as they do on ancient Greek and Hindu materials (the "myths of dissent" of Antigone and Mirabai), seem hardly likely to catch the (admittedly narrow!) imaginations of the existing guild of analytic philosophy of religion. [...] But before we deliver some judgments on Anderson's project as a whole, and relate those to some further thoughts of our own on the future relation between feminist thought and analytic philosophy of religion, we must return briefly to the specific criticisms levied against the discipline by Anderson at the opening of her book. These turn out to be revealing, precisely in their *difference* of nuance from those of Jantzen. Although, as we mentioned above, they share the presumption that analytic philosophy of religion is predicated on the dominance of a "disembodied" male subject, in whose image its patriarchal God is idolatrously constructed, Anderson has some more specific criticisms that bear scrutiny. Her main ire is reserved for the empiricist basis of many of the justificatory arguments for theism (1998, 13), which she regards as a front for a discriminatory, male-neutral posture of privilege, covertly erasing the concerns and interests of women. But she also charges the discipline of analytic philosophy of religion with a widespread "naïve realism" (37, 68–9), which not only favors "literal" speech about God over other modes of expression, but also makes spurious claims to "unmediated experience" of the divine, purportedly escaping the Kantian epistemological grid. Indeed, Anderson's *chief* criticism of analytic philosophy of religion, it seems, is not one that is intrinsically tied to feminist concerns; rather, it is that there is a vicious circularity at the heart of analytic philosophy of religion's claims to "justify" belief in God at all. Whether through evidentialism (Swinburne, par excellence), through examination of "doxastic practices" (Alston), or through the "proper basicality" of Reformed epistemology (Wolterstorff, Plantinga), all these philosophers, claims Anderson, are really appealing to an "experience" into which their Christian belief has already been smuggled (ch. 1). The resultant "scandal of circular reasoning" simultaneously

occludes what has been pushed to the margins by privileged, white male philosophers: the concerns of women, blacks, the poor, and the non-western world disappear in a miasma of talk of "justification" and "warrant" (58). Further, the whole enterprise is sustained by a barely perceptible philosophical imaginary, which assumes female desire while also repressing it; when women *do* appear in the texts of analytic philosophers of religion, it is often as "passive items for ... men's seduction" (43). Anderson additionally charges that when women philosophers occasionally manage, *per impossibile*, to succeed professionally in this particular guild, they are often notable examples of Le Doeuff's Héloïse complex: strongly devoted to male mentors or protectors, whose intellectual hegemony and institutional privilege they obligingly do not question (50–2).

Anderson's argument seems to be at its strongest when she is *explicitly* charting the presence of a "myth" of female subordination in the texts of analytic philosophy of religion. In her analysis of Richard Swinburne's earlier work, in particular, she is able to give bountiful, even embarrassing, evidence of a philosophical imaginary of male privilege and female subordination, which is shot through many of his illustrative examples. When women do appear in his text (which is rarely), they feature as potentially seductive sirens or as mutely submissive spouses. Only the hardened could dismiss *this* "evidence" as mere psychological projection on the part of the critic; indeed, it is a sign of the partial success of such criticism that Swinburne has in a number of ways modified his position and mode of expression in recent revisions of his work. But Anderson's more sweeping criticisms of analytic philosophy of religion for its *empiricist* bias (especially its appeals to "religious experience"), its purportedly *naïve realism*, and its *epistemic circularity* seem more problematic, and do not accord well with the position she herself takes up later in the book on standpoint theory. This matter needs some spelling out, but it will lead on naturally to the final, constructive, section of this chapter. Let us then turn a critical eye on Anderson's standpoint theory, which, as I hope to have demonstrated, is the epistemological lynchpin in her whole feminist project and that which most clearly distinguishes her project from that of Jantzen.

There are three main areas of difficulty in the standpoint position of Anderson in *A Feminist Philosophy of Religion*, as I see it. The first relates to her use of Kant's work in support of her view that "perspective" knowledge can achieve "strong objectivity" and hence preserve a commitment to realism. As we have seen, Anderson also believes that Kant shows us that the knower is irretrievably *distanced* from the object of knowledge, and that there is no available God's-eye view from which this distancing could be overcome. Quite apart from the question of whether this is a proper reading of Kant's intentions in the first *Critique* (which is at the very least a moot point), Anderson's dogmatism on this matter of epistemic distancing leaves her in a paradoxical position as far as her equally strong commitment to realism is concerned. If we are *all* distanced, impenetrably, from that which we seek to "know," how can we *also* know that our "perspectives" all participate in some way in that reality? And why would we seek to enter empathetically into the perspective of another (especially a male-neutral other) unless we did know this? Despite Anderson's stated endeavor to cut through the binary between God-like epistemic "privilege" and epistemological relativism, there are times, as we have seen, when she aligns herself, confusingly, with first one and then the other. She wavers, in fact, on whether true epistemological relativism is implied by the perspectivalism she is proposing; this leaves her position in the book puzzlingly inconsistent. Her more recent work on feminist standpoint theory clears up some of the confusion, but in a more consistently realist way: now we are abjured to enter imaginatively into others' standpoints in order to achieve everwidening perspectives on the truth, and "less biased knowledge" (2001, 131). (The perspective of the margins is no longer granted compensatory epistemic privilege, as it was, in Marxist mode, in the book.) However, it is hard to see how we can engage in this ongoing empathetic task without reliance on *evidences*, and without a fundamentally *realist* commitment to universal "truth" as at least a teleological ideal. If so, then much of Anderson's initial animus against analytic philosophy of religion's empiricism and realism must surely fall away.

This first and central epistemological puzzle relates directly to another problem on standpoint that is also not successfully tackled in the book. When Anderson first lays out the three epistemological options open to feminism (see discussion above), she does not sufficiently explain how the adoption of a standpoint epistemology would differ qualitatively from an expanded feminist empiricism that simply takes more *facts* into account. Such a line is in fact notoriously hard to draw, as was demonstrated long ago in Donald Davidson's famous article "On the Very Idea of a 'Conceptual Scheme'" (1984): the bounded edges, so to speak, of a standpoint (or conceptual scheme) are often so difficult to delineate that one is caused to query whether it exists at all as an *identifiable* epistemological filter. But if Anderson cannot say what a feminist standpoint (as opposed to a set of long-neglected facts about women's issues) finally *is*, then she is in a worryingly weakened position philosophically. Her whole project of the distinctiveness of feminist insight is at stake. She would seemingly do better to withdraw to her first feminist epistemological option (feminist empiricism), which would still be fully compatible with the Quinean form of epistemological revisability suggested by the image of the Neurathian ship. However, Anderson's more recent work has clarified the notion of standpoint and thus blocked the reduction to a mere feminist empiricism. Here, Anderson not only helpfully distinguishes a confusing range of possible meanings of standpoint in previous feminist standpoint epistemology (2001, 137–8), but herself now opts for an idea of standpoint as ethical *achievement* rather than as epistemological filter. This signals a considerable shift; no longer is there the hovering suggestion that women possess, qua marginalized, a distinctive epistemological apparatus (a view that tends towards gender essentialism), but rather, "*A standpoint signifies a particular point of view, or . . . epistemically informed perspective, that is achieved – but not without struggle – as a result of gaining awareness of particular positionings within relations of power*" (145). Anderson notes that this definition no longer suggests that "a standpoint necessarily claims any epistemic privilege" (145) – a significant new admission. But it does allow men to share such a standpoint with women, given goodwill and commitment. Presumably, then, the difference from mere feminist empiricism in this new view resides in the *ethical*

dimensions of attempting to take empathetic account of others' perspectives; as such, one might
dub it a "virtue ethics" more than a strictly feminist one. But therein lies the puzzling surd: has
this shift of Anderson's actually taken the teeth
out of an epistemological project that originally
claimed *special* insight from the feminist camp?
The original goal was to release female desire into
an explicit acknowledgment in the discourses of
philosophy of religion; whereas Anderson's more
recent project seems to flatten or sideline gender
difference and aim instead for a greater self-
"reflexivity" and recognition of "partiality" in all
our epistemic negotiations (146–7).

The third critical issue that arises with
Anderson's standpoint epistemology is a pragmatic
one of how to *convert* the luminaries of analytic
philosophy of religion to a perspective cognizant
of female desire. If this is now more a matter of
ethical commitment than the embracing of a
mysterious feminist *blik*, then the burden rests on
Anderson to convince her readership, first, that
the writings of analytic philosophy of religion
have indeed been the products of repressed
female desire, and second, that there is a creative,
indeed *virtuous*, way forward in terms of a re-
negotiated standpoint. My hesitations about the
success of Anderson's existing strategies in this
third area have already been voiced: not only is
it lamentably easy for the analytic philosopher of
religion to express blanket denial of collusion in
sexism (perhaps especially once his pronouns
have been tidied up!), but the loose sort of
appeal that Anderson makes to myth and mimesis in the area of desire is arguably too far
removed from the existing discourses of analytic
philosophy of religion to attract attention,
regrettable as this may be.

What, then, are the alternatives? After this
exacting analysis and critique of Jantzen's
and Anderson's projects, it is time to sketch
some of my own proposals in closing. At the
same time I shall gather up a number of the
loose ends and questions that I have left along
the way.

Feminism and Analytic Philosophy of Religion: Prospects for Rapprochement?

To ask whether there are prospects of rapprochement between analytic philosophy of religion
and feminist theory and philosophy is of course
in one sense to beg the whole question with
which this chapter has been concerned. The
more one's commitments in feminist theory veer
toward the post-Lacanian end of the spectrum (in
which male phallocentrism is deemed a deep
and irremovable feature of Western intellectual
life), the less will one be inclined to seek out opportunities for such rapprochement or expect the
prospects to be fruitful for women – whether
spiritually or professionally. Because my critique
of the epistemological sectarianism of this particular school of feminist theory will by now
be evident, however, what is offered in this last
section is a discernibly different feminist strategy.
It relies neither on the apparently immovable
gender binaries of French psycholinguistic feminist theory (for, contra Jantzen, I urge a more *fluid*
understanding of the negotiations of gender),[3] nor
does it appeal to the brand of feminist standpoint
epistemology that presumes an inexorable *distancing* of the knower from the known (for,
contra Anderson, feminist epistemology may
arguably afford claims to intensified *intimacy*
with the known, rather than the opposite).
However, *with* Jantzen and Anderson, I take it as
read that feminist critiques of analytic philosophy
of religion have, at the very least, established
the existence of a suspicious gender "subtext"
in much writing in the discipline: the making
of "God" in the image of the autonomous,
Enlightenment "generic male," and, as I have
argued elsewhere,[4] the positing of an unconditioned "incompatibilistic" view of freedom as
a supposedly necessary adjunct to the solution
of the problem of evil are just two signs of the
inherent elevation of a certain form of masculinism over the concerns of relationship, closeness, desire, or dependence, which have rightly
exercised feminist theorists and ethicists. Yet it

---

[3]   I develop this argument about gender "fluidity" (a view that owes much to the patristic author Gregory of Nyssa)
in Coakley (2002, ch. 9), and more fully in a forthcoming first volume of "systematics": *God, Sexuality and the
Self: An Essay "On the Trinity."*
[4]   See Coakley (1997, 601–3).

would, I believe, be a caricature to suggest that *all* (and especially all recent) analytic philosophy of religion is subject to these same failings, as seems to be Jantzen's and Anderson's view. On the contrary, there are signs of such masculinist traits already starting to crack under their own weight: the notable recent turn to the discussion of God-as-Trinity, for instance, or of the relationship between the human and the divine in Christ, while also subject potentially to the distortions of the masculinist imaginary, are nonetheless at least telling first signs of an increasing interest in *communion* and *relationship* as philosophical categories.[5]

Thus, I shall be making here some rather different suggestions from those of Jantzen and Anderson for further feminist interrogation of, and interaction with, analytic philosophy of religion. I believe these have greater prospects for pragmatic success in persuading the guild that gender is *already* intrinsic to its operations, and thus urgently in need of the sort of attention and clarification for which its discipline is justly famed. Gender theory cannot then be safely left to angry women who have denounced and left the analytic guild, or to exponents of Eastern myth and mimesis who appear to have departed from the central concerns of the current analytic discussion. Rather, gender *is*, already, at the heart of this discussion. If it be objected that this strategy is objectionably taking up the master's tools, I can only reply that these tools are so powerful and significant already that the demands of Realpolitik drive me to handle, redirect, and imaginatively renegotiate their usage. This indeed is a vital first part of the task of developing a *transformed* rationality. As I suggested at the start of this chapter, clarity, incisiveness, coherence, and philosophical persuasiveness are not in themselves the feminist problem: their valorization should not be the central cause of feminist anguish; rather, it is precisely the attempt to clarify and convict that fuels the feminist attempt to identify the sexisms that lurk in the regnant philosophical discourse in the first place.

Let me then highlight programmatically in closing just three related areas in which a feminist perspective nuanced rather differently from

that of Jantzen's and Anderson's might suggest a fruitful future interchange between analytic philosophy of religion and feminist theory.

The first area concerns the notable and sophisticated developments in recent analytic philosophy of religion in the epistemology of "religious experience," developments that, one might argue, already herald a disturbance or destabilization of masculinist thought patterns. One thinks here of such diverse, but influential, approaches as (1) the appeal to the evidence of religious experience as both the most subjective and yet also the most definitively significant component in a "cumulative case" approach to the existence of God (Swinburne 1979); (2) the development of nonfoundationalist appeals to "proper basicality" in so-called Reformed epistemology, and of the significance granted there to direct intimacy with the Holy Spirit (Plantinga and Wolterstorff 1983; Plantinga 2000); (3) the rehabiliation of the Reidian notion of "credulity" or "trust" (in contradistinction to a fundamental Humean skepticism) as a starting point in reflection on the cultivation of religious affections, and the implicit acknowledgment of the importance of child development in this epistemological move (Wolterstorff 2001); (4) the assessment of "affectivity" as a vital factor in religious epistemology and cognitive regulation (Wainwright 1995); and (5) the attempt to show that *direct* intimacy with, or "perception" of, the divine is a defensible epistemological possibility (contra Kant), and that appeals to the narratives of female mystics (especially Teresa of Avila) can provide significant support for such a position (Alston 1991).

We have already seen how Anderson attacks such epistemological developments as these as signs of a fatal circularity in the guild's thinking, and of its unhealthy obsession with evidences; and how Jantzen is even more dismissive of naïve *feminist* appeals to experience. But my own reading of these highly sophisticated developments in analytic philosophy of religion is a different one. I want to argue, contrariwise, that once some gender sensibility is developed theoretically, this explosion of interest and creativity in recent analytic philosophy of religion in

---

[5] See ibid., 603–5.

religious epistemology is actually already a sign of the discourse covertly "feminizing" itself.[6] By this I mean that we see philosophers of religion already turning away here, in their different ways, from classic Enlightenment epistemological concerns with foundationalism, public evidentialism, and universalizability, and making appeals instead to the more subtle and contestable categories of experience, trust, affectivity, subjectivity, interiority, and mystical theology. Such categories are often, either implicitly or explicitly, founded in *women's* narratives of transformation; but even if they are not, they bear much of the freight of stereotypical femininity. Put thus, we may suggest that these developments constitute not only a "postmodern" disposition, but more pointedly, a sign of the male philosopher of religion now attempting to "tak[e] *her* light to illuminate his path," as Irigaray has charged.

But are these developments then necessarily negative? Must we dismiss them as another suspicious assimilation by the male philosopher of the occluded power of the feminine? Is this just one more way in which male philosophy obliterates the feminist voice by stealing and controlling the insights of women? Much will depend here on our fundamental gender-theoretical perspective; if we presume a fixed, Lacanian binary (which I have progressively critiqued in this chapter), we may remain deeply pessimistic about the sublation of it. But if we have a more fluid and negotiable view of gender, then the way the argument proceeds in each philosophical case, and how much consciousness is evidenced of an implicit gender subtext in the discussion, will become crucial. Even then, there is a great difference between welcoming, and even pedestalizing, the power of femininity to transform the male psyche or religious dilemma (a recurrent theme in Romanticism), and allowing the *woman* to speak for herself and enunciate her particular concerns and interests. As we have demonstrated above, the subtext of gender often laps at the edges of the philosophical argument in the form of tellingly sexist examples that include women in subordinate or stereotypical roles. But once this is demonstrated, it is at least *possible*, I submit, to

imagine a transformed discourse in which these dangers could be consciously named and averted. The problem of gender denial remains a deep one, but the strategy of demonstrating lively current philosophical debates precisely *as* gender-laden holds better prospects of success, I believe, than that of diverting the discourse to completely other fields (as in Anderson).

The second area for possible future rapprochement between analytic philosophy of religion and feminist theory seems to me to reside precisely where Jantzen, for one, finds least hope. This is in the area of apophatic discourse, on which analytic philosophy of religion has made notably little contribution to date, for reasons that might also have connection to its purported masculinism and literalism. It might seem odd that a topic that Jantzen derides as supremely masculinist and elitist (negative theology in the Dionysian tradition) could become a fruitful source of feminist critique of the discourse of analytic philosophy of religion, which, until recently, has been so notably resistant to feminist concerns. But Jantzen's over-hasty dismissal of the negative theology tradition fails to acknowledge the purgative potential of this tradition in confronting sexist idolatry in the naming and desribing of God. It is unfortunate in this regard that a whole generation of "liberal" feminist *theologians* have adopted what William Alston (1989) has called the "pan-metaphorist" strategy where God-talk is concerned; that is, they have declared in a neo-Kantian vein that *all* talk of God is "metaphorical" and (necessarily, for them) "nonliteral," and so subject to revision simply according to the imaginative "construction" of the feminist theologian. Deep issues are of course at stake here concerning the apparent rejection of dominical and biblical authority, the skepticism about the possibility of divine revelation, and a certain cavalier attitude toward the complex nature of religious language. But it should simply be noted that the more it is declared that the Kantian heritage demands an epistemological *distancing* from reality (especially from divine reality) – a trait we have repeatedly commented on in Anderson's work – the more an anthropomorphic or explicitly

---

[6]   This point is argued in more detail in my 1999 Riddell Lectures, in preparation as *Diotima and the Dispossessed: An Essay "On the Contemplative Life."* [. . .]

Feuerbachian projectionism becomes the norm for religious utterance, whether in masculinist or feminist forms. What the Dionysian tradition of apophaticism holds out as an *alternative*, then, is a form of religious speech that rigorously denies not only its positive but its negative statements about God, and simultaneously points to a transformative contemplative *encounter* with God that transcends even this playful language-game of negations. As such, it claims to participate in a consistent exposure of human projectionism and submits itself to an ongoing purgation of human idolatry (whether in masculinist or feminist form). The Thomistic variant of negative theology in contrast, makes an adjustment to Dionysius's own position by allowing, on the basis of revelatory authority, an important distinction between analogical and metaphorical speech for God, the former being "literal" but, at the Godward end, humanly unknowable in its full semantic *richesse*, the latter being "creaturely," and thus technically inappropriate to God. The parody of Thomas's theory of analogy presented by Jantzen (and briefly discussed above) thus fails altogether to consider the feminist *potential* that this theory, too, holds, especially in its apophatic dimensions. That analytic philosophy of religion has attended rather sparingly to the Dionysian tradition of negative theology – whether directly, or as mediated through Thomas's work – seems, among other things, to be an indication of its lack of appreciation of the pervasive problem of idolatry, and hence a sign of its concomitant lack of concern about sexism. That feminist critiques of such a resistance could develop a rigorous and nuanced account of the potential of a Dionysian perspective seems an urgent priority.

The third arena for possible mediation between feminist concerns and analytic philosophy of religion lies in the related area of claims to an immediate contact with the divine. It is here that Jantzen's and Anderson's rightful interests in the category of desire seem to me to come into relation with an important existing epistemological discussion in analytic philosophy of religion about the possibility of direct "perception" of God. If God is to be "perceivable" in some sense analogous to (but not identical with) the direct perception of objects (so Alston, seeking to evade Kant's objections), then certain "doxastic

practices" may, according to Alston (1991), be the crucial means and mediation of such perception. Desire, as a core factor in the quest for God, *cannot* be ignored – indeed, is projected into center-stage – if women mystical theologians such as Teresa of Avila are utilized as key examples of epistemic intimacy with God, as in Alston's work; but nor can the transforming practices of "contemplation" (that are the *means* of that erotic desire being propelled toward God) be pushed to one side epistemically. Here we have a nexus of entangled themes – desire, intimacy, relationship, transformative practice, knowledge of God, and *gender* – which urgently require further analytic explication. Why is it that the woman stars so often as the site of highest intimacy with the divine in the discourses of analytic philosophy of religion? And what can we conclude from this about the necessary *transformation* of existing epistemic categories in the light of gender analysis, reflection on "practice," and an acknowledgment of the centrality of desire for an adequate account of the perception of God? My approach here, unlike Anderson's, again suggests that analytic philosophy of religion is already signaling its *need* of gender analysis if it is even to further its own current projects and disputed issues. But that is a continuing task, and challenge, for the future.

I have attempted in this chapter to give a detailed account of the two most developed feminist critiques of analytic philosophy of religion (to date), and to show how their *particular* understandings of gender theory and of feminist epistemology fuel the accounts they give. As we have seen, both their philosophical presumptions and their pragmatic conclusions are very different from one another, even though they share a number of central themes and influences, and both *claim* to be seeking some sort of bridge between the disciplines of feminism and analytic philosophy. After providing an appreciative, but critical, account of these first two options, I have suggested a third alternative set of ploys to effect a transformation of gender consciousness in the discourses of analytic philosophy of religion. In so doing, I have urged – on rather different gender-theoretical and epistemological grounds— that analytic philosophy of religion may already be well on the way to undoing its own, and deeply rooted, masculinism. And it is notable that this undoing is closely related to a critique of foundationalism (in all its forms), and also, perhaps more surprising, of the neo-Kantian "recession from reality" stance. As the discipline continues to engage the insights of contemporary continental philosophy and social theory, and to begin to interact more deeply with current feminist theory, we may indeed hope for some significant signs of rapprochement and mutual learning. Perhaps only humility is needed.

Works Cited

Alston, William P. 1989. *Divine Nature and Human Language: Essays in Philosophical Theology*. Ithaca, NY: Cornell University Press.

——. 1991. *Perceiving God: The Epistemology of Religious Experience*. Ithaca, NY: Cornell University Press.

Anderson, Pamela Sue. 1993. *Ricoeur and Kant: Philosophy of the Will*. Atlanta: Scholars Press.

——. 1998. *A Feminist Philosophy of Religion*. Oxford: Blackwell.

——. 2001. "'Standpoint': Its Rightful Place in a Realist Epistemology." *Journal of Philosophical Research* 26: 131–53.

Coakley, Sarah. 1997. "Feminism." In *A Companion to Philosophy of Religion*, ed. Charles Taliaferro and Philip Quinn, 601–6. Oxford: Blackwell.

——. 2002. *Powers and Submissions: Spirituality, Philosophy and Gender*. Oxford: Blackwell.

Davidson, Donald. 1984. "On the Very Idea of a 'Conceptual Scheme.'" In *Inquiries into Truth and Interpretation*, 183–98. Oxford: Clarendon Press.

Harding, Sandra. 1993. "Rethinking Standpoint Epistemology: What Is 'Strong Objectivity'?" In *Feminist Epistemologies*, ed. Linda Alcoff and Elizabeth Potter, 49–82. London: Routledge.

Hartsock, Nancy. 1983. "The Feminist Standpoint: Developing the Ground for Specifically Feminist Historical Materialism." In *Discovering Reality: Feminist Perspectives on Epistemology, Metaphysics, Methodology and Philosophy of Science*, ed. Sandra Harding and Merrill Hintikka, 283–310. Dordrecht: Reidel.

Helm, Paul. 1994. *Belief Policies*. Cambridge, England: Cambridge University Press.

Hick, John. 1973. *God and the Universe of Faiths*. Basingstoke, England: Macmillan.

——. 1976. *Death and Eternal Life*. Basingstoke, England: Macmillan.

hooks, bell. 1990. *Yearning: Race, Gender, Cultural Politics*. Boston: South End Press.

Irigaray, Luce. 1985a. *Speculum of the Other Woman*. Trans. Gillian C. Gill. Ithaca, NY: Cornell University Press.

——. 1985b. *This Sex Which Is Not One*. Trans. Catherine Porter. Ithaca, NY: Cornell University Press.

——. 1993. *An Ethics of Sexual Difference*. Trans. Carolyn Burke and Gillian C. Gill. Ithaca, NY: Cornell University Press.

Jantzen, Grace. 1984. *God's World, God's Body*. London: Darton, Longman and Todd.

——. 1995. *Power, Gender and Christian Mysticism*. Cambridge: Cambridge University Press.

——. 1998. *Becoming Divine: Towards a Feminist Philosophy of Religion*. Manchester, England: Manchester University Press.

Le Doeuff, Michèle. 1989. *The Philosophical Imaginary*. Trans. Colin Gordon. London: Athlone Press.

——. 1990. "Women, Reason, Etc." *Differences* 2: 3, 1–13.

——. 1991. *Hipparchia's Choice: An Essay Concerning Women, Philosophy, Etc*. Trans. Trista Selous. Oxford: Blackwell.

Nagel, Thomas. 1986. *The View from Nowhere*. New York: Oxford University Press.

Plantinga, Alvin. 2000. *Warranted Christian Belief*. New York: Oxford University Press.

Plantinga, Alvin, and Nicholas Wolterstorff, eds. 1983. *Faith and Rationality: Reason and Belief in God*. Notre Dame, Ind.: University of Notre Dame Press.

Quine, W. V. O. 1953. *From a Logical Point of View: Logico-Philosophical Essays*. New York: Harper and Row.

Swinburne, Richard. 1979. *The Existence of God*. Oxford: Clarendon Press.

Wainwright, William J. 1995. *Reason and the Heart: A Prolegomenon to a Critique of Passional Reason*. Ithaca, NY: Cornell University Press.

Wolterstorff, Nicholas. 2001. *Thomas Reid and the Story of Epistemology*. Cambridge: Cambridge University Press.

64

Heidegger and Buddhism

Michael E. Zimmerman

Many commentators have remarked on the affinities between Heidegger's thought and East Asian traditions such as Vedanta, Mahayana Buddhism, and Taoism.[1] In this essay, I shall examine critically some aspects of the apparent rapport between Heidegger's thought and Mahayana Buddhism. [...]

In my critical examination of the presumed similarities between Heidegger and Mahayana Buddhism, I shall focus particular attention on the claim advanced both by Heidegger and by Buddhism: that humans can learn to "let beings be" only by gaining insight into the nothingness that pervades all things. Such insight, we are told, spontaneously leads to the overcoming of anthropocentrism and dualism. In what follows, I first touch on the mystical origins of Heidegger's idea of nothingness; then I examine, in turn, his early and later accounts of the role of nothingness in authentic human existence. After some preliminary remarks about Heidegger's interest in Eastern thought, I examine the Buddhist conception of the relation between enlightenment and the revelation of nothingness. Then I compare what Heidegger and

Mahayana Buddhism have to say about the relation between authenticity or enlightenment and insight into one's own nothingness. [...]

Early Heidegger on Nothingness

The reader may be wondering how there can possibly be any philosophical importance to the idea of nothingness. For the most part, when we think of nothingness, we simply think of ... nothing at all! Nothingness, to our minds, is merely the absence of anything: sheer lack, emptiness in a negative sense. Western thinkers who emphasized the importance of nothingness have been primarily mystics such as Meister Eckhart, the latter of whom greatly influenced Heidegger's writings. Eckhart insisted that "God" is far beyond our conceptual categories, which are appropriate only for understanding *creatures*. Instead of speaking of God in positive terms, it is better to speak of Divine Nothingness. The Divine cannot be regarded as a super entity existing somewhere else, but instead constitutes the unconditioned openness or emptiness in

"Heidegger and Buddhism," a selection from "Heidegger, Buddhism, and Deep Ecology" by Michael E. Zimmerman, in *The Cambridge Companion to Heidegger*, 2nd edition, ed. Charles B. Guignon (New York: Cambridge University Press, 2006), pp. 293–325. © Cambridge University Press, 2006. Reprinted by permission of Cambridge University Press and Michael E. Zimmerman.
[1] The best collection on Heidegger's relation to Eastern thinking is *Heidegger and Asian Thought*, ed. Graham Parkes (Honolulu: University of Hawaii Press, 1987). [...]

which all things appear. Meister Eckhart argued that humans are at one with this openness. So lacking is any distinction between one's soul and the Divine, in fact, that one who is awakened to Divine Nothingness forgets all about God and lives a life of releasement (*Gelassenheit*), moved by compassion to free things from suffering.

Heidegger's interest in mystics such as Eckhart was reflected in his hopes of becoming a priest. After these hopes were dashed for health reasons, Heidegger became a professional philosopher. Although increasingly antagonistic toward Christianity, he nevertheless continued to draw upon the insights of Christian mystics in his philosophical writings. In particular, his notion that human existence is the openness, clearing, or nothingness in which things can manifest themselves is deeply indebted to mysticism. For mystics, the "self" is not an entity that stands opposed in a dualistic way to other entities. Instead, it is the clearing in which entities (including thoughts, feelings, perceptions, objects, others) appear. The idea that humans are not entities but the clearing in which entities appear eventually helped Heidegger overcome not only dualism, but also anthropocentrism, the attitude that humankind is the source of all value and that all things must serve human interests. By maintaining that humans are authentic only when they let a thing manifest itself in ways consistent with its own possibilities, not merely in accordance with its instrumental value, Heidegger countered the anthropocentrism of much of Western thought. In examining his conception of nothingness, let us turn first to his early writings, particularly *Being and Time* (1927). Later, we shall consider the role of nothingness in his later (post-1935) writings.

The mystical notion of nothingness is at work in *Being and Time*, despite the fact that it is disguised in the complex vocabulary of philosophers like Kant. Following Kant, Heidegger asked the following sort of question: How is it possible for humans to understand entities *as* entities? To answer this question, he distinguished between the human understanding of things and the understanding we ascribe to

animals. Birds are clearly able to apprehend entities; otherwise, they could not build nests or feed their young. But, so Heidegger argued, birds and other animals are not able to notice explicitly *that* things *are*.[2] Presumably, birds don't step back from their work to say, "Now that is a fine nest I'm building!" Moreover, we assume that birds don't have identity crises; they don't ask, "Why am I here and what will become of me? Who am I?" We humans understand ourselves and other things *as* entities, that is, as things that *are*. Early Heidegger concentrated on the human capacity for understanding the *being* of entities, a capacity revealed in our ability to use the verb "to be" in so many different ways.

Normally, philosophers conceive of understanding as a faculty of the mind, the thinking thing that attempts to comprehend extramental things. Heidegger, however, sharply criticized the Cartesian epistemological tradition, which conceived of humans as self-conscious substances, or as worldless subjects standing over against objects. Drawing on his study of Eckhart and other mystics, as well as on Kant, Heidegger maintained instead that the human being is not a thing but rather a peculiar kind of nothingness: the temporal linguistic clearing, the opening, the absencing in which things can present themselves and thus "be." If humans are not things, then we have to define "knowing" in a different way than before. Knowing is not a relation between two things, mind and object. Rather, knowing occurs because the openness constituting human existence is configured in terms of the three temporal dimensions: past, present, future. These dimensions hold open the horizons on which entities may manifest themselves in determinate ways – for example, as instruments, objects, or persons. Heidegger's talk of the *a priori* character of the temporal horizons of human existence is analogous to Kant's talk of the *a priori* categories of the human understanding.

Human understanding, then, does not take place inside a mind locked in the skull. Instead, understanding occurs because human temporality is receptive to particular ways in which things can present or manifest themselves. Here it is

---

[2]   Heidegger discusses the question of animal understanding in great detail in *Die Grundbegriffe der Metaphysik*: *Welt-Endlichkeit-Einsamkeit*, *Gesamtausgabe* 29/30 (winter semester, 1929–30), ed. Friedrich-Wilhelm von Hermann (Frankfurt am Main: Vittorio Klostermann, 1983).

important to emphasize that what we ordinarily take to be the ultimate constituents of "mind" – thoughts, beliefs, assertions, and so on – are for Heidegger phenomena that occur *within* the temporal clearing constitutive of human understanding. Hence, minds do not make thoughts possible; rather, *a priori* human understanding of being makes it possible for us to encounter and to conceive of ourselves as minds with thoughts separated from the external world. For Heidegger, thoughts are not radically other than allegedly external entities, such as trees, cars, and books. Thoughts and cars are both entities manifesting themselves within and thus being understood as entities within the temporal clearing of human existence.

Just as in the case of understanding, Heidegger defined "being" in a different way than most other philosophers. Traditionally, philosophers have defined the being of an entity as its ground or substance, that which provides the foundation for the thing. Plato called this foundation the eternal form of things; Aristotle their substance; medieval theologians, their Creator. Refusing to conceive of being as a kind of superior entity, an eternal foundation, ground, cause, or origin for things, Heidegger argued that for something "to be" means for it to disclose or to present itself. For this presencing (*Anwesen*) or self-manifesting to occur, there must be a clearing, an opening, an emptiness, a nothingness, an absencing (*Abwesen*). Human existence constitutes the openness necessary for the presencing (being) of entities to take place. When such presencing occurs through the openness that I am, I encounter an entity *as* an entity; that is, I *understand* what it *is*. Heidegger used the term "Dasein" to name this peculiar receptivity of human existence for the being (self-manifesting) of entities. In German, *da* means "here" or "there," while *sein* is the German verb "to be." Hence, Dasein means the place in which being occurs, the openness in which presencing transpires. For Heidegger, neither temporality (absencing, nothingness) nor being (presencing, self-manifesting) is an "entity." Rather, they are the conditions necessary for entities to appear as such. We never "see" time or "touch" the presencing of things; rather, we see and touch the *things* that manifest or present themselves.

In the light of these remarks, the significance of the title of Heidegger's major work, *Being and Time*, becomes comprehensible. His aim here was to study the internal relationship between being and time. Because being and time, presencing and absencing, manifestness and nothingness lack any phenomenal or empirical properties, they seem to be nothing in the merely negative sense of an "empty vapor" (Nietzsche). For Heidegger, however, presencing and absencing "are" that which is most worthy of thinking.

What evidence, we might ask, is there for the claim that humans are really this temporal nothingness through which entities can manifest themselves and thus be? To answer this question, Heidegger appealed in part to an argument taken from Kant: the best way of accounting for the possibility of our understanding of entities is to postulate that we humans simply *are* the temporal openness or nothingness in which entities can appear *as* entities. In addition to such an argument, however, Heidegger maintained that the mood of anxiety reveals the nothingness lying at the heart of human existence. While contending that anxiety is perhaps the most basic human mood, he also observed that it is such a disquieting mood that we spend most of our lives trying to keep it from overtaking us. Our unreflective absorption in the practices of everyday life – family relations, schooling, job activities, entertainment – keep us distracted enough that we manage to conceal from ourselves the weirdness of being human. Anxiety tears us out of everyday absorption in things; it reveals them to be useless in the face of the radical mortality, finitude, and nothingness at the heart of human existence.

Why is human existence weird? Because humans are not things, but the clearing in which things appear. Although we are not fixed things, we define ourselves as if we were simply a more complex version of the things we encounter in the world: rational animals. Ordinarily, we identify ourselves with our thoughts, beliefs, feelings, attitudes, memories, bodies, material possessions, and so on. Such identification gives us a sense of stability and permanence, which covers up the essential groundlessness and emptiness of human existence. There is no ultimate reason for our doing what we do. We have to postulate our own reasons for doing what we do; we invent our own identities, although those identities to a great extent are determined in advance by social practices and norms that have evolved historically. Moreover, as groundless nothingness, humans are essentially dependent and receptive, finite and mortal. The mood of anxiety is so disturbing because it reveals that at bottom we are nothingness, that our existence is ultimately groundless, and that we are essentially finite and mortal. In the face of such disclosures, little wonder that most people flee from the mood of anxiety.

Early Heidegger claimed, however, that if we submit resolutely to what the mood of anxiety wants to reveal to us, we become authentic (*eigentlich*) in the sense of owning our mortal existence. As authentic, we assume responsibility for being the mortal openness that we already are. Assuming such responsibility is essential to human freedom. Instead of existing in a constricted manner – as egos with firm identities – we allow the temporal openness that we are to expand. This expansion allows things and other humans to manifest themselves in more complex, complete, and novel ways, rather than as mere objects or instruments for our ends.[3] Conversely, by fleeing from anxiety into everyday practices and distractions, we conceal the truth about our own mortal nothingness and are thus incapable of allowing things to manifest themselves primordially.

What early Heidegger says about authenticity may be compared to the famous Zen story about the stages of enlightenment. Before enlightenment occurs, mountains are mountains, at the moment of enlightenment, mountains cease being mountains; but then mountains become mountains once again. Zen enlightenment, *satori*, involves direct insight into one's radical groundlessness and nothingness. In the light of

such a revelation, everyday practices (including working and eating) lose their meaning. Afterward, however, one reenters these practices, but in a way no longer burdened by ignorance about what it means to be human. Likewise for Heidegger, before becoming authentic one exists in accord with everyday practices; upon allowing anxiety to reveal one's utter groundlessness and nothingness, everyday practices slide away into meaninglessness; afterward, one takes up everyday-practices once again, but not in a merely conformist manner.[4]

Instead, being authentic means being free to invigorate and to transform practices in light of the realization of their utter groundlessness. As groundless, things could be otherwise than they are at present. It is important to note, however, that for Heidegger freedom did not mean boundless license for the ego, but instead the capacity for human Dasein to "let things be" in ways other than as mere instruments for the ego. As the Zen tradition puts it, being enlightened means chopping wood and carrying water – but in a manner attuned to the presencing of things as it occurs beyond the dualism of mind and body.

Heidegger's notion that humans are most free when they "let beings be" has been taken up as a slogan by some radical environmentalists, who object to treating nature merely as an instrument for human ends. Early Heidegger suggested that the instrumental disclosure of things played a primary role in human existence.[5] Later, however, he concluded that such instrumentalism was in fact a historical feature of Western history that began with the Greeks and culminated in the technological disclosure of things as nothing but raw material for human ends. Moreover, his early instrumentalism was intimately bound up with his twofold attempt to overcome the

---

[3]   On the topic of authenticity, see Michael E. Zimmerman, *Eclipse of the Self: The Development of Heidegger's Concept of Authenticity*, 2nd ed. (Athens: Ohio University Press, 1986). The final chapter includes a comparison of Heidegger and Buddhism.

[4]   On this topic, see Hubert L. Dreyfus and Jane Rubin, "You Can't Get Something for Nothing: Kierkegaard and Heidegger on How Not to Overcome Nihilism," *Inquiry*, 30 (1987): 33–76.

[5]   See Hubert L. Dreyfus, "Between *Techne* and Technology: The Ambiguous Place of Technology in *Being and Time*," in *The Thought of Martin Heidegger*, ed. Michael E. Zimmerman, Tulane Studies in Philosophy, 32 (New Orleans, La.: Tulane University Press, 1984), pp. 23–35. See also idem, *Heidegger's Confrontation with Modernity* (Bloomington: Indiana University Press, 1990), Chaps 10 and 11.

mind-body dualism that – especially in its scientific version – gave rise to the alienation at work in modern society.

One phase in this attempt involved conceiving of humans not as minds in skulls but rather as the temporal clearing or nothingness in which thoughts and trees, beliefs and cars can appear as entities. The other phase in overcoming dualism involved challenging those who privileged theoretical assertions and abstract knowledge over against pragmatic activity. Instead of conceiving of humans as worldless intellects making abstract assertions about external objects, Heidegger defined humans as being always already involved in myriad practices that utilize many different things. These things do not manifest themselves abstractly as objects, but instead as tools involved in a complex set of relationships that constitute the world of human existence. Human existence, temporally oriented toward the future, is always pressing forward into possibilities opened up within the world. The practical involvements and practices of everyday life precede and make possible the theoretical knowledge so prized by philosophers. Heidegger emphasized the practical dimension of human existence by defining the very being of Dasein as "care." To be human means to be concerned about things and to be solicitous toward other people.

While early Heidegger sometimes spoke as if the objectifying tendencies of modernity were a result of humanity's intrinsic tendency to conceal deeper truths, he later concluded that the objectifying scientific view did not result from any human decision or weakness, but was instead a proper part of the technological disclosure of entities, a disclosure that was itself a dimension of the "destiny of being." The famous "turn" in Heidegger's thinking occurred when he concluded that he could no longer conceive of being in terms of human understanding, but instead had to conceive of human understanding as an aspect of being itself.

Later Heidegger's Conception of Nothingness

Following Kant, early Heidegger sometimes spoke of Dasein's temporal openness as if it were a faculty or capacity of humankind. And he often spoke as if the being of entities were somehow a function of human Dasein's understanding. Moreover, he depicted anxiety primarily as a personal phenomenon that called individuals to a less constricted way of understanding things. Later Heidegger altered these views. Ceasing to speak of temporality or nothingness as a dimension of human existence, he made clear that human temporality arises within a more encompassing "openness" or "region" that cannot be reduced to anything merely human. Later Heidegger emphasized that human existence is appropriated as the site for the self-disclosure or being of entities. Instead of conceiving of being from the perspective of human Dasein, then, Heidegger began thinking being in its own terms. This move was central to his attempt to abandon any remaining anthropocentrism discernible in his earlier work. In this connection, he concluded that inauthenticity, that is, understanding things in a superficial and constricted way, was not a problem of individuals, but a widespread social phenomenon resulting from the self-concealment of being. The technological disclosure of entities, then, arose not because individuals were unable to endure anxiety, but instead because, since around Plato's time, being as such had increasingly withdrawn itself from human view. Correlatively, Western humanity was blinded to the fact that human existence is the clearing for the being of entities. Hence, Western humanity increasingly came to understand itself as a peculiar entity – the clever animal – driven to dominate all other entities for the sake of gaining power and security. Heidegger argued that the emergence of the technological age in the twentieth century was the inevitable result of the clever animals' craving for power.

From Heidegger's viewpoint in the thirties, Western humanity could be saved from technological nihilism only if Germany were granted another encounter with being and nothingness that was as powerful as the beginning granted to the ancient Greeks. Such an encounter, so he mistakenly believed, would be made possible by National Socialism, which revealed that the highest obligation and possibility of humanity were not to be the master of entities, but instead to be the historical clearing necessary for entities to manifest themselves in ways other than merely as flexible raw material.[6] Heidegger insisted that such a new beginning would require that humanity cease regarding itself as the lord and master, or the ground, of entities. A transformed humanity would acknowledge its radically receptive, dependent, mortal, and finite status, thereby allowing itself to be appropriated (*ereignet*) as the site required for the presencing or being of entities to occur. Only in this way could humanity learn to "let beings be," that is, to allow things to manifest themselves in accordance with their own limits instead of in accordance with the limits imposed on them by scientific constructs and technological projects. Heidegger eventually concluded that the historical reality of National Socialism betrayed its "inner truth and greatness" by promoting a particularly virulent version of the technological disclosure of things, instead of opening up a new phase of Western history. Heidegger's lifelong refusal to renounce unambiguously his own authentic version of National Socialism is a source of concern for students of his thought.

The fact that modern humanity came to regard itself as the ground or foundation for entities resulted not from human decision, Heidegger maintained, but instead from the self-concealment of being itself. Plato conceived of being not as the dynamic presencing of entities, but rather as the eternally present, unchanging blueprint, form (*eidos*), or model for things in the realm of becoming. By conceiving of being as the permanently present grounding for entities, Plato initiated the 2,500-year history of metaphysics. Heidegger sought to transform this history by revealing that there is no eternal or final "ground" for things, that in fact what we mean by "being" is always shaped by historical factors.

The Romans gave a crucial twist to the metaphysical tradition by depicting the metaphysical ground as that which causes things to come into being. Henceforth, metaphysics became concerned primarily with telling the story of where things came from, how they were produced or created. Appropriating the metaphysical tradition, medieval theologians argued that for something "to be" meant for it to be created (produced) and preserved by the supreme entity, the Creator of biblical faith. In early modern times, human reason arrogated to itself the divine role as the ground of entities. Beginning with Descartes, Western humanity began to encounter entities as objects for the self-certain rational subject. For something to be meant for it to be capable of being represented – measured, quantified, known – by the subject. Modern science forced entities to reveal themselves only in accordance with theoretical presuppositions consistent with Western humanity's ever-increasing drive to gain control of everything. While during the industrial age the achievement of such control could be described as a means for the end of improving the human estate, during the technological era – which may be said to have commenced with the horrors of World War I – humanity itself has become a means to an end without purpose: the quest for power for its own sake, which Heidegger described as the sheer Will to Will.

Later Heidegger differentiated his own meditations on being from theological and scientific accounts that search for the "causes" of things. He focused instead on the manifestness by virtue of which entities can first be encountered and only subsequently interpreted in terms of theoretical categories such as cause and effect, ground and consequent. He insisted that human reason cannot ground or explain the sheer presencing of things. Following the German mystic Angelius Silesius, he spoke of such acausal origination by saying, "The rose is without why; it blooms because it blooms."[7] Moreover, later Heidegger also concluded that the "clearing" necessary for the self-manifesting of entities cannot be understood in terms of the Kantian model of temporal ecstases of human existence. Rather, he argued that the clearing is constituted by a thing – whether natural or artifactual – that gathers mortals and gods, earth and sky into a kind of cosmic dance which frees up the inherent luminosity of things.

---

[6]   See my essays "The Thorn in Heidegger's Side: The Question of National Socialism," *Philosophical Forum*, 20 (Summer 1989): 326–65; and "Philosophy and Politics: The Case of Heidegger," *Philosophy Today*, 33 (Summer 1989): 3–19. Concerning Heidegger's misguided view that National Socialism promised to offer an alternative to industrial nihilism, see my *Heidegger's Confrontation with Modernity*.

[7]   *Der Satz vom Grund* (Pfullingen: Neske, 1971), pp. 101–2.

The world constitutes itself by virtue of the spontaneous coordination or mutual appropriation of the appearances that arise – un-caused, from no-thing – moment by moment. Later Heidegger used the term *logos* to name this mutual coordination of appearances; hence, his claim that language (*logos*) lets things be. This account of the self-organization of uncaused appearances, which is close to Taoism, also provides the key to Heidegger's proximity to Mahayana Buddhism.

Heidegger and Eastern Thought: Preliminary Remarks

We know of Heidegger's debt to Meister Eckhart, whose writings reveal many congruences with Buddhism and other East Asian traditions.[8] And Heidegger himself was interested in Buddhism and Taoism. In one essay, for example, he noted the resonances between the Chinese term *tao* and his own notion of *Ereignis*, the "event of appropriation" that claims humanity as the site for the self-manifesting of entities. Such appropriation would change the course of Western history by freeing humanity from its compulsion to dominate things through technical means and by freeing humanity to adhering to the self-concealing "way" of things themselves.[9] In fact, so intrigued was Heidegger by Taoism that he spent most of the summer in 1946 working with a Chinese student, Paul Shih-yi Hsiao, translating portions of the *Tao Te Ching*.[10] Otto Pöggeler, one of Heidegger's ablest

commentators, reports that as early as 1930, to help settle a dispute on the nature of intersubjectivity, Heidegger cited a famous passage from Chuang-Tsu.[11] And William Barrett reports the possibly apocryphal story that upon reading one of D. T. Suzuki's books on Buddhism, Heidegger exclaimed that Suzuki voiced what Heidegger had been trying to say all along.[12] The fact that the Japanese have published seven translations of *Being and Time* gives credence to the idea that there is an important relation between Heidegger's thought and Buddhism.[13]

Those skeptical of the East Asian influence on Heidegger's thought point out his insistence that the new beginning that he envisioned for the West could arise only from the West itself, since it was in ancient Greece that there arose the first beginning, which culminated in the technological disclosure of all things – including humans – as flexible raw material. In 1966 Heidegger said that the transformation of the technological impulse "cannot happen because of any takeover by Zen Buddhism or any other Eastern experience of the world. . . . Thinking itself can only be transformed by a thinking which has the same origin and calling."[14]

In making such a distinction between East and West, Heidegger not only tended to downplay the impact of Eastern thinking on the German philosophical tradition (beginning with Leibniz and continuing through Nietzsche), but also seemed to be thinking meta-physically in accordance with a binary opposition between East and West, an opposition that seems to privilege the West as the origin of the technological

[8] See, e.g., Rudolf Otto, *Mysticism East and West*, trans. Bertha L. Cracey and Richenda C. Payne (New York: Meridian Books, 1959); S. Radhakrishnan, *Eastern Religious and Western Thought* (Oxford: Oxford University Press, 1974); Daisetz T. Suzuki, *Zen and Japanese Culture* (Princeton, NJ: Princeton University Press, 1970).
[9] *On the Way to Language*, trans. Peter D. Hertz (New York: Harper & Row, 1971), p. 92; *Unterwegs zur Sprache* (Pfullingen: Neske, 1965), p. 198.
[10] Paul Shih-yi Hsiao, "Heidegger and Our Translation of the *Tao Te Ching*," in *Heidegger and Asian Thought*, ed. Parkes, pp. 93–103.
[11] Otto Pöggeler, "West–East Dialogue: Heidegger and Lao-Tzu," trans. Graham Parkes, in *Heidegger and Asian Thought*, p. 53.
[12] William Barrett, Introduction to D. T. Suzuki, *Zen Buddhism* (Garden City, NY: Doubleday, 1956), p. xi.
[13] In an unpublished essay, "Die Übersetzbarkeit Heideggers' ins Japanische," Noriko Idada (Tokyo Metropolitan University) has commented on the difficulty of translating Heidegger into Japanese.
[14] "Only a God Can Save Us: *Der Spiegel's* Interview with Martin Heidegger," trans. Maria P. Alter and John D. Caputo, *Philosophy Today*, 20 (Winter 1976): 267–84 (281); "Nur Noch ein Gott Kann uns retten," *Spiegel*-Gespräch mit Martin Heidegger am 23 September, 1966, *Der Spiegel*, No. 26 (May 31, 1976): 193–219 (214–17).

disclosure of things that now pervades the planet.[15] Nevertheless, in calling for another beginning that would displace the Western metaphysical quest for the ultimate ground of things, Heidegger questioned the validity of the West's claim to cultural superiority. Belief in such superiority hinges on the conviction that Western rationality, especially as manifested in science and technology, constitutes the ground for things: to be means to be a representation for the rational subject. In deconstructing metaphysical foundationalism, however, Heidegger revealed the groundlessness not only of rationality, but also of the historical project of mastery based on such rationality.

Heidegger maintained that, despite pretensions to the contrary, Western humanity never had control over its own destiny, including the rise of planetary technology. If such technology arises from trends in Western history, one might well make the case that it can be thought in terms of Western discourse. While Heidegger himself believed that his own thinking could be enriched by his encounter with Eastern thinking, he also maintained that radically different kinds of languages forced Western and Eastern peoples to live in different "houses of being." His dialogue with the Japanese thinker and his incomplete translation of *Tao Te Ching* were efforts to bridge this linguistic gap. Before moving further into our examination of the Heidegger-Buddhism relation, we must pause to consider major features of Mahayana Buddhism, especially its idea of absolute nothingness.

The Buddhist Conception of Nothingness

Buddhism is a cosmological, psychological, and religious system which maintains that salvation arises from insight into the true nature of reality. A central teaching of Buddhism is *anatman*, the claim that the human being lacks a substantial self. As described in the *Abhidharma* literature, human experience is constituted by the interplay of five impersonal *skandhas* (heaps or collections): matter/form, sensation, perception, volitional elements, and mind. The *skandhas* are

composed of basic units called *dharmas*, of which there are about eighty different kinds. Although *dharmas* arise and disappear rapidly in complex casual relationships, early Buddhists said that the *dharmas* are real "from their own side" (*svabhava*). Hence, *dharmas* are the primary reality out of which the secondary reality of the *skandhas* is constructed. The fourth *skandha*, composed of many kinds of volitional, motivational, and affective *dharmas*, involves karmic actions, that is, actions that affect the subsequent birth. Important examples of volitional *dharmas* are aversion and craving. If these are not extinguished in the present lifetime, they will profoundly influence the composition of the fourth *skandha* – and thus the whole psycho-physical organism – in the subsequent lifetime.

To describe the totally interrelated factors generating the cycle of birth and rebirth (*samsara*), Buddhists speak of a twelve fold process of "conditioned co-production" or "dependent co-origination," *pratitya samutpada*. Conditioned co-production emphasizes the merely constructed and thus empty (*sunya*) nature of all secondary phenomena, that is, phenomena composed of *dharmas*. Despite appearing to be continuous and solid, then, the contents of human experience are "constructed" of *dharmas* that are constantly arising and falling. Flux, not permanence, and conditioning, not independence, characterize all phenomena. *Nirvana* names the one totally unconditioned state, the way to which involves eliminating – step by step – the processes involved in conditioned co-production. Buddhism's major advance over Indian religions 2,500 years ago lay in explaining salvation not in terms of sacrifices made to irrational divinities, but instead in terms of understanding and altering basic causal processes. Expressed succinctly: If one does this, that follows; if one undoes that, this follows.

The great Buddhist philosopher Nagarjuna (c. 150 CE), commenting on the *Prajnaparamita Sutras*, effected an important conceptual shift that is central to Mahayana Buddhism. He concluded that even the *dharmas* are characterized by emptiness (*sunyata*). Instead of being the primary reality forming the basis for phenomena constructed in the five *skandhas*, the *dharmas*

15   On this issue, see Evan Thompson, "Planetary Thinking/Planetary Building: An Essay on Martin Heidegger and Nishitani Keiji," *Philosophy East and West*, 36, No. 3 (1986): 235–52.

themselves arise and fall along with everything else in conditioned co production. All phenomena whatsoever are empty, because they lack independent, substantial existence apart from the totality of mutually conditioned phenomena that arise and fall together. To be empty means to be empty of independent or self-caused reality. In everyday language, we may say that things exist in this way or that, but in language drawn from ultimate insight we say that no-thing exists at all. This distinction between everyday and ultimate ways of seeing phenomena is called the Two Truth doctrine. Seeking to overcome all dualisms, including *nirvana* versus *samsara*, Nagarjuna indicated that there is no perceiving subject and no perceived object.[16] Instead, so one could infer, experience is constituted of self-luminous phenomena that have no substance, origin, or destination.[17] This may amount to a phenomenalism that lacks a perceiver.

The most famous metaphorical expression of this insight, advanced by the Hua-yen school, is the jewel net of the god Indra. Into this infinite net, representing the universe, are set an infinite number of perfect gems, each of which reflects the light given off by all the other gems throughout the expanse of the net. The play of reflected light is codetermined simultaneously by all the gems, no one of which stands in a superior or causal relation to the others. Mahayana Buddhism holds that the phenomenal world is akin to such an interplay of reflected appearances, in which each thing is aware of its relation to all other things. These appearances have no ground; there is nothing behind what appears, no substantial ground or essence to cause them. All things arise together in an internally cosmic event of reflection, which is sentient though not usually self-conscious. Based on the insight that all appearances are ultimately empty, Mahayana Buddhists draw the conclusion that form *is* emptiness and emptiness *is* form, a paradoxical conclusion whose proof demands direct insight, which argument alone cannot provide.

Nagarjuna warned against turning emptiness, the lack of own-self, into a new metaphysical reality or absolute.[18] Nevertheless, some Buddhists moved in this direction, by suggesting that *sunyata* is somehow generative of the phenomenal display. This interpretation may be traced to the fact that the Sanskrit word *sunyata* is derived from a term meaning "to swell." Something that looks swollen is hollow or empty inside. One commentator has noted that "this relationship is made still clearer by the fact that the mathematical symbol for zero was originally none other than the symbol for *sunyata*."[19] Swelling also calls to mind pregnancy, a fact that suggests reading *sunyata* as a somehow the ultimate generative source that, because it transcends all conditions, cannot be said either to cause or *not* to cause anything. Commentators sometimes speak of absolute nothingness – which transcends the polarities of being and nonbeing, cause and effect, subject and object, time and eternity, finitude and infinity – as the groundless ground. This view of *sunyata* became important in Chinese Buddhism, influenced as it was by the notion of the Tao as the groundless ground.

The doctrine of the radical emptiness of all forms, derived from the doctrine of dependent co-production, suggests that every form, every phenomenon, has equal worth. Since there are no essences, there is no hierarchy of phenomenal reality; hence, no one thing is subordinate to or lesser than any other. Each thing is uniquely itself, like a particular jewel reflecting the play of all other jewels in the cosmic phenomenal play. Insight into the interdependency of all things reveals the falsehood of anthropocentrism: humans are not radically different from or better than other beings, but instead are moments in the play of phenomena.

If all things are internally related, there is no internal substance or core of entities, including humans. Human suffering (*dukha*) arises because people posit and identify with a substantial, unchanging ego at the core of the flux of experience.

---

[16] See David Loy's excellent book, *Nonduality: A Study in Comparative Philosophy* (New Haven: Yale University Press, 1988).

[17] For this point, I am indebted to David Loy.

[18] David Loy, personal communication.

[19] Hans Waldenfels, *Absolute Nothingness: Foundations for a Buddhist–Christian Dialogue*, trans. J. W. Heisig (New York: Paulist Press, 1980), 19.

By identifying with this supposedly permanent self, we enter into the state of ignorance known as subject–object dualism. Such dualism is characterized by craving, aversion, and delusion, which combine to produce suffering. From one perspective, of course, there do seem to be individual things (including the ego) that are apparently connected by causal relationships. Hence, we speak of the laws of cause and effect at work among entities. From another perspective, however, as David Loy points out, "every moment and experience is momentary, uncaused because an end in itself, complete and lacking nothing."[20] Nothing here causes something else to happen there. Attempts to explain how anything – including the self or the cosmos – "originates" fail to comprehend the radicality of dependent co-production. There is not even a process that causes one to enter into illusion and suffering, nor can one do anything to free oneself from illusion, for illusion already *is* enlightenment. There is no better "place" at which one should hope to arrive. Ultimately, there is no difference between *nirvana* and *samsara* insofar as both are conditioned and hence empty of self or own-being. That is, form is emptiness, emptiness is form. Recognition of this fact is said to be the source of the extraordinary laughter that often accompanies *satori*, laughter that occurs when one apprehends that all attempts to transcend the phenomenal world in order to become enlightened are profoundly misguided. The longed-for *nirvana* is not other than the world of everyday life, although theoretical constructs prevent us from directly apprehending this liberating insight.

According to Buddhism, Gautama Buddha opposed the traditional doctrine of the Upanishads and Vedas, according to which eternal Atman, the unchanging Divine Self, permeates and sustains things by constituting their ultimate essence, their true "self." For the Vedantic tradition, suffering ends only when one overcomes dualism by ceasing to cling to the illusory ego and identifying instead with the Absolute Self; for Mahayana Buddhism, suffering ends only when one overcomes dualism by

ceasing to cling to the illusory ego and recognizing that there is no Absolute Self either. The conception of Buddhism as a life-denying tradition may be attributed to those adherents of Hinayana Buddhism who conceived of *nirvana*, the cessation of suffering, as being possible only for those few individuals who followed the arduous process of deconstructing the ego, encountering its emptiness, and thereby transcending the illusions of the world of appearance. Mahayana Buddhism affirms the possibility of and the need for saving *all* beings, since all "beings" are internally related – hence, the increasingly active role played by Mahayana Buddhists in the movement to protect nature from human abuse.[21]

The Relation between Heidegger's Thought and Mahayana Buddhism

Heidegger's thought is close to that of Mahayana Buddhism, particularly Zen, in several respects. First, both maintain that inauthenticity or suffering arises from conceiving of oneself in a constricted manner: as an isolated ego craving security, avoiding pain, and seeking distraction. Both maintain that the self is not a thing, but rather the openness or nothingness in which the incessant play of phenomena can occur. Both criticize the dualistic view of the self as a cogitating ego standing apart from the "external" world. Both emphasize that the un-self-conscious nature of everyday practices reveals that people are not separate from things, but are rather directly involved with them. Human hands, diapers, the baby being cleaned up, the mixed feelings of aversion and affection – all these are moments of the same phenomenal event. No particular moment is privileged.

Second, Heidegger's thought is in some ways consistent with the *Heart Sutra's* teaching that form is emptiness and emptiness is form. The proximity of this statement to Heidegger's notion that being and nothingness "are" virtually the same, helps to explain why Buddhist-influenced Japanese thinkers have been so attracted to

---

20   David Loy, personal communication.
21   See Allan Hunt Badiner, ed., *Dharma Gaia* (Berkeley: Parallax Press, 1990), and Mary Evelyn Tucker and Duncan Ryuken Williams, eds, *Buddhism and Ecology* (Cambridge, MA: Harvard University Press, 1996).

Heidegger's thought. Central to such comparisons, however, is the similarity between *sunyata* (emptiness) and *das Nichts* (nothingness). According to Nagarjuna, as we have seen, emptiness refers to the fact that all phenomena are empty of self (*atman*) or substance. Later Buddhists, however, suggested that absolute emptiness had generative ontological significance beyond the *anatman* doctrine. Such views of *sunyata* as the generative "clear light" bear resemblance to Heidegger's idea that nothingness refers to the temporal clearing in which appearing (being) takes place. Neither being nor clearing are entities, but instead constitute the conditions necessary for the possibility for things to manifest *themselves*. Despite differences between later Heidegger and Mahayana Buddhism, both suggest that things are in an important sense self-luminous. They arise and disappear not merely within, but *as* the absolutely clear light of no-thingness. Form or being is not other than emptiness or nothingness; the known is not other than the knower. Absolute non-duality constitutes ultimate realization.

Third, both Heidegger and the Zen tradition maintain that once one is released from the constricted self-understanding associated with dualistic egocentrism, other people and things in the world no longer appear as radically separate and threatening, but instead as profoundly interrelated phenomena. Surrendering one's constricted ego-identity, and thus moving beyond dualism, enables one to become the compassion (Buddhism) or care (Heidegger) that one always already is. "Authenticity" (Heidegger) and "enlightenment" (Buddhism), then, result from the insight into nondualism, the fact that there are "not two," neither an ego-mind here nor objects there.

There is a difference between Heidegger's early and later idea of authenticity. Early Heidegger maintained that the moment of authenticity required resoluteness, a decision to allow human temporality to transform itself into a more radical openness for the self-manifesting of things. Later Heidegger, however, played down the voluntaristic dimension discernible in resoluteness

and conceived of authenticity in terms of *Gelassenheit*, releasement from will. Interestingly, similarities between these two ways of conceiving of authenticity – as resoluteness and as releasement – are detectable in the Rinzai and the Soto Zen traditions, respectively.[22] Rinzai Zen emphasizes resoluteness in the face of the ego's resistance to transformation, while Soto Zen maintains that enlightenment can never be willed but can only be cultivated by learning to "let things be" in everyday life. The differences between the voluntarism of early Heidegger and Rinzai Zen, on the one hand, and the "letting be" of later Heidegger and Soto Zen, on the other, should not obscure their shared belief that enlightenment involves becoming the nothingness that we already are, such that we are open for and responsive to the phenomena that show up moment by moment in everyday life.

While maintaining that one can never *resolve* to become authentic or enlightened, however, both later Heidegger and the Soto Zen master suggest that spiritual practices may help put one in the position of a paradoxical willingness not to will thereby preparing one for the releasement that brings one into the world appropriately for the first time. While we may be familiar with the Zen emphasis on sitting meditation, proper breathing, and working with paradoxical koans, we may be somewhat less familiar with later Heidegger's claim that releasement may be cultivated by meditative practices, by proper breathing, and by contemplating paradoxical questions (Heideggerean "koans"). All of these practices are designed to bring one to the utter silence and stillness needed to become attuned to the openness or nothingness pervading all things.[23]

Fourth, Heidegger and Buddhism emphasize the importance of human existence, without thereby promoting a narrow anthropocentrism. For early Heidegger, because only human Dasein constitutes the clearing through which things can manifest themselves, only human Dasein can be authentic (*eigentlich*). Later on, however, he indicated that the clearing cannot be understood as a strictly human capacity. Instead, Dasein exists authentically insofar as it

[22]   See Zimmerman, *Eclipse of the Self*, Chap. 8.
[23]   On these issues, see my essay "Heidegger and Heraclitus on Spiritual Practice," *Philosophy Today*, 27, No. 2 (1983): 87–103.

is appropriated (*vereignet*) as a partner in the world-opening dance of the fourfold that grants to all things their appropriate place. Early Buddhism asserts that enlightenment is possible only if one has been born a human being. Mahayana Buddhism emphasizes, however, that the wisdom accompanying enlightenment simultaneously gives rise to compassion for all beings. Moreover, according to the Mahayana doctrine of Buddha nature (*tathagatagarbha*) *all* sentient beings are endowed with the possibility of attaining supreme enlightenment as Buddhas.

Fifth, both Heidegger and the Zen master suggest that, when authentic or enlightened, the individual exists beyond dualistic constraints, including those imposed by the distinction between good and evil. In many different traditions, mystics have said – in effect – "Love God, and do what you will." The danger here, of course, is that a person may transgress moral boundaries when under the illusion that he or she has become enlightened or authentic. Heidegger seems to have been gripped by such an illusion during support for National Socialism, as did many leading Japanese Zen masters during their support of Japanese nationalism and militarism leading up to World War II.[24] Zeal for the mystical ideal of anarchy,[25] which allegedly brings forth boundless compassion, must be tempered by insight into humanity's enormous capacity for self-delusion.

Despite similarities, there are also important differences between Heidegger's thought and Mahayana Buddhism. Members of Japan's famous Kyoto school, such as Keiji Nishitani[26] and Masao Abe,[27] have offered the most extensive Buddhist discussions of the limits of Heidegger's thought. Nishitani and Abe are interested in Heidegger partly because his rigorous meditation

upon nothingness may help to galvanize a Zen tradition that has become intellectually flabby. If Zen practitioners are willing to learn from Heidegger, however, Nishitana and Abe also suggest that Western proponents of his thought learn from Zen experience regarding the futility of metaphysical speculation.

Masao Abe argues that Heidegger, despite his interest in nothingness, never arrived at absolute nothingness because even his meditative thinking was still too connected with the metaphysical tradition.[28] Presumably, in the Zen Buddhist tradition someone truly enlightened would no longer think, even in Heidegger's meditative manner, but would instead live a life without goal or purpose, although a life of profound compassion as well. Heidegger's continued insistence on the importance of thinking also differentiates him from Meister Eckhart. As Rciner Schürmann points out, "For Meister Eckhart *geläzenheit* as an attitude of man refers to thought only secondarily. Primarily it is a matter of a way of life – a life without representation of ends and purposes."[29]

According to Masao Abe, what follows the direct experience of absolute nothingness may be called Non-thinking to distinguish it from the usual opposition between thinking and non-thinking. Despite his critique of Heidegger's adherence to thinking, Masao Abe warns that

because of its standpoint of Non-thinking, Zen has in fact not fully realized the positive and creative aspects of thinking and their significance which have been especially developed in the West. Logic and scientific cognition based on substantive objective thinking, and moral principles and ethical realization based on Subjective practical thinking, have been very

---

[24]   See James W. Heisig and John C. Maraldo, eds, *Rude Awakenings: Zen, the Kyoto School, and the Question of Nationalism* (Honolulu: University of Hawaii Press, 1994), and Brian A. Victoria, *Zen at War* (New York and Tokyo: Weatherhill, 1997).

[25]   In his book *Heidegger on Being and Acting: From Principles to Anarchy*, trans. Christine-Marie Gros (Bloomington: Indiana University Press, 1987), Schürmann draws from Heidegger's writings the possibility of an anarchistic life, a life led "without why."

[26]   Keiji Nishitani, *Religion and Nothingness*, trans. Jan Van Bragt (Berkeley and Los Angeles: University of California Press, 1982).

[27]   Masao Abe, *Zen and Western Thought*, ed. William R. LaFleur (Honolulu: University of Hawaii Press, 1985).

[28]   Ibid., p. 119.

[29]   Schürmann, *Meister Eckhart*, p. 204.

conspicuous in the West. In contrast to this, some of these things have been vague or lacking in the world of Zen. [Hence, Zen's] position in Not-thinking always harbours the danger of degenerating into mere not thinking.[30]

Masao Abe charges that in spite of Heidegger's talk of nothingness, his emphasis on human existence "does not necessarily lead him to the completely dehomocentric, cosmological dimension alone in which the impermanence of all beings in the universe is fully realized."[31] Heidegger's own student, Karl Löwith, also argued that his mentor remained trapped within an anthropocentrism that blinded him to the cosmocentrism of ancient Greek thinkers such as Heraclitus.[32] Nevertheless, later Heidegger's notion of the "event of appropriation" (Ereignis), which gathers mortals together into the luminous cosmic dance with gods, earth, and sky, bears important similarities to Buddhism's dependent coproduction and Lao Tsu's tao, both of which are nonanthropocentric. Ereignis, sun-yata. tao: these may be different names for the acausal, spontaneous arising and mutually appropriating play of phenomena. In suggesting that Ereignis "gives" time and being, however, Heidegger opens himself to the criticism that he is inventing a metaphysics of nothingness. Nevertheless, Dogen (1200–53 AD), founder of Zen's Soto sect, analyzed the temporality of nothingness in a way that has significant affinities both with early Heidegger's notion or temporality as the "clearing" for presencing and with later Heidegger's notion of the mutually appropriative play of appearances.[33]

Another apparent difference between Ereignis and sunyata is that the former supposedly "sends" the different modes of presencing that have shaped Western history in its Greek, Roman, medieval, modern, and technological eras.[34]

Some Mahayana Buddhists think that Ereignis, understood in this manner, becomes a metaphysical category inconsistent with Heidegger's non-dualism. One could reply in a number of ways.[35] First, instead of interpreting sunyata to mean simply that all things are empty of own-being or self, some Mahayanists themselves – despite Nagarjuna's warning – have turned sunyata into a metaphysical category, for example, the generative matrix for all phenomena. Other Buddhists, however, largely avoided such metaphysical tendencies and succeeded in interpreting sunyata as absolute non-duality. Second, precisely because Mahayana lacks the conceptual resources needed to confront planetary technology, Nishitani and other members of the Kyoto school looked to Heidegger's thought for insight into an alternative to the technological understanding of the being of beings. [...]

Conclusion

The foregoing remarks do not purport to offer an exhaustive treatment of the complexities involved in laying out parallel themes in Heidegger and Mahayana Buddhism. Comparisons of modern Western philosophy and Buddhism are difficult not only because of significant differences in language and culture, but also because of differences in motivation. Whereas modern Western thought is typically motivated by knowledge as an end in itself, Buddhism's primary motivation is soteriological, that is, to help make all sentient beings happy. For Buddhism, philosophical reflection occurs in the service of a transformational process. Starting with Plato and going through the of the European middle ages, Western philosophy, too, was often implicitly or explicitly aligned with transformation and soteriological goals. These aims are still

30   Masao Abe, *Zen and Western Thought*, pp. 119–20.
31   Ibid., p. 67.
32   See, e.g., Karl Löwith, "Zu Heideggers Seinsfrage: Die Natur des Menschen und die Welt der Natur," *Aufsätze und Vorträge, 1930–1970* (Stuttgart: W. Kohlhammer, 1971), pp. 189–203.
33   On this topic, see Steven Heine, *Existential and Ontological Dimensions of Time in Heidegger and Dogen* (Albany: State University of New York Press, 1985). While his book is informative, Heine sometimes promotes Dogen's views at the expense of Heidegger's.
34   See Charles Wei-hsun Fu, "The Trans-onto-theo-logical Foundations of Language in Heidegger and Taoism," *Journal of Chinese Philosophy*, 1 (1975): 130–61.
35   See, e.g., Nishitani, *Religion and Nothingness*, Chap. 6.

discernible in the work of thinkers such as Descartes, Spinoza, Hegel, and Nietzsche. By the twentieth century, however, these aims were increasingly displaced, as philosophy conceived of itself as a kind of science. Heidegger, too, was influenced by Husserl's intention to make philosophy a "rigorous science." With his notions of authenticity and releasement, however, Heidegger also renewed the transformational goal of Western philosophy. This fact explains why he is regarded with suspicion on the part of many contemporary Western philosophers, and with interest on the part of Asian Buddhist philosophers. Whether Western philosophy will regain an interest in how philosophy can shed light on leading the good life remains to be seen.

Li and the A-theistic Religiousness of Classical Confucianism

Roger T. Ames

Classical confucianism is at once a-theistic and profoundly religious. It is a religion without a God, a religion that affirms the cumulative human experience itself. Confucianism celebrates the way in which the process of human growth and extension both is shaped by and contributes to the meaning of the totality – what I will call human "co-creativity." In the classical literature the process of "co-creativity" has many related expressions (*ren, junzi, shengren, shen, he, zhongyong*), but in all cases it is, to use John Dewey's expression, "doing and undergoing" in the effort to get the most out of one's experiences.

There are several profound differences between this kind of religiousness and that of the Abrahamic traditions that have defined the meaning of religion in the Western cultural experience. In this essay, I will argue that, unlike the "worship" model, which defers to the ultimate meaning of some temporally prior, independent, external agency – what Friedrich Schleiermacher has called "absolute dependence" – Confucian religious experience is itself a *product* of the flourishing community, where the quality of the religious life is a direct consequence of the quality of communal living. Religion is not the root of the flourishing community, not the foundation on which it is built, but rather is its product, its flower.

A second important distinction is that Confucian religiousness is neither salvific nor eschatological. While it does entail a kind of transformation, this is specifically a transformation of the quality of one's life in the ordinary business of the day.

The definition of this "a-theistic," *li*-centered religiousness that I will attempt to elicit from the *Analects* and from its even more explicit statement in the *Zhongyong* will challenge both the familiar "Heaven (*tian*)"-centered "christianized" interpretation of classical Confucianism and the default claim that Confucianism is merely a secular humanism. This discussion is particularly relevant to our contemporary world, I believe, because it provides us with a sophisticated example of a kind of nontheistic religious "humanism," or better, "naturalism," that was advanced with little success by an American movement that included Felix Adler, Curtis W. Reese, Charles Francis Potter, and John Dewey early in the twentieth century. These philosophers believed that recent developments in human culture and in the sciences in particular, have placed humanity at a crossroads, making the supernatural dimensions of religious practices such as a theistic "God" not only obsolete but degrading, thus requiring a wholesale revisioning of religious sensibilities

"A-theistic Religiousness of Classical Confucianism" by Roger T. Ames, in *Confucian Spirituality*, Vol. 1 (New York: Crossroad Press, 2003), pp. 165–78; 180–2.

that celebrates the unqualified value of the human community. The failure of this religious humanism to win an audience was as much due to the vagaries that attended its articulation as it was to the inability of a population with allegiance to the supernaturalism of the dominant theistic religions to hear this new message. Perhaps the classical Chinese experience will enable us to understand better these religious reformers.

To bring classical Confucian religiousness into focus, I will begin by distinguishing the Confucian sense of "co-creativity" (*zhongyong*) – getting the most out of one's experience – from "creation-as-power" as it has been largely understood within the context of those religions that appeal to a transcendent, supernatural source of meaning. This fundamental distinction between "creativity" and "power" will enable us to generate an alternative vocabulary for Confucian religiousness and to understand better how ordinary human experience – ritualized living through the roles and relationships of family and community – can be the creative source of intense religious experience. I will explore the way in which the process of *li*, as a dynamic social grammar, not only locates but also creates meaningful human beings that are able to live profoundly religious lives. *Li*, I will claim, is quite literally the process of human "education" that "extends" otherwise inchoate persons into thriving centers of spiritual experience.

Creativity versus Power

David Hall appeals to the *wu*-form Daoist sensibilities (*wuwei*, *wuzhi*, and *wuyu*) in his attempt to bring the very recent Whiteheadian process notion of "creativity" into clearer focus:

... "creativity" is a notion that can be characterized only in terms of self-actualization. Unlike power relationships that require that tensions among component elements be resolved in favor of one of the components, in relations

defined by creativity there is no otherness, no separation or distancing, nothing to be overcome.[1]

Such a definition of "creativity" cannot be reconciled with absolutist religious doctrines that appeal to determination by external agency. In fact, Hall worries over what he takes to be a persistent confusion that has attended all but the most recent thinking about religious experience within the *creatio ex nihilo* doctrines familiar to the Western religious culture: "*Creatio ex nihilo*, as it is normally understood, is in fact the paradigm of all power relationships since the 'creative' element of the relation is completely in control of its 'other,' which is in itself literally *nothing*."[2] It is this "power" relationship that introduces an ontological distinction between reality and appearance, the One and the many – a distinction that reduces "creativity" to "power" (in the sense of the power of one thing to determine another), and, in so doing, precludes the very possibility of "creativity" as self-actualization. As Zarathustra says: "What would it then mean to create, if there were – gods!"[3]

This "power/creativity" distinction is what for Steve Owen is at stake in his reluctance to use the English word "poem" to translate *shi*:

If we translate *shih* [*shi*] as "poem," it is merely for the sake of convenience. *Shih* is not a "poem"; *shih* is not a "thing made" like in the same way one makes a bed or a painting or a shoe. A *shih* can be worked on, polished, and crafted; but that has nothing to do with what a *shih* fundamentally "is.". . . *Shih* is not the "object" of its writer; it *is* the writer, the outside of an inside.[4]

Owen's point is that a poem is not artistic "power" creating something other than itself; it is a creative process of self-actualization. Owen would dissociate *shi* from Aristotle's "productive science (*poietikē technē*)" – the lowest of the sciences, actually, of which "poetics" is his example par excellence.

[1]   See David L. Hall, *Uncertain Phoenix*, 249. See a more recent discussion of these ideas in David L. Hall and Roger T. Ames, *Thinking from the Han*.
[2]   Hall, *Uncertain Phoenix*, 249.
[3]   *Thus Spake Zarathustra* II, 2, trans. Graham Parkes in Ken Nishitani, *The Self-Overcoming of Nihilism*, 49.
[4]   Stephen Owen, *Readings in Chinese Literary Thought*, 27 [. . .].

In the end, it is only a process of "co-creativity" in which ontological distinctions are abandoned in favor of cosmological parity among all things, and in which the unique particular and its environments are seen as mutually shaping, that can be meaningfully construed as "creativity." Said another way, "creativity" is always "co-creativity" since there can be no creativity that is not a transactional, processive, and cooperative endeavor. In fact, this process notion of creativity as a spontaneously emerging novelty is such a recent development in Western philosophical thinking that it is not until the 1971 "Dictionary Supplement" to the *Oxford English Dictionary* that this hallowed record of Western civilization includes this new entry, with two of its three illustrations directing the curious reader explicitly to Whitehead's *Religion in the Making* (1926).

By contrast, in the noncosmogonic traditions of China – Confucianism as well as Daoism – this notion of "co-creativity" is a familiar if not the defining sensibility. In Daoism, it is captured in the notion of "non-coercive action (*wuwei*)," and in Confucianism it has many expressions. For example, in the *Analects*:

Authoritative persons establish others in seeking to establish themselves and promote others in seeking to get there themselves. Correlating one's conduct with those near at hand can be said to be the method of becoming an authoritative person (*ren*). (6:30)

The Co-creativity (*Cheng*) of the Unique Narrative

Cheng – "co-creativity" – is most often translated as "sincerity" or "integrity." The notion of integrity can have at least two very different meanings that are corollary to the power/creativity distinction. The first belongs to objects as integers in the creativity-as-power worldview. The second refers to the persistence and continuity of changing events within the co-creativity model as they shape and are shaped by their circumstances. As such, it is at once integrity and "integration."

In the absence of the two-world reality/appearance distinction, the classical Chinese tradition does not generate the dualistic worldview necessary to sponsor the notion of the real as the *objective*. Without this notion of *objectivity* that provides a perspective outside of "objects" and thus creates them as objects (they "object"), there can only be a stream of passing circumstances. Without *objectivity*, objects dissolve into the flux and flow, the changefulness of our surroundings. They are not objects but events, and as events they are continuous with other events, thus dissolving into the transactional processes of our experience. A deobjectified, defactualized discourse is the language of process, and to speak and hear that language is to experience the flow of things.

In a world of objects defined as integers by their endowed essences, integrity is the self-same identical characteristic shared by natural kinds that makes each of them one-of-a-*kind*. They are thus meaningful in themselves.

Cheng, then, is the process analogue of this notion of essence defined by the uniqueness and persistence of the constitutive relationships that define a particular "event." "Event" is a more felicitous term than "object" or "thing" because it suggests that such experiences are *one-of-a-kind* and that, in this world, their meaning is something achieved in their relationships. The *Zhongyong* speaks to this question directly:

Co-creativity [*cheng*] is self-realizing [*zicheng*], and its way [*dao*] is self-advancing [*zidao*]. Co-creativity is an event [*wu*] taken from its beginning to its end, and without this co-creativity, there are no events. It is thus that, for exemplary persons [*junzi*] it is co-creativity that is prized. But co-creativity is not simply the self-realization of one's own person; it is what realizes events. Realizing oneself is authoritative conduct [*ren*]; realizing events is wisdom [*zhi*]. This is the excellence [*de*] of one's natural tendencies and is the way of integrating what is more internal and what is more external. Thus, whenever one applies this excellence, it is fitting. (25)

There is no genetic fallacy entailed by *cheng*, in which there is assumed to be some essential and unchanging element that persists throughout the narrative of any particular. Co-creativity is the coherence of the narrative itself – its persistence and continuity – as it shapes and is shaped by its ever-changing context.

Translating this metaphysical distinction into more concrete terms, the tendency of philosophy to reify human nature and assume it to be ready-made is challenged by human nature as process, an aggregate of human experience. The basis of community is not a metaphysically identical, ready-made mind, but rather a "functional" or "instrumental" inchoate heart-mind (*xin*) expressed in the language of relations that, through communication, produces the aims, beliefs, aspirations, and knowledge necessary to establish the like-mindedness of effective community. Human realization is achieved not by wholehearted participation in communal life forms but by life in community that forms one wholeheartedly.

This idea of constructing the mind out of social transactions and effective communication suggests a further dimension of *cheng* that is not expressed fully by the translation "integrity," and is not made explicit in the translation "co-creativity." As we know, an alternative, perhaps more familiar rendering of *cheng* is "sincerity." The virtue of the term "sincerity" is that it describes a commitment to one's purposes, a quality of action, a solemn affirmation of one's process of self-actualization, a Confucian statement of *amor fati*.

Zhongyong as Staying Centered in Familiar Affairs

In addition to *ren*, another one of the early Confucian expressions for this "co-creativity" on which I have chosen to focus in this essay is *zhongyong*, which first appears in *Analects* 6:29:

The Master said, "The excellence born of staying centered in familiar affairs is of the highest order. It is rare among the people to be able to sustain it for long."

Given the processional and aggregating nature of our narratives as human beings, it is incumbent upon the person who would flourish in the world that appropriate adjustments be made *mutatis mutandis* along the way. In fact, it is the sustained attention to achieving equilibrium by staying centered in the familiar affairs of one's life that leads ultimately to religious experience and

pays off in religious dividends. Equilibrium (*zhong*) – the studied ability to remain centered within those natural, social, and cultural environments that both contextualize and constitute one – is productive of a thriving harmony (*he*) achieved through patterns of deference. And as one becomes increasingly extended in the world through these patterns of deference, this centeredness enables one ultimately to become a co-creator of cosmic proportions in the nurturing processes of the heavens and the earth:

> When equilibrium [*zhong*] and harmony [*he*] are fully realized, the heavens and earth maintain their proper places and all things flourish in the world. . . . Only those in the world of the utmost co-creativity are able to separate out and braid together the many threads on the great loom of the world. Only they set the great root of the world and realize the transforming and nourishing processes of heaven and earth.
>> How could there be anything on which they depend?
>> So earnest, they are authoritative [*ren*];
>> So profound, they are a bottomless abyss [*yuan*];
>> So pervasive, they are *tian* [*tian*]. (*Zhongyong* 2 and 32)

The Process of Education: *Educere* or *Educare*?

The growth and extension that occur within these patterns of deference are the product of education. The etymology of the English word "educate" provides us with a useful distinction that is again corollary to the power/creativity distinction. It can mean *educare*, "to cultivate, to rear, to bring up," suggesting growth in the sense of a process of discovery, the actualizing of a given potential, where the role of teacher, like Meno's Socrates, is only catalytic to something already there. However, "educate" can also mean *educere*, "to educe, elicit, evoke, lead forth, draw out," a collaborative effort on the part of *this* mentor and *this* student in which there is a focus on the particular conditions of the relationship, and their creative possibilities. While the first sense is perhaps more familiar in Western usage, appealing as it does to the articulation of ideal types, the second sense gives us "to educe" in the sense of assisting in "extending one's way" through a process of modeling and emulation that must be tailored to one's own specific conditions:

In striving to be authoritative in your conduct, do not yield even to your teacher. (*Analects* 15:36)

Education so construed is a transactional process that entails both continuity and creativity – the growth of both *this* able teacher and *that* able student. It is this sense of education that is captured in the *Zhongyong*'s expression an "advancing pathway (*dadao*)" (*Zhongyong* 1 and 20).

A classic statement that illustrates this second meaning of "leading forth" and "extending the way" is *Analects* 9:11, a wonderful passage in which Yan Hui recounts the process through which he is being led forward by Confucius one step at a time, creating his way in the very walking:

Yan Hui, with a deep sigh, said, "The more I look up at it, the higher it soars; the more I penetrate into, the harder it becomes. I am looking at it in front of me, and suddenly it is behind me. The Master is good at drawing me forward a step at a time; he broadens me with culture (*wen*) and disciplines my behavior through the observance of ritual propriety (*li*). Even if I wanted to quit, I could not. And when I have exhausted my abilities, it is as though something rises up right in front of me, and even though I want to follow it, there is no road to take."

The Family as Governing Metaphor

The family as an institution, and the nexus of ritualized roles and relationships that define it (*li*), provides the model for this optimizing process of making one's way by both giving and getting the most out of the human experience.

Exemplary persons (*junzi*) concentrate their efforts on the root, for the root having taken hold, the way (*dao*) will grow therefrom. As for filial and fraternal responsibility, it is, I suspect, the root of authoritative conduct (*ren*). (*Analects* 1.2)

The assumption is that persons are more likely to give themselves utterly and unconditionally to their families than to any other human institution. Promoting the centrality of family relations is an attempt to assure that entire persons without remainder are invested in each of their actions.

The power of the family to function as the radial locus for human growth is much enhanced when natural family and communal relations are not perceived as being in competition with, a distraction from, or dependent on some higher supernatural relations. It is from the family expanding outward that persons emerge as objects of profound communal, cultural, and ultimately religious deference. Beyond the achievement of an intense religious quality felt in the everyday experience of their lives, these exemplary persons emerge as ancestors for their families and communities, and as contributors to the ancestral legacy – *tian* – that defines Chinese culture more broadly construed.

The etymology of the Chinese term most often translated as "education" or "teaching" (*jiao*), is also suggestive, focusing the process of education squarely within the family context. According to the *Shuowen*, "education [*jiao*]" "is what the elders dispense and on which the juniors model," with the two elements of the character itself being explained as "those above providing culture [*wen*] with those below responding with filiality [*xiao*]." It should not go unnoticed that this same term *jiao* came to carry strong religious connotations early in the tradition, especially in its associations with both religious Daoism (*daojiao*) and Confucianism (*rujiao*) as a state ideology.

Speaking generally, it is the patterns of deference that make up the family itself and the appropriate transactions among its members that give rise to, define, and authorize the specific ritualized roles and relationships (*li*) through which the process of refinement is pursued. As *Zhongyong* 20 explains:

The degree of love due different kin and the graduated esteem due those who are qualitatively different in their character is what gives rise to the observance of ritual propriety (*li*).

What makes these ritualized roles and relationships fundamentally different from rules or laws

is the fact that not only must they be personalized, but the quality of the particular person
invested in these *li* is the ultimate criterion of their
efficacy.

The Process and Content of Education

In our recent translation of the Dingzhou
Analects, Henry Rosemont and I began our discussion of *li* with the following disclaimer:

> Perhaps the greatest obstacle to understanding
> what *li* means in the world of Confucius is
> thinking that "ritual" is a familiar dimension of
> our own world, and [that] ... we [thus] fully
> understand what it entails. (52)

The *Shuowen* lexicon defines *li* paronomasti-
cally as *lu*, "to tread a path." In reading the
Analects, there is a tendency to give short shrift
to the middle books 9–11, which are primarily a
series of intimate snapshots depicting the historical person Confucius. Yet it is precisely these
passages that are most revealing of the extent to
which the appropriate behaviors of a scholar-
official participating in the daily life of the court
were choreographed: the slightest gesture, the
cut of one's clothes, the cadence of one's stride,
one's posture and facial expression, one's tone of
voice, even the rhythm of one's breathing:

> On passing through the entrance way to the
> Duke's court, he would bow forward from the waist,
> as though the gateway were not high enough.
> While in attendance, he would not stand in the
> middle of the entranceway; on passing through,
> he would not step on the raised threshold. On
> passing by the empty throne, his countenance
> would change visibly, his legs would bend, and
> in his speech he would seem to be breathless. He
> would lift the hem of his skirts in ascending the
> hall, bow forward from the waist, and hold in his
> breath as though ceasing to breathe. On leaving
> and descending the first steps, he would relax his
> expression and regain his composure. He would
> glide briskly from the bottom of the steps, and
> returning to his place, he would resume a rev-
> erent posture. (*Analects* 10:4)

From this passage and many others like it, it
should be clear that *li* do not reduce to generic,

formally prescribed "rites" and "rituals," performed at stipulated times to announce status and
to punctuate the seasons of one's life. The *li* are
more, much more. The performance of *li* must
be understood in light of the uniqueness of each
participant and the profoundly aesthetic project
of becoming a person. *Li* is a process of personal
refinement – an achieved disposition, an attitude,
a posture, a signature, an identity. Entailing the
cognate notions of proper, appropriate, propriety, "a making one's own," *li* is a resolutely
personal performance revealing one's worth to
oneself and one's community. *Li* is both a personal and a public discourse through which one
constitutes and reveals oneself qualitatively as a
unique individual, a whole person. Importantly,
there is no respite; *li* requires the utmost attention in every detail of what one does at every
moment that one is doing it, from the drama of
the high court to the posture one assumes in going
to sleep, from the reception of different guests to
the proper way to comport oneself when alone;
from how one behaves in formal dining situations
to appropriate one-off extemporaneous gestures.
One expression of the intensity of this attention
is *shen qi du*:

> It is for this reason that exemplary persons
> (*junzi*) are so cautious about what is not seen,
> and so anxious about what is not heard. It is
> because there is nothing more present than
> what is hidden, and nothing more manifest than
> what is inchoate that exemplary persons are
> ever circumspect in their uniqueness.

Li is at once cognitive and aesthetic, moral and
religious, physical and spiritual. It is singular as
the narrative of this specific person, Confucius,
and plural as the many consummate events that
make up the business of the day. *Li* are learned
patterns of deference performed individually
and elegantly. They are value-revealing life forms
that attract emulation and inspire religious
devotion, fostering the like-mindedness necessary for a flourishing community. The cognate
relationship between *li* and *ti*, from high religious
performance to its physical embodiment, from *tian*
to *di*, suggests the pervasiveness of *li* in the particular human experience. In the absence of a
ready-made essence, a human being is ultimately
an aggregate of experience, and *li* is a medium that

ensures that this cumulative experience is refined and substantial.[5]

Growth and Extension

The life of *li* is a process of continuing growth and extension. One amplifies the scope and intensity of one's experience through sustaining a steady equilibrium in the process of advancing one's way on the journey of life, a life informed by and performed ceremoniously within the familiar bonds of *li*.

Most of the terms invoked to describe Confucian religious experience connote this process of growth and extension explicitly. For example, as we have seen, productive familial relations are the "root (*ben*)" whence one's way (*dao*) advances (*Analects* 1:2; see also *Zhongyong* 1.29, 32, and esp. 17). The repeated contrast between the exemplary person (*junzi*) and the petty person (*xiaoren*), the inclusiveness of appropriateness (*yi*) as opposed to the exclusiveness of personal benefit (*li*), and the emergence of the authoritative person (*ren*) from individuated persons (*ren*) and from the common masses (*min*) – all of these expressions entail growth and extension through patterns of deference. Even the term "spirituality" itself, *shen*, crosses the divide between "human spirituality" and "divinity," between "human clairvoyance" and the "mysteries." *Shen* is itself cognate with the terms "to extend, to prolong (*shen*)."

The metaphors used to describe those ancestors and cultural heroes who have become "god-like" are frequently celestial – "the sun and moon," "the heavens," "the north star," and so on, expressing in a figurative way the familiar assumption that there is a "continuity between the human being and the ancestral realm (*tianren heyi*)." For example,

> Zhongni [Confucius] . . . is comparable to the heavens and the earth, sheltering and supporting everything that is. He is comparable to the progress of the four seasons, and the alternating brightness of the sun and moon. (*Zhongyong* 30;

see also *Analects* 2:1; 19:21, 23, 24, 25)

The intensity of such religious experience is the measure of one's personal growth; it is the creative elaboration of oneself within one's narrative that is the source of one's religious experience.

Harmonized *Qing* as a Confucian *Amor Fati*

The motive, self-affirming aspect in this process of self-actualization is often understated. The *Zhongyong* defines harmony itself as the achievement of proper measure in one's feelings so as to sustain equilibrium and advance one's way in the world:

> The feelings of joy and anger, of grief and pleasure, not yet having arisen is called nascent equilibrium (*zhong*); once the emotions have arisen, that they all achieve appropriate measure is called harmony (*he*). This notion of equilibrium (*zhong*) is the great root of the world; harmony then is the advancing way (*dadao*). When equilibrium and harmony are fully realized, the heavens and earth maintain their proper places and all things flourish in the world.

One term that has particular prominence in the Zisizi Confucian documents recently uncovered at Mawangdui and Guodian is *qing*. In fact, these recovered texts have not only reinstated the "emotions" as an important factor in self-actualization, but will help to resolve a longstanding dispute over the meaning of this recondite term itself.

A. C. Graham has defined *qing* as "how things and situation are in themselves, independently of how we name or describe them," as "fact," or "essentials," contending that it is Xunzi who first uses this term as "the passions."[6] In the early corpus, *qing* often appears with *xing*, "natural tendencies," and it is in this context that it seems to mean "how things are in themselves." The problem, however, has been, How can the same term mean both the facts of a situation and the

---

[5] Herb Fingarette underscores the way in which *li* becomes a medium of religious expression for Confucius (*Confucius*).

[6] See A. C. Graham, *Disputers of the Tao*, 97–100, 242–5.

emotions that attend it, both fact and value? Graham's answer, now demonstrably incorrect, is that chronologically it first meant "how things are" and only later came to mean "emotions."

A persistent feature of classical Confucianism corollary to the absence of "objectivity," is an unwillingness to separate description and prescription, reality and its interpretation. Everything is always experienced from one perspective or another, where both experiencer and experience are implicated in the event. And there is no design beyond how the sum of these particular perspectives construe their worlds. This prescriptive feature of the tradition is immediately apparent in the use of *shifei*, which means both "this/not-this" (fact), and "approve/disapprove" (value). *Qing* then is not simply "how things are in themselves" but entails the emotional character of the situation and one's role in it. Importantly, emotions are in the events themselves, not simply a response to something "other." And when these emotions are harmonious and one is fully co-creator, giving the most and getting the most out of experience, this achievement is attended by a Confucian version of *amor fati*: the unconditional affirmation of the facts of one's existence as they are. Nietzsche calls *amor fati* "my innermost nature," "height and a bird's eye view in observation."[7] Co-creativity (*cheng*) as a transactional, processive, cooperative endeavor always has the element of affirming things as they are and participating in the process of *educere*. An individual does not bring novel things out of old situations – novelty is brought out cooperatively. And as with *ziran*, "none can tell how it is so" (*Zhuangzi* 5/2/37). It is this sensibility, then, that is the stuff of religious experience.

In comparison with the other Zisizi documents, the *Zhongyong* makes such infrequent reference to *qing* that it raises the question as to whether the *Zhongyong* belongs to the same lineage. I would suggest that the relative absence of explicit reference to *qing* is because, as noted above, *cheng* has an important emotional aspect which justifies its translation as "sincerity," and is thus doing the work *of qing*.

Rethinking the *Zhongyong*

It is the extended discussion of this notion, *zhongyong* "co-creativity," that serves as an illuminating commentary on the ambiguous opening passage of the *Zhongyong*, and which, by virtue of its signal importance as the method of becoming human, gives this text its title. And one despairs at those uncritical interpretations of key philosophical terms such as *tian*, *dao*, and *xing*, conventionally translated as "Heaven," "the Way," and "inborn nature," respectively, that would construe these ideas metaphysically as fixed and determinative principles, and in so doing, vitiate precisely that notion of co-creativity which is such a basic feature of classical Chinese philosophy.

The standard rendering of the opening passage of the *Zhongyong* is a case in point. It is the translation by James Legge which itself references the earlier Jesuit translations and which most subsequent translations, both in English and modern Chinese, follow rather closely:

> What Heaven has conferred is called THE NATURE; an accordance with this nature is called THE PATH *of duty*; the regulation of this path is called INSTRUCTION.

Legge counterbalances the high estimate that the tradition has lavished on the *Zhongyong* as one of the Four Books, with his own pious reservations about it:

> It begins sufficiently well, but the author has hardly enunciated his preliminary apophthegms, when he conducts into an obscurity where we can hardly grope our way, and when we emerge from that, it is to be bewildered by his gorgeous but unsubstantial pictures of sagely perfection. He has eminently contributed to nourish the pride of his countrymen. He has exalted their sages above all that is called God or is worshipped, and taught the masses of the people that with them they have need of nothing from without. In the meantime it is antagonistic to Christianity. By-and-by, when Christianity has prevailed in China, men will

---

[7]   Friedrich Nietzsche, *Will to Power*, 520; and *Nietzsche contra Wagner*, trans. Graham Parkes, cited in Nishitani, *Self-Overcoming of Nihilism*, 50–1.

refer to it as a striking proof how their fathers by their wisdom know neither God nor themselves.[8]

What is particularly telling about Legge's evaluation here is that in spite of the overtly "Christian" interpretation he wants to give to this opening passage, he is entirely aware of the incongruency of this theistic interpretation with the human-centered thrust of the ideas conveyed in the remainder of the text. Legge's interpretation of the text, while wishing that it were otherwise, is not only that human beings have everything necessary to achieve realization without reference to some transcendent deity, but further, that the world itself is sufficiently served by human creativity that it need not appeal beyond itself for divine intervention.

We have a choice. We can follow those commentators who, under the influence of Neo-Confucianism and Christian doctrine, take this opening passage to be confounded by the text that follows from it. Or we can attempt to understand this passage in a way consistent with the philosophical thrust of the document as a whole. A more nuanced reading of this opening passage that would accommodate the commitment to co-creativity without violating the tolerance of the language might be the following:

What *tian* promotes is called natural tendencies; tutoring these natural tendencies is called advancing the way; improving this roadway is called education.

Co-creativity as Religiousness

For classical Confucianism, "religiousness" in its most fundamental sense refers to a person's attainment of a focused appreciation of the complex meaning and value of the total field of existing things through a reflexive awakening to the awesomeness of one's own participatory role as co-creator. It is only in discovering and investing in the connections among things that one becomes aware of, and adds to, the meaning of things. This "standing together" with all things is effected through an achieved and sustained equilibrium in the familiar experiences of our everyday lives that, in the absence of any coercion that would detract from their possibilities, allows for optimum creativity in every act. It is this quality of self-affirming religiousness that Confucius is referring to in reflecting on the progress of his own life:

... from fifty I realized the propensities of *tian* (*tianming*); from sixty my ear was attuned; from seventy I could give my heart-and-mind free rein without overstepping the boundaries. (*Analects* 2:4)

The vocabulary in this passage appeals to the pervasive "path (*dao*)" metaphor: striking out in a direction, taking one's place, knowing which way to go, realizing the terrain around one, following along (there has been speculation that "ear" here might be a corruption, but the Dingzhou text has this character), and then making one's way wherever one wants to go without going astray.

References

Ames, Roger T., and David L. Hall. *Focusing the Familiar: A Translation and Philosophical Interpretation of the Zhongyong*. Honolulu: University of Hawaii Press, 2001 (translations modified).

Ames, Roger T., and Henry Rosemont, Jr. *The Analects of Confucius: A Philosophical Translation*. New York: Ramdom House, 1998 (translations modified).

Fingarette, Herbert. *Confucius: The Secular as Sacred*. New York: Harper Torchbooks, 1972.

Graham, A. C. *Disputers of the Tao: Philosophical Argument in Ancient China*. Lasalle, Ill.: Open Court, 1989.

Hall, David L. *The Uncertain Phoenix*. New York: Fordham University Press, 1982.

Hall, David L., and Roger T. Ames. *Thinking from the Han: Self, Truth, and Transcendence in Chinese and Western Culture*. Albany: State University of New York Press, 1998.

Legge, James. *The Chinese Classics*, Volume 1. Hong Kong: Hong Kong University Press, 1960.

[8]   Legge, *Chinese Classics*, 1:55.

Nietzsche, Friedrich. *The Will to Power*. Translated by Walter Kaufmann and R. J. Hollingdale. New York: Vintage Books, 1968.

Nishitani, Keiji. *The Self-Overcoming of Nihilism*. Translated by Graham Parkes with Setsuko Aihara. Albany: State University of New York Press, 1990.

Owen, Stephen. *Readings in Chinese Literary Thought*. Cambridge, Mass.: Council on East Asian Studies, Harvard University, 1992.

Whitehead, A. N. *Religion in the Making*. New York: Meridian Books, 1960.

Glossary

Advaita Vedanta: a Hindu non-dual (*advaita* = "non-dual") school of thought, according to which Brahman is the only one true reality.

al-Ghazali (also Abu Hamid): influential Muslim Sufi philosopher-theologian (1058–1111), author of the *Incoherence of Philosophers*, amongst other works.

Analects: the collected sayings of Confucius (*Kongzi*).

anatman: literally, "no-self," a Buddhist term used to both deny the existence of an independently existing and unchanging self and to refer to the self as characterized by dependent co-origination.

Anselm of Canterbury: influential Christian philosopher-theologian (1033–1109), author of the *Proslogian*, amongst other works.

Aquinas, Thomas: influential Christian philosopher-theologian (1225–74), author of the *Summa Theologica*, amongst other works.

atheism: the view that there is no God as characterized in theism.

atman: literally, "self," a Hindu term for one's most essential or fundamental self – that which persists through time unchanged, despite changes occurring in one's more superficial aspects – and which is identified with Brahman in the *Upanishads*.

Augustine of Hippo: influential Christian philosopher-theologian (354–430), author of *On Christian Doctrine*, amongst other works.

Avicenna (also Ibn Sina): influential Muslim philosopher-theologian (980–1037), author of *The Book of Healing*, amongst other works.

Avverroes (also Ibn Rushd): influential Muslim philosopher-theologian (1126–98), author of *The Incoherence of the Incoherence*, amongst other works.

basic belief: a belief that is not held on the basis of other beliefs.

bodhisattva: in Mahayana Buddhism, the ideal to which one aspires – one who is motivated by compassion to postpone one's own final *nirvana* in order to foster the liberation of others.

Brahma: a Hindu deity responsible for the creation of the cosmos.

Brahman: a term first introduced in the *Upanishads* that refers to that one Ultimate Sacred Reality from which the existence of everything else derives.

brahmin: refers: (a) to the priest, since early Vedic times, who presides over sacrificial rites; and (b) to the class of people from which priests are drawn in the Hindu caste system.

buddha: literally, "one who is awake, or enlightened," a term which refers to: (a) the historical (fifth century BCE) figure Siddhartha Gautama (also known as Shakyamuni), who is regarded as the founder of Buddhism; and (b) any enlightened individual.

Confucius (also Kongzi): philosopher in ancient China (c. 551–479 BCE) whose sayings are collected in *The Analects*, the foundational text for Confucianism.

contingent existence: to say that something exists in this manner is to say that its existence depends upon something else, and that though it does exist, it might not have existed (contrasted with necessary existence).

cosmological argument: a kind of argument wherein the conclusion – God exists – is offered as the best explanation for the existence of the universe.

dao (tao): literally, "way" or "path," the term is central for all forms of Chinese philosophy originating in the ancient period, including Daoism and Confucianism.

Daodejing (also Tao-te-Ching): literally, "The Way and its Power," an early Daoist classic attributed to Laozi (Lau-tzu).

dependent co-origination: see *patitya-samutpada*.

design argument: a kind of argument wherein the conclusion – God exists – is offered as the best explanation for the fact that some aspects of the universe appear to have a function, or be purpose-serving.

dharma: a term with multiple meanings in Indian philosophy, including: (a) the law or fundamental principle underlying all else; (b) one's duty as defined by caste, sex, and stage in life; (c) the teachings of the Buddha; and (d) a fundamental constituent in the process of dependent co-origination.

dharma-kaya: in Mahayana Buddhism, the highest of the three "bodies (*tri-kaya*)," or ways in which the Buddha may be said to exist – here as formless, or non-dual Truth itself, or Emptiness (*sunyata*).

Dogen: thirteenth-century Japanese Buddhist religious philosopher, founder of the Soto school of Zen Buddhism, and author of the *Shobogenzo*, amongst other works.

dualism: a term used variously but often to assert some version of the metaphysical thesis that there are two distinct types of substance: matter and spirit (or mind).

dukkha: a term used in religions originating in ancient India (Hinduism, Buddhism, Jainism) to refer to the central human problem – that of overcoming a sense of dis-ease in the face of one's inability to achieve lasting satisfaction.

emptiness: see *sunyata*.

evidentialism: the view that one ought to believe only those things for which one has sufficient supporting evidence.

exclusivism: a position on the issue of religious diversity according to which one religious perspective is correct and that those conflicting with it are incorrect.

ex nihilo: literally, "out of nothing." Many Western theists hold that God created the cosmos in this manner, without utilizing any pre-existent material.

fallibilism: the view that certainty, or final confirmation, is elusive on most matters.

fideism: the view that religious belief rests on faith alone and thus that reason has no useful role to play in discerning religious truth.

foundationalism: the view that some properly basic beliefs serve as the rational foundation for all knowledge. In its classical forms, these beliefs are properly basic because they are either: (a) self-evident, (b) impossible to doubt, and/or (c) evident to the senses.

free will defense: a response to the logical problem of evil, according to which it is claimed that: (a) the existence of free agents is of great value; (b) that insofar as such agents are genuinely free, it is logically impossible to guarantee that they will avoid evil; and thus (c) that is logically possible that the God of theism exists, that God created free agents, and that some evil exists for which God is not responsible.

gender: sometimes used as a synonym for the sexual differentiation sense of "sex" (male/female), but more often used to refer to those socially constructed traits (masculine/feminine) often associated with being male or female.

Great Ultimate: see *taiji.*

henotheism: a form of religion which involves belief in many gods but that recognizes one deity as supreme.

hermeneutics: a philosophical approach that focuses on the role of interpretation in all human thinking and communication. Two forms are often emphasized: (a) the hermeneutics of finitude, which claims that human reflection can never extract itself from the limitations imposed by its socio-historical embeddedness; and (b) the hermeneutics of suspicion, which emphasizes the way in which personal and group interests/desires are often, if not always, reflected in one's thinking.

inclusivism: a position on the issue of religious diversity according to which those in some traditions may have grasped aspects of those central religious truths that are most accurately and completely apprehended in one tradition alone.

Ishvara: the name given to Ultimate Sacred Reality when conceived as personal Lord in the *Upanishads.*

jiva (also jivatman): the individuated soul-self that is reborn in Jain and some Hindu models of reincarnation.

junzi (also, chung-tzu): literally, "superior or noble gentleman," a Confucian term that refers to the person who has cultivated exemplary virtue.

kalam: philosophical theology in Islam.

karma (also kamma): literally, "action," refers in Indian philosophy to several aspects of the doctrine that every ego-motivated action of moral significance generates consequences for the agent who performed it. For example, the term may refer to the causal principle, or mechanism, embedded in the structure of the universe that determines the consequences of an action or to the effects experienced by the individual on the basis of his/her prior actions.

koan: literally "public case," these are anecdotes about exchanges between Chinese Zen masters and their monastic disciples that are often paradoxical in character. Once collected together, they began to be used by later Zen masters as a tool for fostering enlightenment in their own disciples.

Laozi (also Lao-tzu): the largely mythological author of the *Daodejing (Tao-te-Ching).*

li: the ritualized roles and relationships in Confucian society.

Mahayana: literally, "great vehicle," a form of Buddhism that arose several centuries after the death of the historical Buddha and one that remains popular in East Asia, emphasizing: (a) that Gautama Buddha was a manifestation of a cosmic Buddha nature; (b) the Bodhisattva ideal of realizing universal compassion in oneself; and (c) the myriad of skillful means (*upaya*) available for bringing about salvation/liberation.

materialism: the metaphysical thesis that only matter exists.

maya: the illusory or distorted appearance of things in Indian philosophy that prevents one from seeing the true nature of things.

metaphysics: inquiry into the general nature, fundamental constituents, and structure of reality.

metaphysics of presence: a phrase coined by Jacques Derrida to capture what he regarded as a misguided and pervasive ambition in the Western philosophical tradition to unite the mind with truth and reality in a pure fashion, unmediated by any possibly distorting influence.

moksha: in Hinduism, the notion of spiritual liberation from dis-ease (*dukkha*) and rebirth (*samsara*), based on enlightened awareness of one's true nature.

monism: the metaphysical view that either: (a) there is only one type of substance; and/or (b) there is only one substance.

monotheism: a form of religion that involves belief that there is but one real God. See also *theism.*

Nagarjuna: influential Mahayana Buddhist philosopher (c. 150–250), and author of *Fundamentals of the Middle Way,* amongst other works.

natural theology: the attempt to establish the existence of God and a systematic understanding of God's nature through reason alone.

necessary existence: to say that something exists in this way is to say that given its nature it could not but exist (contrasted with contingent existence). This is often said to be true of God (as conceived according to traditional theism) as well as *atman* and *Brahman*.

Neo-Confucianism: the dominant religious philosophy of China, Korea, Vietnam, and Japan from the eleventh to the nineteenth centuries, which involved a revival of and elaboration on traditional Confucian teachings concerning the self-in-society.

nihilism: the view that nothing exists or that no objective values/meaning exists.

nirguna Brahman: literally, "Brahman without qualities," this is used to refer to formless non-dual Brahman, as it exists in itself.

nirvana (also nibbana): literally, "extinction," a term referring in Buddhism both to the state of those in this life who have grasped their true nature as *anatman* and so live free from dis-ease (*dukkha*), as well as to their final liberation from rebirth (*samsara*) at the time of their death.

non-realism (or anti-realism): Generally, a view that rejects the possibility of making objectively true/false statements about a mind-independent reality. In philosophy of religion, it is a view about religious statements which involves the denial of one or both of: (a) that such statements assert something to be true or false; and/or (b) that they refer to a transcendent mind-independent Ultimate Sacred Reality.

omnibenevolent: literally, "all-good," one of the central attributes of God, according to classical Western theism.

omnipotent: literally, "all-powerful," one of the central attributes of God, according to classical Western theism.

omniscient: literally, "all-knowing," one of the central attributes of God, according to classical Western theism.

ontological argument: an argument that seeks to establish that God must exist based simply on the idea of what God is thought to be.

ontology: an area of metaphysics devoted to the study of existence, or being itself – that is, the most general and unifying characteristics shared by all things that exist.

ontotheology: a term used by Martin Heidegger for the thesis that theology became illegitimately united with ontology beginning in ancient Greece, when it was assumed that what unifies all that exists and renders it rationally intelligible must at the same time be its divine creative source.

panentheism: literally "all is in God," a view according to which the universe exists within Ultimate Sacred Reality.

pantheism: literally, "all is God." On this view, there is only one thing that truly exists: Ultimate Sacred Reality. All else – the universe itself – is an expression or manifestation of this one reality.

patitya-samupada: the Buddhist teaching that the fundamental constituents of reality are constantly changing processes (rather than substance-like things) that continually come into being and pass away because of their causal dependence on other such processes.

pluralism: a position on the issue of religious diversity according to which many (if not all) of the world religions are authentic responses to Ultimate Sacred Reality and thus that each of their religious perspectives is roughly equally true.

polytheism: a form of religion that involves belief in many gods.

properly basic belief: a basic belief that is rational to treat as such.

qi (also ch'i): literally, "material force," a term in ancient Chinese philosophy that refers to the energy circulating in the universe and associated with the breath in human beings.

Ramanuja: influential Hindu philosopher of the "Qualified Non-Dualistic" school of Vedanta (*Vivishadvaita Vedanta*) (c. 1077–c. 1157), author of the *Shri Bhashya* (a commentary on the central Vedanta scriptures), amongst other works.

reincarnation: refers to the cyclical re-embodiment of a self, as in the doctrine of *samsara* in Hinduism, Buddhism, and Jainism.

relativism: a type of view according to which justified belief or truth is determined from within a perspective – for example, that of a particular subject or a community of subjects – rather than being the sort of thing that is determined by objective factors.

religious realism: a view about religious statements, according to which they are held to: (a) assert something to be objectively true or false; (b) refer to the existence of a mind-independent transcendent Ultimate Sacred Reality; and (c) at least sometimes succeed in saying something true about the existence of an Ultimate Sacred Reality.

ren (also jen): the central virtue to be cultivated in Confucianism, involving both compassion and a concern for the moral completion of others.

resurrection: a view in some forms of Western theism whereby one's afterlife existence involves a restoration of one's embodied existence.

Saccidananda (also Sat-Chit-Ananda): a popular characterization of Ultimate Reality in Hindu philosophy – literally, "being, consciousness, bliss."

saguna Brahman: literally, "Brahman with qualities," this is used to refer to Brahman when worshiped in the form of a personal deity.

samsara: literally, "wandering across or through," it refers in Hinduism, Buddhism, and Jainism, to the realm of repeated rebirth and its accompanying experience of dis-ease (*dukkha*).

satori: Japanese Zen term for direct insight into one's true nature as emptiness (*sunyata*).

self-existent: If an individual exists in this way, then its existence does not in any way depend upon anyone or anything else. This is often attributed to God (as conceived according to traditional theism) as well as *atman* and *Brahman*.

Shankara (also Samkara): influential Hindu religious philosopher (788–820) and one of the founding figures of the Advaita Vedanta school of thought.

sheng: a Confucian term that refers to the true sage – one who has not only cultivated exemplary virtue (the *junzi*), and seeks the well-being and moral completion of others in one's circle (*ren*), but also fosters the flourishing of the multitudes.

skandhas: Buddhist term for the dependently co-originating constituents of the non-substantial self, or a*natman:* material form, sensation, perception, volitions, and consciousness.

standpoint epistemology: a theory according to which individuals inhabiting a particular socially situated perspective, or standpoint (typically that of socially marginalized groups), are said to have an epistemic advantage over those from other perspectives (typically that of socially dominant groups).

Sufism: the tradition of mysticism within Islam.

sunyata (also shunyata): literally, "emptiness," an interpretation of the Buddha's teaching of dependent co-origination (*patitya-samupada*), which emphasized that nowhere in reality are there self-existent and unchanging *things*.

sutra: literally, "thread," this term refers to strands of teaching, or verses, in Indian sacred texts.

taiji: a term in the Yijing (I-Ching) and in Neo-Confucianism that refers to Ultimate Sacred Reality as "The Great Ultimate."

theism: a form of religion in which God is represented as: (a) one, (b) personal, (c) creator of all that is not God, (d) eternal, and (e) perfect in goodness, power, and knowledge.

theodicy: the attempt to give a plausible explanation of how the existence, amount, and type of evil found in the world is consistent with the existence of the God of traditional theism.

theology: the systematic attempt to spell out the nature of God and God's relationship with the world from within a theistic religion.

Theravada: literally, "Tradition of the Elders," one of surviving schools of early Buddhism that flourishes in Southeast Asia and that seeks to preserve the teachings and form of Buddhist practice as closely as possible to that of the historical Buddha.

tri-kaya: literally, "three bodies," a Mahayana Buddhist doctrine that distinguishes three forms in which Buddha nature is manifested: (a) as physical and historical figures (*nirmana-kaya*) , e.g., Gautama Buddha; (b) as cosmic trans-historical personal beings to whom one may direct devotional practice (*sambogha-kaya*), e.g., Amida Buddha; and at the most fundamental level (c) as formless Truth itself (*dharma-kaya*).

Upanishads (also Upanisads): the set of texts that comprise the final section of the most sacred of Hindu texts – the *Vedas* – and which serve as the foundation for much of Hindu philosophy.

upaya: literally, "skillful means," a term emphasized in Mahayana Buddhism in order to highlight that teachings and practices are to be judged by their usefulness in moving one toward a direct grasp of one's true nature.

Vedas: the most sacred collection of ancient Hindu scriptural texts.

wu-wei: literally, "no-action," a term in Chinese philosophy that refers to the developed capacity to respond spontaneously and appropriately to the circumstances at hand.

Yijing (also I Ching): literally, "The Book of Changes," this ancient (2000–500 BCE) divination manual provides the cosmological foundation for both Daoism and Confucianism.

yin/yang: two opposing and oscillating forces, or forms of energy, in ancient Chinese philosophy that serve to explain the nature and behavior of the universe.

yoga: a spiritual path, or discipline, in Hinduism leading to enlightenment (*moksha*).

zazen: sitting meditation in Zen Buddhism.

Zen: an iconoclastic form of Mahayana Buddhism that has sought to distill what it regards as the essence of Buddhism – a direct (apart from words-concepts) grasp of one's Buddha nature.

Zhongyong (also Chung yung, or The Doctrine of the Mean): a classic text of later Confucianism that aims to articulate the co-creative means of becoming fully human.

Zhouyi: the earliest strata of the ancient Chinese text that comes later to be the *Yijing*.

Text Sources and Credits

The editor and publisher gratefully acknowledge the permission granted to reproduce the copyright material in this book:

Chapter 1: "The Divine Attributes: What is God Like?" from *Reason and Religious Belief*, 3rd edition, by Michael Peterson, William Hasker, Bruce Reichenbach, and David Basinger (Oxford: Oxford University Press, 2003), pp. 58–75. By permission of Oxford University Press Inc.

Chapter 2: "The Female Nature of God: A Problem in Contemporary Religious Life" by Rosemary Radford Ruether, *Concilium* 143 (1981): 61–6. Reprinted by permission of Stichting Concilium.

Chapter 3: "God as Creative Responsive Love" by John B. Cobb, Jr and David Ray Griffin in *Process Theology: An Introductory Exposition* (Philadelphia: Westminster Press, 1976), pp. 44–57; 61–2.

Chapter 4: "The Vedic-Upanisadic Concept of *Brahman* (The Highest God)" by Sushanta Sen in *Concepts of the Ultimate*, ed. Linda Tessier (New York: St Martin's Press, 1989), pp. 83–97.

Chapter 5: "Emptiness in Mahayana Buddhism," a selection from "Emptiness: Soteriology and Ethics in Mahayana Buddhism" by Christopher Ives in *Concepts of the Ultimate*, ed. Linda Tessier (New York: St Martin's Press, 1989), pp. 113–22; 125–6.

Chapter 6: "Reality and Divinity in Chinese Philosophy" by Chung-Ying Cheng in *A Companion to World Philosophies*, ed. Eliot Deutsch and Ron Bontekoe (Malden, MA: Blackwell Publishers, Inc, 1997), pp. 185–97. Reprinted by permission of the publishers, Blackwell Publishing.

Chapter 7: "How the Supreme Nature Exists through Itself" from *Monologion*, section VI, by Anselm of Canterbury, in *Proslogium; Monologium; an Appendix in Behalf of the Fool by Gaunilon; and Cur Deus Homo*, trans. Sydney Norton Deane (Chicago: Open Court Publishing, 1903, reprinted 1948), pp. 46–9. Reprinted by permission of Open Court Publishing Company, a division of Carus Publishing Company, Peru, IL, from *St Anselm Basic Writings*, trans. S.N. Deane, copyright © 1903 (reprinted 1948) by Open Court Publishing.

Chapter 8: "Of the Unicity of God" by Avicenna (Ibn Sina) from *Avicenna on Theology*, trans. and ed. Arthur J. Arberry (Westport, CT: Hyperion Press, Inc. 1951), pp. 25–6.

Chapter 9: "The Omnipotence of God," Part I, Question 25, 3rd article of *The Summa Theologica* by Thomas Aquinas, trans. Fathers of the English Dominican Province, 2nd revised edition (London: Burns Oates & Washbourne, 1920), pp. 350–2.

Chapter 10: "Thinking and Speaking about God by Analogy," Part I, Question 13, 5th article of *The Summa Theologica*, by Thomas Aquinas, trans. Fathers of the English Dominican Province, 2nd revised edition (London: Burns Oates & Washbourne, 1920), pp. 159–61.

Chapter 11: "Everything has its Self in Brahman" from *Brahmasutrabhasya*, II.1.13–14 by Shankara (Samkara), in *A Sourcebook of Advaita Vedanta*, ed. Eliot Deutsch and J. A. B. van Buitenen (Honolulu: University of Hawaii Press, 1971), pp. 177–9. Reprinted by permission of Professor Eliot Deutsch.

Chapter 31: "Mystical Knowledge: Knowledge by Identity" by Robert K. C. Forman, *Journal of the American Academy of Religion* 61:4 (Winter 1993): 705–32; 734–8. Reprinted by permission of the American Academy of Religion.

Chapter 32: "The Difference between Union and Rapture" by Teresa of Ávila, from *The Collected Works of St Teresa of Ávila*, Vol. 1, trans. Kieran Kavanaugh and Otilio Rodriguez (Washington, DC: ICS Publications, 1976), pp. 161–2; 172–5; 179–80. Reprinted by permission of ICS Publications.

Chapter 33: "Divine Intoxication" from *The Niche of Lights*, by al-Ghazali (Abu Hamid), trans. David Buchman (Provo, UT: Brigham Young University Press, 1998), pp. 17–18. Reprinted by permission of Brigham Young University.

Chapter 34: "Manifesting Suchness" by Ehei Dogen, in *The Heart of Dogen's Shobogenzo*, trans. Norman Waddell and Masao Abe (Albany, NY: SUNY Press, 2002), pp. 41–4.

Chapter 35: "Evil and Omnipotence" by J. L. Mackie, *Mind* 64 (1954): 200–12.

Chapter 36: "The Logical Problem of Evil" from *Philosophy of Religion: An Introduction*, 3rd edition, by William Rowe (Belmont, CA: Wadsworth, 2001), pp. 92–8; 109. Reprinted with permission of Wadsworth, a division of Thomson Learning.

Chapter 37: "An Irenaean Theodicy" by John Hick from *Encountering Evil: Live Options in Theodicy*, new edition, ed. Stephen T. Davis (Atlanta: John Knox/Westminster, 2001), pp. 38–52; 213.

Chapter 38: "The Evidential Problem of Evil" from *Philosophy of Religion: An Introduction*, 3rd edition, by William Rowe (Belmont, CA: Wadsworth, 2001), pp. 98–110. Reprinted with permission of Wadsworth, a division of Thomson Learning.

Chapter 39: "The Concept of God after Auschwitz: A Jewish Voice" by Hans Jonas, *The Journal of Religion* 67:1 (January 1987): 1–13. Reprinted by permission of the publisher, The University of Chicago Press.

Chapter 40: "Śaṃkara's Theodicy" by Bimal K. Matilal, *Journal of Indian Philosophy* 20 (1992): 363–76. With kind permission from Springer Science and Business Media.

Chapter 41: "Karma, Rebirth, and the Problem of Evil" by Whitley R. P. Kaufman, *Philosophy East & West* 59:1 (January 2005): 15–32. Reprinted by permission of the University of Hawaii Press.

Chapter 42: "Evil as a Privation of Good" from sections 10–13 of *The Enchiridion* by Aurelius Augustine, trans. S. D. Salmond, in *The Works of Aurelius Augustine, Bishop of Hippo*, ed. Marcus Dods (Edinburgh: T. & T. Clark, George Street, 1877), pp. 181–3.

Chapter 43: "The Argument from Evil" from Part X of *Dialogues Concerning Natural Religion* by David Hume, in *A Treatise of Human Nature and Dialogues Concerning Natural Religion*, Vol. II, ed. T. H. Green and T. H. Grose (New York: Longmans, Green, and Co., 1898), pp. 439–43.

Chapter 44: "Brahman, Creation, and Evil" by Shankara, *Brahmasutrabhasya*, II.1.34–6, *A Sourcebook of Advaita Vedenta*, ed. Eliot Deutsch and J. A. B. van Buitenen (Honolulu: University of Hawaii Press, 1971), pp. 191–2. Reprinted by permission of Professor Eliot Deutsch.

Chapter 45: "A Naturalistic Case for Extinction" by Linda Badham, in *Death and Immortality in the Religions of the World*, ed. Linda and Paul Badham (St Paul, MN: Paragon House Publishers, 1987), pp. 158–66; 168–9. Reprinted by permission of Paragon House Publishers.

Chapter 46: "Brain Science and the Soul" by Donald MacKay in *The Oxford Companion to the Mind*, ed. Richard L. Gregory (New York: Oxford University Press, 1987), pp. 723–5.

Chapter 47: "The Resurrection of the Dead" by Stephen T. Davis in *Death and Afterlife*, ed. Stephen T. Davis (New York: St Martin's Press, 1989), pp. 119–44.

Chapter 48: "The Idea of Reincarnation" by Joseph Prabhu, in *Death and Afterlife*, ed. Stephen T. Davis (New York: St Martin's Press, 1989), pp. 65–80.

Chapter 49: "Not-Self, *Kamma*, and Rebirth," from *Philosophy of the Buddha* by Christopher Gowans (New York: Routledge, 2003), pp. xi; 69–74; 104–8. Copyright © 2003, Routledge. Reproduced by permission of Taylor & Francis Books UK.

Chapter 50: "Nondualistic Problems of Immortality," a selection from "Dualistic and Nondualistic Problems of Immortality" by Roy W. Perrett, in *Philosophy East and West* 35:4 (October 1985): 341–50. Reprinted by permission of the University of Hawai'i Press.

Chapter 51: "The Immortality of the Soul" from the *Phaedo* by Plato, in *Dialogues of Plato*, trans. Benjamin Jowett (New York: D. Appleton and Co., 1898), pp. 414–16; 421; 432–5.

Chapter 52: "The Conscious Subject Persists in the State of Release" by Ramanuja, in *A Sourcebook in Indian Philosophy*, ed. Sarvepalli Radhakrishan and

Charles A. Moore (Princeton, NJ: Princeton University Press, 1957), pp. 547–8. © 1957 Princeton University Press, 1985 renewed PUP. Reprinted by permission of Princeton University Press.

Chapter 53: "What is Reborn is Neither the Same Nor Another" from the *Questions of King Milinda*, trans. T. W. Rhys Davids (Delhi: Motilal Banarsidass Publishers, 1890/1992), pp. 63–4; 71–4. Reprinted by permission of Motilal Banarsidass Publishers (P) Ltd.

Chapter 54: "A Religious Understanding of Religion: A Model of the Relationship between Traditions" by John Hick, in *Inter-Religious Models and Criteria*, ed. James Kellenberger (New York: St Martins Press, 1993), pp. 21–36.

Chapter 55: "In Defence of a Contented Religious Exclusivism" by Jerome Gellman, *Religious Studies* 36 (2000): 401–10; 414–17.

Chapter 56: "John Hick and the Question of Truth in Religion" by Brian Hebblethwaite, in *God, Truth, and Reality: Essays in Honour of John Hick*, ed. Arvind Sharma (New York: St Martins Press, 1993), pp. 124–34.

Chapter 57: "A Process Approach to Pluralism," a selection from "Metaphysical Pluralism" by John B. Cobb, Jr in *The Intercultural Challenge of Raimon Panikkar*, ed. Joseph Prabhu (Maryknoll, NY: Orbis Books, 1996), pp. 49–54. Reprinted by permission of Orbis Books.

Chapter 58: "A Dynamic Unity in Religious Pluralism: A Proposal from the Buddhist Point of View" by Masao Abe, in *The Experience of Religious Diversity*, ed. John Hick and Hasan Askari (Brookfield, VT: Gower Publishing Co., 1985), pp. 167–80; 182–90; 225–7.

Chapter 59: "Anti-Realist Faith" by Don Cupitt, in *Is God Real?*, ed. Joseph Runzo (New York: St Martin's Press, 1993), pp. 45–55.

Chapter 60: "The Religious Necessity of Realism" by Paul Badham, in *Is God Real?*, ed. Joseph Runzo (New York: St Martin's Press, 1993), pp. 183–92.

Chapter 61: "Postmodernism and Religious Reflection" by Merold Westphal, *International Journal for Philosophy of Religion* 38 (1995): 127–37; 140–2. With kind permission from Springer Science and Business Media. Reprinted by permission of Merold Westphal.

Chapter 62: "The Ends of Metaphysics" by Robert Kane, *International Philosophical Quarterly* 33:4 (December 1993): 413–28. Reprinted by permission of Philosophy Documentation Center, on behalf of *International Philosophical Quarterly*.

Chapter 63: "Feminism and Analytic Philosophy of Religion" by Sarah Coakley in *The Oxford Handbook of Philosophy of Religion*, ed. William J. Wainwright (New York: Oxford University Press, 2005), pp. 494–525. Reprinted by permission of Oxford University Press Inc.

Chapter 64: "Heidegger and Buddhism," a selection from "Heidegger, Buddhism, and Deep Ecology" by Michael E. Zimmerman, in *The Cambridge Companion to Heidegger*, 2nd edition, ed. Charles B. Guignon (New York: Cambridge University Press, 2006), pp. 293–325. © Cambridge University Press, 2006. Reprinted by permission of Cambridge University Press and Michael E. Zimmerman.

Chapter 65: "A-theistic Religiousness of Classical Confucianism" by Roger T. Ames, in *Confucian Spirituality*, Vol. 1 (New York: Crossroad Press, 2003), pp. 165–78; 180–2.